I have to admit it: when I first opened the Bible, I thought it was a collection of myths and legends, of inaccurate history and wishful thinking, of fanciful exaggerations and hopeless contradictions.

As an atheist, I was convinced that God didn't create people, but that people created God. In other words, they had been so afraid of death that they decided to manufacture a feel-good fairy tale about a benevolent deity and a blissful afterlife awaiting them on the other side of the grave.

Surely the Gospels didn't accurately record anything about the life of the itinerant revolutionary named Jesus of Nazareth, who met his gruesome demise at the hands of the Romans. And doesn't everyone know that the Old Testament merely contains the wild superstitions and fables of an ancient and irrelevant tribe from the Middle East?

After all, how can modern, scientifically informed people believe in the supernatural? As the liberal Jesus Seminar said: "The Christ of creed and dogma, who had been firmly in place in the Middle Ages, can no longer command the assent of those who have seen the heavens through Galileo's telescope . . . Copernicus, Kepler, and Galileo have dismantled the mythological abodes of the gods and Satan, and bequeathed us secular heavens."[1]

In spite of my skeptical predisposition, however, I eventually became a "seeker," someone open-minded and inquisitive enough to sincerely investigate the claims of this bestselling book of all time. I decided at the outset to follow the facts wherever they would lead. So for nearly two years, I studied archaeology and ancient history, interviewed scholars and scientists, and combed through these pages with an attitude of curiosity and growing expectancy. Putting my background in journalism and law to use, I scrutinized the words of the Bible and tested the evidence for and against it.

[1] Robert W. Funk, et al, editors, *The Five Gospels* (San Francisco: HarperSanFrancisco, 1997, paperback ed.), 2.

What I found changed my mind and, ultimately, transformed my life.

Maybe you're spiritually curious as well. Perhaps you've been a skeptic like I was or you're an adherent of another religion. Perhaps you were once a follower of Jesus but your faith has grown cold, and now you're determined to find answers to the deepest questions of your mind and soul. Or maybe you're already a committed Christian and want to grow in your understanding of God's Word and how you can share its message with others.

Regardless of your motivation for picking up this volume, there's something in this unique book for you. It includes the text of the New Testament, Psalms and Proverbs in the reliable and readable New International Version; these words of Scripture are the first place to start your investigation, so read them thoughtfully and carefully. Alongside of these readings you'll find intriguing questions answered by information designed to facilitate your investigation[2] into the person of Jesus.

Along the way, you'll learn fascinating details about the Christ of Christianity. You'll start to discover why Christians are convinced that history points powerfully and persuasively toward Jesus as being God's unique Son. In the process, you'll discover some of the facts that pointed a cynic like me to the life-changing and eternity-altering reality of Jesus Christ.

So welcome to the adventure of investigating faith! My prayer is that the context and background in this small book will deepen your confidence in the trustworthiness of the Bible and solidify your commitment to the One who lovingly wants to adopt each of us as his own—for all of eternity.

— Lee Strobel

[2] Editor's Note: The readings in this book come from a larger work entitled *The Case for Christ* (Grand Rapids, MI: Zondervan, 2002, 2016). You can continue your research with that and many related "Case for" books written by Lee Strobel.

What Does the Old Testament Prophesy About Jesus Christ?

"I will put enmity between you and the woman, and between your offspring and hers; he will crush your head, and you will strike his heel." Genesis 3:15

The first prophecy about Jesus comes in Genesis 3:15, shortly after the creation story. After Adam and Eve's rebellion, God doled out punishments to those involved: first to the serpent, then to Eve and finally to Adam. When God told the serpent that he would "put enmity" between the serpent and Eve, he was referring not only to their story but also to the story of all of humankind—a story plagued by the evil one, Satan. Only Christ himself, a descendant of Eve, would ever be powerful enough to overcome Satan. It is a victory in which all believers share (see Romans 16:20).

When the time was right, Jesus came into the world (see John 1:14; 3:16; Romans 1:1–6; Galatians 4:4; 1 John 4:14). He came to crush the evil that humans had allowed Satan to usher into the world, close the deep chasm that had separated humanity from God, destroy Satan, and free those imprisoned by sin and their fear of death (see Hebrews 2:14–15).

For to us a child is born, to us a son is given, and the government will be on his shoulders. And he will be called Wonderful Counselor, Mighty God, Everlasting Father, Prince of Peace. Isaiah 9:6

Isaiah 9:1–7 is full of prophecies concerning the coming Messiah; these include details about where he would live and minister, what people would call him, and the significance of his kingdom. Are these predictions consistent with the description of Jesus found in the Gospels?

Isaiah 9:1–2 foretells that the Messiah will live in the lands of Zebulun, Naphtali and Galilee. The Gospels recount that Jesus' ministry started in Galilee (see Matthew 4:12,23) after he heard the news of John the Baptist's imprisonment. He left Nazareth and "went and lived in Capernaum, which was by the lake in the area of Zebulun and Naphtali" (Matthew 4:13). Matthew recognizes that this fulfilled prophecy and quotes Isaiah 9:1–2 (see Matthew 4:14–16).

Isaiah also prophesies about the birth of this future king, calling him the "Wonderful Counselor" and "Prince of Peace" who will reign on David's throne forever with justice and righteousness (see Isaiah 9:6–7). Before Jesus' birth, an angel tells Mary the importance of the baby she is carrying; he will reign forever on the throne of David (see Luke 1:32–33). Because Jesus is a descendant of David, this kingship rightfully belongs to him.

The accounts of the Gospels confirm that Jesus fulfilled the Messianic prophecies, including those found in Isaiah 9:1–7, further confirming his identity as the long-awaited Messiah.

"But you, Bethlehem Ephrathah, though you are small among the clans of Judah, out of you will come for me one who will be ruler over Israel, whose origins are from of old, from ancient times." Micah 5:2

Hundreds of years before Jesus' birth, prophets foretold the coming of the Messiah, or the Anointed One, who would redeem God's people. One prophecy, found in Micah 5:2, was fulfilled when Jesus was born in Bethlehem (see Matthew 2:1,6; Luke 2:4–7). In addition to this prophecy, dozens of other Old Testament prophecies created a fingerprint that only the true Messiah could fit. This gave Israel a way to rule out impostors and validate the credentials of the authentic Messiah.

Against astronomical odds—according to one estimate, a single chance in a trillion, trillion, trillion, trillion, trillion, trillion, trillion, trillion, trillion, trillion, trillion, trillion, trillion[1]—Jesus, and only Jesus throughout history, matched this prophetic fingerprint. This confirms Jesus' identity to an incredible degree of certainty.

---

[1] Peter W. Stoner, *Science Speaks* (Chicago: Moody Press, 1969), 109.

What Do the Psalms and Proverbs Say About Jesus Christ?

My God, my God, why have you forsaken me? Psalm 22:1 (Read Psalm 22:1-31)

From its opening sentence to its very last verse, Psalm 22 prophesies in painstaking detail Jesus' acceptance of his fate, his rejection by his persecutors, his crucifixion and his glorification because of it all (see also John 17:4–5).

Before ,Jesus' arrest, he prays and likens his suffering to a cup (see Luke 22:42); in the same way, David, the author of Psalm 22, expresses his anguish by saying that he is "poured out like water" (verse 14).

Also, as Jesus was being taken to be crucified, "those who passed by hurled insults at him, shaking their heads" (Matthew 27:39). This verse in Matthew corresponds almost verbatim with Psalm 22:7, which says David's enemies "hurl insults, shaking their heads." The crucifixion itself is described in vivid detail in Psalm 22:16: "they pierce my hands and my feet." Psalm 22:16–17 also predicts the multitude of people who will mock Jesus as he hangs from the cross (see Matthew 27:39–44).

Additionally, the description in John 19:23–24 of the soldiers who cast lots for Jesus' clothing is mirrored by the words of Psalm 22:18, and the prophecy itself is mentioned in the description in John 19.

Finally, Jesus' last words on the cross, "My God, my God, why have you forsaken me?" (Matthew 27:46), echo the very first line of Psalm 22. These words would have reminded those nearby during the crucifixion of the psalm's prophecy, which they had just seen fulfilled.

———————

For the LORD gives wisdom; from his mouth come knowledge and understanding. Proverbs 2:6

Proverbs 2:1–11 extols the value of wisdom and the necessity of searching for it as "hidden treasure" (Proverbs 2:4). It is the Lord who initiates the search. He gives us wisdom and knowledge, as well as discretion and understanding to guard and protect us.

Jesus is wisdom incarnate. As the Word of God, he is the very nature of truth (see John 1:1,14). Because Jesus came from God and is one with him, he embodies the spirit of truth and wisdom. Jesus is called "wisdom from God" (1 Corinthians 1:30), and in him "are hidden all the treasures of wisdom and knowledge" (Colossians 2:3). Jesus himself said that he is greater than Solomon, who composed much of the book of Proverbs and whose wisdom the Queen of Sheba came to listen to (see Matthew 12:42).

Witnesses confirmed that Jesus' words were beyond anything they had heard before (see Mark 1:21–22). When Jesus was only 12 years old, he engaged the teachers in the temple and asked them insightful questions, astonishing the crowds with his understanding and answers. This episode was followed by a rare comment on Jesus' childhood: "Jesus grew in wisdom and stature, and in favor with God and man" (Luke 2:52).

The book of Proverbs shows what a life of true wisdom looks like, and only one person has ever lived it: Jesus. Wisdom guards us from foolish choices, helping us to navigate the temptations of this world and to avoid sin and its consequences. We look to Jesus to show us wisdom's hidden treasures.

NEW INTERNATIONAL VERSION

HOLY BIBLE

ZONDERVAN®

NIV New Testament with Psalms and Proverbs
Published by Zondervan, 2020
Grand Rapids, Michigan 49546
All rights reserved

Printed in India

N120712

22 23 24 25 26 /THI/ 20 19 18 17 16 15 14 13 12 11 10 9 8 7 6 5 4 3 2 1

A portion of the purchase price of your NIV® Bible is provided to Biblica so together we support the mission of *Transforming lives through God's Word.*

Biblica provides God's Word to people through translation, publishing and Bible engagement in Africa, Asia Pacific, Europe, Latin America, Middle East, and North America. Through its worldwide reach, Biblica engages people with God's Word so that their lives are transformed through a relationship with Jesus Christ.

Table of Contents

New Testament

Psalms and Proverbs

New Testament

Matthew

The Genealogy of Jesus the Messiah

1 This is the genealogy[a] of Jesus the Messiah[b] the son of David, the son of Abraham:

2 Abraham was the father of Isaac,
Isaac the father of Jacob,
Jacob the father of Judah and his brothers,
3 Judah the father of Perez and Zerah, whose mother was Tamar,
Perez the father of Hezron,
Hezron the father of Ram,
4 Ram the father of Amminadab,
Amminadab the father of Nahshon,
Nahshon the father of Salmon,
5 Salmon the father of Boaz, whose mother was Rahab,
Boaz the father of Obed, whose mother was Ruth,
Obed the father of Jesse,
6 and Jesse the father of King David.

David was the father of Solomon, whose mother had been Uriah's wife,
7 Solomon the father of Rehoboam,
Rehoboam the father of Abijah,
Abijah the father of Asa,
8 Asa the father of Jehoshaphat,
Jehoshaphat the father of Jehoram,
Jehoram the father of Uzziah,
9 Uzziah the father of Jotham,
Jotham the father of Ahaz,
Ahaz the father of Hezekiah,
10 Hezekiah the father of Manasseh,
Manasseh the father of Amon,
Amon the father of Josiah,
11 and Josiah the father of Jeconiah[c] and his brothers at the time of the exile to Babylon.

12 After the exile to Babylon:
Jeconiah was the father of Shealtiel,
Shealtiel the father of Zerubbabel,
13 Zerubbabel the father of Abihud,
Abihud the father of Eliakim,
Eliakim the father of Azor,
14 Azor the father of Zadok,
Zadok the father of Akim,
Akim the father of Elihud,
15 Elihud the father of Eleazar,
Eleazar the father of Matthan,
Matthan the father of Jacob,
16 and Jacob the father of Joseph, the husband of Mary, and Mary was the mother of Jesus who is called the Messiah.

17 Thus there were fourteen generations in all from Abraham to David, fourteen from David to the exile to Babylon, and fourteen from the exile to the Messiah.

Joseph Accepts Jesus as His Son

18 This is how the birth of Jesus the Messiah came about[d]: His mother

---

a 1 Or is an account of the origin   b 1 Or Jesus Christ. Messiah (Hebrew) and Christ (Greek) both mean Anointed One; also in verse 18.
c 11 That is, Jehoiachin; also in verse 12
d 18 Or The origin of Jesus the Messiah was like this

Mary was pledged to be married to Joseph, but before they came together, she was found to be pregnant through the Holy Spirit. ¹⁹Because Joseph her husband was faithful to the law, and yet*ᵃ* did not want to expose her to public disgrace, he had in mind to divorce her quietly.

²⁰But after he had considered this, an angel of the Lord appeared to him in a dream and said, "Joseph son of David, do not be afraid to take Mary home as your wife, because what is conceived in her is from the Holy Spirit. ²¹She will give birth to a son, and you are to give him the name Jesus,*ᵇ* because he will save his people from their sins."

²²All this took place to fulfill what the Lord had said through the prophet: ²³"The virgin will conceive and give birth to a son, and they will call him Immanuel"*ᶜ* (which means "God with us").

²⁴When Joseph woke up, he did what the angel of the Lord had commanded him and took Mary home as his wife. ²⁵But he did not consummate their marriage until she gave birth to a son. And he gave him the name Jesus.

The Magi Visit the Messiah

2 After Jesus was born in Bethlehem in Judea, during the time of King Herod, Magi*ᵈ* from the east came to Jerusalem ²and asked, "Where is the one who has been born king of the Jews? We saw his star when it rose and have come to worship him."

³When King Herod heard this he was disturbed, and all Jerusalem with him. ⁴When he had called together all the people's chief priests and teachers of the law, he asked them where the Messiah was to be born. ⁵"In Bethlehem in Judea," they replied, "for this is what the prophet has written:

⁶ "'But you, Bethlehem, in the
        land of Judah,
    are by no means least among
        the rulers of Judah;
for out of you will come a ruler
    who will shepherd my people
        Israel.'*ᵉ*"

⁷Then Herod called the Magi secretly and found out from them the exact time the star had appeared. ⁸He sent them to Bethlehem and said, "Go and search carefully for the child. As soon as you find him, report to me, so that I too may go and worship him."

⁹After they had heard the king, they went on their way, and the star they had seen when it rose went ahead of them until it stopped over the place where the child was. ¹⁰When they saw the star, they were overjoyed. ¹¹On coming to the house, they saw the child with his mother Mary, and they bowed down and worshiped him. Then they opened their treasures and presented him with gifts of gold, frankincense and myrrh. ¹²And having been warned in a dream not to go back to Herod, they returned to their country by another route.

The Escape to Egypt

¹³When they had gone, an angel of the Lord appeared to Joseph in a dream. "Get up," he said, "take the child and his mother and escape to Egypt. Stay there until I tell you, for Herod is going to search for the child to kill him."

¹⁴So he got up, took the child and his mother during the night and left for Egypt, ¹⁵where he stayed until the death of Herod. And so was fulfilled

---

ᵃ 19 Or was a righteous man and   *ᵇ 21 Jesus* is the Greek form of *Joshua,* which means *the* LORD *saves.*   *ᶜ 23 Isaiah 7:14*   *ᵈ 1 Traditionally wise men*   *ᵉ 6 Micah 5:2,4* what the Lord had said through the prophet: "Out of Egypt I called my son."[a]

[16]When Herod realized that he had been outwitted by the Magi, he was furious, and he gave orders to kill all the boys in Bethlehem and its vicinity who were two years old and under, in accordance with the time he had learned from the Magi. [17]Then what was said through the prophet Jeremiah was fulfilled:

[18] "A voice is heard in Ramah,
      weeping and great mourning,
   Rachel weeping for her children
      and refusing to be comforted,
      because they are no more."[b]

The Return to Nazareth

[19]After Herod died, an angel of the Lord appeared in a dream to Joseph in Egypt [20]and said, "Get up, take the child and his mother and go to the land of Israel, for those who were trying to take the child's life are dead."

[21]So he got up, took the child and his mother and went to the land of Israel. [22]But when he heard that Archelaus was reigning in Judea in place of his father Herod, he was afraid to go there. Having been warned in a dream, he withdrew to the district of Galilee, [23]and he went and lived in a town called Nazareth. So was fulfilled what was said through the prophets, that he would be called a Nazarene.

John the Baptist Prepares the Way

3 In those days John the Baptist came, preaching in the wilderness of Judea [2]and saying, "Repent, for the kingdom of heaven has come near." [3]This is he who was spoken of through the prophet Isaiah:

"A voice of one calling in the wilderness,
   'Prepare the way for the Lord,
      make straight paths for him.'"[c]

[4]John's clothes were made of camel's hair, and he had a leather belt around his waist. His food was locusts and wild honey. [5]People went out to him from Jerusalem and all Judea and the whole region of the Jordan. [6]Confessing their sins, they were baptized by him in the Jordan River.

[7]But when he saw many of the Pharisees and Sadducees coming to where he was baptizing, he said to them: "You brood of vipers! Who warned you to flee from the coming wrath? [8]Produce fruit in keeping with repentance. [9]And do not think you can say to yourselves, 'We have Abraham as our father.' I tell you that out of these stones God can raise up children for Abraham. [10]The ax is already at the root of the trees, and every tree that does not produce good fruit will be cut down and thrown into the fire.

[11]"I baptize you with[d] water for repentance. But after me comes one who is more powerful than I, whose sandals I am not worthy to carry. He will baptize you with[d] the Holy Spirit and fire. [12]His winnowing fork is in his hand, and he will clear his threshing floor, gathering his wheat into the barn and burning up the chaff with unquenchable fire."

The Baptism of Jesus

[13]Then Jesus came from Galilee to the Jordan to be baptized by John. [14]But John tried to deter him, saying, "I need to be baptized by you, and do you come to me?"

[a] 15 Hosea 11:1   [b] 18 Jer. 31:15
[c] 3 Isaiah 40:3   [d] 11 Or in

¹⁵Jesus replied, "Let it be so now; it is proper for us to do this to fulfill all righteousness." Then John consented.

¹⁶As soon as Jesus was baptized, he went up out of the water. At that moment heaven was opened, and he saw the Spirit of God descending like a dove and alighting on him. ¹⁷And a voice from heaven said, "This is my Son, whom I love; with him I am well pleased."

Jesus Is Tested in the Wilderness

4 Then Jesus was led by the Spirit into the wilderness to be tempted[a] by the devil. ²After fasting forty days and forty nights, he was hungry. ³The tempter came to him and said, "If you are the Son of God, tell these stones to become bread."

⁴Jesus answered, "It is written: 'Man shall not live on bread alone, but on every word that comes from the mouth of God.'[b]"

⁵Then the devil took him to the holy city and had him stand on the highest point of the temple. ⁶"If you are the Son of God," he said, "throw yourself down. For it is written:

" 'He will command his angels
concerning you,
and they will lift you up in
their hands,
so that you will not strike your
foot against a stone.'[c]"

⁷Jesus answered him, "It is also written: 'Do not put the Lord your God to the test.'[d]"

⁸Again, the devil took him to a very high mountain and showed him all the kingdoms of the world and their splendor. ⁹"All this I will give you," he said, "if you will bow down and worship me."

¹⁰Jesus said to him, "Away from me,

Satan! For it is written: 'Worship the Lord your God, and serve him only.'[e]"

¹¹Then the devil left him, and angels came and attended him.

Jesus Begins to Preach

¹²When Jesus heard that John had been put in prison, he withdrew to Galilee. ¹³Leaving Nazareth, he went and lived in Capernaum, which was by the lake in the area of Zebulun and Naphtali — ¹⁴to fulfill what was said through the prophet Isaiah:

¹⁵ "Land of Zebulun and land
of Naphtali,
the Way of the Sea, beyond
the Jordan,
Galilee of the Gentiles —
¹⁶ the people living in darkness
have seen a great light;
on those living in the land
of the shadow of death
a light has dawned."[f]

¹⁷From that time on Jesus began to preach, "Repent, for the kingdom of heaven has come near."

Jesus Calls His First Disciples

¹⁸As Jesus was walking beside the Sea of Galilee, he saw two brothers, Simon called Peter and his brother Andrew. They were casting a net into the lake, for they were fishermen. ¹⁹"Come, follow me," Jesus said, "and I will send you out to fish for people." ²⁰At once they left their nets and followed him.

²¹Going on from there, he saw two other brothers, James son of Zebedee and his brother John. They were in a boat with their father Zebedee, preparing their nets. Jesus called them,

---

[a] 1 The Greek for *tempted* can also mean *tested*.   [b] 4 Deut. 8:3   [c] 6 Psalm 91:11,12   [d] 7 Deut. 6:16   [e] 10 Deut. 6:13   [f] 16 Isaiah 9:1,2

22and immediately they left the boat and their father and followed him.

Jesus Heals the Sick

23 Jesus went throughout Galilee, teaching in their synagogues, proclaiming the good news of the kingdom, and healing every disease and sickness among the people. 24News about him spread all over Syria, and people brought to him all who were ill with various diseases, those suffering severe pain, the demon-possessed, those having seizures, and the paralyzed; and he healed them. 25Large crowds from Galilee, the Decapolis,ᵃ Jerusalem, Judea and the region across the Jordan followed him.

Introduction to the Sermon on the Mount

5 Now when Jesus saw the crowds, he went up on a mountainside and sat down. His disciples came to him, 2and he began to teach them.

The Beatitudes

He said:

³ "Blessed are the poor in spirit,
    for theirs is the kingdom of
       heaven.
⁴ Blessed are those who mourn,
    for they will be comforted.
⁵ Blessed are the meek,
    for they will inherit the earth.
⁶ Blessed are those who
       hunger and thirst for
       righteousness,
    for they will be filled.
⁷ Blessed are the merciful,
    for they will be shown mercy.
⁸ Blessed are the pure in heart,
    for they will see God.
⁹ Blessed are the peacemakers,
    for they will be called children
       of God.

¹⁰ Blessed are those who are
       persecuted because of
       righteousness,
    for theirs is the kingdom of
       heaven.

¹¹"Blessed are you when people insult you, persecute you and falsely say all kinds of evil against you because of me. ¹²Rejoice and be glad, because great is your reward in heaven, for in the same way they persecuted the prophets who were before you.

Salt and Light

¹³"You are the salt of the earth. But if the salt loses its saltiness, how can it be made salty again? It is no longer good for anything, except to be thrown out and trampled underfoot. ¹⁴"You are the light of the world. A town built on a hill cannot be hidden. ¹⁵Neither do people light a lamp and put it under a bowl. Instead they put it on its stand, and it gives light to everyone in the house. ¹⁶In the same way, let your light shine before others, that they may see your good deeds and glorify your Father in heaven.

The Fulfillment of the Law

¹⁷"Do not think that I have come to abolish the Law or the Prophets; I have not come to abolish them but to fulfill them. ¹⁸For truly I tell you, until heaven and earth disappear, not the smallest letter, not the least stroke of a pen, will by any means disappear from the Law until everything is accomplished. ¹⁹Therefore anyone who sets aside one of the least of these commands and teaches others accordingly will be called least in the kingdom of heaven, but whoever practices and teaches these commands will be called great in the

---

ᵃ 25 That is, the Ten Cities

kingdom of heaven. [20]For I tell you that unless your righteousness surpasses that of the Pharisees and the teachers of the law, you will certainly not enter the kingdom of heaven.

Murder

[21]"You have heard that it was said to the people long ago, 'You shall not murder,[b] and anyone who murders will be subject to judgment.' [22]But I tell you that anyone who is angry with a brother or sister[b,c] will be subject to judgment. Again, anyone who says to a brother or sister, 'Raca,'[d] is answerable to the court. And anyone who says, 'You fool!' will be in danger of the fire of hell.

[23]"Therefore, if you are offering your gift at the altar and there remember that your brother or sister has something against you, [24]leave your gift in front of the altar. First go and be reconciled to them; then come and offer your gift.

[25]"Settle matters quickly with your adversary who is taking you to court. Do it while you are still together on the way, or your adversary may hand you over to the judge, and the judge may hand you over to the officer, and you may be thrown into prison. [26]Truly I tell you, you will not get out until you have paid the last penny.

Adultery

[27]"You have heard that it was said, 'You shall not commit adultery.'[e] [28]But I tell you that anyone who looks at a woman lustfully has already committed adultery with her in his heart. [29]If your right eye causes you to stumble, gouge it out and throw it away. It is better for you to lose one part of your body than for your whole body to be thrown into hell. [30]And if your right hand causes

you to stumble, cut it off and throw it away. It is better for you to lose one part of your body than for your whole body to go into hell.

Divorce

[31]"It has been said, 'Anyone who divorces his wife must give her a certificate of divorce.'[f] [32]But I tell you that anyone who divorces his wife, except for sexual immorality, makes her the victim of adultery, and anyone who marries a divorced woman commits adultery.

Oaths

[33]"Again, you have heard that it was said to the people long ago, 'Do not break your oath, but fulfill to the Lord the vows you have made.' [34]But I tell you, do not swear an oath at all: either by heaven, for it is God's throne; [35]or by the earth, for it is his footstool; or by Jerusalem, for it is the city of the Great King. [36]And do not swear by your head, for you cannot make even one hair white or black. [37]All you need to say is simply 'Yes' or 'No'; anything beyond this comes from the evil one.[g]

Eye for Eye

[38]"You have heard that it was said, 'Eye for eye, and tooth for tooth.'[h] [39]But I tell you, do not resist an evil person. If anyone slaps you on the right cheek, turn to them the other cheek also. [40]And if anyone wants to sue you and take your shirt, hand over your coat as well. [41]If anyone forces you to go one mile, go with them two

---

[a] 21 Exodus 20:13   [b] 22 The Greek word for *brother or sister* (*adelphos*) refers here to a fellow disciple, whether man or woman; also in verse 23.   [c] 22 Some manuscripts *brother or sister without cause*   [d] 22 An Aramaic term of contempt   [e] 27 Exodus 20:14   [f] 31 Deut. 24:1   [g] 37 Or *from evil*   [h] 38 Exodus 21:24; Lev. 24:20; Deut. 19:21

miles. ⁴²Give to the one who asks you, and do not turn away from the one who wants to borrow from you.

Love for Enemies

⁴³"You have heard that it was said, 'Love your neighbor*ᵃ* and hate your enemy.' ⁴⁴But I tell you, love your enemies and pray for those who persecute you, ⁴⁵that you may be children of your Father in heaven. He causes his sun to rise on the evil and the good, and sends rain on the righteous and the unrighteous. ⁴⁶If you love those who love you, what reward will you get? Are not even the tax collectors doing that? ⁴⁷And if you greet only your own people, what are you doing more than others? Do not even pagans do that? ⁴⁸Be perfect, therefore, as your heavenly Father is perfect.

Giving to the Needy

6 "Be careful not to practice your righteousness in front of others to be seen by them. If you do, you will have no reward from your Father in heaven.

²"So when you give to the needy, do not announce it with trumpets, as the hypocrites do in the synagogues and on the streets, to be honored by others. Truly I tell you, they have received their reward in full. ³But when you give to the needy, do not let your left hand know what your right hand is doing, ⁴so that your giving may be in secret. Then your Father, who sees what is done in secret, will reward you.

Prayer

⁵"And when you pray, do not be like the hypocrites, for they love to pray standing in the synagogues and on the street corners to be seen by others. Truly I tell you, they have received their reward in full. ⁶But when you pray, go into your room, close the door and pray to your Father, who is unseen. Then your Father, who sees what is done in secret, will reward you. ⁷And when you pray, do not keep on babbling like pagans, for they think they will be heard because of their many words. ⁸Do not be like them, for your Father knows what you need before you ask him.

⁹"This, then, is how you should pray:

"'Our Father in heaven,
   hallowed be your name,
¹⁰ your kingdom come,
   your will be done,
     on earth as it is in heaven.
¹¹ Give us today our daily
     bread.
¹² And forgive us our debts,
     as we also have forgiven our
      debtors.
¹³ And lead us not into temptation,*ᵇ*
     but deliver us from the evil
      one.*ᶜ*'

¹⁴For if you forgive other people when they sin against you, your heavenly Father will also forgive you. ¹⁵But if you do not forgive others their sins, your Father will not forgive your sins.

Fasting

¹⁶"When you fast, do not look somber as the hypocrites do, for they disfigure their faces to show others they are fasting. Truly I tell you, they have received their reward in full. ¹⁷But when you fast, put oil on your head and wash your face, ¹⁸so that

---

ᵃ 43 Lev. 19:18   *ᵇ 13* The Greek for *temptation* can also mean *testing.*   *ᶜ 13* Or *from evil;* some late manuscripts *one, / for yours is the kingdom and the power and the glory forever. Amen.*

it will not be obvious to others that you are fasting, but only to your Father, who is unseen; and your Father, who sees what is done in secret, will reward you.

Treasures in Heaven

¹⁹"Do not store up for yourselves treasures on earth, where moths and vermin destroy, and where thieves break in and steal. ²⁰But store up for yourselves treasures in heaven, where moths and vermin do not destroy, and where thieves do not break in and steal. ²¹For where your treasure is, there your heart will be also.

²²"The eye is the lamp of the body. If your eyes are healthy,ᵃ your whole body will be full of light. ²³But if your eyes are unhealthy,ᵇ your whole body will be full of darkness. If then the light within you is darkness, how great is that darkness!

²⁴"No one can serve two masters. Either you will hate the one and love the other, or you will be devoted to the one and despise the other. You cannot serve both God and money.

Do Not Worry

²⁵"Therefore I tell you, do not worry about your life, what you will eat or drink; or about your body, what you will wear. Is not life more than food, and the body more than clothes? ²⁶Look at the birds of the air; they do not sow or reap or store away in barns, and yet your heavenly Father feeds them. Are you not much more valuable than they? ²⁷Can any one of you by worrying add a single hour to your life?ᶜ

²⁸"And why do you worry about clothes? See how the flowers of the field grow. They do not labor or spin. ²⁹Yet I tell you that not even Solomon in all his splendor was dressed like one of these. ³⁰If that is how God clothes the grass of the field, which is here today and tomorrow is thrown into the fire, will he not much more clothe you — you of little faith? ³¹So do not worry, saying, 'What shall we eat?' or 'What shall we drink?' or 'What shall we wear?' ³²For the pagans run after all these things, and your heavenly Father knows that you need them. ³³But seek first his kingdom and his righteousness, and all these things will be given to you as well. ³⁴Therefore do not worry about tomorrow, for tomorrow will worry about itself. Each day has enough trouble of its own.

Judging Others

7 "Do not judge, or you too will be judged. ²For in the same way you judge others, you will be judged, and with the measure you use, it will be measured to you.

³"Why do you look at the speck of sawdust in your brother's eye and pay no attention to the plank in your own eye? ⁴How can you say to your brother, 'Let me take the speck out of your eye,' when all the time there is a plank in your own eye? ⁵You hypocrite, first take the plank out of your own eye, and then you will see clearly to remove the speck from your brother's eye.

⁶"Do not give dogs what is sacred; do not throw your pearls to pigs. If you do, they may trample them under their feet, and turn and tear you to pieces.

Ask, Seek, Knock

⁷"Ask and it will be given to you; seek and you will find; knock and

---

ᵃ *22* The Greek for *healthy* here implies *generous.*　　ᵇ *23* The Greek for *unhealthy* here implies *stingy.*　　ᶜ *27* Or *single cubit to your height* the door will be opened to you. ⁸For everyone who asks receives; the one who seeks finds; and to the one who knocks, the door will be opened.

⁹"Which of you, if your son asks for bread, will give him a stone? ¹⁰Or if he asks for a fish, will give him a snake? ¹¹If you, then, though you are evil, know how to give good gifts to your children, how much more will your Father in heaven give good gifts to those who ask him! ¹²So in everything, do to others what you would have them do to you, for this sums up the Law and the Prophets.

The Narrow and Wide Gates

¹³"Enter through the narrow gate. For wide is the gate and broad is the road that leads to destruction, and many enter through it. ¹⁴But small is the gate and narrow the road that leads to life, and only a few find it.

True and False Prophets

¹⁵"Watch out for false prophets. They come to you in sheep's clothing, but inwardly they are ferocious wolves. ¹⁶By their fruit you will recognize them. Do people pick grapes from thornbushes, or figs from thistles? ¹⁷Likewise, every good tree bears good fruit, but a bad tree bears bad fruit. ¹⁸A good tree cannot bear bad fruit, and a bad tree cannot bear good fruit. ¹⁹Every tree that does not bear good fruit is cut down and thrown into the fire. ²⁰Thus, by their fruit you will recognize them.

True and False Disciples

²¹"Not everyone who says to me, 'Lord, Lord,' will enter the kingdom of heaven, but only the one who does the will of my Father who is in heaven. ²²Many will say to me on that day, 'Lord, Lord, did we not prophesy in your name and in your name drive out demons and in your name perform many miracles?' ²³Then I will tell them plainly, 'I never knew you. Away from me, you evildoers!'

The Wise and Foolish Builders

²⁴"Therefore everyone who hears these words of mine and puts them into practice is like a wise man who built his house on the rock. ²⁵The rain came down, the streams rose, and the winds blew and beat against that house; yet it did not fall, because it had its foundation on the rock. ²⁶But everyone who hears these words of mine and does not put them into practice is like a foolish man who built his house on sand. ²⁷The rain came down, the streams rose, and the winds blew and beat against that house, and it fell with a great crash."

²⁸When Jesus had finished saying these things, the crowds were amazed at his teaching, ²⁹because he taught as one who had authority, and not as their teachers of the law.

Jesus Heals a Man With Leprosy

8 When Jesus came down from the mountainside, large crowds followed him. ²A man with leprosy* came and knelt before him and said, "Lord, if you are willing, you can make me clean."

³Jesus reached out his hand and touched the man. "I am willing," he said. "Be clean!" Immediately he was cleansed of his leprosy. ⁴Then Jesus said to him, "See that you don't tell anyone. But go, show yourself to the

---

*2 The Greek word traditionally translated *leprosy* was used for various diseases affecting the skin.

priest and offer the gift Moses commanded, as a testimony to them."

The Faith of the Centurion

⁵When Jesus had entered Capernaum, a centurion came to him, asking for help. ⁶"Lord," he said, "my servant lies at home paralyzed, suffering terribly."

⁷Jesus said to him, "Shall I come and heal him?"

⁸The centurion replied, "Lord, I do not deserve to have you come under my roof. But just say the word, and my servant will be healed. ⁹For I myself am a man under authority, with soldiers under me. I tell this one, 'Go,' and he goes; and that one, 'Come,' and he comes. I say to my servant, 'Do this,' and he does it."

¹⁰When Jesus heard this, he was amazed and said to those following him, "Truly I tell you, I have not found anyone in Israel with such great faith. ¹¹I say to you that many will come from the east and the west, and will take their places at the feast with Abraham, Isaac and Jacob in the kingdom of heaven. ¹²But the subjects of the kingdom will be thrown outside, into the darkness, where there will be weeping and gnashing of teeth."

¹³Then Jesus said to the centurion, "Go! Let it be done just as you believed it would." And his servant was healed at that moment.

Jesus Heals Many

¹⁴When Jesus came into Peter's house, he saw Peter's mother-in-law lying in bed with a fever. ¹⁵He touched her hand and the fever left her, and she got up and began to wait on him.

¹⁶When evening came, many who were demon-possessed were brought to him, and he drove out the spirits with a word and healed all the sick.

¹⁷This was to fulfill what was spoken through the prophet Isaiah:

"He took up our infirmities
and bore our diseases."ᵃ

The Cost of Following Jesus

¹⁸When Jesus saw the crowd around him, he gave orders to cross to the other side of the lake. ¹⁹Then a teacher of the law came to him and said, "Teacher, I will follow you wherever you go."

²⁰Jesus replied, "Foxes have dens and birds have nests, but the Son of Man has no place to lay his head."

²¹Another disciple said to him, "Lord, first let me go and bury my father."

²²But Jesus told him, "Follow me, and let the dead bury their own dead."

Jesus Calms the Storm

²³Then he got into the boat and his disciples followed him. ²⁴Suddenly a furious storm came up on the lake, so that the waves swept over the boat. But Jesus was sleeping. ²⁵The disciples went and woke him, saying, "Lord, save us! We're going to drown!"

²⁶He replied, "You of little faith, why are you so afraid?" Then he got up and rebuked the winds and the waves, and it was completely calm.

²⁷The men were amazed and asked, "What kind of man is this? Even the winds and the waves obey him!"

Jesus Restores Two Demon-Possessed Men

²⁸When he arrived at the other side in the region of the Gadarenes,ᵇ two demon-possessed men coming from the tombs met him. They were so vi-

---

ᵃ 17 Isaiah 53:4 (see Septuagint)   ᵇ 28 Some manuscripts *Gergesenes*; other manuscripts *Gerasenes* olent that no one could pass that way. ²⁹"What do you want with us, Son of God?" they shouted. "Have you come here to torture us before the appointed time?"

³⁰Some distance from them a large herd of pigs was feeding. ³¹The demons begged Jesus, "If you drive us out, send us into the herd of pigs."

³²He said to them, "Go!" So they came out and went into the pigs, and the whole herd rushed down the steep bank into the lake and died in the water. ³³Those tending the pigs ran off, went into the town and reported all this, including what had happened to the demon-possessed men. ³⁴Then the whole town went out to meet Jesus. And when they saw him, they pleaded with him to leave their region.

Jesus Forgives and Heals a Paralyzed Man

9 Jesus stepped into a boat, crossed over and came to his own town. ²Some men brought to him a paralyzed man, lying on a mat. When Jesus saw their faith, he said to the man, "Take heart, son; your sins are forgiven."

³At this, some of the teachers of the law said to themselves, "This fellow is blaspheming!"

⁴Knowing their thoughts, Jesus said, "Why do you entertain evil thoughts in your hearts? ⁵Which is easier: to say, 'Your sins are forgiven,' or to say, 'Get up and walk'? ⁶But I want you to know that the Son of Man has authority on earth to forgive sins." So he said to the paralyzed man, "Get up, take your mat and go home." ⁷Then the man got up and went home. ⁸When the crowd saw this, they were filled with awe; and they praised God, who had given such authority to man.

The Calling of Matthew

⁹As Jesus went on from there, he saw a man named Matthew sitting at the tax collector's booth. "Follow me," he told him, and Matthew got up and followed him.

¹⁰While Jesus was having dinner at Matthew's house, many tax collectors and sinners came and ate with him and his disciples. ¹¹When the Pharisees saw this, they asked his disciples, "Why does your teacher eat with tax collectors and sinners?"

¹²On hearing this, Jesus said, "It is not the healthy who need a doctor, but the sick. ¹³But go and learn what this means: 'I desire mercy, not sacrifice.'ᵃ For I have not come to call the righteous, but sinners."

Jesus Questioned About Fasting

¹⁴Then John's disciples came and asked him, "How is it that we and the Pharisees fast often, but your disciples do not fast?"

¹⁵Jesus answered, "How can the guests of the bridegroom mourn while he is with them? The time will come when the bridegroom will be taken from them; then they will fast.

¹⁶"No one sews a patch of unshrunk cloth on an old garment, for the patch will pull away from the garment, making the tear worse. ¹⁷Neither do people pour new wine into old wineskins. If they do, the skins will burst; the wine will run out and the wineskins will be ruined. No, they pour new wine into new wineskins, and both are preserved."

Jesus Raises a Dead Girl and Heals a Sick Woman

¹⁸While he was saying this, a synagogue leader came and knelt before

ᵃ 13 Hosea 6:6

him and said, "My daughter has just died. But come and put your hand on her, and she will live." [19]Jesus got up and went with him, and so did his disciples.

[20]Just then a woman who had been subject to bleeding for twelve years came up behind him and touched the edge of his cloak. [21]She said to herself, "If I only touch his cloak, I will be healed."

[22]Jesus turned and saw her. "Take heart, daughter," he said, "your faith has healed you." And the woman was healed at that moment.

[23]When Jesus entered the synagogue leader's house and saw the noisy crowd and people playing pipes, [24]he said, "Go away. The girl is not dead but asleep." But they laughed at him. [25]After the crowd had been put outside, he went in and took the girl by the hand, and she got up. [26]News of this spread through all that region.

Jesus Heals the Blind and the Mute

[27]As Jesus went on from there, two blind men followed him, calling out, "Have mercy on us, Son of David!"

[28]When he had gone indoors, the blind men came to him, and he asked them, "Do you believe that I am able to do this?"

"Yes, Lord," they replied.

[29]Then he touched their eyes and said, "According to your faith let it be done to you"; [30]and their sight was restored. Jesus warned them sternly, "See that no one knows about this." [31]But they went out and spread the news about him all over that region.

[32]While they were going out, a man who was demon-possessed and could not talk was brought to Jesus. [33]And when the demon was driven out, the man who had been mute spoke. The crowd was amazed and said, "Nothing like this has ever been seen in Israel."

[34]But the Pharisees said, "It is by the prince of demons that he drives out demons."

The Workers Are Few

[35]Jesus went through all the towns and villages, teaching in their synagogues, proclaiming the good news of the kingdom and healing every disease and sickness. [36]When he saw the crowds, he had compassion on them, because they were harassed and helpless, like sheep without a shepherd. [37]Then he said to his disciples, "The harvest is plentiful but the workers are few. [38]Ask the Lord of the harvest, therefore, to send out workers into his harvest field."

Jesus Sends Out the Twelve

10 Jesus called his twelve disciples to him and gave them authority to drive out impure spirits and to heal every disease and sickness.

[2]These are the names of the twelve apostles: first, Simon (who is called Peter) and his brother Andrew; James son of Zebedee, and his brother John; [3]Philip and Bartholomew; Thomas and Matthew the tax collector; James son of Alphaeus, and Thaddaeus; [4]Simon the Zealot and Judas Iscariot, who betrayed him.

[5]These twelve Jesus sent out with the following instructions: "Do not go among the Gentiles or enter any town of the Samaritans. [6]Go rather to the lost sheep of Israel. [7]As you go, proclaim this message: 'The kingdom of heaven has come near.' [8]Heal the sick, raise the dead, cleanse those who have leprosy,[a] drive out demons. Freely you have received; freely give.

---

[a] 8 The Greek word traditionally translated *leprosy* was used for various diseases affecting the skin.

⁹"Do not get any gold or silver or copper to take with you in your belts — ¹⁰no bag for the journey or extra shirt or sandals or a staff, for the worker is worth his keep. ¹¹Whatever town or village you enter, search there for some worthy person and stay at their house until you leave. ¹²As you enter the home, give it your greeting. ¹³If the home is deserving, let your peace rest on it; if it is not, let your peace return to you. ¹⁴If anyone will not welcome you or listen to your words, leave that home or town and shake the dust off your feet. ¹⁵Truly I tell you, it will be more bearable for Sodom and Gomorrah on the day of judgment than for that town.

¹⁶"I am sending you out like sheep among wolves. Therefore be as shrewd as snakes and as innocent as doves. ¹⁷Be on your guard; you will be handed over to the local councils and be flogged in the synagogues. ¹⁸On my account you will be brought before governors and kings as witnesses to them and to the Gentiles. ¹⁹But when they arrest you, do not worry about what to say or how to say it. At that time you will be given what to say, ²⁰for it will not be you speaking, but the Spirit of your Father speaking through you.

²¹"Brother will betray brother to death, and a father his child; children will rebel against their parents and have them put to death. ²²You will be hated by everyone because of me, but the one who stands firm to the end will be saved. ²³When you are persecuted in one place, flee to another. Truly I tell you, you will not finish going through the towns of Israel before the Son of Man comes.

²⁴"The student is not above the teacher, nor a servant above his master. ²⁵It is enough for students to be like their teachers, and servants like their masters. If the head of the house has been called Beelzebul, how much more the members of his household!

²⁶"So do not be afraid of them, for there is nothing concealed that will not be disclosed, or hidden that will not be made known. ²⁷What I tell you in the dark, speak in the daylight; what is whispered in your ear, proclaim from the roofs. ²⁸Do not be afraid of those who kill the body but cannot kill the soul. Rather, be afraid of the One who can destroy both soul and body in hell. ²⁹Are not two sparrows sold for a penny? Yet not one of them will fall to the ground outside your Father's care.ᵃ ³⁰And even the very hairs of your head are all numbered. ³¹So don't be afraid; you are worth more than many sparrows.

³²"Whoever acknowledges me before others, I will also acknowledge before my Father in heaven. ³³But whoever disowns me before others, I will disown before my Father in heaven.

³⁴"Do not suppose that I have come to bring peace to the earth. I did not come to bring peace, but a sword. ³⁵For I have come to turn

"'a man against his father,
        a daughter against her mother,
    a daughter-in-law against her
            mother-in-law —
³⁶   a man's enemies will be the
            members of his own
            household.'ᵇ

³⁷"Anyone who loves their father or mother more than me is not worthy of me; anyone who loves their son or daughter more than me is not worthy of me. ³⁸Whoever does not take up their cross and follow me is

---

ᵃ 29 Or will; or knowledge   ᵇ 36 Micah 7:6

not worthy of me. ³⁹Whoever finds their life will lose it, and whoever loses their life for my sake will find it.

⁴⁰"Anyone who welcomes you welcomes me, and anyone who welcomes me welcomes the one who sent me. ⁴¹Whoever welcomes a prophet as a prophet will receive a prophet's reward, and whoever welcomes a righteous person as a righteous person will receive a righteous person's reward. ⁴²And if anyone gives even a cup of cold water to one of these little ones who is my disciple, truly I tell you, that person will certainly not lose their reward."

Jesus and John the Baptist

11 After Jesus had finished instructing his twelve disciples, he went on from there to teach and preach in the towns of Galilee.ᵃ

²When John, who was in prison, heard about the deeds of the Messiah, he sent his disciples ³to ask him, "Are you the one who is to come, or should we expect someone else?"

⁴Jesus replied, "Go back and report to John what you hear and see: ⁵The blind receive sight, the lame walk, those who have leprosyᵇ are cleansed, the deaf hear, the dead are raised, and the good news is proclaimed to the poor. ⁶Blessed is anyone who does not stumble on account of me."

⁷As John's disciples were leaving, Jesus began to speak to the crowd about John: "What did you go out into the wilderness to see? A reed swayed by the wind? ⁸If not, what did you go out to see? A man dressed in fine clothes? No, those who wear fine clothes are in kings' palaces. ⁹Then what did you go out to see? A prophet? Yes, I tell you, and more than a prophet. ¹⁰This is the one about whom it is written:

" 'I will send my messenger
ahead of you,
who will prepare your way
before you.'ᶜ

¹¹Truly I tell you, among those born of women there has not risen anyone greater than John the Baptist; yet whoever is least in the kingdom of heaven is greater than he. ¹²From the days of John the Baptist until now, the kingdom of heaven has been subjected to violence,ᵈ and violent people have been raiding it. ¹³For all the Prophets and the Law prophesied until John. ¹⁴And if you are willing to accept it, he is the Elijah who was to come. ¹⁵Whoever has ears, let them hear.

¹⁶"To what can I compare this generation? They are like children sitting in the marketplaces and calling out to others:

¹⁷" 'We played the pipe for you,
and you did not dance;
we sang a dirge,
and you did not mourn.'

¹⁸For John came neither eating nor drinking, and they say, 'He has a demon.' ¹⁹The Son of Man came eating and drinking, and they say, 'Here is a glutton and a drunkard, a friend of tax collectors and sinners.' But wisdom is proved right by her deeds."

Woe on Unrepentant Towns

²⁰Then Jesus began to denounce the towns in which most of his miracles had been performed, because they did not repent. ²¹"Woe to you, Chorazin! Woe to you, Bethsaida! For if the miracles that were performed in

---

ᵃ 1 Greek *in their towns*   ᵇ 5 The Greek word traditionally translated *leprosy* was used for various diseases affecting the skin.
ᶜ 10 Mal. 3:1   ᵈ 12 Or *been forcefully advancing*

you had been performed in Tyre and Sidon, they would have repented long ago in sackcloth and ashes. 22But I tell you, it will be more bearable for Tyre and Sidon on the day of judgment than for you. 23And you, Capernaum, will you be lifted to the heavens? No, you will go down to Hades.[a] For if the miracles that were performed in you had been performed in Sodom, it would have remained to this day. 24But I tell you that it will be more bearable for Sodom on the day of judgment than for you."

The Father Revealed in the Son

25At that time Jesus said, "I praise you, Father, Lord of heaven and earth, because you have hidden these things from the wise and learned, and revealed them to little children. 26Yes, Father, for this is what you were pleased to do.

27"All things have been committed to me by my Father. No one knows the Son except the Father, and no one knows the Father except the Son and those to whom the Son chooses to reveal him.

28"Come to me, all you who are weary and burdened, and I will give you rest. 29Take my yoke upon you and learn from me, for I am gentle and humble in heart, and you will find rest for your souls. 30For my yoke is easy and my burden is light."

Jesus Is Lord of the Sabbath

12 At that time Jesus went through the grainfields on the Sabbath. His disciples were hungry and began to pick some heads of grain and eat them. 2When the Pharisees saw this, they said to him, "Look! Your disciples are doing what is unlawful on the Sabbath."

3He answered, "Haven't you read what David did when he and his companions were hungry? 4He entered the house of God, and he and his companions ate the consecrated bread — which was not lawful for them to do, but only for the priests. 5Or haven't you read in the Law that the priests on Sabbath duty in the temple desecrate the Sabbath and yet are innocent? 6I tell you that something greater than the temple is here. 7If you had known what these words mean, 'I desire mercy, not sacrifice,'[b] you would not have condemned the innocent. 8For the Son of Man is Lord of the Sabbath."

9Going on from that place, he went into their synagogue, 10and a man with a shriveled hand was there. Looking for a reason to bring charges against Jesus, they asked him, "Is it lawful to heal on the Sabbath?"

11He said to them, "If any of you has a sheep and it falls into a pit on the Sabbath, will you not take hold of it and lift it out? 12How much more valuable is a person than a sheep! Therefore it is lawful to do good on the Sabbath."

13Then he said to the man, "Stretch out your hand." So he stretched it out and it was completely restored, just as sound as the other. 14But the Pharisees went out and plotted how they might kill Jesus.

God's Chosen Servant

15Aware of this, Jesus withdrew from that place. A large crowd followed him, and he healed all who were ill. 16He warned them not to tell others about him. 17This was to fulfill what was spoken through the prophet Isaiah:

---

[a] 23 That is, the realm of the dead
[b] 7 Hosea 6:6

18 "Here is my servant whom I have
    chosen,
   the one I love, in whom I
       delight;
   I will put my Spirit on him,
       and he will proclaim justice to
       the nations.
19 He will not quarrel or cry out;
   no one will hear his voice in
       the streets.
20 A bruised reed he will not break,
   and a smoldering wick he will
       not snuff out,
   till he has brought justice
       through to victory.
21   In his name the nations will
       put their hope."[a]

Jesus and Beelzebul

22 Then they brought him a demon-possessed man who was blind
and mute, and Jesus healed him, so
that he could both talk and see. 23 All
the people were astonished and said,
"Could this be the Son of David?"

24 But when the Pharisees heard
this, they said, "It is only by Beelzebul, the prince of demons, that this
fellow drives out demons."

25 Jesus knew their thoughts and
said to them, "Every kingdom divided
against itself will be ruined, and every city or household divided against
itself will not stand. 26 If Satan drives
out Satan, he is divided against himself. How then can his kingdom stand?
27 And if I drive out demons by Beelzebul, by whom do your people drive
them out? So then, they will be your
judges. 28 But if it is by the Spirit of
God that I drive out demons, then the
kingdom of God has come upon you.

29 "Or again, how can anyone enter
a strong man's house and carry off
his possessions unless he first ties up
the strong man? Then he can plunder
his house.

30 "Whoever is not with me is
against me, and whoever does not
gather with me scatters. 31 And so I
tell you, every kind of sin and slander can be forgiven, but blasphemy
against the Spirit will not be forgiven.
32 Anyone who speaks a word against
the Son of Man will be forgiven, but
anyone who speaks against the Holy
Spirit will not be forgiven, either in
this age or in the age to come.

33 "Make a tree good and its fruit
will be good, or make a tree bad and
its fruit will be bad, for a tree is recognized by its fruit. 34 You brood of
vipers, how can you who are evil
say anything good? For the mouth
speaks what the heart is full of. 35 A
good man brings good things out of
the good stored up in him, and an evil
man brings evil things out of the evil
stored up in him. 36 But I tell you that
everyone will have to give account on
the day of judgment for every empty
word they have spoken. 37 For by your
words you will be acquitted, and by
your words you will be condemned."

The Sign of Jonah

38 Then some of the Pharisees
and teachers of the law said to him,
"Teacher, we want to see a sign from
you."

39 He answered, "A wicked and adulterous generation asks for a sign! But
none will be given it except the sign
of the prophet Jonah. 40 For as Jonah was
three days and three nights in the belly
of a huge fish, so the Son of Man will
be three days and three nights in the
heart of the earth. 41 The men of Nineveh will stand up at the judgment with
this generation and condemn it; for
they repented at the preaching of Jonah, and now something greater than

[a] 21 Isaiah 42:1-4

Jonah is here. ⁴²The Queen of the South will rise at the judgment with this generation and condemn it; for she came from the ends of the earth to listen to Solomon's wisdom, and now something greater than Solomon is here.

⁴³"When an impure spirit comes out of a person, it goes through arid places seeking rest and does not find it. ⁴⁴Then it says, 'I will return to the house I left.' When it arrives, it finds the house unoccupied, swept clean and put in order. ⁴⁵Then it goes and takes with it seven other spirits more wicked than itself, and they go in and live there. And the final condition of that person is worse than the first. That is how it will be with this wicked generation."

Jesus' Mother and Brothers

⁴⁶While Jesus was still talking to the crowd, his mother and brothers stood outside, wanting to speak to him. ⁴⁷Someone told him, "Your mother and brothers are standing outside, wanting to speak to you."

⁴⁸He replied to him, "Who is my mother, and who are my brothers?" ⁴⁹Pointing to his disciples, he said, "Here are my mother and my brothers. ⁵⁰For whoever does the will of my Father in heaven is my brother and sister and mother."

The Parable of the Sower

13 That same day Jesus went out of the house and sat by the lake. ²Such large crowds gathered around him that he got into a boat and sat in it, while all the people stood on the shore. ³Then he told them many things in parables, saying: "A farmer went out to sow his seed. ⁴As he was scattering the seed, some fell along the path, and the birds came and ate it up. ⁵Some fell on rocky places, where it did not have much soil. It sprang up quickly, because the soil was shallow. ⁶But when the sun came up, the plants were scorched, and they withered because they had no root. ⁷Other seed fell among thorns, which grew up and choked the plants. ⁸Still other seed fell on good soil, where it produced a crop—a hundred, sixty or thirty times what was sown. ⁹Whoever has ears, let them hear."

¹⁰The disciples came to him and asked, "Why do you speak to the people in parables?"

¹¹He replied, "Because the knowledge of the secrets of the kingdom of heaven has been given to you, but not to them. ¹²Whoever has will be given more, and they will have an abundance. Whoever does not have, even what they have will be taken from them. ¹³This is why I speak to them in parables:

"Though seeing, they do not
  see;
  though hearing, they do not
    hear or understand.

¹⁴In them is fulfilled the prophecy of Isaiah:

"'You will be ever hearing but
    never understanding;
  you will be ever seeing but
    never perceiving.
¹⁵ For this people's heart has
    become calloused;
  they hardly hear with their
    ears,
  and they have closed their eyes.
Otherwise they might see with
    their eyes,
  hear with their ears,
  understand with their hearts
and turn, and I would heal
    them.'ᵃ

ᵃ 15 Isaiah 6:9,10 (see Septuagint)

16But blessed are your eyes because they see, and your ears because they hear. 17For truly I tell you, many prophets and righteous people longed to see what you see but did not see it, and to hear what you hear but did not hear it.

18"Listen then to what the parable of the sower means: 19When anyone hears the message about the kingdom and does not understand it, the evil one comes and snatches away what was sown in their heart. This is the seed sown along the path. 20The seed falling on rocky ground refers to someone who hears the word and at once receives it with joy. 21But since they have no root, they last only a short time. When trouble or persecution comes because of the word, they quickly fall away. 22The seed falling among the thorns refers to someone who hears the word, but the worries of this life and the deceitfulness of wealth choke the word, making it unfruitful. 23But the seed falling on good soil refers to someone who hears the word and understands it. This is the one who produces a crop, yielding a hundred, sixty or thirty times what was sown."

The Parable of the Weeds

24Jesus told them another parable: "The kingdom of heaven is like a man who sowed good seed in his field. 25But while everyone was sleeping, his enemy came and sowed weeds among the wheat, and went away. 26When the wheat sprouted and formed heads, then the weeds also appeared.

27"The owner's servants came to him and said, 'Sir, didn't you sow good seed in your field? Where then did the weeds come from?'

28"'An enemy did this,' he replied.

"The servants asked him, 'Do you want us to go and pull them up?'

29"'No,' he answered, 'because while you are pulling the weeds, you may uproot the wheat with them. 30Let both grow together until the harvest. At that time I will tell the harvesters: First collect the weeds and tie them in bundles to be burned; then gather the wheat and bring it into my barn.'"

The Parables of the Mustard Seed and the Yeast

31He told them another parable: "The kingdom of heaven is like a mustard seed, which a man took and planted in his field. 32Though it is the smallest of all seeds, yet when it grows, it is the largest of garden plants and becomes a tree, so that the birds come and perch in its branches."

33He told them still another parable: "The kingdom of heaven is like yeast that a woman took and mixed into about sixty pounds[a] of flour until it worked all through the dough."

34Jesus spoke all these things to the crowd in parables; he did not say anything to them without using a parable. 35So was fulfilled what was spoken through the prophet:

"I will open my mouth in
    parables,
I will utter things hidden
    since the creation of the
    world."[b]

The Parable of the Weeds Explained

36Then he left the crowd and went into the house. His disciples came to him and said, "Explain to us the parable of the weeds in the field."

37He answered, "The one who sowed

---

[a] 33 Or about 27 kilograms   [b] 35 Psalm 78:2

the good seed is the Son of Man. 38The field is the world, and the good seed stands for the people of the kingdom. The weeds are the people of the evil one, 39and the enemy who sows them is the devil. The harvest is the end of the age, and the harvesters are angels.

40"As the weeds are pulled up and burned in the fire, so it will be at the end of the age. 41The Son of Man will send out his angels, and they will weed out of his kingdom everything that causes sin and all who do evil. 42They will throw them into the blazing furnace, where there will be weeping and gnashing of teeth. 43Then the righteous will shine like the sun in the kingdom of their Father. Whoever has ears, let them hear.

The Parables of the Hidden Treasure and the Pearl

44"The kingdom of heaven is like treasure hidden in a field. When a man found it, he hid it again, and then in his joy went and sold all he had and bought that field.

45"Again, the kingdom of heaven is like a merchant looking for fine pearls. 46When he found one of great value, he went away and sold everything he had and bought it.

The Parable of the Net

47"Once again, the kingdom of heaven is like a net that was let down into the lake and caught all kinds of fish. 48When it was full, the fishermen pulled it up on the shore. Then they sat down and collected the good fish in baskets, but threw the bad away. 49This is how it will be at the end of the age. The angels will come and separate the wicked from the righteous 50and throw them into the blazing furnace, where there will be weeping and gnashing of teeth.

51"Have you understood all these things?" Jesus asked.

"Yes," they replied.

52He said to them, "Therefore every teacher of the law who has become a disciple in the kingdom of heaven is like the owner of a house who brings out of his storeroom new treasures as well as old."

A Prophet Without Honor

53When Jesus had finished these parables, he moved on from there. 54Coming to his hometown, he began teaching the people in their synagogue, and they were amazed. "Where did this man get this wisdom and these miraculous powers?" they asked. 55"Isn't this the carpenter's son? Isn't his mother's name Mary, and aren't his brothers James, Joseph, Simon and Judas? 56Aren't all his sisters with us? Where then did this man get all these things?" 57And they took offense at him.

But Jesus said to them, "A prophet is not without honor except in his own town and in his own home."

58And he did not do many miracles there because of their lack of faith.

John the Baptist Beheaded

14 At that time Herod the tetrarch heard the reports about Jesus, 2and he said to his attendants, "This is John the Baptist; he has risen from the dead! That is why miraculous powers are at work in him."

3Now Herod had arrested John and bound him and put him in prison because of Herodias, his brother Philip's wife, 4for John had been saying to him: "It is not lawful for you to have her." 5Herod wanted to kill John, but he was afraid of the people, because they considered John a prophet.

6On Herod's birthday the daughter

of Herodias danced for the guests and pleased Herod so much [7]that he promised with an oath to give her whatever she asked. [8]Prompted by her mother, she said, "Give me here on a platter the head of John the Baptist." [9]The king was distressed, but because of his oaths and his dinner guests, he ordered that her request be granted [10]and had John beheaded in the prison. [11]His head was brought in on a platter and given to the girl, who carried it to her mother. [12]John's disciples came and took his body and buried it. Then they went and told Jesus.

Jesus Feeds the Five Thousand

[13]When Jesus heard what had happened, he withdrew by boat privately to a solitary place. Hearing of this, the crowds followed him on foot from the towns. [14]When Jesus landed and saw a large crowd, he had compassion on them and healed their sick.

[15]As evening approached, the disciples came to him and said, "This is a remote place, and it's already getting late. Send the crowds away, so they can go to the villages and buy themselves some food."

[16]Jesus replied, "They do not need to go away. You give them something to eat."

[17]"We have here only five loaves of bread and two fish," they answered.

[18]"Bring them here to me," he said. [19]And he directed the people to sit down on the grass. Taking the five loaves and the two fish and looking up to heaven, he gave thanks and broke the loaves. Then he gave them to the disciples, and the disciples gave them to the people. [20]They all ate and were satisfied, and the disciples picked up twelve basketfuls of broken pieces that were left over. [21]The number of those who ate was about five thousand men, besides women and children.

Jesus Walks on the Water

[22]Immediately Jesus made the disciples get into the boat and go on ahead of him to the other side, while he dismissed the crowd. [23]After he had dismissed them, he went up on a mountainside by himself to pray. Later that night, he was there alone, [24]and the boat was already a considerable distance from land, buffeted by the waves because the wind was against it.

[25]Shortly before dawn Jesus went out to them, walking on the lake. [26]When the disciples saw him walking on the lake, they were terrified. "It's a ghost," they said, and cried out in fear.

[27]But Jesus immediately said to them: "Take courage! It is I. Don't be afraid."

[28]"Lord, if it's you," Peter replied, "tell me to come to you on the water."

[29]"Come," he said.

Then Peter got down out of the boat, walked on the water and came toward Jesus. [30]But when he saw the wind, he was afraid and, beginning to sink, cried out, "Lord, save me!"

[31]Immediately Jesus reached out his hand and caught him. "You of little faith," he said, "why did you doubt?"

[32]And when they climbed into the boat, the wind died down. [33]Then those who were in the boat worshiped him, saying, "Truly you are the Son of God."

[34]When they had crossed over, they landed at Gennesaret. [35]And when the men of that place recognized Jesus, they sent word to all the surrounding country. People brought all their sick to him [36]and begged him to let the

sick just touch the edge of his cloak, and all who touched it were healed.

That Which Defiles

15 Then some Pharisees and teachers of the law came to Jesus from Jerusalem and asked, ²"Why do your disciples break the tradition of the elders? They don't wash their hands before they eat!"

³Jesus replied, "And why do you break the command of God for the sake of your tradition? ⁴For God said, 'Honor your father and mother'ᵃ and 'Anyone who curses their father or mother is to be put to death.'ᵇ ⁵But you say that if anyone declares that what might have been used to help their father or mother is 'devoted to God,' ⁶they are not to 'honor their father or mother' with it. Thus you nullify the word of God for the sake of your tradition. ⁷You hypocrites! Isaiah was right when he prophesied about you:

⁸ "'These people honor me with
     their lips,
  but their hearts are far from
     me.
⁹ They worship me in vain;
  their teachings are merely
     human rules.'ᶜ"

¹⁰Jesus called the crowd to him and said, "Listen and understand. ¹¹What goes into someone's mouth does not defile them, but what comes out of their mouth, that is what defiles them."

¹²Then the disciples came to him and asked, "Do you know that the Pharisees were offended when they heard this?"

¹³He replied, "Every plant that my heavenly Father has not planted will be pulled up by the roots. ¹⁴Leave them; they are blind guides.ᵈ If the blind lead the blind, both will fall into a pit."

¹⁵Peter said, "Explain the parable to us."

¹⁶"Are you still so dull?" Jesus asked them. ¹⁷"Don't you see that whatever enters the mouth goes into the stomach and then out of the body? ¹⁸But the things that come out of a person's mouth come from the heart, and these defile them. ¹⁹For out of the heart come evil thoughts — murder, adultery, sexual immorality, theft, false testimony, slander. ²⁰These are what defile a person; but eating with unwashed hands does not defile them."

The Faith of a Canaanite Woman

²¹Leaving that place, Jesus withdrew to the region of Tyre and Sidon. ²²A Canaanite woman from that vicinity came to him, crying out, "Lord, Son of David, have mercy on me! My daughter is demon-possessed and suffering terribly."

²³Jesus did not answer a word. So his disciples came to him and urged him, "Send her away, for she keeps crying out after us."

²⁴He answered, "I was sent only to the lost sheep of Israel."

²⁵The woman came and knelt before him. "Lord, help me!" she said.

²⁶He replied, "It is not right to take the children's bread and toss it to the dogs."

²⁷"Yes it is, Lord," she said. "Even the dogs eat the crumbs that fall from their master's table."

²⁸Then Jesus said to her, "Woman, you have great faith! Your request is granted." And her daughter was healed at that moment.

ᵃ 4 Exodus 20:12; Deut. 5:16   ᵇ 4 Exodus 21:17;
Lev. 20:9   ᶜ 9 Isaiah 29:13   ᵈ 14 Some
manuscripts *blind guides of the blind*

Jesus Feeds the Four Thousand

29Jesus left there and went along the Sea of Galilee. Then he went up on a mountainside and sat down. 30Great crowds came to him, bringing the lame, the blind, the crippled, the mute and many others, and laid them at his feet; and he healed them. 31The people were amazed when they saw the mute speaking, the crippled made well, the lame walking and the blind seeing. And they praised the God of Israel.

32Jesus called his disciples to him and said, "I have compassion for these people; they have already been with me three days and have nothing to eat. I do not want to send them away hungry, or they may collapse on the way."

33His disciples answered, "Where could we get enough bread in this remote place to feed such a crowd?"

34"How many loaves do you have?" Jesus asked.

"Seven," they replied, "and a few small fish."

35He told the crowd to sit down on the ground. 36Then he took the seven loaves and the fish, and when he had given thanks, he broke them and gave them to the disciples, and they in turn to the people. 37They all ate and were satisfied. Afterward the disciples picked up seven basketfuls of broken pieces that were left over. 38The number of those who ate was four thousand men, besides women and children. 39After Jesus had sent the crowd away, he got into the boat and went to the vicinity of Magadan.

The Demand for a Sign

16 The Pharisees and Sadducees came to Jesus and tested him by asking him to show them a sign from heaven.

2He replied, "When evening comes, you say, 'It will be fair weather, for the sky is red,' 3and in the morning, 'Today it will be stormy, for the sky is red and overcast.' You know how to interpret the appearance of the sky, but you cannot interpret the signs of the times.ᵃ 4A wicked and adulterous generation looks for a sign, but none will be given it except the sign of Jonah." Jesus then left them and went away.

The Yeast of the Pharisees and Sadducees

5When they went across the lake, the disciples forgot to take bread. 6"Be careful," Jesus said to them. "Be on your guard against the yeast of the Pharisees and Sadducees."

7They discussed this among themselves and said, "It is because we didn't bring any bread."

8Aware of their discussion, Jesus asked, "You of little faith, why are you talking among yourselves about having no bread? 9Do you still not understand? Don't you remember the five loaves for the five thousand, and how many basketfuls you gathered? 10Or the seven loaves for the four thousand, and how many basketfuls you gathered? 11How is it you don't understand that I was not talking to you about bread? But be on your guard against the yeast of the Pharisees and Sadducees." 12Then they understood that he was not telling them to guard against the yeast used in bread, but against the teaching of the Pharisees and Sadducees.

Peter Declares That Jesus Is the Messiah

13When Jesus came to the region of Caesarea Philippi, he asked his dis-

---

ᵃ 2,3 Some early manuscripts do not have *When evening comes . . . of the times.*

ciples, "Who do people say the Son of Man is?"

¹⁴They replied, "Some say John the Baptist; others say Elijah; and still others, Jeremiah or one of the prophets."

¹⁵"But what about you?" he asked. "Who do you say I am?"

¹⁶Simon Peter answered, "You are the Messiah, the Son of the living God."

¹⁷Jesus replied, "Blessed are you, Simon son of Jonah, for this was not revealed to you by flesh and blood, but by my Father in heaven. ¹⁸And I tell you that you are Peter,ᵃ and on this rock I will build my church, and the gates of Hadesᵇ will not overcome it. ¹⁹I will give you the keys of the kingdom of heaven; whatever you bind on earth will beᶜ bound in heaven, and whatever you loose on earth will beᶜ loosed in heaven." ²⁰Then he ordered his disciples not to tell anyone that he was the Messiah.

Jesus Predicts His Death

²¹From that time on Jesus began to explain to his disciples that he must go to Jerusalem and suffer many things at the hands of the elders, the chief priests and the teachers of the law, and that he must be killed and on the third day be raised to life.

²²Peter took him aside and began to rebuke him. "Never, Lord!" he said. "This shall never happen to you!"

²³Jesus turned and said to Peter, "Get behind me, Satan! You are a stumbling block to me; you do not have in mind the concerns of God, but merely human concerns."

²⁴Then Jesus said to his disciples, "Whoever wants to be my disciple must deny themselves and take up their cross and follow me. ²⁵For whoever wants to save their lifeᵈ will lose

it, but whoever loses their life for me will find it. ²⁶What good will it be for someone to gain the whole world, yet forfeit their soul? Or what can anyone give in exchange for their soul? ²⁷For the Son of Man is going to come in his Father's glory with his angels, and then he will reward each person according to what they have done.

²⁸"Truly I tell you, some who are standing here will not taste death before they see the Son of Man coming in his kingdom."

The Transfiguration

17 After six days Jesus took with him Peter, James and John the brother of James, and led them up a high mountain by themselves. ²There he was transfigured before them. His face shone like the sun, and his clothes became as white as the light. ³Just then there appeared before them Moses and Elijah, talking with Jesus.

⁴Peter said to Jesus, "Lord, it is good for us to be here. If you wish, I will put up three shelters — one for you, one for Moses and one for Elijah."

⁵While he was still speaking, a bright cloud covered them, and a voice from the cloud said, "This is my Son, whom I love; with him I am well pleased. Listen to him!"

⁶When the disciples heard this, they fell facedown to the ground, terrified. ⁷But Jesus came and touched them. "Get up," he said. "Don't be afraid." ⁸When they looked up, they saw no one except Jesus.

⁹As they were coming down the mountain, Jesus instructed them, "Don't tell anyone what you have

ᵃ 18 The Greek word for *Peter* means *rock*.
ᵇ 18 That is, the realm of the dead   ᶜ 19 Or *will have been*   ᵈ 25 The Greek word means either *life* or *soul*; also in verse 26.

seen, until the Son of Man has been raised from the dead."

¹⁰The disciples asked him, "Why then do the teachers of the law say that Elijah must come first?"

¹¹Jesus replied, "To be sure, Elijah comes and will restore all things. ¹²But I tell you, Elijah has already come, and they did not recognize him, but have done to him everything they wished. In the same way the Son of Man is going to suffer at their hands." ¹³Then the disciples understood that he was talking to them about John the Baptist.

Jesus Heals a Demon-Possessed Boy

¹⁴When they came to the crowd, a man approached Jesus and knelt before him. ¹⁵"Lord, have mercy on my son," he said. "He has seizures and is suffering greatly. He often falls into the fire or into the water. ¹⁶I brought him to your disciples, but they could not heal him."

¹⁷"You unbelieving and perverse generation," Jesus replied, "how long shall I stay with you? How long shall I put up with you? Bring the boy here to me." ¹⁸Jesus rebuked the demon, and it came out of the boy, and he was healed at that moment.

¹⁹Then the disciples came to Jesus in private and asked, "Why couldn't we drive it out?"

²⁰He replied, "Because you have so little faith. Truly I tell you, if you have faith as small as a mustard seed, you can say to this mountain, 'Move from here to there,' and it will move. Nothing will be impossible for you." [21]ᵃ

Jesus Predicts His Death a Second Time

²²When they came together in Galilee, he said to them, "The Son of Man is going to be delivered into the hands of men. ²³They will kill him, and on the third day he will be raised to life." And the disciples were filled with grief.

The Temple Tax

²⁴After Jesus and his disciples arrived in Capernaum, the collectors of the two-drachma temple tax came to Peter and asked, "Doesn't your teacher pay the temple tax?"

²⁵"Yes, he does," he replied.

When Peter came into the house, Jesus was the first to speak. "What do you think, Simon?" he asked. "From whom do the kings of the earth collect duty and taxes — from their own children or from others?"

²⁶"From others," Peter answered.

"Then the children are exempt," Jesus said to him. ²⁷"But so that we may not cause offense, go to the lake and throw out your line. Take the first fish you catch; open its mouth and you will find a four-drachma coin. Take it and give it to them for my tax and yours."

The Greatest in the Kingdom of Heaven

18 At that time the disciples came to Jesus and asked, "Who, then, is the greatest in the kingdom of heaven?"

²He called a little child to him, and placed the child among them. ³And he said: "Truly I tell you, unless you change and become like little children, you will never enter the kingdom of heaven. ⁴Therefore, whoever takes the lowly position of this child is the greatest in the kingdom of heaven. ⁵And whoever welcomes one such child in my name welcomes me.

ᵃ 21 Some manuscripts include here words similar to Mark 9:29.

Causing to Stumble

6"If anyone causes one of these little ones — those who believe in me — to stumble, it would be better for them to have a large millstone hung around their neck and to be drowned in the depths of the sea. 7Woe to the world because of the things that cause people to stumble! Such things must come, but woe to the person through whom they come! 8If your hand or your foot causes you to stumble, cut it off and throw it away. It is better for you to enter life maimed or crippled than to have two hands or two feet and be thrown into eternal fire. 9And if your eye causes you to stumble, gouge it out and throw it away. It is better for you to enter life with one eye than to have two eyes and be thrown into the fire of hell.

The Parable of the Wandering Sheep

10"See that you do not despise one of these little ones. For I tell you that their angels in heaven always see the face of my Father in heaven. [11]ª

12"What do you think? If a man owns a hundred sheep, and one of them wanders away, will he not leave the ninety-nine on the hills and go to look for the one that wandered off? 13And if he finds it, truly I tell you, he is happier about that one sheep than about the ninety-nine that did not wander off. 14In the same way your Father in heaven is not willing that any of these little ones should perish.

Dealing With Sin in the Church

15"If your brother or sisterᵇ sinsᶜ go and point out their fault, just between the two of you. If they listen to you, you have won them over. 16But if they will not listen, take one or two oth-

ers along, so that 'every matter may be established by the testimony of two or three witnesses.'ᵈ 17If they still refuse to listen, tell it to the church; and if they refuse to listen even to the church, treat them as you would a pagan or a tax collector.

18"Truly I tell you, whatever you bind on earth will beᵉ bound in heaven, and whatever you loose on earth will beᵉ loosed in heaven.

19"Again, truly I tell you that if two of you on earth agree about anything they ask for, it will be done for them by my Father in heaven. 20For where two or three gather in my name, there am I with them."

The Parable of the Unmerciful Servant

21Then Peter came to Jesus and asked, "Lord, how many times shall I forgive my brother or sister who sins against me? Up to seven times?"

22Jesus answered, "I tell you, not seven times, but seventy-seven times.ᶠ

23"Therefore, the kingdom of heaven is like a king who wanted to settle accounts with his servants. 24As he began the settlement, a man who owed him ten thousand bags of goldᵍ was brought to him. 25Since he was not able to pay, the master ordered that he and his wife and his children and all that he had be sold to repay the debt.

26"At this the servant fell on his knees before him. 'Be patient with me,' he begged, 'and I will pay back

---

ᵉ 11 Some manuscripts include here the words of Luke 19:10.   ᵇ 15 The Greek word for *brother or sister* (*adelphos*) refers here to a fellow disciple, whether man or woman; also in verses 21 and 35.   ᶜ 15 Some manuscripts *sins against you*   ᵈ 16 Deut. 19:15   ᵉ 18 Or *will have been*   ᶠ 22 Or *seventy times seven*   ᵍ 24 Greek *ten thousand talents*; a talent was worth about 20 years of a day laborer's wages.

everything.' 27The servant's master took pity on him, canceled the debt and let him go.

28"But when that servant went out, he found one of his fellow servants who owed him a hundred silver coins.ᵍ He grabbed him and began to choke him. 'Pay back what you owe me!' he demanded.

29"His fellow servant fell to his knees and begged him, 'Be patient with me, and I will pay it back.'

30"But he refused. Instead, he went off and had the man thrown into prison until he could pay the debt. 31When the other servants saw what had happened, they were outraged and went and told their master everything that had happened.

32"Then the master called the servant in. 'You wicked servant,' he said, 'I canceled all that debt of yours because you begged me to. 33Shouldn't you have had mercy on your fellow servant just as I had on you?' 34In anger his master handed him over to the jailers to be tortured, until he should pay back all he owed.

35"This is how my heavenly Father will treat each of you unless you forgive your brother or sister from your heart."

Divorce

19 When Jesus had finished saying these things, he left Galilee and went into the region of Judea to the other side of the Jordan. 2Large crowds followed him, and he healed them there.

3Some Pharisees came to him to test him. They asked, "Is it lawful for a man to divorce his wife for any and every reason?"

4"Haven't you read," he replied, "that at the beginning the Creator 'made them male and female,'ʰ 5and said, 'For this reason a man will leave his father and mother and be united to his wife, and the two will become one flesh'ⁱ? 6So they are no longer two, but one flesh. Therefore what God has joined together, let no one separate."

7"Why then," they asked, "did Moses command that a man give his wife a certificate of divorce and send her away?"

8Jesus replied, "Moses permitted you to divorce your wives because your hearts were hard. But it was not this way from the beginning. 9I tell you that anyone who divorces his wife, except for sexual immorality, and marries another woman commits adultery."

10The disciples said to him, "If this is the situation between a husband and wife, it is better not to marry."

11Jesus replied, "Not everyone can accept this word, but only those to whom it has been given. 12For there are eunuchs who were born that way, and there are eunuchs who have been made eunuchs by others — and there are those who choose to live like eunuchs for the sake of the kingdom of heaven. The one who can accept this should accept it."

The Little Children and Jesus

13Then people brought little children to Jesus for him to place his hands on them and pray for them. But the disciples rebuked them.

14Jesus said, "Let the little children come to me, and do not hinder them, for the kingdom of heaven belongs to such as these." 15When he had placed his hands on them, he went on from there.

ᵍ 28 Greek *a hundred denarii*; a denarius was the usual daily wage of a day laborer (see 20:2).   ʰ 4 Gen. 1:27   ⁱ 5 Gen. 2:24

The Rich and the Kingdom of God

16 Just then a man came up to Jesus and asked, "Teacher, what good thing must I do to get eternal life?"

17 "Why do you ask me about what is good?" Jesus replied. "There is only One who is good. If you want to enter life, keep the commandments."

18 "Which ones?" he inquired.

Jesus replied, " 'You shall not murder, you shall not commit adultery, you shall not steal, you shall not give false testimony, 19 honor your father and mother,'[a] and 'love your neighbor as yourself.'[b]"

20 "All these I have kept," the young man said. "What do I still lack?"

21 Jesus answered, "If you want to be perfect, go, sell your possessions and give to the poor, and you will have treasure in heaven. Then come, follow me."

22 When the young man heard this, he went away sad, because he had great wealth.

23 Then Jesus said to his disciples, "Truly I tell you, it is hard for someone who is rich to enter the kingdom of heaven. 24 Again I tell you, it is easier for a camel to go through the eye of a needle than for someone who is rich to enter the kingdom of God."

25 When the disciples heard this, they were greatly astonished and asked, "Who then can be saved?"

26 Jesus looked at them and said, "With man this is impossible, but with God all things are possible."

27 Peter answered him, "We have left everything to follow you! What then will there be for us?"

28 Jesus said to them, "Truly I tell you, at the renewal of all things, when the Son of Man sits on his glorious throne, you who have followed me will also sit on twelve thrones, judging the twelve tribes of Israel. 29 And everyone who has left houses or brothers or sisters or father or mother or wife[c] or children or fields for my sake will receive a hundred times as much and will inherit eternal life. 30 But many who are first will be last, and many who are last will be first.

The Parable of the Workers in the Vineyard

20 "For the kingdom of heaven is like a landowner who went out early in the morning to hire workers for his vineyard. 2 He agreed to pay them a denarius[d] for the day and sent them into his vineyard.

3 "About nine in the morning he went out and saw others standing in the marketplace doing nothing. 4 He told them, 'You also go and work in my vineyard, and I will pay you whatever is right.' 5 So they went.

"He went out again about noon and about three in the afternoon and did the same thing. 6 About five in the afternoon he went out and found still others standing around. He asked them, 'Why have you been standing here all day long doing nothing?'

7 " 'Because no one has hired us,' they answered.

"He said to them, 'You also go and work in my vineyard.'

8 "When evening came, the owner of the vineyard said to his foreman, 'Call the workers and pay them their wages, beginning with the last ones hired and going on to the first.'

9 "The workers who were hired about five in the afternoon came and each received a denarius. 10 So when those came who were hired first, they expected to

---

a 19 Exodus 20:12-16; Deut. 5:16-20
b 19 Lev. 19:18   c 29 Some manuscripts do not have *or wife*.   d 2 A denarius was the usual daily wage of a day laborer.

receive more. But each one of them also received a denarius. ¹¹When they received it, they began to grumble against the landowner. ¹²'These who were hired last worked only one hour,' they said, 'and you have made them equal to us who have borne the burden of the work and the heat of the day.'

¹³"But he answered one of them, 'I am not being unfair to you, friend. Didn't you agree to work for a denarius? ¹⁴Take your pay and go. I want to give the one who was hired last the same as I gave you. ¹⁵Don't I have the right to do what I want with my own money? Or are you envious because I am generous?'

¹⁶"So the last will be first, and the first will be last."

Jesus Predicts His Death a Third Time

¹⁷Now Jesus was going up to Jerusalem. On the way, he took the Twelve aside and said to them, ¹⁸"We are going up to Jerusalem, and the Son of Man will be delivered over to the chief priests and the teachers of the law. They will condemn him to death ¹⁹and will hand him over to the Gentiles to be mocked and flogged and crucified. On the third day he will be raised to life!"

A Mother's Request

²⁰Then the mother of Zebedee's sons came to Jesus with her sons and, kneeling down, asked a favor of him.

²¹"What is it you want?" he asked.

She said, "Grant that one of these two sons of mine may sit at your right and the other at your left in your kingdom."

²²"You don't know what you are asking," Jesus said to them. "Can you drink the cup I am going to drink?"

"We can," they answered.

²³Jesus said to them, "You will indeed drink from my cup, but to sit at my right or left is not for me to grant. These places belong to those for whom they have been prepared by my Father."

²⁴When the ten heard about this, they were indignant with the two brothers. ²⁵Jesus called them together and said, "You know that the rulers of the Gentiles lord it over them, and their high officials exercise authority over them. ²⁶Not so with you. Instead, whoever wants to become great among you must be your servant, ²⁷and whoever wants to be first must be your slave — ²⁸just as the Son of Man did not come to be served, but to serve, and to give his life as a ransom for many."

Two Blind Men Receive Sight

²⁹As Jesus and his disciples were leaving Jericho, a large crowd followed him. ³⁰Two blind men were sitting by the roadside, and when they heard that Jesus was going by, they shouted, "Lord, Son of David, have mercy on us!"

³¹The crowd rebuked them and told them to be quiet, but they shouted all the louder, "Lord, Son of David, have mercy on us!"

³²Jesus stopped and called them. "What do you want me to do for you?" he asked.

³³"Lord," they answered, "we want our sight."

³⁴Jesus had compassion on them and touched their eyes. Immediately they received their sight and followed him.

Jesus Comes to Jerusalem as King

21 As they approached Jerusalem and came to Bethphage on the Mount of Olives, Jesus sent two disciples, ²saying to them, "Go to the village ahead of you, and at once you will find a donkey tied there, with her colt by her. Untie them and bring them to me. ³If anyone says anything to you, say that the Lord needs them, and he will send them right away."

⁴This took place to fulfill what was spoken through the prophet:

⁵ "Say to Daughter Zion,
    'See, your king comes to you,
        gentle and riding on a donkey,
        and on a colt, the foal of a
            donkey.'"ᵃ

⁶The disciples went and did as Jesus had instructed them. ⁷They brought the donkey and the colt and placed their cloaks on them for Jesus to sit on. ⁸A very large crowd spread their cloaks on the road, while others cut branches from the trees and spread them on the road. ⁹The crowds that went ahead of him and those that followed shouted,

"Hosannaᵇ to the Son of David!"

"Blessed is he who comes in the name of the Lord!"ᶜ

"Hosannaᵇ in the highest heaven!"

¹⁰When Jesus entered Jerusalem, the whole city was stirred and asked, "Who is this?"

¹¹The crowds answered, "This is Jesus, the prophet from Nazareth in Galilee."

Jesus at the Temple

¹²Jesus entered the temple courts and drove out all who were buying and selling there. He overturned the tables of the money changers and the benches of those selling doves. ¹³"It is written," he said to them, "'My house will be called a house of prayer,'ᵈ but you are making it 'a den of robbers.'ᵉ"

¹⁴The blind and the lame came to him at the temple, and he healed them. ¹⁵But when the chief priests and the teachers of the law saw the wonderful things he did and the children shouting in the temple courts, "Hosanna to the Son of David," they were indignant.

¹⁶"Do you hear what these children are saying?" they asked him.

"Yes," replied Jesus, "have you never read,

"'From the lips of children and
        infants
    you, Lord, have called forth
        your praise'ᶠ?"

¹⁷And he left them and went out of the city to Bethany, where he spent the night.

Jesus Curses a Fig Tree

¹⁸Early in the morning, as Jesus was on his way back to the city, he was hungry. ¹⁹Seeing a fig tree by the road, he went up to it but found nothing on it except leaves. Then he said to it, "May you never bear fruit again!" Immediately the tree withered.

²⁰When the disciples saw this, they were amazed. "How did the fig tree wither so quickly?" they asked.

²¹Jesus replied, "Truly I tell you, if you have faith and do not doubt, not only can you do what was done to the fig tree, but also you can say to this mountain, 'Go, throw yourself into the sea,' and it will be done. ²²If you believe, you will receive whatever you ask for in prayer."

ᵃ 5 Zech. 9:9   ᵇ 9 A Hebrew expression meaning "Save!" which became an exclamation of praise; also in verse 15   ᶜ 9 Psalm 118:25,26   ᵈ 13 Isaiah 56:7   ᵉ 13 Jer. 7:11   ᶠ 16 Psalm 8:2 (see Septuagint)

The Authority of Jesus Questioned

23 Jesus entered the temple courts, and, while he was teaching, the chief priests and the elders of the people came to him. "By what authority are you doing these things?" they asked. "And who gave you this authority?"

24 Jesus replied, "I will also ask you one question. If you answer me, I will tell you by what authority I am doing these things. 25 John's baptism — where did it come from? Was it from heaven, or of human origin?"

They discussed it among themselves and said, "If we say, 'From heaven,' he will ask, 'Then why didn't you believe him?' 26 But if we say, 'Of human origin' — we are afraid of the people, for they all hold that John was a prophet."

27 So they answered Jesus, "We don't know."

Then he said, "Neither will I tell you by what authority I am doing these things.

The Parable of the Two Sons

28 "What do you think? There was a man who had two sons. He went to the first and said, 'Son, go and work today in the vineyard.'

29 "'I will not,' he answered, but later he changed his mind and went.

30 "Then the father went to the other son and said the same thing. He answered, 'I will, sir,' but he did not go.

31 "Which of the two did what his father wanted?"

"The first," they answered.

Jesus said to them, "Truly I tell you, the tax collectors and the prostitutes are entering the kingdom of God ahead of you. 32 For John came to you to show you the way of righteousness, and you did not believe him, but the tax collectors and the prostitutes did. And even after you saw this, you did not repent and believe him.

The Parable of the Tenants

33 "Listen to another parable: There was a landowner who planted a vineyard. He put a wall around it, dug a winepress in it and built a watchtower. Then he rented the vineyard to some farmers and moved to another place. 34 When the harvest time approached, he sent his servants to the tenants to collect his fruit.

35 "The tenants seized his servants; they beat one, killed another, and stoned a third. 36 Then he sent other servants to them, more than the first time, and the tenants treated them the same way. 37 Last of all, he sent his son to them. 'They will respect my son,' he said.

38 "But when the tenants saw the son, they said to each other, 'This is the heir. Come, let's kill him and take his inheritance.' 39 So they took him and threw him out of the vineyard and killed him.

40 "Therefore, when the owner of the vineyard comes, what will he do to those tenants?"

41 "He will bring those wretches to a wretched end," they replied, "and he will rent the vineyard to other tenants, who will give him his share of the crop at harvest time."

42 Jesus said to them, "Have you never read in the Scriptures:

"'The stone the builders rejected
    has become the cornerstone;
the Lord has done this,
    and it is marvelous in our
        eyes'[a]?

43 "Therefore I tell you that the kingdom of God will be taken away from

---

[a] 42 Psalm 118:22,23

you and given to a people who will produce its fruit. ⁴⁴Anyone who falls on this stone will be broken to pieces; anyone on whom it falls will be crushed."ᵃ

⁴⁵When the chief priests and the Pharisees heard Jesus' parables, they knew he was talking about them. ⁴⁶They looked for a way to arrest him, but they were afraid of the crowd because the people held that he was a prophet.

The Parable of the Wedding Banquet

22 Jesus spoke to them again in parables, saying: ²"The kingdom of heaven is like a king who prepared a wedding banquet for his son. ³He sent his servants to those who had been invited to the banquet to tell them to come, but they refused to come.

⁴"Then he sent some more servants and said, 'Tell those who have been invited that I have prepared my dinner: My oxen and fattened cattle have been butchered, and everything is ready. Come to the wedding banquet.'

⁵"But they paid no attention and went off — one to his field, another to his business. ⁶The rest seized his servants, mistreated them and killed them. ⁷The king was enraged. He sent his army and destroyed those murderers and burned their city.

⁸"Then he said to his servants, 'The wedding banquet is ready, but those I invited did not deserve to come. ⁹So go to the street corners and invite to the banquet anyone you find.' ¹⁰So the servants went out into the streets and gathered all the people they could find, the bad as well as the good, and the wedding hall was filled with guests.

¹¹"But when the king came in to see the guests, he noticed a man there who was not wearing wedding clothes. ¹²He asked, 'How did you get in here without wedding clothes, friend?' The man was speechless.

¹³"Then the king told the attendants, 'Tie him hand and foot, and throw him outside, into the darkness, where there will be weeping and gnashing of teeth.'

¹⁴"For many are invited, but few are chosen."

Paying the Imperial Tax to Caesar

¹⁵Then the Pharisees went out and laid plans to trap him in his words. ¹⁶They sent their disciples to him along with the Herodians. "Teacher," they said, "we know that you are a man of integrity and that you teach the way of God in accordance with the truth. You aren't swayed by others, because you pay no attention to who they are. ¹⁷Tell us then, what is your opinion? Is it right to pay the imperial taxᵇ to Caesar or not?"

¹⁸But Jesus, knowing their evil intent, said, "You hypocrites, why are you trying to trap me? ¹⁹Show me the coin used for paying the tax." They brought him a denarius, ²⁰and he asked them, "Whose image is this? And whose inscription?"

²¹"Caesar's," they replied.

Then he said to them, "So give back to Caesar what is Caesar's, and to God what is God's."

²²When they heard this, they were amazed. So they left him and went away.

Marriage at the Resurrection

²³That same day the Sadducees, who say there is no resurrection,

---

ᵃ 44 Some manuscripts do not have verse 44.
ᵇ 17 A special tax levied on subject peoples, not on Roman citizens

came to him with a question. ²⁴"Teacher," they said, "Moses told us that if a man dies without having children, his brother must marry the widow and raise up offspring for him. ²⁵Now there were seven brothers among us. The first one married and died, and since he had no children, he left his wife to his brother. ²⁶The same thing happened to the second and third brother, right on down to the seventh. ²⁷Finally, the woman died. ²⁸Now then, at the resurrection, whose wife will she be of the seven, since all of them were married to her?"

²⁹Jesus replied, "You are in error because you do not know the Scriptures or the power of God. ³⁰At the resurrection people will neither marry nor be given in marriage; they will be like the angels in heaven. ³¹But about the resurrection of the dead — have you not read what God said to you, ³²'I am the God of Abraham, the God of Isaac, and the God of Jacob'ᵃ? He is not the God of the dead but of the living."

³³When the crowds heard this, they were astonished at his teaching.

The Greatest Commandment

³⁴Hearing that Jesus had silenced the Sadducees, the Pharisees got together. ³⁵One of them, an expert in the law, tested him with this question: ³⁶"Teacher, which is the greatest commandment in the Law?"

³⁷Jesus replied: "'Love the Lord your God with all your heart and with all your soul and with all your mind.'ᵇ ³⁸This is the first and greatest commandment. ³⁹And the second is like it: 'Love your neighbor as yourself.'ᶜ ⁴⁰All the Law and the Prophets hang on these two commandments."

Whose Son Is the Messiah?

⁴¹While the Pharisees were gathered together, Jesus asked them, ⁴²"What do you think about the Messiah? Whose son is he?"

"The son of David," they replied.

⁴³He said to them, "How is it then that David, speaking by the Spirit, calls him 'Lord'? For he says,

⁴⁴ " 'The Lord said to my Lord:
  "Sit at my right hand
until I put your enemies
  under your feet." 'ᵈ

⁴⁵If then David calls him 'Lord,' how can he be his son?" ⁴⁶No one could say a word in reply, and from that day on no one dared to ask him any more questions.

A Warning Against Hypocrisy

23 Then Jesus said to the crowds and to his disciples: ²"The teachers of the law and the Pharisees sit in Moses' seat. ³So you must be careful to do everything they tell you. But do not do what they do, for they do not practice what they preach. ⁴They tie up heavy, cumbersome loads and put them on other people's shoulders, but they themselves are not willing to lift a finger to move them.

⁵"Everything they do is done for people to see: They make their phylacteriesᵉ wide and the tassels on their garments long; ⁶they love the place of honor at banquets and the most important seats in the synagogues; ⁷they love to be greeted with respect in the marketplaces and to be called 'Rabbi' by others.

⁸"But you are not to be called 'Rabbi,' for you have one Teacher, and you

---

ᵃ 32 Exodus 3:6   ᵇ 37 Deut. 6:5   ᶜ 39 Lev. 19:18   ᵈ 44 Psalm 110:1   ᵉ 5 That is, boxes containing Scripture verses, worn on forehead and arm are all brothers. 9And do not call anyone on earth 'father,' for you have one Father, and he is in heaven. 10Nor are you to be called instructors, for you have one Instructor, the Messiah. 11The greatest among you will be your servant. 12For those who exalt themselves will be humbled, and those who humble themselves will be exalted.

Seven Woes on the Teachers of the Law and the Pharisees

13"Woe to you, teachers of the law and Pharisees, you hypocrites! You shut the door of the kingdom of heaven in people's faces. You yourselves do not enter, nor will you let those enter who are trying to. [14] *a*

15"Woe to you, teachers of the law and Pharisees, you hypocrites! You travel over land and sea to win a single convert, and when you have succeeded, you make them twice as much a child of hell as you are.

16"Woe to you, blind guides! You say, 'If anyone swears by the temple, it means nothing; but anyone who swears by the gold of the temple is bound by that oath.' 17You blind fools! Which is greater: the gold, or the temple that makes the gold sacred? 18You also say, 'If anyone swears by the altar, it means nothing; but anyone who swears by the gift on the altar is bound by that oath.' 19You blind men! Which is greater: the gift, or the altar that makes the gift sacred? 20Therefore, anyone who swears by the altar swears by it and by everything on it. 21And anyone who swears by the temple swears by it and by the one who dwells in it. 22And anyone who swears by heaven swears by God's throne and by the one who sits on it.

23"Woe to you, teachers of the law and Pharisees, you hypocrites! You

give a tenth of your spices — mint, dill and cumin. But you have neglected the more important matters of the law — justice, mercy and faithfulness. You should have practiced the latter, without neglecting the former. 24You blind guides! You strain out a gnat but swallow a camel.

25"Woe to you, teachers of the law and Pharisees, you hypocrites! You clean the outside of the cup and dish, but inside they are full of greed and self-indulgence. 26Blind Pharisee! First clean the inside of the cup and dish, and then the outside also will be clean.

27"Woe to you, teachers of the law and Pharisees, you hypocrites! You are like whitewashed tombs, which look beautiful on the outside but on the inside are full of the bones of the dead and everything unclean. 28In the same way, on the outside you appear to people as righteous but on the inside you are full of hypocrisy and wickedness.

29"Woe to you, teachers of the law and Pharisees, you hypocrites! You build tombs for the prophets and decorate the graves of the righteous. 30And you say, 'If we had lived in the days of our ancestors, we would not have taken part with them in shedding the blood of the prophets.' 31So you testify against yourselves that you are the descendants of those who murdered the prophets. 32Go ahead, then, and complete what your ancestors started!

33"You snakes! You brood of vipers! How will you escape being condemned to hell? 34Therefore I am sending you prophets and sages and teachers. Some of them you will kill and crucify; others you will flog

a 14 Some manuscripts include here words similar to Mark 12:40 and Luke 20:47.

in your synagogues and pursue from town to town. ³⁵And so upon you will come all the righteous blood that has been shed on earth, from the blood of righteous Abel to the blood of Zechariah son of Berekiah, whom you murdered between the temple and the altar. ³⁶Truly I tell you, all this will come on this generation.

³⁷"Jerusalem, Jerusalem, you who kill the prophets and stone those sent to you, how often I have longed to gather your children together, as a hen gathers her chicks under her wings, and you were not willing. ³⁸Look, your house is left to you desolate. ³⁹For I tell you, you will not see me again until you say, 'Blessed is he who comes in the name of the Lord.'ᵃ"

The Destruction of the Temple and Signs of the End Times

24 Jesus left the temple and was walking away when his disciples came up to him to call his attention to its buildings. ²"Do you see all these things?" he asked. "Truly I tell you, not one stone here will be left on another; every one will be thrown down."

³As Jesus was sitting on the Mount of Olives, the disciples came to him privately. "Tell us," they said, "when will this happen, and what will be the sign of your coming and of the end of the age?"

⁴Jesus answered: "Watch out that no one deceives you. ⁵For many will come in my name, claiming, 'I am the Messiah,' and will deceive many. ⁶You will hear of wars and rumors of wars, but see to it that you are not alarmed. Such things must happen, but the end is still to come. ⁷Nation will rise against nation, and kingdom against kingdom. There will be

famines and earthquakes in various places. ⁸All these are the beginning of birth pains.

⁹"Then you will be handed over to be persecuted and put to death, and you will be hated by all nations because of me. ¹⁰At that time many will turn away from the faith and will betray and hate each other, ¹¹and many false prophets will appear and deceive many people. ¹²Because of the increase of wickedness, the love of most will grow cold, ¹³but the one who stands firm to the end will be saved. ¹⁴And this gospel of the kingdom will be preached in the whole world as a testimony to all nations, and then the end will come.

¹⁵"So when you see standing in the holy place 'the abomination that causes desolation,'ᵇ spoken of through the prophet Daniel — let the reader understand — ¹⁶then let those who are in Judea flee to the mountains. ¹⁷Let no one on the housetop go down to take anything out of the house. ¹⁸Let no one in the field go back to get their cloak. ¹⁹How dreadful it will be in those days for pregnant women and nursing mothers! ²⁰Pray that your flight will not take place in winter or on the Sabbath. ²¹For then there will be great distress, unequaled from the beginning of the world until now — and never to be equaled again.

²²"If those days had not been cut short, no one would survive, but for the sake of the elect those days will be shortened. ²³At that time if anyone says to you, 'Look, here is the Messiah!' or, 'There he is!' do not believe it. ²⁴For false messiahs and false prophets will appear and perform great signs and wonders to

ᵃ 39 Psalm 118:26   ᵇ 15 Daniel 9:27; 11:31; 12:11

deceive, if possible, even the elect. ²⁵See, I have told you ahead of time.

²⁶"So if anyone tells you, 'There he is, out in the wilderness,' do not go out; or, 'Here he is, in the inner rooms,' do not believe it. ²⁷For as lightning that comes from the east is visible even in the west, so will be the coming of the Son of Man. ²⁸Wherever there is a carcass, there the vultures will gather.

²⁹"Immediately after the distress of those days

" 'the sun will be darkened,
    and the moon will not give its
        light;
the stars will fall from the sky,
    and the heavenly bodies will
        be shaken.'^a

³⁰"Then will appear the sign of the Son of Man in heaven. And then all the peoples of the earth^b will mourn when they see the Son of Man coming on the clouds of heaven, with power and great glory.^c ³¹And he will send his angels with a loud trumpet call, and they will gather his elect from the four winds, from one end of the heavens to the other.

³²"Now learn this lesson from the fig tree: As soon as its twigs get tender and its leaves come out, you know that summer is near. ³³Even so, when you see all these things, you know that it^d is near, right at the door. ³⁴Truly I tell you, this generation will certainly not pass away until all these things have happened. ³⁵Heaven and earth will pass away, but my words will never pass away.

The Day and Hour Unknown

³⁶"But about that day or hour no one knows, not even the angels in heaven, nor the Son,^e but only the Father. ³⁷As it was in the days of Noah, so it will be at the coming of the Son of Man. ³⁸For

in the days before the flood, people were eating and drinking, marrying and giving in marriage, up to the day Noah entered the ark; ³⁹and they knew nothing about what would happen until the flood came and took them all away. That is how it will be at the coming of the Son of Man. ⁴⁰Two men will be in the field; one will be taken and the other left. ⁴¹Two women will be grinding with a hand mill; one will be taken and the other left.

⁴²"Therefore keep watch, because you do not know on what day your Lord will come. ⁴³But understand this: If the owner of the house had known at what time of night the thief was coming, he would have kept watch and would not have let his house be broken into. ⁴⁴So you also must be ready, because the Son of Man will come at an hour when you do not expect him.

⁴⁵"Who then is the faithful and wise servant, whom the master has put in charge of the servants in his household to give them their food at the proper time? ⁴⁶It will be good for that servant whose master finds him doing so when he returns. ⁴⁷Truly I tell you, he will put him in charge of all his possessions. ⁴⁸But suppose that servant is wicked and says to himself, 'My master is staying away a long time,' ⁴⁹and he then begins to beat his fellow servants and to eat and drink with drunkards. ⁵⁰The master of that servant will come on a day when he does not expect him and at an hour he is not aware of. ⁵¹He will cut him to pieces and assign him a place with the hypocrites, where there will be weeping and gnashing of teeth.

---

^a 29 Isaiah 13:10; 34:4   ^b 30 Or the tribes of the land   ^c 30 See Daniel 7:13-14.   ^d 33 Or he   ^e 36 Some manuscripts do not have nor the Son.

The Parable of the Ten Virgins

25 "At that time the kingdom of heaven will be like ten virgins who took their lamps and went out to meet the bridegroom. ²Five of them were foolish and five were wise. ³The foolish ones took their lamps but did not take any oil with them. ⁴The wise ones, however, took oil in jars along with their lamps. ⁵The bridegroom was a long time in coming, and they all became drowsy and fell asleep.

⁶"At midnight the cry rang out: 'Here's the bridegroom! Come out to meet him!'

⁷"Then all the virgins woke up and trimmed their lamps. ⁸The foolish ones said to the wise, 'Give us some of your oil; our lamps are going out.'

⁹" 'No,' they replied, 'there may not be enough for both us and you. Instead, go to those who sell oil and buy some for yourselves.'

¹⁰"But while they were on their way to buy the oil, the bridegroom arrived. The virgins who were ready went in with him to the wedding banquet. And the door was shut.

¹¹"Later the others also came. 'Lord, Lord,' they said, 'open the door for us!'

¹²"But he replied, 'Truly I tell you, I don't know you.'

¹³"Therefore keep watch, because you do not know the day or the hour.

The Parable of the Bags of Gold

¹⁴"Again, it will be like a man going on a journey, who called his servants and entrusted his wealth to them. ¹⁵To one he gave five bags of gold, to another two bags, and to another one bag,ᵉ each according to his ability. Then he went on his journey. ¹⁶The man who had received five bags of gold went at once and put his money to work and gained five bags more.

¹⁷So also, the one with two bags of gold gained two more. ¹⁸But the man who had received one bag went off, dug a hole in the ground and hid his master's money.

¹⁹"After a long time the master of those servants returned and settled accounts with them. ²⁰The man who had received five bags of gold brought the other five. 'Master,' he said, 'you entrusted me with five bags of gold. See, I have gained five more.'

²¹"His master replied, 'Well done, good and faithful servant! You have been faithful with a few things; I will put you in charge of many things. Come and share your master's happiness!'

²²"The man with two bags of gold also came. 'Master,' he said, 'you entrusted me with two bags of gold; see, I have gained two more.'

²³"His master replied, 'Well done, good and faithful servant! You have been faithful with a few things; I will put you in charge of many things. Come and share your master's happiness!'

²⁴"Then the man who had received one bag of gold came. 'Master,' he said, 'I knew that you are a hard man, harvesting where you have not sown and gathering where you have not scattered seed. ²⁵So I was afraid and went out and hid your gold in the ground. See, here is what belongs to you.'

²⁶"His master replied, 'You wicked, lazy servant! So you knew that I harvest where I have not sown and gather where I have not scattered seed? ²⁷Well then, you should have put my money on deposit with the bankers,

---

ᵉ 15 Greek *five talents . . . two talents . . . one talent*; also throughout this parable; a talent was worth about 20 years of a day laborer's wage.

so that when I returned I would have received it back with interest.

28 "'So take the bag of gold from him and give it to the one who has ten bags. 29For whoever has will be given more, and they will have an abundance. Whoever does not have, even what they have will be taken from them. 30And throw that worthless servant outside, into the darkness, where there will be weeping and gnashing of teeth.'

The Sheep and the Goats

31"When the Son of Man comes in his glory, and all the angels with him, he will sit on his glorious throne. 32All the nations will be gathered before him, and he will separate the people one from another as a shepherd separates the sheep from the goats. 33He will put the sheep on his right and the goats on his left.

34"Then the King will say to those on his right, 'Come, you who are blessed by my Father; take your inheritance, the kingdom prepared for you since the creation of the world. 35For I was hungry and you gave me something to eat, I was thirsty and you gave me something to drink, I was a stranger and you invited me in, 36I needed clothes and you clothed me, I was sick and you looked after me, I was in prison and you came to visit me.'

37"Then the righteous will answer him, 'Lord, when did we see you hungry and feed you, or thirsty and give you something to drink? 38When did we see you a stranger and invite you in, or needing clothes and clothe you? 39When did we see you sick or in prison and go to visit you?'

40"The King will reply, 'Truly I tell you, whatever you did for one of the least of these brothers and sisters of mine, you did for me.'

41"Then he will say to those on his left, 'Depart from me, you who are cursed, into the eternal fire prepared for the devil and his angels. 42For I was hungry and you gave me nothing to eat, I was thirsty and you gave me nothing to drink, 43I was a stranger and you did not invite me in, I needed clothes and you did not clothe me, I was sick and in prison and you did not look after me.'

44"They also will answer, 'Lord, when did we see you hungry or thirsty or a stranger or needing clothes or sick or in prison, and did not help you?'

45"He will reply, 'Truly I tell you, whatever you did not do for one of the least of these, you did not do for me.'

46"Then they will go away to eternal punishment, but the righteous to eternal life."

The Plot Against Jesus

26 When Jesus had finished saying all these things, he said to his disciples, 2"As you know, the Passover is two days away — and the Son of Man will be handed over to be crucified."

3Then the chief priests and the elders of the people assembled in the palace of the high priest, whose name was Caiaphas, 4and they schemed to arrest Jesus secretly and kill him. 5"But not during the festival," they said, "or there may be a riot among the people."

Jesus Anointed at Bethany

6While Jesus was in Bethany in the home of Simon the Leper, 7a woman came to him with an alabaster jar of very expensive perfume, which she poured on his head as he was reclining at the table.

8When the disciples saw this, they

were indignant. "Why this waste?" they asked. 9"This perfume could have been sold at a high price and the money given to the poor."

10Aware of this, Jesus said to them, "Why are you bothering this woman? She has done a beautiful thing to me. 11The poor you will always have with you,ᵃ but you will not always have me. 12When she poured this perfume on my body, she did it to prepare me for burial. 13Truly I tell you, wherever this gospel is preached throughout the world, what she has done will also be told, in memory of her."

Judas Agrees to Betray Jesus

14Then one of the Twelve — the one called Judas Iscariot — went to the chief priests 15and asked, "What are you willing to give me if I deliver him over to you?" So they counted out for him thirty pieces of silver. 16From then on Judas watched for an opportunity to hand him over.

The Last Supper

17On the first day of the Festival of Unleavened Bread, the disciples came to Jesus and asked, "Where do you want us to make preparations for you to eat the Passover?"

18He replied, "Go into the city to a certain man and tell him, 'The Teacher says: My appointed time is near. I am going to celebrate the Passover with my disciples at your house.'" 19So the disciples did as Jesus had directed them and prepared the Passover.

20When evening came, Jesus was reclining at the table with the Twelve. 21And while they were eating, he said, "Truly I tell you, one of you will betray me."

22They were very sad and began to say to him one after the other, "Surely you don't mean me, Lord?"

23Jesus replied, "The one who has dipped his hand into the bowl with me will betray me. 24The Son of Man will go just as it is written about him. But woe to that man who betrays the Son of Man! It would be better for him if he had not been born."

25Then Judas, the one who would betray him, said, "Surely you don't mean me, Rabbi?"

Jesus answered, "You have said so."

26While they were eating, Jesus took bread, and when he had given thanks, he broke it and gave it to his disciples, saying, "Take and eat; this is my body."

27Then he took a cup, and when he had given thanks, he gave it to them, saying, "Drink from it, all of you. 28This is my blood of theᵇ covenant, which is poured out for many for the forgiveness of sins. 29I tell you, I will not drink from this fruit of the vine from now on until that day when I drink it new with you in my Father's kingdom."

30When they had sung a hymn, they went out to the Mount of Olives.

Jesus Predicts Peter's Denial

31Then Jesus told them, "This very night you will all fall away on account of me, for it is written:

" 'I will strike the shepherd,
     and the sheep of the flock will
        be scattered.'ᶜ

32But after I have risen, I will go ahead of you into Galilee."

33Peter replied, "Even if all fall away on account of you, I never will."

34"Truly I tell you," Jesus answered, "this very night, before the rooster crows, you will disown me three times."

ᵃ 11 See Deut. 15:11.   ᵇ 28 Some manuscripts the new   ᶜ 31 Zech. 13:7

35But Peter declared, "Even if I have to die with you, I will never disown you." And all the other disciples said the same.

Gethsemane

36Then Jesus went with his disciples to a place called Gethsemane, and he said to them, "Sit here while I go over there and pray." 37He took Peter and the two sons of Zebedee along with him, and he began to be sorrowful and troubled. 38Then he said to them, "My soul is overwhelmed with sorrow to the point of death. Stay here and keep watch with me."

39Going a little farther, he fell with his face to the ground and prayed, "My Father, if it is possible, may this cup be taken from me. Yet not as I will, but as you will."

40Then he returned to his disciples and found them sleeping. "Couldn't you men keep watch with me for one hour?" he asked Peter. 41"Watch and pray so that you will not fall into temptation. The spirit is willing, but the flesh is weak."

42He went away a second time and prayed, "My Father, if it is not possible for this cup to be taken away unless I drink it, may your will be done."

43When he came back, he again found them sleeping, because their eyes were heavy. 44So he left them and went away once more and prayed the third time, saying the same thing.

45Then he returned to the disciples and said to them, "Are you still sleeping and resting? Look, the hour has come, and the Son of Man is delivered into the hands of sinners. 46Rise! Let us go! Here comes my betrayer!"

Jesus Arrested

47While he was still speaking, Judas, one of the Twelve, arrived. With him was a large crowd armed with swords and clubs, sent from the chief priests and the elders of the people. 48Now the betrayer had arranged a signal with them: "The one I kiss is the man; arrest him." 49Going at once to Jesus, Judas said, "Greetings, Rabbi!" and kissed him.

50Jesus replied, "Do what you came for, friend."[a]

Then the men stepped forward, seized Jesus and arrested him. 51With that, one of Jesus' companions reached for his sword, drew it out and struck the servant of the high priest, cutting off his ear.

52"Put your sword back in its place," Jesus said to him, "for all who draw the sword will die by the sword. 53Do you think I cannot call on my Father, and he will at once put at my disposal more than twelve legions of angels? 54But how then would the Scriptures be fulfilled that say it must happen in this way?"

55In that hour Jesus said to the crowd, "Am I leading a rebellion, that you have come out with swords and clubs to capture me? Every day I sat in the temple courts teaching, and you did not arrest me. 56But this has all taken place that the writings of the prophets might be fulfilled." Then all the disciples deserted him and fled.

Jesus Before the Sanhedrin

57Those who had arrested Jesus took him to Caiaphas the high priest, where the teachers of the law and the elders had assembled. 58But Peter followed him at a distance, right up to the courtyard of the high priest. He entered and sat down with the guards to see the outcome.

59The chief priests and the whole

---

a 50 Or "Why have you come, friend?"

Sanhedrin were looking for false evidence against Jesus so that they could put him to death. [60]But they did not find any, though many false witnesses came forward.

Finally two came forward [61]and declared, "This fellow said, 'I am able to destroy the temple of God and rebuild it in three days.'"

[62]Then the high priest stood up and said to Jesus, "Are you not going to answer? What is this testimony that these men are bringing against you?" [63]But Jesus remained silent.

The high priest said to him, "I charge you under oath by the living God: Tell us if you are the Messiah, the Son of God."

[64]"You have said so," Jesus replied. "But I say to all of you: From now on you will see the Son of Man sitting at the right hand of the Mighty One and coming on the clouds of heaven."[c]

[65]Then the high priest tore his clothes and said, "He has spoken blasphemy! Why do we need any more witnesses? Look, now you have heard the blasphemy. [66]What do you think?"

"He is worthy of death," they answered.

[67]Then they spit in his face and struck him with their fists. Others slapped him [68]and said, "Prophesy to us, Messiah. Who hit you?"

Peter Disowns Jesus

[69]Now Peter was sitting out in the courtyard, and a servant girl came to him. "You also were with Jesus of Galilee," she said.

[70]But he denied it before them all. "I don't know what you're talking about," he said.

[71]Then he went out to the gateway, where another servant girl saw him and said to the people there, "This fellow was with Jesus of Nazareth."

[72]He denied it again, with an oath: "I don't know the man!"

[73]After a little while, those standing there went up to Peter and said, "Surely you are one of them; your accent gives you away."

[74]Then he began to call down curses, and he swore to them, "I don't know the man!"

Immediately a rooster crowed. [75]Then Peter remembered the word Jesus had spoken: "Before the rooster crows, you will disown me three times." And he went outside and wept bitterly.

Judas Hangs Himself

27 Early in the morning, all the chief priests and the elders of the people made their plans how to have Jesus executed. [2]So they bound him, led him away and handed him over to Pilate the governor.

[3]When Judas, who had betrayed him, saw that Jesus was condemned, he was seized with remorse and returned the thirty pieces of silver to the chief priests and the elders. [4]"I have sinned," he said, "for I have betrayed innocent blood."

"What is that to us?" they replied. "That's your responsibility."

[5]So Judas threw the money into the temple and left. Then he went away and hanged himself.

[6]The chief priests picked up the coins and said, "It is against the law to put this into the treasury, since it is blood money." [7]So they decided to use the money to buy the potter's field as a burial place for foreigners. [8]That is why it has been called the Field of Blood to this day. [9]Then what was spoken by Jeremiah the prophet was fulfilled: "They took the thirty

---

[c] 64 See Psalm 110:1; Daniel 7:13.

pieces of silver, the price set on him by the people of Israel, [10] and they used them to buy the potter's field, as the Lord commanded me."[a]

Jesus Before Pilate

[11] Meanwhile Jesus stood before the governor, and the governor asked him, "Are you the king of the Jews?"

"You have said so," Jesus replied.

[12] When he was accused by the chief priests and the elders, he gave no answer. [13] Then Pilate asked him, "Don't you hear the testimony they are bringing against you?" [14] But Jesus made no reply, not even to a single charge — to the great amazement of the governor.

[15] Now it was the governor's custom at the festival to release a prisoner chosen by the crowd. [16] At that time they had a well-known prisoner whose name was Jesus[b] Barabbas. [17] So when the crowd had gathered, Pilate asked them, "Which one do you want me to release to you: Jesus Barabbas, or Jesus who is called the Messiah?" [18] For he knew it was out of self-interest that they had handed Jesus over to him.

[19] While Pilate was sitting on the judge's seat, his wife sent him this message: "Don't have anything to do with that innocent man, for I have suffered a great deal today in a dream because of him."

[20] But the chief priests and the elders persuaded the crowd to ask for Barabbas and to have Jesus executed.

[21] "Which of the two do you want me to release to you?" asked the governor.

"Barabbas," they answered.

[22] "What shall I do, then, with Jesus who is called the Messiah?" Pilate asked.

They all answered, "Crucify him!"

[23] "Why? What crime has he committed?" asked Pilate.

But they shouted all the louder, "Crucify him!"

[24] When Pilate saw that he was getting nowhere, but that instead an uproar was starting, he took water and washed his hands in front of the crowd. "I am innocent of this man's blood," he said. "It is your responsibility!"

[25] All the people answered, "His blood is on us and on our children!"

[26] Then he released Barabbas to them. But he had Jesus flogged, and handed him over to be crucified.

The Soldiers Mock Jesus

[27] Then the governor's soldiers took Jesus into the Praetorium and gathered the whole company of soldiers around him. [28] They stripped him and put a scarlet robe on him, [29] and then twisted together a crown of thorns and set it on his head. They put a staff in his right hand. Then they knelt in front of him and mocked him. "Hail, king of the Jews!" they said. [30] They spit on him, and took the staff and struck him on the head again and again. [31] After they had mocked him, they took off the robe and put his own clothes on him. Then they led him away to crucify him.

The Crucifixion of Jesus

[32] As they were going out, they met a man from Cyrene, named Simon, and they forced him to carry the cross. [33] They came to a place called Golgotha (which means "the place of the skull"). [34] There they offered Jesus wine to drink, mixed with gall; but after tasting it, he refused to drink

---

[a] 10 See Zech. 11:12,13; Jer. 19:1-13; 32:6-9.
[b] 16 Many manuscripts do not have *Jesus*; also in verse 17.

it. 35When they had crucified him, they divided up his clothes by casting lots. 36And sitting down, they kept watch over him there. 37Above his head they placed the written charge against him: THIS IS JESUS, THE KING OF THE JEWS.

38Two rebels were crucified with him, one on his right and one on his left. 39Those who passed by hurled insults at him, shaking their heads 40and saying, "You who are going to destroy the temple and build it in three days, save yourself! Come down from the cross, if you are the Son of God!" 41In the same way the chief priests, the teachers of the law and the elders mocked him. 42"He saved others," they said, "but he can't save himself! He's the king of Israel! Let him come down now from the cross, and we will believe in him. 43He trusts in God. Let God rescue him now if he wants him, for he said, 'I am the Son of God.'" 44In the same way the rebels who were crucified with him also heaped insults on him.

The Death of Jesus

45From noon until three in the afternoon darkness came over all the land. 46About three in the afternoon Jesus cried out in a loud voice, *"Eli, Eli,[a] lema sabachthani?"* (which means "My God, my God, why have you forsaken me?").[b]

47When some of those standing there heard this, they said, "He's calling Elijah."

48Immediately one of them ran and got a sponge. He filled it with wine vinegar, put it on a staff, and offered it to Jesus to drink. 49The rest said, "Now leave him alone. Let's see if Elijah comes to save him."

50And when Jesus had cried out again in a loud voice, he gave up his spirit.

51At that moment the curtain of the temple was torn in two from top to bottom. The earth shook, the rocks split 52and the tombs broke open. The bodies of many holy people who had died were raised to life. 53They came out of the tombs after Jesus' resurrection and[c] went into the holy city and appeared to many people.

54When the centurion and those with him who were guarding Jesus saw the earthquake and all that had happened, they were terrified, and exclaimed, "Surely he was the Son of God!"

55Many women were there, watching from a distance. They had followed Jesus from Galilee to care for his needs. 56Among them were Mary Magdalene, Mary the mother of James and Joseph,[d] and the mother of Zebedee's sons.

The Burial of Jesus

57As evening approached, there came a rich man from Arimathea, named Joseph, who had himself become a disciple of Jesus. 58Going to Pilate, he asked for Jesus' body, and Pilate ordered that it be given to him. 59Joseph took the body, wrapped it in a clean linen cloth, 60and placed it in his own new tomb that he had cut out of the rock. He rolled a big stone in front of the entrance to the tomb and went away. 61Mary Magdalene and the other Mary were sitting there opposite the tomb.

The Guard at the Tomb

62The next day, the one after Preparation Day, the chief priests and the Pharisees went to Pilate. 63"Sir,"

---

[a] 46 Some manuscripts *Eloi, Eloi*   [b] 46 Psalm 22:1   [c] 53 Or *tombs, and after Jesus' resurrection they*   [d] 56 Greek *Joses,* a variant of *Joseph*

they said, "we remember that while he was still alive that deceiver said, 'After three days I will rise again.' [64]So give the order for the tomb to be made secure until the third day. Otherwise, his disciples may come and steal the body and tell the people that he has been raised from the dead. This last deception will be worse than the first."

[65]"Take a guard," Pilate answered. "Go, make the tomb as secure as you know how." [66]So they went and made the tomb secure by putting a seal on the stone and posting the guard.

Jesus Has Risen

28 After the Sabbath, at dawn on the first day of the week, Mary Magdalene and the other Mary went to look at the tomb.

[2]There was a violent earthquake, for an angel of the Lord came down from heaven and, going to the tomb, rolled back the stone and sat on it. [3]His appearance was like lightning, and his clothes were white as snow. [4]The guards were so afraid of him that they shook and became like dead men.

[5]The angel said to the women, "Do not be afraid, for I know that you are looking for Jesus, who was crucified. [6]He is not here; he has risen, just as he said. Come and see the place where he lay. [7]Then go quickly and tell his disciples: 'He has risen from the dead and is going ahead of you into Galilee. There you will see him.' Now I have told you."

[8]So the women hurried away from the tomb, afraid yet filled with joy, and ran to tell his disciples. [9]Suddenly Jesus met them. "Greetings," he said. They came to him, clasped his feet and worshiped him. [10]Then Jesus said to them, "Do not be afraid. Go and tell my brothers to go to Galilee; there they will see me."

The Guards' Report

[11]While the women were on their way, some of the guards went into the city and reported to the chief priests everything that had happened. [12]When the chief priests had met with the elders and devised a plan, they gave the soldiers a large sum of money, [13]telling them, "You are to say, 'His disciples came during the night and stole him away while we were asleep.' [14]If this report gets to the governor, we will satisfy him and keep you out of trouble." [15]So the soldiers took the money and did as they were instructed. And this story has been widely circulated among the Jews to this very day.

The Great Commission

[16]Then the eleven disciples went to Galilee, to the mountain where Jesus had told them to go. [17]When they saw him, they worshiped him; but some doubted. [18]Then Jesus came to them and said, "All authority in heaven and on earth has been given to me. [19]Therefore go and make disciples of all nations, baptizing them in the name of the Father and of the Son and of the Holy Spirit, [20]and teaching them to obey everything I have commanded you. And surely I am with you always, to the very end of the age."

Mark

John the Baptist Prepares the Way

1 The beginning of the good news about Jesus the Messiah,[a] the Son of God,[b] 2as it is written in Isaiah the prophet:

"I will send my messenger ahead of you,
who will prepare your way"[c] —
3 "a voice of one calling in the wilderness,
'Prepare the way for the Lord,
make straight paths for him.'"[d]

4And so John the Baptist appeared in the wilderness, preaching a baptism of repentance for the forgiveness of sins. 5The whole Judean countryside and all the people of Jerusalem went out to him. Confessing their sins, they were baptized by him in the Jordan River. 6John wore clothing made of camel's hair, with a leather belt around his waist, and he ate locusts and wild honey. 7And this was his message: "After me comes the one more powerful than I, the straps of whose sandals I am not worthy to stoop down and untie. 8I baptize you with[e] water, but he will baptize you with[e] the Holy Spirit."

The Baptism and Testing of Jesus

9At that time Jesus came from Nazareth in Galilee and was baptized by John in the Jordan. 10Just as Jesus was coming up out of the water, he saw heaven being torn open and the Spirit descending on him like a dove. 11And a voice came from heaven: "You are my Son, whom I love; with you I am well pleased."

12At once the Spirit sent him out into the wilderness, 13and he was in the wilderness forty days, being tempted[f] by Satan. He was with the wild animals, and angels attended him.

Jesus Announces the Good News

14After John was put in prison, Jesus went into Galilee, proclaiming the good news of God. 15"The time has come," he said. "The kingdom of God has come near. Repent and believe the good news!"

Jesus Calls His First Disciples

16As Jesus walked beside the Sea of Galilee, he saw Simon and his brother Andrew casting a net into the lake, for they were fishermen. 17"Come, follow me," Jesus said, "and I will send you out to fish for people." 18At once they left their nets and followed him.

19When he had gone a little farther, he saw James son of Zebedee and his brother John in a boat, preparing their nets. 20Without delay he called them, and they left their father Zebedee in the boat with the hired men and followed him.

Jesus Drives Out an Impure Spirit

21They went to Capernaum, and when the Sabbath came, Jesus went

---

into the synagogue and began to teach. [22]The people were amazed at his teaching, because he taught them as one who had authority, not as the teachers of the law. [23]Just then a man in their synagogue who was possessed by an impure spirit cried out, [24]"What do you want with us, Jesus of Nazareth? Have you come to destroy us? I know who you are — the Holy One of God!"

[25]"Be quiet!" said Jesus sternly. "Come out of him!" [26]The impure spirit shook the man violently and came out of him with a shriek.

[27]The people were all so amazed that they asked each other, "What is this? A new teaching — and with authority! He even gives orders to impure spirits and they obey him." [28]News about him spread quickly over the whole region of Galilee.

Jesus Heals Many

[29]As soon as they left the synagogue, they went with James and John to the home of Simon and Andrew. [30]Simon's mother-in-law was in bed with a fever, and they immediately told Jesus about her. [31]So he went to her, took her hand and helped her up. The fever left her and she began to wait on them.

[32]That evening after sunset the people brought to Jesus all the sick and demon-possessed. [33]The whole town gathered at the door, [34]and Jesus healed many who had various diseases. He also drove out many demons, but he would not let the demons speak because they knew who he was.

Jesus Prays in a Solitary Place

[35]Very early in the morning, while it was still dark, Jesus got up, left the house and went off to a solitary place, where he prayed. [36]Simon and his companions went to look for him, [37]and when they found him, they exclaimed: "Everyone is looking for you!"

[38]Jesus replied, "Let us go somewhere else — to the nearby villages — so I can preach there also. That is why I have come." [39]So he traveled throughout Galilee, preaching in their synagogues and driving out demons.

Jesus Heals a Man With Leprosy

[40]A man with leprosy[a] came to him and begged him on his knees, "If you are willing, you can make me clean."

[41]Jesus was indignant.[b] He reached out his hand and touched the man. "I am willing," he said. "Be clean!" [42]Immediately the leprosy left him and he was cleansed.

[43]Jesus sent him away at once with a strong warning: [44]"See that you don't tell this to anyone. But go, show yourself to the priest and offer the sacrifices that Moses commanded for your cleansing, as a testimony to them." [45]Instead he went out and began to talk freely, spreading the news. As a result, Jesus could no longer enter a town openly but stayed outside in lonely places. Yet the people still came to him from everywhere.

Jesus Forgives and Heals a Paralyzed Man

2 A few days later, when Jesus again entered Capernaum, the people heard that he had come home. [2]They gathered in such large numbers that there was no room left, not even outside the door, and he preached the

---

[a] 40 The Greek word traditionally translated *leprosy* was used for various diseases affecting the skin. [b] 41 Many manuscripts *Jesus was filled with compassion*

word to them. ³Some men came, bringing to him a paralyzed man, carried by four of them. ⁴Since they could not get him to Jesus because of the crowd, they made an opening in the roof above Jesus by digging through it and then lowered the mat the man was lying on. ⁵When Jesus saw their faith, he said to the paralyzed man, "Son, your sins are forgiven."

⁶Now some teachers of the law were sitting there, thinking to themselves, ⁷"Why does this fellow talk like that? He's blaspheming! Who can forgive sins but God alone?"

⁸Immediately Jesus knew in his spirit that this was what they were thinking in their hearts, and he said to them, "Why are you thinking these things? ⁹Which is easier: to say to this paralyzed man, 'Your sins are forgiven,' or to say, 'Get up, take your mat and walk'? ¹⁰But I want you to know that the Son of Man has authority on earth to forgive sins." So he said to the man, ¹¹"I tell you, get up, take your mat and go home." ¹²He got up, took his mat and walked out in full view of them all. This amazed everyone and they praised God, saying, "We have never seen anything like this!"

Jesus Calls Levi and Eats With Sinners

¹³Once again Jesus went out beside the lake. A large crowd came to him, and he began to teach them. ¹⁴As he walked along, he saw Levi son of Alphaeus sitting at the tax collector's booth. "Follow me," Jesus told him, and Levi got up and followed him.

¹⁵While Jesus was having dinner at Levi's house, many tax collectors and sinners were eating with him and his disciples, for there were many who followed him. ¹⁶When the teachers of the law who were Pharisees saw him eating with the sinners and tax collectors, they asked his disciples: "Why does he eat with tax collectors and sinners?"

¹⁷On hearing this, Jesus said to them, "It is not the healthy who need a doctor, but the sick. I have not come to call the righteous, but sinners."

Jesus Questioned About Fasting

¹⁸Now John's disciples and the Pharisees were fasting. Some people came and asked Jesus, "How is it that John's disciples and the disciples of the Pharisees are fasting, but yours are not?"

¹⁹Jesus answered, "How can the guests of the bridegroom fast while he is with them? They cannot, so long as they have him with them. ²⁰But the time will come when the bridegroom will be taken from them, and on that day they will fast.

²¹"No one sews a patch of unshrunk cloth on an old garment. Otherwise, the new piece will pull away from the old, making the tear worse. ²²And no one pours new wine into old wineskins. Otherwise, the wine will burst the skins, and both the wine and the wineskins will be ruined. No, they pour new wine into new wineskins."

Jesus Is Lord of the Sabbath

²³One Sabbath Jesus was going through the grainfields, and as his disciples walked along, they began to pick some heads of grain. ²⁴The Pharisees said to him, "Look, why are they doing what is unlawful on the Sabbath?"

²⁵He answered, "Have you never read what David did when he and his companions were hungry and in need? ²⁶In the days of Abiathar the high priest, he entered the house of God and ate the consecrated bread,

which is lawful only for priests to eat. And he also gave some to his companions."

²⁷Then he said to them, "The Sabbath was made for man, not man for the Sabbath. ²⁸So the Son of Man is Lord even of the Sabbath."

Jesus Heals on the Sabbath

3 Another time Jesus went into the synagogue, and a man with a shriveled hand was there. ²Some of them were looking for a reason to accuse Jesus, so they watched him closely to see if he would heal him on the Sabbath. ³Jesus said to the man with the shriveled hand, "Stand up in front of everyone."

⁴Then Jesus asked them, "Which is lawful on the Sabbath: to do good or to do evil, to save life or to kill?" But they remained silent.

⁵He looked around at them in anger and, deeply distressed at their stubborn hearts, said to the man, "Stretch out your hand." He stretched it out, and his hand was completely restored. ⁶Then the Pharisees went out and began to plot with the Herodians how they might kill Jesus.

Crowds Follow Jesus

⁷Jesus withdrew with his disciples to the lake, and a large crowd from Galilee followed. ⁸When they heard about all he was doing, many people came to him from Judea, Jerusalem, Idumea, and the regions across the Jordan and around Tyre and Sidon. ⁹Because of the crowd he told his disciples to have a small boat ready for him, to keep the people from crowding him. ¹⁰For he had healed many, so that those with diseases were pushing forward to touch him. ¹¹Whenever the impure spirits saw him, they fell down before him and

cried out, "You are the Son of God." ¹²But he gave them strict orders not to tell others about him.

Jesus Appoints the Twelve

¹³Jesus went up on a mountainside and called to him those he wanted, and they came to him. ¹⁴He appointed twelveᵃ that they might be with him and that he might send them out to preach ¹⁵and to have authority to drive out demons. ¹⁶These are the twelve he appointed: Simon (to whom he gave the name Peter), ¹⁷James son of Zebedee and his brother John (to them he gave the name Boanerges, which means "sons of thunder"), ¹⁸Andrew, Philip, Bartholomew, Matthew, Thomas, James son of Alphaeus, Thaddaeus, Simon the Zealot ¹⁹and Judas Iscariot, who betrayed him.

Jesus Accused by His Family and by Teachers of the Law

²⁰Then Jesus entered a house, and again a crowd gathered, so that he and his disciples were not even able to eat. ²¹When his familyᵇ heard about this, they went to take charge of him, for they said, "He is out of his mind."

²²And the teachers of the law who came down from Jerusalem said, "He is possessed by Beelzebul! By the prince of demons he is driving out demons."

²³So Jesus called them over to him and began to speak to them in parables: "How can Satan drive out Satan? ²⁴If a kingdom is divided against itself, that kingdom cannot stand. ²⁵If a house is divided against itself, that house cannot stand. ²⁶And if Satan opposes himself and is divided, he cannot stand; his end has come.

ᵃ 14 Some manuscripts twelve — *designating them apostles —*   ᵇ 21 Or *his associates*

²⁷In fact, no one can enter a strong man's house without first tying him up. Then he can plunder the strong man's house. ²⁸Truly I tell you, people can be forgiven all their sins and every slander they utter, ²⁹but whoever blasphemes against the Holy Spirit will never be forgiven; they are guilty of an eternal sin."

³⁰He said this because they were saying, "He has an impure spirit."

³¹Then Jesus' mother and brothers arrived. Standing outside, they sent someone in to call him. ³²A crowd was sitting around him, and they told him, "Your mother and brothers are outside looking for you."

³³"Who are my mother and my brothers?" he asked.

³⁴Then he looked at those seated in a circle around him and said, "Here are my mother and my brothers! ³⁵Whoever does God's will is my brother and sister and mother."

The Parable of the Sower

4 Again Jesus began to teach by the lake. The crowd that gathered around him was so large that he got into a boat and sat in it out on the lake, while all the people were along the shore at the water's edge. ²He taught them many things by parables, and in his teaching said: ³"Listen! A farmer went out to sow his seed. ⁴As he was scattering the seed, some fell along the path, and the birds came and ate it up. ⁵Some fell on rocky places, where it did not have much soil. It sprang up quickly, because the soil was shallow. ⁶But when the sun came up, the plants were scorched, and they withered because they had no root. ⁷Other seed fell among thorns, which grew up and choked the plants, so that they did not bear grain. ⁸Still other seed fell on good soil. It came up, grew and produced a crop, some multiplying thirty, some sixty, some a hundred times."

⁹Then Jesus said, "Whoever has ears to hear, let them hear."

¹⁰When he was alone, the Twelve and the others around him asked him about the parables. ¹¹He told them, "The secret of the kingdom of God has been given to you. But to those on the outside everything is said in parables ¹²so that,

"'they may be ever seeing but
      never perceiving,
  and ever hearing but never
      understanding;
  otherwise they might turn and
      be forgiven!'^a

¹³Then Jesus said to them, "Don't you understand this parable? How then will you understand any parable? ¹⁴The farmer sows the word. ¹⁵Some people are like seed along the path, where the word is sown. As soon as they hear it, Satan comes and takes away the word that was sown in them. ¹⁶Others, like seed sown on rocky places, hear the word and at once receive it with joy. ¹⁷But since they have no root, they last only a short time. When trouble or persecution comes because of the word, they quickly fall away. ¹⁸Still others, like seed sown among thorns, hear the word; ¹⁹but the worries of this life, the deceitfulness of wealth and the desires for other things come in and choke the word, making it unfruitful. ²⁰Others, like seed sown on good soil, hear the word, accept it, and produce a crop — some thirty, some sixty, some a hundred times what was sown."

---

^a 12 Isaiah 6:9,10

A Lamp on a Stand

²¹He said to them, "Do you bring in a lamp to put it under a bowl or a bed? Instead, don't you put it on its stand? ²²For whatever is hidden is meant to be disclosed, and whatever is concealed is meant to be brought out into the open. ²³If anyone has ears to hear, let them hear."

²⁴"Consider carefully what you hear," he continued. "With the measure you use, it will be measured to you — and even more. ²⁵Whoever has will be given more; whoever does not have, even what they have will be taken from them."

The Parable of the Growing Seed

²⁶He also said, "This is what the kingdom of God is like. A man scatters seed on the ground. ²⁷Night and day, whether he sleeps or gets up, the seed sprouts and grows, though he does not know how. ²⁸All by itself the soil produces grain — first the stalk, then the head, then the full kernel in the head. ²⁹As soon as the grain is ripe, he puts the sickle to it, because the harvest has come."

The Parable of the Mustard Seed

³⁰Again he said, "What shall we say the kingdom of God is like, or what parable shall we use to describe it? ³¹It is like a mustard seed, which is the smallest of all seeds on earth. ³²Yet when planted, it grows and becomes the largest of all garden plants, with such big branches that the birds can perch in its shade."

³³With many similar parables Jesus spoke the word to them, as much as they could understand. ³⁴He did not say anything to them without using a parable. But when he was alone with his own disciples, he explained everything.

Jesus Calms the Storm

³⁵That day when evening came, he said to his disciples, "Let us go over to the other side." ³⁶Leaving the crowd behind, they took him along, just as he was, in the boat. There were also other boats with him. ³⁷A furious squall came up, and the waves broke over the boat, so that it was nearly swamped. ³⁸Jesus was in the stern, sleeping on a cushion. The disciples woke him and said to him, "Teacher, don't you care if we drown?"

³⁹He got up, rebuked the wind and said to the waves, "Quiet! Be still!" Then the wind died down and it was completely calm.

⁴⁰He said to his disciples, "Why are you so afraid? Do you still have no faith?"

⁴¹They were terrified and asked each other, "Who is this? Even the wind and the waves obey him!"

Jesus Restores a Demon-Possessed Man

5 They went across the lake to the region of the Gerasenes.[a] ²When Jesus got out of the boat, a man with an impure spirit came from the tombs to meet him. ³This man lived in the tombs, and no one could bind him anymore, not even with a chain. ⁴For he had often been chained hand and foot, but he tore the chains apart and broke the irons on his feet. No one was strong enough to subdue him. ⁵Night and day among the tombs and in the hills he would cry out and cut himself with stones.

---

[a] 1 Some manuscripts *Gadarenes*; other manuscripts *Gergesenes*

⁶When he saw Jesus from a distance, he ran and fell on his knees in front of him. ⁷He shouted at the top of his voice, "What do you want with me, Jesus, Son of the Most High God? In God's name don't torture me!" ⁸For Jesus had said to him, "Come out of this man, you impure spirit!"

⁹Then Jesus asked him, "What is your name?"

"My name is Legion," he replied, "for we are many." ¹⁰And he begged Jesus again and again not to send them out of the area.

¹¹A large herd of pigs was feeding on the nearby hillside. ¹²The demons begged Jesus, "Send us among the pigs; allow us to go into them." ¹³He gave them permission, and the impure spirits came out and went into the pigs. The herd, about two thousand in number, rushed down the steep bank into the lake and were drowned.

¹⁴Those tending the pigs ran off and reported this in the town and countryside, and the people went out to see what had happened. ¹⁵When they came to Jesus, they saw the man who had been possessed by the legion of demons, sitting there, dressed and in his right mind; and they were afraid. ¹⁶Those who had seen it told the people what had happened to the demon-possessed man — and told about the pigs as well. ¹⁷Then the people began to plead with Jesus to leave their region.

¹⁸As Jesus was getting into the boat, the man who had been demon-possessed begged to go with him. ¹⁹Jesus did not let him, but said, "Go home to your own people and tell them how much the Lord has done for you, and how he has had mercy on you." ²⁰So the man went away and began to tell in the Decapolisᵃ how much Jesus had done for him. And all the people were amazed.

Jesus Raises a Dead Girl and Heals a Sick Woman

²¹When Jesus had again crossed over by boat to the other side of the lake, a large crowd gathered around him while he was by the lake. ²²Then one of the synagogue leaders, named Jairus, came, and when he saw Jesus, he fell at his feet. ²³He pleaded earnestly with him, "My little daughter is dying. Please come and put your hands on her so that she will be healed and live." ²⁴So Jesus went with him.

A large crowd followed and pressed around him. ²⁵And a woman was there who had been subject to bleeding for twelve years. ²⁶She had suffered a great deal under the care of many doctors and had spent all she had, yet instead of getting better she grew worse. ²⁷When she heard about Jesus, she came up behind him in the crowd and touched his cloak, ²⁸because she thought, "If I just touch his clothes, I will be healed." ²⁹Immediately her bleeding stopped and she felt in her body that she was freed from her suffering.

³⁰At once Jesus realized that power had gone out from him. He turned around in the crowd and asked, "Who touched my clothes?"

³¹"You see the people crowding against you," his disciples answered, "and yet you can ask, 'Who touched me?'"

³²But Jesus kept looking around to see who had done it. ³³Then the woman, knowing what had happened to her, came and fell at his feet and, trembling with fear, told

---

ᵃ 20 That is, the Ten Cities

him the whole truth. ³⁴He said to her, "Daughter, your faith has healed you. Go in peace and be freed from your suffering."

³⁵While Jesus was still speaking, some people came from the house of Jairus, the synagogue leader. "Your daughter is dead," they said. "Why bother the teacher anymore?"

³⁶Overhearing⁰ what they said, Jesus told him, "Don't be afraid; just believe."

³⁷He did not let anyone follow him except Peter, James and John the brother of James. ³⁸When they came to the home of the synagogue leader, Jesus saw a commotion, with people crying and wailing loudly. ³⁹He went in and said to them, "Why all this commotion and wailing? The child is not dead but asleep." ⁴⁰But they laughed at him.

After he put them all out, he took the child's father and mother and the disciples who were with him, and went in where the child was. ⁴¹He took her by the hand and said to her, "Talitha koum!" (which means "Little girl, I say to you, get up!"). ⁴²Immediately the girl stood up and began to walk around (she was twelve years old). At this they were completely astonished. ⁴³He gave strict orders not to let anyone know about this, and told them to give her something to eat.

A Prophet Without Honor

6 Jesus left there and went to his hometown, accompanied by his disciples. ²When the Sabbath came, he began to teach in the synagogue, and many who heard him were amazed.

"Where did this man get these things?" they asked. "What's this wisdom that has been given him? What are these remarkable miracles he is performing? ³Isn't this the carpenter? Isn't this Mary's son and the brother of James, Joseph,ᵇ Judas and Simon? Aren't his sisters here with us?" And they took offense at him.

⁴Jesus said to them, "A prophet is not without honor except in his own town, among his relatives and in his own home." ⁵He could not do any miracles there, except lay his hands on a few sick people and heal them. ⁶He was amazed at their lack of faith.

Jesus Sends Out the Twelve

Then Jesus went around teaching from village to village. ⁷Calling the Twelve to him, he began to send them out two by two and gave them authority over impure spirits.

⁸These were his instructions: "Take nothing for the journey except a staff—no bread, no bag, no money in your belts. ⁹Wear sandals but not an extra shirt. ¹⁰Whenever you enter a house, stay there until you leave that town. ¹¹And if any place will not welcome you or listen to you, leave that place and shake the dust off your feet as a testimony against them."

¹²They went out and preached that people should repent. ¹³They drove out many demons and anointed many sick people with oil and healed them.

John the Baptist Beheaded

¹⁴King Herod heard about this, for Jesus' name had become well known. Some were saying,ᶜ "John the Baptist has been raised from the dead, and that is why miraculous powers are at work in him."

¹⁵Others said, "He is Elijah."

And still others claimed, "He is a

ᵃ 36 Or Ignoring   ᵇ 3 Greek Joses, a variant of Joseph   ᶜ 14 Some early manuscripts He was saying

prophet, like one of the prophets of long ago."

[16]But when Herod heard this, he said, "John, whom I beheaded, has been raised from the dead!"

[17]For Herod himself had given orders to have John arrested, and he had him bound and put in prison. He did this because of Herodias, his brother Philip's wife, whom he had married. [18]For John had been saying to Herod, "It is not lawful for you to have your brother's wife." [19]So Herodias nursed a grudge against John and wanted to kill him. But she was not able to, [20]because Herod feared John and protected him, knowing him to be a righteous and holy man. When Herod heard John, he was greatly puzzled[a]; yet he liked to listen to him.

[21]Finally the opportune time came. On his birthday Herod gave a banquet for his high officials and military commanders and the leading men of Galilee. [22]When the daughter of[b] Herodias came in and danced, she pleased Herod and his dinner guests.

The king said to the girl, "Ask me for anything you want, and I'll give it to you." [23]And he promised her with an oath, "Whatever you ask I will give you, up to half my kingdom."

[24]She went out and said to her mother, "What shall I ask for?"

"The head of John the Baptist," she answered.

[25]At once the girl hurried in to the king with the request: "I want you to give me right now the head of John the Baptist on a platter."

[26]The king was greatly distressed, but because of his oaths and his dinner guests, he did not want to refuse her. [27]So he immediately sent an executioner with orders to bring John's head. The man went, beheaded John in the prison, [28]and brought back his head on a platter. He presented it to the girl, and she gave it to her mother. [29]On hearing of this, John's disciples came and took his body and laid it in a tomb.

Jesus Feeds the Five Thousand

[30]The apostles gathered around Jesus and reported to him all they had done and taught. [31]Then, because so many people were coming and going that they did not even have a chance to eat, he said to them, "Come with me by yourselves to a quiet place and get some rest."

[32]So they went away by themselves in a boat to a solitary place. [33]But many who saw them leaving recognized them and ran on foot from all the towns and got there ahead of them. [34]When Jesus landed and saw a large crowd, he had compassion on them, because they were like sheep without a shepherd. So he began teaching them many things.

[35]By this time it was late in the day, so his disciples came to him. "This is a remote place," they said, "and it's already very late. [36]Send the people away so that they can go to the surrounding countryside and villages and buy themselves something to eat."

[37]But he answered, "You give them something to eat."

They said to him, "That would take more than half a year's wages[c]! Are we to go and spend that much on bread and give it to them to eat?"

[38]"How many loaves do you have?" he asked. "Go and see."

When they found out, they said, "Five — and two fish."

---

[a] 20 Some early manuscripts *he did many things*　　[b] 22 Some early manuscripts *When his daughter*　　[c] 37 Greek *take two hundred denarii*

[39]Then Jesus directed them to have all the people sit down in groups on the green grass. [40]So they sat down in groups of hundreds and fifties. [41]Taking the five loaves and the two fish and looking up to heaven, he gave thanks and broke the loaves. Then he gave them to his disciples to distribute to the people. He also divided the two fish among them all. [42]They all ate and were satisfied, [43]and the disciples picked up twelve basketfuls of broken pieces of bread and fish. [44]The number of the men who had eaten was five thousand.

Jesus Walks on the Water

[45]Immediately Jesus made his disciples get into the boat and go on ahead of him to Bethsaida, while he dismissed the crowd. [46]After leaving them, he went up on a mountainside to pray.

[47]Later that night, the boat was in the middle of the lake, and he was alone on land. [48]He saw the disciples straining at the oars, because the wind was against them. Shortly before dawn he went out to them, walking on the lake. He was about to pass by them, [49]but when they saw him walking on the lake, they thought he was a ghost. They cried out, [50]because they all saw him and were terrified.

Immediately he spoke to them and said, "Take courage! It is I. Don't be afraid." [51]Then he climbed into the boat with them, and the wind died down. They were completely amazed, [52]for they had not understood about the loaves; their hearts were hardened.

[53]When they had crossed over, they landed at Gennesaret and anchored there. [54]As soon as they got out of the boat, people recognized Jesus. [55]They ran throughout that whole region and carried the sick on mats to wherever they heard he was. [56]And wherever he went — into villages, towns or countryside — they placed the sick in the marketplaces. They begged him to let them touch even the edge of his cloak, and all who touched it were healed.

That Which Defiles

7 The Pharisees and some of the teachers of the law who had come from Jerusalem gathered around Jesus [2]and saw some of his disciples eating food with hands that were defiled, that is, unwashed. [3](The Pharisees and all the Jews do not eat unless they give their hands a ceremonial washing, holding to the tradition of the elders. [4]When they come from the marketplace they do not eat unless they wash. And they observe many other traditions, such as the washing of cups, pitchers and kettles.[a])

[5]So the Pharisees and teachers of the law asked Jesus, "Why don't your disciples live according to the tradition of the elders instead of eating their food with defiled hands?"

[6]He replied, "Isaiah was right when he prophesied about you hypocrites; as it is written:

> "'These people honor me with
> their lips,
>   but their hearts are far from
>   me.
> [7] They worship me in vain;
>   their teachings are merely
>   human rules.'[b]

[8]You have let go of the commands of God and are holding on to human traditions."

[9]And he continued, "You have a

---

[a] 4 Some early manuscripts *pitchers, kettles and dining couches*   [b] 6,7 Isaiah 29:13

fine way of setting aside the commands of God in order to observe[a] your own traditions! 10For Moses said, 'Honor your father and mother,'[b] and, 'Anyone who curses their father or mother is to be put to death.'[c] 11But you say that if anyone declares that what might have been used to help their father or mother is Corban (that is, devoted to God) — 12then you no longer let them do anything for their father or mother. 13Thus you nullify the word of God by your tradition that you have handed down. And you do many things like that."

14Again Jesus called the crowd to him and said, "Listen to me, everyone, and understand this. 15Nothing outside a person can defile them by going into them. Rather, it is what comes out of a person that defiles them." [16] [d]

17After he had left the crowd and entered the house, his disciples asked him about this parable. 18"Are you so dull?" he asked. "Don't you see that nothing that enters a person from the outside can defile them? 19For it doesn't go into their heart but into their stomach, and then out of the body." (In saying this, Jesus declared all foods clean.)

20He went on: "What comes out of a person is what defiles them. 21For it is from within, out of a person's heart, that evil thoughts come — sexual immorality, theft, murder, 22adultery, greed, malice, deceit, lewdness, envy, slander, arrogance and folly. 23All these evils come from inside and defile a person."

Jesus Honors a Syrophoenician Woman's Faith

24Jesus left that place and went to the vicinity of Tyre.[e] He entered a house and did not want anyone to know it; yet he could not keep his presence secret. 25In fact, as soon as she heard about him, a woman whose little daughter was possessed by an impure spirit came and fell at his feet. 26The woman was a Greek, born in Syrian Phoenicia. She begged Jesus to drive the demon out of her daughter.

27"First let the children eat all they want," he told her, "for it is not right to take the children's bread and toss it to the dogs."

28"Lord," she replied, "even the dogs under the table eat the children's crumbs."

29Then he told her, "For such a reply, you may go; the demon has left your daughter."

30She went home and found her child lying on the bed, and the demon gone.

Jesus Heals a Deaf and Mute Man

31Then Jesus left the vicinity of Tyre and went through Sidon, down to the Sea of Galilee and into the region of the Decapolis.[f] 32There some people brought to him a man who was deaf and could hardly talk, and they begged Jesus to place his hand on him.

33After he took him aside, away from the crowd, Jesus put his fingers into the man's ears. Then he spit and touched the man's tongue. 34He looked up to heaven and with a deep sigh said to him, "Ephphatha!" (which means "Be opened!"). 35At this, the man's ears were opened, his tongue was loosened and he began to speak plainly.

---

[a] 9 Some manuscripts set up   [b] 10 Exodus 20:12; Deut. 5:16   [c] 10 Exodus 21:17; Lev. 20:9   [d] 16 Some manuscripts include here the words of 4:23.   [e] 24 Many early manuscripts Tyre and Sidon   [f] 31 That is, the Ten Cities

³⁶Jesus commanded them not to tell anyone. But the more he did so, the more they kept talking about it. ³⁷People were overwhelmed with amazement. "He has done everything well," they said. "He even makes the deaf hear and the mute speak."

Jesus Feeds the Four Thousand

8 During those days another large crowd gathered. Since they had nothing to eat, Jesus called his disciples to him and said, ²"I have compassion for these people; they have already been with me three days and have nothing to eat. ³If I send them home hungry, they will collapse on the way, because some of them have come a long distance."

⁴His disciples answered, "But where in this remote place can anyone get enough bread to feed them?"

⁵"How many loaves do you have?" Jesus asked.

"Seven," they replied.

⁶He told the crowd to sit down on the ground. When he had taken the seven loaves and given thanks, he broke them and gave them to his disciples to distribute to the people, and they did so. ⁷They had a few small fish as well; he gave thanks for them also and told the disciples to distribute them. ⁸The people ate and were satisfied. Afterward the disciples picked up seven basketfuls of broken pieces that were left over. ⁹About four thousand were present. After he had sent them away, ¹⁰he got into the boat with his disciples and went to the region of Dalmanutha.

¹¹The Pharisees came and began to question Jesus. To test him, they asked him for a sign from heaven. ¹²He sighed deeply and said, "Why does this generation ask for a sign? Truly I tell you, no sign will be given to it." ¹³Then he left them, got back into the boat and crossed to the other side.

The Yeast of the Pharisees and Herod

¹⁴The disciples had forgotten to bring bread, except for one loaf they had with them in the boat. ¹⁵"Be careful," Jesus warned them. "Watch out for the yeast of the Pharisees and that of Herod."

¹⁶They discussed this with one another and said, "It is because we have no bread."

¹⁷Aware of their discussion, Jesus asked them: "Why are you talking about having no bread? Do you still not see or understand? Are your hearts hardened? ¹⁸Do you have eyes but fail to see, and ears but fail to hear? And don't you remember? ¹⁹When I broke the five loaves for the five thousand, how many basketfuls of pieces did you pick up?"

"Twelve," they replied.

²⁰"And when I broke the seven loaves for the four thousand, how many basketfuls of pieces did you pick up?"

They answered, "Seven."

²¹He said to them, "Do you still not understand?"

Jesus Heals a Blind Man at Bethsaida

²²They came to Bethsaida, and some people brought a blind man and begged Jesus to touch him. ²³He took the blind man by the hand and led him outside the village. When he had spit on the man's eyes and put his hands on him, Jesus asked, "Do you see anything?"

²⁴He looked up and said, "I see people; they look like trees walking around."

25 Once more Jesus put his hands on the man's eyes. Then his eyes were opened, his sight was restored, and he saw everything clearly. 26 Jesus sent him home, saying, "Don't even go into*a* the village."

Peter Declares That Jesus Is the Messiah

27 Jesus and his disciples went on to the villages around Caesarea Philippi. On the way he asked them, "Who do people say I am?"

28 They replied, "Some say John the Baptist; others say Elijah; and still others, one of the prophets."

29 "But what about you?" he asked. "Who do you say I am?"

Peter answered, "You are the Messiah."

30 Jesus warned them not to tell anyone about him.

Jesus Predicts His Death

31 He then began to teach them that the Son of Man must suffer many things and be rejected by the elders, the chief priests and the teachers of the law, and that he must be killed and after three days rise again. 32 He spoke plainly about this, and Peter took him aside and began to rebuke him.

33 But when Jesus turned and looked at his disciples, he rebuked Peter. "Get behind me, Satan!" he said. "You do not have in mind the concerns of God, but merely human concerns."

The Way of the Cross

34 Then he called the crowd to him along with his disciples and said: "Whoever wants to be my disciple must deny themselves and take up their cross and follow me. 35 For whoever wants to save their life*b* will lose

it, but whoever loses their life for me and for the gospel will save it. 36 What good is it for someone to gain the whole world, yet forfeit their soul? 37 Or what can anyone give in exchange for their soul? 38 If anyone is ashamed of me and my words in this adulterous and sinful generation, the Son of Man will be ashamed of them when he comes in his Father's glory with the holy angels.

9 And he said to them, "Truly I tell you, some who are standing here will not taste death before they see that the kingdom of God has come with power."

The Transfiguration

2 After six days Jesus took Peter, James and John with him and led them up a high mountain, where they were all alone. There he was transfigured before them. 3 His clothes became dazzling white, whiter than anyone in the world could bleach them. 4 And there appeared before them Elijah and Moses, who were talking with Jesus.

5 Peter said to Jesus, "Rabbi, it is good for us to be here. Let us put up three shelters — one for you, one for Moses and one for Elijah." 6 (He did not know what to say, they were so frightened.)

7 Then a cloud appeared and covered them, and a voice came from the cloud: "This is my Son, whom I love. Listen to him!"

8 Suddenly, when they looked around, they no longer saw anyone with them except Jesus.

9 As they were coming down the mountain, Jesus gave them orders not to tell anyone what they had seen

a 26 Some manuscripts *go and tell anyone in*
b 35 The Greek word means either *life* or *soul*; also in verses 36 and 37.

until the Son of Man had risen from the dead. 10They kept the matter to themselves, discussing what "rising from the dead" meant.

11And they asked him, "Why do the teachers of the law say that Elijah must come first?"

12Jesus replied, "To be sure, Elijah does come first, and restores all things. Why then is it written that the Son of Man must suffer much and be rejected? 13But I tell you, Elijah has come, and they have done to him everything they wished, just as it is written about him."

Jesus Heals a Boy Possessed by an Impure Spirit

14When they came to the other disciples, they saw a large crowd around them and the teachers of the law arguing with them. 15As soon as all the people saw Jesus, they were overwhelmed with wonder and ran to greet him.

16"What are you arguing with them about?" he asked.

17A man in the crowd answered, "Teacher, I brought you my son, who is possessed by a spirit that has robbed him of speech. 18Whenever it seizes him, it throws him to the ground. He foams at the mouth, gnashes his teeth and becomes rigid. I asked your disciples to drive out the spirit, but they could not."

19"You unbelieving generation," Jesus replied, "how long shall I stay with you? How long shall I put up with you? Bring the boy to me."

20So they brought him. When the spirit saw Jesus, it immediately threw the boy into a convulsion. He fell to the ground and rolled around, foaming at the mouth.

21Jesus asked the boy's father, "How long has he been like this?"

"From childhood," he answered. 22"It has often thrown him into fire or water to kill him. But if you can do anything, take pity on us and help us."

23"'If you can'?" said Jesus. "Everything is possible for one who believes."

24Immediately the boy's father exclaimed, "I do believe; help me overcome my unbelief!"

25When Jesus saw that a crowd was running to the scene, he rebuked the impure spirit. "You deaf and mute spirit," he said, "I command you, come out of him and never enter him again."

26The spirit shrieked, convulsed him violently and came out. The boy looked so much like a corpse that many said, "He's dead." 27But Jesus took him by the hand and lifted him to his feet, and he stood up.

28After Jesus had gone indoors, his disciples asked him privately, "Why couldn't we drive it out?"

29He replied, "This kind can come out only by prayer.ᵃ"

Jesus Predicts His Death a Second Time

30They left that place and passed through Galilee. Jesus did not want anyone to know where they were, 31because he was teaching his disciples. He said to them, "The Son of Man is going to be delivered into the hands of men. They will kill him, and after three days he will rise." 32But they did not understand what he meant and were afraid to ask him about it.

33They came to Capernaum. When he was in the house, he asked them, "What were you arguing about on the road?" 34But they kept quiet because on the way they had argued about who was the greatest.

ᵃ 29 Some manuscripts *prayer and fasting*

³⁵Sitting down, Jesus called the Twelve and said, "Anyone who wants to be first must be the very last, and the servant of all."

³⁶He took a little child whom he placed among them. Taking the child in his arms, he said to them, ³⁷"Whoever welcomes one of these little children in my name welcomes me; and whoever welcomes me does not welcome me but the one who sent me."

Whoever Is Not Against Us Is for Us

³⁸"Teacher," said John, "we saw someone driving out demons in your name and we told him to stop, because he was not one of us."

³⁹"Do not stop him," Jesus said. "For no one who does a miracle in my name can in the next moment say anything bad about me, ⁴⁰for whoever is not against us is for us. ⁴¹Truly I tell you, anyone who gives you a cup of water in my name because you belong to the Messiah will certainly not lose their reward.

Causing to Stumble

⁴²"If anyone causes one of these little ones — those who believe in me — to stumble, it would be better for them if a large millstone were hung around their neck and they were thrown into the sea. ⁴³If your hand causes you to stumble, cut it off. It is better for you to enter life maimed than with two hands to go into hell, where the fire never goes out. [⁴⁴]ᵃ ⁴⁵And if your foot causes you to stumble, cut it off. It is better for you to enter life crippled than to have two feet and be thrown into hell. [⁴⁶]ᵃ ⁴⁷And if your eye causes you to stumble, pluck it out. It is better for you to enter the kingdom of God with one eye than to have two eyes and be thrown into hell, ⁴⁸where

" 'the worms that eat them do
        not die,
    and the fire is not quenched.'ᵇ

⁴⁹Everyone will be salted with fire.

⁵⁰"Salt is good, but if it loses its saltiness, how can you make it salty again? Have salt among yourselves, and be at peace with each other."

Divorce

10 Jesus then left that place and went into the region of Judea and across the Jordan. Again crowds of people came to him, and as was his custom, he taught them.

²Some Pharisees came and tested him by asking, "Is it lawful for a man to divorce his wife?"

³"What did Moses command you?" he replied.

⁴They said, "Moses permitted a man to write a certificate of divorce and send her away."

⁵"It was because your hearts were hard that Moses wrote you this law," Jesus replied. ⁶"But at the beginning of creation God 'made them male and female.'ᶜ ⁷'For this reason a man will leave his father and mother and be united to his wife,ᵈ ⁸and the two will become one flesh.'ᵉ So they are no longer two, but one flesh. ⁹Therefore what God has joined together, let no one separate.

¹⁰When they were in the house again, the disciples asked Jesus about this. ¹¹He answered, "Anyone who divorces his wife and marries another woman commits adultery against her. ¹²And if she divorces her husband and marries another man, she commits adultery."

ᵃ 44,46 Some manuscripts include here the words of verse 48.   ᵇ 48 Isaiah 66:24   ᶜ 6 Gen. 1:27   ᵈ 7 Some early manuscripts do not have *and be united to his wife*.   ᵉ 8 Gen. 2:24

The Little Children and Jesus

¹³People were bringing little children to Jesus for him to place his hands on them, but the disciples rebuked them. ¹⁴When Jesus saw this, he was indignant. He said to them, "Let the little children come to me, and do not hinder them, for the kingdom of God belongs to such as these. ¹⁵Truly I tell you, anyone who will not receive the kingdom of God like a little child will never enter it." ¹⁶And he took the children in his arms, placed his hands on them and blessed them.

The Rich and the Kingdom of God

¹⁷As Jesus started on his way, a man ran up to him and fell on his knees before him. "Good teacher," he asked, "what must I do to inherit eternal life?"

¹⁸"Why do you call me good?" Jesus answered. "No one is good — except God alone. ¹⁹You know the commandments: 'You shall not murder, you shall not commit adultery, you shall not steal, you shall not give false testimony, you shall not defraud, honor your father and mother.'ᵃ"

²⁰"Teacher," he declared, "all these I have kept since I was a boy."

²¹Jesus looked at him and loved him. "One thing you lack," he said. "Go, sell everything you have and give to the poor, and you will have treasure in heaven. Then come, follow me."

²²At this the man's face fell. He went away sad, because he had great wealth.

²³Jesus looked around and said to his disciples, "How hard it is for the rich to enter the kingdom of God!"

²⁴The disciples were amazed at his words. But Jesus said again, "Children, how hard it isᵇ to enter the kingdom of God! ²⁵It is easier for a camel to go through the eye of a needle than

for someone who is rich to enter the kingdom of God."

²⁶The disciples were even more amazed, and said to each other, "Who then can be saved?"

²⁷Jesus looked at them and said, "With man this is impossible, but not with God; all things are possible with God."

²⁸Then Peter spoke up, "We have left everything to follow you!"

²⁹"Truly I tell you," Jesus replied, "no one who has left home or brothers or sisters or mother or father or children or fields for me and the gospel ³⁰will fail to receive a hundred times as much in this present age: homes, brothers, sisters, mothers, children and fields — along with persecutions — and in the age to come eternal life. ³¹But many who are first will be last, and the last first.

Jesus Predicts His Death a Third Time

³²They were on their way up to Jerusalem, with Jesus leading the way, and the disciples were astonished, while those who followed were afraid. Again he took the Twelve aside and told them what was going to happen to him. ³³"We are going up to Jerusalem," he said, "and the Son of Man will be delivered over to the chief priests and the teachers of the law. They will condemn him to death and will hand him over to the Gentiles, ³⁴who will mock him and spit on him, flog him and kill him. Three days later he will rise."

The Request of James and John

³⁵Then James and John, the sons of Zebedee, came to him. "Teacher," they said, "we want you to do for us whatever we ask."

ᵃ 19 Exodus 20:12-16; Deut. 5:16-20
ᵇ 24 Some manuscripts *is for those who trust in riches*

³⁶"What do you want me to do for you?" he asked.

³⁷They replied, "Let one of us sit at your right and the other at your left in your glory."

³⁸"You don't know what you are asking," Jesus said. "Can you drink the cup I drink or be baptized with the baptism I am baptized with?"

³⁹"We can," they answered.

Jesus said to them, "You will drink the cup I drink and be baptized with the baptism I am baptized with, ⁴⁰but to sit at my right or left is not for me to grant. These places belong to those for whom they have been prepared."

⁴¹When the ten heard about this, they became indignant with James and John. ⁴²Jesus called them together and said, "You know that those who are regarded as rulers of the Gentiles lord it over them, and their high officials exercise authority over them. ⁴³Not so with you. Instead, whoever wants to become great among you must be your servant, ⁴⁴and whoever wants to be first must be slave of all. ⁴⁵For even the Son of Man did not come to be served, but to serve, and to give his life as a ransom for many."

Blind Bartimaeus Receives His Sight

⁴⁶Then they came to Jericho. As Jesus and his disciples, together with a large crowd, were leaving the city, a blind man, Bartimaeus (which means "son of Timaeus"), was sitting by the roadside begging. ⁴⁷When he heard that it was Jesus of Nazareth, he began to shout, "Jesus, Son of David, have mercy on me!"

⁴⁸Many rebuked him and told him to be quiet, but he shouted all the more, "Son of David, have mercy on me!"

⁴⁹Jesus stopped and said, "Call him."

So they called to the blind man, "Cheer up! On your feet! He's calling you." ⁵⁰Throwing his cloak aside, he jumped to his feet and came to Jesus.

⁵¹"What do you want me to do for you?" Jesus asked him.

The blind man said, "Rabbi, I want to see."

⁵²"Go," said Jesus, "your faith has healed you." Immediately he received his sight and followed Jesus along the road.

Jesus Comes to Jerusalem as King

11 As they approached Jerusalem and came to Bethphage and Bethany at the Mount of Olives, Jesus sent two of his disciples, ²saying to them, "Go to the village ahead of you, and just as you enter it, you will find a colt tied there, which no one has ever ridden. Untie it and bring it here. ³If anyone asks you, 'Why are you doing this?' say, 'The Lord needs it and will send it back here shortly.'"

⁴They went and found a colt outside in the street, tied at a doorway. As they untied it, ⁵some people standing there asked, "What are you doing, untying that colt?" ⁶They answered as Jesus had told them to, and the people let them go. ⁷When they brought the colt to Jesus and threw their cloaks over it, he sat on it. ⁸Many people spread their cloaks on the road, while others spread branches they had cut in the fields. ⁹Those who went ahead and those who followed shouted,

"Hosanna!ᵃ"

"Blessed is he who comes in the
name of the Lord!"ᵇ

ᵃ 9 A Hebrew expression meaning "Save!" which became an exclamation of praise; also in verse 10   ᵇ 9 Psalm 118:25,26

10 "Blessed is the coming kingdom
of our father David!"

"Hosanna in the highest
heaven!"

11 Jesus entered Jerusalem and went
into the temple courts. He looked
around at everything, but since it was
already late, he went out to Bethany
with the Twelve.

Jesus Curses a Fig Tree and Clears the Temple Courts

12 The next day as they were leaving
Bethany, Jesus was hungry. 13 Seeing
in the distance a fig tree in leaf, he
went to find out if it had any fruit.
When he reached it, he found nothing but leaves, because it was not the
season for figs. 14 Then he said to the
tree, "May no one ever eat fruit from
you again." And his disciples heard
him say it.

15 On reaching Jerusalem, Jesus entered the temple courts and began
driving out those who were buying
and selling there. He overturned the
tables of the money changers and the
benches of those selling doves, 16 and
would not allow anyone to carry mer-
chandise through the temple courts.
17 And as he taught them, he said, "Is it
not written: 'My house will be called a
house of prayer for all nations'ᵃ? But
you have made it 'a den of robbers.'ᵇ"

18 The chief priests and the teachers of the law heard this and began
looking for a way to kill him, for they
feared him, because the whole crowd
was amazed at his teaching.

19 When evening came, Jesus and
his disciplesᶜ went out of the city.

20 In the morning, as they went
along, they saw the fig tree withered
from the roots. 21 Peter remembered
and said to Jesus, "Rabbi, look! The
fig tree you cursed has withered!"

22 "Have faith in God," Jesus answered. 23 "Trulyᵈ I tell you, if anyone says to this mountain, 'Go, throw
yourself into the sea,' and does not
doubt in their heart but believes that
what they say will happen, it will be
done for them. 24 Therefore I tell you,
whatever you ask for in prayer, believe that you have received it, and it
will be yours. 25 And when you stand
praying, if you hold anything against
anyone, forgive them, so that your
Father in heaven may forgive you
your sins." [26]ᵉ

The Authority of Jesus Questioned

27 They arrived again in Jerusalem,
and while Jesus was walking in the
temple courts, the chief priests, the
teachers of the law and the elders
came to him. 28 "By what authority
are you doing these things?" they
asked. "And who gave you authority
to do this?"

29 Jesus replied, "I will ask you one
question. Answer me, and I will tell
you by what authority I am doing
these things. 30 John's baptism — was
it from heaven, or of human origin?
Tell me!"

31 They discussed it among themselves and said, "If we say, 'From
heaven,' he will ask, 'Then why didn't
you believe him?' 32 But if we say, 'Of
human origin' . . ." (They feared the
people, for everyone held that John
really was a prophet.)

33 So they answered Jesus, "We
don't know."

Jesus said, "Neither will I tell you

ᵃ 17 Isaiah 56:7   ᵇ 17 Jer. 7:11   ᶜ 19 Some
early manuscripts came, Jesus   ᵈ 22,23 Some
early manuscripts "If you have faith in God,"
Jesus answered, 23"truly   ᵉ 26 Some
manuscripts include here words similar to
Matt. 6:15.

by what authority I am doing these things."

The Parable of the Tenants

12 Jesus then began to speak to them in parables: "A man planted a vineyard. He put a wall around it, dug a pit for the winepress and built a watchtower. Then he rented the vineyard to some farmers and moved to another place. ²At harvest time he sent a servant to the tenants to collect from them some of the fruit of the vineyard. ³But they seized him, beat him and sent him away empty-handed. ⁴Then he sent another servant to them; they struck this man on the head and treated him shamefully. ⁵He sent still another, and that one they killed. He sent many others; some of them they beat, others they killed.

⁶"He had one left to send, a son, whom he loved. He sent him last of all, saying, 'They will respect my son.'

⁷"But the tenants said to one another, 'This is the heir. Come, let's kill him, and the inheritance will be ours.' ⁸So they took him and killed him, and threw him out of the vineyard.

⁹"What then will the owner of the vineyard do? He will come and kill those tenants and give the vineyard to others. ¹⁰Haven't you read this passage of Scripture:

" 'The stone the builders rejected
   has become the cornerstone;
¹¹ the Lord has done this,
   and it is marvelous in our
     eyes'ᵃ?"

¹²Then the chief priests, the teachers of the law and the elders looked for a way to arrest him because they knew he had spoken the parable against them. But they were afraid of the crowd; so they left him and went away.

Paying the Imperial Tax to Caesar

¹³Later they sent some of the Pharisees and Herodians to Jesus to catch him in his words. ¹⁴They came to him and said, "Teacher, we know that you are a man of integrity. You aren't swayed by others, because you pay no attention to who they are; but you teach the way of God in accordance with the truth. Is it right to pay the imperial taxᵇ to Caesar or not? ¹⁵Should we pay or shouldn't we?"

But Jesus knew their hypocrisy. "Why are you trying to trap me?" he asked. "Bring me a denarius and let me look at it." ¹⁶They brought the coin, and he asked them, "Whose image is this? And whose inscription?"

"Caesar's," they replied.

¹⁷Then Jesus said to them, "Give back to Caesar what is Caesar's and to God what is God's."

And they were amazed at him.

Marriage at the Resurrection

¹⁸Then the Sadducees, who say there is no resurrection, came to him with a question. ¹⁹"Teacher," they said, "Moses wrote for us that if a man's brother dies and leaves a wife but no children, the man must marry the widow and raise up offspring for his brother. ²⁰Now there were seven brothers. The first one married and died without leaving any children. ²¹The second one married the widow, but he also died, leaving no child. It was the same with the third. ²²In fact, none of the seven left any children. Last of all, the woman died too. ²³At the resurrectionᶜ whose wife will she be, since the seven were married to her?"

ᵃ *11* Psalm 118:22,23   ᵇ *14* A special tax levied on subject peoples, not on Roman citizens   ᶜ *23* Some manuscripts *resurrection, when people rise from the dead,*

²⁴Jesus replied, "Are you not in error because you do not know the Scriptures or the power of God? ²⁵When the dead rise, they will neither marry nor be given in marriage; they will be like the angels in heaven. ²⁶Now about the dead rising — have you not read in the Book of Moses, in the account of the burning bush, how God said to him, 'I am the God of Abraham, the God of Isaac, and the God of Jacob'ᵃ? ²⁷He is not the God of the dead, but of the living. You are badly mistaken!"

The Greatest Commandment

²⁸One of the teachers of the law came and heard them debating. Noticing that Jesus had given them a good answer, he asked him, "Of all the commandments, which is the most important?"

²⁹"The most important one," answered Jesus, "is this: 'Hear, O Israel: The Lord our God, the Lord is one.ᵇ ³⁰Love the Lord your God with all your heart and with all your soul and with all your mind and with all your strength.'ᶜ ³¹The second is this: 'Love your neighbor as yourself.'ᵈ There is no commandment greater than these."

³²"Well said, teacher," the man replied. "You are right in saying that God is one and there is no other but him. ³³To love him with all your heart, with all your understanding and with all your strength, and to love your neighbor as yourself is more important than all burnt offerings and sacrifices."

³⁴When Jesus saw that he had answered wisely, he said to him, "You are not far from the kingdom of God." And from then on no one dared ask him any more questions.

Whose Son Is the Messiah?

³⁵While Jesus was teaching in the temple courts, he asked, "Why do the teachers of the law say that the Messiah is the son of David? ³⁶David himself, speaking by the Holy Spirit, declared:

"'The Lord said to my Lord:
    "Sit at my right hand
until I put your enemies
    under your feet."'ᵉ

³⁷David himself calls him 'Lord.' How then can he be his son?"

The large crowd listened to him with delight.

Warning Against the Teachers of the Law

³⁸As he taught, Jesus said, "Watch out for the teachers of the law. They like to walk around in flowing robes and be greeted with respect in the marketplaces, ³⁹and have the most important seats in the synagogues and the places of honor at banquets. ⁴⁰They devour widows' houses and for a show make lengthy prayers. These men will be punished most severely."

The Widow's Offering

⁴¹Jesus sat down opposite the place where the offerings were put and watched the crowd putting their money into the temple treasury. Many rich people threw in large amounts. ⁴²But a poor widow came and put in two very small copper coins, worth only a few cents.

⁴³Calling his disciples to him, Jesus said, "Truly I tell you, this poor widow has put more into the treasury than all the others. ⁴⁴They all gave out of their wealth; but she, out of her poverty, put in everything — all she had to live on."

ᵃ 26 Exodus 3:6   ᵇ 29 Or The Lord our God is one Lord   ᶜ 30 Deut. 6:4,5   ᵈ 31 Lev. 19:18   ᵉ 36 Psalm 110:1

The Destruction of the Temple and Signs of the End Times

13 As Jesus was leaving the temple, one of his disciples said to him, "Look, Teacher! What massive stones! What magnificent buildings!"

[2] "Do you see all these great buildings?" replied Jesus. "Not one stone here will be left on another; every one will be thrown down."

[3] As Jesus was sitting on the Mount of Olives opposite the temple, Peter, James, John and Andrew asked him privately, [4] "Tell us, when will these things happen? And what will be the sign that they are all about to be fulfilled?"

[5] Jesus said to them: "Watch out that no one deceives you. [6] Many will come in my name, claiming, 'I am he,' and will deceive many. [7] When you hear of wars and rumors of wars, do not be alarmed. Such things must happen, but the end is still to come. [8] Nation will rise against nation, and kingdom against kingdom. There will be earthquakes in various places, and famines. These are the beginning of birth pains.

[9] "You must be on your guard. You will be handed over to the local councils and flogged in the synagogues. On account of me you will stand before governors and kings as witnesses to them. [10] And the gospel must first be preached to all nations. [11] Whenever you are arrested and brought to trial, do not worry beforehand about what to say. Just say whatever is given you at the time, for it is not you speaking, but the Holy Spirit.

[12] "Brother will betray brother to death, and a father his child. Children will rebel against their parents and have them put to death. [13] Everyone will hate you because of me, but the one who stands firm to the end will be saved.

[14] "When you see 'the abomination that causes desolation'[a] standing where it[b] does not belong — let the reader understand — then let those who are in Judea flee to the mountains. [15] Let no one on the housetop go down or enter the house to take anything out. [16] Let no one in the field go back to get their cloak. [17] How dreadful it will be in those days for pregnant women and nursing mothers! [18] Pray that this will not take place in winter, [19] because those will be days of distress unequaled from the beginning, when God created the world, until now — and never to be equaled again.

[20] "If the Lord had not cut short those days, no one would survive. But for the sake of the elect, whom he has chosen, he has shortened them. [21] At that time if anyone says to you, 'Look, here is the Messiah!' or, 'Look, there he is!' do not believe it. [22] For false messiahs and false prophets will appear and perform signs and wonders to deceive, if possible, even the elect. [23] So be on your guard; I have told you everything ahead of time.

[24] "But in those days, following that distress,

"'the sun will be darkened,
    and the moon will not give its
        light;
[25] the stars will fall from the sky,
    and the heavenly bodies will
        be shaken.'[c]

[26] "At that time people will see the Son of Man coming in clouds with great power and glory. [27] And he will send his angels and gather his elect from the four winds, from the ends of the earth to the ends of the heavens.

[28] "Now learn this lesson from the fig tree: As soon as its twigs get tender

---

[a] 14 Daniel 9:27; 11:31; 12:11   [b] 14 Or *he*
[c] 25 Isaiah 13:10; 34:4

and its leaves come out, you know that summer is near. ²⁹Even so, when you see these things happening, you know that it[a] is near, right at the door. ³⁰Truly I tell you, this generation will certainly not pass away until all these things have happened. ³¹Heaven and earth will pass away, but my words will never pass away.

The Day and Hour Unknown

³²"But about that day or hour no one knows, not even the angels in heaven, nor the Son, but only the Father. ³³Be on guard! Be alert[b]! You do not know when that time will come. ³⁴It's like a man going away: He leaves his house and puts his servants in charge, each with their assigned task, and tells the one at the door to keep watch.

³⁵"Therefore keep watch because you do not know when the owner of the house will come back — whether in the evening, or at midnight, or when the rooster crows, or at dawn. ³⁶If he comes suddenly, do not let him find you sleeping. ³⁷What I say to you, I say to everyone: 'Watch!'"

Jesus Anointed at Bethany

14 Now the Passover and the Festival of Unleavened Bread were only two days away, and the chief priests and the teachers of the law were scheming to arrest Jesus secretly and kill him. ²"But not during the festival," they said, "or the people may riot."

³While he was in Bethany, reclining at the table in the home of Simon the Leper, a woman came with an alabaster jar of very expensive perfume, made of pure nard. She broke the jar and poured the perfume on his head.

⁴Some of those present were saying indignantly to one another, "Why this waste of perfume? ⁵It could have been sold for more than a year's wages[c] and the money given to the poor." And they rebuked her harshly.

⁶"Leave her alone," said Jesus. "Why are you bothering her? She has done a beautiful thing to me. ⁷The poor you will always have with you,[d] and you can help them any time you want. But you will not always have me. ⁸She did what she could. She poured perfume on my body beforehand to prepare for my burial. ⁹Truly I tell you, wherever the gospel is preached throughout the world, what she has done will also be told, in memory of her."

¹⁰Then Judas Iscariot, one of the Twelve, went to the chief priests to betray Jesus to them. ¹¹They were delighted to hear this and promised to give him money. So he watched for an opportunity to hand him over.

The Last Supper

¹²On the first day of the Festival of Unleavened Bread, when it was customary to sacrifice the Passover lamb, Jesus' disciples asked him, "Where do you want us to go and make preparations for you to eat the Passover?"

¹³So he sent two of his disciples, telling them, "Go into the city, and a man carrying a jar of water will meet you. Follow him. ¹⁴Say to the owner of the house he enters, 'The Teacher asks: Where is my guest room, where I may eat the Passover with my disciples?' ¹⁵He will show you a large room upstairs, furnished and ready. Make preparations for us there."

¹⁶The disciples left, went into the city and found things just as Jesus had told them. So they prepared the Passover.

---

[a] 29 Or he   [b] 33 Some manuscripts alert and pray   [c] 5 Greek than three hundred denarii   [d] 7 See Deut. 15:11.

¹⁷When evening came, Jesus arrived with the Twelve. ¹⁸While they were reclining at the table eating, he said, "Truly I tell you, one of you will betray me — one who is eating with me."

¹⁹They were saddened, and one by one they said to him, "Surely you don't mean me?"

²⁰"It is one of the Twelve," he replied, "one who dips bread into the bowl with me. ²¹The Son of Man will go just as it is written about him. But woe to that man who betrays the Son of Man! It would be better for him if he had not been born."

²²While they were eating, Jesus took bread, and when he had given thanks, he broke it and gave it to his disciples, saying, "Take it; this is my body."

²³Then he took a cup, and when he had given thanks, he gave it to them, and they all drank from it.

²⁴"This is my blood of the[a] covenant, which is poured out for many," he said to them. ²⁵"Truly I tell you, I will not drink again from the fruit of the vine until that day when I drink it new in the kingdom of God."

²⁶When they had sung a hymn, they went out to the Mount of Olives.

Jesus Predicts Peter's Denial

²⁷"You will all fall away," Jesus told them, "for it is written:

" 'I will strike the shepherd,
    and the sheep will be
        scattered.'[b]

²⁸But after I have risen, I will go ahead of you into Galilee."

²⁹Peter declared, "Even if all fall away, I will not."

³⁰"Truly I tell you," Jesus answered, "today — yes, tonight — before the rooster crows twice[c] you yourself will disown me three times."

³¹But Peter insisted emphatically, "Even if I have to die with you, I will never disown you." And all the others said the same.

Gethsemane

³²They went to a place called Gethsemane, and Jesus said to his disciples, "Sit here while I pray." ³³He took Peter, James and John along with him, and he began to be deeply distressed and troubled. ³⁴"My soul is overwhelmed with sorrow to the point of death," he said to them. "Stay here and keep watch."

³⁵Going a little farther, he fell to the ground and prayed that if possible the hour might pass from him. ³⁶"Abba,[d] Father," he said, "everything is possible for you. Take this cup from me. Yet not what I will, but what you will."

³⁷Then he returned to his disciples and found them sleeping. "Simon," he said to Peter, "are you asleep? Couldn't you keep watch for one hour? ³⁸Watch and pray so that you will not fall into temptation. The spirit is willing, but the flesh is weak."

³⁹Once more he went away and prayed the same thing. ⁴⁰When he came back, he again found them sleeping, because their eyes were heavy. They did not know what to say to him.

⁴¹Returning the third time, he said to them, "Are you still sleeping and resting? Enough! The hour has come. Look, the Son of Man is delivered into the hands of sinners. ⁴²Rise! Let us go! Here comes my betrayer!"

Jesus Arrested

⁴³Just as he was speaking, Judas, one of the Twelve, appeared. With

a 24 Some manuscripts the new   b 27 Zech. 13:7   c 30 Some early manuscripts do not have twice.   d 36 Aramaic for father him was a crowd armed with swords and clubs, sent from the chief priests, the teachers of the law, and the elders.

44 Now the betrayer had arranged a signal with them: "The one I kiss is the man; arrest him and lead him away under guard." 45 Going at once to Jesus, Judas said, "Rabbi!" and kissed him. 46 The men seized Jesus and arrested him. 47 Then one of those standing near drew his sword and struck the servant of the high priest, cutting off his ear.

48 "Am I leading a rebellion," said Jesus, "that you have come out with swords and clubs to capture me? 49 Every day I was with you, teaching in the temple courts, and you did not arrest me. But the Scriptures must be fulfilled." 50 Then everyone deserted him and fled.

51 A young man, wearing nothing but a linen garment, was following Jesus. When they seized him, 52 he fled naked, leaving his garment behind.

Jesus Before the Sanhedrin

53 They took Jesus to the high priest, and all the chief priests, the elders and the teachers of the law came together. 54 Peter followed him at a distance, right into the courtyard of the high priest. There he sat with the guards and warmed himself at the fire.

55 The chief priests and the whole Sanhedrin were looking for evidence against Jesus so that they could put him to death, but they did not find any. 56 Many testified falsely against him, but their statements did not agree.

57 Then some stood up and gave this false testimony against him: 58 "We heard him say, 'I will destroy this temple made with human hands and in three days will build another,

not made with hands.'" 59 Yet even then their testimony did not agree.

60 Then the high priest stood up before them and asked Jesus, "Are you not going to answer? What is this testimony that these men are bringing against you?" 61 But Jesus remained silent and gave no answer.

Again the high priest asked him, "Are you the Messiah, the Son of the Blessed One?"

62 "I am," said Jesus. "And you will see the Son of Man sitting at the right hand of the Mighty One and coming on the clouds of heaven."

63 The high priest tore his clothes. "Why do we need any more witnesses?" he asked. 64 "You have heard the blasphemy. What do you think?"

They all condemned him as worthy of death. 65 Then some began to spit at him; they blindfolded him, struck him with their fists, and said, "Prophesy!" And the guards took him and beat him.

Peter Disowns Jesus

66 While Peter was below in the courtyard, one of the servant girls of the high priest came by. 67 When she saw Peter warming himself, she looked closely at him.

"You also were with that Nazarene, Jesus," she said.

68 But he denied it. "I don't know or understand what you're talking about," he said, and went out into the entryway.[a]

69 When the servant girl saw him there, she said again to those standing around, "This fellow is one of them." 70 Again he denied it.

After a little while, those standing near said to Peter, "Surely you are one of them, for you are a Galilean."

[a] 68 Some early manuscripts *entryway and the rooster crowed*

⁷¹He began to call down curses, and he swore to them, "I don't know this man you're talking about."

⁷²Immediately the rooster crowed the second time.ᵃ Then Peter remembered the word Jesus had spoken to him: "Before the rooster crowsᵇ you will disown me three times." And he broke down and wept.

Jesus Before Pilate

15 Very early in the morning, the chief priests, with the elders, the teachers of the law and the whole Sanhedrin, made their plans. So they bound Jesus, led him away and handed him over to Pilate.

²"Are you the king of the Jews?" asked Pilate.

"You have said so," Jesus replied.

³The chief priests accused him of many things. ⁴So again Pilate asked him, "Aren't you going to answer? See how many things they are accusing you of."

⁵But Jesus still made no reply, and Pilate was amazed.

⁶Now it was the custom at the festival to release a prisoner whom the people requested. ⁷A man called Barabbas was in prison with the insurrectionists who had committed murder in the uprising. ⁸The crowd came up and asked Pilate to do for them what he usually did.

⁹"Do you want me to release to you the king of the Jews?" asked Pilate, ¹⁰knowing it was out of self-interest that the chief priests had handed Jesus over to him. ¹¹But the chief priests stirred up the crowd to have Pilate release Barabbas instead.

¹²"What shall I do, then, with the one you call the king of the Jews?" Pilate asked them.

¹³"Crucify him!" they shouted.

¹⁴"Why? What crime has he committed?" asked Pilate.

But they shouted all the louder, "Crucify him!"

¹⁵Wanting to satisfy the crowd, Pilate released Barabbas to them. He had Jesus flogged, and handed him over to be crucified.

The Soldiers Mock Jesus

¹⁶The soldiers led Jesus away into the palace (that is, the Praetorium) and called together the whole company of soldiers. ¹⁷They put a purple robe on him, then twisted together a crown of thorns and set it on him. ¹⁸And they began to call out to him, "Hail, king of the Jews!" ¹⁹Again and again they struck him on the head with a staff and spit on him. Falling on their knees, they paid homage to him. ²⁰And when they had mocked him, they took off the purple robe and put his own clothes on him. Then they led him out to crucify him.

The Crucifixion of Jesus

²¹A certain man from Cyrene, Simon, the father of Alexander and Rufus, was passing by on his way in from the country, and they forced him to carry the cross. ²²They brought Jesus to the place called Golgotha (which means "the place of the skull"). ²³Then they offered him wine mixed with myrrh, but he did not take it. ²⁴And they crucified him. Dividing up his clothes, they cast lots to see what each would get.

²⁵It was nine in the morning when they crucified him. ²⁶The written notice of the charge against him read: THE KING OF THE JEWS.

²⁷They crucified two rebels with him, one on his right and one on

---

ᵃ 72 Some early manuscripts do not have the second time.　ᵇ 72 Some early manuscripts do not have twice.

his left. [28]ᵃ ²⁹Those who passed by hurled insults at him, shaking their heads and saying, "So! You who are going to destroy the temple and build it in three days, ³⁰come down from the cross and save yourself!" ³¹In the same way the chief priests and the teachers of the law mocked him among themselves. "He saved others," they said, "but he can't save himself! ³²Let this Messiah, this king of Israel, come down now from the cross, that we may see and believe." Those crucified with him also heaped insults on him.

The Death of Jesus

³³At noon, darkness came over the whole land until three in the afternoon. ³⁴And at three in the afternoon Jesus cried out in a loud voice, *"Eloi, Eloi, lema sabachthani?"* (which means "My God, my God, why have you forsaken me?").ᵇ

³⁵When some of those standing near heard this, they said, "Listen, he's calling Elijah."

³⁶Someone ran, filled a sponge with wine vinegar, put it on a staff, and offered it to Jesus to drink. "Now leave him alone. Let's see if Elijah comes to take him down," he said.

³⁷With a loud cry, Jesus breathed his last.

³⁸The curtain of the temple was torn in two from top to bottom. ³⁹And when the centurion, who stood there in front of Jesus, saw how he died,ᶜ he said, "Surely this man was the Son of God!"

⁴⁰Some women were watching from a distance. Among them were Mary Magdalene, Mary the mother of James the younger and of Joseph,ᵈ and Salome. ⁴¹In Galilee these women had followed him and cared for his needs. Many other women who had

come up with him to Jerusalem were also there.

The Burial of Jesus

⁴²It was Preparation Day (that is, the day before the Sabbath). So as evening approached, ⁴³Joseph of Arimathea, a prominent member of the Council, who was himself waiting for the kingdom of God, went boldly to Pilate and asked for Jesus' body. ⁴⁴Pilate was surprised to hear that he was already dead. Summoning the centurion, he asked him if Jesus had already died. ⁴⁵When he learned from the centurion that it was so, he gave the body to Joseph. ⁴⁶So Joseph bought some linen cloth, took down the body, wrapped it in the linen, and placed it in a tomb cut out of rock. Then he rolled a stone against the entrance of the tomb. ⁴⁷Mary Magdalene and Mary the mother of Joseph saw where he was laid.

Jesus Has Risen

16 When the Sabbath was over, Mary Magdalene, Mary the mother of James, and Salome bought spices so that they might go to anoint Jesus' body. ²Very early on the first day of the week, just after sunrise, they were on their way to the tomb ³and they asked each other, "Who will roll the stone away from the entrance of the tomb?"

⁴But when they looked up, they saw that the stone, which was very large, had been rolled away. ⁵As they entered the tomb, they saw a young man dressed in a white robe sitting on the right side, and they were alarmed.

ᵃ 28 Some manuscripts include here words similar to Luke 22:37.   ᵇ 34 Psalm 22:1
ᶜ 39 Some manuscripts *saw that he died with such a cry*   ᵈ 40 Greek *Joses*, a variant of *Joseph*; also in verse 47

⁶"Don't be alarmed," he said. "You are looking for Jesus the Nazarene, who was crucified. He has risen! He is not here. See the place where they laid him. ⁷But go, tell his disciples and Peter, 'He is going ahead of you into Galilee. There you will see him, just as he told you.'"

⁸Trembling and bewildered, the women went out and fled from the tomb. They said nothing to anyone, because they were afraid.ᵃ

[The earliest manuscripts and some other ancient witnesses do not have verses 9 – 20.]

⁹When Jesus rose early on the first day of the week, he appeared first to Mary Magdalene, out of whom he had driven seven demons. ¹⁰She went and told those who had been with him and who were mourning and weeping.

¹¹When they heard that Jesus was alive and that she had seen him, they did not believe it.

¹²Afterward Jesus appeared in a different form to two of them while they were walking in the country. ¹³These returned and reported it to the rest; but they did not believe them either.

¹⁴Later Jesus appeared to the Eleven as they were eating; he rebuked them for their lack of faith and their stubborn refusal to believe those who had seen him after he had risen.

¹⁵He said to them, "Go into all the world and preach the gospel to all creation. ¹⁶Whoever believes and is baptized will be saved, but whoever does not believe will be condemned. ¹⁷And these signs will accompany those who believe: In my name they will drive out demons; they will speak in new tongues; ¹⁸they will pick up snakes with their hands; and when they drink deadly poison, it will not hurt them at all; they will place their hands on sick people, and they will get well."

¹⁹After the Lord Jesus had spoken to them, he was taken up into heaven and he sat at the right hand of God. ²⁰Then the disciples went out and preached everywhere, and the Lord worked with them and confirmed his word by the signs that accompanied it.

Luke

Introduction

1 Many have undertaken to draw up an account of the things that have been fulfilledᵇ among us, ²just as they were handed down to us by those who from the first were eyewitnesses and servants of the word. ³With this in mind, since I myself have carefully investigated everything from the beginning, I too decided to write an orderly account for you, most excellent Theophilus, ⁴so that you may know the certainty of the things you have been taught.

The Birth of John the Baptist Foretold

⁵In the time of Herod king of Judea there was a priest named Zechariah, who belonged to the priestly division of Abijah; his wife Elizabeth was also

---

ᵃ 8 Some manuscripts have the following ending between verses 8 and 9, and one manuscript has it after verse 8 (omitting verses 9-20): Then they quickly reported all these instructions to those around Peter. After this, Jesus himself also sent out through them from east to west the sacred and imperishable proclamation of eternal salvation. Amen.
ᵇ 1 Or been surely believed

a descendant of Aaron. 6Both of them were righteous in the sight of God, observing all the Lord's commands and decrees blamelessly. 7But they were childless because Elizabeth was not able to conceive, and they were both very old.

8Once when Zechariah's division was on duty and he was serving as priest before God, 9he was chosen by lot, according to the custom of the priesthood, to go into the temple of the Lord and burn incense. 10And when the time for the burning of incense came, all the assembled worshipers were praying outside.

11Then an angel of the Lord appeared to him, standing at the right side of the altar of incense. 12When Zechariah saw him, he was startled and was gripped with fear. 13But the angel said to him: "Do not be afraid, Zechariah; your prayer has been heard. Your wife Elizabeth will bear you a son, and you are to call him John. 14He will be a joy and delight to you, and many will rejoice because of his birth, 15for he will be great in the sight of the Lord. He is never to take wine or other fermented drink, and he will be filled with the Holy Spirit even before he is born. 16He will bring back many of the people of Israel to the Lord their God. 17And he will go on before the Lord, in the spirit and power of Elijah, to turn the hearts of the parents to their children and the disobedient to the wisdom of the righteous — to make ready a people prepared for the Lord."

18Zechariah asked the angel, "How can I be sure of this? I am an old man and my wife is well along in years."

19The angel said to him, "I am Gabriel. I stand in the presence of God, and I have been sent to speak to you and to tell you this good news. 20And now you will be silent and not able to speak until the day this happens, because you did not believe my words, which will come true at their appointed time."

21Meanwhile, the people were waiting for Zechariah and wondering why he stayed so long in the temple. 22When he came out, he could not speak to them. They realized he had seen a vision in the temple, for he kept making signs to them but remained unable to speak.

23When his time of service was completed, he returned home. 24After this his wife Elizabeth became pregnant and for five months remained in seclusion. 25"The Lord has done this for me," she said. "In these days he has shown his favor and taken away my disgrace among the people."

The Birth of Jesus Foretold

26In the sixth month of Elizabeth's pregnancy, God sent the angel Gabriel to Nazareth, a town in Galilee, 27to a virgin pledged to be married to a man named Joseph, a descendant of David. The virgin's name was Mary. 28The angel went to her and said, "Greetings, you who are highly favored! The Lord is with you."

29Mary was greatly troubled at his words and wondered what kind of greeting this might be. 30But the angel said to her, "Do not be afraid, Mary; you have found favor with God. 31You will conceive and give birth to a son, and you are to call him Jesus. 32He will be great and will be called the Son of the Most High. The Lord God will give him the throne of his father David, 33and he will reign over Jacob's descendants forever; his kingdom will never end."

34"How will this be," Mary asked the angel, "since I am a virgin?"

³⁵The angel answered, "The Holy Spirit will come on you, and the power of the Most High will overshadow you. So the holy one to be born will be called*ᵉ* the Son of God. ³⁶Even Elizabeth your relative is going to have a child in her old age, and she who was said to be unable to conceive is in her sixth month. ³⁷For no word from God will ever fail."

³⁸"I am the Lord's servant," Mary answered. "May your word to me be fulfilled." Then the angel left her.

Mary Visits Elizabeth

³⁹At that time Mary got ready and hurried to a town in the hill country of Judea, ⁴⁰where she entered Zechariah's home and greeted Elizabeth. ⁴¹When Elizabeth heard Mary's greeting, the baby leaped in her womb, and Elizabeth was filled with the Holy Spirit. ⁴²In a loud voice she exclaimed: "Blessed are you among women, and blessed is the child you will bear! ⁴³But why am I so favored, that the mother of my Lord should come to me? ⁴⁴As soon as the sound of your greeting reached my ears, the baby in my womb leaped for joy. ⁴⁵Blessed is she who has believed that the Lord would fulfill his promises to her!"

Mary's Song

⁴⁶And Mary said:

"My soul glorifies the Lord
⁴⁷   and my spirit rejoices in God
        my Savior,
⁴⁸ for he has been mindful
        of the humble state of his
        servant.
    From now on all generations will
        call me blessed,
⁴⁹   for the Mighty One has done
        great things for me —
        holy is his name.

⁵⁰ His mercy extends to those who
        fear him,
    from generation to generation.
⁵¹ He has performed mighty deeds
        with his arm;
    he has scattered those who
        are proud in their inmost
        thoughts.
⁵² He has brought down rulers from
        their thrones
    but has lifted up the humble.
⁵³ He has filled the hungry with
        good things
    but has sent the rich away
        empty.
⁵⁴ He has helped his servant Israel,
    remembering to be merciful
⁵⁵ to Abraham and his descendants
        forever,
    just as he promised our
        ancestors."

⁵⁶Mary stayed with Elizabeth for about three months and then returned home.

The Birth of John the Baptist

⁵⁷When it was time for Elizabeth to have her baby, she gave birth to a son. ⁵⁸Her neighbors and relatives heard that the Lord had shown her great mercy, and they shared her joy.

⁵⁹On the eighth day they came to circumcise the child, and they were going to name him after his father Zechariah, ⁶⁰but his mother spoke up and said, "No! He is to be called John."

⁶¹They said to her, "There is no one among your relatives who has that name."

⁶²Then they made signs to his father, to find out what he would like to name the child. ⁶³He asked for a writing tablet, and to everyone's astonishment he wrote, "His name is

---

ᵉ 35 Or So the child to be born will be called holy,

John." ⁶⁴Immediately his mouth was opened and his tongue set free, and he began to speak, praising God. ⁶⁵All the neighbors were filled with awe, and throughout the hill country of Judea people were talking about all these things. ⁶⁶Everyone who heard this wondered about it, asking, "What then is this child going to be?" For the Lord's hand was with him.

Zechariah's Song

⁶⁷His father Zechariah was filled with the Holy Spirit and prophesied:

⁶⁸ "Praise be to the Lord, the God of
 Israel,
  because he has come to his
   people and redeemed
   them.
⁶⁹ He has raised up a horn^a of
  salvation for us
  in the house of his servant
   David
⁷⁰ (as he said through his holy
   prophets of long ago),
⁷¹ salvation from our enemies
  and from the hand of all who
   hate us —
⁷² to show mercy to our ancestors
  and to remember his holy
   covenant,
⁷³ the oath he swore to our father
   Abraham:
⁷⁴ to rescue us from the hand of our
   enemies,
  and to enable us to serve him
   without fear
⁷⁵ in holiness and righteousness
  before him all our days.

⁷⁶ And you, my child, will be called
  a prophet of the Most
   High;
 for you will go on before the
   Lord to prepare the way
   for him,

⁷⁷ to give his people the knowledge
  of salvation
 through the forgiveness of
  their sins,
⁷⁸ because of the tender mercy of
  our God,
 by which the rising sun will
  come to us from heaven
⁷⁹ to shine on those living in
  darkness
 and in the shadow of death,
 to guide our feet into the path of
  peace."

⁸⁰And the child grew and became strong in spirit^b; and he lived in the wilderness until he appeared publicly to Israel.

The Birth of Jesus

2 In those days Caesar Augustus issued a decree that a census should be taken of the entire Roman world. ²(This was the first census that took place while^c Quirinius was governor of Syria.) ³And everyone went to their own town to register.

⁴So Joseph also went up from the town of Nazareth in Galilee to Judea, to Bethlehem the town of David, because he belonged to the house and line of David. ⁵He went there to register with Mary, who was pledged to be married to him and was expecting a child. ⁶While they were there, the time came for the baby to be born, ⁷and she gave birth to her firstborn, a son. She wrapped him in cloths and placed him in a manger, because there was no guest room available for them.

⁸And there were shepherds living out in the fields nearby, keeping watch over their flocks at night.

---
^a 69 *Horn* here symbolizes a strong king.
^b 80 Or *in the Spirit*   ^c 2 Or *This census took place before*

9An angel of the Lord appeared to them, and the glory of the Lord shone around them, and they were terrified. 10But the angel said to them, "Do not be afraid. I bring you good news that will cause great joy for all the people. 11Today in the town of David a Savior has been born to you; he is the Messiah, the Lord. 12This will be a sign to you: You will find a baby wrapped in cloths and lying in a manger."

13Suddenly a great company of the heavenly host appeared with the angel, praising God and saying,

14 "Glory to God in the highest
        heaven,
    and on earth peace to those on
        whom his favor rests."

15When the angels had left them and gone into heaven, the shepherds said to one another, "Let's go to Bethlehem and see this thing that has happened, which the Lord has told us about."

16So they hurried off and found Mary and Joseph, and the baby, who was lying in the manger. 17When they had seen him, they spread the word concerning what had been told them about this child, 18and all who heard it were amazed at what the shepherds said to them. 19But Mary treasured up all these things and pondered them in her heart. 20The shepherds returned, glorifying and praising God for all the things they had heard and seen, which were just as they had been told.

21On the eighth day, when it was time to circumcise the child, he was named Jesus, the name the angel had given him before he was conceived.

Jesus Presented in the Temple

22When the time came for the purification rites required by the Law of Moses, Joseph and Mary took him to Jerusalem to present him to the Lord 23(as it is written in the Law of the Lord, "Every firstborn male is to be consecrated to the Lord"a), 24and to offer a sacrifice in keeping with what is said in the Law of the Lord: "a pair of doves or two young pigeons."b

25Now there was a man in Jerusalem called Simeon, who was righteous and devout. He was waiting for the consolation of Israel, and the Holy Spirit was on him. 26It had been revealed to him by the Holy Spirit that he would not die before he had seen the Lord's Messiah. 27Moved by the Spirit, he went into the temple courts. When the parents brought in the child Jesus to do for him what the custom of the Law required, 28Simeon took him in his arms and praised God, saying:

29 "Sovereign Lord, as you have
        promised,
    you may now dismissc your
        servant in peace.
30 For my eyes have seen your
        salvation,
31   which you have prepared in
        the sight of all nations:
32 a light for revelation to the
        Gentiles,
    and the glory of your people
        Israel."

33The child's father and mother marveled at what was said about him. 34Then Simeon blessed them and said to Mary, his mother: "This child is destined to cause the falling and rising of many in Israel, and to be a sign that will be spoken against, 35so that the thoughts of many hearts will be revealed. And a sword will pierce your own soul too."

36There was also a prophet, Anna,

a 23 Exodus 13:2,12   b 24 Lev. 12:8   c 29 Or promised, / now dismiss the daughter of Penuel, of the tribe of Asher. She was very old; she had lived with her husband seven years after her marriage, [37]and then was a widow until she was eighty-four.[a] She never left the temple but worshiped night and day, fasting and praying. [38]Coming up to them at that very moment, she gave thanks to God and spoke about the child to all who were looking forward to the redemption of Jerusalem.

[39]When Joseph and Mary had done everything required by the Law of the Lord, they returned to Galilee to their own town of Nazareth. [40]And the child grew and became strong; he was filled with wisdom, and the grace of God was on him.

The Boy Jesus at the Temple

[41]Every year Jesus' parents went to Jerusalem for the Festival of the Passover. [42]When he was twelve years old, they went up to the festival, according to the custom. [43]After the festival was over, while his parents were returning home, the boy Jesus stayed behind in Jerusalem, but they were unaware of it. [44]Thinking he was in their company, they traveled on for a day. Then they began looking for him among their relatives and friends. [45]When they did not find him, they went back to Jerusalem to look for him. [46]After three days they found him in the temple courts, sitting among the teachers, listening to them and asking them questions. [47]Everyone who heard him was amazed at his understanding and his answers. [48]When his parents saw him, they were astonished. His mother said to him, "Son, why have you treated us like this? Your father and I have been anxiously searching for you."

[49]"Why were you looking for me?" he asked. "Didn't you know I had to be in my Father's house?"[b] [50]But they did not understand what he was saying to them.

[51]Then he went down to Nazareth with them and was obedient to them. But his mother treasured all these things in her heart. [52]And Jesus grew in wisdom and stature, and in favor with God and man.

John the Baptist Prepares the Way

3 In the fifteenth year of the reign of Tiberius Caesar — when Pontius Pilate was governor of Judea, Herod tetrarch of Galilee, his brother Philip tetrarch of Iturea and Traconitis, and Lysanias tetrarch of Abilene — [2]during the high-priesthood of Annas and Caiaphas, the word of God came to John son of Zechariah in the wilderness. [3]He went into all the country around the Jordan, preaching a baptism of repentance for the forgiveness of sins. [4]As it is written in the book of the words of Isaiah the prophet:

"A voice of one calling in the
    wilderness,
'Prepare the way for the Lord,
    make straight paths for him.
[5] Every valley shall be filled in,
    every mountain and hill made
    low.
The crooked roads shall become
    straight,
    the rough ways smooth.
[6] And all people will see God's
    salvation.'"[c]

[7]John said to the crowds coming out to be baptized by him, "You brood of vipers! Who warned you to flee from the coming wrath? [8]Produce

---

[a] 37 Or Then had been a widow for eighty-four years.   [b] 49 Or be about my Father's business
[c] 6 Isaiah 40:3-5

fruit in keeping with repentance. And do not begin to say to yourselves, 'We have Abraham as our father.' For I tell you that out of these stones God can raise up children for Abraham. ⁹The ax is already at the root of the trees, and every tree that does not produce good fruit will be cut down and thrown into the fire."

¹⁰"What should we do then?" the crowd asked.

¹¹John answered, "Anyone who has two shirts should share with the one who has none, and anyone who has food should do the same."

¹²Even tax collectors came to be baptized. "Teacher," they asked, "what should we do?"

¹³"Don't collect any more than you are required to," he told them.

¹⁴Then some soldiers asked him, "And what should we do?"

He replied, "Don't extort money and don't accuse people falsely — be content with your pay."

¹⁵The people were waiting expectantly and were all wondering in their hearts if John might possibly be the Messiah. ¹⁶John answered them all, "I baptize you with⁶ water. But one who is more powerful than I will come, the straps of whose sandals I am not worthy to untie. He will baptize you with⁶ the Holy Spirit and fire. ¹⁷His winnowing fork is in his hand to clear his threshing floor and to gather the wheat into his barn, but he will burn up the chaff with unquenchable fire." ¹⁸And with many other words John exhorted the people and proclaimed the good news to them.

¹⁹But when John rebuked Herod the tetrarch because of his marriage to Herodias, his brother's wife, and all the other evil things he had done, ²⁰Herod added this to them all: He locked John up in prison.

The Baptism and Genealogy of Jesus

²¹When all the people were being baptized, Jesus was baptized too. And as he was praying, heaven was opened ²²and the Holy Spirit descended on him in bodily form like a dove. And a voice came from heaven: "You are my Son, whom I love; with you I am well pleased."

²³Now Jesus himself was about thirty years old when he began his ministry. He was the son, so it was thought, of Joseph,

the son of Heli, ²⁴the son of Matthat,

the son of Levi, the son of Melki, the son of Jannai, the son of Joseph,

²⁵ the son of Mattathias, the son of Amos,

the son of Nahum, the son of Esli, the son of Naggai, ²⁶the son of Maath,

the son of Mattathias, the son of Semein,

the son of Josek, the son of Joda, ²⁷the son of Joanan, the son of Rhesa,

the son of Zerubbabel, the son of Shealtiel,

the son of Neri, ²⁸the son of Melki, the son of Addi, the son of Cosam, the son of Elmadam, the son of Er,

²⁹the son of Joshua, the son of Eliezer,

the son of Jorim, the son of Matthat,

the son of Levi, ³⁰the son of Simeon,

the son of Judah, the son of Joseph,

the son of Jonam, the son of Eliakim,

---

⁶ 16 *in* or *in*

³¹ the son of Melea, the son of Menna,

the son of Mattatha, the son of Nathan,

the son of David, ³² the son of Jesse,

the son of Obed, the son of Boaz,

the son of Salmon,ᵃ the son of Nahshon,

³³ the son of Amminadab, the son of Ram,ᵇ

the son of Hezron, the son of Perez,

the son of Judah, ³⁴ the son of Jacob,

the son of Isaac, the son of Abraham,

the son of Terah, the son of Nahor,

³⁵ the son of Serug, the son of Reu,

the son of Peleg, the son of Eber,

the son of Shelah, ³⁶ the son of Cainan,

the son of Arphaxad, the son of Shem,

the son of Noah, the son of Lamech,

³⁷ the son of Methuselah, the son of Enoch,

the son of Jared, the son of Mahalalel,

the son of Kenan, ³⁸ the son of Enosh,

the son of Seth, the son of Adam,

the son of God.

Jesus Is Tested in the Wilderness

4 Jesus, full of the Holy Spirit, left the Jordan and was led by the Spirit into the wilderness, ² where for forty days he was temptedᶜ by the devil. He ate nothing during those days, and at the end of them he was hungry.

³ The devil said to him, "If you are the Son of God, tell this stone to become bread."

⁴ Jesus answered, "It is written: 'Man shall not live on bread alone.'ᵈ"

⁵ The devil led him up to a high place and showed him in an instant all the kingdoms of the world. ⁶ And he said to him, "I will give you all their authority and splendor; it has been given to me, and I can give it to anyone I want to. ⁷ If you worship me, it will all be yours."

⁸ Jesus answered, "It is written: 'Worship the Lord your God and serve him only.'ᵉ"

⁹ The devil led him to Jerusalem and had him stand on the highest point of the temple. "If you are the Son of God," he said, "throw yourself down from here. ¹⁰ For it is written:

"'He will command his angels concerning you
to guard you carefully;
¹¹ they will lift you up in their hands,
so that you will not strike your foot against a stone.'ᶠ"

¹² Jesus answered, "It is said: 'Do not put the Lord your God to the test.'ᵍ"

¹³ When the devil had finished all this tempting, he left him until an opportune time.

Jesus Rejected at Nazareth

¹⁴ Jesus returned to Galilee in the power of the Spirit, and news about him spread through the whole countryside. ¹⁵ He was teaching in their synagogues, and everyone praised him.

¹⁶ He went to Nazareth, where he had been brought up, and on the Sabbath day he went into the synagogue,

---

ᵃ 32 Some early manuscripts *Sala*
ᵇ 33 Some manuscripts *Amminadab, the son of Admin, the son of Arni*; other manuscripts vary widely.   ᶜ 2 The Greek for *tempted* can also mean *tested*.   ᵈ 4 Deut. 8:3   ᵉ 8 Deut. 6:13
ᶠ 11 Psalm 91:11,12   ᵍ 12 Deut. 6:16

as was his custom. He stood up to read, [17]and the scroll of the prophet Isaiah was handed to him. Unrolling it, he found the place where it is written:

[18] "The Spirit of the Lord is on me,
  because he has anointed me
    to proclaim good news to the
      poor.
He has sent me to proclaim
    freedom for the prisoners
  and recovery of sight for the
      blind,
  to set the oppressed free,
[19]   to proclaim the year of the
      Lord's favor."[a]

[20]Then he rolled up the scroll, gave it back to the attendant and sat down. The eyes of everyone in the synagogue were fastened on him. [21]He began by saying to them, "Today this scripture is fulfilled in your hearing."

[22]All spoke well of him and were amazed at the gracious words that came from his lips. "Isn't this Joseph's son?" they asked.

[23]Jesus said to them, "Surely you will quote this proverb to me: 'Physician, heal yourself!' And you will tell me, 'Do here in your hometown what we have heard that you did in Capernaum.' "

[24]"Truly I tell you," he continued, "no prophet is accepted in his hometown. [25]I assure you that there were many widows in Israel in Elijah's time, when the sky was shut for three and a half years and there was a severe famine throughout the land. [26]Yet Elijah was not sent to any of them, but to a widow in Zarephath in the region of Sidon. [27]And there were many in Israel with leprosy[b] in the time of Elisha the prophet, yet not one of them was cleansed — only Naaman the Syrian."

[28]All the people in the synagogue were furious when they heard this. [29]They got up, drove him out of the town, and took him to the brow of the hill on which the town was built, in order to throw him off the cliff. [30]But he walked right through the crowd and went on his way.

Jesus Drives Out an Impure Spirit

[31]Then he went down to Capernaum, a town in Galilee, and on the Sabbath he taught the people. [32]They were amazed at his teaching, because his words had authority.

[33]In the synagogue there was a man possessed by a demon, an impure spirit. He cried out at the top of his voice, [34]"Go away! What do you want with us, Jesus of Nazareth? Have you come to destroy us? I know who you are — the Holy One of God!"

[35]"Be quiet!" Jesus said sternly. "Come out of him!" Then the demon threw the man down before them all and came out without injuring him.

[36]All the people were amazed and said to each other, "What words these are! With authority and power he gives orders to impure spirits and they come out!" [37]And the news about him spread throughout the surrounding area.

Jesus Heals Many

[38]Jesus left the synagogue and went to the home of Simon. Now Simon's mother-in-law was suffering from a high fever, and they asked Jesus to help her. [39]So he bent over her and rebuked the fever, and it left her. She got up at once and began to wait on them.

---

[a] 19 Isaiah 61:1,2 (see Septuagint); Isaiah 58:6
[b] 27 The Greek word traditionally translated *leprosy* was used for various diseases affecting the skin.

⁴⁰At sunset, the people brought to Jesus all who had various kinds of sickness, and laying his hands on each one, he healed them. ⁴¹Moreover, demons came out of many people, shouting, "You are the Son of God!" But he rebuked them and would not allow them to speak, because they knew he was the Messiah.

⁴²At daybreak, Jesus went out to a solitary place. The people were looking for him and when they came to where he was, they tried to keep him from leaving them. ⁴³But he said, "I must proclaim the good news of the kingdom of God to the other towns also, because that is why I was sent." ⁴⁴And he kept on preaching in the synagogues of Judea.

Jesus Calls His First Disciples

5 One day as Jesus was standing by the Lake of Gennesaret,ᵃ the people were crowding around him and listening to the word of God. ²He saw at the water's edge two boats, left there by the fishermen, who were washing their nets. ³He got into one of the boats, the one belonging to Simon, and asked him to put out a little from shore. Then he sat down and taught the people from the boat.

⁴When he had finished speaking, he said to Simon, "Put out into deep water, and let down the nets for a catch."

⁵Simon answered, "Master, we've worked hard all night and haven't caught anything. But because you say so, I will let down the nets."

⁶When they had done so, they caught such a large number of fish that their nets began to break. ⁷So they signaled their partners in the other boat to come and help them, and they came and filled both boats so full that they began to sink.

⁸When Simon Peter saw this, he fell at Jesus' knees and said, "Go away from me, Lord; I am a sinful man!" ⁹For he and all his companions were astonished at the catch of fish they had taken, ¹⁰and so were James and John, the sons of Zebedee, Simon's partners.

Then Jesus said to Simon, "Don't be afraid; from now on you will fish for people." ¹¹So they pulled their boats up on shore, left everything and followed him.

Jesus Heals a Man With Leprosy

¹²While Jesus was in one of the towns, a man came along who was covered with leprosy.ᵇ When he saw Jesus, he fell with his face to the ground and begged him, "Lord, if you are willing, you can make me clean."

¹³Jesus reached out his hand and touched the man. "I am willing," he said. "Be clean!" And immediately the leprosy left him.

¹⁴Then Jesus ordered him, "Don't tell anyone, but go, show yourself to the priest and offer the sacrifices that Moses commanded for your cleansing, as a testimony to them."

¹⁵Yet the news about him spread all the more, so that crowds of people came to hear him and to be healed of their sicknesses. ¹⁶But Jesus often withdrew to lonely places and prayed.

Jesus Forgives and Heals a Paralyzed Man

¹⁷One day Jesus was teaching, and Pharisees and teachers of the law were sitting there. They had come from every village of Galilee and from Judea and Jerusalem. And the power of

---

ᵃ 1 That is, the Sea of Galilee   ᵇ 12 The Greek word traditionally translated *leprosy* was used for various diseases affecting the skin.

the Lord was with Jesus to heal the sick. ¹⁸Some men came carrying a paralyzed man on a mat and tried to take him into the house to lay him before Jesus. ¹⁹When they could not find a way to do this because of the crowd, they went up on the roof and lowered him on his mat through the tiles into the middle of the crowd, right in front of Jesus.

²⁰When Jesus saw their faith, he said, "Friend, your sins are forgiven."

²¹The Pharisees and the teachers of the law began thinking to themselves, "Who is this fellow who speaks blasphemy? Who can forgive sins but God alone?"

²²Jesus knew what they were thinking and asked, "Why are you thinking these things in your hearts? ²³Which is easier: to say, 'Your sins are forgiven,' or to say, 'Get up and walk'? ²⁴But I want you to know that the Son of Man has authority on earth to forgive sins." So he said to the paralyzed man, "I tell you, get up, take your mat and go home." ²⁵Immediately he stood up in front of them, took what he had been lying on and went home praising God. ²⁶Everyone was amazed and gave praise to God. They were filled with awe and said, "We have seen remarkable things today."

Jesus Calls Levi and Eats With Sinners

²⁷After this, Jesus went out and saw a tax collector by the name of Levi sitting at his tax booth. "Follow me," Jesus said to him, ²⁸and Levi got up, left everything and followed him.

²⁹Then Levi held a great banquet for Jesus at his house, and a large crowd of tax collectors and others were eating with them. ³⁰But the Pharisees and the teachers of the law who belonged to their sect com-plained to his disciples, "Why do you eat and drink with tax collectors and sinners?"

³¹Jesus answered them, "It is not the healthy who need a doctor, but the sick. ³²I have not come to call the righteous, but sinners to repentance."

Jesus Questioned About Fasting

³³They said to him, "John's disciples often fast and pray, and so do the disciples of the Pharisees, but yours go on eating and drinking."

³⁴Jesus answered, "Can you make the friends of the bridegroom fast while he is with them? ³⁵But the time will come when the bridegroom will be taken from them; in those days they will fast."

³⁶He told them this parable: "No one tears a piece out of a new garment to patch an old one. Otherwise, they will have torn the new garment, and the patch from the new will not match the old. ³⁷And no one pours new wine into old wineskins. Otherwise, the new wine will burst the skins; the wine will run out and the wineskins will be ruined. ³⁸No, new wine must be poured into new wineskins. ³⁹And no one after drinking old wine wants the new, for they say, 'The old is better.'"

Jesus Is Lord of the Sabbath

6 One Sabbath Jesus was going through the grainfields, and his disciples began to pick some heads of grain, rub them in their hands and eat the kernels. ²Some of the Pharisees asked, "Why are you doing what is unlawful on the Sabbath?"

³Jesus answered them, "Have you never read what David did when he and his companions were hungry? ⁴He entered the house of God, and taking the consecrated bread, he ate

what is lawful only for priests to eat. And he also gave some to his companions." ⁵Then Jesus said to them, "The Son of Man is Lord of the Sabbath."

⁶On another Sabbath he went into the synagogue and was teaching, and a man was there whose right hand was shriveled. ⁷The Pharisees and the teachers of the law were looking for a reason to accuse Jesus, so they watched him closely to see if he would heal on the Sabbath. ⁸But Jesus knew what they were thinking and said to the man with the shriveled hand, "Get up and stand in front of everyone." So he got up and stood there.

⁹Then Jesus said to them, "I ask you, which is lawful on the Sabbath: to do good or to do evil, to save life or to destroy it?"

¹⁰He looked around at them all, and then said to the man, "Stretch out your hand." He did so, and his hand was completely restored. ¹¹But the Pharisees and the teachers of the law were furious and began to discuss with one another what they might do to Jesus.

The Twelve Apostles

¹²One of those days Jesus went out to a mountainside to pray, and spent the night praying to God. ¹³When morning came, he called his disciples to him and chose twelve of them, whom he also designated apostles: ¹⁴Simon (whom he named Peter), his brother Andrew, James, John, Philip, Bartholomew, ¹⁵Matthew, Thomas, James son of Alphaeus, Simon who was called the Zealot, ¹⁶Judas son of James, and Judas Iscariot, who became a traitor.

Blessings and Woes

¹⁷He went down with them and stood on a level place. A large crowd of his disciples was there and a great number of people from all over Judea, from Jerusalem, and from the coastal region around Tyre and Sidon, ¹⁸who had come to hear him and to be healed of their diseases. Those troubled by impure spirits were cured, ¹⁹and the people all tried to touch him, because power was coming from him and healing them all.

²⁰Looking at his disciples, he said:

"Blessed are you who are poor,
   for yours is the kingdom of God.
²¹ Blessed are you who hunger now,
   for you will be satisfied.
Blessed are you who weep now,
   for you will laugh.
²² Blessed are you when people hate you,
   when they exclude you and insult you
   and reject your name as evil,
      because of the Son of Man.

²³"Rejoice in that day and leap for joy, because great is your reward in heaven. For that is how their ancestors treated the prophets.

²⁴ "But woe to you who are rich,
   for you have already received your comfort.
²⁵ Woe to you who are well fed now,
   for you will go hungry.
Woe to you who laugh now,
   for you will mourn and weep.
²⁶ Woe to you when everyone speaks well of you,
   for that is how their ancestors treated the false prophets.

Love for Enemies

²⁷"But to you who are listening I say: Love your enemies, do good to those who hate you, ²⁸bless those who curse you, pray for those who mistreat you. ²⁹If someone slaps you

on one cheek, turn to them the other also. If someone takes your coat, do not withhold your shirt from them. ³⁰Give to everyone who asks you, and if anyone takes what belongs to you, do not demand it back. ³¹Do to others as you would have them do to you.

³²"If you love those who love you, what credit is that to you? Even sinners love those who love them. ³³And if you do good to those who are good to you, what credit is that to you? Even sinners do that. ³⁴And if you lend to those from whom you expect repayment, what credit is that to you? Even sinners lend to sinners, expecting to be repaid in full. ³⁵But love your enemies, do good to them, and lend to them without expecting to get anything back. Then your reward will be great, and you will be children of the Most High, because he is kind to the ungrateful and wicked. ³⁶Be merciful, just as your Father is merciful.

Judging Others

³⁷"Do not judge, and you will not be judged. Do not condemn, and you will not be condemned. Forgive, and you will be forgiven. ³⁸Give, and it will be given to you. A good measure, pressed down, shaken together and running over, will be poured into your lap. For with the measure you use, it will be measured to you."

³⁹He also told them this parable: "Can the blind lead the blind? Will they not both fall into a pit? ⁴⁰The student is not above the teacher, but everyone who is fully trained will be like their teacher.

⁴¹"Why do you look at the speck of sawdust in your brother's eye and pay no attention to the plank in your own eye? ⁴²How can you say to your brother, 'Brother, let me take the speck out of your eye,' when you yourself fail to see the plank in your own eye? You hypocrite, first take the plank out of your eye, and then you will see clearly to remove the speck from your brother's eye.

A Tree and Its Fruit

⁴³"No good tree bears bad fruit, nor does a bad tree bear good fruit. ⁴⁴Each tree is recognized by its own fruit. People do not pick figs from thornbushes, or grapes from briers. ⁴⁵A good man brings good things out of the good stored up in his heart, and an evil man brings evil things out of the evil stored up in his heart. For the mouth speaks what the heart is full of.

The Wise and Foolish Builders

⁴⁶"Why do you call me, 'Lord, Lord,' and do not do what I say? ⁴⁷As for everyone who comes to me and hears my words and puts them into practice, I will show you what they are like. ⁴⁸They are like a man building a house, who dug down deep and laid the foundation on rock. When a flood came, the torrent struck that house but could not shake it, because it was well built. ⁴⁹But the one who hears my words and does not put them into practice is like a man who built a house on the ground without a foundation. The moment the torrent struck that house, it collapsed and its destruction was complete."

The Faith of the Centurion

7 When Jesus had finished saying all this to the people who were listening, he entered Capernaum. ²There a centurion's servant, whom his master valued highly, was sick and about to die. ³The centurion heard of Jesus and sent some elders of the Jews to him, asking him to come and heal his servant. [4]When they came to Jesus, they pleaded earnestly with him, "This man deserves to have you do this, [5]because he loves our nation and has built our synagogue." [6]So Jesus went with them.

He was not far from the house when the centurion sent friends to say to him: "Lord, don't trouble yourself, for I do not deserve to have you come under my roof. [7]That is why I did not even consider myself worthy to come to you. But say the word, and my servant will be healed. [8]For I myself am a man under authority, with soldiers under me. I tell this one, 'Go,' and he goes; and that one, 'Come,' and he comes. I say to my servant, 'Do this,' and he does it."

[9]When Jesus heard this, he was amazed at him, and turning to the crowd following him, he said, "I tell you, I have not found such great faith even in Israel." [10]Then the men who had been sent returned to the house and found the servant well.

Jesus Raises a Widow's Son

[11]Soon afterward, Jesus went to a town called Nain, and his disciples and a large crowd went along with him. [12]As he approached the town gate, a dead person was being carried out — the only son of his mother, and she was a widow. And a large crowd from the town was with her. [13]When the Lord saw her, his heart went out to her and he said, "Don't cry."

[14]Then he went up and touched the bier they were carrying him on, and the bearers stood still. He said, "Young man, I say to you, get up!" [15]The dead man sat up and began to talk, and Jesus gave him back to his mother.

[16]They were all filled with awe and praised God. "A great prophet has appeared among us," they said. "God has come to help his people." [17]This news about Jesus spread throughout Judea and the surrounding country.

Jesus and John the Baptist

[18]John's disciples told him about all these things. Calling two of them, [19]he sent them to the Lord to ask, "Are you the one who is to come, or should we expect someone else?"

[20]When the men came to Jesus, they said, "John the Baptist sent us to you to ask, 'Are you the one who is to come, or should we expect someone else?'"

[21]At that very time Jesus cured many who had diseases, sicknesses and evil spirits, and gave sight to many who were blind. [22]So he replied to the messengers, "Go back and report to John what you have seen and heard: The blind receive sight, the lame walk, those who have leprosy[a] are cleansed, the deaf hear, the dead are raised, and the good news is proclaimed to the poor. [23]Blessed is anyone who does not stumble on account of me."

[24]After John's messengers left, Jesus began to speak to the crowd about John: "What did you go out into the wilderness to see? A reed swayed by the wind? [25]If not, what did you go out to see? A man dressed in fine clothes? No, those who wear expensive clothes and indulge in luxury are in palaces. [26]But what did you go out to see? A prophet? Yes, I tell you, and more than a prophet. [27]This is the one about whom it is written:

"'I will send my messenger
   ahead of you,
who will prepare your way
   before you.'[b]

[a] 22 The Greek word traditionally translated *leprosy* was used for various diseases affecting the skin. [b] 27 Mal. 3:1

²⁸I tell you, among those born of women there is no one greater than John; yet the one who is least in the kingdom of God is greater than he."

²⁹(All the people, even the tax collectors, when they heard Jesus' words, acknowledged that God's way was right, because they had been baptized by John. ³⁰But the Pharisees and the experts in the law rejected God's purpose for themselves, because they had not been baptized by John.)

³¹Jesus went on to say, "To what, then, can I compare the people of this generation? What are they like? ³²They are like children sitting in the marketplace and calling out to each other:

" 'We played the pipe for you,
      and you did not dance;
  we sang a dirge,
      and you did not cry.'

³³For John the Baptist came neither eating bread nor drinking wine, and you say, 'He has a demon.' ³⁴The Son of Man came eating and drinking, and you say, 'Here is a glutton and a drunkard, a friend of tax collectors and sinners.' ³⁵But wisdom is proved right by all her children."

Jesus Anointed by a Sinful Woman

³⁶When one of the Pharisees invited Jesus to have dinner with him, he went to the Pharisee's house and reclined at the table. ³⁷A woman in that town who lived a sinful life learned that Jesus was eating at the Pharisee's house, so she came there with an alabaster jar of perfume. ³⁸As she stood behind him at his feet weeping, she began to wet his feet with her tears. Then she wiped them with her hair, kissed them and poured perfume on them.

³⁹When the Pharisee who had invited him saw this, he said to himself, "If this man were a prophet, he would know who is touching him and what kind of woman she is — that she is a sinner."

⁴⁰Jesus answered him, "Simon, I have something to tell you."

"Tell me, teacher," he said.

⁴¹"Two people owed money to a certain moneylender. One owed him five hundred denarii,ᵃ and the other fifty. ⁴²Neither of them had the money to pay him back, so he forgave the debts of both. Now which of them will love him more?"

⁴³Simon replied, "I suppose the one who had the bigger debt forgiven."

"You have judged correctly," Jesus said.

⁴⁴Then he turned toward the woman and said to Simon, "Do you see this woman? I came into your house. You did not give me any water for my feet, but she wet my feet with her tears and wiped them with her hair. ⁴⁵You did not give me a kiss, but this woman, from the time I entered, has not stopped kissing my feet. ⁴⁶You did not put oil on my head, but she has poured perfume on my feet. ⁴⁷Therefore, I tell you, her many sins have been forgiven — as her great love has shown. But whoever has been forgiven little loves little."

⁴⁸Then Jesus said to her, "Your sins are forgiven."

⁴⁹The other guests began to say among themselves, "Who is this who even forgives sins?"

⁵⁰Jesus said to the woman, "Your faith has saved you; go in peace."

The Parable of the Sower

8 After this, Jesus traveled about from one town and village to another, proclaiming the good news of

---

ᵃ 41 A denarius was the usual daily wage of a day laborer (see Matt. 20:2).

the kingdom of God. The Twelve were with him, ²and also some women who had been cured of evil spirits and diseases: Mary (called Magdalene) from whom seven demons had come out; ³Joanna the wife of Chuza, the manager of Herod's household; Susanna; and many others. These women were helping to support them out of their own means.

⁴While a large crowd was gathering and people were coming to Jesus from town after town, he told this parable: ⁵"A farmer went out to sow his seed. As he was scattering the seed, some fell along the path; it was trampled on, and the birds ate it up. ⁶Some fell on rocky ground, and when it came up, the plants withered because they had no moisture. ⁷Other seed fell among thorns, which grew up with it and choked the plants. ⁸Still other seed fell on good soil. It came up and yielded a crop, a hundred times more than was sown."

When he said this, he called out, "Whoever has ears to hear, let them hear."

⁹His disciples asked him what this parable meant. ¹⁰He said, "The knowledge of the secrets of the kingdom of God has been given to you, but to others I speak in parables, so that,

"'though seeing, they may not
    see;
though hearing, they may not
    understand.'ᵃ

¹¹"This is the meaning of the parable: The seed is the word of God. ¹²Those along the path are the ones who hear, and then the devil comes and takes away the word from their hearts, so that they may not believe and be saved. ¹³Those on the rocky ground are the ones who receive the word with joy when they hear it, but

they have no root. They believe for a while, but in the time of testing they fall away. ¹⁴The seed that fell among thorns stands for those who hear, but as they go on their way they are choked by life's worries, riches and pleasures, and they do not mature. ¹⁵But the seed on good soil stands for those with a noble and good heart, who hear the word, retain it, and by persevering produce a crop.

A Lamp on a Stand

¹⁶"No one lights a lamp and hides it in a clay jar or puts it under a bed. Instead, they put it on a stand, so that those who come in can see the light. ¹⁷For there is nothing hidden that will not be disclosed, and nothing concealed that will not be known or brought out into the open. ¹⁸Therefore consider carefully how you listen. Whoever has will be given more; whoever does not have, even what they think they have will be taken from them."

Jesus' Mother and Brothers

¹⁹Now Jesus' mother and brothers came to see him, but they were not able to get near him because of the crowd. ²⁰Someone told him, "Your mother and brothers are standing outside, wanting to see you."

²¹He replied, "My mother and brothers are those who hear God's word and put it into practice."

Jesus Calms the Storm

²²One day Jesus said to his disciples, "Let us go over to the other side of the lake." So they got into a boat and set out. ²³As they sailed, he fell asleep. A squall came down on the lake, so that the boat was being

---

ᵃ 10 Isaiah 6:9

swamped, and they were in great danger.

²⁴The disciples went and woke him, saying, "Master, Master, we're going to drown!"

He got up and rebuked the wind and the raging waters; the storm subsided, and all was calm. ²⁵"Where is your faith?" he asked his disciples.

In fear and amazement they asked one another, "Who is this? He commands even the winds and the water, and they obey him."

Jesus Restores a Demon-Possessed Man

²⁶They sailed to the region of the Gerasenes,ᵃ which is across the lake from Galilee. ²⁷When Jesus stepped ashore, he was met by a demon-possessed man from the town. For a long time this man had not worn clothes or lived in a house, but had lived in the tombs. ²⁸When he saw Jesus, he cried out and fell at his feet, shouting at the top of his voice, "What do you want with me, Jesus, Son of the Most High God? I beg you, don't torture me!" ²⁹For Jesus had commanded the impure spirit to come out of the man. Many times it had seized him, and though he was chained hand and foot and kept under guard, he had broken his chains and had been driven by the demon into solitary places.

³⁰Jesus asked him, "What is your name?"

"Legion," he replied, because many demons had gone into him. ³¹And they begged Jesus repeatedly not to order them to go into the Abyss.

³²A large herd of pigs was feeding there on the hillside. The demons begged Jesus to let them go into the pigs, and he gave them permission. ³³When the demons came out of the man, they went into the pigs, and the herd rushed down the steep bank into the lake and was drowned.

³⁴When those tending the pigs saw what had happened, they ran off and reported this in the town and countryside, ³⁵and the people went out to see what had happened. When they came to Jesus, they found the man from whom the demons had gone out, sitting at Jesus' feet, dressed and in his right mind; and they were afraid. ³⁶Those who had seen it told the people how the demon-possessed man had been cured. ³⁷Then all the people of the region of the Gerasenes asked Jesus to leave them, because they were overcome with fear. So he got into the boat and left.

³⁸The man from whom the demons had gone out begged to go with him, but Jesus sent him away, saying, ³⁹"Return home and tell how much God has done for you." So the man went away and told all over town how much Jesus had done for him.

Jesus Raises a Dead Girl and Heals a Sick Woman

⁴⁰Now when Jesus returned, a crowd welcomed him, for they were all expecting him. ⁴¹Then a man named Jairus, a synagogue leader, came and fell at Jesus' feet, pleading with him to come to his house ⁴²because his only daughter, a girl of about twelve, was dying.

As Jesus was on his way, the crowds almost crushed him. ⁴³And a woman was there who had been subject to bleeding for twelve years,ᵇ but no one could heal her. ⁴⁴She came up behind him and touched the edge of his cloak, and immediately her bleeding stopped.

ᵃ 26 Some manuscripts *Gadarenes*; other manuscripts *Gergesenes*; also in verse 37
ᵇ 43 Many manuscripts *years, and she had spent all she had on doctors*

⁴⁵"Who touched me?" Jesus asked.

When they all denied it, Peter said, "Master, the people are crowding and pressing against you."

⁴⁶But Jesus said, "Someone touched me; I know that power has gone out from me."

⁴⁷Then the woman, seeing that she could not go unnoticed, came trembling and fell at his feet. In the presence of all the people, she told why she had touched him and how she had been instantly healed. ⁴⁸Then he said to her, "Daughter, your faith has healed you. Go in peace."

⁴⁹While Jesus was still speaking, someone came from the house of Jairus, the synagogue leader. "Your daughter is dead," he said. "Don't bother the teacher anymore."

⁵⁰Hearing this, Jesus said to Jairus, "Don't be afraid; just believe, and she will be healed."

⁵¹When he arrived at the house of Jairus, he did not let anyone go in with him except Peter, John and James, and the child's father and mother. ⁵²Meanwhile, all the people were wailing and mourning for her. "Stop wailing," Jesus said. "She is not dead but asleep."

⁵³They laughed at him, knowing that she was dead. ⁵⁴But he took her by the hand and said, "My child, get up!" ⁵⁵Her spirit returned, and at once she stood up. Then Jesus told them to give her something to eat. ⁵⁶Her parents were astonished, but he ordered them not to tell anyone what had happened.

Jesus Sends Out the Twelve

9 When Jesus had called the Twelve together, he gave them power and authority to drive out all demons and to cure diseases, ²and he sent them out to proclaim the kingdom of God

and to heal the sick. ³He told them: "Take nothing for the journey — no staff, no bag, no bread, no money, no extra shirt. ⁴Whatever house you enter, stay there until you leave that town. ⁵If people do not welcome you, leave their town and shake the dust off your feet as a testimony against them." ⁶So they set out and went from village to village, proclaiming the good news and healing people everywhere.

⁷Now Herod the tetrarch heard about all that was going on. And he was perplexed because some were saying that John had been raised from the dead, ⁸others that Elijah had appeared, and still others that one of the prophets of long ago had come back to life. ⁹But Herod said, "I beheaded John. Who, then, is this I hear such things about?" And he tried to see him.

Jesus Feeds the Five Thousand

¹⁰When the apostles returned, they reported to Jesus what they had done. Then he took them with him and they withdrew by themselves to a town called Bethsaida, ¹¹but the crowds learned about it and followed him. He welcomed them and spoke to them about the kingdom of God, and healed those who needed healing.

¹²Late in the afternoon the Twelve came to him and said, "Send the crowd away so they can go to the surrounding villages and countryside and find food and lodging, because we are in a remote place here."

¹³He replied, "You give them something to eat."

They answered, "We have only five loaves of bread and two fish — unless we go and buy food for all this crowd." ¹⁴(About five thousand men were there.)

But he said to his disciples, "Have them sit down in groups of about fifty each." ¹⁵The disciples did so, and everyone sat down. ¹⁶Taking the five loaves and the two fish and looking up to heaven, he gave thanks and broke them. Then he gave them to the disciples to distribute to the people. ¹⁷They all ate and were satisfied, and the disciples picked up twelve basketfuls of broken pieces that were left over.

Peter Declares That Jesus Is the Messiah

¹⁸Once when Jesus was praying in private and his disciples were with him, he asked them, "Who do the crowds say I am?"

¹⁹They replied, "Some say John the Baptist; others say Elijah; and still others, that one of the prophets of long ago has come back to life."

²⁰"But what about you?" he asked. "Who do you say I am?"

Peter answered, "God's Messiah."

Jesus Predicts His Death

²¹Jesus strictly warned them not to tell this to anyone. ²²And he said, "The Son of Man must suffer many things and be rejected by the elders, the chief priests and the teachers of the law, and he must be killed and on the third day be raised to life."

²³Then he said to them all: "Whoever wants to be my disciple must deny themselves and take up their cross daily and follow me. ²⁴For whoever wants to save their life will lose it, but whoever loses their life for me will save it. ²⁵What good is it for someone to gain the whole world, and yet lose or forfeit their very self? ²⁶Whoever is ashamed of me and my words, the Son of Man will be ashamed of them when he comes in his glory and in the glory of the Father and of the holy angels.

²⁷"Truly I tell you, some who are standing here will not taste death before they see the kingdom of God."

The Transfiguration

²⁸About eight days after Jesus said this, he took Peter, John and James with him and went up onto a mountain to pray. ²⁹As he was praying, the appearance of his face changed, and his clothes became as bright as a flash of lightning. ³⁰Two men, Moses and Elijah, appeared in glorious splendor, talking with Jesus. ³¹They spoke about his departure,ᵃ which he was about to bring to fulfillment at Jerusalem. ³²Peter and his companions were very sleepy, but when they became fully awake, they saw his glory and the two men standing with him. ³³As the men were leaving Jesus, Peter said to him, "Master, it is good for us to be here. Let us put up three shelters — one for you, one for Moses and one for Elijah." (He did not know what he was saying.)

³⁴While he was speaking, a cloud appeared and covered them, and they were afraid as they entered the cloud. ³⁵A voice came from the cloud, saying, "This is my Son, whom I have chosen; listen to him." ³⁶When the voice had spoken, they found that Jesus was alone. The disciples kept this to themselves and did not tell anyone at that time what they had seen.

Jesus Heals a Demon-Possessed Boy

³⁷The next day, when they came down from the mountain, a large crowd met him. ³⁸A man in the crowd called out, "Teacher, I beg you to look at my son, for he is my only child. ³⁹A spirit seizes him and

---

ᵃ 31 Greek *exodos*

he suddenly screams; it throws him into convulsions so that he foams at the mouth. It scarcely ever leaves him, and is destroying him. ⁴⁰I begged your disciples to drive it out, but they could not."

⁴¹"You unbelieving and perverse generation," Jesus replied, "how long shall I stay with you and put up with you? Bring your son here."

⁴²Even while the boy was coming, the demon threw him to the ground in a convulsion. But Jesus rebuked the impure spirit, healed the boy and gave him back to his father. ⁴³And they were all amazed at the greatness of God.

Jesus Predicts His Death a Second Time

While everyone was marveling at all that Jesus did, he said to his disciples, ⁴⁴"Listen carefully to what I am about to tell you: The Son of Man is going to be delivered into the hands of men." ⁴⁵But they did not understand what this meant. It was hidden from them, so that they did not grasp it, and they were afraid to ask him about it.

⁴⁶An argument started among the disciples as to which of them would be the greatest. ⁴⁷Jesus, knowing their thoughts, took a little child and had him stand beside him. ⁴⁸Then he said to them, "Whoever welcomes this little child in my name welcomes me; and whoever welcomes me welcomes the one who sent me. For it is the one who is least among you all who is the greatest."

⁴⁹"Master," said John, "we saw someone driving out demons in your name and we tried to stop him, because he is not one of us."

⁵⁰"Do not stop him," Jesus said, "for whoever is not against you is for you."

Samaritan Opposition

⁵¹As the time approached for him to be taken up to heaven, Jesus resolutely set out for Jerusalem. ⁵²And he sent messengers on ahead, who went into a Samaritan village to get things ready for him; ⁵³but the people there did not welcome him, because he was heading for Jerusalem. ⁵⁴When the disciples James and John saw this, they asked, "Lord, do you want us to call fire down from heaven to destroy them*ᵃ*?" ⁵⁵But Jesus turned and rebuked them. ⁵⁶Then he and his disciples went to another village.

The Cost of Following Jesus

⁵⁷As they were walking along the road, a man said to him, "I will follow you wherever you go."

⁵⁸Jesus replied, "Foxes have dens and birds have nests, but the Son of Man has no place to lay his head."

⁵⁹He said to another man, "Follow me."

But he replied, "Lord, first let me go and bury my father."

⁶⁰Jesus said to him, "Let the dead bury their own dead, but you go and proclaim the kingdom of God."

⁶¹Still another said, "I will follow you, Lord; but first let me go back and say goodbye to my family."

⁶²Jesus replied, "No one who puts a hand to the plow and looks back is fit for service in the kingdom of God."

Jesus Sends Out the Seventy-Two

10 After this the Lord appointed seventy-twoᵇ others and sent them two by two ahead of him to every town and place where he was about to go. ²He told them, "The

---

ᵃ 54 Some manuscripts *them, just as Elijah did*
ᵇ 1 Some manuscripts *seventy*; also in verse 17

harvest is plentiful, but the workers are few. Ask the Lord of the harvest, therefore, to send out workers into his harvest field. ³Go! I am sending you out like lambs among wolves. ⁴Do not take a purse or bag or sandals; and do not greet anyone on the road.

⁵"When you enter a house, first say, 'Peace to this house.' ⁶If someone who promotes peace is there, your peace will rest on them; if not, it will return to you. ⁷Stay there, eating and drinking whatever they give you, for the worker deserves his wages. Do not move around from house to house.

⁸"When you enter a town and are welcomed, eat what is offered to you. ⁹Heal the sick who are there and tell them, 'The kingdom of God has come near to you.' ¹⁰But when you enter a town and are not welcomed, go into its streets and say, ¹¹'Even the dust of your town we wipe from our feet as a warning to you. Yet be sure of this: The kingdom of God has come near.' ¹²I tell you, it will be more bearable on that day for Sodom than for that town.

¹³"Woe to you, Chorazin! Woe to you, Bethsaida! For if the miracles that were performed in you had been performed in Tyre and Sidon, they would have repented long ago, sitting in sackcloth and ashes. ¹⁴But it will be more bearable for Tyre and Sidon at the judgment than for you. ¹⁵And you, Capernaum, will you be lifted to the heavens? No, you will go down to Hades.ᵃ

¹⁶"Whoever listens to you listens to me; whoever rejects you rejects me; but whoever rejects me rejects him who sent me."

¹⁷The seventy-two returned with joy and said, "Lord, even the demons submit to us in your name."

¹⁸He replied, "I saw Satan fall like lightning from heaven. ¹⁹I have given you authority to trample on snakes and scorpions and to overcome all the power of the enemy; nothing will harm you. ²⁰However, do not rejoice that the spirits submit to you, but rejoice that your names are written in heaven."

²¹At that time Jesus, full of joy through the Holy Spirit, said, "I praise you, Father, Lord of heaven and earth, because you have hidden these things from the wise and learned, and revealed them to little children. Yes, Father, for this is what you were pleased to do.

²²"All things have been committed to me by my Father. No one knows who the Son is except the Father, and no one knows who the Father is except the Son and those to whom the Son chooses to reveal him."

²³Then he turned to his disciples and said privately, "Blessed are the eyes that see what you see. ²⁴For I tell you that many prophets and kings wanted to see what you see but did not see it, and to hear what you hear but did not hear it."

The Parable of the Good Samaritan

²⁵On one occasion an expert in the law stood up to test Jesus. "Teacher," he asked, "what must I do to inherit eternal life?"

²⁶"What is written in the Law?" he replied. "How do you read it?"

²⁷He answered, "'Love the Lord your God with all your heart and with all your soul and with all your strength and with all your mind'ᵇ; and, 'Love your neighbor as yourself.'ᶜ"

²⁸"You have answered correctly,"

ᵃ 15 That is, the realm of the dead   ᵇ 27 Deut. 6:5   ᶜ 27 Lev. 19:18

Jesus replied. "Do this and you will live."

[29]But he wanted to justify himself, so he asked Jesus, "And who is my neighbor?"

[30]In reply Jesus said: "A man was going down from Jerusalem to Jericho, when he was attacked by robbers. They stripped him of his clothes, beat him and went away, leaving him half dead. [31]A priest happened to be going down the same road, and when he saw the man, he passed by on the other side. [32]So too, a Levite, when he came to the place and saw him, passed by on the other side. [33]But a Samaritan, as he traveled, came where the man was; and when he saw him, he took pity on him. [34]He went to him and bandaged his wounds, pouring on oil and wine. Then he put the man on his own donkey, brought him to an inn and took care of him. [35]The next day he took out two denarii[a] and gave them to the innkeeper. 'Look after him,' he said, 'and when I return, I will reimburse you for any extra expense you may have.'

[36]"Which of these three do you think was a neighbor to the man who fell into the hands of robbers?"

[37]The expert in the law replied, "The one who had mercy on him."

Jesus told him, "Go and do likewise."

At the Home of Martha and Mary

[38]As Jesus and his disciples were on their way, he came to a village where a woman named Martha opened her home to him. [39]She had a sister called Mary, who sat at the Lord's feet listening to what he said. [40]But Martha was distracted by all the preparations that had to be made. She came to him and asked, "Lord, don't you care that my sister has left me to do the work by myself? Tell her to help me!"

[41]"Martha, Martha," the Lord answered, "you are worried and upset about many things, [42]but few things are needed — or indeed only one.[b] Mary has chosen what is better, and it will not be taken away from her."

Jesus' Teaching on Prayer

11 One day Jesus was praying in a certain place. When he finished, one of his disciples said to him, "Lord, teach us to pray, just as John taught his disciples."

[2]He said to them, "When you pray, say:

"'Father,[c]
hallowed be your name,
    your kingdom come.[d]
[3] Give us each day our daily bread.
[4] Forgive us our sins,
        for we also forgive everyone
            who sins against us.[e]
    And lead us not into
            temptation.'"

[5]Then Jesus said to them, "Suppose you have a friend, and you go to him at midnight and say, 'Friend, lend me three loaves of bread; [6]a friend of mine on a journey has come to me, and I have no food to offer him.' [7]And suppose the one inside answers, 'Don't bother me. The door is already locked, and my children and I are in bed. I can't get up and give you anything.' [8]I tell you, even though he will not get up and give you the bread

---

[a] 35 A denarius was the usual daily wage of a day laborer (see Matt. 20:2).   [b] 42 Some manuscripts *but only one thing is needed*   [c] 2 Some manuscripts *Our Father in heaven*   [d] 2 Some manuscripts *May your will be done on earth as it is in heaven.*   [e] 4 Greek *everyone who is indebted to us*   [f] 4 Some manuscripts *temptation, but deliver us from the evil one*

because of friendship, yet because of your shameless audacity[a] he will surely get up and give you as much as you need.

⁹"So I say to you: Ask and it will be given to you; seek and you will find; knock and the door will be opened to you. ¹⁰For everyone who asks receives; the one who seeks finds; and to the one who knocks, the door will be opened.

¹¹"Which of you fathers, if your son asks for[b] a fish, will give him a snake instead? ¹²Or if he asks for an egg, will give him a scorpion? ¹³If you then, though you are evil, know how to give good gifts to your children, how much more will your Father in heaven give the Holy Spirit to those who ask him!"

Jesus and Beelzebul

¹⁴Jesus was driving out a demon that was mute. When the demon left, the man who had been mute spoke, and the crowd was amazed. ¹⁵But some of them said, "By Beelzebul, the prince of demons, he is driving out demons." ¹⁶Others tested him by asking for a sign from heaven.

¹⁷Jesus knew their thoughts and said to them: "Any kingdom divided against itself will be ruined, and a house divided against itself will fall. ¹⁸If Satan is divided against himself, how can his kingdom stand? I say this because you claim that I drive out demons by Beelzebul. ¹⁹Now if I drive out demons by Beelzebul, by whom do your followers drive them out? So then, they will be your judges. ²⁰But if I drive out demons by the finger of God, then the kingdom of God has come upon you.

²¹"When a strong man, fully armed, guards his own house, his possessions are safe. ²²But when someone stronger attacks and overpowers him, he takes away the armor in which the man trusted and divides up his plunder.

²³"Whoever is not with me is against me, and whoever does not gather with me scatters.

²⁴"When an impure spirit comes out of a person, it goes through arid places seeking rest and does not find it. Then it says, 'I will return to the house I left.' ²⁵When it arrives, it finds the house swept clean and put in order. ²⁶Then it goes and takes seven other spirits more wicked than itself, and they go in and live there. And the final condition of that person is worse than the first."

²⁷As Jesus was saying these things, a woman in the crowd called out, "Blessed is the mother who gave you birth and nursed you."

²⁸He replied, "Blessed rather are those who hear the word of God and obey it."

The Sign of Jonah

²⁹As the crowds increased, Jesus said, "This is a wicked generation. It asks for a sign, but none will be given it except the sign of Jonah. ³⁰For as Jonah was a sign to the Ninevites, so also will the Son of Man be to this generation. ³¹The Queen of the South will rise at the judgment with the people of this generation and condemn them, for she came from the ends of the earth to listen to Solomon's wisdom; and now something greater than Solomon is here. ³²The men of Nineveh will stand up at the judgment with this generation and condemn it, for they repented at the preaching of Jonah; and now something greater than Jonah is here.

---

[a] 8 Or yet to preserve his good name
[b] 11 Some manuscripts for bread, will give him a stone? Or if he asks for

The Lamp of the Body

³³"No one lights a lamp and puts it in a place where it will be hidden, or under a bowl. Instead they put it on its stand, so that those who come in may see the light. ³⁴Your eye is the lamp of your body. When your eyes are healthy,[a] your whole body also is full of light. But when they are unhealthy,[b] your body also is full of darkness. ³⁵See to it, then, that the light within you is not darkness. ³⁶Therefore, if your whole body is full of light, and no part of it dark, it will be just as full of light as when a lamp shines its light on you."

Woes on the Pharisees and the Experts in the Law

³⁷When Jesus had finished speaking, a Pharisee invited him to eat with him; so he went in and reclined at the table. ³⁸But the Pharisee was surprised when he noticed that Jesus did not first wash before the meal.

³⁹Then the Lord said to him, "Now then, you Pharisees clean the outside of the cup and dish, but inside you are full of greed and wickedness. ⁴⁰You foolish people! Did not the one who made the outside make the inside also? ⁴¹But now as for what is inside you — be generous to the poor, and everything will be clean for you.

⁴²"Woe to you Pharisees, because you give God a tenth of your mint, rue and all other kinds of garden herbs, but you neglect justice and the love of God. You should have practiced the latter without leaving the former undone.

⁴³"Woe to you Pharisees, because you love the most important seats in the synagogues and respectful greetings in the marketplaces.

⁴⁴"Woe to you, because you are like unmarked graves, which people walk over without knowing it."

⁴⁵One of the experts in the law answered him, "Teacher, when you say these things, you insult us also."

⁴⁶Jesus replied, "And you experts in the law, woe to you, because you load people down with burdens they can hardly carry, and you yourselves will not lift one finger to help them.

⁴⁷"Woe to you, because you build tombs for the prophets, and it was your ancestors who killed them. ⁴⁸So you testify that you approve of what your ancestors did; they killed the prophets, and you build their tombs. ⁴⁹Because of this, God in his wisdom said, 'I will send them prophets and apostles, some of whom they will kill and others they will persecute.' ⁵⁰Therefore this generation will be held responsible for the blood of all the prophets that has been shed since the beginning of the world, ⁵¹from the blood of Abel to the blood of Zechariah, who was killed between the altar and the sanctuary. Yes, I tell you, this generation will be held responsible for it all.

⁵²"Woe to you experts in the law, because you have taken away the key to knowledge. You yourselves have not entered, and you have hindered those who were entering."

⁵³When Jesus went outside, the Pharisees and the teachers of the law began to oppose him fiercely and to besiege him with questions, ⁵⁴waiting to catch him in something he might say.

Warnings and Encouragements

12 Meanwhile, when a crowd of many thousands had gathered, so that they were trampling on one

---

[a] 34 The Greek for *healthy* here implies *generous*.   [b] 34 The Greek for *unhealthy* here implies *stingy*.

another, Jesus began to speak first to his disciples, saying: "Be[a] on your guard against the yeast of the Pharisees, which is hypocrisy. [2]There is nothing concealed that will not be disclosed, or hidden that will not be made known. [3]What you have said in the dark will be heard in the daylight, and what you have whispered in the ear in the inner rooms will be proclaimed from the roofs.

[4]"I tell you, my friends, do not be afraid of those who kill the body and after that can do no more. [5]But I will show you whom you should fear: Fear him who, after your body has been killed, has authority to throw you into hell. Yes, I tell you, fear him. [6]Are not five sparrows sold for two pennies? Yet not one of them is forgotten by God. [7]Indeed, the very hairs of your head are all numbered. Don't be afraid; you are worth more than many sparrows.

[8]"I tell you, whoever publicly acknowledges me before others, the Son of Man will also acknowledge before the angels of God. [9]But whoever disowns me before others will be disowned before the angels of God. [10]And everyone who speaks a word against the Son of Man will be forgiven, but anyone who blasphemes against the Holy Spirit will not be forgiven.

[11]"When you are brought before synagogues, rulers and authorities, do not worry about how you will defend yourselves or what you will say, [12]for the Holy Spirit will teach you at that time what you should say."

The Parable of the Rich Fool

[13]Someone in the crowd said to him, "Teacher, tell my brother to divide the inheritance with me."

[14]Jesus replied, "Man, who appointed me a judge or an arbiter between you?" [15]Then he said to them, "Watch out! Be on your guard against all kinds of greed; life does not consist in an abundance of possessions."

[16]And he told them this parable: "The ground of a certain rich man yielded an abundant harvest. [17]He thought to himself, 'What shall I do? I have no place to store my crops.'

[18]"Then he said, 'This is what I'll do. I will tear down my barns and build bigger ones, and there I will store my surplus grain. [19]And I'll say to myself, "You have plenty of grain laid up for many years. Take life easy; eat, drink and be merry."'

[20]"But God said to him, 'You fool! This very night your life will be demanded from you. Then who will get what you have prepared for yourself?'

[21]"This is how it will be with whoever stores up things for themselves but is not rich toward God."

Do Not Worry

[22]Then Jesus said to his disciples: "Therefore I tell you, do not worry about your life, what you will eat; or about your body, what you will wear. [23]For life is more than food, and the body more than clothes. [24]Consider the ravens: They do not sow or reap, they have no storeroom or barn; yet God feeds them. And how much more valuable you are than birds! [25]Who of you by worrying can add a single hour to your life[b]? [26]Since you cannot do this very little thing, why do you worry about the rest?

[27]"Consider how the wild flowers grow. They do not labor or spin. Yet I tell you, not even Solomon in all his splendor was dressed like one of these. [28]If that is how God clothes the grass of the field, which is here to-

---

[a] 1 Or speak to his disciples, saying: "First of all, be   [b] 25 Or single cubit to your height

day, and tomorrow is thrown into the fire, how much more will he clothe you — you of little faith! ²⁹And do not set your heart on what you will eat or drink; do not worry about it. ³⁰For the pagan world runs after all such things, and your Father knows that you need them. ³¹But seek his kingdom, and these things will be given to you as well.

³²"Do not be afraid, little flock, for your Father has been pleased to give you the kingdom. ³³Sell your possessions and give to the poor. Provide purses for yourselves that will not wear out, a treasure in heaven that will never fail, where no thief comes near and no moth destroys. ³⁴For where your treasure is, there your heart will be also.

Watchfulness

³⁵"Be dressed ready for service and keep your lamps burning, ³⁶like servants waiting for their master to return from a wedding banquet, so that when he comes and knocks they can immediately open the door for him. ³⁷It will be good for those servants whose master finds them watching when he comes. Truly I tell you, he will dress himself to serve, will have them recline at the table and will come and wait on them. ³⁸It will be good for those servants whose master finds them ready, even if he comes in the middle of the night or toward daybreak. ³⁹But understand this: If the owner of the house had known at what hour the thief was coming, he would not have let his house be broken into. ⁴⁰You also must be ready, because the Son of Man will come at an hour when you do not expect him."

⁴¹Peter asked, "Lord, are you telling this parable to us, or to everyone?"

⁴²The Lord answered, "Who then is the faithful and wise manager, whom the master puts in charge of his servants to give them their food allowance at the proper time? ⁴³It will be good for that servant whom the master finds doing so when he returns. ⁴⁴Truly I tell you, he will put him in charge of all his possessions. ⁴⁵But suppose the servant says to himself, 'My master is taking a long time in coming,' and he then begins to beat the other servants, both men and women, and to eat and drink and get drunk. ⁴⁶The master of that servant will come on a day when he does not expect him and at an hour he is not aware of. He will cut him to pieces and assign him a place with the unbelievers.

⁴⁷"The servant who knows the master's will and does not get ready or does not do what the master wants will be beaten with many blows. ⁴⁸But the one who does not know and does things deserving punishment will be beaten with few blows. From everyone who has been given much, much will be demanded; and from the one who has been entrusted with much, much more will be asked.

Not Peace but Division

⁴⁹"I have come to bring fire on the earth, and how I wish it were already kindled! ⁵⁰But I have a baptism to undergo, and what constraint I am under until it is completed! ⁵¹Do you think I came to bring peace on earth? No, I tell you, but division. ⁵²From now on there will be five in one family divided against each other, three against two and two against three. ⁵³They will be divided, father against son and son against father, mother against daughter and daughter against mother, mother-in-law against daughter-in-law and daughter-in-law against mother-in-law."

Interpreting the Times

⁵⁴He said to the crowd: "When you see a cloud rising in the west, immediately you say, 'It's going to rain,' and it does. ⁵⁵And when the south wind blows, you say, 'It's going to be hot,' and it is. ⁵⁶Hypocrites! You know how to interpret the appearance of the earth and the sky. How is it that you don't know how to interpret this present time?

⁵⁷"Why don't you judge for yourselves what is right? ⁵⁸As you are going with your adversary to the magistrate, try hard to be reconciled on the way, or your adversary may drag you off to the judge, and the judge turn you over to the officer, and the officer throw you into prison. ⁵⁹I tell you, you will not get out until you have paid the last penny."

Repent or Perish

13 Now there were some present at that time who told Jesus about the Galileans whose blood Pilate had mixed with their sacrifices. ²Jesus answered, "Do you think that these Galileans were worse sinners than all the other Galileans because they suffered this way? ³I tell you, no! But unless you repent, you too will all perish. ⁴Or those eighteen who died when the tower in Siloam fell on them — do you think they were more guilty than all the others living in Jerusalem? ⁵I tell you, no! But unless you repent, you too will all perish.

⁶Then he told this parable: "A man had a fig tree growing in his vineyard, and he went to look for fruit on it but did not find any. ⁷So he said to the man who took care of the vineyard, 'For three years now I've been coming to look for fruit on this fig tree and haven't found any. Cut it down! Why should it use up the soil?'

⁸"'Sir,' the man replied, 'leave it alone for one more year, and I'll dig around it and fertilize it. ⁹If it bears fruit next year, fine! If not, then cut it down.'"

Jesus Heals a Crippled Woman on the Sabbath

¹⁰On a Sabbath Jesus was teaching in one of the synagogues, ¹¹and a woman was there who had been crippled by a spirit for eighteen years. She was bent over and could not straighten up at all. ¹²When Jesus saw her, he called her forward and said to her, "Woman, you are set free from your infirmity." ¹³Then he put his hands on her, and immediately she straightened up and praised God.

¹⁴Indignant because Jesus had healed on the Sabbath, the synagogue leader said to the people, "There are six days for work. So come and be healed on those days, not on the Sabbath."

¹⁵The Lord answered him, "You hypocrites! Doesn't each of you on the Sabbath untie your ox or donkey from the stall and lead it out to give it water? ¹⁶Then should not this woman, a daughter of Abraham, whom Satan has kept bound for eighteen long years, be set free on the Sabbath day from what bound her?"

¹⁷When he said this, all his opponents were humiliated, but the people were delighted with all the wonderful things he was doing.

The Parables of the Mustard Seed and the Yeast

¹⁸Then Jesus asked, "What is the kingdom of God like? What shall I compare it to? ¹⁹It is like a mustard seed, which a man took and planted in his garden. It grew and became a tree, and the birds perched in its branches."

²⁰Again he asked, "What shall I compare the kingdom of God to? ²¹It is like yeast that a woman took and mixed into about sixty pounds*ᵃ* of flour until it worked all through the dough."

The Narrow Door

²²Then Jesus went through the towns and villages, teaching as he made his way to Jerusalem. ²³Someone asked him, "Lord, are only a few people going to be saved?"

He said to them, ²⁴"Make every effort to enter through the narrow door, because many, I tell you, will try to enter and will not be able to. ²⁵Once the owner of the house gets up and closes the door, you will stand outside knocking and pleading, 'Sir, open the door for us.'

"But he will answer, 'I don't know you or where you come from.'

²⁶"Then you will say, 'We ate and drank with you, and you taught in our streets.'

²⁷"But he will reply, 'I don't know you or where you come from. Away from me, all you evildoers!'

²⁸"There will be weeping there, and gnashing of teeth, when you see Abraham, Isaac and Jacob and all the prophets in the kingdom of God, but you yourselves thrown out. ²⁹People will come from east and west and north and south, and will take their places at the feast in the kingdom of God. ³⁰Indeed there are those who are last who will be first, and first who will be last."

Jesus' Sorrow for Jerusalem

³¹At that time some Pharisees came to Jesus and said to him, "Leave this place and go somewhere else. Herod wants to kill you."

³²He replied, "Go tell that fox, 'I will keep on driving out demons and healing people today and tomorrow, and on the third day I will reach my goal.' ³³In any case, I must press on today and tomorrow and the next day—for surely no prophet can die outside Jerusalem!

³⁴"Jerusalem, Jerusalem, you who kill the prophets and stone those sent to you, how often I have longed to gather your children together, as a hen gathers her chicks under her wings, and you were not willing. ³⁵Look, your house is left to you desolate. I tell you, you will not see me again until you say, 'Blessed is he who comes in the name of the Lord.'*ᵇ*

Jesus at a Pharisee's House

14 One Sabbath, when Jesus went to eat in the house of a prominent Pharisee, he was being carefully watched. ²There in front of him was a man suffering from abnormal swelling of his body. ³Jesus asked the Pharisees and experts in the law, "Is it lawful to heal on the Sabbath or not?" ⁴But they remained silent. So taking hold of the man, he healed him and sent him on his way.

⁵Then he asked them, "If one of you has a child*ᶜ* or an ox that falls into a well on the Sabbath day, will you not immediately pull it out?" ⁶And they had nothing to say.

⁷When he noticed how the guests picked the places of honor at the table, he told them this parable: ⁸"When someone invites you to a wedding feast, do not take the place of honor, for a person more distinguished than you may have been invited. ⁹If so, the host who invited both of you will come and say to you, 'Give this person your seat.' Then, humiliated, you will

---

ᵃ 21 Or about 27 kilograms   *ᵇ 35* Psalm 118:26
ᶜ 5 Some manuscripts *donkey*

have to take the least important place. ¹⁰But when you are invited, take the lowest place, so that when your host comes, he will say to you, 'Friend, move up to a better place.' Then you will be honored in the presence of all the other guests. ¹¹For all those who exalt themselves will be humbled, and those who humble themselves will be exalted."

¹²Then Jesus said to his host, "When you give a luncheon or dinner, do not invite your friends, your brothers or sisters, your relatives, or your rich neighbors; if you do, they may invite you back and so you will be repaid. ¹³But when you give a banquet, invite the poor, the crippled, the lame, the blind, ¹⁴and you will be blessed. Although they cannot repay you, you will be repaid at the resurrection of the righteous."

The Parable of the Great Banquet

¹⁵When one of those at the table with him heard this, he said to Jesus, "Blessed is the one who will eat at the feast in the kingdom of God."

¹⁶Jesus replied: "A certain man was preparing a great banquet and invited many guests. ¹⁷At the time of the banquet he sent his servant to tell those who had been invited, 'Come, for everything is now ready.'

¹⁸"But they all alike began to make excuses. The first said, 'I have just bought a field, and I must go and see it. Please excuse me.'

¹⁹"Another said, 'I have just bought five yoke of oxen, and I'm on my way to try them out. Please excuse me.'

²⁰"Still another said, 'I just got married, so I can't come.'

²¹"The servant came back and reported this to his master. Then the owner of the house became angry and ordered his servant, 'Go out quickly into the streets and alleys of the town and bring in the poor, the crippled, the blind and the lame.'

²²"'Sir,' the servant said, 'what you ordered has been done, but there is still room.'

²³"Then the master told his servant, 'Go out to the roads and country lanes and compel them to come in, so that my house will be full. ²⁴I tell you, not one of those who were invited will get a taste of my banquet.'"

The Cost of Being a Disciple

²⁵Large crowds were traveling with Jesus, and turning to them he said: ²⁶"If anyone comes to me and does not hate father and mother, wife and children, brothers and sisters — yes, even their own life — such a person cannot be my disciple. ²⁷And whoever does not carry their cross and follow me cannot be my disciple.

²⁸"Suppose one of you wants to build a tower. Won't you first sit down and estimate the cost to see if you have enough money to complete it? ²⁹For if you lay the foundation and are not able to finish it, everyone who sees it will ridicule you, ³⁰saying, 'This person began to build and wasn't able to finish.'

³¹"Or suppose a king is about to go to war against another king. Won't he first sit down and consider whether he is able with ten thousand men to oppose the one coming against him with twenty thousand? ³²If he is not able, he will send a delegation while the other is still a long way off and will ask for terms of peace. ³³In the same way, those of you who do not give up everything you have cannot be my disciples.

³⁴"Salt is good, but if it loses its saltiness, how can it be made salty

again? ³⁵It is fit neither for the soil nor for the manure pile; it is thrown out.

"Whoever has ears to hear, let them hear."

The Parable of the Lost Sheep

15 Now the tax collectors and sinners were all gathering around to hear Jesus. ²But the Pharisees and the teachers of the law muttered, "This man welcomes sinners and eats with them."

³Then Jesus told them this parable: ⁴"Suppose one of you has a hundred sheep and loses one of them. Doesn't he leave the ninety-nine in the open country and go after the lost sheep until he finds it? ⁵And when he finds it, he joyfully puts it on his shoulders ⁶and goes home. Then he calls his friends and neighbors together and says, 'Rejoice with me; I have found my lost sheep.' ⁷I tell you that in the same way there will be more rejoicing in heaven over one sinner who repents than over ninety-nine righteous persons who do not need to repent.

The Parable of the Lost Coin

⁸"Or suppose a woman has ten silver coins⁶ and loses one. Doesn't she light a lamp, sweep the house and search carefully until she finds it? ⁹And when she finds it, she calls her friends and neighbors together and says, 'Rejoice with me; I have found my lost coin.' ¹⁰In the same way, I tell you, there is rejoicing in the presence of the angels of God over one sinner who repents."

The Parable of the Lost Son

¹¹Jesus continued: "There was a man who had two sons. ¹²The younger one said to his father, 'Father, give me my share of the estate.' So he divided his property between them.

¹³"Not long after that, the younger son got together all he had, set off for a distant country and there squandered his wealth in wild living. ¹⁴After he had spent everything, there was a severe famine in that whole country, and he began to be in need. ¹⁵So he went and hired himself out to a citizen of that country, who sent him to his fields to feed pigs. ¹⁶He longed to fill his stomach with the pods that the pigs were eating, but no one gave him anything.

¹⁷"When he came to his senses, he said, 'How many of my father's hired servants have food to spare, and here I am starving to death! ¹⁸I will set out and go back to my father and say to him: Father, I have sinned against heaven and against you. ¹⁹I am no longer worthy to be called your son; make me like one of your hired servants.' ²⁰So he got up and went to his father.

"But while he was still a long way off, his father saw him and was filled with compassion for him; he ran to his son, threw his arms around him and kissed him.

²¹"The son said to him, 'Father, I have sinned against heaven and against you. I am no longer worthy to be called your son.'

²²"But the father said to his servants, 'Quick! Bring the best robe and put it on him. Put a ring on his finger and sandals on his feet. ²³Bring the fattened calf and kill it. Let's have a feast and celebrate. ²⁴For this son of mine was dead and is alive again; he was lost and is found.' So they began to celebrate.

²⁵"Meanwhile, the older son was in the field. When he came near the house, he heard music and dancing.

---

⁶ 8 Greek *ten drachmas*, each worth about a day's wages

26So he called one of the servants and asked him what was going on. 27'Your brother has come,' he replied, 'and your father has killed the fattened calf because he has him back safe and sound.'

28"The older brother became angry and refused to go in. So his father went out and pleaded with him. 29But he answered his father, 'Look! All these years I've been slaving for you and never disobeyed your orders. Yet you never gave me even a young goat so I could celebrate with my friends. 30But when this son of yours who has squandered your property with prostitutes comes home, you kill the fattened calf for him!'

31"'My son,' the father said, 'you are always with me, and everything I have is yours. 32But we had to celebrate and be glad, because this brother of yours was dead and is alive again; he was lost and is found.'"

The Parable of the Shrewd Manager

16 Jesus told his disciples: "There was a rich man whose manager was accused of wasting his possessions. 2So he called him in and asked him, 'What is this I hear about you? Give an account of your management, because you cannot be manager any longer.'

3"The manager said to himself, 'What shall I do now? My master is taking away my job. I'm not strong enough to dig, and I'm ashamed to beg— 4I know what I'll do so that, when I lose my job here, people will welcome me into their houses.'

5"So he called in each one of his master's debtors. He asked the first, 'How much do you owe my master?'

6"'Nine hundred gallons[a] of olive oil,' he replied.

"The manager told him, 'Take your bill, sit down quickly, and make it four hundred and fifty.'

7"Then he asked the second, 'And how much do you owe?'

"'A thousand bushels[b] of wheat,' he replied.

"He told him, 'Take your bill and make it eight hundred.'

8"The master commended the dishonest manager because he had acted shrewdly. For the people of this world are more shrewd in dealing with their own kind than are the people of the light. 9I tell you, use worldly wealth to gain friends for yourselves, so that when it is gone, you will be welcomed into eternal dwellings.

10"Whoever can be trusted with very little can also be trusted with much, and whoever is dishonest with very little will also be dishonest with much. 11So if you have not been trustworthy in handling worldly wealth, who will trust you with true riches? 12And if you have not been trustworthy with someone else's property, who will give you property of your own?

13"No one can serve two masters. Either you will hate the one and love the other, or you will be devoted to the one and despise the other. You cannot serve both God and money."

14The Pharisees, who loved money, heard all this and were sneering at Jesus. 15He said to them, "You are the ones who justify yourselves in the eyes of others, but God knows your hearts. What people value highly is detestable in God's sight.

Additional Teachings

16"The Law and the Prophets were proclaimed until John. Since that time, the good news of the kingdom

---

[a] 6 Or about 3,000 liters   [b] 7 Or about 30 tons

of God is being preached, and everyone is forcing their way into it. ¹⁷It is easier for heaven and earth to disappear than for the least stroke of a pen to drop out of the Law.

¹⁸"Anyone who divorces his wife and marries another woman commits adultery, and the man who marries a divorced woman commits adultery.

The Rich Man and Lazarus

¹⁹"There was a rich man who was dressed in purple and fine linen and lived in luxury every day. ²⁰At his gate was laid a beggar named Lazarus, covered with sores ²¹and longing to eat what fell from the rich man's table. Even the dogs came and licked his sores.

²²"The time came when the beggar died and the angels carried him to Abraham's side. The rich man also died and was buried. ²³In Hades, where he was in torment, he looked up and saw Abraham far away, with Lazarus by his side. ²⁴So he called to him, 'Father Abraham, have pity on me and send Lazarus to dip the tip of his finger in water and cool my tongue, because I am in agony in this fire.'

²⁵"But Abraham replied, 'Son, remember that in your lifetime you received your good things, while Lazarus received bad things, but now he is comforted here and you are in agony. ²⁶And besides all this, between us and you a great chasm has been set in place, so that those who want to go from here to you cannot, nor can anyone cross over from there to us.'

²⁷"He answered, 'Then I beg you, father, send Lazarus to my family, ²⁸for I have five brothers. Let him warn them, so that they will not also come to this place of torment.'

²⁹"Abraham replied, 'They have

Moses and the Prophets; let them listen to them.'

³⁰"'No, father Abraham,' he said, 'but if someone from the dead goes to them, they will repent.'

³¹"He said to him, 'If they do not listen to Moses and the Prophets, they will not be convinced even if someone rises from the dead.'"

Sin, Faith, Duty

17 Jesus said to his disciples: "Things that cause people to stumble are bound to come, but woe to anyone through whom they come. ²It would be better for them to be thrown into the sea with a millstone tied around their neck than to cause one of these little ones to stumble. ³So watch yourselves.

"If your brother or sister *a* sins against you, rebuke them; and if they repent, forgive them. ⁴Even if they sin against you seven times in a day and seven times come back to you saying 'I repent,' you must forgive them."

⁵The apostles said to the Lord, "Increase our faith!"

⁶He replied, "If you have faith as small as a mustard seed, you can say to this mulberry tree, 'Be uprooted and planted in the sea,' and it will obey you.

⁷"Suppose one of you has a servant plowing or looking after the sheep. Will he say to the servant when he comes in from the field, 'Come along now and sit down to eat'? ⁸Won't he rather say, 'Prepare my supper, get yourself ready and wait on me while I eat and drink; after that you may eat and drink'? ⁹Will he thank the servant because he did what he was told to do? ¹⁰So you also, when you have

---

a 3 The Greek word for *brother or sister* (*adelphos*) refers here to a fellow disciple, whether man or woman.

done everything you were told to do, should say, 'We are unworthy servants; we have only done our duty.'"

Jesus Heals Ten Men With Leprosy

¹¹Now on his way to Jerusalem, Jesus traveled along the border between Samaria and Galilee. ¹²As he was going into a village, ten men who had leprosy[a] met him. They stood at a distance ¹³and called out in a loud voice, "Jesus, Master, have pity on us!"

¹⁴When he saw them, he said, "Go, show yourselves to the priests." And as they went, they were cleansed.

¹⁵One of them, when he saw he was healed, came back, praising God in a loud voice. ¹⁶He threw himself at Jesus' feet and thanked him — and he was a Samaritan.

¹⁷Jesus asked, "Were not all ten cleansed? Where are the other nine? ¹⁸Has no one returned to give praise to God except this foreigner?" ¹⁹Then he said to him, "Rise and go; your faith has made you well."

The Coming of the Kingdom of God

²⁰Once, on being asked by the Pharisees when the kingdom of God would come, Jesus replied, "The coming of the kingdom of God is not something that can be observed, ²¹nor will people say, 'Here it is,' or 'There it is,' because the kingdom of God is in your midst."[b]

²²Then he said to his disciples, "The time is coming when you will long to see one of the days of the Son of Man, but you will not see it. ²³People will tell you, 'There he is!' or 'Here he is!' Do not go running off after them. ²⁴For the Son of Man in his day[c] will be like the lightning, which flashes and lights up the sky from one end to the other. ²⁵But first he must suffer

many things and be rejected by this generation.

²⁶"Just as it was in the days of Noah, so also will it be in the days of the Son of Man. ²⁷People were eating, drinking, marrying and being given in marriage up to the day Noah entered the ark. Then the flood came and destroyed them all.

²⁸"It was the same in the days of Lot. People were eating and drinking, buying and selling, planting and building. ²⁹But the day Lot left Sodom, fire and sulfur rained down from heaven and destroyed them all.

³⁰"It will be just like this on the day the Son of Man is revealed. ³¹On that day no one who is on the housetop, with possessions inside, should go down to get them. Likewise, no one in the field should go back for anything. ³²Remember Lot's wife! ³³Whoever tries to keep their life will lose it, and whoever loses their life will preserve it. ³⁴I tell you, on that night two people will be in one bed; one will be taken and the other left. ³⁵Two women will be grinding grain together; one will be taken and the other left. [³⁶][d]

³⁷"Where, Lord?" they asked.

He replied, "Where there is a dead body, there the vultures will gather."

The Parable of the Persistent Widow

18 Then Jesus told his disciples a parable to show them that they should always pray and not give up. ²He said: "In a certain town there was a judge who neither feared God

---

[a] 12 The Greek word traditionally translated *leprosy* was used for various diseases affecting the skin.   [b] 21 Or *is within you*   [c] 24 Some manuscripts do not have *in his day*.   [d] 36 Some manuscripts include here words similar to Matt. 24:40.

nor cared what people thought. ³And there was a widow in that town who kept coming to him with the plea, 'Grant me justice against my adversary.'

⁴"For some time he refused. But finally he said to himself, 'Even though I don't fear God or care what people think, ⁵yet because this widow keeps bothering me, I will see that she gets justice, so that she won't eventually come and attack me!'"

⁶And the Lord said, "Listen to what the unjust judge says. ⁷And will not God bring about justice for his chosen ones, who cry out to him day and night? Will he keep putting them off? ⁸I tell you, he will see that they get justice, and quickly. However, when the Son of Man comes, will he find faith on the earth?"

The Parable of the Pharisee and the Tax Collector

⁹To some who were confident of their own righteousness and looked down on everyone else, Jesus told this parable: ¹⁰"Two men went up to the temple to pray, one a Pharisee and the other a tax collector. ¹¹The Pharisee stood by himself and prayed: 'God, I thank you that I am not like other people—robbers, evildoers, adulterers—or even like this tax collector. ¹²I fast twice a week and give a tenth of all I get.'

¹³"But the tax collector stood at a distance. He would not even look up to heaven, but beat his breast and said, 'God, have mercy on me, a sinner.'

¹⁴"I tell you that this man, rather than the other, went home justified before God. For all those who exalt themselves will be humbled, and those who humble themselves will be exalted."

The Little Children and Jesus

¹⁵People were also bringing babies to Jesus for him to place his hands on them. When the disciples saw this, they rebuked them. ¹⁶But Jesus called the children to him and said, "Let the little children come to me, and do not hinder them, for the kingdom of God belongs to such as these. ¹⁷Truly I tell you, anyone who will not receive the kingdom of God like a little child will never enter it."

The Rich and the Kingdom of God

¹⁸A certain ruler asked him, "Good teacher, what must I do to inherit eternal life?"

¹⁹"Why do you call me good?" Jesus answered. "No one is good—except God alone. ²⁰You know the commandments: 'You shall not commit adultery, you shall not murder, you shall not steal, you shall not give false testimony, honor your father and mother.'ᵒ"

²¹"All these I have kept since I was a boy," he said.

²²When Jesus heard this, he said to him, "You still lack one thing. Sell everything you have and give to the poor, and you will have treasure in heaven. Then come, follow me."

²³When he heard this, he became very sad, because he was very wealthy. ²⁴Jesus looked at him and said, "How hard it is for the rich to enter the kingdom of God! ²⁵Indeed, it is easier for a camel to go through the eye of a needle than for someone who is rich to enter the kingdom of God."

²⁶Those who heard this asked, "Who then can be saved?"

²⁷Jesus replied, "What is impossible with man is possible with God."

ᵒ 20 Exodus 20:12-16; Deut. 5:16-20

²⁸Peter said to him, "We have left all we had to follow you!"

²⁹"Truly I tell you," Jesus said to them, "no one who has left home or wife or brothers or sisters or parents or children for the sake of the kingdom of God ³⁰will fail to receive many times as much in this age, and in the age to come eternal life."

Jesus Predicts His Death a Third Time

³¹Jesus took the Twelve aside and told them, "We are going up to Jerusalem, and everything that is written by the prophets about the Son of Man will be fulfilled. ³²He will be delivered over to the Gentiles. They will mock him, insult him and spit on him; ³³they will flog him and kill him. On the third day he will rise again." ³⁴The disciples did not understand any of this. Its meaning was hidden from them, and they did not know what he was talking about.

A Blind Beggar Receives His Sight

³⁵As Jesus approached Jericho, a blind man was sitting by the roadside begging. ³⁶When he heard the crowd going by, he asked what was happening. ³⁷They told him, "Jesus of Nazareth is passing by."

³⁸He called out, "Jesus, Son of David, have mercy on me!"

³⁹Those who led the way rebuked him and told him to be quiet, but he shouted all the more, "Son of David, have mercy on me!"

⁴⁰Jesus stopped and ordered the man to be brought to him. When he came near, Jesus asked him, ⁴¹"What do you want me to do for you?"

"Lord, I want to see," he replied.

⁴²Jesus said to him, "Receive your sight; your faith has healed you."

⁴³Immediately he received his sight and followed Jesus, praising God. When all the people saw it, they also praised God.

Zacchaeus the Tax Collector

19 Jesus entered Jericho and was passing through. ²A man was there by the name of Zacchaeus; he was a chief tax collector and was wealthy. ³He wanted to see who Jesus was, but because he was short he could not see over the crowd. ⁴So he ran ahead and climbed a sycamore-fig tree to see him, since Jesus was coming that way.

⁵When Jesus reached the spot, he looked up and said to him, "Zacchaeus, come down immediately. I must stay at your house today." ⁶So he came down at once and welcomed him gladly.

⁷All the people saw this and began to mutter, "He has gone to be the guest of a sinner."

⁸But Zacchaeus stood up and said to the Lord, "Look, Lord! Here and now I give half of my possessions to the poor, and if I have cheated anybody out of anything, I will pay back four times the amount."

⁹Jesus said to him, "Today salvation has come to this house, because this man, too, is a son of Abraham. ¹⁰For the Son of Man came to seek and to save the lost."

The Parable of the Ten Minas

¹¹While they were listening to this, he went on to tell them a parable, because he was near Jerusalem and the people thought that the kingdom of God was going to appear at once. ¹²He said: "A man of noble birth went to a distant country to have himself appointed king and then to return. ¹³So he called ten of his

servants and gave them ten minas.ᵃ 'Put this money to work,' he said, 'until I come back.'

¹⁴"But his subjects hated him and sent a delegation after him to say, 'We don't want this man to be our king.'

¹⁵"He was made king, however, and returned home. Then he sent for the servants to whom he had given the money, in order to find out what they had gained with it.

¹⁶"The first one came and said, 'Sir, your mina has earned ten more.'

¹⁷"'Well done, my good servant!' his master replied. 'Because you have been trustworthy in a very small matter, take charge of ten cities.'

¹⁸"The second came and said, 'Sir, your mina has earned five more.'

¹⁹"His master answered, 'You take charge of five cities.'

²⁰"Then another servant came and said, 'Sir, here is your mina; I have kept it laid away in a piece of cloth. ²¹I was afraid of you, because you are a hard man. You take out what you did not put in and reap what you did not sow.'

²²"His master replied, 'I will judge you by your own words, you wicked servant! You knew, did you, that I am a hard man, taking out what I did not put in, and reaping what I did not sow? ²³Why then didn't you put my money on deposit, so that when I came back, I could have collected it with interest?'

²⁴"Then he said to those standing by, 'Take his mina away from him and give it to the one who has ten minas.'

²⁵"'Sir,' they said, 'he already has ten!'

²⁶"He replied, 'I tell you that to everyone who has, more will be given, but as for the one who has nothing, even what they have will be taken away. ²⁷But those enemies of mine who did not want me to be king over them — bring them here and kill them in front of me.'"

Jesus Comes to Jerusalem as King

²⁸After Jesus had said this, he went on ahead, going up to Jerusalem. ²⁹As he approached Bethphage and Bethany at the hill called the Mount of Olives, he sent two of his disciples, saying to them, ³⁰"Go to the village ahead of you, and as you enter it, you will find a colt tied there, which no one has ever ridden. Untie it and bring it here. ³¹If anyone asks you, 'Why are you untying it?' say, 'The Lord needs it.'"

³²Those who were sent ahead went and found it just as he had told them. ³³As they were untying the colt, its owners asked them, "Why are you untying the colt?"

³⁴They replied, "The Lord needs it."

³⁵They brought it to Jesus, threw their cloaks on the colt and put Jesus on it. ³⁶As he went along, people spread their cloaks on the road.

³⁷When he came near the place where the road goes down the Mount of Olives, the whole crowd of disciples began joyfully to praise God in loud voices for all the miracles they had seen:

³⁸ "Blessed is the king who comes
        in the name of the Lord!"ᵇ

    "Peace in heaven and glory in the
        highest!"

³⁹Some of the Pharisees in the crowd said to Jesus, "Teacher, rebuke your disciples!"

⁴⁰"I tell you," he replied, "if they keep quiet, the stones will cry out."

⁴¹As he approached Jerusalem and

ᵃ 13 A mina was about three months' wages.
ᵇ 38 Psalm 118:26

saw the city, he wept over it [42] and said, "If you, even you, had only known on this day what would bring you peace—but now it is hidden from your eyes. [43] The days will come upon you when your enemies will build an embankment against you and encircle you and hem you in on every side. [44] They will dash you to the ground, you and the children within your walls. They will not leave one stone on another, because you did not recognize the time of God's coming to you."

Jesus at the Temple

[45] When Jesus entered the temple courts, he began to drive out those who were selling. [46] "It is written," he said to them, "'My house will be a house of prayer'[a]; but you have made it 'a den of robbers.'[b]"

[47] Every day he was teaching at the temple. But the chief priests, the teachers of the law and the leaders among the people were trying to kill him. [48] Yet they could not find any way to do it, because all the people hung on his words.

The Authority of Jesus Questioned

20 One day as Jesus was teaching the people in the temple courts and proclaiming the good news, the chief priests and the teachers of the law, together with the elders, came up to him. [2] "Tell us by what authority you are doing these things," they said. "Who gave you this authority?"

[3] He replied, "I will also ask you a question. Tell me: [4] John's baptism—was it from heaven, or of human origin?"

[5] They discussed it among themselves and said, "If we say, 'From heaven,' he will ask, 'Why didn't you believe him?' [6] But if we say, 'Of human origin,' all the people will stone us, because they are persuaded that John was a prophet."

[7] So they answered, "We don't know where it is from."

[8] Jesus said, "Neither will I tell you by what authority I am doing these things."

The Parable of the Tenants

[9] He went on to tell the people this parable: "A man planted a vineyard, rented it to some farmers and went away for a long time. [10] At harvest time he sent a servant to the tenants so they would give him some of the fruit of the vineyard. But the tenants beat him and sent him away empty-handed. [11] He sent another servant, but that one also they beat and treated shamefully and sent away empty-handed. [12] He sent still a third, and they wounded him and threw him out.

[13] "Then the owner of the vineyard said, 'What shall I do? I will send my son, whom I love; perhaps they will respect him.'

[14] "But when the tenants saw him, they talked the matter over. 'This is the heir,' they said. 'Let's kill him, and the inheritance will be ours.' [15] So they threw him out of the vineyard and killed him.

"What then will the owner of the vineyard do to them? [16] He will come and kill those tenants and give the vineyard to others."

When the people heard this, they said, "God forbid!"

[17] Jesus looked directly at them and asked, "Then what is the meaning of that which is written:

"'The stone the builders rejected
    has become the cornerstone'[c]?

---

[a] 46 Isaiah 56:7   [b] 46 Jer. 7:11
[c] 17 Psalm 118:22

18Everyone who falls on that stone will be broken to pieces; anyone on whom it falls will be crushed."

19The teachers of the law and the chief priests looked for a way to arrest him immediately, because they knew he had spoken this parable against them. But they were afraid of the people.

Paying Taxes to Caesar

20Keeping a close watch on him, they sent spies, who pretended to be sincere. They hoped to catch Jesus in something he said, so that they might hand him over to the power and authority of the governor. 21So the spies questioned him: "Teacher, we know that you speak and teach what is right, and that you do not show partiality but teach the way of God in accordance with the truth. 22Is it right for us to pay taxes to Caesar or not?"

23He saw through their duplicity and said to them, 24"Show me a denarius. Whose image and inscription are on it?"

"Caesar's," they replied.

25He said to them, "Then give back to Caesar what is Caesar's, and to God what is God's."

26They were unable to trap him in what he had said there in public. And astonished by his answer, they became silent.

The Resurrection and Marriage

27Some of the Sadducees, who say there is no resurrection, came to Jesus with a question. 28"Teacher," they said, "Moses wrote for us that if a man's brother dies and leaves a wife but no children, the man must marry the widow and raise up offspring for his brother. 29Now there were seven brothers. The first one married a woman and died childless. 30The second 31and then the third married her, and in the same way the seven died, leaving no children. 32Finally, the woman died too. 33Now then, at the resurrection whose wife will she be, since the seven were married to her?"

34Jesus replied, "The people of this age marry and are given in marriage. 35But those who are considered worthy of taking part in the age to come and in the resurrection from the dead will neither marry nor be given in marriage, 36and they can no longer die; for they are like the angels. They are God's children, since they are children of the resurrection. 37But in the account of the burning bush, even Moses showed that the dead rise, for he calls the Lord 'the God of Abraham, and the God of Isaac, and the God of Jacob.'a 38He is not the God of the dead, but of the living, for to him all are alive."

39Some of the teachers of the law responded, "Well said, teacher!" 40And no one dared to ask him any more questions.

Whose Son Is the Messiah?

41Then Jesus said to them, "Why is it said that the Messiah is the son of David? 42David himself declares in the Book of Psalms:

" 'The Lord said to my Lord:
    "Sit at my right hand
43 until I make your enemies
    a footstool for your feet." 'b

44David calls him 'Lord.' How then can he be his son?"

Warning Against the Teachers of the Law

45While all the people were listening, Jesus said to his disciples, 46"Beware of the teachers of the law. They

---

a 37 Exodus 3:6   b 43 Psalm 110:1

like to walk around in flowing robes and love to be greeted with respect in the marketplaces and have the most important seats in the synagogues and the places of honor at banquets. 47They devour widows' houses and for a show make lengthy prayers. These men will be punished most severely."

The Widow's Offering

21 As Jesus looked up, he saw the rich putting their gifts into the temple treasury. 2He also saw a poor widow put in two very small copper coins. 3"Truly I tell you," he said, "this poor widow has put in more than all the others. 4All these people gave their gifts out of their wealth; but she out of her poverty put in all she had to live on."

The Destruction of the Temple and Signs of the End Times

5Some of his disciples were remarking about how the temple was adorned with beautiful stones and with gifts dedicated to God. But Jesus said, 6"As for what you see here, the time will come when not one stone will be left on another; every one of them will be thrown down."

7"Teacher," they asked, "when will these things happen? And what will be the sign that they are about to take place?"

8He replied: "Watch out that you are not deceived. For many will come in my name, claiming, 'I am he,' and, 'The time is near.' Do not follow them. 9When you hear of wars and uprisings, do not be frightened. These things must happen first, but the end will not come right away."

10Then he said to them: "Nation will rise against nation, and kingdom against kingdom. 11There will be great earthquakes, famines and pestilences in various places, and fearful events and great signs from heaven.

12"But before all this, they will seize you and persecute you. They will hand you over to synagogues and put you in prison, and you will be brought before kings and governors, and all on account of my name. 13And so you will bear testimony to me. 14But make up your mind not to worry beforehand how you will defend yourselves. 15For I will give you words and wisdom that none of your adversaries will be able to resist or contradict. 16You will be betrayed even by parents, brothers and sisters, relatives and friends, and they will put some of you to death. 17Everyone will hate you because of me. 18But not a hair of your head will perish. 19Stand firm, and you will win life.

20"When you see Jerusalem being surrounded by armies, you will know that its desolation is near. 21Then let those who are in Judea flee to the mountains, let those in the city get out, and let those in the country not enter the city. 22For this is the time of punishment in fulfillment of all that has been written. 23How dreadful it will be in those days for pregnant women and nursing mothers! There will be great distress in the land and wrath against this people. 24They will fall by the sword and will be taken as prisoners to all the nations. Jerusalem will be trampled on by the Gentiles until the times of the Gentiles are fulfilled.

25"There will be signs in the sun, moon and stars. On the earth, nations will be in anguish and perplexity at the roaring and tossing of the sea. 26People will faint from terror, apprehensive of what is coming on the world, for the heavenly bodies will be shaken. 27At that time they will see the Son of Man coming in a cloud with power and great glory. ²⁸When these things begin to take place, stand up and lift up your heads, because your redemption is drawing near."

²⁹He told them this parable: "Look at the fig tree and all the trees. ³⁰When they sprout leaves, you can see for yourselves and know that summer is near. ³¹Even so, when you see these things happening, you know that the kingdom of God is near.

³²"Truly I tell you, this generation will certainly not pass away until all these things have happened. ³³Heaven and earth will pass away, but my words will never pass away.

³⁴"Be careful, or your hearts will be weighed down with carousing, drunkenness and the anxieties of life, and that day will close on you suddenly like a trap. ³⁵For it will come on all those who live on the face of the whole earth. ³⁶Be always on the watch, and pray that you may be able to escape all that is about to happen, and that you may be able to stand before the Son of Man."

³⁷Each day Jesus was teaching at the temple, and each evening he went out to spend the night on the hill called the Mount of Olives, ³⁸and all the people came early in the morning to hear him at the temple.

Judas Agrees to Betray Jesus

22 Now the Festival of Unleavened Bread, called the Passover, was approaching, ²and the chief priests and the teachers of the law were looking for some way to get rid of Jesus, for they were afraid of the people. ³Then Satan entered Judas, called Iscariot, one of the Twelve. ⁴And Judas went to the chief priests and the officers of the temple guard and discussed with them how he might betray Jesus. ⁵They were delighted

and agreed to give him money. ⁶He consented, and watched for an opportunity to hand Jesus over to them when no crowd was present.

The Last Supper

⁷Then came the day of Unleavened Bread on which the Passover lamb had to be sacrificed. ⁸Jesus sent Peter and John, saying, "Go and make preparations for us to eat the Passover."

⁹"Where do you want us to prepare for it?" they asked.

¹⁰He replied, "As you enter the city, a man carrying a jar of water will meet you. Follow him to the house that he enters, ¹¹and say to the owner of the house, 'The Teacher asks: Where is the guest room, where I may eat the Passover with my disciples?' ¹²He will show you a large room upstairs, all furnished. Make preparations there."

¹³They left and found things just as Jesus had told them. So they prepared the Passover.

¹⁴When the hour came, Jesus and his apostles reclined at the table. ¹⁵And he said to them, "I have eagerly desired to eat this Passover with you before I suffer. ¹⁶For I tell you, I will not eat it again until it finds fulfillment in the kingdom of God."

¹⁷After taking the cup, he gave thanks and said, "Take this and divide it among you. ¹⁸For I tell you I will not drink again from the fruit of the vine until the kingdom of God comes."

¹⁹And he took bread, gave thanks and broke it, and gave it to them, saying, "This is my body given for you; do this in remembrance of me."

²⁰In the same way, after the supper he took the cup, saying, "This cup is the new covenant in my blood, which is poured out for you.ᵃ ²¹But the hand

---

ᵃ *19,20 Some manuscripts do not have given for you . . . poured out for you.*

of him who is going to betray me is with mine on the table. ²²The Son of Man will go as it has been decreed. But woe to that man who betrays him!" ²³They began to question among themselves which of them it might be who would do this.

²⁴A dispute also arose among them as to which of them was considered to be greatest. ²⁵Jesus said to them, "The kings of the Gentiles lord it over them; and those who exercise authority over them call themselves Benefactors. ²⁶But you are not to be like that. Instead, the greatest among you should be like the youngest, and the one who rules like the one who serves. ²⁷For who is greater, the one who is at the table or the one who serves? Is it not the one who is at the table? But I am among you as one who serves. ²⁸You are those who have stood by me in my trials. ²⁹And I confer on you a kingdom, just as my Father conferred one on me, ³⁰so that you may eat and drink at my table in my kingdom and sit on thrones, judging the twelve tribes of Israel.

³¹"Simon, Simon, Satan has asked to sift all of you as wheat. ³²But I have prayed for you, Simon, that your faith may not fail. And when you have turned back, strengthen your brothers."

³³But he replied, "Lord, I am ready to go with you to prison and to death."

³⁴Jesus answered, "I tell you, Peter, before the rooster crows today, you will deny three times that you know me."

³⁵Then Jesus asked them, "When I sent you without purse, bag or sandals, did you lack anything?"

"Nothing," they answered.

³⁶He said to them, "But now if you have a purse, take it, and also a bag; and if you don't have a sword, sell your cloak and buy one. ³⁷It is written: 'And he was numbered with the transgressors'ᵃ; and I tell you that this must be fulfilled in me. Yes, what is written about me is reaching its fulfillment."

³⁸The disciples said, "See, Lord, here are two swords."

"That's enough!" he replied.

Jesus Prays on the Mount of Olives

³⁹Jesus went out as usual to the Mount of Olives, and his disciples followed him. ⁴⁰On reaching the place, he said to them, "Pray that you will not fall into temptation." ⁴¹He withdrew about a stone's throw beyond them, knelt down and prayed, ⁴²"Father, if you are willing, take this cup from me; yet not my will, but yours be done." ⁴³An angel from heaven appeared to him and strengthened him. ⁴⁴And being in anguish, he prayed more earnestly, and his sweat was like drops of blood falling to the ground.ᵇ

⁴⁵When he rose from prayer and went back to the disciples, he found them asleep, exhausted from sorrow. ⁴⁶"Why are you sleeping?" he asked them. "Get up and pray so that you will not fall into temptation."

Jesus Arrested

⁴⁷While he was still speaking a crowd came up, and the man who was called Judas, one of the Twelve, was leading them. He approached Jesus to kiss him, ⁴⁸but Jesus asked him, "Judas, are you betraying the Son of Man with a kiss?"

⁴⁹When Jesus' followers saw what was going to happen, they said, "Lord, should we strike with our swords?" ⁵⁰And one of them struck the ser-

ᵃ 37 Isaiah 53:12   ᵇ 43,44 Many early manuscripts do not have verses 43 and 44.

vant of the high priest, cutting off his right ear.

⁵¹But Jesus answered, "No more of this!" And he touched the man's ear and healed him.

⁵²Then Jesus said to the chief priests, the officers of the temple guard, and the elders, who had come for him, "Am I leading a rebellion, that you have come with swords and clubs? ⁵³Every day I was with you in the temple courts, and you did not lay a hand on me. But this is your hour — when darkness reigns."

Peter Disowns Jesus

⁵⁴Then seizing him, they led him away and took him into the house of the high priest. Peter followed at a distance. ⁵⁵And when some there had kindled a fire in the middle of the courtyard and had sat down together, Peter sat down with them. ⁵⁶A servant girl saw him seated there in the firelight. She looked closely at him and said, "This man was with him."

⁵⁷But he denied it. "Woman, I don't know him," he said.

⁵⁸A little later someone else saw him and said, "You also are one of them."

"Man, I am not!" Peter replied.

⁵⁹About an hour later another asserted, "Certainly this fellow was with him, for he is a Galilean."

⁶⁰Peter replied, "Man, I don't know what you're talking about!" Just as he was speaking, the rooster crowed. ⁶¹The Lord turned and looked straight at Peter. Then Peter remembered the word the Lord had spoken to him: "Before the rooster crows today, you will disown me three times." ⁶²And he went outside and wept bitterly.

The Guards Mock Jesus

⁶³The men who were guarding Jesus began mocking and beating him. ⁶⁴They blindfolded him and demanded, "Prophesy! Who hit you?" ⁶⁵And they said many other insulting things to him.

Jesus Before Pilate and Herod

⁶⁶At daybreak the council of the elders of the people, both the chief priests and the teachers of the law, met together, and Jesus was led before them. ⁶⁷"If you are the Messiah," they said, "tell us."

Jesus answered, "If I tell you, you will not believe me, ⁶⁸and if I asked you, you would not answer. ⁶⁹But from now on, the Son of Man will be seated at the right hand of the mighty God."

⁷⁰They all asked, "Are you then the Son of God?"

He replied, "You say that I am."

⁷¹Then they said, "Why do we need any more testimony? We have heard it from his own lips."

23 Then the whole assembly rose and led him off to Pilate. ²And they began to accuse him, saying, "We have found this man subverting our nation. He opposes payment of taxes to Caesar and claims to be Messiah, a king."

³So Pilate asked Jesus, "Are you the king of the Jews?"

"You have said so," Jesus replied.

⁴Then Pilate announced to the chief priests and the crowd, "I find no basis for a charge against this man."

⁵But they insisted, "He stirs up the people all over Judea by his teaching. He started in Galilee and has come all the way here."

⁶On hearing this, Pilate asked if the man was a Galilean. ⁷When he learned that Jesus was under Herod's jurisdiction, he sent him to Herod, who was also in Jerusalem at that time.

[8]When Herod saw Jesus, he was greatly pleased, because for a long time he had been wanting to see him. From what he had heard about him, he hoped to see him perform a sign of some sort. [9]He plied him with many questions, but Jesus gave him no answer. [10]The chief priests and the teachers of the law were standing there, vehemently accusing him. [11]Then Herod and his soldiers ridiculed and mocked him. Dressing him in an elegant robe, they sent him back to Pilate. [12]That day Herod and Pilate became friends — before this they had been enemies.

[13]Pilate called together the chief priests, the rulers and the people, [14]and said to them, "You brought me this man as one who was inciting the people to rebellion. I have examined him in your presence and have found no basis for your charges against him. [15]Neither has Herod, for he sent him back to us; as you can see, he has done nothing to deserve death. [16]Therefore, I will punish him and then release him." [[17]][a]

[18]But the whole crowd shouted, "Away with this man! Release Barabbas to us!" [19](Barabbas had been thrown into prison for an insurrection in the city, and for murder.)

[20]Wanting to release Jesus, Pilate appealed to them again. [21]But they kept shouting, "Crucify him! Crucify him!"

[22]For the third time he spoke to them: "Why? What crime has this man committed? I have found in him no grounds for the death penalty. Therefore I will have him punished and then release him."

[23]But with loud shouts they insistently demanded that he be crucified, and their shouts prevailed. [24]So Pilate decided to grant their demand.

[25]He released the man who had been thrown into prison for insurrection and murder, the one they asked for, and surrendered Jesus to their will.

The Crucifixion of Jesus

[26]As the soldiers led him away, they seized Simon from Cyrene, who was on his way in from the country, and put the cross on him and made him carry it behind Jesus. [27]A large number of people followed him, including women who mourned and wailed for him. [28]Jesus turned and said to them, "Daughters of Jerusalem, do not weep for me; weep for yourselves and for your children. [29]For the time will come when you will say, 'Blessed are the childless women, the wombs that never bore and the breasts that never nursed!' [30]Then

"'they will say to the mountains,
    "Fall on us!"
  and to the hills, "Cover us!"'[b]

[31]For if people do these things when the tree is green, what will happen when it is dry?"

[32]Two other men, both criminals, were also led out with him to be executed. [33]When they came to the place called the Skull, they crucified him there, along with the criminals — one on his right, the other on his left. [34]Jesus said, "Father, forgive them, for they do not know what they are doing."[c] And they divided up his clothes by casting lots.

[35]The people stood watching, and the rulers even sneered at him. They said, "He saved others; let him save himself if he is God's Messiah, the Chosen One."

---

[a] 17 Some manuscripts include here words similar to Matt. 27:15 and Mark 15:6.
[b] 30 Hosea 10:8   [c] 34 Some early manuscripts do not have this sentence.

³⁶The soldiers also came up and mocked him. They offered him wine vinegar ³⁷and said, "If you are the king of the Jews, save yourself."

³⁸There was a written notice above him, which read: THIS IS THE KING OF THE JEWS.

³⁹One of the criminals who hung there hurled insults at him: "Aren't you the Messiah? Save yourself and us!"

⁴⁰But the other criminal rebuked him. "Don't you fear God," he said, "since you are under the same sentence? ⁴¹We are punished justly, for we are getting what our deeds deserve. But this man has done nothing wrong."

⁴²Then he said, "Jesus, remember me when you come into your kingdom.ᵃ"

⁴³Jesus answered him, "Truly I tell you, today you will be with me in paradise."

The Death of Jesus

⁴⁴It was now about noon, and darkness came over the whole land until three in the afternoon, ⁴⁵for the sun stopped shining. And the curtain of the temple was torn in two. ⁴⁶Jesus called out with a loud voice, "Father, into your hands I commit my spirit."ᵇ When he had said this, he breathed his last.

⁴⁷The centurion, seeing what had happened, praised God and said, "Surely this was a righteous man." ⁴⁸When all the people who had gathered to witness this sight saw what took place, they beat their breasts and went away. ⁴⁹But all those who knew him, including the women who had followed him from Galilee, stood at a distance, watching these things.

The Burial of Jesus

⁵⁰Now there was a man named Joseph, a member of the Council, a good and upright man, ⁵¹who had not consented to their decision and action. He came from the Judean town of Arimathea, and he himself was waiting for the kingdom of God. ⁵²Going to Pilate, he asked for Jesus' body. ⁵³Then he took it down, wrapped it in linen cloth and placed it in a tomb cut in the rock, one in which no one had yet been laid. ⁵⁴It was Preparation Day, and the Sabbath was about to begin.

⁵⁵The women who had come with Jesus from Galilee followed Joseph and saw the tomb and how his body was laid in it. ⁵⁶Then they went home and prepared spices and perfumes. But they rested on the Sabbath in obedience to the commandment.

Jesus Has Risen

24 On the first day of the week, very early in the morning, the women took the spices they had prepared and went to the tomb. ²They found the stone rolled away from the tomb, ³but when they entered, they did not find the body of the Lord Jesus. ⁴While they were wondering about this, suddenly two men in clothes that gleamed like lightning stood beside them. ⁵In their fright the women bowed down with their faces to the ground, but the men said to them, "Why do you look for the living among the dead? ⁶He is not here; he has risen! Remember how he told you, while he was still with you in Galilee: ⁷'The Son of Man must be delivered over to the hands of sinners, be crucified and on the third day be raised again.' " ⁸Then they remembered his words.

⁹When they came back from the tomb, they told all these things to the

---

ᵃ 42 Some manuscripts *come with your kingly power*   ᵇ 46 Psalm 31:5

Eleven and to all the others. [10]It was Mary Magdalene, Joanna, Mary the mother of James, and the others with them who told this to the apostles. [11]But they did not believe the women, because their words seemed to them like nonsense. [12]Peter, however, got up and ran to the tomb. Bending over, he saw the strips of linen lying by themselves, and he went away, wondering to himself what had happened.

On the Road to Emmaus

[13]Now that same day two of them were going to a village called Emmaus, about seven miles[e] from Jerusalem. [14]They were talking with each other about everything that had happened. [15]As they talked and discussed these things with each other, Jesus himself came up and walked along with them; [16]but they were kept from recognizing him.

[17]He asked them, "What are you discussing together as you walk along?"

They stood still, their faces downcast. [18]One of them, named Cleopas, asked him, "Are you the only one visiting Jerusalem who does not know the things that have happened there in these days?"

[19]"What things?" he asked.

"About Jesus of Nazareth," they replied. "He was a prophet, powerful in word and deed before God and all the people. [20]The chief priests and our rulers handed him over to be sentenced to death, and they crucified him; [21]but we had hoped that he was the one who was going to redeem Israel. And what is more, it is the third day since all this took place. [22]In addition, some of our women amazed us. They went to the tomb early this morning [23]but didn't find his body. They came and told us that they had seen a vision of angels, who said he was alive. [24]Then some of our companions went to the tomb and found it just as the women had said, but they did not see Jesus."

[25]He said to them, "How foolish you are, and how slow to believe all that the prophets have spoken! [26]Did not the Messiah have to suffer these things and then enter his glory?" [27]And beginning with Moses and all the Prophets, he explained to them what was said in all the Scriptures concerning himself.

[28]As they approached the village to which they were going, Jesus continued on as if he were going farther. [29]But they urged him strongly, "Stay with us, for it is nearly evening; the day is almost over." So he went in to stay with them.

[30]When he was at the table with them, he took bread, gave thanks, broke it and began to give it to them. [31]Then their eyes were opened and they recognized him, and he disappeared from their sight. [32]They asked each other, "Were not our hearts burning within us while he talked with us on the road and opened the Scriptures to us?"

[33]They got up and returned at once to Jerusalem. There they found the Eleven and those with them, assembled together [34]and saying, "It is true! The Lord has risen and has appeared to Simon." [35]Then the two told what had happened on the way, and how Jesus was recognized by them when he broke the bread.

Jesus Appears to the Disciples

[36]While they were still talking about this, Jesus himself stood among them and said to them, "Peace be with you."

---

[e] 13 Or about 11 kilometers

³⁷They were startled and frightened, thinking they saw a ghost. ³⁸He said to them, "Why are you troubled, and why do doubts rise in your minds? ³⁹Look at my hands and my feet. It is I myself! Touch me and see; a ghost does not have flesh and bones, as you see I have."

⁴⁰When he had said this, he showed them his hands and feet. ⁴¹And while they still did not believe it because of joy and amazement, he asked them, "Do you have anything here to eat?" ⁴²They gave him a piece of broiled fish, ⁴³and he took it and ate it in their presence.

⁴⁴He said to them, "This is what I told you while I was still with you: Everything must be fulfilled that is written about me in the Law of Moses, the Prophets and the Psalms."

⁴⁵Then he opened their minds so they could understand the Scriptures. ⁴⁶He told them, "This is what is written: The Messiah will suffer and rise from the dead on the third day, ⁴⁷and repentance for the forgiveness of sins will be preached in his name to all nations, beginning at Jerusalem. ⁴⁸You are witnesses of these things. ⁴⁹I am going to send you what my Father has promised; but stay in the city until you have been clothed with power from on high."

The Ascension of Jesus

⁵⁰When he had led them out to the vicinity of Bethany, he lifted up his hands and blessed them. ⁵¹While he was blessing them, he left them and was taken up into heaven. ⁵²Then they worshiped him and returned to Jerusalem with great joy. ⁵³And they stayed continually at the temple, praising God.

John

The Word Became Flesh

1 In the beginning was the Word, and the Word was with God, and the Word was God. ²He was with God in the beginning. ³Through him all things were made; without him nothing was made that has been made. ⁴In him was life, and that life was the light of all mankind. ⁵The light shines in the darkness, and the darkness has not overcome[a] it.

⁶There was a man sent from God whose name was John. ⁷He came as a witness to testify concerning that light, so that through him all might believe. ⁸He himself was not the light; he came only as a witness to the light.

⁹The true light that gives light to everyone was coming into the world. ¹⁰He was in the world, and though the world was made through him, the world did not recognize him. ¹¹He came to that which was his own, but his own did not receive him. ¹²Yet to all who did receive him, to those who believed in his name, he gave the right to become children of God — ¹³children born not of natural descent,

---

[a] 5 Or *understood*

nor of human decision or a husband's will, but born of God.

[14]The Word became flesh and made his dwelling among us. We have seen his glory, the glory of the one and only Son, who came from the Father, full of grace and truth.

[15](John testified concerning him. He cried out, saying, "This is the one I spoke about when I said, 'He who comes after me has surpassed me because he was before me.' ")[16]Out of his fullness we have all received grace in place of grace already given. [17]For the law was given through Moses; grace and truth came through Jesus Christ. [18]No one has ever seen God, but the one and only Son, who is himself God and[a] is in closest relationship with the Father, has made him known.

John the Baptist Denies Being the Messiah

[19]Now this was John's testimony when the Jewish leaders[b] in Jerusalem sent priests and Levites to ask him who he was. [20]He did not fail to confess, but confessed freely, "I am not the Messiah."

[21]They asked him, "Then who are you? Are you Elijah?"

He said, "I am not."

"Are you the Prophet?"

He answered, "No."

[22]Finally they said, "Who are you? Give us an answer to take back to those who sent us. What do you say about yourself?"

[23]John replied in the words of Isaiah the prophet, "I am the voice of one calling in the wilderness, 'Make straight the way for the Lord.' "[c]

[24]Now the Pharisees who had been sent [25]questioned him, "Why then do you baptize if you are not the Messiah, nor Elijah, nor the Prophet?"

[26]"I baptize with[d] water," John re-

plied, "but among you stands one you do not know. [27]He is the one who comes after me, the straps of whose sandals I am not worthy to untie."

[28]This all happened at Bethany on the other side of the Jordan, where John was baptizing.

John Testifies About Jesus

[29]The next day John saw Jesus coming toward him and said, "Look, the Lamb of God, who takes away the sin of the world! [30]This is the one I meant when I said, 'A man who comes after me has surpassed me because he was before me.' [31]I myself did not know him, but the reason I came baptizing with water was that he might be revealed to Israel."

[32]Then John gave this testimony: "I saw the Spirit come down from heaven as a dove and remain on him. [33]And I myself did not know him, but the one who sent me to baptize with water told me, 'The man on whom you see the Spirit come down and remain is the one who will baptize with the Holy Spirit.' [34]I have seen and I testify that this is God's Chosen One."[e]

John's Disciples Follow Jesus

[35]The next day John was there again with two of his disciples. [36]When he saw Jesus passing by, he said, "Look, the Lamb of God!"

[37]When the two disciples heard him say this, they followed Jesus. [38]Turning around, Jesus saw them following and asked, "What do you want?"

---

[a] 18 Some manuscripts *but the only Son, who*   [b] 19 The Greek term traditionally translated *the Jews* (*hoi Ioudaioi*) refers here and elsewhere in John's Gospel to those Jewish leaders who opposed Jesus; also in 5:10, 15, 16; 7:1, 11, 13; 9:22; 18:14, 28, 36; 19:7, 12, 31, 38; 20:19.   [c] 23 Isaiah 40:3   [d] 26 Or *in*; also in verses 31 and 33 (twice)   [e] 34 See Isaiah 42:1; many manuscripts *is the Son of God*.

They said, "Rabbi" (which means "Teacher"), "where are you staying?"
39 "Come," he replied, "and you will see."

So they went and saw where he was staying, and they spent that day with him. It was about four in the afternoon.

40 Andrew, Simon Peter's brother, was one of the two who heard what John had said and who had followed Jesus. **41** The first thing Andrew did was to find his brother Simon and tell him, "We have found the Messiah" (that is, the Christ). **42** And he brought him to Jesus.

Jesus looked at him and said, "You are Simon son of John. You will be called Cephas" (which, when translated, is Peter[a]).

Jesus Calls Philip and Nathanael

43 The next day Jesus decided to leave for Galilee. Finding Philip, he said to him, "Follow me."

44 Philip, like Andrew and Peter, was from the town of Bethsaida. **45** Philip found Nathanael and told him, "We have found the one Moses wrote about in the Law, and about whom the prophets also wrote — Jesus of Nazareth, the son of Joseph."

46 "Nazareth! Can anything good come from there?" Nathanael asked.

"Come and see," said Philip.

47 When Jesus saw Nathanael approaching, he said of him, "Here truly is an Israelite in whom there is no deceit."

48 "How do you know me?" Nathanael asked.

Jesus answered, "I saw you while you were still under the fig tree before Philip called you."

49 Then Nathanael declared, "Rabbi, you are the Son of God; you are the king of Israel."

50 Jesus said, "You believe[b] because I told you I saw you under the fig tree. You will see greater things than that." **51** He then added, "Very truly I tell you,[c] you[c] will see 'heaven open, and the angels of God ascending and descending on'[d] the Son of Man."

Jesus Changes Water Into Wine

2 On the third day a wedding took place at Cana in Galilee. Jesus' mother was there, **2** and Jesus and his disciples had also been invited to the wedding. **3** When the wine was gone, Jesus' mother said to him, "They have no more wine."

4 "Woman,[e] why do you involve me?" Jesus replied. "My hour has not yet come."

5 His mother said to the servants, "Do whatever he tells you."

6 Nearby stood six stone water jars, the kind used by the Jews for ceremonial washing, each holding from twenty to thirty gallons.[f]

7 Jesus said to the servants, "Fill the jars with water"; so they filled them to the brim.

8 Then he told them, "Now draw some out and take it to the master of the banquet."

They did so, **9** and the master of the banquet tasted the water that had been turned into wine. He did not realize where it had come from, though the servants who had drawn the water knew. Then he called the bridegroom aside **10** and said, "Everyone brings out the choice wine first and then the cheaper wine after the guests have had too much to drink; but you have saved the best till now."

---

[a] 42 *Cephas* (Aramaic) and *Peter* (Greek) both mean *rock*.   [b] 50 Or *Do you believe . . . ?*
[c] 51 The Greek is plural.   [d] 51 Gen. 28:12
[e] 4 The Greek for *Woman* does not denote any disrespect.   [f] 6 Or from about 75 to about 115 liters

¹¹What Jesus did here in Cana of Galilee was the first of the signs through which he revealed his glory; and his disciples believed in him.

¹²After this he went down to Capernaum with his mother and brothers and his disciples. There they stayed for a few days.

Jesus Clears the Temple Courts

¹³When it was almost time for the Jewish Passover, Jesus went up to Jerusalem. ¹⁴In the temple courts he found people selling cattle, sheep and doves, and others sitting at tables exchanging money. ¹⁵So he made a whip out of cords, and drove all from the temple courts, both sheep and cattle; he scattered the coins of the money changers and overturned their tables. ¹⁶To those who sold doves he said, "Get these out of here! Stop turning my Father's house into a market!" ¹⁷His disciples remembered that it is written: "Zeal for your house will consume me."ᵃ

¹⁸The Jews then responded to him, "What sign can you show us to prove your authority to do all this?"

¹⁹Jesus answered them, "Destroy this temple, and I will raise it again in three days."

²⁰They replied, "It has taken forty-six years to build this temple, and you are going to raise it in three days?" ²¹But the temple he had spoken of was his body. ²²After he was raised from the dead, his disciples recalled what he had said. Then they believed the scripture and the words that Jesus had spoken.

²³Now while he was in Jerusalem at the Passover Festival, many people saw the signs he was performing and believed in his name.ᵇ ²⁴But Jesus would not entrust himself to them,

for he knew all people. ²⁵He did not need any testimony about mankind, for he knew what was in each person.

Jesus Teaches Nicodemus

3 Now there was a Pharisee, a man named Nicodemus who was a member of the Jewish ruling council. ²He came to Jesus at night and said, "Rabbi, we know that you are a teacher who has come from God. For no one could perform the signs you are doing if God were not with him."

³Jesus replied, "Very truly I tell you, no one can see the kingdom of God unless they are born again.ᶜ"

⁴"How can someone be born when they are old?" Nicodemus asked. "Surely they cannot enter a second time into their mother's womb to be born!"

⁵Jesus answered, "Very truly I tell you, no one can enter the kingdom of God unless they are born of water and the Spirit. ⁶Flesh gives birth to flesh, but the Spiritᵈ gives birth to spirit. ⁷You should not be surprised at my saying, 'Youᵉ must be born again.' ⁸The wind blows wherever it pleases. You hear its sound, but you cannot tell where it comes from or where it is going. So it is with everyone born of the Spirit."ᶠ

⁹"How can this be?" Nicodemus asked.

¹⁰"You are Israel's teacher," said Jesus, "and do you not understand these things? ¹¹Very truly I tell you, we speak of what we know, and we testify to what we have seen, but still you people do not accept our testimony. ¹²I have spoken to you of earthly

---

ᵃ 17 Psalm 69:9   ᵇ 23 Or *in him*   ᶜ 3 The Greek for *again* also means *from above*; also in verse 7.   ᵈ 6 Or *but spirit*   ᵉ 7 The Greek is plural.   ᶠ 8 The Greek for *Spirit* is the same as that for *wind*.

³³Then his disciples said to each other, "Could someone have brought him food?"

³⁴"My food," said Jesus, "is to do the will of him who sent me and to finish his work. ³⁵Don't you have a saying, 'It's still four months until harvest'? I tell you, open your eyes and look at the fields! They are ripe for harvest. ³⁶Even now the one who reaps draws a wage and harvests a crop for eternal life, so that the sower and the reaper may be glad together. ³⁷Thus the saying 'One sows and another reaps' is true. ³⁸I sent you to reap what you have not worked for. Others have done the hard work, and you have reaped the benefits of their labor."

Many Samaritans Believe

³⁹Many of the Samaritans from that town believed in him because of the woman's testimony, "He told me everything I ever did." ⁴⁰So when the Samaritans came to him, they urged him to stay with them, and he stayed two days. ⁴¹And because of his words many more became believers.

⁴²They said to the woman, "We no longer believe just because of what you said; now we have heard for ourselves, and we know that this man really is the Savior of the world."

Jesus Heals an Official's Son

⁴³After the two days he left for Galilee. ⁴⁴(Now Jesus himself had pointed out that a prophet has no honor in his own country.) ⁴⁵When he arrived in Galilee, the Galileans welcomed him. They had seen all that he had done in Jerusalem at the Passover Festival, for they also had been there.

⁴⁶Once more he visited Cana in Galilee, where he had turned the water into wine. And there was a certain royal official whose son lay sick at Capernaum. ⁴⁷When this man heard that Jesus had arrived in Galilee from Judea, he went to him and begged him to come and heal his son, who was close to death.

⁴⁸"Unless you people see signs and wonders," Jesus told him, "you will never believe."

⁴⁹The royal official said, "Sir, come down before my child dies."

⁵⁰"Go," Jesus replied, "your son will live."

The man took Jesus at his word and departed. ⁵¹While he was still on the way, his servants met him with the news that his boy was living. ⁵²When he inquired as to the time when his son got better, they said to him, "Yesterday, at one in the afternoon, the fever left him."

⁵³Then the father realized that this was the exact time at which Jesus had said to him, "Your son will live." So he and his whole household believed.

⁵⁴This was the second sign Jesus performed after coming from Judea to Galilee.

The Healing at the Pool

5 Some time later, Jesus went up to Jerusalem for one of the Jewish festivals. ²Now there is in Jerusalem near the Sheep Gate a pool, which in Aramaic is called Bethesdaᵃ and which is surrounded by five covered colonnades. ³Here a great number of disabled people used to lie — the blind, the lame, the paralyzed. [4] ᵇ ⁵One who was there had been an

ᵃ 2 Some manuscripts Bethzatha; other manuscripts Bethsaida ᵇ 3,4 Some manuscripts include here, wholly or in part, paralyzed — and they waited for the moving of the waters. ⁴From time to time an angel of the Lord would come down and stir up the waters. The first one into the pool after each such disturbance would be cured of whatever disease they had.

invalid for thirty-eight years. [6]When Jesus saw him lying there and learned that he had been in this condition for a long time, he asked him, "Do you want to get well?"

[7]"Sir," the invalid replied, "I have no one to help me into the pool when the water is stirred. While I am trying to get in, someone else goes down ahead of me."

[8]Then Jesus said to him, "Get up! Pick up your mat and walk." [9]At once the man was cured; he picked up his mat and walked.

The day on which this took place was a Sabbath, [10]and so the Jewish leaders said to the man who had been healed, "It is the Sabbath; the law forbids you to carry your mat."

[11]But he replied, "The man who made me well said to me, 'Pick up your mat and walk.' "

[12]So they asked him, "Who is this fellow who told you to pick it up and walk?"

[13]The man who was healed had no idea who it was, for Jesus had slipped away into the crowd that was there.

[14]Later Jesus found him at the temple and said to him, "See, you are well again. Stop sinning or something worse may happen to you." [15]The man went away and told the Jewish leaders that it was Jesus who had made him well.

The Authority of the Son

[16]So, because Jesus was doing these things on the Sabbath, the Jewish leaders began to persecute him. [17]In his defense Jesus said to them, "My Father is always at his work to this very day, and I too am working." [18]For this reason they tried all the more to kill him; not only was he breaking the Sabbath, but he was even calling God his own Father, making himself equal with God.

[19]Jesus gave them this answer: "Very truly I tell you, the Son can do nothing by himself; he can do only what he sees his Father doing, because whatever the Father does the Son also does. [20]For the Father loves the Son and shows him all he does. Yes, and he will show him even greater works than these, so that you will be amazed. [21]For just as the Father raises the dead and gives them life, even so the Son gives life to whom he is pleased to give it. [22]Moreover, the Father judges no one, but has entrusted all judgment to the Son, [23]that all may honor the Son just as they honor the Father. Whoever does not honor the Son does not honor the Father, who sent him.

[24]"Very truly I tell you, whoever hears my word and believes him who sent me has eternal life and will not be judged but has crossed over from death to life. [25]Very truly I tell you, a time is coming and has now come when the dead will hear the voice of the Son of God and those who hear will live. [26]For as the Father has life in himself, so he has granted the Son also to have life in himself. [27]And he has given him authority to judge because he is the Son of Man.

[28]"Do not be amazed at this, for a time is coming when all who are in their graves will hear his voice [29]and come out — those who have done what is good will rise to live, and those who have done what is evil will rise to be condemned. [30]By myself I can do nothing; I judge only as I hear, and my judgment is just, for I seek not to please myself but him who sent me.

Testimonies About Jesus

[31]"If I testify about myself, my testimony is not true. [32]There is another

who testifies in my favor, and I know that his testimony about me is true. 33"You have sent to John and he has testified to the truth. 34Not that I accept human testimony; but I mention it that you may be saved. 35John was a lamp that burned and gave light, and you chose for a time to enjoy his light.

36"I have testimony weightier than that of John. For the works that the Father has given me to finish — the very works that I am doing — testify that the Father has sent me. 37And the Father who sent me has testified concerning me. You have never heard his voice nor seen his form, 38nor does his word dwell in you, for you do not believe the one he sent. 39You study[a] the Scriptures diligently because you think that in them you have eternal life. These are the very Scriptures that testify about me, 40yet you refuse to come to me to have life.

41"I do not accept glory from human beings, 42but I know you. I know that you do not have the love of God in your hearts. 43I have come in my Father's name, and you do not accept me; but if someone else comes in his own name, you will accept him. 44How can you believe since you accept glory from one another but do not seek the glory that comes from the only God[b]?

45"But do not think I will accuse you before the Father. Your accuser is Moses, on whom your hopes are set. 46If you believed Moses, you would believe me, for he wrote about me. 47But since you do not believe what he wrote, how are you going to believe what I say?"

Jesus Feeds the Five Thousand

6 Some time after this, Jesus crossed to the far shore of the Sea of Galilee (that is, the Sea of Tiberias), 2and a great crowd of people followed him because they saw the signs he had performed by healing the sick. 3Then Jesus went up on a mountainside and sat down with his disciples. 4The Jewish Passover Festival was near.

5When Jesus looked up and saw a great crowd coming toward him, he said to Philip, "Where shall we buy bread for these people to eat?" 6He asked this only to test him, for he already had in mind what he was going to do.

7Philip answered him, "It would take more than half a year's wages[c] to buy enough bread for each one to have a bite!"

8Another of his disciples, Andrew, Simon Peter's brother, spoke up, 9"Here is a boy with five small barley loaves and two small fish, but how far will they go among so many?"

10Jesus said, "Have the people sit down." There was plenty of grass in that place, and they sat down (about five thousand men were there). 11Jesus then took the loaves, gave thanks, and distributed to those who were seated as much as they wanted. He did the same with the fish.

12When they had all had enough to eat, he said to his disciples, "Gather the pieces that are left over. Let nothing be wasted." 13So they gathered them and filled twelve baskets with the pieces of the five barley loaves left over by those who had eaten.

14After the people saw the sign Jesus performed, they began to say, "Surely this is the Prophet who is to come into the world." 15Jesus, knowing that they intended to come and make him king by force, withdrew again to a mountain by himself.

---

[a] 39 Or *Study*   [b] 44 Some early manuscripts *the Only One*   [c] 7 Greek *take two hundred denarii*

Jesus Walks on the Water

[16]When evening came, his disciples went down to the lake, [17]where they got into a boat and set off across the lake for Capernaum. By now it was dark, and Jesus had not yet joined them. [18]A strong wind was blowing and the waters grew rough. [19]When they had rowed about three or four miles,[a] they saw Jesus approaching the boat, walking on the water; and they were frightened. [20]But he said to them, "It is I; don't be afraid." [21]Then they were willing to take him into the boat, and immediately the boat reached the shore where they were heading.

[22]The next day the crowd that had stayed on the opposite shore of the lake realized that only one boat had been there, and that Jesus had not entered it with his disciples, but that they had gone away alone. [23]Then some boats from Tiberias landed near the place where the people had eaten the bread after the Lord had given thanks. [24]Once the crowd realized that neither Jesus nor his disciples were there, they got into the boats and went to Capernaum in search of Jesus.

Jesus the Bread of Life

[25]When they found him on the other side of the lake, they asked him, "Rabbi, when did you get here?"

[26]Jesus answered, "Very truly I tell you, you are looking for me, not because you saw the signs I performed but because you ate the loaves and had your fill. [27]Do not work for food that spoils, but for food that endures to eternal life, which the Son of Man will give you. For on him God the Father has placed his seal of approval."

[28]Then they asked him, "What must we do to do the works God requires?"

[29]Jesus answered, "The work of God is this: to believe in the one he has sent."

[30]So they asked him, "What sign then will you give that we may see it and believe you? What will you do? [31]Our ancestors ate the manna in the wilderness; as it is written: 'He gave them bread from heaven to eat.'[b]"

[32]Jesus said to them, "Very truly I tell you, it is not Moses who has given you the bread from heaven, but it is my Father who gives you the true bread from heaven. [33]For the bread of God is the bread that comes down from heaven and gives life to the world."

[34]"Sir," they said, "always give us this bread."

[35]Then Jesus declared, "I am the bread of life. Whoever comes to me will never go hungry, and whoever believes in me will never be thirsty. [36]But as I told you, you have seen me and still you do not believe. [37]All those the Father gives me will come to me, and whoever comes to me I will never drive away. [38]For I have come down from heaven not to do my will but to do the will of him who sent me. [39]And this is the will of him who sent me, that I shall lose none of all those he has given me, but raise them up at the last day. [40]For my Father's will is that everyone who looks to the Son and believes in him shall have eternal life, and I will raise them up at the last day."

[41]At this the Jews there began to grumble about him because he said, "I am the bread that came down from heaven." [42]They said, "Is this not Jesus, the son of Joseph, whose father and mother we know? How can he now say, 'I came down from heaven'?"

[43]"Stop grumbling among yourselves," Jesus answered. [44]"No one

[a] 19 Or about 5 or 6 kilometers
[b] 31 Exodus 16:4; Neh. 9:15; Psalm 78:24,25

can come to me unless the Father who sent me draws them, and I will raise them up at the last day. ⁴⁵It is written in the Prophets: 'They will all be taught by God.'ᵃ Everyone who has heard the Father and learned from him comes to me. ⁴⁶No one has seen the Father except the one who is from God; only he has seen the Father. ⁴⁷Very truly I tell you, the one who believes has eternal life. ⁴⁸I am the bread of life. ⁴⁹Your ancestors ate the manna in the wilderness, yet they died. ⁵⁰But here is the bread that comes down from heaven, which anyone may eat and not die. ⁵¹I am the living bread that came down from heaven. Whoever eats this bread will live forever. This bread is my flesh, which I will give for the life of the world."

⁵²Then the Jews began to argue sharply among themselves, "How can this man give us his flesh to eat?"

⁵³Jesus said to them, "Very truly I tell you, unless you eat the flesh of the Son of Man and drink his blood, you have no life in you. ⁵⁴Whoever eats my flesh and drinks my blood has eternal life, and I will raise them up at the last day. ⁵⁵For my flesh is real food and my blood is real drink. ⁵⁶Whoever eats my flesh and drinks my blood remains in me, and I in them. ⁵⁷Just as the living Father sent me and I live because of the Father, so the one who feeds on me will live because of me. ⁵⁸This is the bread that came down from heaven. Your ancestors ate manna and died, but whoever feeds on this bread will live forever." ⁵⁹He said this while teaching in the synagogue in Capernaum.

Many Disciples Desert Jesus

⁶⁰On hearing it, many of his disciples said, "This is a hard teaching. Who can accept it?"

⁶¹Aware that his disciples were grumbling about this, Jesus said to them, "Does this offend you? ⁶²Then what if you see the Son of Man ascend to where he was before! ⁶³The Spirit gives life; the flesh counts for nothing. The words I have spoken to you — they are full of the Spiritᵇ and life. ⁶⁴Yet there are some of you who do not believe." For Jesus had known from the beginning which of them did not believe and who would betray him. ⁶⁵He went on to say, "This is why I told you that no one can come to me unless the Father has enabled them."

⁶⁶From this time many of his disciples turned back and no longer followed him.

⁶⁷"You do not want to leave too, do you?" Jesus asked the Twelve.

⁶⁸Simon Peter answered him, "Lord, to whom shall we go? You have the words of eternal life. ⁶⁹We have come to believe and to know that you are the Holy One of God."

⁷⁰Then Jesus replied, "Have I not chosen you, the Twelve? Yet one of you is a devil!" ⁷¹(He meant Judas, the son of Simon Iscariot, who, though one of the Twelve, was later to betray him.)

Jesus Goes to the Festival of Tabernacles

7 After this, Jesus went around in Galilee. He did not wantᶜ to go about in Judea because the Jewish leaders there were looking for a way to kill him. ²But when the Jewish Festival of Tabernacles was near, ³Jesus' brothers said to him, "Leave Galilee and go to Judea, so that your disciples there may see the works you do. ⁴No one who wants to become a public

---

ᵃ 45 Isaiah 54:13   ᵇ 63 Or are Spirit; or are spirit   ᶜ 1 Some manuscripts not have authority figure acts in secret. Since you are doing these things, show yourself to the world." ⁵For even his own brothers did not believe in him.

⁶Therefore Jesus told them, "My time is not yet here; for you any time will do. ⁷The world cannot hate you, but it hates me because I testify that its works are evil. ⁸You go to the festival. I am not*ᵃ* going up to this festival, because my time has not yet fully come." ⁹After he had said this, he stayed in Galilee.

¹⁰However, after his brothers had left for the festival, he went also, not publicly, but in secret. ¹¹Now at the festival the Jewish leaders were watching for Jesus and asking, "Where is he?"

¹²Among the crowds there was widespread whispering about him. Some said, "He is a good man."

Others replied, "No, he deceives the people." ¹³But no one would say anything publicly about him for fear of the leaders.

Jesus Teaches at the Festival

¹⁴Not until halfway through the festival did Jesus go up to the temple courts and begin to teach. ¹⁵The Jews there were amazed and asked, "How did this man get such learning without having been taught?"

¹⁶Jesus answered, "My teaching is not my own. It comes from the one who sent me. ¹⁷Anyone who chooses to do the will of God will find out whether my teaching comes from God or whether I speak on my own. ¹⁸Whoever speaks on their own does so to gain personal glory, but he who seeks the glory of the one who sent him is a man of truth; there is nothing false about him. ¹⁹Has not Moses given you the law? Yet not one of you keeps the law. Why are you trying to kill me?"

²⁰"You are demon-possessed," the crowd answered. "Who is trying to kill you?"

²¹Jesus said to them, "I did one miracle, and you are all amazed. ²²Yet, because Moses gave you circumcision (though actually it did not come from Moses, but from the patriarchs), you circumcise a boy on the Sabbath. ²³Now if a boy can be circumcised on the Sabbath so that the law of Moses may not be broken, why are you angry with me for healing a man's whole body on the Sabbath? ²⁴Stop judging by mere appearances, but instead judge correctly."

Division Over Who Jesus Is

²⁵At that point some of the people of Jerusalem began to ask, "Isn't this the man they are trying to kill? ²⁶Here he is, speaking publicly, and they are not saying a word to him. Have the authorities really concluded that he is the Messiah? ²⁷But we know where this man is from; when the Messiah comes, no one will know where he is from."

²⁸Then Jesus, still teaching in the temple courts, cried out, "Yes, you know me, and you know where I am from. I am not here on my own authority, but he who sent me is true. You do not know him, ²⁹but I know him because I am from him and he sent me."

³⁰At this they tried to seize him, but no one laid a hand on him, because his hour had not yet come. ³¹Still, many in the crowd believed in him. They said, "When the Messiah comes, will he perform more signs than this man?"

³²The Pharisees heard the crowd whispering such things about him. Then the chief priests and the Pharisees sent temple guards to arrest him.

ᵃ 8 Some manuscripts not yet

³³Jesus said, "I am with you for only a short time, and then I am going to the one who sent me. ³⁴You will look for me, but you will not find me; and where I am, you cannot come."

³⁵The Jews said to one another, "Where does this man intend to go that we cannot find him? Will he go where our people live scattered among the Greeks, and teach the Greeks? ³⁶What did he mean when he said, 'You will look for me, but you will not find me,' and 'Where I am, you cannot come'?"

³⁷On the last and greatest day of the festival, Jesus stood and said in a loud voice, "Let anyone who is thirsty come to me and drink. ³⁸Whoever believes in me, as Scripture has said, rivers of living water will flow from within them."ᵃ ³⁹By this he meant the Spirit, whom those who believed in him were later to receive. Up to that time the Spirit had not been given, since Jesus had not yet been glorified.

⁴⁰On hearing his words, some of the people said, "Surely this man is the Prophet."

⁴¹Others said, "He is the Messiah."

Still others asked, "How can the Messiah come from Galilee? ⁴²Does not Scripture say that the Messiah will come from David's descendants and from Bethlehem, the town where David lived?" ⁴³Thus the people were divided because of Jesus. ⁴⁴Some wanted to seize him, but no one laid a hand on him.

Unbelief of the Jewish Leaders

⁴⁵Finally the temple guards went back to the chief priests and the Pharisees, who asked them, "Why didn't you bring him in?"

⁴⁶"No one ever spoke the way this man does," the guards replied.

⁴⁷"You mean he has deceived you also?" the Pharisees retorted. ⁴⁸"Have any of the rulers or of the Pharisees believed in him? ⁴⁹No! But this mob that knows nothing of the law — there is a curse on them."

⁵⁰Nicodemus, who had gone to Jesus earlier and who was one of their own number, asked, ⁵¹"Does our law condemn a man without first hearing him to find out what he has been doing?"

⁵²They replied, "Are you from Galilee, too? Look into it, and you will find that a prophet does not come out of Galilee."

[The earliest manuscripts and many other ancient witnesses do not have John 7:53 — 8:11. A few manuscripts include these verses, wholly or in part, after John 7:36, John 21:25, Luke 21:38 or Luke 24:53.]

S ⁵³Then they all went home, ¹but Jesus went to the Mount of Olives.

²At dawn he appeared again in the temple courts, where all the people gathered around him, and he sat down to teach them. ³The teachers of the law and the Pharisees brought in a woman caught in adultery. They made her stand before the group ⁴and said to Jesus, "Teacher, this woman was caught in the act of adultery. ⁵In the Law Moses commanded us to stone such women. Now what do you say?" ⁶They were using this question as a trap, in order to have a basis for accusing him.

But Jesus bent down and started to write on the ground with his finger. ⁷When they kept on questioning him, he straightened up and said to them, "Let any one of you who is without sin be the first to throw a stone at her." ⁸Again he stooped down and wrote on the ground.

⁹At this, those who heard began to go away one at a time, the older ones first, until only Jesus was left, with the woman still standing there. ¹⁰Jesus straightened up and asked her,

ᵃ 37,38 Or me. And let anyone drink ³⁸who believes in me." As Scripture has said, "Out of him (or them) will flow rivers of living water."

*"Woman, where are they? Has no one con-
demned you?"*

¹¹*"No one, sir," she said.*

*"Then neither do I condemn you," Jesus
declared. "Go now and leave your life of sin."*

Dispute Over Jesus' Testimony

¹²When Jesus spoke again to the
people, he said, "I am the light of the
world. Whoever follows me will never
walk in darkness, but will have the
light of life."

¹³The Pharisees challenged him,
"Here you are, appearing as your own
witness; your testimony is not valid."

¹⁴Jesus answered, "Even if I testify
on my own behalf, my testimony is
valid, for I know where I came from
and where I am going. But you have
no idea where I come from or where
I am going. ¹⁵You judge by human
standards; I pass judgment on no one.
¹⁶But if I do judge, my decisions are
true, because I am not alone. I stand
with the Father, who sent me. ¹⁷In
your own Law it is written that the
testimony of two witnesses is true.
¹⁸I am one who testifies for myself;
my other witness is the Father, who
sent me."

¹⁹Then they asked him, "Where is
your father?"

"You do not know me or my Father," Jesus replied. "If you knew me,
you would know my Father also." ²⁰He
spoke these words while teaching in
the temple courts near the place
where the offerings were put. Yet
no one seized him, because his hour
had not yet come.

Dispute Over Who Jesus Is

²¹Once more Jesus said to them,
"I am going away, and you will look
for me, and you will die in your sin.
Where I go, you cannot come."

²²This made the Jews ask, "Will
he kill himself? Is that why he says,
'Where I go, you cannot come'?"

²³But he continued, "You are from
below; I am from above. You are of
this world; I am not of this world. ²⁴I
told you that you would die in your
sins; if you do not believe that I am
he, you will indeed die in your sins."

²⁵"Who are you?" they asked.

"Just what I have been telling you
from the beginning," Jesus replied.
²⁶"I have much to say in judgment
of you. But he who sent me is trustworthy, and what I have heard from
him I tell the world."

²⁷They did not understand that he
was telling them about his Father.
²⁸So Jesus said, "When you have lift-
ed up^a the Son of Man, then you will
know that I am he and that I do nothing on my own but speak just what
the Father has taught me. ²⁹The one
who sent me is with me; he has not
left me alone, for I always do what
pleases him." ³⁰Even as he spoke,
many believed in him.

Dispute Over Whose Children Jesus' Opponents Are

³¹To the Jews who had believed
him, Jesus said, "If you hold to my
teaching, you are really my disciples.
³²Then you will know the truth, and
the truth will set you free."

³³They answered him, "We are
Abraham's descendants and have
never been slaves of anyone. How
can you say that we shall be set free?"

³⁴Jesus replied, "Very truly I tell
you, everyone who sins is a slave to
sin. ³⁵Now a slave has no permanent
place in the family, but a son belongs
to it forever. ³⁶So if the Son sets you
free, you will be free indeed. ³⁷I know
that you are Abraham's descendants.

---

^a 28 The Greek for *lifted up* also means *exalted*.

Yet you are looking for a way to kill me, because you have no room for my word. [38]I am telling you what I have seen in the Father's presence, and you are doing what you have heard from your father.ª"

[39]"Abraham is our father," they answered.

"If you were Abraham's children," said Jesus, "then you wouldᵇ do what Abraham did. [40]As it is, you are looking for a way to kill me, a man who has told you the truth that I heard from God. Abraham did not do such things. [41]You are doing the works of your own father."

"We are not illegitimate children," they protested. "The only Father we have is God himself."

[42]Jesus said to them, "If God were your Father, you would love me, for I have come here from God. I have not come on my own; God sent me. [43]Why is my language not clear to you? Because you are unable to hear what I say. [44]You belong to your father, the devil, and you want to carry out your father's desires. He was a murderer from the beginning, not holding to the truth, for there is no truth in him. When he lies, he speaks his native language, for he is a liar and the father of lies. [45]Yet because I tell the truth, you do not believe me! [46]Can any of you prove me guilty of sin? If I am telling the truth, why don't you believe me? [47]Whoever belongs to God hears what God says. The reason you do not hear is that you do not belong to God."

Jesus' Claims About Himself

[48]The Jews answered him, "Aren't we right in saying that you are a Samaritan and demon-possessed?"

[49]"I am not possessed by a demon," said Jesus, "but I honor my Father and

you dishonor me. [50]I am not seeking glory for myself; but there is one who seeks it, and he is the judge. [51]Very truly I tell you, whoever obeys my word will never see death."

[52]At this they exclaimed, "Now we know that you are demon-possessed! Abraham died and so did the prophets, yet you say that whoever obeys your word will never taste death. [53]Are you greater than our father Abraham? He died, and so did the prophets. Who do you think you are?"

[54]Jesus replied, "If I glorify myself, my glory means nothing. My Father, whom you claim as your God, is the one who glorifies me. [55]Though you do not know him, I know him. If I said I did not, I would be a liar like you, but I do know him and obey his word. [56]Your father Abraham rejoiced at the thought of seeing my day; he saw it and was glad."

[57]"You are not yet fifty years old," they said to him, "and you have seen Abraham!"

[58]"Very truly I tell you," Jesus answered, "before Abraham was born, I am!" [59]At this, they picked up stones to stone him, but Jesus hid himself, slipping away from the temple grounds.

Jesus Heals a Man Born Blind

9 As he went along, he saw a man blind from birth. [2]His disciples asked him, "Rabbi, who sinned, this man or his parents, that he was born blind?"

[3]"Neither this man nor his parents sinned," said Jesus, "but this happened so that the works of God might be displayed in him. [4]As long

---

ª 38 Or *presence. Therefore do what you have heard from the Father.*   ᵇ 39 Some early manuscripts *"If you are Abraham's children," said Jesus, "then* as it is day, we must do the works of him who sent me. Night is coming, when no one can work. [5]While I am in the world, I am the light of the world."

[6]After saying this, he spit on the ground, made some mud with the saliva, and put it on the man's eyes. [7]"Go," he told him, "wash in the Pool of Siloam" (this word means "Sent"). So the man went and washed, and came home seeing.

[8]His neighbors and those who had formerly seen him begging asked, "Isn't this the same man who used to sit and beg?" [9]Some claimed that he was.

Others said, "No, he only looks like him."

But he himself insisted, "I am the man."

[10]"How then were your eyes opened?" they asked.

[11]He replied, "The man they call Jesus made some mud and put it on my eyes. He told me to go to Siloam and wash. So I went and washed, and then I could see."

[12]"Where is this man?" they asked him.

"I don't know," he said.

The Pharisees Investigate the Healing

[13]They brought to the Pharisees the man who had been blind. [14]Now the day on which Jesus had made the mud and opened the man's eyes was a Sabbath. [15]Therefore the Pharisees also asked him how he had received his sight. "He put mud on my eyes," the man replied, "and I washed, and now I see."

[16]Some of the Pharisees said, "This man is not from God, for he does not keep the Sabbath."

But others asked, "How can a sinner perform such signs?" So they were divided.

[17]Then they turned again to the blind man, "What have you to say about him? It was your eyes he opened."

The man replied, "He is a prophet."

[18]They still did not believe that he had been blind and had received his sight until they sent for the man's parents. [19]"Is this your son?" they asked. "Is this the one you say was born blind? How is it that now he can see?"

[20]"We know he is our son," the parents answered, "and we know he was born blind. [21]But how he can see now, or who opened his eyes, we don't know. Ask him. He is of age; he will speak for himself." [22]His parents said this because they were afraid of the Jewish leaders, who already had decided that anyone who acknowledged that Jesus was the Messiah would be put out of the synagogue. [23]That was why his parents said, "He is of age; ask him."

[24]A second time they summoned the man who had been blind. "Give glory to God by telling the truth," they said. "We know this man is a sinner."

[25]He replied, "Whether he is a sinner or not, I don't know. One thing I do know. I was blind but now I see!"

[26]Then they asked him, "What did he do to you? How did he open your eyes?"

[27]He answered, "I have told you already and you did not listen. Why do you want to hear it again? Do you want to become his disciples too?"

[28]Then they hurled insults at him and said, "You are this fellow's disciple! We are disciples of Moses! [29]We know that God spoke to Moses, but as for this fellow, we don't even know where he comes from."

[30]The man answered, "Now that is remarkable! You don't know where he

comes from, yet he opened my eyes. [31]We know that God does not listen to sinners. He listens to the godly person who does his will. [32]Nobody has ever heard of opening the eyes of a man born blind. [33]If this man were not from God, he could do nothing."

[34]To this they replied, "You were steeped in sin at birth; how dare you lecture us!" And they threw him out.

Spiritual Blindness

[35]Jesus heard that they had thrown him out, and when he found him, he said, "Do you believe in the Son of Man?"

[36]"Who is he, sir?" the man asked. "Tell me so that I may believe in him."

[37]Jesus said, "You have now seen him; in fact, he is the one speaking with you."

[38]Then the man said, "Lord, I believe," and he worshiped him.

[39]Jesus said,[a] "For judgment I have come into this world, so that the blind will see and those who see will become blind."

[40]Some Pharisees who were with him heard him say this and asked, "What? Are we blind too?"

[41]Jesus said, "If you were blind, you would not be guilty of sin; but now that you claim you can see, your guilt remains.

The Good Shepherd and His Sheep

10 "Very truly I tell you Pharisees, anyone who does not enter the sheep pen by the gate, but climbs in by some other way, is a thief and a robber. [2]The one who enters by the gate is the shepherd of the sheep. [3]The gatekeeper opens the gate for him, and the sheep listen to his voice. He calls his own sheep by name and leads them out. [4]When he has brought out all his own, he goes on ahead of them, and his sheep follow him because they know his voice. [5]But they will never follow a stranger; in fact, they will run away from him because they do not recognize a stranger's voice." [6]Jesus used this figure of speech, but the Pharisees did not understand what he was telling them.

[7]Therefore Jesus said again, "Very truly I tell you, I am the gate for the sheep. [8]All who have come before me are thieves and robbers, but the sheep have not listened to them. [9]I am the gate; whoever enters through me will be saved.[b] They will come in and go out, and find pasture. [10]The thief comes only to steal and kill and destroy; I have come that they may have life, and have it to the full.

[11]"I am the good shepherd. The good shepherd lays down his life for the sheep. [12]The hired hand is not the shepherd and does not own the sheep. So when he sees the wolf coming, he abandons the sheep and runs away. Then the wolf attacks the flock and scatters it. [13]The man runs away because he is a hired hand and cares nothing for the sheep.

[14]"I am the good shepherd; I know my sheep and my sheep know me — [15]just as the Father knows me and I know the Father — and I lay down my life for the sheep. [16]I have other sheep that are not of this sheep pen. I must bring them also. They too will listen to my voice, and there shall be one flock and one shepherd. [17]The reason my Father loves me is that I lay down my life — only to take it up again. [18]No one takes it from me, but I lay it down of my own accord. I have authority to lay it down and authority

---

[a] 38,39 Some early manuscripts do not have Then the man said . . . [39]Jesus said.   [b] 9 Or kept safe

to take it up again. This command I received from my Father."

¹⁹The Jews who heard these words were again divided. ²⁰Many of them said, "He is demon-possessed and raving mad. Why listen to him?"

²¹But others said, "These are not the sayings of a man possessed by a demon. Can a demon open the eyes of the blind?"

Further Conflict Over Jesus' Claims

²²Then came the Festival of Dedication[c] at Jerusalem. It was winter, ²³and Jesus was in the temple courts walking in Solomon's Colonnade. ²⁴The Jews who were there gathered around him, saying, "How long will you keep us in suspense? If you are the Messiah, tell us plainly."

²⁵Jesus answered, "I did tell you, but you do not believe. The works I do in my Father's name testify about me, ²⁶but you do not believe because you are not my sheep. ²⁷My sheep listen to my voice; I know them, and they follow me. ²⁸I give them eternal life, and they shall never perish; no one will snatch them out of my hand. ²⁹My Father, who has given them to me, is greater than all[b]; no one can snatch them out of my Father's hand. ³⁰I and the Father are one."

³¹Again his Jewish opponents picked up stones to stone him, ³²but Jesus said to them, "I have shown you many good works from the Father. For which of these do you stone me?"

³³"We are not stoning you for any good work," they replied, "but for blasphemy, because you, a mere man, claim to be God."

³⁴Jesus answered them, "Is it not written in your Law, 'I have said you are "gods"'[c]? ³⁵If he called them 'gods,' to whom the word of God

came — and Scripture cannot be set aside — ³⁶what about the one whom the Father set apart as his very own and sent into the world? Why then do you accuse me of blasphemy because I said, 'I am God's Son'? ³⁷Do not believe me unless I do the works of my Father. ³⁸But if I do them, even though you do not believe me, believe the works, that you may know and understand that the Father is in me, and I in the Father." ³⁹Again they tried to seize him, but he escaped their grasp.

⁴⁰Then Jesus went back across the Jordan to the place where John had been baptizing in the early days. There he stayed, ⁴¹and many people came to him. They said, "Though John never performed a sign, all that John said about this man was true." ⁴²And in that place many believed in Jesus.

The Death of Lazarus

11 Now a man named Lazarus was sick. He was from Bethany, the village of Mary and her sister Martha. ²(This Mary, whose brother Lazarus now lay sick, was the same one who poured perfume on the Lord and wiped his feet with her hair.) ³So the sisters sent word to Jesus, "Lord, the one you love is sick."

⁴When he heard this, Jesus said, "This sickness will not end in death. No, it is for God's glory so that God's Son may be glorified through it." ⁵Now Jesus loved Martha and her sister and Lazarus. ⁶So when he heard that Lazarus was sick, he stayed where he was two more days, ⁷and then he said to his disciples, "Let us go back to Judea."

⁸"But Rabbi," they said, "a short while ago the Jews there tried to stone you, and yet you are going back?"

ᶜ 22 That is, Hanukkah   ᵇ 29 Many early manuscripts *What my Father has given me is greater than all*   ᶜ 34 Psalm 82:6

[9] Jesus answered, "Are there not twelve hours of daylight? Anyone who walks in the daytime will not stumble, for they see by this world's light. [10] It is when a person walks at night that they stumble, for they have no light."

[11] After he had said this, he went on to tell them, "Our friend Lazarus has fallen asleep; but I am going there to wake him up."

[12] His disciples replied, "Lord, if he sleeps, he will get better." [13] Jesus had been speaking of his death, but his disciples thought he meant natural sleep.

[14] So then he told them plainly, "Lazarus is dead, [15] and for your sake I am glad I was not there, so that you may believe. But let us go to him."

[16] Then Thomas (also known as Didymus[c]) said to the rest of the disciples, "Let us also go, that we may die with him."

Jesus Comforts the Sisters of Lazarus

[17] On his arrival, Jesus found that Lazarus had already been in the tomb for four days. [18] Now Bethany was less than two miles[b] from Jerusalem, [19] and many Jews had come to Martha and Mary to comfort them in the loss of their brother. [20] When Martha heard that Jesus was coming, she went out to meet him, but Mary stayed at home.

[21] "Lord," Martha said to Jesus, "if you had been here, my brother would not have died. [22] But I know that even now God will give you whatever you ask."

[23] Jesus said to her, "Your brother will rise again."

[24] Martha answered, "I know he will rise again in the resurrection at the last day."

[25] Jesus said to her, "I am the resurrection and the life. The one who believes in me will live, even though they die; [26] and whoever lives by believing in me will never die. Do you believe this?"

[27] "Yes, Lord," she replied, "I believe that you are the Messiah, the Son of God, who is to come into the world."

[28] After she had said this, she went back and called her sister Mary aside. "The Teacher is here," she said, "and is asking for you." [29] When Mary heard this, she got up quickly and went to him. [30] Now Jesus had not yet entered the village, but was still at the place where Martha had met him. [31] When the Jews who had been with Mary in the house, comforting her, noticed how quickly she got up and went out, they followed her, supposing she was going to the tomb to mourn there.

[32] When Mary reached the place where Jesus was and saw him, she fell at his feet and said, "Lord, if you had been here, my brother would not have died."

[33] When Jesus saw her weeping, and the Jews who had come along with her also weeping, he was deeply moved in spirit and troubled. [34] "Where have you laid him?" he asked.

"Come and see, Lord," they replied.

[35] Jesus wept.

[36] Then the Jews said, "See how he loved him!"

[37] But some of them said, "Could not he who opened the eyes of the blind man have kept this man from dying?"

Jesus Raises Lazarus From the Dead

[38] Jesus, once more deeply moved, came to the tomb. It was a cave with a stone laid across the entrance. [39] "Take away the stone," he said.

---

[c] 16 *Thomas* (Aramaic) and *Didymus* (Greek) both mean *twin*.   [b] 18 Or about 3 kilometers

"But, Lord," said Martha, the sister of the dead man, "by this time there is a bad odor, for he has been there four days."

[40]Then Jesus said, "Did I not tell you that if you believe, you will see the glory of God?"

[41]So they took away the stone. Then Jesus looked up and said, "Father, I thank you that you have heard me. [42]I knew that you always hear me, but I said this for the benefit of the people standing here, that they may believe that you sent me."

[43]When he had said this, Jesus called in a loud voice, "Lazarus, come out!" [44]The dead man came out, his hands and feet wrapped with strips of linen, and a cloth around his face.

Jesus said to them, "Take off the grave clothes and let him go."

The Plot to Kill Jesus

[45]Therefore many of the Jews who had come to visit Mary, and had seen what Jesus did, believed in him. [46]But some of them went to the Pharisees and told them what Jesus had done. [47]Then the chief priests and the Pharisees called a meeting of the Sanhedrin.

"What are we accomplishing?" they asked. "Here is this man performing many signs. [48]If we let him go on like this, everyone will believe in him, and then the Romans will come and take away both our temple and our nation."

[49]Then one of them, named Caiaphas, who was high priest that year, spoke up, "You know nothing at all! [50]You do not realize that it is better for you that one man die for the people than that the whole nation perish."

[51]He did not say this on his own, but as high priest that year he prophesied that Jesus would die for the Jewish nation, [52]and not only for that nation but also for the scattered children of God, to bring them together and make them one. [53]So from that day on they plotted to take his life.

[54]Therefore Jesus no longer moved about publicly among the people of Judea. Instead he withdrew to a region near the wilderness, to a village called Ephraim, where he stayed with his disciples.

[55]When it was almost time for the Jewish Passover, many went up from the country to Jerusalem for their ceremonial cleansing before the Passover. [56]They kept looking for Jesus, and as they stood in the temple courts they asked one another, "What do you think? Isn't he coming to the festival at all?" [57]But the chief priests and the Pharisees had given orders that anyone who found out where Jesus was should report it so that they might arrest him.

Jesus Anointed at Bethany

12 Six days before the Passover, Jesus came to Bethany, where Lazarus lived, whom Jesus had raised from the dead. [2]Here a dinner was given in Jesus' honor. Martha served, while Lazarus was among those reclining at the table with him. [3]Then Mary took about a pint[a] of pure nard, an expensive perfume; she poured it on Jesus' feet and wiped his feet with her hair. And the house was filled with the fragrance of the perfume.

[4]But one of his disciples, Judas Iscariot, who was later to betray him, objected, [5]"Why wasn't this perfume sold and the money given to the poor? It was worth a year's wages.[b]" [6]He did not say this because he cared about the poor but because he was a thief; as

---

[a] 3 Or about 0.5 liter   [b] 5 Greek *three hundred denarii*

keeper of the money bag, he used to help himself to what was put into it.

7"Leave her alone," Jesus replied. "It was intended that she should save this perfume for the day of my burial. 8You will always have the poor among you,[a] but you will not always have me."

9Meanwhile a large crowd of Jews found out that Jesus was there and came, not only because of him but also to see Lazarus, whom he had raised from the dead. 10So the chief priests made plans to kill Lazarus as well, 11for on account of him many of the Jews were going over to Jesus and believing in him.

Jesus Comes to Jerusalem as King

12The next day the great crowd that had come for the festival heard that Jesus was on his way to Jerusalem. 13They took palm branches and went out to meet him, shouting,

"Hosanna!"

"Blessed is he who comes in the name of the Lord!"[c]

"Blessed is the king of Israel!"

14Jesus found a young donkey and sat on it, as it is written:

15 "Do not be afraid, Daughter Zion;
　　see, your king is coming,
　　seated on a donkey's colt."[d]

16At first his disciples did not understand all this. Only after Jesus was glorified did they realize that these things had been written about him and that these things had been done to him.

17Now the crowd that was with him when he called Lazarus from the tomb and raised him from the dead continued to spread the word. 18Many

people, because they had heard that he had performed this sign, went out to meet him. 19So the Pharisees said to one another, "See, this is getting us nowhere. Look how the whole world has gone after him!"

Jesus Predicts His Death

20Now there were some Greeks among those who went up to worship at the festival. 21They came to Philip, who was from Bethsaida in Galilee, with a request. "Sir," they said, "we would like to see Jesus." 22Philip went to tell Andrew; Andrew and Philip in turn told Jesus.

23Jesus replied, "The hour has come for the Son of Man to be glorified. 24Very truly I tell you, unless a kernel of wheat falls to the ground and dies, it remains only a single seed. But if it dies, it produces many seeds. 25Anyone who loves their life will lose it, while anyone who hates their life in this world will keep it for eternal life. 26Whoever serves me must follow me; and where I am, my servant also will be. My Father will honor the one who serves me.

27"Now my soul is troubled, and what shall I say? 'Father, save me from this hour'? No, it was for this very reason I came to this hour. 28Father, glorify your name!"

Then a voice came from heaven, "I have glorified it, and will glorify it again." 29The crowd that was there and heard it said it had thundered; others said an angel had spoken to him.

30Jesus said, "This voice was for your benefit, not mine. 31Now is the time for judgment on this world; now the prince of this world will be driven out. ³²And I, when I am lifted up[a] from the earth, will draw all people to myself." ³³He said this to show the kind of death he was going to die.

³⁴The crowd spoke up, "We have heard from the Law that the Messiah will remain forever, so how can you say, 'The Son of Man must be lifted up'? Who is this 'Son of Man'?"

³⁵Then Jesus told them, "You are going to have the light just a little while longer. Walk while you have the light, before darkness overtakes you. Whoever walks in the dark does not know where they are going. ³⁶Believe in the light while you have the light, so that you may become children of light." When he had finished speaking, Jesus left and hid himself from them.

Belief and Unbelief Among the Jews

³⁷Even after Jesus had performed so many signs in their presence, they still would not believe in him. ³⁸This was to fulfill the word of Isaiah the prophet:

"Lord, who has believed our
        message
    and to whom has the arm of
        the Lord been revealed?"[b]

³⁹For this reason they could not believe, because, as Isaiah says elsewhere:

⁴⁰ "He has blinded their eyes
        and hardened their hearts,
    so they can neither see with their
        eyes,
    nor understand with their
        hearts,
    nor turn—and I would heal
        them."[c]

⁴¹Isaiah said this because he saw Jesus' glory and spoke about him.

⁴²Yet at the same time many even among the leaders believed in him. But because of the Pharisees they would not openly acknowledge their faith for fear they would be put out of the synagogue; ⁴³for they loved human praise more than praise from God.

⁴⁴Then Jesus cried out, "Whoever believes in me does not believe in me only, but in the one who sent me. ⁴⁵The one who looks at me is seeing the one who sent me. ⁴⁶I have come into the world as a light, so that no one who believes in me should stay in darkness.

⁴⁷"If anyone hears my words but does not keep them, I do not judge that person. For I did not come to judge the world, but to save the world. ⁴⁸There is a judge for the one who rejects me and does not accept my words; the very words I have spoken will condemn them at the last day. ⁴⁹For I did not speak on my own, but the Father who sent me commanded me to say all that I have spoken. ⁵⁰I know that his command leads to eternal life. So whatever I say is just what the Father has told me to say."

Jesus Washes His Disciples' Feet

13 It was just before the Passover Festival. Jesus knew that the hour had come for him to leave this world and go to the Father. Having loved his own who were in the world, he loved them to the end.

²The evening meal was in progress, and the devil had already prompted Judas, the son of Simon Iscariot, to betray Jesus. ³Jesus knew that the Father had put all things under his power, and that he had come from God and was returning to God; ⁴so he got

---

[a] 32 The Greek for *lifted up* also means *exalted.*
[b] 38 Isaiah 53:1   [c] 40 Isaiah 6:10

up from the meal, took off his outer clothing, and wrapped a towel around his waist. [5]After that, he poured water into a basin and began to wash his disciples' feet, drying them with the towel that was wrapped around him.

[6]He came to Simon Peter, who said to him, "Lord, are you going to wash my feet?"

[7]Jesus replied, "You do not realize now what I am doing, but later you will understand."

[8]"No," said Peter, "you shall never wash my feet."

Jesus answered, "Unless I wash you, you have no part with me."

[9]"Then, Lord," Simon Peter replied, "not just my feet but my hands and my head as well!"

[10]Jesus answered, "Those who have had a bath need only to wash their feet; their whole body is clean. And you are clean, though not every one of you." [11]For he knew who was going to betray him, and that was why he said not every one was clean.

[12]When he had finished washing their feet, he put on his clothes and returned to his place. "Do you understand what I have done for you?" he asked them. [13]"You call me 'Teacher' and 'Lord,' and rightly so, for that is what I am. [14]Now that I, your Lord and Teacher, have washed your feet, you also should wash one another's feet. [15]I have set you an example that you should do as I have done for you. [16]Very truly I tell you, no servant is greater than his master, nor is a messenger greater than the one who sent him. [17]Now that you know these things, you will be blessed if you do them.

Jesus Predicts His Betrayal

[18]"I am not referring to all of you; I know those I have chosen. But this is to fulfill this passage of Scripture: 'He who shared my bread has turned[a] against me.'[b]

[19]"I am telling you now before it happens, so that when it does happen you will believe that I am who I am. [20]Very truly I tell you, whoever accepts anyone I send accepts me; and whoever accepts me accepts the one who sent me."

[21]After he had said this, Jesus was troubled in spirit and testified, "Very truly I tell you, one of you is going to betray me."

[22]His disciples stared at one another, at a loss to know which of them he meant. [23]One of them, the disciple whom Jesus loved, was reclining next to him. [24]Simon Peter motioned to this disciple and said, "Ask him which one he means."

[25]Leaning back against Jesus, he asked him, "Lord, who is it?"

[26]Jesus answered, "It is the one to whom I will give this piece of bread when I have dipped it in the dish." Then, dipping the piece of bread, he gave it to Judas, the son of Simon Iscariot. [27]As soon as Judas took the bread, Satan entered into him.

So Jesus told him, "What you are about to do, do quickly." [28]But no one at the meal understood why Jesus said this to him. [29]Since Judas had charge of the money, some thought Jesus was telling him to buy what was needed for the festival, or to give something to the poor. [30]As soon as Judas had taken the bread, he went out. And it was night.

Jesus Predicts Peter's Denial

[31]When he was gone, Jesus said, "Now the Son of Man is glorified and God is glorified in him. [32]If God is glorified in him,[c] God will glorify

---

[a] 18 Greek has lifted up his heel
[b] 18 Psalm 41:9   [c] 32 Many early manuscripts do not have If God is glorified in him.

the Son in himself, and will glorify him at once.

33"My children, I will be with you only a little longer. You will look for me, and just as I told the Jews, so I tell you now: Where I am going, you cannot come.

34"A new command I give you: Love one another. As I have loved you, so you must love one another. 35By this everyone will know that you are my disciples, if you love one another."

36Simon Peter asked him, "Lord, where are you going?"

Jesus replied, "Where I am going, you cannot follow now, but you will follow later."

37Peter asked, "Lord, why can't I follow you now? I will lay down my life for you."

38Then Jesus answered, "Will you really lay down your life for me? Very truly I tell you, before the rooster crows, you will disown me three times!

Jesus Comforts His Disciples

14 "Do not let your hearts be troubled. You believe in God[a]; believe also in me. 2My Father's house has many rooms; if that were not so, would I have told you that I am going there to prepare a place for you? 3And if I go and prepare a place for you, I will come back and take you to be with me that you also may be where I am. 4You know the way to the place where I am going."

Jesus the Way to the Father

5Thomas said to him, "Lord, we don't know where you are going, so how can we know the way?"

6Jesus answered, "I am the way and the truth and the life. No one comes to the Father except through me. 7If you really know me, you will know[b]

my Father as well. From now on, you do know him and have seen him."

8Philip said, "Lord, show us the Father and that will be enough for us."

9Jesus answered: "Don't you know me, Philip, even after I have been among you such a long time? Anyone who has seen me has seen the Father. How can you say, 'Show us the Father'? 10Don't you believe that I am in the Father, and that the Father is in me? The words I say to you I do not speak on my own authority. Rather, it is the Father, living in me, who is doing his work. 11Believe me when I say that I am in the Father and the Father is in me; or at least believe on the evidence of the works themselves. 12Very truly I tell you, whoever believes in me will do the works I have been doing, and they will do even greater things than these, because I am going to the Father. 13And I will do whatever you ask in my name, so that the Father may be glorified in the Son. 14You may ask me for anything in my name, and I will do it.

Jesus Promises the Holy Spirit

15"If you love me, keep my commands. 16And I will ask the Father, and he will give you another advocate to help you and be with you forever — 17the Spirit of truth. The world cannot accept him, because it neither sees him nor knows him. But you know him, for he lives with you and will be[c] in you. 18I will not leave you as orphans; I will come to you. 19Before long, the world will not see me anymore, but you will see me. Because I live, you also will live. 20On that day you will realize that I am in my Father, and you are in me, and I am in you.

---

[a] 1 Or *Believe in God*   [b] 7 Some manuscripts *If you really knew me, you would know*   [c] 17 Some early manuscripts *and is*

²¹Whoever has my commands and keeps them is the one who loves me. The one who loves me will be loved by my Father, and I too will love them and show myself to them."

²²Then Judas (not Judas Iscariot) said, "But, Lord, why do you intend to show yourself to us and not to the world?"

²³Jesus replied, "Anyone who loves me will obey my teaching. My Father will love them, and we will come to them and make our home with them. ²⁴Anyone who does not love me will not obey my teaching. These words you hear are not my own; they belong to the Father who sent me.

²⁵"All this I have spoken while still with you. ²⁶But when the Advocate, the Holy Spirit, whom the Father will send in my name, will teach you all things and will remind you of everything I have said to you. ²⁷Peace I leave with you; my peace I give you. I do not give to you as the world gives. Do not let your hearts be troubled and do not be afraid.

²⁸"You heard me say, 'I am going away and I am coming back to you.' If you loved me, you would be glad that I am going to the Father, for the Father is greater than I. ²⁹I have told you now before it happens, so that when it does happen you will believe. ³⁰I will not say much more to you, for the prince of this world is coming. He has no hold over me, ³¹but he comes so that the world may learn that I love the Father and do exactly what my Father has commanded me.

"Come now; let us leave.

The Vine and the Branches

15 "I am the true vine, and my Father is the gardener. ²He cuts off every branch in me that bears no fruit, while every branch that does bear fruit he prunes*ᵃ* so that it will be even more fruitful. ³You are already clean because of the word I have spoken to you. ⁴Remain in me, as I also remain in you. No branch can bear fruit by itself; it must remain in the vine. Neither can you bear fruit unless you remain in me.

⁵"I am the vine; you are the branches. If you remain in me and I in you, you will bear much fruit; apart from me you can do nothing. ⁶If you do not remain in me, you are like a branch that is thrown away and withers; such branches are picked up, thrown into the fire and burned. ⁷If you remain in me and my words remain in you, ask whatever you wish, and it will be done for you. ⁸This is to my Father's glory, that you bear much fruit, showing yourselves to be my disciples.

⁹"As the Father has loved me, so have I loved you. Now remain in my love. ¹⁰If you keep my commands, you will remain in my love, just as I have kept my Father's commands and remain in his love. ¹¹I have told you this so that my joy may be in you and that your joy may be complete. ¹²My command is this: Love each other as I have loved you. ¹³Greater love has no one than this: to lay down one's life for one's friends. ¹⁴You are my friends if you do what I command. ¹⁵I no longer call you servants, because a servant does not know his master's business. Instead, I have called you friends, for everything that I learned from my Father I have made known to you. ¹⁶You did not choose me, but I chose you and appointed you so that you might go and bear fruit — fruit that will last — and so that whatever you ask in my name the Father will give you. ¹⁷This is my command: Love each other.

ᵃ 2 The Greek for he prunes also means he cleans.

The World Hates the Disciples

¹⁸"If the world hates you, keep in mind that it hated me first. ¹⁹If you belonged to the world, it would love you as its own. As it is, you do not belong to the world, but I have chosen you out of the world. That is why the world hates you. ²⁰Remember what I told you: 'A servant is not greater than his master.'ᵃ If they persecuted me, they will persecute you also. If they obeyed my teaching, they will obey yours also. ²¹They will treat you this way because of my name, for they do not know the one who sent me. ²²If I had not come and spoken to them, they would not be guilty of sin; but now they have no excuse for their sin. ²³Whoever hates me hates my Father as well. ²⁴If I had not done among them the works no one else did, they would not be guilty of sin. As it is, they have seen, and yet they have hated both me and my Father. ²⁵But this is to fulfill what is written in their Law: 'They hated me without reason.'ᵇ

The Work of the Holy Spirit

²⁶"When the Advocate comes, whom I will send to you from the Father — the Spirit of truth who goes out from the Father — he will testify about me. ²⁷And you also must testify, for you have been with me from the beginning.

16 "All this I have told you so that you will not fall away. ²They will put you out of the synagogue; in fact, the time is coming when anyone who kills you will think they are offering a service to God. ³They will do such things because they have not known the Father or me. ⁴I have told you this, so that when their time comes you will remember that I warned you about them. I did not tell you this

from the beginning because I was with you, ⁵but now I am going to him who sent me. None of you asks me, 'Where are you going?' ⁶Rather, you are filled with grief because I have said these things. ⁷But very truly I tell you, it is for your good that I am going away. Unless I go away, the Advocate will not come to you; but if I go, I will send him to you. ⁸When he comes, he will prove the world to be in the wrong about sin and righteousness and judgment: ⁹about sin, because people do not believe in me; ¹⁰about righteousness, because I am going to the Father, where you can see me no longer; ¹¹and about judgment, because the prince of this world now stands condemned.

¹²"I have much more to say to you, more than you can now bear. ¹³But when he, the Spirit of truth, comes, he will guide you into all the truth. He will not speak on his own; he will speak only what he hears, and he will tell you what is yet to come. ¹⁴He will glorify me because it is from me that he will receive what he will make known to you. ¹⁵All that belongs to the Father is mine. That is why I said the Spirit will receive from me what he will make known to you."

The Disciples' Grief Will Turn to Joy

¹⁶Jesus went on to say, "In a little while you will see me no more, and then after a little while you will see me."

¹⁷At this, some of his disciples said to one another, "What does he mean by saying, 'In a little while you will see me no more, and then after a little while you will see me,' and 'Because I am going to the Father'?" ¹⁸They kept asking, "What does he mean by

ᵃ 20 John 13:16   ᵇ 25 Psalms 35:19; 69:4

'a little while'? We don't understand what he is saying."

[19] Jesus saw that they wanted to ask him about this, so he said to them, "Are you asking one another what I meant when I said, 'In a little while you will see me no more, and then after a little while you will see me'? [20] Very truly I tell you, you will weep and mourn while the world rejoices. You will grieve, but your grief will turn to joy. [21] A woman giving birth to a child has pain because her time has come; but when her baby is born she forgets the anguish because of her joy that a child is born into the world. [22] So with you: Now is your time of grief, but I will see you again and you will rejoice, and no one will take away your joy. [23] In that day you will no longer ask me anything. Very truly I tell you, my Father will give you whatever you ask in my name. [24] Until now you have not asked for anything in my name. Ask and you will receive, and your joy will be complete.

[25] "Though I have been speaking figuratively, a time is coming when I will no longer use this kind of language but will tell you plainly about my Father. [26] In that day you will ask in my name. I am not saying that I will ask the Father on your behalf. [27] No, the Father himself loves you because you have loved me and have believed that I came from God. [28] I came from the Father and entered the world; now I am leaving the world and going back to the Father."

[29] Then Jesus' disciples said, "Now you are speaking clearly and without figures of speech. [30] Now we can see that you know all things and that you do not even need to have anyone ask you questions. This makes us believe that you came from God."

[31] "Do you now believe?" Jesus re-plied. [32] "A time is coming and in fact has come when you will be scattered, each to your own home. You will leave me all alone. Yet I am not alone, for my Father is with me.

[33] "I have told you these things, so that in me you may have peace. In this world you will have trouble. But take heart! I have overcome the world."

Jesus Prays to Be Glorified

17 After Jesus said this, he looked toward heaven and prayed:

"Father, the hour has come. Glorify your Son, that your Son may glorify you. [2] For you granted him authority over all people that he might give eternal life to all those you have given him. [3] Now this is eternal life: that they know you, the only true God, and Jesus Christ, whom you have sent. [4] I have brought you glory on earth by finishing the work you gave me to do. [5] And now, Father, glorify me in your presence with the glory I had with you before the world began.

Jesus Prays for His Disciples

[6] "I have revealed you[a] to those whom you gave me out of the world. They were yours; you gave them to me and they have obeyed your word. [7] Now they know that everything you have given me comes from you. [8] For I gave them the words you gave me and they accepted them. They knew with certainty that I came from you, and they believed that you sent me. [9] I pray for them. I am not praying for the world, but for those you have given me, for they are yours. [10] All

---
[a] 6 Greek *your name*

I have is yours, and all you have is mine. And glory has come to me through them. [11]I will remain in the world no longer, but they are still in the world, and I am coming to you. Holy Father, protect them by the power of[a] your name, the name you gave me, so that they may be one as we are one. [12]While I was with them, I protected them and kept them safe by[b] that name you gave me. None has been lost except the one doomed to destruction so that Scripture would be fulfilled.

[13]"I am coming to you now, but I say these things while I am still in the world, so that they may have the full measure of my joy within them. [14]I have given them your word and the world has hated them, for they are not of the world any more than I am of the world. [15]My prayer is not that you take them out of the world but that you protect them from the evil one. [16]They are not of the world, even as I am not of it. [17]Sanctify them by[c] the truth; your word is truth. [18]As you sent me into the world, I have sent them into the world. [19]For them I sanctify myself, that they too may be truly sanctified.

Jesus Prays for All Believers

[20]"My prayer is not for them alone. I pray also for those who will believe in me through their message, [21]that all of them may be one, Father, just as you are in me and I am in you. May they also be in us so that the world may believe that you have sent me. [22]I have given them the glory that you gave me, that they may be one as we are one — [23]I in them and you in me — so that they may be brought to complete unity. Then the world will know that you sent me and have loved them even as you have loved me.

[24]"Father, I want those you have given me to be with me where I am, and to see my glory, the glory you have given me because you loved me before the creation of the world.

[25]"Righteous Father, though the world does not know you, I know you, and they know that you have sent me. [26]I have made you[d] known to them, and will continue to make you known in order that the love you have for me may be in them and that I myself may be in them."

Jesus Arrested

18 When he had finished praying, Jesus left with his disciples and crossed the Kidron Valley. On the other side there was a garden, and he and his disciples went into it.

[2]Now Judas, who betrayed him, knew the place, because Jesus had often met there with his disciples. [3]So Judas came to the garden, guiding a detachment of soldiers and some officials from the chief priests and the Pharisees. They were carrying torches, lanterns and weapons.

[4]Jesus, knowing all that was going to happen to him, went out and asked them, "Who is it you want?"

[5]"Jesus of Nazareth," they replied.

"I am he," Jesus said. (And Judas the traitor was standing there with them.) [6]When Jesus said, "I am he," they drew back and fell to the ground.

[7]Again he asked them, "Who is it you want?"

"Jesus of Nazareth," they said.

---

[a] 11 Or *Father, keep them faithful to*　　[b] 12 Or *kept them faithful to*　　[c] 17 Or *them to live in accordance with*　　[d] 26 Greek *your name*

⁸Jesus answered, "I told you that I am he. If you are looking for me, then let these men go." ⁹This happened so that the words he had spoken would be fulfilled: "I have not lost one of those you gave me."ᵍ

¹⁰Then Simon Peter, who had a sword, drew it and struck the high priest's servant, cutting off his right ear. (The servant's name was Malchus.)

¹¹Jesus commanded Peter, "Put your sword away! Shall I not drink the cup the Father has given me?"

¹²Then the detachment of soldiers with its commander and the Jewish officials arrested Jesus. They bound him ¹³and brought him first to Annas, who was the father-in-law of Caiaphas, the high priest that year. ¹⁴Caiaphas was the one who had advised the Jewish leaders that it would be good if one man died for the people.

Peter's First Denial

¹⁵Simon Peter and another disciple were following Jesus. Because this disciple was known to the high priest, he went with Jesus into the high priest's courtyard, ¹⁶but Peter had to wait outside at the door. The other disciple, who was known to the high priest, came back, spoke to the servant girl on duty there and brought Peter in.

¹⁷"You aren't one of this man's disciples, are you?" she asked Peter.

He replied, "I am not."

¹⁸It was cold, and the servants and officials stood around a fire they had made to keep warm. Peter also was standing with them, warming himself.

The High Priest Questions Jesus

¹⁹Meanwhile, the high priest questioned Jesus about his disciples and his teaching.

²⁰"I have spoken openly to the world," Jesus replied. "I always taught in synagogues or at the temple, where all the Jews come together. I said nothing in secret. ²¹Why question me? Ask those who heard me. Surely they know what I said."

²²When Jesus said this, one of the officials nearby slapped him in the face. "Is this the way you answer the high priest?" he demanded.

²³"If I said something wrong," Jesus replied, "testify as to what is wrong. But if I spoke the truth, why did you strike me?" ²⁴Then Annas sent him bound to Caiaphas the high priest.

Peter's Second and Third Denials

²⁵Meanwhile, Simon Peter was still standing there warming himself. So they asked him, "You aren't one of his disciples too, are you?"

He denied it, saying, "I am not."

²⁶One of the high priest's servants, a relative of the man whose ear Peter had cut off, challenged him, "Didn't I see you with him in the garden?" ²⁷Again Peter denied it, and at that moment a rooster began to crow.

Jesus Before Pilate

²⁸Then the Jewish leaders took Jesus from Caiaphas to the palace of the Roman governor. By now it was early morning, and to avoid ceremonial uncleanness they did not enter the palace, because they wanted to be able to eat the Passover. ²⁹So Pilate came out to them and asked, "What charges are you bringing against this man?"

³⁰"If he were not a criminal," they replied, "we would not have handed him over to you."

³¹Pilate said, "Take him yourselves and judge him by your own law."

ᵍ 9 John 6:39

"But we have no right to execute anyone," they objected. ³²This took place to fulfill what Jesus had said about the kind of death he was going to die.

³³Pilate then went back inside the palace, summoned Jesus and asked him, "Are you the king of the Jews?"

³⁴"Is that your own idea," Jesus asked, "or did others talk to you about me?"

³⁵"Am I a Jew?" Pilate replied. "Your own people and chief priests handed you over to me. What is it you have done?"

³⁶Jesus said, "My kingdom is not of this world. If it were, my servants would fight to prevent my arrest by the Jewish leaders. But now my kingdom is from another place."

³⁷"You are a king, then!" said Pilate. Jesus answered, "You say that I am a king. In fact, the reason I was born and came into the world is to testify to the truth. Everyone on the side of truth listens to me."

³⁸"What is truth?" retorted Pilate. With this he went out again to the Jews gathered there and said, "I find no basis for a charge against him. ³⁹But it is your custom for me to release to you one prisoner at the time of the Passover. Do you want me to release 'the king of the Jews'?"

⁴⁰They shouted back, "No, not him! Give us Barabbas!" Now Barabbas had taken part in an uprising.

Jesus Sentenced to Be Crucified

19 Then Pilate took Jesus and had him flogged. ²The soldiers twisted together a crown of thorns and put it on his head. They clothed him in a purple robe ³and went up to him again and again, saying, "Hail, king of the Jews!" And they slapped him in the face.

⁴Once more Pilate came out and said to the Jews gathered there, "Look, I am bringing him out to you to let you know that I find no basis for a charge against him." ⁵When Jesus came out wearing the crown of thorns and the purple robe, Pilate said to them, "Here is the man!"

⁶As soon as the chief priests and their officials saw him, they shouted, "Crucify! Crucify!"

But Pilate answered, "You take him and crucify him. As for me, I find no basis for a charge against him."

⁷The Jewish leaders insisted, "We have a law, and according to that law he must die, because he claimed to be the Son of God."

⁸When Pilate heard this, he was even more afraid, ⁹and he went back inside the palace. "Where do you come from?" he asked Jesus, but Jesus gave him no answer. ¹⁰"Do you refuse to speak to me?" Pilate said. "Don't you realize I have power either to free you or to crucify you?"

¹¹Jesus answered, "You would have no power over me if it were not given to you from above. Therefore the one who handed me over to you is guilty of a greater sin."

¹²From then on, Pilate tried to set Jesus free, but the Jewish leaders kept shouting, "If you let this man go, you are no friend of Caesar. Anyone who claims to be a king opposes Caesar."

¹³When Pilate heard this, he brought Jesus out and sat down on the judge's seat at a place known as the Stone Pavement (which in Aramaic is Gabbatha). ¹⁴It was the day of Preparation of the Passover; it was about noon.

"Here is your king," Pilate said to the Jews.

¹⁵But they shouted, "Take him away! Take him away! Crucify him!"

"Shall I crucify your king?" Pilate asked.

"We have no king but Caesar," the chief priests answered.

16 Finally Pilate handed him over to them to be crucified.

The Crucifixion of Jesus

So the soldiers took charge of Jesus. 17 Carrying his own cross, he went out to the place of the Skull (which in Aramaic is called Golgotha). 18 There they crucified him, and with him two others — one on each side and Jesus in the middle.

19 Pilate had a notice prepared and fastened to the cross. It read: JESUS OF NAZARETH, THE KING OF THE JEWS. 20 Many of the Jews read this sign, for the place where Jesus was crucified was near the city, and the sign was written in Aramaic, Latin and Greek. 21 The chief priests of the Jews protested to Pilate, "Do not write 'The King of the Jews,' but that this man claimed to be king of the Jews."

22 Pilate answered, "What I have written, I have written."

23 When the soldiers crucified Jesus, they took his clothes, dividing them into four shares, one for each of them, with the undergarment remaining. This garment was seamless, woven in one piece from top to bottom.

24 "Let's not tear it," they said to one another. "Let's decide by lot who will get it."

This happened that the scripture might be fulfilled that said,

"They divided my clothes among them
    and cast lots for my garment."[a]

So this is what the soldiers did.

25 Near the cross of Jesus stood his mother, his mother's sister, Mary the wife of Clopas, and Mary Magdalene. 26 When Jesus saw his mother there, and the disciple whom he loved standing nearby, he said to her, "Woman,[b] here is your son," 27 and to the disciple, "Here is your mother." From that time on, this disciple took her into his home.

The Death of Jesus

28 Later, knowing that everything had now been finished, and so that Scripture would be fulfilled, Jesus said, "I am thirsty." 29 A jar of wine vinegar was there, so they soaked a sponge in it, put the sponge on a stalk of the hyssop plant, and lifted it to Jesus' lips. 30 When he had received the drink, Jesus said, "It is finished." With that, he bowed his head and gave up his spirit.

31 Now it was the day of Preparation, and the next day was to be a special Sabbath. Because the Jewish leaders did not want the bodies left on the crosses during the Sabbath, they asked Pilate to have the legs broken and the bodies taken down. 32 The soldiers therefore came and broke the legs of the first man who had been crucified with Jesus, and then those of the other. 33 But when they came to Jesus and found that he was already dead, they did not break his legs. 34 Instead, one of the soldiers pierced Jesus' side with a spear, bringing a sudden flow of blood and water. 35 The man who saw it has given testimony, and his testimony is true. He knows that he tells the truth, and he testifies so that you also may believe. 36 These things happened so that the scripture would be fulfilled: "Not one of his bones will be broken,"[c] 37 and, as another

---

[a] 24 Psalm 22:18   [b] 26 The Greek for *Woman* does not denote any disrespect.
[c] 36 Exodus 12:46; Num. 9:12; Psalm 34:20

scripture says, "They will look on the one they have pierced."[a]

The Burial of Jesus

38Later, Joseph of Arimathea asked Pilate for the body of Jesus. Now Joseph was a disciple of Jesus, but secretly because he feared the Jewish leaders. With Pilate's permission, he came and took the body away. 39He was accompanied by Nicodemus, the man who earlier had visited Jesus at night. Nicodemus brought a mixture of myrrh and aloes, about seventy-five pounds.[b] 40Taking Jesus' body, the two of them wrapped it, with the spices, in strips of linen. This was in accordance with Jewish burial customs. 41At the place where Jesus was crucified, there was a garden, and in the garden a new tomb, in which no one had ever been laid. 42Because it was the Jewish day of Preparation and since the tomb was nearby, they laid Jesus there.

The Empty Tomb

20 Early on the first day of the week, while it was still dark, Mary Magdalene went to the tomb and saw that the stone had been removed from the entrance. 2So she came running to Simon Peter and the other disciple, the one Jesus loved, and said, "They have taken the Lord out of the tomb, and we don't know where they have put him!"

3So Peter and the other disciple started for the tomb. 4Both were running, but the other disciple outran Peter and reached the tomb first. 5He bent over and looked in at the strips of linen lying there but did not go in. 6Then Simon Peter came along behind him and went straight into the tomb. He saw the strips of linen lying there, 7as well as the cloth that had been wrapped around Jesus' head. The cloth was still lying in its place, separate from the linen. 8Finally the other disciple, who had reached the tomb first, also went inside. He saw and believed. 9(They still did not understand from Scripture that Jesus had to rise from the dead.) 10Then the disciples went back to where they were staying.

Jesus Appears to Mary Magdalene

11Now Mary stood outside the tomb crying. As she wept, she bent over to look into the tomb 12and saw two angels in white, seated where Jesus' body had been, one at the head and the other at the foot.

13They asked her, "Woman, why are you crying?"

"They have taken my Lord away," she said, "and I don't know where they have put him." 14At this, she turned around and saw Jesus standing there, but she did not realize that it was Jesus.

15He asked her, "Woman, why are you crying? Who is it you are looking for?"

Thinking he was the gardener, she said, "Sir, if you have carried him away, tell me where you have put him, and I will get him."

16Jesus said to her, "Mary."

She turned toward him and cried out in Aramaic, "Rabboni!" (which means "Teacher").

17Jesus said, "Do not hold on to me, for I have not yet ascended to the Father. Go instead to my brothers and tell them, 'I am ascending to my Father and your Father, to my God and your God.'"

18Mary Magdalene went to the disciples with the news: "I have seen the

---

[a] 37 Zech. 12:10　　[b] 39 Or about 34 kilograms

Lord!" And she told them that he had said these things to her.

Jesus Appears to His Disciples

¹⁹On the evening of that first day of the week, when the disciples were together, with the doors locked for fear of the Jewish leaders, Jesus came and stood among them and said, "Peace be with you!" ²⁰After he said this, he showed them his hands and side. The disciples were overjoyed when they saw the Lord.

²¹Again Jesus said, "Peace be with you! As the Father has sent me, I am sending you." ²²And with that he breathed on them and said, "Receive the Holy Spirit. ²³If you forgive anyone's sins, their sins are forgiven; if you do not forgive them, they are not forgiven."

Jesus Appears to Thomas

²⁴Now Thomas (also known as Didymusᵃ), one of the Twelve, was not with the disciples when Jesus came. ²⁵So the other disciples told him, "We have seen the Lord!"

But he said to them, "Unless I see the nail marks in his hands and put my finger where the nails were, and put my hand into his side, I will not believe."

²⁶A week later his disciples were in the house again, and Thomas was with them. Though the doors were locked, Jesus came and stood among them and said, "Peace be with you!" ²⁷Then he said to Thomas, "Put your finger here; see my hands. Reach out your hand and put it into my side. Stop doubting and believe."

²⁸Thomas said to him, "My Lord and my God!"

²⁹Then Jesus told him, "Because you have seen me, you have believed; blessed are those who have not seen and yet have believed."

The Purpose of John's Gospel

³⁰Jesus performed many other signs in the presence of his disciples, which are not recorded in this book. ³¹But these are written that you may believeᵇ that Jesus is the Messiah, the Son of God, and that by believing you may have life in his name.

Jesus and the Miraculous Catch of Fish

21 Afterward Jesus appeared again to his disciples, by the Sea of Galilee.ᶜ It happened this way: ²Simon Peter, Thomas (also known as Didymusᵈ), Nathanael from Cana in Galilee, the sons of Zebedee, and two other disciples were together. ³"I'm going out to fish," Simon Peter told them, and they said, "We'll go with you." So they went out and got into the boat, but that night they caught nothing.

⁴Early in the morning, Jesus stood on the shore, but the disciples did not realize that it was Jesus.

⁵He called out to them, "Friends, haven't you any fish?"

"No," they answered.

⁶He said, "Throw your net on the right side of the boat and you will find some." When they did, they were unable to haul the net in because of the large number of fish.

⁷Then the disciple whom Jesus loved said to Peter, "It is the Lord!" As soon as Simon Peter heard him say, "It is the Lord," he wrapped his outer garment around him (for he had taken it off) and jumped into the water. ⁸The other disciples followed in the boat, towing the net full of fish, for they were not far from shore, about a hundred yards.ᵈ ⁹When they landed,

ᵃ 24,2 *Thomas* (Aramaic) and *Didymus* (Greek) both mean *twin.*   ᵇ 31 Or *may continue to believe*   ᶜ 1 Greek *Tiberias*   ᵈ 8 Or about 90 meters they saw a fire of burning coals there with fish on it, and some bread. ¹⁰Jesus said to them, "Bring some of the fish you have just caught." ¹¹So Simon Peter climbed back into the boat and dragged the net ashore. It was full of large fish, 153, but even with so many the net was not torn. ¹²Jesus said to them, "Come and have breakfast." None of the disciples dared ask him, "Who are you?" They knew it was the Lord. ¹³Jesus came, took the bread and gave it to them, and did the same with the fish. ¹⁴This was now the third time Jesus appeared to his disciples after he was raised from the dead.

Jesus Reinstates Peter

¹⁵When they had finished eating, Jesus said to Simon Peter, "Simon son of John, do you love me more than these?"

"Yes, Lord," he said, "you know that I love you."

Jesus said, "Feed my lambs."

¹⁶Again Jesus said, "Simon son of John, do you love me?"

He answered, "Yes, Lord, you know that I love you."

Jesus said, "Take care of my sheep."

¹⁷The third time he said to him, "Simon son of John, do you love me?"

Peter was hurt because Jesus asked him the third time, "Do you love me?" He said, "Lord, you know all things; you know that I love you."

Jesus said, "Feed my sheep. ¹⁸Very truly I tell you, when you were younger you dressed yourself and went where you wanted; but when you are old you will stretch out your hands, and someone else will dress you and lead you where you do not want to go." ¹⁹Jesus said this to indicate the kind of death by which Peter would glorify God. Then he said to him, "Follow me!"

²⁰Peter turned and saw that the disciple whom Jesus loved was following them. (This was the one who had leaned back against Jesus at the supper and had said, "Lord, who is going to betray you?") ²¹When Peter saw him, he asked, "Lord, what about him?"

²²Jesus answered, "If I want him to remain alive until I return, what is that to you? You must follow me." ²³Because of this, the rumor spread among the believers that this disciple would not die. But Jesus did not say that he would not die; he only said, "If I want him to remain alive until I return, what is that to you?"

²⁴This is the disciple who testifies to these things and who wrote them down. We know that his testimony is true.

²⁵Jesus did many other things as well. If every one of them were written down, I suppose that even the whole world would not have room for the books that would be written.

Acts

Jesus Taken Up Into Heaven

1 In my former book, Theophilus, I wrote about all that Jesus began to do and to teach [2]until the day he was taken up to heaven, after giving instructions through the Holy Spirit to the apostles he had chosen. [3]After his suffering, he presented himself to them and gave many convincing proofs that he was alive. He appeared to them over a period of forty days and spoke about the kingdom of God. [4]On one occasion, while he was eating with them, he gave them this command: "Do not leave Jerusalem, but wait for the gift my Father promised, which you have heard me speak about. [5]For John baptized with[a] water, but in a few days you will be baptized with[a] the Holy Spirit."

[6]Then they gathered around him and asked him, "Lord, are you at this time going to restore the kingdom to Israel?"

[7]He said to them: "It is not for you to know the times or dates the Father has set by his own authority. [8]But you will receive power when the Holy Spirit comes on you; and you will be my witnesses in Jerusalem, and in all Judea and Samaria, and to the ends of the earth."

[9]After he said this, he was taken up before their very eyes, and a cloud hid him from their sight.

[10]They were looking intently up into the sky as he was going, when suddenly two men dressed in white stood beside them. [11]"Men of Galilee," they said, "why do you stand here looking into the sky? This same Jesus, who has been taken from you into heaven, will come back in the same way you have seen him go into heaven."

Matthias Chosen to Replace Judas

[12]Then the apostles returned to Jerusalem from the hill called the Mount of Olives, a Sabbath day's walk[b] from the city. [13]When they arrived, they went upstairs to the room where they were staying. Those present were Peter, John, James and Andrew; Philip and Thomas, Bartholomew and Matthew; James son of Alphaeus and Simon the Zealot, and Judas son of James. [14]They all joined together constantly in prayer, along with the women and Mary the mother of Jesus, and with his brothers.

[15]In those days Peter stood up among the believers (a group numbering about a hundred and twenty) [16]and said, "Brothers and sisters,[c] the Scripture had to be fulfilled in which the Holy Spirit spoke long ago through David concerning Judas, who served as guide for those who arrested Jesus. [17]He was one of our number and shared in our ministry."

[18](With the payment he received for his wickedness, Judas bought a field; there he fell headlong, his body burst open and all his intestines spilled out. [19]Everyone in Jerusalem heard about this, so they called that

---

[a] 5 Or *in*   [b] 12 That is, about 5/8 mile or about 1 kilometer   [c] 16 The Greek word for *brothers and sisters* (*adelphoi*) refers here to believers, both men and women, as part of God's family; also in 6:3; 11:29; 12:17; 16:40; 18:18, 27; 21:7, 17; 28:14, 15.

field in their language Akeldama, that is, Field of Blood.)

20 "For," said Peter, "it is written in the Book of Psalms:

> "'May his place be deserted;
>   let there be no one to dwell
>   in it,'[a]

and,

> "'May another take his place of
>   leadership.'[b]

21 Therefore it is necessary to choose one of the men who have been with us the whole time the Lord Jesus was living among us, 22 beginning from John's baptism to the time when Jesus was taken up from us. For one of these must become a witness with us of his resurrection."

23 So they nominated two men: Joseph called Barsabbas (also known as Justus) and Matthias. 24 Then they prayed, "Lord, you know everyone's heart. Show us which of these two you have chosen 25 to take over this apostolic ministry, which Judas left to go where he belongs." 26 Then they cast lots, and the lot fell to Matthias; so he was added to the eleven apostles.

The Holy Spirit Comes at Pentecost

2 When the day of Pentecost came, they were all together in one place. 2 Suddenly a sound like the blowing of a violent wind came from heaven and filled the whole house where they were sitting. 3 They saw what seemed to be tongues of fire that separated and came to rest on each of them. 4 All of them were filled with the Holy Spirit and began to speak in other tongues[c] as the Spirit enabled them.

5 Now there were staying in Jerusalem God-fearing Jews from every nation under heaven. 6 When they heard this sound, a crowd came together in bewilderment, because each one heard their own language being spoken. 7 Utterly amazed, they asked: "Aren't all these who are speaking Galileans? 8 Then how is it that each of us hears them in our native language? 9 Parthians, Medes and Elamites; residents of Mesopotamia, Judea and Cappadocia, Pontus and Asia,[d] 10 Phrygia and Pamphylia, Egypt and the parts of Libya near Cyrene; visitors from Rome 11 (both Jews and converts to Judaism); Cretans and Arabs — we hear them declaring the wonders of God in our own tongues!" 12 Amazed and perplexed, they asked one another, "What does this mean?"

13 Some, however, made fun of them and said, "They have had too much wine."

Peter Addresses the Crowd

14 Then Peter stood up with the Eleven, raised his voice and addressed the crowd: "Fellow Jews and all of you who live in Jerusalem, let me explain this to you; listen carefully to what I say. 15 These people are not drunk, as you suppose. It's only nine in the morning! 16 No, this is what was spoken by the prophet Joel:

> 17 "'In the last days, God says,
>   I will pour out my Spirit on all
>   people.
> Your sons and daughters will
>   prophesy,
>   your young men will see
>   visions,
>   your old men will dream
>   dreams.

---

[a] 20 Psalm 69:25   [b] 20 Psalm 109:8   [c] 4 Or languages; also in verse 11   [d] 9 That is, the Roman province by that name

18 Even on my servants, both men
      and women,
   I will pour out my Spirit in
      those days,
   and they will prophesy.
19 I will show wonders in the
      heavens above
   and signs on the earth
      below,
   blood and fire and billows of
      smoke.
20 The sun will be turned to
      darkness
   and the moon to blood
   before the coming of the great
      and glorious day of the
      Lord.
21 And everyone who calls
   on the name of the Lord will
      be saved.'ᵃ

22"Fellow Israelites, listen to this:
Jesus of Nazareth was a man accredit-
ed by God to you by miracles, wonders
and signs, which God did among you
through him, as you yourselves know.
23This man was handed over to you
by God's deliberate plan and foreknowledge; and you, with the help
of wicked men,ᵇ put him to death by
nailing him to the cross. 24But God
raised him from the dead, freeing him
from the agony of death, because it
was impossible for death to keep its
hold on him. 25David said about him:

" 'I saw the Lord always
      before me.
   Because he is at my right
      hand,
   I will not be shaken.
26 Therefore my heart is glad and
      my tongue rejoices;
   my body also will rest in hope,
27 because you will not abandon me
      to the realm of the dead,
   you will not let your holy one
      see decay.

28 You have made known to me the
      paths of life;
   you will fill me with joy in
      your presence.'ᶜ

29"Fellow Israelites, I can tell you
confidently that the patriarch David
died and was buried, and his tomb is
here to this day. 30But he was a prophet and knew that God had promised
him on oath that he would place one
of his descendants on his throne.
31Seeing what was to come, he spoke
of the resurrection of the Messiah,
that he was not abandoned to the
realm of the dead, nor did his body
see decay. 32God has raised this Jesus
to life, and we are all witnesses of it.
33Exalted to the right hand of God,
he has received from the Father the
promised Holy Spirit and has poured
out what you now see and hear. 34For
David did not ascend to heaven, and
yet he said,

" 'The Lord said to my Lord:
      "Sit at my right hand
35 until I make your enemies
      a footstool for your feet." 'ᵈ

36"Therefore let all Israel be assured of this: God has made this Jesus,
whom you crucified, both Lord and
Messiah."

37When the people heard this, they
were cut to the heart and said to Peter and the other apostles, "Brothers,
what shall we do?"

38Peter replied, "Repent and be
baptized, every one of you, in the
name of Jesus Christ for the forgiveness of your sins. And you will
receive the gift of the Holy Spirit. 39The promise is for you and your children and
for all who are far off — for all whom
the Lord our God will call."

ᵃ 21 Joel 2:28-32   ᵇ 23 Or of those not having
the law (that is, Gentiles)   ᶜ 28 Psalm 16:8-11
(see Septuagint)   ᵈ 35 Psalm 110:1

⁴⁰With many other words he warned them; and he pleaded with them, "Save yourselves from this corrupt generation." ⁴¹Those who accepted his message were baptized, and about three thousand were added to their number that day.

The Fellowship of the Believers

⁴²They devoted themselves to the apostles' teaching and to fellowship, to the breaking of bread and to prayer. ⁴³Everyone was filled with awe at the many wonders and signs performed by the apostles. ⁴⁴All the believers were together and had everything in common. ⁴⁵They sold property and possessions to give to anyone who had need. ⁴⁶Every day they continued to meet together in the temple courts. They broke bread in their homes and ate together with glad and sincere hearts, ⁴⁷praising God and enjoying the favor of all the people. And the Lord added to their number daily those who were being saved.

Peter Heals a Lame Beggar

3 One day Peter and John were going up to the temple at the time of prayer — at three in the afternoon. ²Now a man who was lame from birth was being carried to the temple gate called Beautiful, where he was put every day to beg from those going into the temple courts. ³When he saw Peter and John about to enter, he asked them for money. ⁴Peter looked straight at him, as did John. Then Peter said, "Look at us!" ⁵So the man gave them his attention, expecting to get something from them.

⁶Then Peter said, "Silver or gold I do not have, but what I do have I give you. In the name of Jesus Christ of Nazareth, walk." ⁷Taking him by the right hand, he helped him up, and instantly the man's feet and ankles became strong. ⁸He jumped to his feet and began to walk. Then he went with them into the temple courts, walking and jumping, and praising God. ⁹When all the people saw him walking and praising God, ¹⁰they recognized him as the same man who used to sit begging at the temple gate called Beautiful, and they were filled with wonder and amazement at what had happened to him.

Peter Speaks to the Onlookers

¹¹While the man held on to Peter and John, all the people were astonished and came running to them in the place called Solomon's Colonnade. ¹²When Peter saw this, he said to them: "Fellow Israelites, why does this surprise you? Why do you stare at us as if by our own power or godliness we had made this man walk? ¹³The God of Abraham, Isaac and Jacob, the God of our fathers, has glorified his servant Jesus. You handed him over to be killed, and you disowned him before Pilate, though he had decided to let him go. ¹⁴You disowned the Holy and Righteous One and asked that a murderer be released to you. ¹⁵You killed the author of life, but God raised him from the dead. We are witnesses of this. ¹⁶By faith in the name of Jesus, this man whom you see and know was made strong. It is Jesus' name and the faith that comes through him that has completely healed him, as you can all see.

¹⁷"Now, fellow Israelites, I know that you acted in ignorance, as did your leaders. ¹⁸But this is how God fulfilled what he had foretold through all the prophets, saying that his Messiah would suffer. ¹⁹Repent, then, and turn to God, so that your sins may

be wiped out, that times of refreshing may come from the Lord, ²⁰and that he may send the Messiah, who has been appointed for you — even Jesus. ²¹Heaven must receive him until the time comes for God to restore everything, as he promised long ago through his holy prophets. ²²For Moses said, 'The Lord your God will raise up for you a prophet like me from among your own people; you must listen to everything he tells you. ²³Anyone who does not listen to him will be completely cut off from their people.'ᵃ

²⁴"Indeed, beginning with Samuel, all the prophets who have spoken have foretold these days. ²⁵And you are heirs of the prophets and of the covenant God made with your fathers. He said to Abraham, 'Through your offspring all peoples on earth will be blessed.'ᵇ ²⁶When God raised up his servant, he sent him first to you to bless you by turning each of you from your wicked ways."

Peter and John Before the Sanhedrin

4 The priests and the captain of the temple guard and the Sadducees came up to Peter and John while they were speaking to the people. ²They were greatly disturbed because the apostles were teaching the people, proclaiming in Jesus the resurrection of the dead. ³They seized Peter and John and, because it was evening, they put them in jail until the next day. ⁴But many who heard the message believed; so the number of men who believed grew to about five thousand.

⁵The next day the rulers, the elders and the teachers of the law met in Jerusalem. ⁶Annas the high priest was there, and so were Caiaphas, John,

Alexander and others of the high priest's family. ⁷They had Peter and John brought before them and began to question them: "By what power or what name did you do this?"

⁸Then Peter, filled with the Holy Spirit, said to them: "Rulers and elders of the people! ⁹If we are being called to account today for an act of kindness shown to a man who was lame and are being asked how he was healed, ¹⁰then know this, you and all the people of Israel: It is by the name of Jesus Christ of Nazareth, whom you crucified but whom God raised from the dead, that this man stands before you healed. ¹¹Jesus is

" 'the stone you builders rejected,
   which has become the
      cornerstone.'ᶜ

¹²Salvation is found in no one else, for there is no other name under heaven given to mankind by which we must be saved."

¹³When they saw the courage of Peter and John and realized that they were unschooled, ordinary men, they were astonished and they took note that these men had been with Jesus. ¹⁴But since they could see the man who had been healed standing there with them, there was nothing they could say. ¹⁵So they ordered them to withdraw from the Sanhedrin and then conferred together. ¹⁶"What are we going to do with these men?" they asked. "Everyone living in Jerusalem knows they have performed a notable sign, and we cannot deny it. ¹⁷But to stop this thing from spreading any further among the people, we must warn them to speak no longer to anyone in this name."

¹⁸Then they called them in again

ᵃ 23 Deut. 18:15,18,19   ᵇ 25 Gen. 22:18; 26:4
ᶜ 11 Psalm 118:22

and commanded them not to speak or teach at all in the name of Jesus. [19]But Peter and John replied, "Which is right in God's eyes: to listen to you, or to him? You be the judges! [20]As for us, we cannot help speaking about what we have seen and heard."

[21]After further threats they let them go. They could not decide how to punish them, because all the people were praising God for what had happened. [22]For the man who was miraculously healed was over forty years old.

The Believers Pray

[23]On their release, Peter and John went back to their own people and reported all that the chief priests and the elders had said to them. [24]When they heard this, they raised their voices together in prayer to God. "Sovereign Lord," they said, "you made the heavens and the earth and the sea, and everything in them. [25]You spoke by the Holy Spirit through the mouth of your servant, our father David:

"'Why do the nations rage
    and the peoples plot in vain?
[26] The kings of the earth rise up
    and the rulers band together
against the Lord
    and against his anointed
        one.'[a][b]

[27]Indeed Herod and Pontius Pilate met together with the Gentiles and the people of Israel in this city to conspire against your holy servant Jesus, whom you anointed. [28]They did what your power and will had decided beforehand should happen. [29]Now, Lord, consider their threats and enable your servants to speak your word with great boldness. [30]Stretch out your hand to heal and perform signs and wonders through the name of your holy servant Jesus."

[31]After they prayed, the place where they were meeting was shaken. And they were all filled with the Holy Spirit and spoke the word of God boldly.

The Believers Share Their Possessions

[32]All the believers were one in heart and mind. No one claimed that any of their possessions was their own, but they shared everything they had. [33]With great power the apostles continued to testify to the resurrection of the Lord Jesus. And God's grace was so powerfully at work in them all [34]that there were no needy persons among them. For from time to time those who owned land or houses sold them, brought the money from the sales [35]and put it at the apostles' feet, and it was distributed to anyone who had need.

[36]Joseph, a Levite from Cyprus, whom the apostles called Barnabas (which means "son of encouragement"), [37]sold a field he owned and brought the money and put it at the apostles' feet.

Ananias and Sapphira

5 Now a man named Ananias, together with his wife Sapphira, also sold a piece of property. [2]With his wife's full knowledge he kept back part of the money for himself, but brought the rest and put it at the apostles' feet.

[3]Then Peter said, "Ananias, how is it that Satan has so filled your heart that you have lied to the Holy Spirit and have kept for yourself some of the money you received for the land? [4]Didn't it belong to you before it was sold? And after it was sold, wasn't the money at your disposal? What made

---

[a] 26 That is, Messiah or Christ
[b] 26 Psalm 2:1,2

you think of doing such a thing? You have not lied just to human beings but to God."

⁵When Ananias heard this, he fell down and died. And great fear seized all who heard what had happened. ⁶Then some young men came forward, wrapped up his body, and carried him out and buried him.

⁷About three hours later his wife came in, not knowing what had happened. ⁸Peter asked her, "Tell me, is this the price you and Ananias got for the land?"

"Yes," she said, "that is the price."

⁹Peter said to her, "How could you conspire to test the Spirit of the Lord? Listen! The feet of the men who buried your husband are at the door, and they will carry you out also."

¹⁰At that moment she fell down at his feet and died. Then the young men came in and, finding her dead, carried her out and buried her beside her husband. ¹¹Great fear seized the whole church and all who heard about these events.

The Apostles Heal Many

¹²The apostles performed many signs and wonders among the people. And all the believers used to meet together in Solomon's Colonnade. ¹³No one else dared join them, even though they were highly regarded by the people. ¹⁴Nevertheless, more and more men and women believed in the Lord and were added to their number. ¹⁵As a result, people brought the sick into the streets and laid them on beds and mats so that at least Peter's shadow might fall on some of them as he passed by. ¹⁶Crowds gathered also from the towns around Jerusalem, bringing their sick and those tormented by impure spirits, and all of them were healed.

The Apostles Persecuted

¹⁷Then the high priest and all his associates, who were members of the party of the Sadducees, were filled with jealousy. ¹⁸They arrested the apostles and put them in the public jail. ¹⁹But during the night an angel of the Lord opened the doors of the jail and brought them out. ²⁰"Go, stand in the temple courts," he said, "and tell the people all about this new life."

²¹At daybreak they entered the temple courts, as they had been told, and began to teach the people.

When the high priest and his associates arrived, they called together the Sanhedrin — the full assembly of the elders of Israel — and sent to the jail for the apostles. ²²But on arriving at the jail, the officers did not find them there. So they went back and reported, ²³"We found the jail securely locked, with the guards standing at the doors; but when we opened them, we found no one inside." ²⁴On hearing this report, the captain of the temple guard and the chief priests were at a loss, wondering what this might lead to.

²⁵Then someone came and said, "Look! The men you put in jail are standing in the temple courts teaching the people." ²⁶At that, the captain went with his officers and brought the apostles. They did not use force, because they feared that the people would stone them.

²⁷The apostles were brought in and made to appear before the Sanhedrin to be questioned by the high priest. ²⁸"We gave you strict orders not to teach in this name," he said. "Yet you have filled Jerusalem with your teaching and are determined to make us guilty of this man's blood."

²⁹Peter and the other apostles replied: "We must obey God rather than

human beings! 30 The God of our ancestors raised Jesus from the dead — whom you killed by hanging him on a cross. 31 God exalted him to his own right hand as Prince and Savior that he might bring Israel to repentance and forgive their sins. 32 We are witnesses of these things, and so is the Holy Spirit, whom God has given to those who obey him."

33 When they heard this, they were furious and wanted to put them to death. 34 But a Pharisee named Gamaliel, a teacher of the law, who was honored by all the people, stood up in the Sanhedrin and ordered that the men be put outside for a little while. 35 Then he addressed the Sanhedrin: "Men of Israel, consider carefully what you intend to do to these men. 36 Some time ago Theudas appeared, claiming to be somebody, and about four hundred men rallied to him. He was killed, all his followers were dispersed, and it all came to nothing. 37 After him, Judas the Galilean appeared in the days of the census and led a band of people in revolt. He too was killed, and all his followers were scattered. 38 Therefore, in the present case I advise you: Leave these men alone! Let them go! For if their purpose or activity is of human origin, it will fail. 39 But if it is from God, you will not be able to stop these men; you will only find yourselves fighting against God."

40 His speech persuaded them. They called the apostles in and had them flogged. Then they ordered them not to speak in the name of Jesus, and let them go.

41 The apostles left the Sanhedrin, rejoicing because they had been counted worthy of suffering disgrace for the Name. 42 Day after day, in the temple courts and from house to house, they never stopped teaching and proclaiming the good news that Jesus is the Messiah.

The Choosing of the Seven

6 In those days when the number of disciples was increasing, the Hellenistic Jews[a] among them complained against the Hebraic Jews because their widows were being overlooked in the daily distribution of food. 2 So the Twelve gathered all the disciples together and said, "It would not be right for us to neglect the ministry of the word of God in order to wait on tables. 3 Brothers and sisters, choose seven men from among you who are known to be full of the Spirit and wisdom. We will turn this responsibility over to them 4 and will give our attention to prayer and the ministry of the word."

5 This proposal pleased the whole group. They chose Stephen, a man full of faith and of the Holy Spirit; also Philip, Procorus, Nicanor, Timon, Parmenas, and Nicolas from Antioch, a convert to Judaism. 6 They presented these men to the apostles, who prayed and laid their hands on them.

7 So the word of God spread. The number of disciples in Jerusalem increased rapidly, and a large number of priests became obedient to the faith.

Stephen Seized

8 Now Stephen, a man full of God's grace and power, performed great wonders and signs among the people. 9 Opposition arose, however, from members of the Synagogue of the Freedmen (as it was called) — Jews of Cyrene and Alexandria as well as the provinces of Cilicia and Asia — who began to argue with Stephen.

---

a 1 That is, Jews who had adopted the Greek language and culture

[10]But they could not stand up against the wisdom the Spirit gave him as he spoke.

[11]Then they secretly persuaded some men to say, "We have heard Stephen speak blasphemous words against Moses and against God."

[12]So they stirred up the people and the elders and the teachers of the law. They seized Stephen and brought him before the Sanhedrin. [13]They produced false witnesses, who testified, "This fellow never stops speaking against this holy place and against the law. [14]For we have heard him say that this Jesus of Nazareth will destroy this place and change the customs Moses handed down to us."

[15]All who were sitting in the Sanhedrin looked intently at Stephen, and they saw that his face was like the face of an angel.

Stephen's Speech to the Sanhedrin

7 Then the high priest asked Stephen, "Are these charges true?"

[2]To this he replied: "Brothers and fathers, listen to me! The God of glory appeared to our father Abraham while he was still in Mesopotamia, before he lived in Harran. [3]'Leave your country and your people,' God said, 'and go to the land I will show you.'[a]

[4]"So he left the land of the Chaldeans and settled in Harran. After the death of his father, God sent him to this land where you are now living. [5]He gave him no inheritance here, not even enough ground to set his foot on. But God promised him that he and his descendants after him would possess the land, even though at that time Abraham had no child. [6]God spoke to him in this way: 'For four hundred years your descendants will be strangers in a country not their own, and they will be enslaved and mistreated. [7]But I will punish the nation they serve as slaves,' God said, 'and afterward they will come out of that country and worship me in this place.'[b] [8]Then he gave Abraham the covenant of circumcision. And Abraham became the father of Isaac and circumcised him eight days after his birth. Later Isaac became the father of Jacob, and Jacob became the father of the twelve patriarchs.

[9]"Because the patriarchs were jealous of Joseph, they sold him as a slave into Egypt. But God was with him [10]and rescued him from all his troubles. He gave Joseph wisdom and enabled him to gain the goodwill of Pharaoh king of Egypt. So Pharaoh made him ruler over Egypt and all his palace.

[11]"Then a famine struck all Egypt and Canaan, bringing great suffering, and our ancestors could not find food. [12]When Jacob heard that there was grain in Egypt, he sent our forefathers on their first visit. [13]On their second visit, Joseph told his brothers who he was, and Pharaoh learned about Joseph's family. [14]After this, Joseph sent for his father Jacob and his whole family, seventy-five in all. [15]Then Jacob went down to Egypt, where he and our ancestors died. [16]Their bodies were brought back to Shechem and placed in the tomb that Abraham had bought from the sons of Hamor at Shechem for a certain sum of money.

[17]"As the time drew near for God to fulfill his promise to Abraham, the number of our people in Egypt had greatly increased. [18]Then 'a new king, to whom Joseph meant nothing, came to power in Egypt.'[c] [19]He dealt treacherously with our people and

___
[a] 3 Gen. 12:1   [b] 7 Gen. 15:13,14
[c] 18 Exodus 1:8

oppressed our ancestors by forcing them to throw out their newborn babies so that they would die.

²⁰"At that time Moses was born, and he was no ordinary child.ᵉ For three months he was cared for by his family. ²¹When he was placed outside, Pharaoh's daughter took him and brought him up as her own son. ²²Moses was educated in all the wisdom of the Egyptians and was powerful in speech and action.

²³"When Moses was forty years old, he decided to visit his own people, the Israelites. ²⁴He saw one of them being mistreated by an Egyptian, so he went to his defense and avenged him by killing the Egyptian. ²⁵Moses thought that his own people would realize that God was using him to rescue them, but they did not. ²⁶The next day Moses came upon two Israelites who were fighting. He tried to reconcile them by saying, 'Men, you are brothers; why do you want to hurt each other?'

²⁷"But the man who was mistreating the other pushed Moses aside and said, 'Who made you ruler and judge over us? ²⁸Are you thinking of killing me as you killed the Egyptian yesterday?'ᵇ ²⁹When Moses heard this, he fled to Midian, where he settled as a foreigner and had two sons.

³⁰"After forty years had passed, an angel appeared to Moses in the flames of a burning bush in the desert near Mount Sinai. ³¹When he saw this, he was amazed at the sight. As he went over to get a closer look, he heard the Lord say: ³²'I am the God of your fathers, the God of Abraham, Isaac and Jacob.'ᶜ Moses trembled with fear and did not dare to look.

³³"Then the Lord said to him, 'Take off your sandals, for the place where you are standing is holy ground. ³⁴I

have indeed seen the oppression of my people in Egypt. I have heard their groaning and have come down to set them free. Now come, I will send you back to Egypt.'ᵈ

³⁵"This is the same Moses they had rejected with the words, 'Who made you ruler and judge?' He was sent to be their ruler and deliverer by God himself, through the angel who appeared to him in the bush. ³⁶He led them out of Egypt and performed wonders and signs in Egypt, at the Red Sea and for forty years in the wilderness.

³⁷"This is the Moses who told the Israelites, 'God will raise up for you a prophet like me from your own people.'ᵉ ³⁸He was in the assembly in the wilderness, with the angel who spoke to him on Mount Sinai, and with our ancestors; and he received living words to pass on to us.

³⁹"But our ancestors refused to obey him. Instead, they rejected him and in their hearts turned back to Egypt. ⁴⁰They told Aaron, 'Make us gods who will go before us. As for this fellow Moses who led us out of Egypt—we don't know what has happened to him!'ᶠ ⁴¹That was the time they made an idol in the form of a calf. They brought sacrifices to it and reveled in what their own hands had made. ⁴²But God turned away from them and gave them over to the worship of the sun, moon and stars. This agrees with what is written in the book of the prophets:

" 'Did you bring me sacrifices and
      offerings
   forty years in the wilderness,
   people of Israel?

ᵉ 20 Or *was fair in the sight of God*   ᵇ 28 Exodus 2:14   ᶜ 32 Exodus 3:6
ᵈ 34 Exodus 3:5,7,8,10   ᵉ 37 Deut. 18:15
ᶠ 40 Exodus 32:1

43 You have taken up the tabernacle
　　　　of Molek
　　and the star of your god
　　　　Rephan,
　　the idols you made to worship.
Therefore I will send you into
exile'[a] beyond Babylon.

44 "Our ancestors had the tabernacle of the covenant law with them
in the wilderness. It had been made
as God directed Moses, according to
the pattern he had seen. 45 After receiving the tabernacle, our ancestors
under Joshua brought it with them
when they took the land from the
nations God drove out before them.
It remained in the land until the time
of David, 46 who enjoyed God's favor
and asked that he might provide a
dwelling place for the God of Jacob.[b]
47 But it was Solomon who built a
house for him.

48 "However, the Most High does
not live in houses made by human
hands. As the prophet says:

49 " 'Heaven is my throne,
　　and the earth is my footstool.
　What kind of house will you
　　　　build for me?
　　　says the Lord.
　Or where will my resting place
　　　　be?
50 Has not my hand made all these
　　　　things?'[c]

51 "You stiff-necked people! Your
hearts and ears are still uncircumcised. You are just like your ancestors: You always resist the Holy Spirit! 52 Was there ever a prophet your
ancestors did not persecute? They
even killed those who predicted the
coming of the Righteous One. And
now you have betrayed and murdered
him — 53 you who have received the
law that was given through angels
but have not obeyed it."

The Stoning of Stephen

54 When the members of the Sanhedrin heard this, they were furious
and gnashed their teeth at him. 55 But
Stephen, full of the Holy Spirit, looked
up to heaven and saw the glory of God,
and Jesus standing at the right hand
of God. 56 "Look," he said, "I see heaven
open and the Son of Man standing at
the right hand of God."

57 At this they covered their ears
and, yelling at the top of their voices,
they all rushed at him, 58 dragged him
out of the city and began to stone
him. Meanwhile, the witnesses laid
their coats at the feet of a young man
named Saul.

59 While they were stoning him, Stephen prayed, "Lord Jesus, receive my
spirit." 60 Then he fell on his knees and
cried out, "Lord, do not hold this sin
against them." When he had said this,
he fell asleep.

8 And Saul approved of their killing him.

The Church Persecuted and Scattered

On that day a great persecution
broke out against the church in Jerusalem, and all except the apostles
were scattered throughout Judea and
Samaria. 2 Godly men buried Stephen
and mourned deeply for him. 3 But
Saul began to destroy the church. Going from house to house, he dragged
off both men and women and put
them in prison.

Philip in Samaria

4 Those who had been scattered
preached the word wherever they
went. 5 Philip went down to a city in
Samaria and proclaimed the Messiah

---

[a] 43 Amos 5:25-27 (see Septuagint)　[b] 46 Some early manuscripts the house of Jacob　[c] 50 Isaiah 66:1,2

there. 6When the crowds heard Philip and saw the signs he performed, they all paid close attention to what he said. 7For with shrieks, impure spirits came out of many, and many who were paralyzed or lame were healed. 8So there was great joy in that city.

Simon the Sorcerer

9Now for some time a man named Simon had practiced sorcery in the city and amazed all the people of Samaria. He boasted that he was someone great, 10and all the people, both high and low, gave him their attention and exclaimed, "This man is rightly called the Great Power of God." 11They followed him because he had amazed them for a long time with his sorcery. 12But when they believed Philip as he proclaimed the good news of the kingdom of God and the name of Jesus Christ, they were baptized, both men and women. 13Simon himself believed and was baptized. And he followed Philip everywhere, astonished by the great signs and miracles he saw.

14When the apostles in Jerusalem heard that Samaria had accepted the word of God, they sent Peter and John to Samaria. 15When they arrived, they prayed for the new believers there that they might receive the Holy Spirit, 16because the Holy Spirit had not yet come on any of them; they had simply been baptized in the name of the Lord Jesus. 17Then Peter and John placed their hands on them, and they received the Holy Spirit.

18When Simon saw that the Spirit was given at the laying on of the apostles' hands, he offered them money 19and said, "Give me also this ability so that everyone on whom I lay my hands may receive the Holy Spirit."

20Peter answered: "May your money perish with you, because you thought you could buy the gift of God with money! 21You have no part or share in this ministry, because your heart is not right before God. 22Repent of this wickedness and pray to the Lord in the hope that he may forgive you for having such a thought in your heart. 23For I see that you are full of bitterness and captive to sin."

24Then Simon answered, "Pray to the Lord for me so that nothing you have said may happen to me."

25After they had further proclaimed the word of the Lord and testified about Jesus, Peter and John returned to Jerusalem, preaching the gospel in many Samaritan villages.

Philip and the Ethiopian

26Now an angel of the Lord said to Philip, "Go south to the road — the desert road — that goes down from Jerusalem to Gaza." 27So he started out, and on his way he met an Ethiopian*a* eunuch, an important official in charge of all the treasury of the Kandake (which means "queen of the Ethiopians"). This man had gone to Jerusalem to worship, 28and on his way home was sitting in his chariot reading the Book of Isaiah the prophet. 29The Spirit told Philip, "Go to that chariot and stay near it."

30Then Philip ran up to the chariot and heard the man reading Isaiah the prophet. "Do you understand what you are reading?" Philip asked.

31"How can I," he said, "unless someone explains it to me?" So he invited Philip to come up and sit with him.

32This is the passage of Scripture the eunuch was reading:

---

a 27 That is, from the southern Nile region

"He was led like a sheep to the
    slaughter,
and as a lamb before its
    shearer is silent,
so he did not open his mouth.
33 In his humiliation he was
    deprived of justice.
Who can speak of his
    descendants?
For his life was taken from the
    earth."[a]

34 The eunuch asked Philip, "Tell me, please, who is the prophet talking about, himself or someone else?" 35 Then Philip began with that very passage of Scripture and told him the good news about Jesus.

36 As they traveled along the road, they came to some water and the eunuch said, "Look, here is water. What can stand in the way of my being baptized?" [37][b] 38 And he gave orders to stop the chariot. Then both Philip and the eunuch went down into the water and Philip baptized him. 39 When they came up out of the water, the Spirit of the Lord suddenly took Philip away, and the eunuch did not see him again, but went on his way rejoicing. 40 Philip, however, appeared at Azotus and traveled about, preaching the gospel in all the towns until he reached Caesarea.

Saul's Conversion

9 Meanwhile, Saul was still breathing out murderous threats against the Lord's disciples. He went to the high priest 2 and asked him for letters to the synagogues in Damascus, so that if he found any there who belonged to the Way, whether men or women, he might take them as prisoners to Jerusalem. 3 As he neared Damascus on his journey, suddenly a light from heaven flashed around him. 4 He fell to the ground and heard

a voice say to him, "Saul, Saul, why do you persecute me?"

5 "Who are you, Lord?" Saul asked.
"I am Jesus, whom you are persecuting," he replied. 6 "Now get up and go into the city, and you will be told what you must do."

7 The men traveling with Saul stood there speechless; they heard the sound but did not see anyone. 8 Saul got up from the ground, but when he opened his eyes he could see nothing. So they led him by the hand into Damascus. 9 For three days he was blind, and did not eat or drink anything.

10 In Damascus there was a disciple named Ananias. The Lord called to him in a vision, "Ananias!"
"Yes, Lord," he answered.

11 The Lord told him, "Go to the house of Judas on Straight Street and ask for a man from Tarsus named Saul, for he is praying. 12 In a vision he has seen a man named Ananias come and place his hands on him to restore his sight."

13 "Lord," Ananias answered, "I have heard many reports about this man and all the harm he has done to your holy people in Jerusalem. 14 And he has come here with authority from the chief priests to arrest all who call on your name."

15 But the Lord said to Ananias, "Go! This man is my chosen instrument to proclaim my name to the Gentiles and their kings and to the people of Israel. 16 I will show him how much he must suffer for my name."

17 Then Ananias went to the house and entered it. Placing his hands

a 33 Isaiah 53:7,8 (see Septuagint)   b 37 Some manuscripts include here Philip said, "If you believe with all your heart, you may." The eunuch answered, "I believe that Jesus Christ is the Son of God."

on Saul, he said, "Brother Saul, the Lord — Jesus, who appeared to you on the road as you were coming here — has sent me so that you may see again and be filled with the Holy Spirit." ¹⁸Immediately, something like scales fell from Saul's eyes, and he could see again. He got up and was baptized, ¹⁹and after taking some food, he regained his strength.

Saul in Damascus and Jerusalem

Saul spent several days with the disciples in Damascus. ²⁰At once he began to preach in the synagogues that Jesus is the Son of God. ²¹All those who heard him were astonished and asked, "Isn't he the man who raised havoc in Jerusalem among those who call on this name? And hasn't he come here to take them as prisoners to the chief priests?" ²²Yet Saul grew more and more powerful and baffled the Jews living in Damascus by proving that Jesus is the Messiah.

²³After many days had gone by, there was a conspiracy among the Jews to kill him, ²⁴but Saul learned of their plan. Day and night they kept close watch on the city gates in order to kill him. ²⁵But his followers took him by night and lowered him in a basket through an opening in the wall.

²⁶When he came to Jerusalem, he tried to join the disciples, but they were all afraid of him, not believing that he really was a disciple. ²⁷But Barnabas took him and brought him to the apostles. He told them how Saul on his journey had seen the Lord and that the Lord had spoken to him, and how in Damascus he had preached fearlessly in the name of Jesus. ²⁸So Saul stayed with them and moved about freely in Jerusalem, speaking boldly in the name of the Lord. ²⁹He talked and debated with the Hellenistic Jews,ᵃ but they tried to kill him. ³⁰When the believers learned of this, they took him down to Caesarea and sent him off to Tarsus.

³¹Then the church throughout Judea, Galilee and Samaria enjoyed a time of peace and was strengthened. Living in the fear of the Lord and encouraged by the Holy Spirit, it increased in numbers.

Aeneas and Dorcas

³²As Peter traveled about the country, he went to visit the Lord's people who lived in Lydda. ³³There he found a man named Aeneas, who was paralyzed and had been bedridden for eight years. ³⁴"Aeneas," Peter said to him, "Jesus Christ heals you. Get up and roll up your mat." Immediately Aeneas got up. ³⁵All those who lived in Lydda and Sharon saw him and turned to the Lord.

³⁶In Joppa there was a disciple named Tabitha (in Greek her name is Dorcas); she was always doing good and helping the poor. ³⁷About that time she became sick and died, and her body was washed and placed in an upstairs room. ³⁸Lydda was near Joppa; so when the disciples heard that Peter was in Lydda, they sent two men to him and urged him, "Please come at once!"

³⁹Peter went with them, and when he arrived he was taken upstairs to the room. All the widows stood around him, crying and showing him the robes and other clothing that Dorcas had made while she was still with them.

⁴⁰Peter sent them all out of the room; then he got down on his knees

ᵃ 29 That is, Jews who had adopted the Greek language and culture and prayed. Turning toward the dead woman, he said, "Tabitha, get up." She opened her eyes, and seeing Peter she sat up. ⁴¹He took her by the hand and helped her to her feet. Then he called for the believers, especially the widows, and presented her to them alive. ⁴²This became known all over Joppa, and many people believed in the Lord. ⁴³Peter stayed in Joppa for some time with a tanner named Simon.

Cornelius Calls for Peter

10 At Caesarea there was a man named Cornelius, a centurion in what was known as the Italian Regiment. ²He and all his family were devout and God-fearing; he gave generously to those in need and prayed to God regularly. ³One day at about three in the afternoon he had a vision. He distinctly saw an angel of God, who came to him and said, "Cornelius!"

⁴Cornelius stared at him in fear. "What is it, Lord?" he asked.

The angel answered, "Your prayers and gifts to the poor have come up as a memorial offering before God. ⁵Now send men to Joppa to bring back a man named Simon who is called Peter. ⁶He is staying with Simon the tanner, whose house is by the sea."

⁷When the angel who spoke to him had gone, Cornelius called two of his servants and a devout soldier who was one of his attendants. ⁸He told them everything that had happened and sent them to Joppa.

Peter's Vision

⁹About noon the following day as they were on their journey and approaching the city, Peter went up on the roof to pray. ¹⁰He became hungry and wanted something to eat, and while the meal was being prepared, he fell into a trance. ¹¹He saw heaven opened and something like a large sheet being let down to earth by its four corners. ¹²It contained all kinds of four-footed animals, as well as reptiles and birds. ¹³Then a voice told him, "Get up, Peter. Kill and eat."

¹⁴"Surely not, Lord!" Peter replied. "I have never eaten anything impure or unclean."

¹⁵The voice spoke to him a second time, "Do not call anything impure that God has made clean."

¹⁶This happened three times, and immediately the sheet was taken back to heaven.

¹⁷While Peter was wondering about the meaning of the vision, the men sent by Cornelius found out where Simon's house was and stopped at the gate. ¹⁸They called out, asking if Simon who was known as Peter was staying there.

¹⁹While Peter was still thinking about the vision, the Spirit said to him, "Simon, three[a] men are looking for you. ²⁰So get up and go downstairs. Do not hesitate to go with them, for I have sent them."

²¹Peter went down and said to the men, "I'm the one you're looking for. Why have you come?"

²²The men replied, "We have come from Cornelius the centurion. He is a righteous and God-fearing man, who is respected by all the Jewish people. A holy angel told him to ask you to come to his house so that he could hear what you have to say." ²³Then Peter invited the men into the house to be his guests.

Peter at Cornelius's House

The next day Peter started out with them, and some of the believers from Joppa went along. ²⁴The

---

[a] 19 One early manuscript *two*; other manuscripts do not have the number.

following day he arrived in Caesarea. Cornelius was expecting them and had called together his relatives and close friends. ²⁵As Peter entered the house, Cornelius met him and fell at his feet in reverence. ²⁶But Peter made him get up. "Stand up," he said, "I am only a man myself."

²⁷While talking with him, Peter went inside and found a large gathering of people. ²⁸He said to them: "You are well aware that it is against our law for a Jew to associate with or visit a Gentile. But God has shown me that I should not call anyone impure or unclean. ²⁹So when I was sent for, I came without raising any objection. May I ask why you sent for me?"

³⁰Cornelius answered: "Three days ago I was in my house praying at this hour, at three in the afternoon. Suddenly a man in shining clothes stood before me ³¹and said, 'Cornelius, God has heard your prayer and remembered your gifts to the poor. ³²Send to Joppa for Simon who is called Peter. He is a guest in the home of Simon the tanner, who lives by the sea.' ³³So I sent for you immediately, and it was good of you to come. Now we are all here in the presence of God to listen to everything the Lord has commanded you to tell us."

³⁴Then Peter began to speak: "I now realize how true it is that God does not show favoritism ³⁵but accepts from every nation the one who fears him and does what is right. ³⁶You know the message God sent to the people of Israel, announcing the good news of peace through Jesus Christ, who is Lord of all. ³⁷You know what has happened throughout the province of Judea, beginning in Galilee after the baptism that John preached — ³⁸how God anointed Jesus of Nazareth with the Holy Spirit and power, and how he went around doing good and healing all who were under the power of the devil, because God was with him.

³⁹"We are witnesses of everything he did in the country of the Jews and in Jerusalem. They killed him by hanging him on a cross, ⁴⁰but God raised him from the dead on the third day and caused him to be seen. ⁴¹He was not seen by all the people, but by witnesses whom God had already chosen — by us who ate and drank with him after he rose from the dead. ⁴²He commanded us to preach to the people and to testify that he is the one whom God appointed as judge of the living and the dead. ⁴³All the prophets testify about him that everyone who believes in him receives forgiveness of sins through his name."

⁴⁴While Peter was still speaking these words, the Holy Spirit came on all who heard the message. ⁴⁵The circumcised believers who had come with Peter were astonished that the gift of the Holy Spirit had been poured out even on Gentiles. ⁴⁶For they heard them speaking in tongues*ᵃ* and praising God.

Then Peter said, ⁴⁷"Surely no one can stand in the way of their being baptized with water. They have received the Holy Spirit just as we have." ⁴⁸So he ordered that they be baptized in the name of Jesus Christ. Then they asked Peter to stay with them for a few days.

Peter Explains His Actions

11 The apostles and the believers throughout Judea heard that the Gentiles also had received the word of God. ²So when Peter went up to Jerusalem, the circumcised believers criticized him ³and said, "You went

---

ᵃ 46 Or other languages

into the house of uncircumcised men and ate with them."

⁴Starting from the beginning, Peter told them the whole story: ⁵"I was in the city of Joppa praying, and in a trance I saw a vision. I saw something like a large sheet being let down from heaven by its four corners, and it came down to where I was. ⁶I looked into it and saw four-footed animals of the earth, wild beasts, reptiles and birds. ⁷Then I heard a voice telling me, 'Get up, Peter. Kill and eat.'

⁸"I replied, 'Surely not, Lord! Nothing impure or unclean has ever entered my mouth.'

⁹"The voice spoke from heaven a second time, 'Do not call anything impure that God has made clean.' ¹⁰This happened three times, and then it was all pulled up to heaven again.

¹¹"Right then three men who had been sent to me from Caesarea stopped at the house where I was staying. ¹²The Spirit told me to have no hesitation about going with them. These six brothers also went with me, and we entered the man's house. ¹³He told us how he had seen an angel appear in his house and say, 'Send to Joppa for Simon who is called Peter. ¹⁴He will bring you a message through which you and all your household will be saved.'

¹⁵"As I began to speak, the Holy Spirit came on them as he had come on us at the beginning. ¹⁶Then I remembered what the Lord had said: 'John baptized with[c] water, but you will be baptized with[c] the Holy Spirit.' ¹⁷So if God gave them the same gift he gave us who believed in the Lord Jesus Christ, who was I to think that I could stand in God's way?"

¹⁸When they heard this, they had no further objections and praised God, saying, "So then, even to Gen-

tiles God has granted repentance that leads to life."

The Church in Antioch

¹⁹Now those who had been scattered by the persecution that broke out when Stephen was killed traveled as far as Phoenicia, Cyprus and Antioch, spreading the word only among Jews. ²⁰Some of them, however, men from Cyprus and Cyrene, went to Antioch and began to speak to Greeks also, telling them the good news about the Lord Jesus. ²¹The Lord's hand was with them, and a great number of people believed and turned to the Lord.

²²News of this reached the church in Jerusalem, and they sent Barnabas to Antioch. ²³When he arrived and saw what the grace of God had done, he was glad and encouraged them all to remain true to the Lord with all their hearts. ²⁴He was a good man, full of the Holy Spirit and faith, and a great number of people were brought to the Lord.

²⁵Then Barnabas went to Tarsus to look for Saul, ²⁶and when he found him, he brought him to Antioch. So for a whole year Barnabas and Saul met with the church and taught great numbers of people. The disciples were called Christians first at Antioch.

²⁷During this time some prophets came down from Jerusalem to Antioch. ²⁸One of them, named Agabus, stood up and through the Spirit predicted that a severe famine would spread over the entire Roman world. (This happened during the reign of Claudius.) ²⁹The disciples, as each one was able, decided to provide help for the brothers and sisters living in Judea. ³⁰This they did, sending their gift to the elders by Barnabas and Saul.

---

[c] 16 Or *in*

Peter's Miraculous Escape From Prison

12 It was about this time that King Herod arrested some who belonged to the church, intending to persecute them. ²He had James, the brother of John, put to death with the sword. ³When he saw that this met with approval among the Jews, he proceeded to seize Peter also. This happened during the Festival of Unleavened Bread. ⁴After arresting him, he put him in prison, handing him over to be guarded by four squads of four soldiers each. Herod intended to bring him out for public trial after the Passover.

⁵So Peter was kept in prison, but the church was earnestly praying to God for him.

⁶The night before Herod was to bring him to trial, Peter was sleeping between two soldiers, bound with two chains, and sentries stood guard at the entrance. ⁷Suddenly an angel of the Lord appeared and a light shone in the cell. He struck Peter on the side and woke him up. "Quick, get up!" he said, and the chains fell off Peter's wrists.

⁸Then the angel said to him, "Put on your clothes and sandals." And Peter did so. "Wrap your cloak around you and follow me," the angel told him. ⁹Peter followed him out of the prison, but he had no idea that what the angel was doing was really happening; he thought he was seeing a vision. ¹⁰They passed the first and second guards and came to the iron gate leading to the city. It opened for them by itself, and they went through it. When they had walked the length of one street, suddenly the angel left him.

¹¹Then Peter came to himself and said, "Now I know without a doubt that the Lord has sent his angel and rescued me from Herod's clutches and from everything the Jewish people were hoping would happen."

¹²When this had dawned on him, he went to the house of Mary the mother of John, also called Mark, where many people had gathered and were praying. ¹³Peter knocked at the outer entrance, and a servant named Rhoda came to answer the door. ¹⁴When she recognized Peter's voice, she was so overjoyed she ran back without opening it and exclaimed, "Peter is at the door!"

¹⁵"You're out of your mind," they told her. When she kept insisting that it was so, they said, "It must be his angel."

¹⁶But Peter kept on knocking, and when they opened the door and saw him, they were astonished. ¹⁷Peter motioned with his hand for them to be quiet and described how the Lord had brought him out of prison. "Tell James and the other brothers and sisters about this," he said, and then he left for another place.

¹⁸In the morning, there was no small commotion among the soldiers as to what had become of Peter. ¹⁹After Herod had a thorough search made for him and did not find him, he cross-examined the guards and ordered that they be executed.

Herod's Death

Then Herod went from Judea to Caesarea and stayed there. ²⁰He had been quarreling with the people of Tyre and Sidon; they now joined together and sought an audience with him. After securing the support of Blastus, a trusted personal servant of the king, they asked for peace, because they depended on the king's country for their food supply.

²¹On the appointed day Herod, wearing his royal robes, sat on his throne and delivered a public address to the people. ²²They shouted, "This is the voice of a god, not of a man." ²³Immediately, because Herod did not give praise to God, an angel of the Lord struck him down, and he was eaten by worms and died.

²⁴But the word of God continued to spread and flourish.

Barnabas and Saul Sent Off

²⁵When Barnabas and Saul finished their mission, they returned from⁰ Jerusalem, taking with them John, also called Mark. ¹Now in the church at Antioch there were prophets and teachers: Barnabas, Simeon called Niger, Lucius of Cyrene, Manaen (who had been brought up with Herod the tetrarch) and Saul. ²While they were worshiping the Lord and fasting, the Holy Spirit said, "Set apart for me Barnabas and Saul for the work to which I have called them." ³So after they had fasted and prayed, they placed their hands on them and sent them off.

On Cyprus

⁴The two of them, sent on their way by the Holy Spirit, went down to Seleucia and sailed from there to Cyprus. ⁵When they arrived at Salamis, they proclaimed the word of God in the Jewish synagogues. John was with them as their helper.

⁶They traveled through the whole island until they came to Paphos. There they met a Jewish sorcerer and false prophet named Bar-Jesus, ⁷who was an attendant of the proconsul, Sergius Paulus. The proconsul, an intelligent man, sent for Barnabas and Saul because he wanted to hear the word of God. ⁸But Elymas the sorcer-

er (for that is what his name means) opposed them and tried to turn the proconsul from the faith. ⁹Then Saul, who was also called Paul, filled with the Holy Spirit, looked straight at Elymas and said, ¹⁰"You are a child of the devil and an enemy of everything that is right! You are full of all kinds of deceit and trickery. Will you never stop perverting the right ways of the Lord? ¹¹Now the hand of the Lord is against you. You are going to be blind for a time, not even able to see the light of the sun."

Immediately mist and darkness came over him, and he groped about, seeking someone to lead him by the hand. ¹²When the proconsul saw what had happened, he believed, for he was amazed at the teaching about the Lord.

In Pisidian Antioch

¹³From Paphos, Paul and his companions sailed to Perga in Pamphylia, where John left them to return to Jerusalem. ¹⁴From Perga they went on to Pisidian Antioch. On the Sabbath they entered the synagogue and sat down. ¹⁵After the reading from the Law and the Prophets, the leaders of the synagogue sent word to them, saying, "Brothers, if you have a word of exhortation for the people, please speak."

¹⁶Standing up, Paul motioned with his hand and said: "Fellow Israelites and you Gentiles who worship God, listen to me! ¹⁷The God of the people of Israel chose our ancestors; he made the people prosper during their stay in Egypt; with mighty power he led them out of that country; ¹⁸for about forty years he endured their conduct⁰ in the wilderness; ¹⁹and he overthrew

---

⁰ 25 Some manuscripts *to*   ᵇ 18 Some manuscripts *he cared for them*

seven nations in Canaan, giving their land to his people as their inheritance. [20] All this took about 450 years.

"After this, God gave them judges until the time of Samuel the prophet. [21] Then the people asked for a king, and he gave them Saul son of Kish, of the tribe of Benjamin, who ruled forty years. [22] After removing Saul, he made David their king. God testified concerning him: 'I have found David son of Jesse, a man after my own heart; he will do everything I want him to do.'

[23] "From this man's descendants God has brought to Israel the Savior Jesus, as he promised. [24] Before the coming of Jesus, John preached repentance and baptism to all the people of Israel. [25] As John was completing his work, he said: 'Who do you suppose I am? I am not the one you are looking for. But there is one coming after me whose sandals I am not worthy to untie.'

[26] "Fellow children of Abraham and you God-fearing Gentiles, it is to us that this message of salvation has been sent. [27] The people of Jerusalem and their rulers did not recognize Jesus, yet in condemning him they fulfilled the words of the prophets that are read every Sabbath. [28] Though they found no proper ground for a death sentence, they asked Pilate to have him executed. [29] When they had carried out all that was written about him, they took him down from the cross and laid him in a tomb. [30] But God raised him from the dead, [31] and for many days he was seen by those who had traveled with him from Galilee to Jerusalem. They are now his witnesses to our people.

[32] "We tell you the good news: What God promised our ancestors [33] he has fulfilled for us, their children, by raising up Jesus. As it is written in the second Psalm:

"'You are my son;
    today I have become your
        father.'[a]

[34] God raised him from the dead so that he will never be subject to decay. As God has said,

"'I will give you the holy and
    sure blessings promised
        to David.'[b]

[35] So it is also stated elsewhere:

"'You will not let your holy one
    see decay.'[c]

[36] "Now when David had served God's purpose in his own generation, he fell asleep; he was buried with his ancestors and his body decayed. [37] But the one whom God raised from the dead did not see decay.

[38] "Therefore, my friends, I want you to know that through Jesus the forgiveness of sins is proclaimed to you. [39] Through him everyone who believes is set free from every sin, a justification you were not able to obtain under the law of Moses. [40] Take care that what the prophets have said does not happen to you:

[41] "'Look, you scoffers,
    wonder and perish,
for I am going to do something
        in your days
    that you would never believe,
    even if someone told you.'[d]"

[42] As Paul and Barnabas were leaving the synagogue, the people invited them to speak further about these things on the next Sabbath. [43] When the congregation was dismissed,

----

[a] 33 Psalm 2:7   [b] 34 Isaiah 55:3
[c] 35 Psalm 16:10 (see Septuagint)
[d] 41 Hab. 1:5

many of the Jews and devout converts to Judaism followed Paul and Barnabas, who talked with them and urged them to continue in the grace of God.

⁴⁴On the next Sabbath almost the whole city gathered to hear the word of the Lord. ⁴⁵When the Jews saw the crowds, they were filled with jealousy. They began to contradict what Paul was saying and heaped abuse on him.

⁴⁶Then Paul and Barnabas answered them boldly: "We had to speak the word of God to you first. Since you reject it and do not consider yourselves worthy of eternal life, we now turn to the Gentiles. ⁴⁷For this is what the Lord has commanded us:

"'I have made you[a] a light for the
    Gentiles,
  that you[a] may bring salvation
    to the ends of the earth.'[b]"

⁴⁸When the Gentiles heard this, they were glad and honored the word of the Lord; and all who were appointed for eternal life believed.

⁴⁹The word of the Lord spread through the whole region. ⁵⁰But the Jewish leaders incited the God-fearing women of high standing and the leading men of the city. They stirred up persecution against Paul and Barnabas, and expelled them from their region. ⁵¹So they shook the dust off their feet as a warning to them and went to Iconium. ⁵²And the disciples were filled with joy and with the Holy Spirit.

In Iconium

14 At Iconium Paul and Barnabas went as usual into the Jewish synagogue. There they spoke so effectively that a great number of Jews and Greeks believed. ²But the Jews who refused to believe stirred up the other Gentiles and poisoned their minds

against the brothers. ³So Paul and Barnabas spent considerable time there, speaking boldly for the Lord, who confirmed the message of his grace by enabling them to perform signs and wonders. ⁴The people of the city were divided; some sided with the Jews, others with the apostles. ⁵There was a plot afoot among both Gentiles and Jews, together with their leaders, to mistreat them and stone them. ⁶But they found out about it and fled to the Lycaonian cities of Lystra and Derbe and to the surrounding country, ⁷where they continued to preach the gospel.

In Lystra and Derbe

⁸In Lystra there sat a man who was lame. He had been that way from birth and had never walked. ⁹He listened to Paul as he was speaking. Paul looked directly at him, saw that he had faith to be healed ¹⁰and called out, "Stand up on your feet!" At that, the man jumped up and began to walk.

¹¹When the crowd saw what Paul had done, they shouted in the Lycaonian language, "The gods have come down to us in human form!" ¹²Barnabas they called Zeus, and Paul they called Hermes because he was the chief speaker. ¹³The priest of Zeus, whose temple was just outside the city, brought bulls and wreaths to the city gates because he and the crowd wanted to offer sacrifices to them.

¹⁴But when the apostles Barnabas and Paul heard of this, they tore their clothes and rushed out into the crowd, shouting: ¹⁵"Friends, why are you doing this? We too are only human, like you. We are bringing you good news, telling you to turn from these worthless things to the living

[a] 47 The Greek is singular.   [b] 47 Isaiah 49:6

God, who made the heavens and the earth and the sea and everything in them. ¹⁶In the past, he let all nations go their own way. ¹⁷Yet he has not left himself without testimony: He has shown kindness by giving you rain from heaven and crops in their seasons; he provides you with plenty of food and fills your hearts with joy." ¹⁸Even with these words, they had difficulty keeping the crowd from sacrificing to them.

¹⁹Then some Jews came from Antioch and Iconium and won the crowd over. They stoned Paul and dragged him outside the city, thinking he was dead. ²⁰But after the disciples had gathered around him, he got up and went back into the city. The next day he and Barnabas left for Derbe.

The Return to Antioch in Syria

²¹They preached the gospel in that city and won a large number of disciples. Then they returned to Lystra, Iconium and Antioch, ²²strengthening the disciples and encouraging them to remain true to the faith. "We must go through many hardships to enter the kingdom of God," they said. ²³Paul and Barnabas appointed elders[a] for them in each church and, with prayer and fasting, committed them to the Lord, in whom they had put their trust. ²⁴After going through Pisidia, they came into Pamphylia, ²⁵and when they had preached the word in Perga, they went down to Attalia.

²⁶From Attalia they sailed back to Antioch, where they had been committed to the grace of God for the work they had now completed. ²⁷On arriving there, they gathered the church together and reported all that God had done through them and how he had opened a door of faith to

the Gentiles. ²⁸And they stayed there a long time with the disciples.

The Council at Jerusalem

15 Certain people came down from Judea to Antioch and were teaching the believers: "Unless you are circumcised, according to the custom taught by Moses, you cannot be saved." ²This brought Paul and Barnabas into sharp dispute and debate with them. So Paul and Barnabas were appointed, along with some other believers, to go up to Jerusalem to see the apostles and elders about this question. ³The church sent them on their way, and as they traveled through Phoenicia and Samaria, they told how the Gentiles had been converted. This news made all the believers very glad. ⁴When they came to Jerusalem, they were welcomed by the church and the apostles and elders, to whom they reported everything God had done through them.

⁵Then some of the believers who belonged to the party of the Pharisees stood up and said, "The Gentiles must be circumcised and required to keep the law of Moses."

⁶The apostles and elders met to consider this question. ⁷After much discussion, Peter got up and addressed them: "Brothers, you know that some time ago God made a choice among you that the Gentiles might hear from my lips the message of the gospel and believe. ⁸God, who knows the heart, showed that he accepted them by giving the Holy Spirit to them, just as he did to us. ⁹He did not discriminate between us and them, for he purified their hearts by faith. ¹⁰Now then, why do you try to test God by putting on the necks of

---

[a] 23 Or Barnabas ordained elders; or Barnabas had elders elected

Gentiles a yoke that neither we nor our ancestors have been able to bear? [11] No! We believe it is through the grace of our Lord Jesus that we are saved, just as they are."

[12] The whole assembly became silent as they listened to Barnabas and Paul telling about the signs and wonders God had done among the Gentiles through them. [13] When they finished, James spoke up. "Brothers," he said, "listen to me. [14] Simon[e] has described to us how God first intervened to choose a people for his name from the Gentiles. [15] The words of the prophets are in agreement with this, as it is written:

[16] " 'After this I will return
        and rebuild David's fallen tent.
    Its ruins I will rebuild,
        and I will restore it,
[17] that the rest of mankind may
        seek the Lord,
    even all the Gentiles who bear
        my name,
    says the Lord, who does these
        things'[b] —
[18]   things known from long ago.[c]

[19] "It is my judgment, therefore, that we should not make it difficult for the Gentiles who are turning to God. [20] Instead we should write to them, telling them to abstain from food polluted by idols, from sexual immorality, from the meat of strangled animals and from blood. [21] For the law of Moses has been preached in every city from the earliest times and is read in the synagogues on every Sabbath."

The Council's Letter to Gentile Believers

[22] Then the apostles and elders, with the whole church, decided to choose some of their own men and send them to Antioch with Paul and Barnabas. They chose Judas (called Barsabbas) and Silas, men who were leaders among the believers. [23] With them they sent the following letter:

The apostles and elders, your brothers,

To the Gentile believers in Antioch, Syria and Cilicia:

Greetings.

[24] We have heard that some went out from us without our authorization and disturbed you, troubling your minds by what they said. [25] So we all agreed to choose some men and send them to you with our dear friends Barnabas and Paul — [26] men who have risked their lives for the name of our Lord Jesus Christ. [27] Therefore we are sending Judas and Silas to confirm by word of mouth what we are writing. [28] It seemed good to the Holy Spirit and to us not to burden you with anything beyond the following requirements: [29] You are to abstain from food sacrificed to idols, from blood, from the meat of strangled animals and from sexual immorality. You will do well to avoid these things.

Farewell.

[30] So the men were sent off and went down to Antioch, where they gathered the church together and delivered the letter. [31] The people read it and were glad for its encouraging

---

[e] 14 Greek *Simeon*, a variant of *Simon*; that is, Peter   [b] 17 Amos 9:11,12 (see Septuagint)
[c] 17,18 Some manuscripts *things'* — / *[18] the Lord's work is known to him from long ago*

message. ³²Judas and Silas, who themselves were prophets, said much to encourage and strengthen the believers. ³³After spending some time there, they were sent off by the believers with the blessing of peace to return to those who had sent them. [³⁴]ᵃ ³⁵But Paul and Barnabas remained in Antioch, where they and many others taught and preached the word of the Lord.

Disagreement Between Paul and Barnabas

³⁶Some time later Paul said to Barnabas, "Let us go back and visit the believers in all the towns where we preached the word of the Lord and see how they are doing." ³⁷Barnabas wanted to take John, also called Mark, with them, ³⁸but Paul did not think it wise to take him, because he had deserted them in Pamphylia and had not continued with them in the work. ³⁹They had such a sharp disagreement that they parted company. Barnabas took Mark and sailed for Cyprus, ⁴⁰but Paul chose Silas and left, commended by the believers to the grace of the Lord. ⁴¹He went through Syria and Cilicia, strengthening the churches.

Timothy Joins Paul and Silas

16 Paul came to Derbe and then to Lystra, where a disciple named Timothy lived, whose mother was Jewish and a believer but whose father was a Greek. ²The believers at Lystra and Iconium spoke well of him. ³Paul wanted to take him along on the journey, so he circumcised him because of the Jews who lived in that area, for they all knew that his father was a Greek. ⁴As they traveled from town to town, they delivered the decisions reached by the apostles and elders in Jerusalem for the

people to obey. ⁵So the churches were strengthened in the faith and grew daily in numbers.

Paul's Vision of the Man of Macedonia

⁶Paul and his companions traveled throughout the region of Phrygia and Galatia, having been kept by the Holy Spirit from preaching the word in the province of Asia. ⁷When they came to the border of Mysia, they tried to enter Bithynia, but the Spirit of Jesus would not allow them to. ⁸So they passed by Mysia and went down to Troas. ⁹During the night Paul had a vision of a man of Macedonia standing and begging him, "Come over to Macedonia and help us." ¹⁰After Paul had seen the vision, we got ready at once to leave for Macedonia, concluding that God had called us to preach the gospel to them.

Lydia's Conversion in Philippi

¹¹From Troas we put out to sea and sailed straight for Samothrace, and the next day we went on to Neapolis. ¹²From there we traveled to Philippi, a Roman colony and the leading city of that districtᵇ of Macedonia. And we stayed there several days.

¹³On the Sabbath we went outside the city gate to the river, where we expected to find a place of prayer. We sat down and began to speak to the women who had gathered there. ¹⁴One of those listening was a woman from the city of Thyatira named Lydia, a dealer in purple cloth. She was a worshiper of God. The Lord opened her heart to respond to Paul's message. ¹⁵When she and the members

ᵃ 34 Some manuscripts include here *But Silas decided to remain there.*   ᵇ 12 The text and meaning of the Greek for *the leading city of that district* are uncertain.

of her household were baptized, she invited us to her home. "If you consider me a believer in the Lord," she said, "come and stay at my house." And she persuaded us.

Paul and Silas in Prison

16Once when we were going to the place of prayer, we were met by a female slave who had a spirit by which she predicted the future. She earned a great deal of money for her owners by fortune-telling. 17She followed Paul and the rest of us, shouting, "These men are servants of the Most High God, who are telling you the way to be saved." 18She kept this up for many days. Finally Paul became so annoyed that he turned around and said to the spirit, "In the name of Jesus Christ I command you to come out of her!" At that moment the spirit left her.

19When her owners realized that their hope of making money was gone, they seized Paul and Silas and dragged them into the marketplace to face the authorities. 20They brought them before the magistrates and said, "These men are Jews, and are throwing our city into an uproar 21by advocating customs unlawful for us Romans to accept or practice."

22The crowd joined in the attack against Paul and Silas, and the magistrates ordered them to be stripped and beaten with rods. 23After they had been severely flogged, they were thrown into prison, and the jailer was commanded to guard them carefully. 24When he received these orders, he put them in the inner cell and fastened their feet in the stocks.

25About midnight Paul and Silas were praying and singing hymns to God, and the other prisoners were listening to them. 26Suddenly there was such a violent earthquake that

the foundations of the prison were shaken. At once all the prison doors flew open, and everyone's chains came loose. 27The jailer woke up, and when he saw the prison doors open, he drew his sword and was about to kill himself because he thought the prisoners had escaped. 28But Paul shouted, "Don't harm yourself! We are all here!"

29The jailer called for lights, rushed in and fell trembling before Paul and Silas. 30He then brought them out and asked, "Sirs, what must I do to be saved?"

31They replied, "Believe in the Lord Jesus, and you will be saved — you and your household." 32Then they spoke the word of the Lord to him and to all the others in his house. 33At that hour of the night the jailer took them and washed their wounds; then immediately he and all his household were baptized. 34The jailer brought them into his house and set a meal before them; he was filled with joy because he had come to believe in God — he and his whole household.

35When it was daylight, the magistrates sent their officers to the jailer with the order: "Release those men." 36The jailer told Paul, "The magistrates have ordered that you and Silas be released. Now you can leave. Go in peace."

37But Paul said to the officers: "They beat us publicly without a trial, even though we are Roman citizens, and threw us into prison. And now do they want to get rid of us quietly? No! Let them come themselves and escort us out."

38The officers reported this to the magistrates, and when they heard that Paul and Silas were Roman citizens, they were alarmed. 39They came to appease them and escorted them from the prison, requesting them to leave the city. 40After Paul and Silas came out of the prison, they went to Lydia's house, where they met with the brothers and sisters and encouraged them. Then they left.

In Thessalonica

17 When Paul and his companions had passed through Amphipolis and Apollonia, they came to Thessalonica, where there was a Jewish synagogue. 2As was his custom, Paul went into the synagogue, and on three Sabbath days he reasoned with them in the Scriptures, 3explaining and proving that the Messiah had to suffer and rise from the dead. "This Jesus I am proclaiming to you is the Messiah," he said. 4Some of the Jews were persuaded and joined Paul and Silas, as did a large number of God-fearing Greeks and quite a few prominent women.

5But other Jews were jealous; so they rounded up some bad characters from the marketplace, formed a mob and started a riot in the city. They rushed to Jason's house in search of Paul and Silas in order to bring them out to the crowd.ᵃ 6But when they did not find them, they dragged Jason and some other believers before the city officials, shouting: "These men who have caused trouble all over the world have now come here, 7and Jason has welcomed them into his house. They are all defying Caesar's decrees, saying that there is another king, one called Jesus." 8When they heard this, the crowd and the city officials were thrown into turmoil. 9Then they made Jason and the others post bond and let them go.

In Berea

10As soon as it was night, the believers sent Paul and Silas away to Berea. On arriving there, they went to the Jewish synagogue. 11Now the Berean Jews were of more noble character than those in Thessalonica, for they received the message with great eagerness and examined the Scriptures every day to see if what Paul said was true. 12As a result, many of them believed, as did also a number of prominent Greek women and many Greek men.

13But when the Jews in Thessalonica learned that Paul was preaching the word of God at Berea, some of them went there too, agitating the crowds and stirring them up. 14The believers immediately sent Paul to the coast, but Silas and Timothy stayed at Berea. 15Those who escorted him brought him to Athens and then left with instructions for Silas and Timothy to join him as soon as possible.

In Athens

16While Paul was waiting for them in Athens, he was greatly distressed to see that the city was full of idols. 17So he reasoned in the synagogue with both Jews and God-fearing Greeks, as well as in the marketplace day by day with those who happened to be there. 18A group of Epicurean and Stoic philosophers began to debate with him. Some of them asked, "What is this babbler trying to say?" Others remarked, "He seems to be advocating foreign gods." They said this because Paul was preaching the good news about Jesus and the resurrection. 19Then they took him and brought him to a meeting of the Areopagus, where they said to him, "May we know what this new teaching is that you are presenting? 20You are bringing some strange ideas to our ears,

---

ᵃ 5 Or the assembly of the people

and we would like to know what they mean." ²¹(All the Athenians and the foreigners who lived there spent their time doing nothing but talking about and listening to the latest ideas.)

²²Paul then stood up in the meeting of the Areopagus and said: "People of Athens! I see that in every way you are very religious. ²³For as I walked around and looked carefully at your objects of worship, I even found an altar with this inscription: TO AN UNKNOWN GOD. So you are ignorant of the very thing you worship—and this is what I am going to proclaim to you.

²⁴"The God who made the world and everything in it is the Lord of heaven and earth and does not live in temples built by human hands. ²⁵And he is not served by human hands, as if he needed anything. Rather, he himself gives everyone life and breath and everything else. ²⁶From one man he made all the nations, that they should inhabit the whole earth; and he marked out their appointed times in history and the boundaries of their lands. ²⁷God did this so that they would seek him and perhaps reach out for him and find him, though he is not far from any one of us. ²⁸'For in him we live and move and have our being.'ᵃ As some of your own poets have said, 'We are his offspring.'ᵇ

²⁹"Therefore since we are God's offspring, we should not think that the divine being is like gold or silver or stone—an image made by human design and skill. ³⁰In the past God overlooked such ignorance, but now he commands all people everywhere to repent. ³¹For he has set a day when he will judge the world with justice by the man he has appointed. He has given proof of this to everyone by raising him from the dead."

³²When they heard about the resurrection of the dead, some of them sneered, but others said, "We want to hear you again on this subject." ³³At that, Paul left the Council. ³⁴Some of the people became followers of Paul and believed. Among them was Dionysius, a member of the Areopagus, also a woman named Damaris, and a number of others.

In Corinth

18 After this, Paul left Athens and went to Corinth. ²There he met a Jew named Aquila, a native of Pontus, who had recently come from Italy with his wife Priscilla, because Claudius had ordered all Jews to leave Rome. Paul went to see them, ³and because he was a tentmaker as they were, he stayed and worked with them. ⁴Every Sabbath he reasoned in the synagogue, trying to persuade Jews and Greeks.

⁵When Silas and Timothy came from Macedonia, Paul devoted himself exclusively to preaching, testifying to the Jews that Jesus was the Messiah. ⁶But when they opposed Paul and became abusive, he shook out his clothes in protest and said to them, "Your blood be on your own heads! I am innocent of it. From now on I will go to the Gentiles."

⁷Then Paul left the synagogue and went next door to the house of Titius Justus, a worshiper of God. ⁸Crispus, the synagogue leader, and his entire household believed in the Lord; and many of the Corinthians who heard Paul believed and were baptized.

⁹One night the Lord spoke to Paul in a vision: "Do not be afraid; keep on speaking, do not be silent. ¹⁰For I am

---

ᵃ 28 From the Cretan philosopher Epimenides
ᵇ 28 From the Cilician Stoic philosopher Aratus

with you, and no one is going to attack and harm you, because I have many people in this city." 11So Paul stayed in Corinth for a year and a half, teaching them the word of God.

12While Gallio was proconsul of Achaia, the Jews of Corinth made a united attack on Paul and brought him to the place of judgment. 13"This man," they charged, "is persuading the people to worship God in ways contrary to the law."

14Just as Paul was about to speak, Gallio said to them, "If you Jews were making a complaint about some misdemeanor or serious crime, it would be reasonable for me to listen to you. 15But since it involves questions about words — names and your own law — settle the matter yourselves. I will not be a judge of such things." 16So he drove them off. 17Then the crowd there turned on Sosthenes the synagogue leader and beat him in front of the proconsul; and Gallio showed no concern whatever.

Priscilla, Aquila and Apollos

18Paul stayed on in Corinth for some time. Then he left the brothers and sisters and sailed for Syria, accompanied by Priscilla and Aquila. Before he sailed, he had his hair cut off at Cenchreae because of a vow he had taken. 19They arrived at Ephesus, where Paul left Priscilla and Aquila. He himself went into the synagogue and reasoned with the Jews. 20When they asked him to spend more time with them, he declined. 21But as he left, he promised, "I will come back if it is God's will." Then he set sail from Ephesus. 22When he landed at Caesarea, he went up to Jerusalem and greeted the church and then went down to Antioch.

23After spending some time in Antioch, Paul set out from there and traveled from place to place throughout the region of Galatia and Phrygia, strengthening all the disciples.

24Meanwhile a Jew named Apollos, a native of Alexandria, came to Ephesus. He was a learned man, with a thorough knowledge of the Scriptures. 25He had been instructed in the way of the Lord, and he spoke with great fervor[a] and taught about Jesus accurately, though he knew only the baptism of John. 26He began to speak boldly in the synagogue. When Priscilla and Aquila heard him, they invited him to their home and explained to him the way of God more adequately.

27When Apollos wanted to go to Achaia, the brothers and sisters encouraged him and wrote to the disciples there to welcome him. When he arrived, he was a great help to those who by grace had believed. 28For he vigorously refuted his Jewish opponents in public debate, proving from the Scriptures that Jesus was the Messiah.

Paul in Ephesus

19 While Apollos was at Corinth, Paul took the road through the interior and arrived at Ephesus. There he found some disciples 2and asked them, "Did you receive the Holy Spirit when[b] you believed?"

They answered, "No, we have not even heard that there is a Holy Spirit."

3So Paul asked, "Then what baptism did you receive?"

"John's baptism," they replied.

4Paul said, "John's baptism was a baptism of repentance. He told the people to believe in the one coming after him, that is, in Jesus." 5On hear-

---

a 25 Or with fervor in the Spirit   b 2 Or after

ing this, they were baptized in the name of the Lord Jesus. [6]When Paul placed his hands on them, the Holy Spirit came on them, and they spoke in tongues[a] and prophesied. [7]There were about twelve men in all.

[8]Paul entered the synagogue and spoke boldly there for three months, arguing persuasively about the kingdom of God. [9]But some of them became obstinate; they refused to believe and publicly maligned the Way. So Paul left them. He took the disciples with him and had discussions daily in the lecture hall of Tyrannus. [10]This went on for two years, so that all the Jews and Greeks who lived in the province of Asia heard the word of the Lord.

[11]God did extraordinary miracles through Paul, [12]so that even handkerchiefs and aprons that had touched him were taken to the sick, and their illnesses were cured and the evil spirits left them.

[13]Some Jews who went around driving out evil spirits tried to invoke the name of the Lord Jesus over those who were demon-possessed. They would say, "In the name of the Jesus whom Paul preaches, I command you to come out." [14]Seven sons of Sceva, a Jewish chief priest, were doing this. [15]One day the evil spirit answered them, "Jesus I know, and Paul I know about, but who are you?" [16]Then the man who had the evil spirit jumped on them and overpowered them all. He gave them such a beating that they ran out of the house naked and bleeding.

[17]When this became known to the Jews and Greeks living in Ephesus, they were all seized with fear, and the name of the Lord Jesus was held in high honor. [18]Many of those who believed now came and openly confessed what they had done. [19]A number who had practiced sorcery brought their scrolls together and burned them publicly. When they calculated the value of the scrolls, the total came to fifty thousand drachmas.[b] [20]In this way the word of the Lord spread widely and grew in power.

[21]After all this had happened, Paul decided[c] to go to Jerusalem, passing through Macedonia and Achaia. "After I have been there," he said, "I must visit Rome also." [22]He sent two of his helpers, Timothy and Erastus, to Macedonia, while he stayed in the province of Asia a little longer.

The Riot in Ephesus

[23]About that time there arose a great disturbance about the Way. [24]A silversmith named Demetrius, who made silver shrines of Artemis, brought in a lot of business for the craftsmen there. [25]He called them together, along with the workers in related trades, and said: "You know, my friends, that we receive a good income from this business. [26]And you see and hear how this fellow Paul has convinced and led astray large numbers of people here in Ephesus and in practically the whole province of Asia. He says that gods made by human hands are no gods at all. [27]There is danger not only that our trade will lose its good name, but also that the temple of the great goddess Artemis will be discredited; and the goddess herself, who is worshiped throughout the province of Asia and the world, will be robbed of her divine majesty."

[28]When they heard this, they were furious and began shouting: "Great

---

[a] 6 Or other languages   [b] 19 A drachma was a silver coin worth about a day's wages.   [c] 21 Or decided in the Spirit

is Artemis of the Ephesians!" ²⁹Soon the whole city was in an uproar. The people seized Gaius and Aristarchus, Paul's traveling companions from Macedonia, and all of them rushed into the theater together. ³⁰Paul wanted to appear before the crowd, but the disciples would not let him. ³¹Even some of the officials of the province, friends of Paul, sent him a message begging him not to venture into the theater.

³²The assembly was in confusion: Some were shouting one thing, some another. Most of the people did not even know why they were there. ³³The Jews in the crowd pushed Alexander to the front, and they shouted instructions to him. He motioned for silence in order to make a defense before the people. ³⁴But when they realized he was a Jew, they all shouted in unison for about two hours: "Great is Artemis of the Ephesians!"

³⁵The city clerk quieted the crowd and said: "Fellow Ephesians, doesn't all the world know that the city of Ephesus is the guardian of the temple of the great Artemis and of her image, which fell from heaven? ³⁶Therefore, since these facts are undeniable, you ought to calm down and not do anything rash. ³⁷You have brought these men here, though they have neither robbed temples nor blasphemed our goddess. ³⁸If, then, Demetrius and his fellow craftsmen have a grievance against anybody, the courts are open and there are proconsuls. They can press charges. ³⁹If there is anything further you want to bring up, it must be settled in a legal assembly. ⁴⁰As it is, we are in danger of being charged with rioting because of what happened today. In that case we would not be able to account for this commotion, since there is no reason

for it." ⁴¹After he had said this, he dismissed the assembly.

Through Macedonia and Greece

20 When the uproar had ended, Paul sent for the disciples and, after encouraging them, said goodbye and set out for Macedonia. ²He traveled through that area, speaking many words of encouragement to the people, and finally arrived in Greece, ³where he stayed three months. Because some Jews had plotted against him just as he was about to sail for Syria, he decided to go back through Macedonia. ⁴He was accompanied by Sopater son of Pyrrhus from Berea, Aristarchus and Secundus from Thessalonica, Gaius from Derbe, Timothy also, and Tychicus and Trophimus from the province of Asia. ⁵These men went on ahead and waited for us at Troas. ⁶But we sailed from Philippi after the Festival of Unleavened Bread, and five days later joined the others at Troas, where we stayed seven days.

Eutychus Raised From the Dead at Troas

⁷On the first day of the week we came together to break bread. Paul spoke to the people and, because he intended to leave the next day, kept on talking until midnight. ⁸There were many lamps in the upstairs room where we were meeting. ⁹Seated in a window was a young man named Eutychus, who was sinking into a deep sleep as Paul talked on and on. When he was sound asleep, he fell to the ground from the third story and was picked up dead. ¹⁰Paul went down, threw himself on the young man and put his arms around him. "Don't be alarmed," he said. "He's alive!" ¹¹Then he went upstairs again

and broke bread and ate. After talking until daylight, he left. ¹²The people took the young man home alive and were greatly comforted.

Paul's Farewell to the Ephesian Elders

¹³We went on ahead to the ship and sailed for Assos, where we were going to take Paul aboard. He had made this arrangement because he was going there on foot. ¹⁴When he met us at Assos, we took him aboard and went on to Mitylene. ¹⁵The next day we set sail from there and arrived off Chios. The day after that we crossed over to Samos, and on the following day arrived at Miletus. ¹⁶Paul had decided to sail past Ephesus to avoid spending time in the province of Asia, for he was in a hurry to reach Jerusalem, if possible, by the day of Pentecost.

¹⁷From Miletus, Paul sent to Ephesus for the elders of the church. ¹⁸When they arrived, he said to them: "You know how I lived the whole time I was with you, from the first day I came into the province of Asia. ¹⁹I served the Lord with great humility and with tears and in the midst of severe testing by the plots of my Jewish opponents. ²⁰You know that I have not hesitated to preach anything that would be helpful to you but have taught you publicly and from house to house. ²¹I have declared to both Jews and Greeks that they must turn to God in repentance and have faith in our Lord Jesus.

²²"And now, compelled by the Spirit, I am going to Jerusalem, not knowing what will happen to me there. ²³I only know that in every city the Holy Spirit warns me that prison and hardships are facing me. ²⁴However, I consider my life worth nothing to me; my only aim is to finish the race and complete the task the Lord Jesus has given me — the task of testifying to the good news of God's grace.

²⁵"Now I know that none of you among whom I have gone about preaching the kingdom will ever see me again. ²⁶Therefore, I declare to you today that I am innocent of the blood of any of you. ²⁷For I have not hesitated to proclaim to you the whole will of God. ²⁸Keep watch over yourselves and all the flock of which the Holy Spirit has made you overseers. Be shepherds of the church of God,ᵃ which he bought with his own blood.ᵇ ²⁹I know that after I leave, savage wolves will come in among you and will not spare the flock. ³⁰Even from your own number men will arise and distort the truth in order to draw away disciples after them. ³¹So be on your guard! Remember that for three years I never stopped warning each of you night and day with tears.

³²"Now I commit you to God and to the word of his grace, which can build you up and give you an inheritance among all those who are sanctified. ³³I have not coveted anyone's silver or gold or clothing. ³⁴You yourselves know that these hands of mine have supplied my own needs and the needs of my companions. ³⁵In everything I did, I showed you that by this kind of hard work we must help the weak, remembering the words the Lord Jesus himself said: 'It is more blessed to give than to receive.'"

³⁶When Paul had finished speaking, he knelt down with all of them and prayed. ³⁷They all wept as they embraced him and kissed him. ³⁸What grieved them most was his statement that they would never see his face again. Then they accompanied him to the ship.

ᵃ 28 Many manuscripts *of the Lord*   ᵇ 28 Or *with the blood of his own Son.*

On to Jerusalem

21 After we had torn ourselves away from them, we put out to sea and sailed straight to Kos. The next day we went to Rhodes and from there to Patara. ²We found a ship crossing over to Phoenicia, went on board and set sail. ³After sighting Cyprus and passing to the south of it, we sailed on to Syria. We landed at Tyre, where our ship was to unload its cargo. ⁴We sought out the disciples there and stayed with them seven days. Through the Spirit they urged Paul not to go on to Jerusalem. ⁵When it was time to leave, we left and continued on our way. All of them, including wives and children, accompanied us out of the city, and there on the beach we knelt to pray. ⁶After saying goodbye to each other, we went aboard the ship, and they returned home.

⁷We continued our voyage from Tyre and landed at Ptolemais, where we greeted the brothers and sisters and stayed with them for a day. ⁸Leaving the next day, we reached Caesarea and stayed at the house of Philip the evangelist, one of the Seven. ⁹He had four unmarried daughters who prophesied.

¹⁰After we had been there a number of days, a prophet named Agabus came down from Judea. ¹¹Coming over to us, he took Paul's belt, tied his own hands and feet with it and said, "The Holy Spirit says, 'In this way the Jewish leaders in Jerusalem will bind the owner of this belt and will hand him over to the Gentiles.'"

¹²When we heard this, we and the people there pleaded with Paul not to go up to Jerusalem. ¹³Then Paul answered, "Why are you weeping and breaking my heart? I am ready not only to be bound, but also to die in Jerusalem for the name of the Lord Jesus." ¹⁴When he would not be dissuaded, we gave up and said, "The Lord's will be done."

¹⁵After this, we started on our way up to Jerusalem. ¹⁶Some of the disciples from Caesarea accompanied us and brought us to the home of Mnason, where we were to stay. He was a man from Cyprus and one of the early disciples.

Paul's Arrival at Jerusalem

¹⁷When we arrived at Jerusalem, the brothers and sisters received us warmly. ¹⁸The next day Paul and the rest of us went to see James, and all the elders were present. ¹⁹Paul greeted them and reported in detail what God had done among the Gentiles through his ministry.

²⁰When they heard this, they praised God. Then they said to Paul: "You see, brother, how many thousands of Jews have believed, and all of them are zealous for the law. ²¹They have been informed that you teach all the Jews who live among the Gentiles to turn away from Moses, telling them not to circumcise their children or live according to our customs. ²²What shall we do? They will certainly hear that you have come, ²³so do what we tell you. There are four men with us who have made a vow. ²⁴Take these men, join in their purification rites and pay their expenses, so that they can have their heads shaved. Then everyone will know there is no truth in these reports about you, but that you yourself are living in obedience to the law. ²⁵As for the Gentile believers, we have written to them our decision that they should abstain from food sacrificed to idols, from blood, from the meat of strangled animals and from sexual immorality."

26The next day Paul took the men and purified himself along with them. Then he went to the temple to give notice of the date when the days of purification would end and the offering would be made for each of them.

Paul Arrested

27When the seven days were nearly over, some Jews from the province of Asia saw Paul at the temple. They stirred up the whole crowd and seized him, 28shouting, "Fellow Israelites, help us! This is the man who teaches everyone everywhere against our people and our law and this place. And besides, he has brought Greeks into the temple and defiled this holy place." 29(They had previously seen Trophimus the Ephesian in the city with Paul and assumed that Paul had brought him into the temple.)

30The whole city was aroused, and the people came running from all directions. Seizing Paul, they dragged him from the temple, and immediately the gates were shut. 31While they were trying to kill him, news reached the commander of the Roman troops that the whole city of Jerusalem was in an uproar. 32He at once took some officers and soldiers and ran down to the crowd. When the rioters saw the commander and his soldiers, they stopped beating Paul.

33The commander came up and arrested him and ordered him to be bound with two chains. Then he asked who he was and what he had done. 34Some in the crowd shouted one thing and some another, and since the commander could not get at the truth because of the uproar, he ordered that Paul be taken into the barracks. 35When Paul reached the steps, the violence of the mob was so great that he had to be carried by the soldiers. 36The crowd that followed kept shouting, "Get rid of him!"

Paul Speaks to the Crowd

37As the soldiers were about to take Paul into the barracks, he asked the commander, "May I say something to you?"

"Do you speak Greek?" he replied. 38"Aren't you the Egyptian who started a revolt and led four thousand terrorists out into the wilderness some time ago?"

39Paul answered, "I am a Jew, from Tarsus in Cilicia, a citizen of no ordinary city. Please let me speak to the people."

40After receiving the commander's permission, Paul stood on the steps and motioned to the crowd. When they were all silent, he said to them **22** in Aramaic[c]: 1"Brothers and fathers, listen now to my defense."

2When they heard him speak to them in Aramaic, they became very quiet.

Then Paul said: 3"I am a Jew, born in Tarsus of Cilicia, but brought up in this city. I studied under Gamaliel and was thoroughly trained in the law of our ancestors. I was just as zealous for God as any of you are today. 4I persecuted the followers of this Way to their death, arresting both men and women and throwing them into prison, 5as the high priest and all the Council can themselves testify. I even obtained letters from them to their associates in Damascus, and went there to bring these people as prisoners to Jerusalem to be punished.

6"About noon as I came near Damascus, suddenly a bright light from heaven flashed around me. 7I fell to

c 40 Or possibly Hebrew; also in 22:2

the ground and heard a voice say to me, 'Saul! Saul! Why do you persecute me?'

[8]"'Who are you, Lord?' I asked.

"'I am Jesus of Nazareth, whom you are persecuting,' he replied. [9]My companions saw the light, but they did not understand the voice of him who was speaking to me.

[10]"'What shall I do, Lord?' I asked.

"'Get up,' the Lord said, 'and go into Damascus. There you will be told all that you have been assigned to do.' [11]My companions led me by the hand into Damascus, because the brilliance of the light had blinded me.

[12]"A man named Ananias came to see me. He was a devout observer of the law and highly respected by all the Jews living there. [13]He stood beside me and said, 'Brother Saul, receive your sight!' And at that very moment I was able to see him.

[14]"Then he said: 'The God of our ancestors has chosen you to know his will and to see the Righteous One and to hear words from his mouth. [15]You will be his witness to all people of what you have seen and heard. [16]And now what are you waiting for? Get up, be baptized and wash your sins away, calling on his name.'

[17]"When I returned to Jerusalem and was praying at the temple, I fell into a trance [18]and saw the Lord speaking to me. 'Quick!' he said. 'Leave Jerusalem immediately, because the people here will not accept your testimony about me.'

[19]"'Lord,' I replied, 'these people know that I went from one synagogue to another to imprison and beat those who believe in you. [20]And when the blood of your martyr[a] Stephen was shed, I stood there giving my approval and guarding the clothes of those who were killing him.'

[21]"Then the Lord said to me, 'Go; I will send you far away to the Gentiles.'"

Paul the Roman Citizen

[22]The crowd listened to Paul until he said this. Then they raised their voices and shouted, "Rid the earth of him! He's not fit to live!"

[23]As they were shouting and throwing off their cloaks and flinging dust into the air, [24]the commander ordered that Paul be taken into the barracks. He directed that he be flogged and interrogated in order to find out why the people were shouting at him like this. [25]As they stretched him out to flog him, Paul said to the centurion standing there, "Is it legal for you to flog a Roman citizen who hasn't even been found guilty?"

[26]When the centurion heard this, he went to the commander and reported it. "What are you going to do?" he asked. "This man is a Roman citizen."

[27]The commander went to Paul and asked, "Tell me, are you a Roman citizen?"

"Yes, I am," he answered.

[28]Then the commander said, "I had to pay a lot of money for my citizenship."

"But I was born a citizen," Paul replied.

[29]Those who were about to interrogate him withdrew immediately. The commander himself was alarmed when he realized that he had put Paul, a Roman citizen, in chains.

Paul Before the Sanhedrin

[30]The commander wanted to find out exactly why Paul was being accused by the Jews. So the next day he released him and ordered the

---

[a] 20 Or witness

chief priests and all the members of the Sanhedrin to assemble. Then he brought Paul and had him stand before them.

23 Paul looked straight at the Sanhedrin and said, "My brothers, I have fulfilled my duty to God in all good conscience to this day." [2]At this the high priest Ananias ordered those standing near Paul to strike him on the mouth. [3]Then Paul said to him, "God will strike you, you whitewashed wall! You sit there to judge me according to the law, yet you yourself violate the law by commanding that I be struck!"

[4]Those who were standing near Paul said, "How dare you insult God's high priest!"

[5]Paul replied, "Brothers, I did not realize that he was the high priest; for it is written: 'Do not speak evil about the ruler of your people.'ᵃ"

[6]Then Paul, knowing that some of them were Sadducees and the others Pharisees, called out in the Sanhedrin, "My brothers, I am a Pharisee, descended from Pharisees. I stand on trial because of the hope of the resurrection of the dead." [7]When he said this, a dispute broke out between the Pharisees and the Sadducees, and the assembly was divided. [8](The Sadducees say that there is no resurrection, and that there are neither angels nor spirits, but the Pharisees believe all these things.)

[9]There was a great uproar, and some of the teachers of the law who were Pharisees stood up and argued vigorously. "We find nothing wrong with this man," they said. "What if a spirit or an angel has spoken to him?" [10]The dispute became so violent that the commander was afraid Paul would be torn to pieces by them. He ordered the troops to go down and take him away from them by force and bring him into the barracks.

[11]The following night the Lord stood near Paul and said, "Take courage! As you have testified about me in Jerusalem, so you must also testify in Rome."

The Plot to Kill Paul

[12]The next morning some Jews formed a conspiracy and bound themselves with an oath not to eat or drink until they had killed Paul. [13]More than forty men were involved in this plot. [14]They went to the chief priests and the elders and said, "We have taken a solemn oath not to eat anything until we have killed Paul. [15]Now then, you and the Sanhedrin petition the commander to bring him before you on the pretext of wanting more accurate information about his case. We are ready to kill him before he gets here."

[16]But when the son of Paul's sister heard of this plot, he went into the barracks and told Paul.

[17]Then Paul called one of the centurions and said, "Take this young man to the commander; he has something to tell him." [18]So he took him to the commander.

The centurion said, "Paul, the prisoner, sent for me and asked me to bring this young man to you because he has something to tell you."

[19]The commander took the young man by the hand, drew him aside and asked, "What is it you want to tell me?"

[20]He said: "Some Jews have agreed to ask you to bring Paul before the Sanhedrin tomorrow on the pretext of wanting more accurate information about him. [21]Don't give in to them, because more than forty of

---

ᵃ 5 Exodus 22:28

them are waiting in ambush for him. They have taken an oath not to eat or drink until they have killed him. They are ready now, waiting for your consent to their request."

²²The commander dismissed the young man with this warning: "Don't tell anyone that you have reported this to me."

Paul Transferred to Caesarea

²³Then he called two of his centurions and ordered them, "Get ready a detachment of two hundred soldiers, seventy horsemen and two hundred spearmen*a* to go to Caesarea at nine tonight. ²⁴Provide horses for Paul so that he may be taken safely to Governor Felix."

²⁵He wrote a letter as follows:

²⁶Claudius Lysias,

To His Excellency, Governor Felix:

Greetings.

²⁷This man was seized by the Jews and they were about to kill him, but I came with my troops and rescued him, for I had learned that he is a Roman citizen. ²⁸I wanted to know why they were accusing him, so I brought him to their Sanhedrin. ²⁹I found that the accusation had to do with questions about their law, but there was no charge against him that deserved death or imprisonment. ³⁰When I was informed of a plot to be carried out against the man, I sent him to you at once. I also ordered his accusers to present to you their case against him.

³¹So the soldiers, carrying out their orders, took Paul with them during the night and brought him as far as Antipatris. ³²The next day they let the cavalry go on with him, while they returned to the barracks. ³³When the cavalry arrived in Caesarea, they delivered the letter to the governor and handed Paul over to him. ³⁴The governor read the letter and asked what province he was from. Learning that he was from Cilicia, ³⁵he said, "I will hear your case when your accusers get here." Then he ordered that Paul be kept under guard in Herod's palace.

Paul's Trial Before Felix

24 Five days later the high priest Ananias went down to Caesarea with some of the elders and a lawyer named Tertullus, and they brought their charges against Paul before the governor. ²When Paul was called in, Tertullus presented his case before Felix: "We have enjoyed a long period of peace under you, and your foresight has brought about reforms in this nation. ³Everywhere and in every way, most excellent Felix, we acknowledge this with profound gratitude. ⁴But in order not to weary you further, I would request that you be kind enough to hear us briefly.

⁵"We have found this man to be a troublemaker, stirring up riots among the Jews all over the world. He is a ringleader of the Nazarene sect ⁶and even tried to desecrate the temple; so we seized him. [⁷]*b* ⁸By examining him yourself you will be able to learn the truth about all these charges we are bringing against him."

⁹The other Jews joined in the ac-

---

a 23 The meaning of the Greek for this word is uncertain.   *b 6-8* Some manuscripts include here *him, and we would have judged him in accordance with our law.* *⁷But the commander Lysias came and took him from us with much violence,* *⁸ordering his accusers to come before you.*

cusation, asserting that these things were true.

¹⁰When the governor motioned for him to speak, Paul replied: "I know that for a number of years you have been a judge over this nation; so I gladly make my defense. ¹¹You can easily verify that no more than twelve days ago I went up to Jerusalem to worship. ¹²My accusers did not find me arguing with anyone at the temple, or stirring up a crowd in the synagogues or anywhere else in the city. ¹³And they cannot prove to you the charges they are now making against me. ¹⁴However, I admit that I worship the God of our ancestors as a follower of the Way, which they call a sect. I believe everything that is in accordance with the Law and that is written in the Prophets, ¹⁵and I have the same hope in God as these men themselves have, that there will be a resurrection of both the righteous and the wicked. ¹⁶So I strive always to keep my conscience clear before God and man.

¹⁷"After an absence of several years, I came to Jerusalem to bring my people gifts for the poor and to present offerings. ¹⁸I was ceremonially clean when they found me in the temple courts doing this. There was no crowd with me, nor was I involved in any disturbance. ¹⁹But there are some Jews from the province of Asia, who ought to be here before you and bring charges if they have anything against me. ²⁰Or these who are here should state what crime they found in me when I stood before the Sanhedrin — ²¹unless it was this one thing I shouted as I stood in their presence: 'It is concerning the resurrection of the dead that I am on trial before you today.'"

²²Then Felix, who was well acquainted with the Way, adjourned the proceedings. "When Lysias the commander comes," he said, "I will decide your case." ²³He ordered the centurion to keep Paul under guard but to give him some freedom and permit his friends to take care of his needs.

²⁴Several days later Felix came with his wife Drusilla, who was Jewish. He sent for Paul and listened to him as he spoke about faith in Christ Jesus. ²⁵As Paul talked about righteousness, self-control and the judgment to come, Felix was afraid and said, "That's enough for now! You may leave. When I find it convenient, I will send for you." ²⁶At the same time he was hoping that Paul would offer him a bribe, so he sent for him frequently and talked with him.

²⁷When two years had passed, Felix was succeeded by Porcius Festus, but because Felix wanted to grant a favor to the Jews, he left Paul in prison.

Paul's Trial Before Festus

25 Three days after arriving in the province, Festus went up from Caesarea to Jerusalem, ²where the chief priests and the Jewish leaders appeared before him and presented the charges against Paul. ³They requested Festus, as a favor to them, to have Paul transferred to Jerusalem, for they were preparing an ambush to kill him along the way. ⁴Festus answered, "Paul is being held at Caesarea, and I myself am going there soon. ⁵Let some of your leaders come with me, and if the man has done anything wrong, they can press charges against him there."

⁶After spending eight or ten days with them, Festus went down to Caesarea. The next day he convened the court and ordered that Paul be brought before him. ⁷When Paul came

in, the Jews who had come down from Jerusalem stood around him. They brought many serious charges against him, but they could not prove them.

⁸Then Paul made his defense: "I have done nothing wrong against the Jewish law or against the temple or against Caesar."

⁹Festus, wishing to do the Jews a favor, said to Paul, "Are you willing to go up to Jerusalem and stand trial before me there on these charges?"

¹⁰Paul answered: "I am now standing before Caesar's court, where I ought to be tried. I have not done any wrong to the Jews, as you yourself know very well. ¹¹If, however, I am guilty of doing anything deserving death, I do not refuse to die. But if the charges brought against me by these Jews are not true, no one has the right to hand me over to them. I appeal to Caesar!"

¹²After Festus had conferred with his council, he declared: "You have appealed to Caesar. To Caesar you will go!"

Festus Consults King Agrippa

¹³A few days later King Agrippa and Bernice arrived at Caesarea to pay their respects to Festus. ¹⁴Since they were spending many days there, Festus discussed Paul's case with the king. He said: "There is a man here whom Felix left as a prisoner. ¹⁵When I went to Jerusalem, the chief priests and the elders of the Jews brought charges against him and asked that he be condemned.

¹⁶"I told them that it is not the Roman custom to hand over anyone before they have faced their accusers and have had an opportunity to defend themselves against the charges. ¹⁷When they came here with me, I did not delay the case, but convened the court the next day and ordered the man to be brought in. ¹⁸When his accusers got up to speak, they did not charge him with any of the crimes I had expected. ¹⁹Instead, they had some points of dispute with him about their own religion and about a dead man named Jesus who Paul claimed was alive. ²⁰I was at a loss how to investigate such matters; so I asked if he would be willing to go to Jerusalem and stand trial there on these charges. ²¹But when Paul made his appeal to be held over for the Emperor's decision, I ordered him held until I could send him to Caesar."

²²Then Agrippa said to Festus, "I would like to hear this man myself."

He replied, "Tomorrow you will hear him."

Paul Before Agrippa

²³The next day Agrippa and Bernice came with great pomp and entered the audience room with the high-ranking military officers and the prominent men of the city. At the command of Festus, Paul was brought in. ²⁴Festus said: "King Agrippa, and all who are present with us, you see this man! The whole Jewish community has petitioned me about him in Jerusalem and here in Caesarea, shouting that he ought not to live any longer. ²⁵I found he had done nothing deserving of death, but because he made his appeal to the Emperor I decided to send him to Rome. ²⁶But I have nothing definite to write to His Majesty about him. Therefore I have brought him before all of you, and especially before you, King Agrippa, so that as a result of this investigation I may have something to write. ²⁷For I think it is unreasonable to send a prisoner on to Rome without specifying the charges against him."

26

Then Agrippa said to Paul, "You have permission to speak for yourself."

So Paul motioned with his hand and began his defense: ²"King Agrippa, I consider myself fortunate to stand before you today as I make my defense against all the accusations of the Jews, ³and especially so because you are well acquainted with all the Jewish customs and controversies. Therefore, I beg you to listen to me patiently.

⁴"The Jewish people all know the way I have lived ever since I was a child, from the beginning of my life in my own country, and also in Jerusalem. ⁵They have known me for a long time and can testify, if they are willing, that I conformed to the strictest sect of our religion, living as a Pharisee. ⁶And now it is because of my hope in what God has promised our ancestors that I am on trial today. ⁷This is the promise that our twelve tribes are hoping to see fulfilled as they earnestly serve God day and night. King Agrippa, it is because of this hope that these Jews are accusing me. ⁸Why should any of you consider it incredible that God raises the dead?

⁹"I too was convinced that I ought to do all that was possible to oppose the name of Jesus of Nazareth. ¹⁰And that is just what I did in Jerusalem. On the authority of the chief priests I put many of the Lord's people in prison, and when they were put to death, I cast my vote against them. ¹¹Many a time I went from one synagogue to another to have them punished, and I tried to force them to blaspheme. I was so obsessed with persecuting them that I even hunted them down in foreign cities.

¹²"On one of these journeys I was going to Damascus with the authority and commission of the chief priests. ¹³About noon, King Agrippa, as I was on the road, I saw a light from heaven, brighter than the sun, blazing around me and my companions. ¹⁴We all fell to the ground, and I heard a voice saying to me in Aramaic,ᵃ 'Saul, Saul, why do you persecute me? It is hard for you to kick against the goads.'

¹⁵"Then I asked, 'Who are you, Lord?'

" 'I am Jesus, whom you are persecuting,' the Lord replied. ¹⁶'Now get up and stand on your feet. I have appeared to you to appoint you as a servant and as a witness of what you have seen and will see of me. ¹⁷I will rescue you from your own people and from the Gentiles. I am sending you to them ¹⁸to open their eyes and turn them from darkness to light, and from the power of Satan to God, so that they may receive forgiveness of sins and a place among those who are sanctified by faith in me.'

¹⁹"So then, King Agrippa, I was not disobedient to the vision from heaven. ²⁰First to those in Damascus, then to those in Jerusalem and in all Judea, and then to the Gentiles, I preached that they should repent and turn to God and demonstrate their repentance by their deeds. ²¹That is why some Jews seized me in the temple courts and tried to kill me. ²²But God has helped me to this very day; so I stand here and testify to small and great alike. I am saying nothing beyond what the prophets and Moses said would happen — ²³that the Messiah would suffer and, as the first to rise from the dead, would bring the message of light to his own people and to the Gentiles."

²⁴At this point Festus interrupted Paul's defense. "You are out of your

---

ᵃ 14 Or *Hebrew*

mind, Paul!" he shouted. "Your great learning is driving you insane."

25 "I am not insane, most excellent Festus," Paul replied. "What I am saying is true and reasonable. 26 The king is familiar with these things, and I can speak freely to him. I am convinced that none of this has escaped his notice, because it was not done in a corner. 27 King Agrippa, do you believe the prophets? I know you do."

28 Then Agrippa said to Paul, "Do you think that in such a short time you can persuade me to be a Christian?"

29 Paul replied, "Short time or long — I pray to God that not only you but all who are listening to me today may become what I am, except for these chains."

30 The king rose, and with him the governor and Bernice and those sitting with them. 31 After they left the room, they began saying to one another, "This man is not doing anything that deserves death or imprisonment."

32 Agrippa said to Festus, "This man could have been set free if he had not appealed to Caesar."

Paul Sails for Rome

27 When it was decided that we would sail for Italy, Paul and some other prisoners were handed over to a centurion named Julius, who belonged to the Imperial Regiment. 2 We boarded a ship from Adramyttium about to sail for ports along the coast of the province of Asia, and we put out to sea. Aristarchus, a Macedonian from Thessalonica, was with us.

3 The next day we landed at Sidon; and Julius, in kindness to Paul, allowed him to go to his friends so they might provide for his needs. 4 From there we put out to sea again and passed to the lee of Cyprus because the winds were against us. 5 When we had sailed across the open sea off the coast of Cilicia and Pamphylia, we landed at Myra in Lycia. 6 There the centurion found an Alexandrian ship sailing for Italy and put us on board. 7 We made slow headway for many days and had difficulty arriving off Cnidus. When the wind did not allow us to hold our course, we sailed to the lee of Crete, opposite Salmone. 8 We moved along the coast with difficulty and came to a place called Fair Havens, near the town of Lasea.

9 Much time had been lost, and sailing had already become dangerous because by now it was after the Day of Atonement.[a] So Paul warned them, 10 "Men, I can see that our voyage is going to be disastrous and bring great loss to ship and cargo, and to our own lives also." 11 But the centurion, instead of listening to what Paul said, followed the advice of the pilot and of the owner of the ship. 12 Since the harbor was unsuitable to winter in, the majority decided that we should sail on, hoping to reach Phoenix and winter there. This was a harbor in Crete, facing both southwest and northwest.

The Storm

13 When a gentle south wind began to blow, they saw their opportunity; so they weighed anchor and sailed along the shore of Crete. 14 Before very long, a wind of hurricane force, called the Northeaster, swept down from the island. 15 The ship was caught by the storm and could not head into the wind; so we gave way to it and were driven along. 16 As we passed to the lee of a small island called Cauda, we were hardly able to make the lifeboat secure, 17 so the men hoisted

---

[a] 9 That is, Yom Kippur

it aboard. Then they passed ropes under the ship itself to hold it together. Because they were afraid they would run aground on the sandbars of Syrtis, they lowered the sea anchor[a] and let the ship be driven along. [18]We took such a violent battering from the storm that the next day they began to throw the cargo overboard. [19]On the third day, they threw the ship's tackle overboard with their own hands. [20]When neither sun nor stars appeared for many days and the storm continued raging, we finally gave up all hope of being saved.

[21]After they had gone a long time without food, Paul stood up before them and said: "Men, you should have taken my advice not to sail from Crete; then you would have spared yourselves this damage and loss. [22]But now I urge you to keep up your courage, because not one of you will be lost; only the ship will be destroyed. [23]Last night an angel of the God to whom I belong and whom I serve stood beside me [24]and said, 'Do not be afraid, Paul. You must stand trial before Caesar; and God has graciously given you the lives of all who sail with you.' [25]So keep up your courage, men, for I have faith in God that it will happen just as he told me. [26]Nevertheless, we must run aground on some island."

The Shipwreck

[27]On the fourteenth night we were still being driven across the Adriatic[b] Sea, when about midnight the sailors sensed they were approaching land. [28]They took soundings and found that the water was a hundred and twenty feet[c] deep. A short time later they took soundings again and found it was ninety feet[d] deep. [29]Fearing that we would be dashed against the rocks,

they dropped four anchors from the stern and prayed for daylight. [30]In an attempt to escape from the ship, the sailors let the lifeboat down into the sea, pretending they were going to lower some anchors from the bow. [31]Then Paul said to the centurion and the soldiers, "Unless these men stay with the ship, you cannot be saved." [32]So the soldiers cut the ropes that held the lifeboat and let it drift away.

[33]Just before dawn Paul urged them all to eat. "For the last fourteen days," he said, "you have been in constant suspense and have gone without food — you haven't eaten anything. [34]Now I urge you to take some food. You need it to survive. Not one of you will lose a single hair from his head." [35]After he said this, he took some bread and gave thanks to God in front of them all. Then he broke it and began to eat. [36]They were all encouraged and ate some food themselves. [37]Altogether there were 276 of us on board. [38]When they had eaten as much as they wanted, they lightened the ship by throwing the grain into the sea.

[39]When daylight came, they did not recognize the land, but they saw a bay with a sandy beach, where they decided to run the ship aground if they could. [40]Cutting loose the anchors, they left them in the sea and at the same time untied the ropes that held the rudders. Then they hoisted the foresail to the wind and made for the beach. [41]But the ship struck a sandbar and ran aground. The bow stuck fast and would not move, and the stern was broken to pieces by the pounding of the surf.

---

[a] 17 Or the sails [b] 27 In ancient times the name referred to an area extending well south of Italy. [c] 28 Or about 37 meters [d] 28 Or about 27 meters

⁴²The soldiers planned to kill the prisoners to prevent any of them from swimming away and escaping. ⁴³But the centurion wanted to spare Paul's life and kept them from carrying out their plan. He ordered those who could swim to jump overboard first and get to land. ⁴⁴The rest were to get there on planks or on other pieces of the ship. In this way everyone reached land safely.

Paul Ashore on Malta

28 Once safely on shore, we found out that the island was called Malta. ²The islanders showed us unusual kindness. They built a fire and welcomed us all because it was raining and cold. ³Paul gathered a pile of brushwood and, as he put it on the fire, a viper, driven out by the heat, fastened itself on his hand. ⁴When the islanders saw the snake hanging from his hand, they said to each other, "This man must be a murderer; for though he escaped from the sea, the goddess Justice has not allowed him to live." ⁵But Paul shook the snake off into the fire and suffered no ill effects. ⁶The people expected him to swell up or suddenly fall dead; but after waiting a long time and seeing nothing unusual happen to him, they changed their minds and said he was a god.

⁷There was an estate nearby that belonged to Publius, the chief official of the island. He welcomed us to his home and showed us generous hospitality for three days. ⁸His father was sick in bed, suffering from fever and dysentery. Paul went in to see him and, after prayer, placed his hands on him and healed him. ⁹When this had happened, the rest of the sick on the island came and were cured. ¹⁰They honored us in many ways; and when

we were ready to sail, they furnished us with the supplies we needed.

Paul's Arrival at Rome

¹¹After three months we put out to sea in a ship that had wintered in the island — it was an Alexandrian ship with the figurehead of the twin gods Castor and Pollux. ¹²We put in at Syracuse and stayed there three days. ¹³From there we set sail and arrived at Rhegium. The next day the south wind came up, and on the following day we reached Puteoli. ¹⁴There we found some brothers and sisters who invited us to spend a week with them. And so we came to Rome. ¹⁵The brothers and sisters there had heard that we were coming, and they traveled as far as the Forum of Appius and the Three Taverns to meet us. At the sight of these people Paul thanked God and was encouraged. ¹⁶When we got to Rome, Paul was allowed to live by himself, with a soldier to guard him.

Paul Preaches at Rome Under Guard

¹⁷Three days later he called together the local Jewish leaders. When they had assembled, Paul said to them: "My brothers, although I have done nothing against our people or against the customs of our ancestors, I was arrested in Jerusalem and handed over to the Romans. ¹⁸They examined me and wanted to release me, because I was not guilty of any crime deserving death. ¹⁹The Jews objected, so I was compelled to make an appeal to Caesar. I certainly did not intend to bring any charge against my own people. ²⁰For this reason I have asked to see you and talk with you. It is because of the hope of Israel that I am bound with this chain."

²¹They replied, "We have not received any letters from Judea concerning you, and none of our people who have come from there has reported or said anything bad about you. ²²But we want to hear what your views are, for we know that people everywhere are talking against this sect."

²³They arranged to meet Paul on a certain day, and came in even larger numbers to the place where he was staying. He witnessed to them from morning till evening, explaining about the kingdom of God, and from the Law of Moses and from the Prophets he tried to persuade them about Jesus. ²⁴Some were convinced by what he said, but others would not believe. ²⁵They disagreed among themselves and began to leave after Paul had made this final statement: "The Holy Spirit spoke the truth to your ancestors when he said through Isaiah the prophet:

²⁶ " 'Go to this people and say,

"You will be ever hearing but
    never understanding;
you will be ever seeing but
    never perceiving."
²⁷ For this people's heart has
    become calloused;
they hardly hear with their
    ears,
and they have closed their
    eyes.
Otherwise they might see with
    their eyes,
hear with their ears,
    understand with their hearts
and turn, and I would heal
    them.'ᵃ

²⁸"Therefore I want you to know that God's salvation has been sent to the Gentiles, and they will listen!" [²⁹]ᵇ
³⁰For two whole years Paul stayed there in his own rented house and welcomed all who came to see him. ³¹He proclaimed the kingdom of God and taught about the Lord Jesus Christ — with all boldness and without hindrance!

Romans

1 Paul, a servant of Christ Jesus, called to be an apostle and set apart for the gospel of God — ²the gospel he promised beforehand through his prophets in the Holy Scriptures ³regarding his Son, who as to his earthly lifeᶜ was a descendant of David, ⁴and who through the Spirit of holiness was appointed the Son of God in powerᵈ by his resurrection from the dead: Jesus Christ our Lord. ⁵Through him we received grace and apostleship to call all the Gentiles to the obedience that comes fromᵉ faith for his name's sake. ⁶And you also are among those Gentiles who are called to belong to Jesus Christ.

ᵃ 27 Isaiah 6:9,10 (see Septuagint)
ᵇ 29 Some manuscripts include here *After he said this, the Jews left, arguing vigorously among themselves.*   ᶜ 3 Or *who according to the flesh*   ᵈ 4 Or *was declared with power to be the Son of God*   ᵉ 5 Or *that is*

⁷To all in Rome who are loved by God and called to be his holy people:

Grace and peace to you from God our Father and from the Lord Jesus Christ.

Paul's Longing to Visit Rome

⁸First, I thank my God through Jesus Christ for all of you, because your faith is being reported all over the world. ⁹God, whom I serve in my spirit in preaching the gospel of his Son, is my witness how constantly I remember you ¹⁰in my prayers at all times; and I pray that now at last by God's will the way may be opened for me to come to you.

¹¹I long to see you so that I may impart to you some spiritual gift to make you strong — ¹²that is, that you and I may be mutually encouraged by each other's faith. ¹³I do not want you to be unaware, brothers and sisters,ᵃ that I planned many times to come to you (but have been prevented from doing so until now) in order that I might have a harvest among you, just as I have had among the other Gentiles.

¹⁴I am obligated both to Greeks and non-Greeks, both to the wise and the foolish. ¹⁵That is why I am so eager to preach the gospel also to you who are in Rome.

¹⁶For I am not ashamed of the gospel, because it is the power of God that brings salvation to everyone who believes: first to the Jew, then to the Gentile. ¹⁷For in the gospel the righteousness of God is revealed — a righteousness that is by faith from first to last,ᵇ just as it is written: "The righteous will live by faith."ᶜ

God's Wrath Against Sinful Humanity

¹⁸The wrath of God is being revealed from heaven against all the godlessness and wickedness of people, who suppress the truth by their wickedness, ¹⁹since what may be known about God is plain to them, because God has made it plain to them. ²⁰For since the creation of the world God's invisible qualities — his eternal power and divine nature — have been clearly seen, being understood from what has been made, so that people are without excuse.

²¹For although they knew God, they neither glorified him as God nor gave thanks to him, but their thinking became futile and their foolish hearts were darkened. ²²Although they claimed to be wise, they became fools ²³and exchanged the glory of the immortal God for images made to look like a mortal human being and birds and animals and reptiles.

²⁴Therefore God gave them over in the sinful desires of their hearts to sexual impurity for the degrading of their bodies with one another. ²⁵They exchanged the truth about God for a lie, and worshiped and served created things rather than the Creator — who is forever praised. Amen.

²⁶Because of this, God gave them over to shameful lusts. Even their women exchanged natural sexual relations for unnatural ones. ²⁷In the same way the men also abandoned natural relations with women and were inflamed with lust for one another. Men committed shameful acts with other men, and received in themselves the due penalty for their error.

²⁸Furthermore, just as they did not think it worthwhile to retain the

---

ᵃ 13 The Greek word for *brothers and sisters* (*adelphoi*) refers here to believers, both men and women, as part of God's family; also in 7:1, 4; 8:12, 29; 10:1; 11:25; 12:1; 15:14, 30; 16:14, 17.   ᵇ 17 Or *is from faith to faith*   ᶜ 17 Hab. 2:4

knowledge of God, so God gave them
over to a depraved mind, so that they
do what ought not to be done. ²⁹They
have become filled with every kind of
wickedness, evil, greed and depravity.
They are full of envy, murder, strife,
deceit and malice. They are gossips,
³⁰slanderers, God-haters, insolent, arrogant and boastful; they invent ways
of doing evil; they disobey their parents; ³¹they have no understanding,
no fidelity, no love, no mercy. ³²Al-
though they know God's righteous
decree that those who do such things
deserve death, they not only continue to do these very things but also
approve of those who practice them.

God's Righteous Judgment

2 You, therefore, have no excuse,
you who pass judgment on someone else, for at whatever point you
judge another, you are condemning
yourself, because you who pass judgment do the same things. ²Now we
know that God's judgment against
those who do such things is based
on truth. ³So when you, a mere human being, pass judgment on them
and yet do the same things, do you
think you will escape God's judgment?
⁴Or do you show contempt for the
riches of his kindness, forbearance
and patience, not realizing that God's
kindness is intended to lead you to
repentance?

⁵But because of your stubborn-
ness and your unrepentant heart,
you are storing up wrath against
yourself for the day of God's wrath,
when his righteous judgment will
be revealed. ⁶God "will repay each
person according to what they have
done."ᵃ ⁷To those who by persistence
in doing good seek glory, honor and
immortality, he will give eternal life.
⁸But for those who are self-seeking

and who reject the truth and follow
evil, there will be wrath and anger.
⁹There will be trouble and distress
for every human being who does evil:
first for the Jew, then for the Gentile;
¹⁰but glory, honor and peace for everyone who does good: first for the
Jew, then for the Gentile. ¹¹For God
does not show favoritism.

¹²All who sin apart from the law
will also perish apart from the law,
and all who sin under the law will
be judged by the law. ¹³For it is not
those who hear the law who are righteous in God's sight, but it is those
who obey the law who will be declared
righteous. ¹⁴(Indeed, when Gentiles,
who do not have the law, do by nature
things required by the law, they are
a law for themselves, even though
they do not have the law. ¹⁵They show
that the requirements of the law are
written on their hearts, their consciences also bearing witness, and
their thoughts sometimes accusing
them and at other times even defending them.) ¹⁶This will take place
on the day when God judges people's
secrets through Jesus Christ, as my
gospel declares.

The Jews and the Law

¹⁷Now you, if you call yourself a
Jew; if you rely on the law and boast
in God; ¹⁸if you know his will and approve of what is superior because you
are instructed by the law; ¹⁹if you are
convinced that you are a guide for the
blind, a light for those who are in the
dark, ²⁰an instructor of the foolish, a
teacher of little children, because you
have in the law the embodiment of
knowledge and truth — ²¹you, then,
who teach others, do you not teach
yourself? You who preach against
stealing, do you steal? ²²You who

ᵃ 6 Psalm 62:12; Prov. 24:12

say that people should not commit adultery, do you commit adultery? You who abhor idols, do you rob temples? [23]You who boast in the law, do you dishonor God by breaking the law? [24]As it is written: "God's name is blasphemed among the Gentiles because of you."[a]

[25]Circumcision has value if you observe the law, but if you break the law, you have become as though you had not been circumcised. [26]So then, if those who are not circumcised keep the law's requirements, will they not be regarded as though they were circumcised? [27]The one who is not circumcised physically and yet obeys the law will condemn you who, even though you have the[b] written code and circumcision, are a lawbreaker.

[28]A person is not a Jew who is one only outwardly, nor is circumcision merely outward and physical. [29]No, a person is a Jew who is one inwardly; and circumcision is circumcision of the heart, by the Spirit, not by the written code. Such a person's praise is not from other people, but from God.

God's Faithfulness

3 What advantage, then, is there in being a Jew, or what value is there in circumcision? [2]Much in every way! First of all, the Jews have been entrusted with the very words of God.

[3]What if some were unfaithful? Will their unfaithfulness nullify God's faithfulness? [4]Not at all! Let God be true, and every human being a liar. As it is written:

"So that you may be proved right
    when you speak
and prevail when you judge."[c]

[5]But if our unrighteousness brings out God's righteousness more clearly, what shall we say? That God is unjust in bringing his wrath on us? (I am using a human argument.) [6]Certainly not! If that were so, how could God judge the world? [7]Someone might argue, "If my falsehood enhances God's truthfulness and so increases his glory, why am I still condemned as a sinner?" [8]Why not say — as some slanderously claim that we say — "Let us do evil that good may result"? Their condemnation is just!

No One Is Righteous

[9]What shall we conclude then? Do we have any advantage? Not at all! For we have already made the charge that Jews and Gentiles alike are all under the power of sin. [10]As it is written:

"There is no one righteous, not
    even one;
[11]   there is no one who
        understands;
    there is no one who seeks God.
[12] All have turned away,
    they have together become
        worthless;
there is no one who does good,
    not even one."[d]
[13] "Their throats are open graves;
    their tongues practice deceit."[e]
"The poison of vipers is on their
    lips."[f]
[14]   "Their mouths are full of
        cursing and bitterness."[g]
[15] "Their feet are swift to shed blood;
[16]   ruin and misery mark their
        ways,
[17] and the way of peace they do not
        know."[h]
[18]   "There is no fear of God before
        their eyes."[i]

---

[a] 24 Isaiah 52:5 (see Septuagint); Ezek. 36:20,22
[b] 27 Or who, by means of a   [c] 4 Psalm 51:4
[d] 12 Psalms 14:1-3; 53:1-3; Eccles. 7:20
[e] 13 Psalm 5:9   [f] 13 Psalm 140:3
[g] 14 Psalm 10:7 (see Septuagint)
[h] 17 Isaiah 59:7,8   [i] 18 Psalm 36:1

¹⁹Now we know that whatever the law says, it says to those who are under the law, so that every mouth may be silenced and the whole world held accountable to God. ²⁰Therefore no one will be declared righteous in God's sight by the works of the law; rather, through the law we become conscious of our sin.

Righteousness Through Faith

²¹But now apart from the law the righteousness of God has been made known, to which the Law and the Prophets testify. ²²This righteousness is given through faith in[a] Jesus Christ to all who believe. There is no difference between Jew and Gentile, ²³for all have sinned and fall short of the glory of God, ²⁴and all are justified freely by his grace through the redemption that came by Christ Jesus. ²⁵God presented Christ as a sacrifice of atonement,[b] through the shedding of his blood — to be received by faith. He did this to demonstrate his righteousness, because in his forbearance he had left the sins committed beforehand unpunished — ²⁶he did it to demonstrate his righteousness at the present time, so as to be just and the one who justifies those who have faith in Jesus.

²⁷Where, then, is boasting? It is excluded. Because of what law? The law that requires works? No, because of the law that requires faith. ²⁸For we maintain that a person is justified by faith apart from the works of the law. ²⁹Or is God the God of Jews only? Is he not the God of Gentiles too? Yes, of Gentiles too, ³⁰since there is only one God, who will justify the circumcised by faith and the uncircumcised through that same faith. ³¹Do we, then, nullify the law by this faith? Not at all! Rather, we uphold the law.

Abraham Justified by Faith

4 What then shall we say that Abraham, our forefather according to the flesh, discovered in this matter? ²If, in fact, Abraham was justified by works, he had something to boast about — but not before God. ³What does Scripture say? "Abraham believed God, and it was credited to him as righteousness."[c]

⁴Now to the one who works, wages are not credited as a gift but as an obligation. ⁵However, to the one who does not work but trusts God who justifies the ungodly, their faith is credited as righteousness. ⁶David says the same thing when he speaks of the blessedness of the one to whom God credits righteousness apart from works:

⁷"Blessed are those
    whose transgressions are
      forgiven,
    whose sins are covered.
⁸ Blessed is the one
    whose sin the Lord will never
      count against them."[d]

⁹Is this blessedness only for the circumcised, or also for the uncircumcised? We have been saying that Abraham's faith was credited to him as righteousness. ¹⁰Under what circumstances was it credited? Was it after he was circumcised, or before? It was not after, but before! ¹¹And he received circumcision as a sign, a seal of the righteousness that he had by faith while he was still uncircumcised. So then, he is the father of all who believe but have not been circumcised, in order that righteousness might be credited to them. ¹²And he is then also

---

[a] 22 Or *through the faithfulness of*   [b] 25 The Greek for *sacrifice of atonement* refers to the atonement cover on the ark of the covenant (see Lev. 16:15,16).   [c] 3 Gen. 15:6; also in verse 22   [d] 8 Psalm 32:1,2

the father of the circumcised who not only are circumcised but who also follow in the footsteps of the faith that our father Abraham had before he was circumcised.

[13] It was not through the law that Abraham and his offspring received the promise that he would be heir of the world, but through the righteousness that comes by faith. [14] For if those who depend on the law are heirs, faith means nothing and the promise is worthless, [15] because the law brings wrath. And where there is no law there is no transgression.

[16] Therefore, the promise comes by faith, so that it may be by grace and may be guaranteed to all Abraham's offspring — not only to those who are of the law but also to those who have the faith of Abraham. He is the father of us all. [17] As it is written: "I have made you a father of many nations."[a] He is our father in the sight of God, in whom he believed — the God who gives life to the dead and calls into being things that were not.

[18] Against all hope, Abraham in hope believed and so became the father of many nations, just as it had been said to him, "So shall your offspring be."[b] [19] Without weakening in his faith, he faced the fact that his body was as good as dead — since he was about a hundred years old — and that Sarah's womb was also dead. [20] Yet he did not waver through unbelief regarding the promise of God, but was strengthened in his faith and gave glory to God, [21] being fully persuaded that God had power to do what he had promised. [22] This is why "it was credited to him as righteousness." [23] The words "it was credited to him" were written not for him alone, [24] but also for us, to whom God will credit righteousness — for us who believe in him who raised Jesus our Lord from the dead. [25] He was delivered over to death for our sins and was raised to life for our justification.

Peace and Hope

5 Therefore, since we have been justified through faith, we[c] have peace with God through our Lord Jesus Christ, [2] through whom we have gained access by faith into this grace in which we now stand. And we[d] boast in the hope of the glory of God. [3] Not only so, but we[d] also glory in our sufferings, because we know that suffering produces perseverance; [4] perseverance, character; and character, hope. [5] And hope does not put us to shame, because God's love has been poured out into our hearts through the Holy Spirit, who has been given to us.

[6] You see, at just the right time, when we were still powerless, Christ died for the ungodly. [7] Very rarely will anyone die for a righteous person, though for a good person someone might possibly dare to die. [8] But God demonstrates his own love for us in this: While we were still sinners, Christ died for us.

[9] Since we have now been justified by his blood, how much more shall we be saved from God's wrath through him! [10] For if, while we were God's enemies, we were reconciled to him through the death of his Son, how much more, having been reconciled, shall we be saved through his life! [11] Not only is this so, but we also boast in God through our Lord Jesus Christ, through whom we have now received reconciliation.

---

[a] 17 Gen. 17:5   [b] 18 Gen. 15:5   [c] 1 Many manuscripts let us   [d] 2,3 Or let us

Death Through Adam, Life Through Christ

12Therefore, just as sin entered the world through one man, and death through sin, and in this way death came to all people, because all sinned —

13To be sure, sin was in the world before the law was given, but sin is not charged against anyone's account where there is no law. 14Nevertheless, death reigned from the time of Adam to the time of Moses, even over those who did not sin by breaking a command, as did Adam, who is a pattern of the one to come.

15But the gift is not like the trespass. For if the many died by the trespass of the one man, how much more did God's grace and the gift that came by the grace of the one man, Jesus Christ, overflow to the many! 16Nor can the gift of God be compared with the result of one man's sin: The judgment followed one sin and brought condemnation, but the gift followed many trespasses and brought justification. 17For if, by the trespass of the one man, death reigned through that one man, how much more will those who receive God's abundant provision of grace and of the gift of righteousness reign in life through the one man, Jesus Christ!

18Consequently, just as one trespass resulted in condemnation for all people, so also one righteous act resulted in justification and life for all people. 19For just as through the disobedience of the one man the many were made sinners, so also through the obedience of the one man the many will be made righteous.

20The law was brought in so that the trespass might increase. But where sin increased, grace increased all the more, 21so that, just

as sin reigned in death, so also grace might reign through righteousness to bring eternal life through Jesus Christ our Lord.

Dead to Sin, Alive in Christ

6 What shall we say, then? Shall we go on sinning so that grace may increase? 2By no means! We are those who have died to sin; how can we live in it any longer? 3Or don't you know that all of us who were baptized into Christ Jesus were baptized into his death? 4We were therefore buried with him through baptism into death in order that, just as Christ was raised from the dead through the glory of the Father, we too may live a new life.

5For if we have been united with him in a death like his, we will certainly also be united with him in a resurrection like his. 6For we know that our old self was crucified with him so that the body ruled by sin might be done away with,ᵃ that we should no longer be slaves to sin — 7because anyone who has died has been set free from sin.

8Now if we died with Christ, we believe that we will also live with him. 9For we know that since Christ was raised from the dead, he cannot die again; death no longer has mastery over him. 10The death he died, he died to sin once for all; but the life he lives, he lives to God.

11In the same way, count yourselves dead to sin but alive to God in Christ Jesus. 12Therefore do not let sin reign in your mortal body so that you obey its evil desires. 13Do not offer any part of yourself to sin as an instrument of wickedness, but rather offer yourselves to God as those who have been brought from death to life; and offer

ᵃ 6 Or be rendered powerless

every part of yourself to him as an instrument of righteousness. ¹⁴For sin shall no longer be your master, because you are not under the law, but under grace.

Slaves to Righteousness

¹⁵What then? Shall we sin because we are not under the law but under grace? By no means! ¹⁶Don't you know that when you offer yourselves to someone as obedient slaves, you are slaves of the one you obey—whether you are slaves to sin, which leads to death, or to obedience, which leads to righteousness? ¹⁷But thanks be to God that, though you used to be slaves to sin, you have come to obey from your heart the pattern of teaching that has now claimed your allegiance. ¹⁸You have been set free from sin and have become slaves to righteousness.

¹⁹I am using an example from everyday life because of your human limitations. Just as you used to offer yourselves as slaves to impurity and to ever-increasing wickedness, so now offer yourselves as slaves to righteousness leading to holiness. ²⁰When you were slaves to sin, you were free from the control of righteousness. ²¹What benefit did you reap at that time from the things you are now ashamed of? Those things result in death! ²²But now that you have been set free from sin and have become slaves of God, the benefit you reap leads to holiness, and the result is eternal life. ²³For the wages of sin is death, but the gift of God is eternal life in° Christ Jesus our Lord.

Released From the Law, Bound to Christ

7 Do you not know, brothers and sisters—for I am speaking to those who know the law—that the law has authority over someone only as long as that person lives? ²For example, by law a married woman is bound to her husband as long as he is alive, but if her husband dies, she is released from the law that binds her to him. ³So then, if she has sexual relations with another man while her husband is still alive, she is called an adulteress. But if her husband dies, she is released from that law and is not an adulteress if she marries another man.

⁴So, my brothers and sisters, you also died to the law through the body of Christ, that you might belong to another, to him who was raised from the dead, in order that we might bear fruit for God. ⁵For when we were in the realm of the flesh,ᵇ the sinful passions aroused by the law were at work in us, so that we bore fruit for death. ⁶But now, by dying to what once bound us, we have been released from the law so that we serve in the new way of the Spirit, and not in the old way of the written code.

The Law and Sin

⁷What shall we say, then? Is the law sinful? Certainly not! Nevertheless, I would not have known what sin was had it not been for the law. For I would not have known what coveting really was if the law had not said, "You shall not covet."ᶜ ⁸But sin, seizing the opportunity afforded by the commandment, produced in me every kind of coveting. For apart from the law, sin was dead. ⁹Once I was alive apart from the law; but when the commandment came, sin sprang to life and I died. ¹⁰I

° 23 Or through ᵇ 5 In contexts like this, the Greek word for *flesh* (*sarx*) refers to the sinful state of human beings, often presented as a power in opposition to the Spirit.
ᶜ 7 Exodus 20:17; Deut. 5:21

found that the very commandment that was intended to bring life actually brought death. ¹¹For sin, seizing the opportunity afforded by the commandment, deceived me, and through the commandment put me to death. ¹²So then, the law is holy, and the commandment is holy, righteous and good.

¹³Did that which is good, then, become death to me? By no means! Nevertheless, in order that sin might be recognized as sin, it used what is good to bring about my death, so that through the commandment sin might become utterly sinful.

¹⁴We know that the law is spiritual; but I am unspiritual, sold as a slave to sin. ¹⁵I do not understand what I do. For what I want to do I do not do, but what I hate I do. ¹⁶And if I do what I do not want to do, I agree that the law is good. ¹⁷As it is, it is no longer I myself who do it, but it is sin living in me. ¹⁸For I know that good itself does not dwell in me, that is, in my sinful nature.ᶜ For I have the desire to do what is good, but I cannot carry it out. ¹⁹For I do not do the good I want to do, but the evil I do not want to do — this I keep on doing. ²⁰Now if I do what I do not want to do, it is no longer I who do it, but it is sin living in me that does it.

²¹So I find this law at work: Although I want to do good, evil is right there with me. ²²For in my inner being I delight in God's law; ²³but I see another law at work in me, waging war against the law of my mind and making me a prisoner of the law of sin at work within me. ²⁴What a wretched man I am! Who will rescue me from this body that is subject to death? ²⁵Thanks be to God, who delivers me through Jesus Christ our Lord!

So then, I myself in my mind am a slave to God's law, but in my sinful natureᵇ a slave to the law of sin.

Life Through the Spirit

8 Therefore, there is now no condemnation for those who are in Christ Jesus, ²because through Christ Jesus the law of the Spirit who gives life has set youᶜ free from the law of sin and death. ³For what the law was powerless to do because it was weakened by the flesh,ᵈ God did by sending his own Son in the likeness of sinful flesh to be a sin offering.ᵉ And so he condemned sin in the flesh, ⁴in order that the righteous requirement of the law might be fully met in us, who do not live according to the flesh but according to the Spirit.

⁵Those who live according to the flesh have their minds set on what the flesh desires; but those who live in accordance with the Spirit have their minds set on what the Spirit desires. ⁶The mind governed by the flesh is death, but the mind governed by the Spirit is life and peace. ⁷The mind governed by the flesh is hostile to God; it does not submit to God's law, nor can it do so. ⁸Those who are in the realm of the flesh cannot please God.

⁹You, however, are not in the realm of the flesh but are in the realm of the Spirit, if indeed the Spirit of God lives in you. And if anyone does not have the Spirit of Christ, they do not belong to Christ. ¹⁰But if Christ is in you, then even though your body is subject to death because of sin, the Spirit gives lifeᶠ because of righteousness. ¹¹And if

ᵃ 18 Or my flesh   ᵇ 25 Or in the flesh
ᶜ 2 The Greek is singular; some manuscripts me   ᵈ 3 In contexts like this, the Greek word for flesh (sarx) refers to the sinful state of human beings, often presented as a power in opposition to the Spirit; also in verses 4-13.
ᵉ 3 Or flesh, for sin   ᶠ 10 Or you, your body is dead because of sin, yet your spirit is alive

the Spirit of him who raised Jesus from the dead is living in you, he who raised Christ from the dead will also give life to your mortal bodies because of[a] his Spirit who lives in you.

[12] Therefore, brothers and sisters, we have an obligation — but it is not to the flesh, to live according to it. [13] For if you live according to the flesh, you will die; but if by the Spirit you put to death the misdeeds of the body, you will live.

[14] For those who are led by the Spirit of God are the children of God. [15] The Spirit you received does not make you slaves, so that you live in fear again; rather, the Spirit you received brought about your adoption to sonship.[b] And by him we cry, "Abba,[c] Father." [16] The Spirit himself testifies with our spirit that we are God's children. [17] Now if we are children, then we are heirs — heirs of God and co-heirs with Christ, if indeed we share in his sufferings in order that we may also share in his glory.

Present Suffering and Future Glory

[18] I consider that our present sufferings are not worth comparing with the glory that will be revealed in us. [19] For the creation waits in eager expectation for the children of God to be revealed. [20] For the creation was subjected to frustration, not by its own choice, but by the will of the one who subjected it, in hope [21] that[d] the creation itself will be liberated from its bondage to decay and brought into the freedom and glory of the children of God.

[22] We know that the whole creation has been groaning as in the pains of childbirth right up to the present time. [23] Not only so, but we ourselves, who have the firstfruits of the Spirit, groan inwardly as we wait eagerly for our adoption to sonship, the redemption of our bodies. [24] For in this hope we were saved. But hope that is seen is no hope at all. Who hopes for what they already have? [25] But if we hope for what we do not yet have, we wait for it patiently.

[26] In the same way, the Spirit helps us in our weakness. We do not know what we ought to pray for, but the Spirit himself intercedes for us through wordless groans. [27] And he who searches our hearts knows the mind of the Spirit, because the Spirit intercedes for God's people in accordance with the will of God.

[28] And we know that in all things God works for the good of those who love him, who[e] have been called according to his purpose. [29] For those God foreknew he also predestined to be conformed to the image of his Son, that he might be the firstborn among many brothers and sisters. [30] And those he predestined, he also called; those he called, he also justified; those he justified, he also glorified.

More Than Conquerors

[31] What, then, shall we say in response to these things? If God is for us, who can be against us? [32] He who did not spare his own Son, but gave him up for us all — how will he not also, along with him, graciously give us all things? [33] Who will bring any

---

[a] 11 Some manuscripts bodies through
[b] 15 The Greek word for adoption to sonship is a term referring to the full legal standing of an adopted male heir in Roman culture; also in verse 23. [c] 15 Aramaic for father
[d] 20,21 Or subjected it in hope. [21]For   [e] 28 Or that all things work together for good to those who love God, who; or that in all things God works together with those who love him to bring about what is good — with those who

charge against those whom God has chosen? It is God who justifies. ³⁴Who then is the one who condemns? No one. Christ Jesus who died — more than that, who was raised to life — is at the right hand of God and is also interceding for us. ³⁵Who shall separate us from the love of Christ? Shall trouble or hardship or persecution or famine or nakedness or danger or sword? ³⁶As it is written:

> "For your sake we face death all
>   day long;
>   we are considered as sheep to
>   be slaughtered."ᵃ

³⁷No, in all these things we are more than conquerors through him who loved us. ³⁸For I am convinced that neither death nor life, neither angels nor demons,ᵇ neither the present nor the future, nor any powers, ³⁹neither height nor depth, nor anything else in all creation, will be able to separate us from the love of God that is in Christ Jesus our Lord.

Paul's Anguish Over Israel

9 I speak the truth in Christ — I am not lying, my conscience confirms it through the Holy Spirit — ²I have great sorrow and unceasing anguish in my heart. ³For I could wish that I myself were cursed and cut off from Christ for the sake of my people, those of my own race, ⁴the people of Israel. Theirs is the adoption to sonship; theirs the divine glory, the covenants, the receiving of the law, the temple worship and the promises. ⁵Theirs are the patriarchs, and from them is traced the human ancestry of the Messiah, who is God over all, forever praised!ᶜ Amen.

God's Sovereign Choice

⁶It is not as though God's word had failed. For not all who are descended

from Israel are Israel. ⁷Nor because they are his descendants are they all Abraham's children. On the contrary, "It is through Isaac that your offspring will be reckoned."ᵈ ⁸In other words, it is not the children by physical descent who are God's children, but it is the children of the promise who are regarded as Abraham's offspring. ⁹For this was how the promise was stated: "At the appointed time I will return, and Sarah will have a son."ᵉ

¹⁰Not only that, but Rebekah's children were conceived at the same time by our father Isaac. ¹¹Yet, before the twins were born or had done anything good or bad — in order that God's purpose in election might stand: ¹²not by works but by him who calls — she was told, "The older will serve the younger."ᶠ ¹³Just as it is written: "Jacob I loved, but Esau I hated."ᵍ

¹⁴What then shall we say? Is God unjust? Not at all! ¹⁵For he says to Moses,

> "I will have mercy on whom I
>   have mercy,
>   and I will have compassion
>   on whom I have
>   compassion."ʰ

¹⁶It does not, therefore, depend on human desire or effort, but on God's mercy. ¹⁷For Scripture says to Pharaoh: "I raised you up for this very purpose, that I might display my power in you and that my name might be proclaimed in all the earth."ⁱ ¹⁸Therefore God has mercy on whom he wants to have mercy, and he hardens whom he wants to harden.

ᵃ 36 Psalm 44:22   ᵇ 38 Or heavenly rulers
ᶜ 5 Or Messiah, who is over all. God be forever praised! Or Messiah. God who is over all be forever praised!   ᵈ 7 Gen. 21:12
ᵉ 9 Gen. 18:10,14   ᶠ 12 Gen. 25:23
ᵍ 13 Mal. 1:2,3   ʰ 15 Exodus 33:19
ⁱ 17 Exodus 9:16

¹⁹One of you will say to me: "Then why does God still blame us? For who is able to resist his will?" ²⁰But who are you, a human being, to talk back to God? "Shall what is formed say to the one who formed it, 'Why did you make me like this?'"ᵃ ²¹Does not the potter have the right to make out of the same lump of clay some pottery for special purposes and some for common use?

²²What if God, although choosing to show his wrath and make his power known, bore with great patience the objects of his wrath — prepared for destruction? ²³What if he did this to make the riches of his glory known to the objects of his mercy, whom he prepared in advance for glory — ²⁴even us, whom he also called, not only from the Jews but also from the Gentiles? ²⁵As he says in Hosea:

"I will call them 'my people' who
        are not my people;
    and I will call her 'my loved
        one' who is not my loved
        one,"ᵇ

²⁶and,

"In the very place where it was
        said to them,
    'You are not my people,'
    there they will be called
        'children of the living
        God.'"ᶜ

²⁷Isaiah cries out concerning Israel:

"Though the number of the
        Israelites be like the sand
        by the sea,
    only the remnant will be
        saved.
²⁸ For the Lord will carry out
        his sentence on earth with
        speed and finality."ᵈ

²⁹It is just as Isaiah said previously:

"Unless the Lord Almighty
        had left us descendants,
    we would have become like
        Sodom,
    we would have been like
        Gomorrah."ᵉ

Israel's Unbelief

³⁰What then shall we say? That the Gentiles, who did not pursue righteousness, have obtained it, a righteousness that is by faith; ³¹but the people of Israel, who pursued the law as the way of righteousness, have not attained their goal. ³²Why not? Because they pursued it not by faith but as if it were by works. They stumbled over the stumbling stone. ³³As it is written:

"See, I lay in Zion a stone that
        causes people to stumble
    and a rock that makes them
        fall,
    and the one who believes in
        him will never be put to
        shame."ᶠ

10 Brothers and sisters, my heart's desire and prayer to God for the Israelites is that they may be saved. ²For I can testify about them that they are zealous for God, but their zeal is not based on knowledge. ³Since they did not know the righteousness of God and sought to establish their own, they did not submit to God's righteousness. ⁴Christ is the culmination of the law so that there may be righteousness for everyone who believes.

⁵Moses writes this about the righteousness that is by the law: "The person who does these things will

---

ᵃ 20 Isaiah 29:16; 45:9   ᵇ 25 Hosea 2:23
ᶜ 26 Hosea 1:10   ᵈ 28 Isaiah 10:22,23 (see Septuagint)   ᵉ 29 Isaiah 1:9
ᶠ 33 Isaiah 8:14; 28:16

live by them."ᵃ ⁶But the righteousness that is by faith says: "Do not say
in your heart, 'Who will ascend into
heaven?'"ᵇ (that is, to bring Christ
down) ⁷or 'Who will descend into
the deep?'"ᶜ (that is, to bring Christ
up from the dead). ⁸But what does it
say? "The word is near you; it is
in your mouth and in your heart,"ᵈ
that is, the message concerning faith
that we proclaim: ⁹If you declare
with your mouth, "Jesus is Lord,"
and believe in your heart that God
raised him from the dead, you will
be saved. ¹⁰For it is with your heart
that you believe and are justified,
and it is with your mouth that you
profess your faith and are saved. ¹¹As
Scripture says, "Anyone who believes
in him will never be put to shame."ᵉ
¹²For there is no difference between
Jew and Gentile — the same Lord
is Lord of all and richly blesses all
who call on him, ¹³for, "Everyone
who calls on the name of the Lord
will be saved."ᶠ

¹⁴How, then, can they call on the
one they have not believed in? And
how can they believe in the one of
whom they have not heard? And
how can they hear without someone
preaching to them? ¹⁵And how can
anyone preach unless they are sent?
As it is written: "How beautiful are the
feet of those who bring good news!"ᵍ

¹⁶But not all the Israelites accepted the good news. For Isaiah says,
"Lord, who has believed our message?"ʰ ¹⁷Consequently, faith comes
from hearing the message, and the
message is heard through the word
about Christ. ¹⁸But I ask: Did they not
hear? Of course they did:

"Their voice has gone out into all
      the earth,
   their words to the ends of the
      world."ⁱ

¹⁹Again I ask: Did Israel not understand? First, Moses says,

"I will make you envious by
      those who are not a
      nation;
I will make you angry by
      a nation that has no
      understanding."ʲ

²⁰And Isaiah boldly says,

"I was found by those who did
      not seek me;
I revealed myself to those who
      did not ask for me."ᵏ

²¹But concerning Israel he says,

"All day long I have held out my
      hands
   to a disobedient and obstinate
      people."ˡ

The Remnant of Israel

11 I ask then: Did God reject his
people? By no means! I am an
Israelite myself, a descendant of
Abraham, from the tribe of Benjamin. ²God did not reject his people,
whom he foreknew. Don't you know
what Scripture says in the passage
about Elijah — how he appealed to
God against Israel: ³"Lord, they have
killed your prophets and torn down
your altars; I am the only one left,
and they are trying to kill me"ᵐ? ⁴And
what was God's answer to him? "I have
reserved for myself seven thousand
who have not bowed the knee to
Baal."ⁿ ⁵So too, at the present time
there is a remnant chosen by grace.
⁶And if by grace, then it cannot be

ᵃ 5 Lev. 18:5   ᵇ 6 Deut. 30:12   ᶜ 7 Deut. 30:13
ᵈ 8 Deut. 30:14   ᵉ 11 Isaiah 28:16 (see
Septuagint)   ᶠ 13 Joel 2:32   ᵍ 15 Isaiah 52:7
ʰ 16 Isaiah 53:1   ⁱ 18 Psalm 19:4
ʲ 19 Deut. 32:21   ᵏ 20 Isaiah 65:1
ˡ 21 Isaiah 65:2   ᵐ 3 1 Kings 19:10,14
ⁿ 4 1 Kings 19:18

based on works; if it were, grace would no longer be grace.

[7] What then? What the people of Israel sought so earnestly they did not obtain. The elect among them did, but the others were hardened, [8] as it is written:

> "God gave them a spirit of stupor,
>   eyes that could not see
>   and ears that could not hear,
> to this very day."[a]

[9] And David says:

> "May their table become a snare
>   and a trap,
>   a stumbling block and a
>   retribution for them.
> [10] May their eyes be darkened so
>   they cannot see,
>   and their backs be bent
>   forever."[b]

Ingrafted Branches

[11] Again I ask: Did they stumble so as to fall beyond recovery? Not at all! Rather, because of their transgression, salvation has come to the Gentiles to make Israel envious. [12] But if their transgression means riches for the world, and their loss means riches for the Gentiles, how much greater riches will their full inclusion bring!

[13] I am talking to you Gentiles. Inasmuch as I am the apostle to the Gentiles, I take pride in my ministry [14] in the hope that I may somehow arouse my own people to envy and save some of them. [15] For if their rejection brought reconciliation to the world, what will their acceptance be but life from the dead? [16] If the part of the dough offered as firstfruits is holy, then the whole batch is holy; if the root is holy, so are the branches.

[17] If some of the branches have been broken off, and you, though a wild olive shoot, have been grafted in among the others and now share in the nourishing sap from the olive root, [18] do not consider yourself to be superior to those other branches. If you do, consider this: You do not support the root, but the root supports you. [19] You will say then, "Branches were broken off so that I could be grafted in." [20] Granted. But they were broken off because of unbelief, and you stand by faith. Do not be arrogant, but tremble. [21] For if God did not spare the natural branches, he will not spare you either.

[22] Consider therefore the kindness and sternness of God: sternness to those who fell, but kindness to you, provided that you continue in his kindness. Otherwise, you also will be cut off. [23] And if they do not persist in unbelief, they will be grafted in, for God is able to graft them in again. [24] After all, if you were cut out of an olive tree that is wild by nature, and contrary to nature were grafted into a cultivated olive tree, how much more readily will these, the natural branches, be grafted into their own olive tree!

All Israel Will Be Saved

[25] I do not want you to be ignorant of this mystery, brothers and sisters, so that you may not be conceited: Israel has experienced a hardening in part until the full number of the Gentiles has come in, [26] and in this way[c] all Israel will be saved. As it is written:

> "The deliverer will come from
>   Zion;
>   he will turn godlessness away
>   from Jacob.
> [27] And this is[d] my covenant with
>   them
>   when I take away their sins."[e]

---

[a] 8 Deut. 29:4; Isaiah 29:10   [c] 26 Or and so   [d] 27 Or
[b] 10 Psalm 69:22,23   will be   [e] 27 Isaiah 59:20,21; 27:9 (see
Septuagint); Jer. 31:33,34

²⁸As far as the gospel is concerned, they are enemies for your sake; but as far as election is concerned, they are loved on account of the patriarchs, ²⁹for God's gifts and his call are irrevocable. ³⁰Just as you who were at one time disobedient to God have now received mercy as a result of their disobedience, ³¹so they too have now become disobedient in order that they too may now*ᵃ* receive mercy as a result of God's mercy to you. ³²For God has bound everyone over to disobedience so that he may have mercy on them all.

Doxology

³³ Oh, the depth of the riches of the
        wisdom andᵇ knowledge
        of God!
    How unsearchable his
        judgments,
    and his paths beyond tracing
        out!
³⁴ "Who has known the mind of the
        Lord?
    Or who has been his
        counselor?"ᶜ
³⁵ "Who has ever given to God,
        that God should repay them?"ᵈ
³⁶ For from him and through him
        and for him are all things.
    To him be the glory forever!
    Amen.

A Living Sacrifice

12 Therefore, I urge you, brothers and sisters, in view of God's mercy, to offer your bodies as a living sacrifice, holy and pleasing to God — this is your true and proper worship. ²Do not conform to the pattern of this world, but be transformed by the renewing of your mind. Then you will be able to test and approve what God's will is — his good, pleasing and perfect will.

Humble Service in the Body of Christ

³For by the grace given me I say to every one of you: Do not think of yourself more highly than you ought, but rather think of yourself with sober judgment, in accordance with the faith God has distributed to each of you. ⁴For just as each of us has one body with many members, and these members do not all have the same function, ⁵so in Christ we, though many, form one body, and each member belongs to all the others. ⁶We have different gifts, according to the grace given to each of us. If your gift is prophesying, then prophesy in accordance with yourᵉ faith; ⁷if it is serving, then serve; if it is teaching, then teach; ⁸if it is to encourage, then give encouragement; if it is giving, then give generously; if it is to lead,ᶠ do it diligently; if it is to show mercy, do it cheerfully.

Love in Action

⁹Love must be sincere. Hate what is evil; cling to what is good. ¹⁰Be devoted to one another in love. Honor one another above yourselves. ¹¹Never be lacking in zeal, but keep your spiritual fervor, serving the Lord. ¹²Be joyful in hope, patient in affliction, faithful in prayer. ¹³Share with the Lord's people who are in need. Practice hospitality.

¹⁴Bless those who persecute you; bless and do not curse. ¹⁵Rejoice with those who rejoice; mourn with those who mourn. ¹⁶Live in harmony with one another. Do not be proud, but be willing to associate with people of low position.ᵍ Do not be conceited.

ᵃ *31* Some manuscripts do not have *now.*
ᵇ *33* Or *riches and the wisdom and the*
ᶜ *34* Isaiah 40:13   ᵈ *35* Job 41:11   ᵉ *6* Or *the*
ᶠ *8* Or *to provide for others*   ᵍ *16* Or *willing to do menial work*

¹⁷Do not repay anyone evil for evil. Be careful to do what is right in the eyes of everyone. ¹⁸If it is possible, as far as it depends on you, live at peace with everyone. ¹⁹Do not take revenge, my dear friends, but leave room for God's wrath, for it is written: "It is mine to avenge; I will repay,"[a] says the Lord. ²⁰On the contrary:

"If your enemy is hungry, feed
   him;
if he is thirsty, give him
     something to drink.
In doing this, you will heap
   burning coals on his
     head."[b]

²¹Do not be overcome by evil, but overcome evil with good.

Submission to Governing Authorities

13 Let everyone be subject to the governing authorities, for there is no authority except that which God has established. The authorities that exist have been established by God. ²Consequently, whoever rebels against the authority is rebelling against what God has instituted, and those who do so will bring judgment on themselves. ³For rulers hold no terror for those who do right, but for those who do wrong. Do you want to be free from fear of the one in authority? Then do what is right and you will be commended. ⁴For the one in authority is God's servant for your good. But if you do wrong, be afraid, for rulers do not bear the sword for no reason. They are God's servants, agents of wrath to bring punishment on the wrongdoer. ⁵Therefore, it is necessary to submit to the authorities, not only because of possible punishment but also as a matter of conscience.

⁶This is also why you pay taxes, for the authorities are God's servants, who give their full time to governing. ⁷Give to everyone what you owe them: If you owe taxes, pay taxes; if revenue, then revenue; if respect, then respect; if honor, then honor.

Love Fulfills the Law

⁸Let no debt remain outstanding, except the continuing debt to love one another, for whoever loves others has fulfilled the law. ⁹The commandments, "You shall not commit adultery," "You shall not murder," "You shall not steal," "You shall not covet,"[c] and whatever other command there may be, are summed up in this one command: "Love your neighbor as yourself."[d] ¹⁰Love does no harm to a neighbor. Therefore love is the fulfillment of the law.

The Day Is Near

¹¹And do this, understanding the present time: The hour has already come for you to wake up from your slumber, because our salvation is nearer now than when we first believed. ¹²The night is nearly over; the day is almost here. So let us put aside the deeds of darkness and put on the armor of light. ¹³Let us behave decently, as in the daytime, not in carousing and drunkenness, not in sexual immorality and debauchery, not in dissension and jealousy. ¹⁴Rather, clothe yourselves with the Lord Jesus Christ, and do not think about how to gratify the desires of the flesh.[e]

---

[a] 19 Deut. 32:35   [b] 20 Prov. 25:21,22
[c] 9 Exodus 20:13-15,17; Deut. 5:17-19,21
[d] 9 Lev. 19:18   [e] 14 In contexts like this, the Greek word for *flesh* (*sarx*) refers to the sinful state of human beings, often presented as a power in opposition to the Spirit.

The Weak and the Strong

14 Accept the one whose faith is weak, without quarreling over disputable matters. ²One person's faith allows them to eat anything, but another, whose faith is weak, eats only vegetables. ³The one who eats everything must not treat with contempt the one who does not, and the one who does not eat everything must not judge the one who does, for God has accepted them. ⁴Who are you to judge someone else's servant? To their own master, servants stand or fall. And they will stand, for the Lord is able to make them stand.

⁵One person considers one day more sacred than another; another considers every day alike. Each of them should be fully convinced in their own mind. ⁶Whoever regards one day as special does so to the Lord. Whoever eats meat does so to the Lord, for they give thanks to God; and whoever abstains does so to the Lord and gives thanks to God. ⁷For none of us lives for ourselves alone, and none of us dies for ourselves alone. ⁸If we live, we live for the Lord; and if we die, we die for the Lord. So, whether we live or die, we belong to the Lord. ⁹For this very reason, Christ died and returned to life so that he might be the Lord of both the dead and the living.

¹⁰You, then, why do you judge your brother or sister*? Or why do you treat them with contempt? For we will all stand before God's judgment seat. ¹¹It is written:

"'As surely as I live,' says the Lord,
'every knee will bow before me;
    every tongue will acknowledge God.'"*

¹²So then, each of us will give an account of ourselves to God.

¹³Therefore let us stop passing judgment on one another. Instead, make up your mind not to put any stumbling block or obstacle in the way of a brother or sister. ¹⁴I am convinced, being fully persuaded in the Lord Jesus, that nothing is unclean in itself. But if anyone regards something as unclean, then for that person it is unclean. ¹⁵If your brother or sister is distressed because of what you eat, you are no longer acting in love. Do not by your eating destroy someone for whom Christ died. ¹⁶Therefore do not let what you know is good be spoken of as evil. ¹⁷For the kingdom of God is not a matter of eating and drinking, but of righteousness, peace and joy in the Holy Spirit, ¹⁸because anyone who serves Christ in this way is pleasing to God and receives human approval.

¹⁹Let us therefore make every effort to do what leads to peace and to mutual edification. ²⁰Do not destroy the work of God for the sake of food. All food is clean, but it is wrong for a person to eat anything that causes someone else to stumble. ²¹It is better not to eat meat or drink wine or to do anything else that will cause your brother or sister to fall.

²²So whatever you believe about these things keep between yourself and God. Blessed is the one who does not condemn himself by what he approves. ²³But whoever has doubts is condemned if they eat, because their eating is not from faith; and everything that does not come from faith is sin.*

ᵃ 10 The Greek word for *brother or sister* (*adelphos*) refers here to a believer, whether man or woman, as part of God's family; also in verses 13, 15 and 21.   *ᵇ 11* Isaiah 45:23
ᶜ 23 Some manuscripts place 16:25-27 here; others after 15:33.

15 We who are strong ought to bear with the failings of the weak and not to please ourselves. ²Each of us should please our neighbors for their good, to build them up. ³For even Christ did not please himself but, as it is written: "The insults of those who insult you have fallen on me."ᵃ ⁴For everything that was written in the past was written to teach us, so that through the endurance taught in the Scriptures and the encouragement they provide we might have hope.

⁵May the God who gives endurance and encouragement give you the same attitude of mind toward each other that Christ Jesus had, ⁶so that with one mind and one voice you may glorify the God and Father of our Lord Jesus Christ.

⁷Accept one another, then, just as Christ accepted you, in order to bring praise to God. ⁸For I tell you that Christ has become a servant of the Jewsᵇ on behalf of God's truth, so that the promises made to the patriarchs might be confirmed ⁹and, moreover, that the Gentiles might glorify God for his mercy. As it is written:

"Therefore I will praise you
        among the Gentiles;
    I will sing the praises of your
        name."ᶜ

¹⁰Again, it says,

"Rejoice, you Gentiles, with his
        people."ᵈ

¹¹And again,

"Praise the Lord, all you Gentiles;
    let all the peoples extol him."ᵉ

¹²And again, Isaiah says,

"The Root of Jesse will spring up,
    one who will arise to rule over
        the nations;
    in him the Gentiles will hope."ᶠ

¹³May the God of hope fill you with all joy and peace as you trust in him, so that you may overflow with hope by the power of the Holy Spirit.

Paul the Minister to the Gentiles

¹⁴I myself am convinced, my brothers and sisters, that you yourselves are full of goodness, filled with knowledge and competent to instruct one another. ¹⁵Yet I have written you quite boldly on some points to remind you of them again, because of the grace God gave me ¹⁶to be a minister of Christ Jesus to the Gentiles. He gave me the priestly duty of proclaiming the gospel of God, so that the Gentiles might become an offering acceptable to God, sanctified by the Holy Spirit.

¹⁷Therefore I glory in Christ Jesus in my service to God. ¹⁸I will not venture to speak of anything except what Christ has accomplished through me in leading the Gentiles to obey God by what I have said and done — ¹⁹by the power of signs and wonders, through the power of the Spirit of God. So from Jerusalem all the way around to Illyricum, I have fully proclaimed the gospel of Christ. ²⁰It has always been my ambition to preach the gospel where Christ was not known, so that I would not be building on someone else's foundation. ²¹Rather, as it is written:

"Those who were not told about
        him will see,
    and those who have not heard
        will understand."ᵍ

²²This is why I have often been hindered from coming to you.

ᵃ 3 Psalm 69:9   ᵇ 8 Greek *circumcision*
ᶜ 9 2 Samuel 22:50; Psalm 18:49
ᵈ 10 Deut. 32:43   ᵉ 11 Psalm 117:1
ᶠ 12 Isaiah 11:10 (see Septuagint)
ᵍ 21 Isaiah 52:15 (see Septuagint)

Paul's Plan to Visit Rome

23But now that there is no more place for me to work in these regions, and since I have been longing for many years to visit you, 24I plan to do so when I go to Spain. I hope to see you while passing through and to have you assist me on my journey there, after I have enjoyed your company for a while. 25Now, however, I am on my way to Jerusalem in the service of the Lord's people there. 26For Macedonia and Achaia were pleased to make a contribution for the poor among the Lord's people in Jerusalem. 27They were pleased to do it, and indeed they owe it to them. For if the Gentiles have shared in the Jews' spiritual blessings, they owe it to the Jews to share with them their material blessings. 28So after I have completed this task and have made sure that they have received this contribution, I will go to Spain and visit you on the way. 29I know that when I come to you, I will come in the full measure of the blessing of Christ.

30I urge you, brothers and sisters, by our Lord Jesus Christ and by the love of the Spirit, to join me in my struggle by praying to God for me. 31Pray that I may be kept safe from the unbelievers in Judea and that the contribution I take to Jerusalem may be favorably received by the Lord's people there, 32so that I may come to you with joy, by God's will, and in your company be refreshed. 33The God of peace be with you all. Amen.

Personal Greetings

16 I commend to you our sister Phoebe, a deacon*a,b* of the church in Cenchreae. 2I ask you to receive her in the Lord in a way worthy of his people and to give her any help she may need from you, for she has

been the benefactor of many people, including me.

3 Greet Priscilla*c* and Aquila, my co-workers in Christ Jesus. 4They risked their lives for me. Not only I but all the churches of the Gentiles are grateful to them.

5 Greet also the church that meets at their house.

Greet my dear friend Epenetus, who was the first convert to Christ in the province of Asia.

6 Greet Mary, who worked very hard for you.

7 Greet Andronicus and Junia, my fellow Jews who have been in prison with me. They are outstanding among*d* the apostles, and they were in Christ before I was.

8 Greet Ampliatus, my dear friend in the Lord.

9 Greet Urbanus, our co-worker in Christ, and my dear friend Stachys.

10 Greet Apelles, whose fidelity to Christ has stood the test.

Greet those who belong to the household of Aristobulus.

11 Greet Herodion, my fellow Jew.

Greet those in the household of Narcissus who are in the Lord.

12 Greet Tryphena and Tryphosa, those women who work hard in the Lord.

Greet my dear friend Persis, another woman who has worked very hard in the Lord.

13 Greet Rufus, chosen in the Lord, and his mother, who has been a mother to me, too.

---

a 1 Or servant   *b 1 The word deacon refers here to a Christian designated to serve with the overseers/elders of the church in a variety of ways; similarly in Phil. 1:1 and 1 Tim. 3:8,12.*   *c 3 Greek Prisca, a variant of Priscilla*   *d 7 Or are esteemed by*

¹⁴ Greet Asyncritus, Phlegon, Hermes, Patrobas, Hermas and the other brothers and sisters with them. ¹⁵ Greet Philologus, Julia, Nereus and his sister, and Olympas and all the Lord's people who are with them.

¹⁶ Greet one another with a holy kiss. All the churches of Christ send greetings.

¹⁷ I urge you, brothers and sisters, to watch out for those who cause divisions and put obstacles in your way that are contrary to the teaching you have learned. Keep away from them. ¹⁸ For such people are not serving our Lord Christ, but their own appetites. By smooth talk and flattery they deceive the minds of naive people. ¹⁹ Everyone has heard about your obedience, so I rejoice because of you; but I want you to be wise about what is good, and innocent about what is evil.

²⁰ The God of peace will soon crush Satan under your feet.

The grace of our Lord Jesus be with you.

²¹ Timothy, my co-worker, sends his greetings to you, as do Lucius, Jason and Sosipater, my fellow Jews.

²² I, Tertius, who wrote down this letter, greet you in the Lord.

²³ Gaius, whose hospitality I and the whole church here enjoy, sends you his greetings.

Erastus, who is the city's director of public works, and our brother Quartus send you their greetings. [²⁴]ᵃ

²⁵ Now to him who is able to establish you in accordance with my gospel, the message I proclaim about Jesus Christ, in keeping with the revelation of the mystery hidden for long ages past, ²⁶ but now revealed and made known through the prophetic writings by the command of the eternal God, so that all the Gentiles might come to the obedience that comes fromᵇ faith — ²⁷ to the only wise God be glory forever through Jesus Christ! Amen.

1 Corinthians

1 Paul, called to be an apostle of Christ Jesus by the will of God, and our brother Sosthenes,

²To the church of God in Corinth, to those sanctified in Christ Jesus and called to be his holy people, together with all those everywhere who call on the name of our Lord Jesus Christ — their Lord and ours:

³Grace and peace to you from God our Father and the Lord Jesus Christ.

Thanksgiving

⁴I always thank my God for you because of his grace given you in Christ Jesus. ⁵For in him you have been enriched in every way — with all kinds of speech and with all knowledge — ⁶God thus confirming our testimony about Christ among

ᵃ 24 Some manuscripts include here *May the grace of our Lord Jesus Christ be with all of you. Amen.*   ᵇ 26 Or *that is* you. [7] Therefore you do not lack any spiritual gift as you eagerly wait for our Lord Jesus Christ to be revealed. [8] He will also keep you firm to the end, so that you will be blameless on the day of our Lord Jesus Christ. [9] God is faithful, who has called you into fellowship with his Son, Jesus Christ our Lord.

A Church Divided Over Leaders

[10] I appeal to you, brothers and sisters,[a] in the name of our Lord Jesus Christ, that all of you agree with one another in what you say and that there be no divisions among you, but that you be perfectly united in mind and thought. [11] My brothers and sisters, some from Chloe's household have informed me that there are quarrels among you. [12] What I mean is this: One of you says, "I follow Paul"; another, "I follow Apollos"; another, "I follow Cephas[b]"; still another, "I follow Christ."

[13] Is Christ divided? Was Paul crucified for you? Were you baptized in the name of Paul? [14] I thank God that I did not baptize any of you except Crispus and Gaius, [15] so no one can say that you were baptized in my name. [16] (Yes, I also baptized the household of Stephanas; beyond that, I don't remember if I baptized anyone else.) [17] For Christ did not send me to baptize, but to preach the gospel — not with wisdom and eloquence, lest the cross of Christ be emptied of its power.

Christ Crucified Is God's Power and Wisdom

[18] For the message of the cross is foolishness to those who are perishing, but to us who are being saved it is the power of God. [19] For it is written:

"I will destroy the wisdom of the wise;
   the intelligence of the intelligent I will frustrate."[c]

[20] Where is the wise person? Where is the teacher of the law? Where is the philosopher of this age? Has not God made foolish the wisdom of the world? [21] For since in the wisdom of God the world through its wisdom did not know him, God was pleased through the foolishness of what was preached to save those who believe. [22] Jews demand signs and Greeks look for wisdom, [23] but we preach Christ crucified: a stumbling block to Jews and foolishness to Gentiles, [24] but to those whom God has called, both Jews and Greeks, Christ the power of God and the wisdom of God. [25] For the foolishness of God is wiser than human wisdom, and the weakness of God is stronger than human strength.

[26] Brothers and sisters, think of what you were when you were called. Not many of you were wise by human standards; not many were influential; not many were of noble birth. [27] But God chose the foolish things of the world to shame the wise; God chose the weak things of the world to shame the strong. [28] God chose the lowly things of this world and the despised things — and the things that are not — to nullify the things that are, [29] so that no one may boast before him. [30] It is because of him that you are in Christ Jesus, who has become for us wisdom from God — that is,

---

[a] 10 The Greek word for brothers and sisters (adelphoi) refers here to believers, both men and women, as part of God's family; also in verses 11 and 26; and in 2:1; 3:1; 4:6; 6:8; 7:24, 29; 10:1; 11:33; 12:1; 14:6, 20, 26, 39; 15:1, 6, 50, 58; 16:15, 20.   [b] 12 That is, Peter
[c] 19 Isaiah 29:14

our righteousness, holiness and redemption. [31]Therefore, as it is written: "Let the one who boasts boast in the Lord."[a]

2 And so it was with me, brothers and sisters. When I came to you, I did not come with eloquence or human wisdom as I proclaimed to you the testimony about God.[b] [2]For I resolved to know nothing while I was with you except Jesus Christ and him crucified. [3]I came to you in weakness with great fear and trembling. [4]My message and my preaching were not with wise and persuasive words, but with a demonstration of the Spirit's power, [5]so that your faith might not rest on human wisdom, but on God's power.

God's Wisdom Revealed by the Spirit

[6]We do, however, speak a message of wisdom among the mature, but not the wisdom of this age or of the rulers of this age, who are coming to nothing. [7]No, we declare God's wisdom, a mystery that has been hidden and that God destined for our glory before time began. [8]None of the rulers of this age understood it, for if they had, they would not have crucified the Lord of glory. [9]However, as it is written:

"What no eye has seen,
    what no ear has heard,
and what no human mind has
        conceived"[c] —
    the things God has prepared
        for those who love him —

[10]these are the things God has revealed to us by his Spirit.
    The Spirit searches all things, even the deep things of God. [11]For who knows a person's thoughts except their own spirit within them? In the same way no one knows the thoughts

of God except the Spirit of God. [12]What we have received is not the spirit of the world, but the Spirit who is from God, so that we may understand what God has freely given us. [13]This is what we speak, not in words taught us by human wisdom but in words taught by the Spirit, explaining spiritual realities with Spirit-taught words.[d] [14]The person without the Spirit does not accept the things that come from the Spirit of God but considers them foolishness, and cannot understand them because they are discerned only through the Spirit. [15]The person with the Spirit makes judgments about all things, but such a person is not subject to merely human judgments, [16]for,

"Who has known the mind of the
        Lord
    so as to instruct him?"[e]

But we have the mind of Christ.

The Church and Its Leaders

3 Brothers and sisters, I could not address you as people who live by the Spirit but as people who are still worldly — mere infants in Christ. [2]I gave you milk, not solid food, for you were not yet ready for it. Indeed, you are still not ready. [3]You are still worldly. For since there is jealousy and quarreling among you, are you not worldly? Are you not acting like mere humans? [4]For when one says, "I follow Paul," and another, "I follow Apollos," are you not mere human beings?

[5]What, after all, is Apollos? And what is Paul? Only servants, through

---

[a] 31 Jer. 9:24   [b] 1 Some manuscripts
proclaimed to you God's mystery
[c] 9 Isaiah 64:4   [d] 13 Or *Spirit, interpreting*
spiritual truths to those who are spiritual
[e] 16 Isaiah 40:13

whom you came to believe — as the Lord has assigned to each his task. ⁶I planted the seed, Apollos watered it, but God has been making it grow. ⁷So neither the one who plants nor the one who waters is anything, but only God, who makes things grow. ⁸The one who plants and the one who waters have one purpose, and they will each be rewarded according to their own labor. ⁹For we are co-workers in God's service; you are God's field, God's building.

¹⁰By the grace God has given me, I laid a foundation as a wise builder, and someone else is building on it. But each one should build with care. ¹¹For no one can lay any foundation other than the one already laid, which is Jesus Christ. ¹²If anyone builds on this foundation using gold, silver, costly stones, wood, hay or straw, ¹³their work will be shown for what it is, because the Day will bring it to light. It will be revealed with fire, and the fire will test the quality of each person's work. ¹⁴If what has been built survives, the builder will receive a reward. ¹⁵If it is burned up, the builder will suffer loss but yet will be saved — even though only as one escaping through the flames.

¹⁶Don't you know that you yourselves are God's temple and that God's Spirit dwells in your midst? ¹⁷If anyone destroys God's temple, God will destroy that person; for God's temple is sacred, and you together are that temple.

¹⁸Do not deceive yourselves. If any of you think you are wise by the standards of this age, you should become "fools" so that you may become wise. ¹⁹For the wisdom of this world is foolishness in God's sight. As it is written: "He catches the wise in their craftiness"ᵃ; ²⁰and again, "The Lord knows that the thoughts of the wise are futile."ᵇ ²¹So then, no more boasting about human leaders! All things are yours, ²²whether Paul or Apollos or Cephasᶜ or the world or life or death or the present or the future — all are yours, ²³and you are of Christ, and Christ is of God.

The Nature of True Apostleship

4 This, then, is how you ought to regard us: as servants of Christ and as those entrusted with the mysteries God has revealed. ²Now it is required that those who have been given a trust must prove faithful. ³I care very little if I am judged by you or by any human court; indeed, I do not even judge myself. ⁴My conscience is clear, but that does not make me innocent. It is the Lord who judges me. ⁵Therefore judge nothing before the appointed time; wait until the Lord comes. He will bring to light what is hidden in darkness and will expose the motives of the heart. At that time each will receive their praise from God.

⁶Now, brothers and sisters, I have applied these things to myself and Apollos for your benefit, so that you may learn from us the meaning of the saying, "Do not go beyond what is written." Then you will not be puffed up in being a follower of one of us over against the other. ⁷For who makes you different from anyone else? What do you have that you did not receive? And if you did receive it, why do you boast as though you did not?

⁸Already you have all you want! Already you have become rich! You have begun to reign — and that without us!

ᵃ 19 Job 5:13   ᵇ 20 Psalm 94:11   ᶜ 22 That is, Peter

How I wish that you really had begun to reign so that we also might reign with you! ⁹For it seems to me that God has put us apostles on display at the end of the procession, like those condemned to die in the arena. We have been made a spectacle to the whole universe, to angels as well as to human beings. ¹⁰We are fools for Christ, but you are so wise in Christ! We are weak, but you are strong! You are honored, we are dishonored! ¹¹To this very hour we go hungry and thirsty, we are in rags, we are brutally treated, we are homeless. ¹²We work hard with our own hands. When we are cursed, we bless; when we are persecuted, we endure it; ¹³when we are slandered, we answer kindly. We have become the scum of the earth, the garbage of the world — right up to this moment.

Paul's Appeal and Warning

¹⁴I am writing this not to shame you but to warn you as my dear children. ¹⁵Even if you had ten thousand guardians in Christ, you do not have many fathers, for in Christ Jesus I became your father through the gospel. ¹⁶Therefore I urge you to imitate me. ¹⁷For this reason I have sent to you Timothy, my son whom I love, who is faithful in the Lord. He will remind you of my way of life in Christ Jesus, which agrees with what I teach everywhere in every church.

¹⁸Some of you have become arrogant, as if I were not coming to you. ¹⁹But I will come to you very soon, if the Lord is willing, and then I will find out not only how these arrogant people are talking, but what power they have. ²⁰For the kingdom of God is not a matter of talk but of power. ²¹What do you prefer? Shall I come to you with a rod of discipline, or shall I come in love and with a gentle spirit?

Dealing With a Case of Incest

5 It is actually reported that there is sexual immorality among you, and of a kind that even pagans do not tolerate: A man is sleeping with his father's wife. ²And you are proud! Shouldn't you rather have gone into mourning and have put out of your fellowship the man who has been doing this? ³For my part, even though I am not physically present, I am with you in spirit. As one who is present with you in this way, I have already passed judgment in the name of our Lord Jesus on the one who has been doing this. ⁴So when you are assembled and I am with you in spirit, and the power of our Lord Jesus is present, ⁵hand this man over to Satan for the destruction of the flesh,ᵃ,ᵇ so that his spirit may be saved on the day of the Lord.

⁶Your boasting is not good. Don't you know that a little yeast leavens the whole batch of dough? ⁷Get rid of the old yeast, so that you may be a new unleavened batch — as you really are. For Christ, our Passover lamb, has been sacrificed. ⁸Therefore let us keep the Festival, not with the old bread leavened with malice and wickedness, but with the unleavened bread of sincerity and truth.

⁹I wrote to you in my letter not to associate with sexually immoral people — ¹⁰not at all meaning the people of this world who are immoral, or the greedy and swindlers, or idolaters. In that case you would have to leave this world. ¹¹But now I am writing to you that you must not associate with anyone who claims to be a brother

---

ᵃ 5 In contexts like this, the Greek word for *flesh (sarx)* refers to the sinful state of human beings, often presented as a power in opposition to the Spirit.   ᵇ 5 Or *of his body* or sister[a] but is sexually immoral or greedy, an idolater or slanderer, a drunkard or swindler. Do not even eat with such people.

¹²What business is it of mine to judge those outside the church? Are you not to judge those inside? ¹³God will judge those outside. "Expel the wicked person from among you."[b]

Lawsuits Among Believers

6 If any of you has a dispute with another, do you dare to take it before the ungodly for judgment instead of before the Lord's people? ²Or do you not know that the Lord's people will judge the world? And if you are to judge the world, are you not competent to judge trivial cases? ³Do you not know that we will judge angels? How much more the things of this life! ⁴Therefore, if you have disputes about such matters, do you ask for a ruling from those whose way of life is scorned in the church? ⁵I say this to shame you. Is it possible that there is nobody among you wise enough to judge a dispute between believers? ⁶But instead, one brother takes another to court — and this in front of unbelievers!

⁷The very fact that you have lawsuits among you means you have been completely defeated already. Why not rather be wronged? Why not rather be cheated? ⁸Instead, you yourselves cheat and do wrong, and you do this to your brothers and sisters. ⁹Or do you not know that wrongdoers will not inherit the kingdom of God? Do not be deceived: Neither the sexually immoral nor idolaters nor adulterers nor men who have sex with men[c] ¹⁰nor thieves nor the greedy nor drunkards nor slanderers nor swindlers will inherit the kingdom of God. ¹¹And that

is what some of you were. But you were washed, you were sanctified, you were justified in the name of the Lord Jesus Christ and by the Spirit of our God.

Sexual Immorality

¹²"I have the right to do anything," you say — but not everything is beneficial. "I have the right to do anything" — but I will not be mastered by anything. ¹³You say, "Food for the stomach and the stomach for food, and God will destroy them both." The body, however, is not meant for sexual immorality but for the Lord, and the Lord for the body. ¹⁴By his power God raised the Lord from the dead, and he will raise us also. ¹⁵Do you not know that your bodies are members of Christ himself? Shall I then take the members of Christ and unite them with a prostitute? Never! ¹⁶Do you not know that he who unites himself with a prostitute is one with her in body? For it is said, "The two will become one flesh."[d] ¹⁷But whoever is united with the Lord is one with him in spirit.[e]

¹⁸Flee from sexual immorality. All other sins a person commits are outside the body, but whoever sins sexually, sins against their own body. ¹⁹Do you not know that your bodies are temples of the Holy Spirit, who is in you, whom you have received from God? You are not your own; ²⁰you were bought at a price. Therefore honor God with your bodies.

[a] 11 The Greek word for brother or sister (adelphos) refers here to a believer, whether man or woman, as part of God's family; also in 8:11, 13. [b] 13 Deut. 13:5; 17:7; 19:19; 21:21; 22:21,24; 24:7 [c] 9 The words men who have sex with men translate two Greek words that refer to the passive and active participants in homosexual acts. [d] 16 Gen. 2:24 [e] 17 Or in the Spirit

Concerning Married Life

7 Now for the matters you wrote about: "It is good for a man not to have sexual relations with a woman." ²But since sexual immorality is occurring, each man should have sexual relations with his own wife, and each woman with her own husband. ³The husband should fulfill his marital duty to his wife, and likewise the wife to her husband. ⁴The wife does not have authority over her own body but yields it to her husband. In the same way, the husband does not have authority over his own body but yields it to his wife. ⁵Do not deprive each other except perhaps by mutual consent and for a time, so that you may devote yourselves to prayer. Then come together again so that Satan will not tempt you because of your lack of self-control. ⁶I say this as a concession, not as a command. ⁷I wish that all of you were as I am. But each of you has your own gift from God; one has this gift, another has that.

⁸Now to the unmarried⁰ and the widows I say: It is good for them to stay unmarried, as I do. ⁹But if they cannot control themselves, they should marry, for it is better to marry than to burn with passion.

¹⁰To the married I give this command (not I, but the Lord): A wife must not separate from her husband. ¹¹But if she does, she must remain unmarried or else be reconciled to her husband. And a husband must not divorce his wife.

¹²To the rest I say this (I, not the Lord): If any brother has a wife who is not a believer and she is willing to live with him, he must not divorce her. ¹³And if a woman has a husband who is not a believer and he is willing to live with her, she must not divorce him. ¹⁴For the unbelieving husband has been sanctified through his wife, and the unbelieving wife has been sanctified through her believing husband. Otherwise your children would be unclean, but as it is, they are holy.

¹⁵But if the unbeliever leaves, let it be so. The brother or the sister is not bound in such circumstances; God has called us to live in peace. ¹⁶How do you know, wife, whether you will save your husband? Or, how do you know, husband, whether you will save your wife?

Concerning Change of Status

¹⁷Nevertheless, each person should live as a believer in whatever situation the Lord has assigned to them, just as God has called them. This is the rule I lay down in all the churches. ¹⁸Was a man already circumcised when he was called? He should not become uncircumcised. Was a man uncircumcised when he was called? He should not be circumcised. ¹⁹Circumcision is nothing and uncircumcision is nothing. Keeping God's commands is what counts. ²⁰Each person should remain in the situation they were in when God called them.

²¹Were you a slave when you were called? Don't let it trouble you — although if you can gain your freedom, do so. ²²For the one who was a slave when called to faith in the Lord is the Lord's freed person; similarly, the one who was free when called is Christ's slave. ²³You were bought at a price; do not become slaves of human beings. ²⁴Brothers and sisters, each person, as responsible to God, should remain in the situation they were in when God called them.

Concerning the Unmarried

²⁵Now about virgins: I have no command from the Lord, but I give a judgment as one who by the Lord's

⁰ 8 Or *widowers*

mercy is trustworthy. [26]Because of the present crisis, I think that it is good for a man to remain as he is. [27]Are you pledged to a woman? Do not seek to be released. Are you free from such a commitment? Do not look for a wife. [28]But if you do marry, you have not sinned; and if a virgin marries, she has not sinned. But those who marry will face many troubles in this life, and I want to spare you this.

[29]What I mean, brothers and sisters, is that the time is short. From now on those who have wives should live as if they do not; [30]those who mourn, as if they did not; those who are happy, as if they were not; those who buy something, as if it were not theirs to keep; [31]those who use the things of the world, as if not engrossed in them. For this world in its present form is passing away.

[32]I would like you to be free from concern. An unmarried man is concerned about the Lord's affairs — how he can please the Lord. [33]But a married man is concerned about the affairs of this world — how he can please his wife — [34]and his interests are divided. An unmarried woman or virgin is concerned about the Lord's affairs: Her aim is to be devoted to the Lord in both body and spirit. But a married woman is concerned about the affairs of this world — how she can please her husband. [35]I am saying this for your own good, not to restrict you, but that you may live in a right way in undivided devotion to the Lord.

[36]If anyone is worried that he might not be acting honorably toward the virgin he is engaged to, and if his passions are too strong[a] and he feels he ought to marry, he should do as he wants. He is not sinning. They should get married. [37]But the man who has settled the matter in his own mind,

who is under no compulsion but has control over his own will, and who has made up his mind not to marry the virgin — this man also does the right thing. [38]So then, he who marries the virgin does right, but he who does not marry her does better.[b]

[39]A woman is bound to her husband as long as he lives. But if her husband dies, she is free to marry anyone she wishes, but he must belong to the Lord. [40]In my judgment, she is happier if she stays as she is — and I think that I too have the Spirit of God.

Concerning Food Sacrificed to Idols

8 Now about food sacrificed to idols: We know that "We all possess knowledge." But knowledge puffs up while love builds up. [2]Those who think they know something do not yet know as they ought to know. [3]But whoever loves God is known by God.[c]

[4]So then, about eating food sacrificed to idols: We know that "An idol is nothing at all in the world" and that "There is no God but one." [5]For even if there are so-called gods, whether in heaven or on earth (as indeed there are many "gods" and many "lords"), [6]yet for us there is but one God, the

---

[a] 36 Or *if she is getting beyond the usual age for marriage*   [b] 36-38 Or [36]*If anyone thinks he is not treating his daughter properly, and if she is getting along in years (or if her passions are too strong), and he feels she ought to marry, he should do as he wants. He is not sinning. He should let her get married.* [37]*But the man who has settled the matter in his own mind, who is under no compulsion but has control over his own will, and who has made up his mind to keep the virgin unmarried — this man also does the right thing.* [38]*So then, he who gives his virgin in marriage does right, but he who does not give her in marriage does better.*   [c] 2,3 An early manuscript and another ancient witness *think they have knowledge do not yet know as they ought to know.* [3]*But whoever loves truly knows.*

Father, from whom all things came and for whom we live; and there is but one Lord, Jesus Christ, through whom all things came and through whom we live.

⁷But not everyone possesses this knowledge. Some people are still so accustomed to idols that when they eat sacrificial food they think of it as having been sacrificed to a god, and since their conscience is weak, it is defiled. ⁸But food does not bring us near to God; we are no worse if we do not eat, and no better if we do.

⁹Be careful, however, that the exercise of your rights does not become a stumbling block to the weak. ¹⁰For if someone with a weak conscience sees you, with all your knowledge, eating in an idol's temple, won't that person be emboldened to eat what is sacrificed to idols? ¹¹So this weak brother or sister, for whom Christ died, is destroyed by your knowledge. ¹²When you sin against them in this way and wound their weak conscience, you sin against Christ. ¹³Therefore, if what I eat causes my brother or sister to fall into sin, I will never eat meat again, so that I will not cause them to fall.

Paul's Rights as an Apostle

9 Am I not free? Am I not an apostle? Have I not seen Jesus our Lord? Are you not the result of my work in the Lord? ²Even though I may not be an apostle to others, surely I am to you! For you are the seal of my apostleship in the Lord.

³This is my defense to those who sit in judgment on me. ⁴Don't we have the right to food and drink? ⁵Don't we have the right to take a believing wife along with us, as do the other apostles and the Lord's brothers and Cephas*a*? ⁶Or is it only I and Barnabas who lack the right to not work for a living?

⁷Who serves as a soldier at his own expense? Who plants a vineyard and does not eat its grapes? Who tends a flock and does not drink the milk? ⁸Do I say this merely on human authority? Doesn't the Law say the same thing? ⁹For it is written in the Law of Moses: "Do not muzzle an ox while it is treading out the grain."*b* Is it about oxen that God is concerned? ¹⁰Surely he says this for us, doesn't he? Yes, this was written for us, because whoever plows and threshes should be able to do so in the hope of sharing in the harvest. ¹¹If we have sown spiritual seed among you, is it too much if we reap a material harvest from you? ¹²If others have this right of support from you, shouldn't we have it all the more?

But we did not use this right. On the contrary, we put up with anything rather than hinder the gospel of Christ.

¹³Don't you know that those who serve in the temple get their food from the temple, and that those who serve at the altar share in what is offered on the altar? ¹⁴In the same way, the Lord has commanded that those who preach the gospel should receive their living from the gospel.

¹⁵But I have not used any of these rights. And I am not writing this in the hope that you will do such things for me, for I would rather die than allow anyone to deprive me of this boast. ¹⁶For when I preach the gospel, I cannot boast, since I am compelled to preach. Woe to me if I do not preach the gospel! ¹⁷If I preach voluntarily, I have a reward; if not voluntarily, I am simply discharging the trust committed to me. ¹⁸What then is my reward? Just this: that in preaching the gospel I may offer it free of charge, and so

---

a 5 That is, Peter   *b* 9 Deut. 25:4

not make full use of my rights as a preacher of the gospel.

Paul's Use of His Freedom

[19]Though I am free and belong to no one, I have made myself a slave to everyone, to win as many as possible. [20]To the Jews I became like a Jew, to win the Jews. To those under the law I became like one under the law (though I myself am not under the law), so as to win those under the law. [21]To those not having the law I became like one not having the law (though I am not free from God's law but am under Christ's law), so as to win those not having the law. [22]To the weak I became weak, to win the weak. I have become all things to all people so that by all possible means I might save some. [23]I do all this for the sake of the gospel, that I may share in its blessings.

The Need for Self-Discipline

[24]Do you not know that in a race all the runners run, but only one gets the prize? Run in such a way as to get the prize. [25]Everyone who competes in the games goes into strict training. They do it to get a crown that will not last, but we do it to get a crown that will last forever. [26]Therefore I do not run like someone running aimlessly; I do not fight like a boxer beating the air. [27]No, I strike a blow to my body and make it my slave so that after I have preached to others, I myself will not be disqualified for the prize.

Warnings From Israel's History

10 For I do not want you to be ignorant of the fact, brothers and sisters, that our ancestors were all under the cloud and that they all passed through the sea. [2]They were all baptized into Moses in the cloud and in the sea. [3]They all ate the same spiritual food [4]and drank the same spiritual drink; for they drank from the spiritual rock that accompanied them, and that rock was Christ. [5]Nevertheless, God was not pleased with most of them; their bodies were scattered in the wilderness.

[6]Now these things occurred as examples to keep us from setting our hearts on evil things as they did. [7]Do not be idolaters, as some of them were; as it is written: "The people sat down to eat and drink and got up to indulge in revelry."[a] [8]We should not commit sexual immorality, as some of them did — and in one day twenty-three thousand of them died. [9]We should not test Christ,[b] as some of them did — and were killed by snakes. [10]And do not grumble, as some of them did — and were killed by the destroying angel.

[11]These things happened to them as examples and were written down as warnings for us, on whom the culmination of the ages has come. [12]So, if you think you are standing firm, be careful that you don't fall! [13]No temptation[c] has overtaken you except what is common to mankind. And God is faithful; he will not let you be tempted[c] beyond what you can bear. But when you are tempted,[c] he will also provide a way out so that you can endure it.

Idol Feasts and the Lord's Supper

[14]Therefore, my dear friends, flee from idolatry. [15]I speak to sensible people; judge for yourselves what I say. [16]Is not the cup of thanksgiving

---

[a] 7 Exodus 32:6   [b] 9 Some manuscripts test the Lord   [c] 13 The Greek for temptation and tempted can also mean testing and tested.

for which we give thanks a participation in the blood of Christ? And is not the bread that we break a participation in the body of Christ? ¹⁷Because there is one loaf, we, who are many, are one body, for we all share the one loaf.

¹⁸Consider the people of Israel: Do not those who eat the sacrifices participate in the altar? ¹⁹Do I mean then that food sacrificed to an idol is anything, or that an idol is anything? ²⁰No, but the sacrifices of pagans are offered to demons, not to God, and I do not want you to be participants with demons. ²¹You cannot drink the cup of the Lord and the cup of demons too; you cannot have a part in both the Lord's table and the table of demons. ²²Are we trying to arouse the Lord's jealousy? Are we stronger than he?

The Believer's Freedom

²³"I have the right to do anything," you say — but not everything is beneficial. "I have the right to do anything" — but not everything is constructive. ²⁴No one should seek their own good, but the good of others.

²⁵Eat anything sold in the meat market without raising questions of conscience, ²⁶for, "The earth is the Lord's, and everything in it."ᵃ

²⁷If an unbeliever invites you to a meal and you want to go, eat whatever is put before you without raising questions of conscience. ²⁸But if someone says to you, "This has been offered in sacrifice," then do not eat it, both for the sake of the one who told you and for the sake of conscience. ²⁹I am referring to the other person's conscience, not yours. For why is my freedom being judged by another's conscience? ³⁰If I take part in the meal with thankfulness, why am I

denounced because of something I thank God for?

³¹So whether you eat or drink or whatever you do, do it all for the glory of God. ³²Do not cause anyone to stumble, whether Jews, Greeks or the church of God — ³³even as I try to please everyone in every way. For I am not seeking my own good but the good of many, so that they may **11** be saved. ¹Follow my example, as I follow the example of Christ.

On Covering the Head in Worship

²I praise you for remembering me in everything and for holding to the traditions just as I passed them on to you. ³But I want you to realize that the head of every man is Christ, and the head of the woman is man,ᵇ and the head of Christ is God. ⁴Every man who prays or prophesies with his head covered dishonors his head. ⁵But every woman who prays or prophesies with her head uncovered dishonors her head — it is the same as having her head shaved. ⁶For if a woman does not cover her head, she might as well have her hair cut off; but if it is a disgrace for a woman to have her hair cut off or her head shaved, then she should cover her head.

⁷A man ought not to cover his head,ᶜ since he is the image and glory of God; but woman is the glory of man. ⁸For man did not come from woman, but woman from man; ⁹nei-

---

ᵃ 26 Psalm 24:1   ᵇ 3 Or of the wife is her husband   ᶜ 4-7 Or ⁴Every man who prays or prophesies with long hair dishonors his head. ⁵But every woman who prays or prophesies with no covering of hair dishonors her head — she is just like one of the "shorn women." ⁶If a woman has no covering, let her be for now with short hair; but since it is a disgrace for a woman to have her hair shorn or shaved, she should grow it again. ⁷A man ought not to have long hair ther was man created for woman, but woman for man. ¹⁰It is for this reason that a woman ought to have authority over her own* head, because of the angels. ¹¹Nevertheless, in the Lord woman is not independent of man, nor is man independent of woman. ¹²For as woman came from man, so also man is born of woman. But everything comes from God.

¹³Judge for yourselves: Is it proper for a woman to pray to God with her head uncovered? ¹⁴Does not the very nature of things teach you that if a man has long hair, it is a disgrace to him, ¹⁵but that if a woman has long hair, it is her glory? For long hair is given to her as a covering. ¹⁶If anyone wants to be contentious about this, we have no other practice — nor do the churches of God.

Correcting an Abuse of the Lord's Supper

¹⁷In the following directives I have no praise for you, for your meetings do more harm than good. ¹⁸In the first place, I hear that when you come together as a church, there are divisions among you, and to some extent I believe it. ¹⁹No doubt there have to be differences among you to show which of you have God's approval. ²⁰So then, when you come together, it is not the Lord's Supper you eat, ²¹for when you are eating, some of you go ahead with your own private suppers. As a result, one person remains hungry and another gets drunk. ²²Don't you have homes to eat and drink in? Or do you despise the church of God by humiliating those who have nothing? What shall I say to you? Shall I praise you? Certainly not in this matter!

²³For I received from the Lord what I also passed on to you: The Lord Jesus, on the night he was betrayed,

took bread, ²⁴and when he had given thanks, he broke it and said, "This is my body, which is for you; do this in remembrance of me." ²⁵In the same way, after supper he took the cup, saying, "This cup is the new covenant in my blood; do this, whenever you drink it, in remembrance of me." ²⁶For whenever you eat this bread and drink this cup, you proclaim the Lord's death until he comes.

²⁷So then, whoever eats the bread or drinks the cup of the Lord in an unworthy manner will be guilty of sinning against the body and blood of the Lord. ²⁸Everyone ought to examine themselves before they eat of the bread and drink from the cup. ²⁹For those who eat and drink without discerning the body of Christ eat and drink judgment on themselves. ³⁰That is why many among you are weak and sick, and a number of you have fallen asleep. ³¹But if we were more discerning with regard to ourselves, we would not come under such judgment. ³²Nevertheless, when we are judged in this way by the Lord, we are being disciplined so that we will not be finally condemned with the world.

³³So then, my brothers and sisters, when you gather to eat, you should all eat together. ³⁴Anyone who is hungry should eat something at home, so that when you meet together it may not result in judgment.

And when I come I will give further directions.

Concerning Spiritual Gifts

12 Now about the gifts of the Spirit, brothers and sisters, I do not want you to be uninformed. ²You know that when you were pagans, somehow or other you were

---

*10 Or have a sign of authority on her

influenced and led astray to mute idols. ³Therefore I want you to know that no one who is speaking by the Spirit of God says, "Jesus be cursed," and no one can say, "Jesus is Lord," except by the Holy Spirit.

⁴There are different kinds of gifts, but the same Spirit distributes them. ⁵There are different kinds of service, but the same Lord. ⁶There are different kinds of working, but in all of them and in everyone it is the same God at work.

⁷Now to each one the manifestation of the Spirit is given for the common good. ⁸To one there is given through the Spirit a message of wisdom, to another a message of knowledge by means of the same Spirit, ⁹to another faith by the same Spirit, to another gifts of healing by that one Spirit, ¹⁰to another miraculous powers, to another prophecy, to another distinguishing between spirits, to another speaking in different kinds of tongues,ᵃ and to still another the interpretation of tongues.ᵃ ¹¹All these are the work of one and the same Spirit, and he distributes them to each one, just as he determines.

Unity and Diversity in the Body

¹²Just as a body, though one, has many parts, but all its many parts form one body, so it is with Christ. ¹³For we were all baptized byᵇ one Spirit so as to form one body—whether Jews or Gentiles, slave or free—and we were all given the one Spirit to drink. ¹⁴Even so the body is not made up of one part but of many.

¹⁵Now if the foot should say, "Because I am not a hand, I do not belong to the body," it would not for that reason stop being part of the body. ¹⁶And if the ear should say, "Because I am not an eye, I do not belong to the body," it would not for that reason stop being part of the body. ¹⁷If the whole body were an eye, where would the sense of hearing be? If the whole body were an ear, where would the sense of smell be? ¹⁸But in fact God has placed the parts in the body, every one of them, just as he wanted them to be. ¹⁹If they were all one part, where would the body be? ²⁰As it is, there are many parts, but one body.

²¹The eye cannot say to the hand, "I don't need you!" And the head cannot say to the feet, "I don't need you!" ²²On the contrary, those parts of the body that seem to be weaker are indispensable, ²³and the parts that we think are less honorable we treat with special honor. And the parts that are unpresentable are treated with special modesty, ²⁴while our presentable parts need no special treatment. But God has put the body together, giving greater honor to the parts that lacked it, ²⁵so that there should be no division in the body, but that its parts should have equal concern for each other. ²⁶If one part suffers, every part suffers with it; if one part is honored, every part rejoices with it.

²⁷Now you are the body of Christ, and each one of you is a part of it. ²⁸And God has placed in the church first of all apostles, second prophets, third teachers, then miracles, then gifts of healing, of helping, of guidance, and of different kinds of tongues. ²⁹Are all apostles? Are all prophets? Are all teachers? Do all work miracles? ³⁰Do all have gifts of healing? Do all speak in tonguesᶜ? Do all interpret? ³¹Now eagerly desire the greater gifts.

ᵃ 10 Or languages; also in verse 28   ᵇ 13 Or with; or in   ᶜ 30 Or other languages

Love Is Indispensable

And yet I will show you the most excellent way.

13 If I speak in the tongues[a] of men or of angels, but do not have love, I am only a resounding gong or a clanging cymbal. [2]If I have the gift of prophecy and can fathom all mysteries and all knowledge, and if I have a faith that can move mountains, but do not have love, I am nothing. [3]If I give all I possess to the poor and give over my body to hardship that I may boast,[b] but do not have love, I gain nothing.

[4]Love is patient, love is kind. It does not envy, it does not boast, it is not proud. [5]It does not dishonor others, it is not self-seeking, it is not easily angered, it keeps no record of wrongs. [6]Love does not delight in evil but rejoices with the truth. [7]It always protects, always trusts, always hopes, always perseveres.

[8]Love never fails. But where there are prophecies, they will cease; where there are tongues, they will be stilled; where there is knowledge, it will pass away. [9]For we know in part and we prophesy in part, [10]but when completeness comes, what is in part disappears. [11]When I was a child, I talked like a child, I thought like a child, I reasoned like a child. When I became a man, I put the ways of childhood behind me. [12]For now we see only a reflection as in a mirror; then we shall see face to face. Now I know in part; then I shall know fully, even as I am fully known.

[13]And now these three remain: faith, hope and love. But the greatest of these is love.

Intelligibility in Worship

14 Follow the way of love and eagerly desire gifts of the Spirit, especially prophecy. [2]For anyone who speaks in a tongue[c] does not speak to people but to God. Indeed, no one understands them; they utter mysteries by the Spirit. [3]But the one who prophesies speaks to people for their strengthening, encouraging and comfort. [4]Anyone who speaks in a tongue edifies themselves, but the one who prophesies edifies the church. [5]I would like every one of you to speak in tongues,[d] but I would rather have you prophesy. The one who prophesies is greater than the one who speaks in tongues,[d] unless someone interprets, so that the church may be edified.

[6]Now, brothers and sisters, if I come to you and speak in tongues, what good will I be to you, unless I bring you some revelation or knowledge or prophecy or word of instruction? [7]Even in the case of lifeless things that make sounds, such as the pipe or harp, how will anyone know what tune is being played unless there is a distinction in the notes? [8]Again, if the trumpet does not sound a clear call, who will get ready for battle? [9]So it is with you. Unless you speak intelligible words with your tongue, how will anyone know what you are saying? You will just be speaking into the air. [10]Undoubtedly there are all sorts of languages in the world, yet none of them is without meaning. [11]If then I do not grasp the meaning of what someone is saying, I am a foreigner to the speaker, and the speaker is a foreigner to me. [12]So it is with you. Since you are eager for gifts of the Spirit, try to excel in those that build up the church.

---

[a] 1 Or *languages*   [b] 3 Some manuscripts *body to the flames*   [c] 2 Or *in another language*; also in verses 4, 13, 14, 19, 26 and 27   [d] 5 Or *in other languages*; also in verses 6, 18, 22, 23 and 39

For this reason the one who speaks in a tongue should pray that they may interpret what they say. **14**For if I pray in a tongue, my spirit prays, but my mind is unfruitful. **15**So what shall I do? I will pray with my spirit, but I will also pray with my understanding; I will sing with my spirit, but I will also sing with my understanding. **16**Otherwise when you are praising God in the Spirit, how can someone else, who is now put in the position of an inquirer,*ᵃ* say "Amen" to your thanksgiving, since they do not know what you are saying? **17**You are giving thanks well enough, but no one else is edified.

18I thank God that I speak in tongues more than all of you. **19**But in the church I would rather speak five intelligible words to instruct others than ten thousand words in a tongue.

20Brothers and sisters, stop thinking like children. In regard to evil be infants, but in your thinking be adults. **21**In the Law it is written:

"With other tongues
 and through the lips of
  foreigners
I will speak to this people,
 but even then they will not
  listen to me,
   says the Lord."*ᵇ*

22Tongues, then, are a sign, not for believers but for unbelievers; prophecy, however, is not for unbelievers but for believers. **23**So if the whole church comes together and everyone speaks in tongues, and inquirers or unbelievers come in, will they not say that you are out of your mind? **24**But if an unbeliever or an inquirer comes in while everyone is prophesying, they are convicted of sin and are brought under judgment by all, **25**as the secrets of their hearts are laid bare. So they

will fall down and worship God, exclaiming, "God is really among you!"

Good Order in Worship

26What then shall we say, brothers and sisters? When you come together, each of you has a hymn, or a word of instruction, a revelation, a tongue or an interpretation. Everything must be done so that the church may be built up. **27**If anyone speaks in a tongue, two — or at the most three — should speak, one at a time, and someone must interpret. **28**If there is no interpreter, the speaker should keep quiet in the church and speak to himself and to God.

29Two or three prophets should speak, and the others should weigh carefully what is said. **30**And if a revelation comes to someone who is sitting down, the first speaker should stop. **31**For you can all prophesy in turn so that everyone may be instructed and encouraged. **32**The spirits of prophets are subject to the control of prophets. **33**For God is not a God of disorder but of peace — as in all the congregations of the Lord's people.

34Women*ᶜ* should remain silent in the churches. They are not allowed to speak, but must be in submission, as the law says. **35**If they want to inquire about something, they should ask their own husbands at home; for it is disgraceful for a woman to speak in the church.*ᵈ*

36Or did the word of God originate with you? Or are you the only people it has reached? **37**If anyone thinks

---

ᵃ 16 The Greek word for *inquirer* is a technical term for someone not fully initiated into a religion; also in verses 23 and 24.
ᵇ 21 Isaiah 28:11,12   *ᶜ 33,34* Or *peace. As in all the congregations of the Lord's people,* ³⁴*women*
ᵈ 34,35 In a few manuscripts these verses come after verse 40.

they are a prophet or otherwise gifted by the Spirit, let them acknowledge that what I am writing to you is the Lord's command. ³⁸But if anyone ignores this, they will themselves be ignored.^a

³⁹Therefore, my brothers and sisters, be eager to prophesy, and do not forbid speaking in tongues. ⁴⁰But everything should be done in a fitting and orderly way.

The Resurrection of Christ

15 Now, brothers and sisters, I want to remind you of the gospel I preached to you, which you received and on which you have taken your stand. ²By this gospel you are saved, if you hold firmly to the word I preached to you. Otherwise, you have believed in vain.

³For what I received I passed on to you as of first importance^b: that Christ died for our sins according to the Scriptures, ⁴that he was buried, that he was raised on the third day according to the Scriptures, ⁵and that he appeared to Cephas,^c and then to the Twelve. ⁶After that, he appeared to more than five hundred of the brothers and sisters at the same time, most of whom are still living, though some have fallen asleep. ⁷Then he appeared to James, then to all the apostles, ⁸and last of all he appeared to me also, as to one abnormally born.

⁹For I am the least of the apostles and do not even deserve to be called an apostle, because I persecuted the church of God. ¹⁰But by the grace of God I am what I am, and his grace to me was not without effect. No, I worked harder than all of them — yet not I, but the grace of God that was with me. ¹¹Whether, then, it is I or they, this is what we preach, and this is what you believed.

The Resurrection of the Dead

¹²But if it is preached that Christ has been raised from the dead, how can some of you say that there is no resurrection of the dead? ¹³If there is no resurrection of the dead, then not even Christ has been raised. ¹⁴And if Christ has not been raised, our preaching is useless and so is your faith. ¹⁵More than that, we are then found to be false witnesses about God, for we have testified about God that he raised Christ from the dead. But he did not raise him if in fact the dead are not raised. ¹⁶For if the dead are not raised, then Christ has not been raised either. ¹⁷And if Christ has not been raised, your faith is futile; you are still in your sins. ¹⁸Then those also who have fallen asleep in Christ are lost. ¹⁹If only for this life we have hope in Christ, we are of all people most to be pitied.

²⁰But Christ has indeed been raised from the dead, the firstfruits of those who have fallen asleep. ²¹For since death came through a man, the resurrection of the dead comes also through a man. ²²For as in Adam all die, so in Christ all will be made alive. ²³But each in turn: Christ, the firstfruits; then, when he comes, those who belong to him. ²⁴Then the end will come, when he hands over the kingdom to God the Father after he has destroyed all dominion, authority and power. ²⁵For he must reign until he has put all his enemies under his feet. ²⁶The last enemy to be destroyed is death. ²⁷For he "has put everything under his feet."^d Now when it says that "everything" has been put under him, it is clear that this does not include God himself, who put everything under Christ. ²⁸When

^a 38 Some manuscripts *But anyone who is ignorant of this will be ignorant*   ^b 3 Or *you at the first*   ^c 5 That is, Peter   ^d 27 Psalm 8:6

he has done this, then the Son himself will be made subject to him who put everything under him, so that God may be all in all.

[29] Now if there is no resurrection, what will those do who are baptized for the dead? If the dead are not raised at all, why are people baptized for them? [30] And as for us, why do we endanger ourselves every hour? [31] I face death every day — yes, just as surely as I boast about you in Christ Jesus our Lord. [32] If I fought wild beasts in Ephesus with no more than human hopes, what have I gained? If the dead are not raised,

> "Let us eat and drink,
>   for tomorrow we die." [a]

[33] Do not be misled: "Bad company corrupts good character." [b] [34] Come back to your senses as you ought, and stop sinning; for there are some who are ignorant of God — I say this to your shame.

The Resurrection Body

[35] But someone will ask, "How are the dead raised? With what kind of body will they come?" [36] How foolish! What you sow does not come to life unless it dies. [37] When you sow, you do not plant the body that will be, but just a seed, perhaps of wheat or of something else. [38] But God gives it a body as he has determined, and to each kind of seed he gives its own body. [39] Not all flesh is the same: People have one kind of flesh, animals have another, birds another and fish another. [40] There are also heavenly bodies and there are earthly bodies; but the splendor of the heavenly bodies is one kind, and the splendor of the earthly bodies is another. [41] The sun has one kind of splendor, the moon another and the stars another; and star differs from star in splendor.

[42] So will it be with the resurrection of the dead. The body that is sown is perishable, it is raised imperishable; [43] it is sown in dishonor, it is raised in glory; it is sown in weakness, it is raised in power; [44] it is sown a natural body, it is raised a spiritual body.

If there is a natural body, there is also a spiritual body. [45] So it is written: "The first man Adam became a living being" [c]; the last Adam, a life-giving spirit. [46] The spiritual did not come first, but the natural, and after that the spiritual. [47] The first man was of the dust of the earth; the second man is of heaven. [48] As was the earthly man, so are those who are of the earth; and as is the heavenly man, so also are those who are of heaven. [49] And just as we have borne the image of the earthly man, so shall we [d] bear the image of the heavenly man.

[50] I declare to you, brothers and sisters, that flesh and blood cannot inherit the kingdom of God, nor does the perishable inherit the imperishable. [51] Listen, I tell you a mystery: We will not all sleep, but we will all be changed — [52] in a flash, in the twinkling of an eye, at the last trumpet. For the trumpet will sound, the dead will be raised imperishable, and we will be changed. [53] For the perishable must clothe itself with the imperishable, and the mortal with immortality. [54] When the perishable has been clothed with the imperishable, and the mortal with immortality, then the saying that is written will come true: "Death has been swallowed up in victory." [e]

[55] "Where, O death, is your victory?
    Where, O death, is your sting?" [f]

---

[a] 32 Isaiah 22:13 [b] 33 From the Greek poet Menander [c] 45 Gen. 2:7 [d] 49 Some early manuscripts *so let us* [e] 54 Isaiah 25:8 [f] 55 Hosea 13:14

⁵⁶The sting of death is sin, and the power of sin is the law. ⁵⁷But thanks be to God! He gives us the victory through our Lord Jesus Christ.

⁵⁸Therefore, my dear brothers and sisters, stand firm. Let nothing move you. Always give yourselves fully to the work of the Lord, because you know that your labor in the Lord is not in vain.

The Collection for the Lord's People

16 Now about the collection for the Lord's people: Do what I told the Galatian churches to do. ²On the first day of every week, each one of you should set aside a sum of money in keeping with your income, saving it up, so that when I come no collections will have to be made. ³Then, when I arrive, I will give letters of introduction to the men you approve and send them with your gift to Jerusalem. ⁴If it seems advisable for me to go also, they will accompany me.

Personal Requests

⁵After I go through Macedonia, I will come to you — for I will be going through Macedonia. ⁶Perhaps I will stay with you for a while, or even spend the winter, so that you can help me on my journey, wherever I go. ⁷For I do not want to see you now and make only a passing visit; I hope to spend some time with you, if the Lord permits. ⁸But I will stay on at Ephesus until Pentecost, ⁹because a great door for effective work has opened to me, and there are many who oppose me.

¹⁰When Timothy comes, see to it that he has nothing to fear while he is with you, for he is carrying on the work of the Lord, just as I am. ¹¹No one, then, should treat him with contempt. Send him on his way in peace so that he may return to me. I am expecting him along with the brothers.

¹²Now about our brother Apollos: I strongly urged him to go to you with the brothers. He was quite unwilling to go now, but he will go when he has the opportunity.

¹³Be on your guard; stand firm in the faith; be courageous; be strong. ¹⁴Do everything in love.

¹⁵You know that the household of Stephanas were the first converts in Achaia, and they have devoted themselves to the service of the Lord's people. I urge you, brothers and sisters, ¹⁶to submit to such people and to everyone who joins in the work and labors at it. ¹⁷I was glad when Stephanas, Fortunatus and Achaicus arrived, because they have supplied what was lacking from you. ¹⁸For they refreshed my spirit and yours also. Such men deserve recognition.

Final Greetings

¹⁹The churches in the province of Asia send you greetings. Aquila and Priscilla*a* greet you warmly in the Lord, and so does the church that meets at their house. ²⁰All the brothers and sisters here send you greetings. Greet one another with a holy kiss.

²¹I, Paul, write this greeting in my own hand.

²²If anyone does not love the Lord, let that person be cursed! Come, Lord*b*!

²³The grace of the Lord Jesus be with you.

²⁴My love to all of you in Christ Jesus. Amen.*c*

---

a 19 Greek *Prisca*, a variant of *Priscilla*
b 22 The Greek for *Come, Lord* reproduces an Aramaic expression (*Marana tha*) used by early Christians.   *c 24* Some manuscripts do not have *Amen.*

2 Corinthians

1 Paul, an apostle of Christ Jesus by the will of God, and Timothy our brother,

To the church of God in Corinth, together with all his holy people throughout Achaia:

[2] Grace and peace to you from God our Father and the Lord Jesus Christ.

Praise to the God of All Comfort

[3] Praise be to the God and Father of our Lord Jesus Christ, the Father of compassion and the God of all comfort, [4] who comforts us in all our troubles, so that we can comfort those in any trouble with the comfort we ourselves receive from God. [5] For just as we share abundantly in the sufferings of Christ, so also our comfort abounds through Christ. [6] If we are distressed, it is for your comfort and salvation; if we are comforted, it is for your comfort, which produces in you patient endurance of the same sufferings we suffer. [7] And our hope for you is firm, because we know that just as you share in our sufferings, so also you share in our comfort.

[8] We do not want you to be uninformed, brothers and sisters,[a] about the troubles we experienced in the province of Asia. We were under great pressure, far beyond our ability to endure, so that we despaired of life itself. [9] Indeed, we felt we had received the sentence of death. But this happened that we might not rely on ourselves but on God, who raises the dead. [10] He has delivered us from such a deadly peril, and he will deliver us again. On him we have set our hope that he will continue to deliver us, [11] as you help us by your prayers. Then many will give thanks on our behalf for the gracious favor granted us in answer to the prayers of many.

Paul's Change of Plans

[12] Now this is our boast: Our conscience testifies that we have conducted ourselves in the world, and especially in our relations with you, with integrity[b] and godly sincerity. We have done so, relying not on worldly wisdom but on God's grace. [13] For we do not write you anything you cannot read or understand. And I hope that, [14] as you have understood us in part, you will come to understand fully that you can boast of us just as we will boast of you in the day of the Lord Jesus.

[15] Because I was confident of this, I wanted to visit you first so that you might benefit twice. [16] I wanted to visit you on my way to Macedonia and to come back to you from Macedonia, and then to have you send me on my way to Judea. [17] Was I fickle when I intended to do this? Or do I make my plans in a worldly manner so that in the same breath I say both "Yes, yes" and "No, no"?

[18] But as surely as God is faithful, our message to you is not "Yes" and "No." [19] For the Son of God, Jesus Christ, who was preached among you by us — by me and Silas[c] and Timothy — was not "Yes" and "No," but in

---

[a] 8 The Greek word for *brothers and sisters* (*adelphoi*) refers here to believers, both men and women, as part of God's family; also in 8:1; 13:11. [b] 12 Many manuscripts *holiness* [c] 19 Greek *Silvanus*, a variant of *Silas*

him it has always been "Yes." ²⁰For no matter how many promises God has made, they are "Yes" in Christ. And so through him the "Amen" is spoken by us to the glory of God. ²¹Now it is God who makes both us and you stand firm in Christ. He anointed us, ²²set his seal of ownership on us, and put his Spirit in our hearts as a deposit, guaranteeing what is to come.

²³I call God as my witness—and I stake my life on it—that it was in order to spare you that I did not return to Corinth. ²⁴Not that we lord it over your faith, but we work with you for your joy, because it is by faith **2** you stand firm. ¹So I made up my mind that I would not make another painful visit to you. ²For if I grieve you, who is left to make me glad but you whom I have grieved? ³I wrote as I did, so that when I came I would not be distressed by those who should have made me rejoice. I had confidence in all of you, that you would all share my joy. ⁴For I wrote you out of great distress and anguish of heart and with many tears, not to grieve you but to let you know the depth of my love for you.

Forgiveness for the Offender

⁵If anyone has caused grief, he has not so much grieved me as he has grieved all of you to some extent—not to put it too severely. ⁶The punishment inflicted on him by the majority is sufficient. ⁷Now instead, you ought to forgive and comfort him, so that he will not be overwhelmed by excessive sorrow. ⁸I urge you, therefore, to reaffirm your love for him. ⁹Another reason I wrote you was to see if you would stand the test and be obedient in everything. ¹⁰Anyone you forgive, I also forgive. And what I have forgiven—if there was anything to forgive—I have forgiven in the sight of Christ for your sake, ¹¹in order that Satan might not outwit us. For we are not unaware of his schemes.

Ministers of the New Covenant

¹²Now when I went to Troas to preach the gospel of Christ and found that the Lord had opened a door for me, ¹³I still had no peace of mind, because I did not find my brother Titus there. So I said goodbye to them and went on to Macedonia.

¹⁴But thanks be to God, who always leads us as captives in Christ's triumphal procession and uses us to spread the aroma of the knowledge of him everywhere. ¹⁵For we are to God the pleasing aroma of Christ among those who are being saved and those who are perishing. ¹⁶To the one we are an aroma that brings death; to the other, an aroma that brings life. And who is equal to such a task? ¹⁷Unlike so many, we do not peddle the word of God for profit. On the contrary, in Christ we speak before God with sincerity, as those sent from God.

3 Are we beginning to commend ourselves again? Or do we need, like some people, letters of recommendation to you or from you? ²You yourselves are our letter, written on our hearts, known and read by everyone. ³You show that you are a letter from Christ, the result of our ministry, written not with ink but with the Spirit of the living God, not on tablets of stone but on tablets of human hearts.

⁴Such confidence we have through Christ before God. ⁵Not that we are competent in ourselves to claim anything for ourselves, but our competence comes from God. ⁶He has made us competent as ministers of a new covenant—not of the letter but of the Spirit; for the letter kills, but the Spirit gives life.

The Greater Glory of the New Covenant

7 Now if the ministry that brought death, which was engraved in letters on stone, came with glory, so that the Israelites could not look steadily at the face of Moses because of its glory, transitory though it was, 8 will not the ministry of the Spirit be even more glorious? 9 If the ministry that brought condemnation was glorious, how much more glorious is the ministry that brings righteousness! 10 For what was glorious has no glory now in comparison with the surpassing glory. 11 And if what was transitory came with glory, how much greater is the glory of that which lasts!

12 Therefore, since we have such a hope, we are very bold. 13 We are not like Moses, who would put a veil over his face to prevent the Israelites from seeing the end of what was passing away. 14 But their minds were made dull, for to this day the same veil remains when the old covenant is read. It has not been removed, because only in Christ is it taken away. 15 Even to this day when Moses is read, a veil covers their hearts. 16 But whenever anyone turns to the Lord, the veil is taken away. 17 Now the Lord is the Spirit, and where the Spirit of the Lord is, there is freedom. 18 And we all, who with unveiled faces contemplate[a] the Lord's glory, are being transformed into his image with ever-increasing glory, which comes from the Lord, who is the Spirit.

Present Weakness and Resurrection Life

4 Therefore, since through God's mercy we have this ministry, we do not lose heart. 2 Rather, we have renounced secret and shameful ways; we do not use deception, nor do we distort the word of God. On the contrary, by setting forth the truth plainly we commend ourselves to everyone's conscience in the sight of God. 3 And even if our gospel is veiled, it is veiled to those who are perishing. 4 The god of this age has blinded the minds of unbelievers, so that they cannot see the light of the gospel that displays the glory of Christ, who is the image of God. 5 For what we preach is not ourselves, but Jesus Christ as Lord, and ourselves as your servants for Jesus' sake. 6 For God, who said, "Let light shine out of darkness,"[b] made his light shine in our hearts to give us the light of the knowledge of God's glory displayed in the face of Christ.

7 But we have this treasure in jars of clay to show that this all-surpassing power is from God and not from us. 8 We are hard pressed on every side, but not crushed; perplexed, but not in despair; 9 persecuted, but not abandoned; struck down, but not destroyed. 10 We always carry around in our body the death of Jesus, so that the life of Jesus may also be revealed in our body. 11 For we who are alive are always being given over to death for Jesus' sake, so that his life may also be revealed in our mortal body. 12 So then, death is at work in us, but life is at work in you.

13 It is written: "I believed; therefore I have spoken."[c] Since we have that same spirit of[d] faith, we also believe and therefore speak, 14 because we know that the one who raised the Lord Jesus from the dead will also raise us with Jesus and present us with you to himself. 15 All this is for your benefit, so that the grace that is reaching more and more people

---

[a] 18 Or reflect   [b] 6 Gen. 1:3
[c] 13 Psalm 116:10 (see Septuagint)   [d] 13 Or Spirit-given

may cause thanksgiving to overflow to the glory of God.

¹⁶Therefore we do not lose heart. Though outwardly we are wasting away, yet inwardly we are being renewed day by day. ¹⁷For our light and momentary troubles are achieving for us an eternal glory that far outweighs them all. ¹⁸So we fix our eyes not on what is seen, but on what is unseen, since what is seen is temporary, but what is unseen is eternal.

Awaiting the New Body

5 For we know that if the earthly tent we live in is destroyed, we have a building from God, an eternal house in heaven, not built by human hands. ²Meanwhile we groan, longing to be clothed instead with our heavenly dwelling, ³because when we are clothed, we will not be found naked. ⁴For while we are in this tent, we groan and are burdened, because we do not wish to be unclothed but to be clothed instead with our heavenly dwelling, so that what is mortal may be swallowed up by life. ⁵Now the one who has fashioned us for this very purpose is God, who has given us the Spirit as a deposit, guaranteeing what is to come.

⁶Therefore we are always confident and know that as long as we are at home in the body we are away from the Lord. ⁷For we live by faith, not by sight. ⁸We are confident, I say, and would prefer to be away from the body and at home with the Lord. ⁹So we make it our goal to please him, whether we are at home in the body or away from it. ¹⁰For we must all appear before the judgment seat of Christ, so that each of us may receive what is due us for the things done while in the body, whether good or bad.

The Ministry of Reconciliation

¹¹Since, then, we know what it is to fear the Lord, we try to persuade others. What we are is plain to God, and I hope it is also plain to your conscience. ¹²We are not trying to commend ourselves to you again, but are giving you an opportunity to take pride in us, so that you can answer those who take pride in what is seen rather than in what is in the heart. ¹³If we are "out of our mind," as some say, it is for God; if we are in our right mind, it is for you. ¹⁴For Christ's love compels us, because we are convinced that one died for all, and therefore all died. ¹⁵And he died for all, that those who live should no longer live for themselves but for him who died for them and was raised again.

¹⁶So from now on we regard no one from a worldly point of view. Though we once regarded Christ in this way, we do so no longer. ¹⁷Therefore, if anyone is in Christ, the new creation has come:ᵃ The old has gone, the new is here! ¹⁸All this is from God, who reconciled us to himself through Christ and gave us the ministry of reconciliation: ¹⁹that God was reconciling the world to himself in Christ, not counting people's sins against them. And he has committed to us the message of reconciliation. ²⁰We are therefore Christ's ambassadors, as though God were making his appeal through us. We implore you on Christ's behalf: Be reconciled to God. ²¹God made him who had no sin to be sinᵇ for us, so that in him we might become the righteousness of God.

6 As God's co-workers we urge you not to receive God's grace in vain. ²For he says,

---

ᵃ 17 Or *Christ, that person is a new creation.*
ᵇ 21 Or *be a sin offering*

"In the time of my favor I heard
you,
and in the day of salvation I
helped you."[a]

I tell you, now is the time of God's
favor, now is the day of salvation.

Paul's Hardships

[3]We put no stumbling block in anyone's path, so that our ministry will
not be discredited. [4]Rather, as servants of God we commend ourselves
in every way: in great endurance; in
troubles, hardships and distresses; [5]in
beatings, imprisonments and riots;
in hard work, sleepless nights and
hunger; [6]in purity, understanding,
patience and kindness; in the Holy
Spirit and in sincere love; [7]in truthful speech and in the power of God;
with weapons of righteousness in the
right hand and in the left; [8]through
glory and dishonor, bad report and
good report; genuine, yet regarded
as impostors; [9]known, yet regarded
as unknown; dying, and yet we live
on; beaten, and yet not killed; [10]sor-
rowful, yet always rejoicing; poor, yet
making many rich; having nothing,
and yet possessing everything.

[11]We have spoken freely to you,
Corinthians, and opened wide our
hearts to you. [12]We are not withholding our affection from you, but you
are withholding yours from us. [13]As a
fair exchange — I speak as to my children — open wide your hearts also.

Warning Against Idolatry

[14]Do not be yoked together with unbelievers. For what do righteousness
and wickedness have in common? Or
what fellowship can light have with
darkness? [15]What harmony is there
between Christ and Belial[b]? Or what
does a believer have in common with
an unbeliever? [16]What agreement is

there between the temple of God and
idols? For we are the temple of the
living God. As God has said:

"I will live with them
and walk among them,
and I will be their God,
and they will be my people."[c]

[17]Therefore,

"Come out from them
and be separate,
       says the Lord.
Touch no unclean thing,
and I will receive you."[d]

[18]And,

"I will be a Father to you,
and you will be my sons and
daughters,
    says the Lord Almighty."[e]

7 Therefore, since we have these
promises, dear friends, let us
purify ourselves from everything
that contaminates body and spirit,
perfecting holiness out of reverence
for God.

Paul's Joy Over the Church's Repentance

[2]Make room for us in your hearts.
We have wronged no one, we have
corrupted no one, we have exploit-
ed no one. [3]I do not say this to condemn you; I have said before that you
have such a place in our hearts that
we would live or die with you. [4]I have
spoken to you with great frankness; I
take great pride in you. I am greatly
encouraged; in all our troubles my
joy knows no bounds.

[5]For when we came into Macedonia, we had no rest, but we were ha-

---

[a] 2 Isaiah 49:8   [b] 15 Greek *Beliar*, a variant of
Belial   [c] 16 Lev. 26:12; Jer. 32:38; Ezek. 37:27
[d] 17 Isaiah 52:11; Ezek. 20:34,41
[e] 18 2 Samuel 7:14; 7:8

rassed at every turn — conflicts on the outside, fears within. ⁶But God, who comforts the downcast, comforted us by the coming of Titus, ⁷and not only by his coming but also by the comfort you had given him. He told us about your longing for me, your deep sorrow, your ardent concern for me, so that my joy was greater than ever.

⁸Even if I caused you sorrow by my letter, I do not regret it. Though I did regret it — I see that my letter hurt you, but only for a little while — ⁹yet now I am happy, not because you were made sorry, but because your sorrow led you to repentance. For you became sorrowful as God intended and so were not harmed in any way by us. ¹⁰Godly sorrow brings repentance that leads to salvation and leaves no regret, but worldly sorrow brings death. ¹¹See what this godly sorrow has produced in you: what earnestness, what eagerness to clear yourselves, what indignation, what alarm, what longing, what concern, what readiness to see justice done. At every point you have proved yourselves to be innocent in this matter. ¹²So even though I wrote to you, it was neither on account of the one who did the wrong nor on account of the injured party, but rather that before God you could see for yourselves how devoted to us you are. ¹³By all this we are encouraged.

In addition to our own encouragement, we were especially delighted to see how happy Titus was, because his spirit has been refreshed by all of you. ¹⁴I had boasted to him about you, and you have not embarrassed me. But just as everything we said to you was true, so our boasting about you to Titus has proved to be true as well. ¹⁵And his affection for you is all the greater when he remembers that you were all obedient, receiving him with fear and trembling. ¹⁶I am glad I can have complete confidence in you.

The Collection for the Lord's People

SAnd now, brothers and sisters, we want you to know about the grace that God has given the Macedonian churches. ²In the midst of a very severe trial, their overflowing joy and their extreme poverty welled up in rich generosity. ³For I testify that they gave as much as they were able, and even beyond their ability. Entirely on their own, ⁴they urgently pleaded with us for the privilege of sharing in this service to the Lord's people. ⁵And they exceeded our expectations: They gave themselves first of all to the Lord, and then by the will of God also to us. ⁶So we urged Titus, just as he had earlier made a beginning, to bring also to completion this act of grace on your part. ⁷But since you excel in everything — in faith, in speech, in knowledge, in complete earnestness and in the love we have kindled in youᵃ — see that you also excel in this grace of giving.

⁸I am not commanding you, but I want to test the sincerity of your love by comparing it with the earnestness of others. ⁹For you know the grace of our Lord Jesus Christ, that though he was rich, yet for your sake he became poor, so that you through his poverty might become rich.

¹⁰And here is my judgment about what is best for you in this matter. Last year you were the first not only to give but also to have the desire to do so. ¹¹Now finish the work, so that your eager willingness to do it may be matched by your completion of it,

---

ᵃ 7 Some manuscripts *and in your love for us*

according to your means. ¹²For if the willingness is there, the gift is acceptable according to what one has, not according to what one does not have.

¹³Our desire is not that others might be relieved while you are hard pressed, but that there might be equality. ¹⁴At the present time your plenty will supply what they need, so that in turn their plenty will supply what you need. The goal is equality, ¹⁵as it is written: "The one who gathered much did not have too much, and the one who gathered little did not have too little."ᵃ

Titus Sent to Receive the Collection

¹⁶Thanks be to God, who put into the heart of Titus the same concern I have for you. ¹⁷For Titus not only welcomed our appeal, but he is coming to you with much enthusiasm and on his own initiative. ¹⁸And we are sending along with him the brother who is praised by all the churches for his service to the gospel. ¹⁹What is more, he was chosen by the churches to accompany us as we carry the offering, which we administer in order to honor the Lord himself and to show our eagerness to help. ²⁰We want to avoid any criticism of the way we administer this liberal gift. ²¹For we are taking pains to do what is right, not only in the eyes of the Lord but also in the eyes of man.

²²In addition, we are sending with them our brother who has often proved to us in many ways that he is zealous, and now even more so because of his great confidence in you. ²³As for Titus, he is my partner and co-worker among you; as for our brothers, they are representatives of the churches and an honor to Christ. ²⁴Therefore show these men the proof of your love and the reason for our pride in you, so that the churches can see it.

9 There is no need for me to write to you about this service to the Lord's people. ²For I know your eagerness to help, and I have been boasting about it to the Macedonians, telling them that since last year you in Achaia were ready to give; and your enthusiasm has stirred most of them to action. ³But I am sending the brothers in order that our boasting about you in this matter should not prove hollow, but that you may be ready, as I said you would be. ⁴For if any Macedonians come with me and find you unprepared, we — not to say anything about you — would be ashamed of having been so confident. ⁵So I thought it necessary to urge the brothers to visit you in advance and finish the arrangements for the generous gift you had promised. Then it will be ready as a generous gift, not as one grudgingly given.

Generosity Encouraged

⁶Remember this: Whoever sows sparingly will also reap sparingly, and whoever sows generously will also reap generously. ⁷Each of you should give what you have decided in your heart to give, not reluctantly or under compulsion, for God loves a cheerful giver. ⁸And God is able to bless you abundantly, so that in all things at all times, having all that you need, you will abound in every good work. ⁹As it is written:

"They have freely scattered their
    gifts to the poor;
  their righteousness endures
    forever."ᵇ

ᵃ 15 Exodus 16:18   ᵇ 9 Psalm 112:9

¹⁰Now he who supplies seed to the sower and bread for food will also supply and increase your store of seed and will enlarge the harvest of your righteousness. ¹¹You will be enriched in every way so that you can be generous on every occasion, and through us your generosity will result in thanksgiving to God.

¹²This service that you perform is not only supplying the needs of the Lord's people but is also overflowing in many expressions of thanks to God. ¹³Because of the service by which you have proved yourselves, others will praise God for the obedience that accompanies your confession of the gospel of Christ, and for your generosity in sharing with them and with everyone else. ¹⁴And in their prayers for you their hearts will go out to you, because of the surpassing grace God has given you. ¹⁵Thanks be to God for his indescribable gift!

Paul's Defense of His Ministry

10 By the humility and gentleness of Christ, I appeal to you — I, Paul, who am "timid" when face to face with you, but "bold" toward you when away! ²I beg you that when I come I may not have to be as bold as I expect to be toward some people who think that we live by the standards of this world. ³For though we live in the world, we do not wage war as the world does. ⁴The weapons we fight with are not the weapons of the world. On the contrary, they have divine power to demolish strongholds. ⁵We demolish arguments and every pretension that sets itself up against the knowledge of God, and we take captive every thought to make it obedient to Christ. ⁶And we will be ready to punish every act of disobedience, once your obedience is complete.

⁷You are judging by appearances.ᵃ If anyone is confident that they belong to Christ, they should consider again that we belong to Christ just as much as they do. ⁸So even if I boast somewhat freely about the authority the Lord gave us for building you up rather than tearing you down, I will not be ashamed of it. ⁹I do not want to seem to be trying to frighten you with my letters. ¹⁰For some say, "His letters are weighty and forceful, but in person he is unimpressive and his speaking amounts to nothing." ¹¹Such people should realize that what we are in our letters when we are absent, we will be in our actions when we are present.

¹²We do not dare to classify or compare ourselves with some who commend themselves. When they measure themselves by themselves and compare themselves with themselves, they are not wise. ¹³We, however, will not boast beyond proper limits, but will confine our boasting to the sphere of service God himself has assigned to us, a sphere that also includes you. ¹⁴We are not going too far in our boasting, as would be the case if we had not come to you, for we did get as far as you with the gospel of Christ. ¹⁵Neither do we go beyond our limits by boasting of work done by others. Our hope is that, as your faith continues to grow, our sphere of activity among you will greatly expand, ¹⁶so that we can preach the gospel in the regions beyond you. For we do not want to boast about work already done in someone else's territory. ¹⁷But, "Let the one who boasts boast in the Lord."ᵇ ¹⁸For it is not the one who commends himself who is approved, but the one whom the Lord commends.

ᵃ 7 Or Look at the obvious facts   ᵇ 17 Jer. 9:24

Paul and the False Apostles

11 I hope you will put up with me in a little foolishness. Yes, please put up with me! ²I am jealous for you with a godly jealousy. I promised you to one husband, to Christ, so that I might present you as a pure virgin to him. ³But I am afraid that just as Eve was deceived by the serpent's cunning, your minds may somehow be led astray from your sincere and pure devotion to Christ. ⁴For if someone comes to you and preaches a Jesus other than the Jesus we preached, or if you receive a different spirit from the Spirit you received, or a different gospel from the one you accepted, you put up with it easily enough.

⁵I do not think I am in the least inferior to those "super-apostles."ᵃ ⁶I may indeed be untrained as a speaker, but I do have knowledge. We have made this perfectly clear to you in every way. ⁷Was it a sin for me to lower myself in order to elevate you by preaching the gospel of God to you free of charge? ⁸I robbed other churches by receiving support from them so as to serve you. ⁹And when I was with you and needed something, I was not a burden to anyone, for the brothers who came from Macedonia supplied what I needed. I have kept myself from being a burden to you in any way, and will continue to do so. ¹⁰As surely as the truth of Christ is in me, nobody in the regions of Achaia will stop this boasting of mine. ¹¹Why? Because I do not love you? God knows I do!

¹²And I will keep on doing what I am doing in order to cut the ground from under those who want an opportunity to be considered equal with us in the things they boast about. ¹³For such people are false apostles, deceitful workers, masquerading as

apostles of Christ. ¹⁴And no wonder, for Satan himself masquerades as an angel of light. ¹⁵It is not surprising, then, if his servants also masquerade as servants of righteousness. Their end will be what their actions deserve.

Paul Boasts About His Sufferings

¹⁶I repeat: Let no one take me for a fool. But if you do, then tolerate me just as you would a fool, so that I may do a little boasting. ¹⁷In this self-confident boasting I am not talking as the Lord would, but as a fool. ¹⁸Since many are boasting in the way the world does, I too will boast. ¹⁹You gladly put up with fools since you are so wise! ²⁰In fact, you even put up with anyone who enslaves you or exploits you or takes advantage of you or puts on airs or slaps you in the face. ²¹To my shame I admit that we were too weak for that!

Whatever anyone else dares to boast about — I am speaking as a fool — I also dare to boast about. ²²Are they Hebrews? So am I. Are they Israelites? So am I. Are they Abraham's descendants? So am I. ²³Are they servants of Christ? (I am out of my mind to talk like this.) I am more. I have worked much harder, been in prison more frequently, been flogged more severely, and been exposed to death again and again. ²⁴Five times I received from the Jews the forty lashes minus one. ²⁵Three times I was beaten with rods, once I was pelted with stones, three times I was shipwrecked, I spent a night and a day in the open sea, ²⁶I have been constantly on the move. I have been in danger from rivers, in danger from bandits, in danger from my fellow Jews, in danger from Gentiles; in danger in

---

ᵃ 5 Or to the most eminent apostles

the city, in danger in the country, in danger at sea; and in danger from false believers. ²⁷I have labored and toiled and have often gone without sleep; I have known hunger and thirst and have often gone without food; I have been cold and naked. ²⁸Besides everything else, I face daily the pressure of my concern for all the churches. ²⁹Who is weak, and I do not feel weak? Who is led into sin, and I do not inwardly burn?

³⁰If I must boast, I will boast of the things that show my weakness. ³¹The God and Father of the Lord Jesus, who is to be praised forever, knows that I am not lying. ³²In Damascus the governor under King Aretas had the city of the Damascenes guarded in order to arrest me. ³³But I was lowered in a basket from a window in the wall and slipped through his hands.

Paul's Vision and His Thorn

12 I must go on boasting. Although there is nothing to be gained, I will go on to visions and revelations from the Lord. ²I know a man in Christ who fourteen years ago was caught up to the third heaven. Whether it was in the body or out of the body I do not know — God knows. ³And I know that this man — whether in the body or apart from the body I do not know, but God knows — ⁴was caught up to paradise and heard inexpressible things, things that no one is permitted to tell. ⁵I will boast about a man like that, but I will not boast about myself, except about my weaknesses. ⁶Even if I should choose to boast, I would not be a fool, because I would be speaking the truth. But I refrain, so no one will think more of me than is warranted by what I do or say, ⁷or because of these surpassingly great revelations. Therefore, in order

to keep me from becoming conceited, I was given a thorn in my flesh, a messenger of Satan, to torment me. ⁸Three times I pleaded with the Lord to take it away from me. ⁹But he said to me, "My grace is sufficient for you, for my power is made perfect in weakness." Therefore I will boast all the more gladly about my weaknesses, so that Christ's power may rest on me. ¹⁰That is why, for Christ's sake, I delight in weaknesses, in insults, in hardships, in persecutions, in difficulties. For when I am weak, then I am strong.

Paul's Concern for the Corinthians

¹¹I have made a fool of myself, but you drove me to it. I ought to have been commended by you, for I am not in the least inferior to the "super-apostles,"ᵃ even though I am nothing. ¹²I persevered in demonstrating among you the marks of a true apostle, including signs, wonders and miracles. ¹³How were you inferior to the other churches, except that I was never a burden to you? Forgive me this wrong!

¹⁴Now I am ready to visit you for the third time, and I will not be a burden to you, because what I want is not your possessions but you. After all, children should not have to save up for their parents, but parents for their children. ¹⁵So I will very gladly spend for you everything I have and expend myself as well. If I love you more, will you love me less? ¹⁶Be that as it may, I have not been a burden to you. Yet, crafty fellow that I am, I caught you by trickery! ¹⁷Did I exploit you through any of the men I sent to you? ¹⁸I urged Titus to go to

---

ᵃ 11 Or *the most eminent apostles*

you and I sent our brother with him. Titus did not exploit you, did he? Did we not walk in the same footsteps by the same Spirit?

¹⁹Have you been thinking all along that we have been defending ourselves to you? We have been speaking in the sight of God as those in Christ; and everything we do, dear friends, is for your strengthening. ²⁰For I am afraid that when I come I may not find you as I want you to be, and you may not find me as you want me to be. I fear that there may be discord, jealousy, fits of rage, selfish ambition, slander, gossip, arrogance and disorder. ²¹I am afraid that when I come again my God will humble me before you, and I will be grieved over many who have sinned earlier and have not repented of the impurity, sexual sin and debauchery in which they have indulged.

Final Warnings

13 This will be my third visit to you. "Every matter must be established by the testimony of two or three witnesses."ᵃ ²I already gave you a warning when I was with you the second time. I now repeat it while absent: On my return I will not spare those who sinned earlier or any of the others, ³since you are demanding proof that Christ is speaking through me. He is not weak in dealing with you, but is powerful among you. ⁴For to be sure, he was crucified in weakness, yet he lives by God's power. Likewise, we are weak in him, yet by God's power we will live with him in our dealing with you.

⁵Examine yourselves to see whether you are in the faith; test yourselves. Do you not realize that Christ Jesus is in you — unless, of course, you fail the test? ⁶And I trust that you will discover that we have not failed the test. ⁷Now we pray to God that you will not do anything wrong — not so that people will see that we have stood the test but so that you will do what is right even though we may seem to have failed. ⁸For we cannot do anything against the truth, but only for the truth. ⁹We are glad whenever we are weak but you are strong; and our prayer is that you may be fully restored. ¹⁰This is why I write these things when I am absent, that when I come I may not have to be harsh in my use of authority — the authority the Lord gave me for building you up, not for tearing you down.

Final Greetings

¹¹Finally, brothers and sisters, rejoice! Strive for full restoration, encourage one another, be of one mind, live in peace. And the God of love and peace will be with you.

¹²Greet one another with a holy kiss. ¹³All God's people here send their greetings.

¹⁴May the grace of the Lord Jesus Christ, and the love of God, and the fellowship of the Holy Spirit be with you all.

ᵃ 1 Deut. 19:15

Galatians

1

Paul, an apostle — sent not from men nor by a man, but by Jesus Christ and God the Father, who raised him from the dead — ²and all the brothers and sisters[a] with me,

To the churches in Galatia:

³Grace and peace to you from God our Father and the Lord Jesus Christ, ⁴who gave himself for our sins to rescue us from the present evil age, according to the will of our God and Father, ⁵to whom be glory for ever and ever. Amen.

No Other Gospel

⁶I am astonished that you are so quickly deserting the one who called you to live in the grace of Christ and are turning to a different gospel — ⁷which is really no gospel at all. Evidently some people are throwing you into confusion and are trying to pervert the gospel of Christ. ⁸But even if we or an angel from heaven should preach a gospel other than the one we preached to you, let them be under God's curse! ⁹As we have already said, so now I say again: If anybody is preaching to you a gospel other than what you accepted, let them be under God's curse!

¹⁰Am I now trying to win the approval of human beings, or of God? Or am I trying to please people? If I were still trying to please people, I would not be a servant of Christ.

Paul Called by God

¹¹I want you to know, brothers and sisters, that the gospel I preached is not of human origin. ¹²I did not receive it from any man, nor was I taught it; rather, I received it by revelation from Jesus Christ.

¹³For you have heard of my previous way of life in Judaism, how intensely I persecuted the church of God and tried to destroy it. ¹⁴I was advancing in Judaism beyond many of my own age among my people and was extremely zealous for the traditions of my fathers. ¹⁵But when God, who set me apart from my mother's womb and called me by his grace, was pleased ¹⁶to reveal his Son in me so that I might preach him among the Gentiles, my immediate response was not to consult any human being. ¹⁷I did not go up to Jerusalem to see those who were apostles before I was, but I went into Arabia. Later I returned to Damascus.

¹⁸Then after three years, I went up to Jerusalem to get acquainted with Cephas[b] and stayed with him fifteen days. ¹⁹I saw none of the other apostles — only James, the Lord's brother. ²⁰I assure you before God that what I am writing you is no lie.

²¹Then I went to Syria and Cilicia. ²²I was personally unknown to the churches of Judea that are in Christ. ²³They only heard the report: "The man who formerly persecuted us is now preaching the faith he once tried to destroy." ²⁴And they praised God because of me.

Paul Accepted by the Apostles

2

Then after fourteen years, I went up again to Jerusalem, this time with Barnabas. I took Titus along also. ²I went in response to a revelation and, meeting privately with

---

[a] 2 The Greek word for *brothers and sisters* (*adelphoi*) refers here to believers, both men and women, as part of God's family; also in verse 11; and in 3:15; 4:12, 28, 31; 5:11, 13; 6:1, 18.
[b] 18 That is, Peter

those esteemed as leaders, I presented to them the gospel that I preach among the Gentiles. I wanted to be sure I was not running and had not been running my race in vain. ³Yet not even Titus, who was with me, was compelled to be circumcised, even though he was a Greek. ⁴This matter arose because some false believers had infiltrated our ranks to spy on the freedom we have in Christ Jesus and to make us slaves. ⁵We did not give in to them for a moment, so that the truth of the gospel might be preserved for you.

⁶As for those who were held in high esteem — whatever they were makes no difference to me; God does not show favoritism — they added nothing to my message. ⁷On the contrary, they recognized that I had been entrusted with the task of preaching the gospel to the uncircumcised,ᵃ just as Peter had been to the circumcised.ᵇ ⁸For God, who was at work in Peter as an apostle to the circumcised, was also at work in me as an apostle to the Gentiles. ⁹James, Cephasᶜ and John, those esteemed as pillars, gave me and Barnabas the right hand of fellowship when they recognized the grace given to me. They agreed that we should go to the Gentiles, and they to the circumcised. ¹⁰All they asked was that we should continue to remember the poor, the very thing I had been eager to do all along.

Paul Opposes Cephas

¹¹When Cephas came to Antioch, I opposed him to his face, because he stood condemned. ¹²For before certain men came from James, he used to eat with the Gentiles. But when they arrived, he began to draw back and separate himself from the Gentiles because he was afraid of those

who belonged to the circumcision group. The other Jews joined him in his hypocrisy, so that by their hypocrisy even Barnabas was led astray.

¹⁴When I saw that they were not acting in line with the truth of the gospel, I said to Cephas in front of them all, "You are a Jew, yet you live like a Gentile and not like a Jew. How is it, then, that you force Gentiles to follow Jewish customs?

¹⁵"We who are Jews by birth and not sinful Gentiles ¹⁶know that a person is not justified by the works of the law, but by faith in Jesus Christ. So we, too, have put our faith in Christ Jesus that we may be justified by faith inᵈ Christ and not by the works of the law, because by the works of the law no one will be justified.

¹⁷"But if, in seeking to be justified in Christ, we Jews find ourselves also among the sinners, doesn't that mean that Christ promotes sin? Absolutely not! ¹⁸If I rebuild what I destroyed, then I really would be a lawbreaker.

¹⁹"For through the law I died to the law so that I might live for God. ²⁰I have been crucified with Christ and I no longer live, but Christ lives in me. The life I now live in the body, I live by faith in the Son of God, who loved me and gave himself for me. ²¹I do not set aside the grace of God, for if righteousness could be gained through the law, Christ died for nothing!"ᵉ

Faith or Works of the Law

3 You foolish Galatians! Who has bewitched you? Before your very eyes Jesus Christ was clearly portrayed as crucified. ²I would like to

ᵃ 7 That is, Gentiles   ᵇ 7 That is, Jews; also in verses 8 and 9   ᶜ 9 That is, Peter; also in verses 11 and 14   ᵈ 16 Or but through the faithfulness of . . . justified on the basis of the faithfulness of   ᵉ 21 Some interpreters end the quotation after verse 14.

learn just one thing from you: Did you receive the Spirit by the works of the law, or by believing what you heard? ³Are you so foolish? After beginning by means of the Spirit, are you now trying to finish by means of the flesh?ᵃ ⁴Have you experiencedᵇ so much in vain — if it really was in vain? ⁵So again I ask, does God give you his Spirit and work miracles among you by the works of the law, or by your believing what you heard? ⁶So also Abraham "believed God, and it was credited to him as righteousness."ᶜ

⁷Understand, then, that those who have faith are children of Abraham. ⁸Scripture foresaw that God would justify the Gentiles by faith, and announced the gospel in advance to Abraham: "All nations will be blessed through you."ᵈ ⁹So those who rely on faith are blessed along with Abraham, the man of faith.

¹⁰For all who rely on the works of the law are under a curse, as it is written: "Cursed is everyone who does not continue to do everything written in the Book of the Law."ᵉ ¹¹Clearly no one who relies on the law is justified before God, because "the righteous will live by faith."ᶠ ¹²The law is not based on faith; on the contrary, it says, "The person who does these things will live by them."ᵍ ¹³Christ redeemed us from the curse of the law by becoming a curse for us, for it is written: "Cursed is everyone who is hung on a pole."ʰ ¹⁴He redeemed us in order that the blessing given to Abraham might come to the Gentiles through Christ Jesus, so that by faith we might receive the promise of the Spirit.

The Law and the Promise

¹⁵Brothers and sisters, let me take an example from everyday life. Just as no one can set aside or add to a human covenant that has been duly established, so it is in this case. ¹⁶The promises were spoken to Abraham and to his seed. Scripture does not say "and to seeds," meaning many people, but "and to your seed,"ⁱ meaning one person, who is Christ. ¹⁷What I mean is this: The law, introduced 430 years later, does not set aside the covenant previously established by God and thus do away with the promise. ¹⁸For if the inheritance depends on the law, then it no longer depends on the promise; but God in his grace gave it to Abraham through a promise.

¹⁹Why, then, was the law given at all? It was added because of transgressions until the Seed to whom the promise referred had come. The law was given through angels and entrusted to a mediator. ²⁰A mediator, however, implies more than one party; but God is one.

²¹Is the law, therefore, opposed to the promises of God? Absolutely not! For if a law had been given that could impart life, then righteousness would certainly have come by the law. ²²But Scripture has locked up everything under the control of sin, so that what was promised, being given through faith in Jesus Christ, might be given to those who believe.

Children of God

²³Before the coming of this faith,ʲ we were held in custody under the law, locked up until the faith that was to come would be revealed. ²⁴So the

---

ᵃ 3 In contexts like this, the Greek word for *flesh* (sarx) refers to the sinful state of human beings, often presented as a power in opposition to the Spirit.   ᵇ 4 Or *suffered*
ᶜ 6 Gen. 15:6   ᵈ 8 Gen. 12:3; 18:18; 22:18
ᵉ 10 Deut. 27:26   ᶠ 11 Hab. 2:4   ᵍ 12 Lev. 18:5
ʰ 13 Deut. 21:23   ⁱ 16 Gen. 12:7; 13:15; 24:7
ʲ 22,23 Or *through the faithfulness of Jesus* . . .
ᵏ Before faith came

law was our guardian until Christ came that we might be justified by faith. [25]Now that this faith has come, we are no longer under a guardian.

[26]So in Christ Jesus you are all children of God through faith, [27]for all of you who were baptized into Christ have clothed yourselves with Christ. [28]There is neither Jew nor Gentile, neither slave nor free, nor is there male and female, for you are all one in Christ Jesus. [29]If you belong to Christ, then you are Abraham's seed, and heirs according to the promise.

4 What I am saying is that as long as an heir is underage, he is no different from a slave, although he owns the whole estate. [2]The heir is subject to guardians and trustees until the time set by his father. [3]So also, when we were underage, we were in slavery under the elemental spiritual forces[c] of the world. [4]But when the set time had fully come, God sent his Son, born of a woman, born under the law, [5]to redeem those under the law, that we might receive adoption to sonship.[b] [6]Because you are his sons, God sent the Spirit of his Son into our hearts, the Spirit who calls out, "Abba,[c] Father." [7]So you are no longer a slave, but God's child; and since you are his child, God has made you also an heir.

Paul's Concern for the Galatians

[8]Formerly, when you did not know God, you were slaves to those who by nature are not gods. [9]But now that you know God — or rather are known by God — how is it that you are turning back to those weak and miserable forces[d]? Do you wish to be enslaved by them all over again? [10]You are observing special days and months and seasons and years! [11]I fear for you,

that somehow I have wasted my efforts on you.

[12]I plead with you, brothers and sisters, become like me, for I became like you. You did me no wrong. [13]As you know, it was because of an illness that I first preached the gospel to you, [14]and even though my illness was a trial to you, you did not treat me with contempt or scorn. Instead, you welcomed me as if I were an angel of God, as if I were Christ Jesus himself. [15]Where, then, is your blessing of me now? I can testify that, if you could have done so, you would have torn out your eyes and given them to me. [16]Have I now become your enemy by telling you the truth?

[17]Those people are zealous to win you over, but for no good. What they want is to alienate you from us, so that you may have zeal for them. [18]It is fine to be zealous, provided the purpose is good, and to be so always, not just when I am with you. [19]My dear children, for whom I am again in the pains of childbirth until Christ is formed in you, [20]how I wish I could be with you now and change my tone, because I am perplexed about you!

Hagar and Sarah

[21]Tell me, you who want to be under the law, are you not aware of what the law says? [22]For it is written that Abraham had two sons, one by the slave woman and the other by the free woman. [23]His son by the slave woman was born according to the flesh, but his son by the free woman was born as the result of a divine promise. [24]These things are being taken

---

[c] 3 Or under the basic principles   *[b] 5 The Greek word for adoption to sonship is a legal term referring to the full legal standing of an adopted male heir in Roman culture.*   *[c] 6 Aramaic for Father*   *[d] 9 Or principles*

figuratively: The women represent two covenants. One covenant is from Mount Sinai and bears children who are to be slaves: This is Hagar. 25Now Hagar stands for Mount Sinai in Arabia and corresponds to the present city of Jerusalem, because she is in slavery with her children. 26But the Jerusalem that is above is free, and she is our mother. 27For it is written:

> "Be glad, barren woman,
>   you who never bore a child;
> shout for joy and cry aloud,
>   you who were never in labor;
> because more are the children of
>   the desolate woman
>   than of her who has a
>   husband."[a]

28Now you, brothers and sisters, like Isaac, are children of promise. 29At that time the son born according to the flesh persecuted the son born by the power of the Spirit. It is the same now. 30But what does Scripture say? "Get rid of the slave woman and her son, for the slave woman's son will never share in the inheritance with the free woman's son."[b] 31Therefore, brothers and sisters, we are not children of the slave woman, but of the free woman.

Freedom in Christ

5 It is for freedom that Christ has set us free. Stand firm, then, and do not let yourselves be burdened again by a yoke of slavery.

2Mark my words! I, Paul, tell you that if you let yourselves be circumcised, Christ will be of no value to you at all. 3Again I declare to every man who lets himself be circumcised that he is obligated to obey the whole law. 4You who are trying to be justified by the law have been alienated from Christ; you have fallen away

from grace. 5For through the Spirit we eagerly await by faith the righteousness for which we hope. 6For in Christ Jesus neither circumcision nor uncircumcision has any value. The only thing that counts is faith expressing itself through love.

7You were running a good race. Who cut in on you to keep you from obeying the truth? 8That kind of persuasion does not come from the one who calls you. 9"A little yeast works through the whole batch of dough." 10I am confident in the Lord that you will take no other view. The one who is throwing you into confusion, whoever that may be, will have to pay the penalty. 11Brothers and sisters, if I am still preaching circumcision, why am I still being persecuted? In that case the offense of the cross has been abolished. 12As for those agitators, I wish they would go the whole way and emasculate themselves!

Life by the Spirit

13You, my brothers and sisters, were called to be free. But do not use your freedom to indulge the flesh[c]; rather, serve one another humbly in love. 14For the entire law is fulfilled in keeping this one command: "Love your neighbor as yourself."[d] 15If you bite and devour each other, watch out or you will be destroyed by each other.

16So I say, walk by the Spirit, and you will not gratify the desires of the flesh. 17For the flesh desires what is contrary to the Spirit, and the Spirit what is contrary to the flesh. They are in conflict with each other, so that

---

[a] 27 Isaiah 54:1 [b] 30 Gen. 21:10 [c] 13 In contexts like this, the Greek word for *flesh* (*sarx*) refers to the sinful state of human beings, often presented as a power in opposition to the Spirit; also in verses 16, 17, 19 and 24; and in 6:8. [d] 14 Lev. 19:18

you are not to do whatever[a] you want. [18]But if you are led by the Spirit, you are not under the law.

[19]The acts of the flesh are obvious: sexual immorality, impurity and debauchery; [20]idolatry and witchcraft; hatred, discord, jealousy, fits of rage, selfish ambition, dissensions, factions [21]and envy; drunkenness, orgies, and the like. I warn you, as I did before, that those who live like this will not inherit the kingdom of God.

[22]But the fruit of the Spirit is love, joy, peace, forbearance, kindness, goodness, faithfulness, [23]gentleness and self-control. Against such things there is no law. [24]Those who belong to Christ Jesus have crucified the flesh with its passions and desires. [25]Since we live by the Spirit, let us keep in step with the Spirit. [26]Let us not become conceited, provoking and envying each other.

Doing Good to All

6 Brothers and sisters, if someone is caught in a sin, you who live by the Spirit should restore that person gently. But watch yourselves, or you also may be tempted. [2]Carry each other's burdens, and in this way you will fulfill the law of Christ. [3]If anyone thinks they are something when they are not, they deceive themselves. [4]Each one should test their own actions. Then they can take pride in themselves alone, without comparing themselves to someone else, [5]for each one should carry their own load. [6]Nevertheless, the one who receives instruction in the word should share all good things with their instructor.

[7]Do not be deceived: God cannot be mocked. A man reaps what he sows. [8]Whoever sows to please their flesh, from the flesh will reap destruction; whoever sows to please the Spirit, from the Spirit will reap eternal life. [9]Let us not become weary in doing good, for at the proper time we will reap a harvest if we do not give up. [10]Therefore, as we have opportunity, let us do good to all people, especially to those who belong to the family of believers.

Not Circumcision but the New Creation

[11]See what large letters I use as I write to you with my own hand! [12]Those who want to impress people by means of the flesh are trying to compel you to be circumcised. The only reason they do this is to avoid being persecuted for the cross of Christ. [13]Not even those who are circumcised keep the law, yet they want you to be circumcised that they may boast about your circumcision in the flesh. [14]May I never boast except in the cross of our Lord Jesus Christ, through which[b] the world has been crucified to me, and I to the world. [15]Neither circumcision nor uncircumcision means anything; what counts is the new creation. [16]Peace and mercy to all who follow this rule — to[c] the Israel of God.

[17]From now on, let no one cause me trouble, for I bear on my body the marks of Jesus.

[18]The grace of our Lord Jesus Christ be with your spirit, brothers and sisters. Amen.

---

[a] 17 Or *you do not do what*   [b] 14 Or *whom*
[c] 16 Or *rule and to*

Ephesians

1

Paul, an apostle of Christ Jesus by the will of God,

To God's holy people in Ephesus,[a] the faithful in Christ Jesus:

²Grace and peace to you from God our Father and the Lord Jesus Christ.

Praise for Spiritual Blessings in Christ

³Praise be to the God and Father of our Lord Jesus Christ, who has blessed us in the heavenly realms with every spiritual blessing in Christ. ⁴For he chose us in him before the creation of the world to be holy and blameless in his sight. In love ⁵he[b] predestined us for adoption to sonship[c] through Jesus Christ, in accordance with his pleasure and will — ⁶to the praise of his glorious grace, which he has freely given us in the One he loves. ⁷In him we have redemption through his blood, the forgiveness of sins, in accordance with the riches of God's grace ⁸that he lavished on us. With all wisdom and understanding, ⁹he[d] made known to us the mystery of his will according to his good pleasure, which he purposed in Christ, ¹⁰to be put into effect when the times reach their fulfillment — to bring unity to all things in heaven and on earth under Christ.

¹¹In him we were also chosen,[e] having been predestined according to the plan of him who works out everything in conformity with the purpose of his will, ¹²in order that we, who were the first to put our hope in Christ, might be for the praise of his glory. ¹³And you also were included in Christ when you heard the message

of truth, the gospel of your salvation. When you believed, you were marked in him with a seal, the promised Holy Spirit, ¹⁴who is a deposit guaranteeing our inheritance until the redemption of those who are God's possession — to the praise of his glory.

Thanksgiving and Prayer

¹⁵For this reason, ever since I heard about your faith in the Lord Jesus and your love for all God's people, ¹⁶I have not stopped giving thanks for you, remembering you in my prayers. ¹⁷I keep asking that the God of our Lord Jesus Christ, the glorious Father, may give you the Spirit[f] of wisdom and revelation, so that you may know him better. ¹⁸I pray that the eyes of your heart may be enlightened in order that you may know the hope to which he has called you, the riches of his glorious inheritance in his holy people, ¹⁹and his incomparably great power for us who believe. That power is the same as the mighty strength ²⁰he exerted when he raised Christ from the dead and seated him at his right hand in the heavenly realms, ²¹far above all rule and authority, power and dominion, and every name that is invoked, not only in the present age but also in the one to come. ²²And God placed all things under his feet and appointed him to be head over everything for the church, ²³which is his body, the

---

[a] 1 Some early manuscripts do not have *in Ephesus.*   [b] 4,5 Or *sight in love.*   [c] *He*   [c] 5 The Greek word for *adoption to sonship* is a legal term referring to the full legal standing of an adopted male heir in Roman culture.
[d] 8,9 Or *us with all wisdom and understanding.*
[e] *And he*   [e] 11 Or *were made heirs*   [f] 17 Or *a spirit*

fullness of him who fills everything in every way.

Made Alive in Christ

2 As for you, you were dead in your transgressions and sins, [2]in which you used to live when you followed the ways of this world and of the ruler of the kingdom of the air, the spirit who is now at work in those who are disobedient. [3]All of us also lived among them at one time, gratifying the cravings of our flesh[c] and following its desires and thoughts. Like the rest, we were by nature deserving of wrath. [4]But because of his great love for us, God, who is rich in mercy, [5]made us alive with Christ even when we were dead in transgressions — it is by grace you have been saved. [6]And God raised us up with Christ and seated us with him in the heavenly realms in Christ Jesus, [7]in order that in the coming ages he might show the incomparable riches of his grace, expressed in his kindness to us in Christ Jesus. [8]For it is by grace you have been saved, through faith — and this is not from yourselves, it is the gift of God — [9]not by works, so that no one can boast. [10]For we are God's handiwork, created in Christ Jesus to do good works, which God prepared in advance for us to do.

Jew and Gentile Reconciled Through Christ

[11]Therefore, remember that formerly you who are Gentiles by birth and called "uncircumcised" by those who call themselves "the circumcision" (which is done in the body by human hands) — [12]remember that at that time you were separate from Christ, excluded from citizenship in Israel and foreigners to the covenants of the promise, without hope and without God in the world. [13]But now in Christ Jesus you who once were far away have been brought near by the blood of Christ.

[14]For he himself is our peace, who has made the two groups one and has destroyed the barrier, the dividing wall of hostility, [15]by setting aside in his flesh the law with its commands and regulations. His purpose was to create in himself one new humanity out of the two, thus making peace, [16]and in one body to reconcile both of them to God through the cross, by which he put to death their hostility. [17]He came and preached peace to you who were far away and peace to those who were near. [18]For through him we both have access to the Father by one Spirit.

[19]Consequently, you are no longer foreigners and strangers, but fellow citizens with God's people and also members of his household, [20]built on the foundation of the apostles and prophets, with Christ Jesus himself as the chief cornerstone. [21]In him the whole building is joined together and rises to become a holy temple in the Lord. [22]And in him you too are being built together to become a dwelling in which God lives by his Spirit.

God's Marvelous Plan for the Gentiles

3 For this reason I, Paul, the prisoner of Christ Jesus for the sake of you Gentiles —

[2]Surely you have heard about the administration of God's grace that was given to me for you, [3]that is, the mystery made known to me by

---

[c] 3 In contexts like this, the Greek word for *flesh* (*sarx*) refers to the sinful state of human beings, often presented as a power in opposition to the Spirit.

revelation, as I have already written briefly. ⁴In reading this, then, you will be able to understand my insight into the mystery of Christ, ⁵which was not made known to people in other generations as it has now been revealed by the Spirit to God's holy apostles and prophets. ⁶This mystery is that through the gospel the Gentiles are heirs together with Israel, members together of one body, and sharers together in the promise in Christ Jesus.

⁷I became a servant of this gospel by the gift of God's grace given me through the working of his power. ⁸Although I am less than the least of all the Lord's people, this grace was given me: to preach to the Gentiles the boundless riches of Christ, ⁹and to make plain to everyone the administration of this mystery, which for ages past was kept hidden in God, who created all things. ¹⁰His intent was that now, through the church, the manifold wisdom of God should be made known to the rulers and authorities in the heavenly realms, ¹¹according to his eternal purpose that he accomplished in Christ Jesus our Lord. ¹²In him and through faith in him we may approach God with freedom and confidence. ¹³I ask you, therefore, not to be discouraged because of my sufferings for you, which are your glory.

A Prayer for the Ephesians

¹⁴For this reason I kneel before the Father, ¹⁵from whom every family*ᵃ* in heaven and on earth derives its name. ¹⁶I pray that out of his glorious riches he may strengthen you with power through his Spirit in your inner being, ¹⁷so that Christ may dwell in your hearts through faith. And I pray that you, being rooted and established in love, ¹⁸may have power, together with all the Lord's holy people, to grasp how wide and long and high and deep is the love of Christ, ¹⁹and to know this love that surpasses knowledge — that you may be filled to the measure of all the fullness of God.

²⁰Now to him who is able to do immeasurably more than all we ask or imagine, according to his power that is at work within us, ²¹to him be glory in the church and in Christ Jesus throughout all generations, for ever and ever! Amen.

Unity and Maturity in the Body of Christ

4 As a prisoner for the Lord, then, I urge you to live a life worthy of the calling you have received. ²Be completely humble and gentle; be patient, bearing with one another in love. ³Make every effort to keep the unity of the Spirit through the bond of peace. ⁴There is one body and one Spirit, just as you were called to one hope when you were called; ⁵one Lord, one faith, one baptism; ⁶one God and Father of all, who is over all and through all and in all.

⁷But to each one of us grace has been given as Christ apportioned it. ⁸This is why itᵇ says:

"When he ascended on high,
  he took many captives
    and gave gifts to his people."ᶜ

⁹(What does "he ascended" mean except that he also descended to the lower, earthly regionsᵈ? ¹⁰He who descended is the very one who ascended higher than all the heavens, in order to fill the whole universe.)

ᵃ *15* The Greek for *family (patria)* is derived from the Greek for *father (pater).*   ᵇ *8* Or *God*   ᶜ *8* Psalm 68:18   ᵈ *9* Or *the depths of the earth*

¹¹So Christ himself gave the apostles, the prophets, the evangelists, the pastors and teachers, ¹²to equip his people for works of service, so that the body of Christ may be built up ¹³until we all reach unity in the faith and in the knowledge of the Son of God and become mature, attaining to the whole measure of the fullness of Christ.

¹⁴Then we will no longer be infants, tossed back and forth by the waves, and blown here and there by every wind of teaching and by the cunning and craftiness of people in their deceitful scheming. ¹⁵Instead, speaking the truth in love, we will grow to become in every respect the mature body of him who is the head, that is, Christ. ¹⁶From him the whole body, joined and held together by every supporting ligament, grows and builds itself up in love, as each part does its work.

Instructions for Christian Living

¹⁷So I tell you this, and insist on it in the Lord, that you must no longer live as the Gentiles do, in the futility of their thinking. ¹⁸They are darkened in their understanding and separated from the life of God because of the ignorance that is in them due to the hardening of their hearts. ¹⁹Having lost all sensitivity, they have given themselves over to sensuality so as to indulge in every kind of impurity, and they are full of greed.

²⁰That, however, is not the way of life you learned ²¹when you heard about Christ and were taught in him in accordance with the truth that is in Jesus. ²²You were taught, with regard to your former way of life, to put off your old self, which is being corrupted by its deceitful desires; ²³to be made new in the attitude of your minds; ²⁴and to put on the new self, created to be like God in true righteousness and holiness.

²⁵Therefore each of you must put off falsehood and speak truthfully to your neighbor, for we are all members of one body. ²⁶"In your anger do not sin"ᵃ: Do not let the sun go down while you are still angry, ²⁷and do not give the devil a foothold. ²⁸Anyone who has been stealing must steal no longer, but must work, doing something useful with their own hands, that they may have something to share with those in need.

²⁹Do not let any unwholesome talk come out of your mouths, but only what is helpful for building others up according to their needs, that it may benefit those who listen. ³⁰And do not grieve the Holy Spirit of God, with whom you were sealed for the day of redemption. ³¹Get rid of all bitterness, rage and anger, brawling and slander, along with every form of malice. ³²Be kind and compassionate to one another, forgiving each other, just as in Christ God forgave you. ¹Follow God's example, therefore, as dearly loved children ²and walk in the way of love, just as Christ loved us and gave himself up for us as a fragrant offering and sacrifice to God.

³But among you there must not be even a hint of sexual immorality, or of any kind of impurity, or of greed, because these are improper for God's holy people. ⁴Nor should there be obscenity, foolish talk or coarse joking, which are out of place, but rather thanksgiving. ⁵For of this you can be sure: No immoral, impure or greedy person — such a person is

---

ᵃ 26 Psalm 4:4 (see Septuagint)

an idolater — has any inheritance in the kingdom of Christ and of God.[a] [6]Let no one deceive you with empty words, for because of such things God's wrath comes on those who are disobedient. [7]Therefore do not be partners with them.

[8]For you were once darkness, but now you are light in the Lord. Live as children of light [9](for the fruit of the light consists in all goodness, righteousness and truth) [10]and find out what pleases the Lord. [11]Have nothing to do with the fruitless deeds of darkness, but rather expose them. [12]It is shameful even to mention what the disobedient do in secret. [13]But everything exposed by the light becomes visible — and everything that is illuminated becomes a light. [14]This is why it is said:

> "Wake up, sleeper,
>   rise from the dead,
>   and Christ will shine
>   on you."

[15]Be very careful, then, how you live — not as unwise but as wise, [16]making the most of every opportunity, because the days are evil. [17]Therefore do not be foolish, but understand what the Lord's will is. [18]Do not get drunk on wine, which leads to debauchery. Instead, be filled with the Spirit, [19]speaking to one another with psalms, hymns, and songs from the Spirit. Sing and make music from your heart to the Lord, [20]always giving thanks to God the Father for everything, in the name of our Lord Jesus Christ.

Instructions for Christian Households

[21]Submit to one another out of reverence for Christ.

[22]Wives, submit yourselves to your own husbands as you do to the Lord. [23]For the husband is the head of the wife as Christ is the head of the church, his body, of which he is the Savior. [24]Now as the church submits to Christ, so also wives should submit to their husbands in everything.

[25]Husbands, love your wives, just as Christ loved the church and gave himself up for her [26]to make her holy, cleansing[b] her by the washing with water through the word, [27]and to present her to himself as a radiant church, without stain or wrinkle or any other blemish, but holy and blameless. [28]In this same way, husbands ought to love their wives as their own bodies. He who loves his wife loves himself. [29]After all, no one ever hated their own body, but they feed and care for their body, just as Christ does the church — [30]for we are members of his body. [31]"For this reason a man will leave his father and mother and be united to his wife, and the two will become one flesh."[c] [32]This is a profound mystery — but I am talking about Christ and the church. [33]However, each one of you also must love his wife as he loves himself, and the wife must respect her husband.

6 Children, obey your parents in the Lord, for this is right. [2]"Honor your father and mother" — which is the first commandment with a promise — [3]"so that it may go well with you and that you may enjoy long life on the earth."[d]

[4]Fathers,[e] do not exasperate your children; instead, bring them up in the training and instruction of the Lord.

[5]Slaves, obey your earthly masters with respect and fear, and with sincerity of heart, just as you would obey

---

[a] 5 Or *kingdom of the Messiah and God*
[b] 26 Or *having cleansed*   [c] 31 Gen. 2:24
[d] 3 Deut. 5:16   [e] 4 Or *Parents*

Christ. [6]Obey them not only to win their favor when their eye is on you, but as slaves of Christ, doing the will of God from your heart. [7]Serve wholeheartedly, as if you were serving the Lord, not people, [8]because you know that the Lord will reward each one for whatever good they do, whether they are slave or free.

[9]And masters, treat your slaves in the same way. Do not threaten them, since you know that he who is both their Master and yours is in heaven, and there is no favoritism with him.

The Armor of God

[10]Finally, be strong in the Lord and in his mighty power. [11]Put on the full armor of God, so that you can take your stand against the devil's schemes. [12]For our struggle is not against flesh and blood, but against the rulers, against the authorities, against the powers of this dark world and against the spiritual forces of evil in the heavenly realms. [13]Therefore put on the full armor of God, so that when the day of evil comes, you may be able to stand your ground, and after you have done everything, to stand. [14]Stand firm then, with the belt of truth buckled around your waist, with the breastplate of righteousness in place, [15]and with your feet fitted with the readiness that comes from the gospel of peace. [16]In addition to all this, take up the shield of faith, with which you can extinguish all the flaming arrows of the evil one. [17]Take the helmet of salvation and the sword of the Spirit, which is the word of God.

[18]And pray in the Spirit on all occasions with all kinds of prayers and requests. With this in mind, be alert and always keep on praying for all the Lord's people. [19]Pray also for me, that whenever I speak, words may be given me so that I will fearlessly make known the mystery of the gospel, [20]for which I am an ambassador in chains. Pray that I may declare it fearlessly, as I should.

Final Greetings

[21]Tychicus, the dear brother and faithful servant in the Lord, will tell you everything, so that you also may know how I am and what I am doing. [22]I am sending him to you for this very purpose, that you may know how we are, and that he may encourage you.

[23]Peace to the brothers and sisters,[a] and love with faith from God the Father and the Lord Jesus Christ. [24]Grace to all who love our Lord Jesus Christ with an undying love.[b]

---

[a] 23 The Greek word for *brothers and sisters* (*adelphoi*) refers here to believers, both men and women, as part of God's family.　[b] 24 Or *Grace and immortality to all who love our Lord Jesus Christ.*

Philippians

1 Paul and Timothy, servants of Christ Jesus,

To all God's holy people in Christ Jesus at Philippi, together with the overseers and deacons[a]:

2 Grace and peace to you from God our Father and the Lord Jesus Christ.

Thanksgiving and Prayer

3 I thank my God every time I remember you. 4 In all my prayers for all of you, I always pray with joy 5 because of your partnership in the gospel from the first day until now, 6 being confident of this, that he who began a good work in you will carry it on to completion until the day of Christ Jesus.

7 It is right for me to feel this way about all of you, since I have you in my heart and, whether I am in chains or defending and confirming the gospel, all of you share in God's grace with me. 8 God can testify how I long for all of you with the affection of Christ Jesus.

9 And this is my prayer: that your love may abound more and more in knowledge and depth of insight, 10 so that you may be able to discern what is best and may be pure and blameless for the day of Christ, 11 filled with the fruit of righteousness that comes through Jesus Christ — to the glory and praise of God.

Paul's Chains Advance the Gospel

12 Now I want you to know, brothers and sisters,[b] that what has happened to me has actually served to advance the gospel. 13 As a result, it has become clear throughout the whole palace guard[c] and to everyone else that I am in chains for Christ. 14 And because of my chains, most of the brothers and sisters have become confident in the Lord and dare all the more to proclaim the gospel without fear.

15 It is true that some preach Christ out of envy and rivalry, but others out of goodwill. 16 The latter do so out of love, knowing that I am put here for the defense of the gospel. 17 The former preach Christ out of selfish ambition, not sincerely, supposing that they can stir up trouble for me while I am in chains. 18 But what does it matter? The important thing is that in every way, whether from false motives or true, Christ is preached. And because of this I rejoice.

Yes, and I will continue to rejoice, 19 for I know that through your prayers and God's provision of the Spirit of Jesus Christ what has happened to me will turn out for my deliverance.[d] 20 I eagerly expect and hope that I will in no way be ashamed, but will have sufficient courage so that now as always Christ will be exalted in my body, whether by life or by death. 21 For to me, to live is Christ and to die is gain. 22 If I am to go on living in the body, this will mean fruitful labor for me. Yet what shall I choose? I do not know! 23 I am torn between the two:

---

a 1 The word *deacons* refers here to Christians designated to serve with the overseers/elders of the church in a variety of ways; similarly in Romans 16:1 and 1 Tim. 3:8,12.   *b* 12 The Greek word for *brothers and sisters (adelphoi)* refers here to believers, both men and women, as part of God's family; also in verse 14; and in 3:1, 13, 17; 4:1, 8, 21.   *c* 13 Or *whole palace*   *d* 19 Or *vindication;* or *salvation*

I desire to depart and be with Christ, which is better by far; ²⁴but it is more necessary for you that I remain in the body. ²⁵Convinced of this, I know that I will remain, and I will continue with all of you for your progress and joy in the faith, ²⁶so that through my being with you again your boasting in Christ Jesus will abound on account of me.

Life Worthy of the Gospel

²⁷Whatever happens, conduct yourselves in a manner worthy of the gospel of Christ. Then, whether I come and see you or only hear about you in my absence, I will know that you stand firm in the one Spirit,ᵃ striving together as one for the faith of the gospel ²⁸without being frightened in any way by those who oppose you. This is a sign to them that they will be destroyed, but that you will be saved — and that by God. ²⁹For it has been granted to you on behalf of Christ not only to believe in him, but also to suffer for him, ³⁰since you are going through the same struggle you saw I had, and now hear that I still have.

Imitating Christ's Humility

2 Therefore if you have any encouragement from being united with Christ, if any comfort from his love, if any common sharing in the Spirit, if any tenderness and compassion, ²then make my joy complete by being like-minded, having the same love, being one in spirit and of one mind. ³Do nothing out of selfish ambition or vain conceit. Rather, in humility value others above yourselves, ⁴not looking to your own interests but each of you to the interests of the others.

⁵In your relationships with one another, have the same mindset as Christ Jesus:

⁶Who, being in very natureᵇ God,
did not consider equality with
God something to be used
to his own advantage;
⁷rather, he made himself nothing
by taking the very natureᶜ of a
servant,
being made in human
likeness.
⁸And being found in appearance
as a man,
he humbled himself
by becoming obedient to
death —
even death on a cross!

⁹Therefore God exalted him to the
highest place
and gave him the name that is
above every name,
¹⁰that at the name of Jesus every
knee should bow,
in heaven and on earth and
under the earth,
¹¹and every tongue acknowledge
that Jesus Christ
is Lord,
to the glory of God the
Father.

Do Everything Without Grumbling

¹²Therefore, my dear friends, as you have always obeyed — not only in my presence, but now much more in my absence — continue to work out your salvation with fear and trembling, ¹³for it is God who works in you to will and to act in order to fulfill his good purpose.

¹⁴Do everything without grumbling or arguing, ¹⁵so that you may become blameless and pure, "children of God without fault in a warped and crooked generation."ᵈ Then you will shine

---

ᵃ 27 Or in one spirit   ᵇ 6 Or in the form of
ᶜ 7 Or the form   ᵈ 15 Deut. 32:5

among them like stars in the sky [16]as you hold firmly to the word of life. And then I will be able to boast on the day of Christ that I did not run or labor in vain. [17]But even if I am being poured out like a drink offering on the sacrifice and service coming from your faith, I am glad and rejoice with all of you. [18]So you too should be glad and rejoice with me.

Timothy and Epaphroditus

[19]I hope in the Lord Jesus to send Timothy to you soon, that I also may be cheered when I receive news about you. [20]I have no one else like him, who will show genuine concern for your welfare. [21]For everyone looks out for their own interests, not those of Jesus Christ. [22]But you know that Timothy has proved himself, because as a son with his father he has served with me in the work of the gospel. [23]I hope, therefore, to send him as soon as I see how things go with me. [24]And I am confident in the Lord that I myself will come soon.

[25]But I think it is necessary to send back to you Epaphroditus, my brother, co-worker and fellow soldier, who is also your messenger, whom you sent to take care of my needs. [26]For he longs for all of you and is distressed because you heard he was ill. [27]Indeed he was ill, and almost died. But God had mercy on him, and not on him only but also on me, to spare me sorrow upon sorrow. [28]Therefore I am all the more eager to send him, so that when you see him again you may be glad and I may have less anxiety. [29]So then, welcome him in the Lord with great joy, and honor people like him, [30]because he almost died for the work of Christ. He risked his life to make up for the help you yourselves could not give me.

No Confidence in the Flesh

3 Further, my brothers and sisters, rejoice in the Lord! It is no trouble for me to write the same things to you again, and it is a safeguard for you. [2]Watch out for those dogs, those evildoers, those mutilators of the flesh. [3]For it is who we are the circumcision, we who serve God by his Spirit, who boast in Christ Jesus, and who put no confidence in the flesh — [4]though I myself have reasons for such confidence.

If someone else thinks they have reasons to put confidence in the flesh, I have more: [5]circumcised on the eighth day, of the people of Israel, of the tribe of Benjamin, a Hebrew of Hebrews; in regard to the law, a Pharisee; [6]as for zeal, persecuting the church; as for righteousness based on the law, faultless.

[7]But whatever were gains to me I now consider loss for the sake of Christ. [8]What is more, I consider everything a loss because of the surpassing worth of knowing Christ Jesus my Lord, for whose sake I have lost all things. I consider them garbage, that I may gain Christ [9]and be found in him, not having a righteousness of my own that comes from the law, but that which is through faith in[a] Christ — the righteousness that comes from God on the basis of faith. [10]I want to know Christ — yes, to know the power of his resurrection and participation in his sufferings, becoming like him in his death, [11]and so, somehow, attaining to the resurrection from the dead.

[12]Not that I have already obtained all this, or have already arrived at my goal, but I press on to take hold of that for which Christ Jesus took hold of me. [13]Brothers and sisters, I do not

---

[a] 9 Or *through the faithfulness of*

consider myself yet to have taken hold of it. But one thing I do: Forgetting what is behind and straining toward what is ahead, [14]I press on toward the goal to win the prize for which God has called me heavenward in Christ Jesus.

Following Paul's Example

[15]All of us, then, who are mature should take such a view of things. And if on some point you think differently, that too God will make clear to you. [16]Only let us live up to what we have already attained.

[17]Join together in following my example, brothers and sisters, and just as you have us as a model, keep your eyes on those who live as we do. [18]For, as I have often told you before and now tell you again even with tears, many live as enemies of the cross of Christ. [19]Their destiny is destruction, their god is their stomach, and their glory is in their shame. Their mind is set on earthly things. [20]But our citizenship is in heaven. And we eagerly await a Savior from there, the Lord Jesus Christ, [21]who, by the power that enables him to bring everything under his control, will transform our lowly bodies so that they will be like his glorious body.

Closing Appeal for Steadfastness and Unity

4 Therefore, my brothers and sisters, you whom I love and long for, my joy and crown, stand firm in the Lord in this way, dear friends!

[2]I plead with Euodia and I plead with Syntyche to be of the same mind in the Lord. [3]Yes, and I ask you, my true companion, help these women since they have contended at my side in the cause of the gospel, along with Clement and the rest of my co-workers, whose names are in the book of life.

Final Exhortations

[4]Rejoice in the Lord always. I will say it again: Rejoice! [5]Let your gentleness be evident to all. The Lord is near. [6]Do not be anxious about anything, but in every situation, by prayer and petition, with thanksgiving, present your requests to God. [7]And the peace of God, which transcends all understanding, will guard your hearts and your minds in Christ Jesus.

[8]Finally, brothers and sisters, whatever is true, whatever is noble, whatever is right, whatever is pure, whatever is lovely, whatever is admirable — if anything is excellent or praiseworthy — think about such things. [9]Whatever you have learned or received or heard from me, or seen in me — put it into practice. And the God of peace will be with you.

Thanks for Their Gifts

[10]I rejoiced greatly in the Lord that at last you renewed your concern for me. Indeed, you were concerned, but you had no opportunity to show it. [11]I am not saying this because I am in need, for I have learned to be content whatever the circumstances. [12]I know what it is to be in need, and I know what it is to have plenty. I have learned the secret of being content in any and every situation, whether well fed or hungry, whether living in plenty or in want. [13]I can do all this through him who gives me strength.

[14]Yet it was good of you to share in my troubles. [15]Moreover, as you Philippians know, in the early days of your acquaintance with the gospel, when I set out from Macedonia, not one church shared with me in the matter of giving and receiving, except you only; [16]for even when I was in Thessalonica, you sent me aid

more than once when I was in need. [17]Not that I desire your gifts; what I desire is that more be credited to your account. [18]I have received full payment and have more than enough. I am amply supplied, now that I have received from Epaphroditus the gifts you sent. They are a fragrant offering, an acceptable sacrifice, pleasing to God. [19]And my God will meet all your needs according to the riches of his glory in Christ Jesus.

[20]To our God and Father be glory for ever and ever. Amen.

Final Greetings

[21]Greet all God's people in Christ Jesus. The brothers and sisters who are with me send greetings. [22]All God's people here send you greetings, especially those who belong to Caesar's household.

[23]The grace of the Lord Jesus Christ be with your spirit. Amen.[a]

Colossians

1 Paul, an apostle of Christ Jesus by the will of God, and Timothy our brother,

[2]To God's holy people in Colossae, the faithful brothers and sisters[b] in Christ:

Grace and peace to you from God our Father.[c]

Thanksgiving and Prayer

[3]We always thank God, the Father of our Lord Jesus Christ, when we pray for you, [4]because we have heard of your faith in Christ Jesus and of the love you have for all God's people — [5]the faith and love that spring from the hope stored up for you in heaven and about which you have already heard in the true message of the gospel [6]that has come to you. In the same way, the gospel is bearing fruit and growing throughout the whole world — just as it has been doing among you since the day you heard it and truly understood God's grace.

[7]You learned it from Epaphras, our dear fellow servant,[d] who is a faithful minister of Christ on our[e] behalf, [8]and who also told us of your love in the Spirit.

[9]For this reason, since the day we heard about you, we have not stopped praying for you. We continually ask God to fill you with the knowledge of his will through all the wisdom and understanding that the Spirit gives,[f] [10]so that you may live a life worthy of the Lord and please him in every way: bearing fruit in every good work, growing in the knowledge of God, [11]being strengthened with all power according to his glorious might so that you may have great endurance

---

[a] 23 Some manuscripts do not have *Amen.*
[b] 2 The Greek word for *brothers and sisters* (*adelphoi*) refers here to believers, both men and women, as part of God's family; also in 4:15.   [c] 2 Some manuscripts *Father and the Lord Jesus Christ*   [d] 7 Or *slave*   [e] 7 Some manuscripts *your*   [f] 9 Or *all spiritual wisdom and understanding*

and patience, ¹²and giving joyful thanks to the Father, who has qualified you⁶ to share in the inheritance of his holy people in the kingdom of light. ¹³For he has rescued us from the dominion of darkness and brought us into the kingdom of the Son he loves, ¹⁴in whom we have redemption, the forgiveness of sins.

The Supremacy of the Son of God

¹⁵The Son is the image of the invisible God, the firstborn over all creation. ¹⁶For in him all things were created: things in heaven and on earth, visible and invisible, whether thrones or powers or rulers or authorities; all things have been created through him and for him. ¹⁷He is before all things, and in him all things hold together. ¹⁸And he is the head of the body, the church; he is the beginning and the firstborn from among the dead, so that in everything he might have the supremacy. ¹⁹For God was pleased to have all his fullness dwell in him, ²⁰and through him to reconcile to himself all things, whether things on earth or things in heaven, by making peace through his blood, shed on the cross.

²¹Once you were alienated from God and were enemies in your minds because of⁶ your evil behavior. ²²But now he has reconciled you by Christ's physical body through death to present you holy in his sight, without blemish and free from accusation — ²³if you continue in your faith, established and firm, and do not move from the hope held out in the gospel. This is the gospel that you heard and that has been proclaimed to every creature under heaven, and of which I, Paul, have become a servant.

Paul's Labor for the Church

²⁴Now I rejoice in what I am suffering for you, and I fill up in my flesh what is still lacking in regard to Christ's afflictions, for the sake of his body, which is the church. ²⁵I have become its servant by the commission God gave me to present to you the word of God in its fullness — ²⁶the mystery that has been kept hidden for ages and generations, but is now disclosed to the Lord's people. ²⁷To them God has chosen to make known among the Gentiles the glorious riches of this mystery, which is Christ in you, the hope of glory.

²⁸He is the one we proclaim, admonishing and teaching everyone with all wisdom, so that we may present everyone fully mature in Christ. ²⁹To this end I strenuously contend with all the energy Christ so powerfully works in me.

2 I want you to know how hard I am contending for you and for those at Laodicea, and for all who have not met me personally. ²My goal is that they may be encouraged in heart and united in love, so that they may have the full riches of complete understanding, in order that they may know the mystery of God, namely, Christ, ³in whom are hidden all the treasures of wisdom and knowledge. ⁴I tell you this so that no one may deceive you by fine-sounding arguments. ⁵For though I am absent from you in body, I am present with you in spirit and delight to see how disciplined you are and how firm your faith in Christ is.

Spiritual Fullness in Christ

⁶So then, just as you received Christ Jesus as Lord, continue to live your

---

⁶ 12 Some manuscripts *us*   ᵇ 21 *Or minds, as shown by*

lives in him, [7]rooted and built up in him, strengthened in the faith as you were taught, and overflowing with thankfulness.

[8]See to it that no one takes you captive through hollow and deceptive philosophy, which depends on human tradition and the elemental spiritual forces[a] of this world rather than on Christ.

[9]For in Christ all the fullness of the Deity lives in bodily form, [10]and in Christ you have been brought to fullness. He is the head over every power and authority. [11]In him you were also circumcised with a circumcision not performed by human hands. Your whole self ruled by the flesh[b] was put off when you were circumcised by[c] Christ, [12]having been buried with him in baptism, in which you were also raised with him through your faith in the working of God, who raised him from the dead.

[13]When you were dead in your sins and in the uncircumcision of your flesh, God made you[d] alive with Christ. He forgave us all our sins, [14]having canceled the charge of our legal indebtedness, which stood against us and condemned us; he has taken it away, nailing it to the cross. [15]And having disarmed the powers and authorities, he made a public spectacle of them, triumphing over them by the cross.[e]

Freedom From Human Rules

[16]Therefore do not let anyone judge you by what you eat or drink, or with regard to a religious festival, a New Moon celebration or a Sabbath day. [17]These are a shadow of the things that were to come; the reality, however, is found in Christ. [18]Do not let anyone who delights in false humility and the worship of angels disqualify you. Such a person also goes into great detail about what they have seen; they are puffed up with idle notions by their unspiritual mind. [19]They have lost connection with the head, from whom the whole body, supported and held together by its ligaments and sinews, grows as God causes it to grow.

[20]Since you died with Christ to the elemental spiritual forces of this world, why, as though you still belonged to the world, do you submit to its rules: [21]"Do not handle! Do not taste! Do not touch!"? [22]These rules, which have to do with things that are all destined to perish with use, are based on merely human commands and teachings. [23]Such regulations indeed have an appearance of wisdom, with their self-imposed worship, their false humility and their harsh treatment of the body, but they lack any value in restraining sensual indulgence.

Living as Those Made Alive in Christ

3 Since, then, you have been raised with Christ, set your hearts on things above, where Christ is, seated at the right hand of God. [2]Set your minds on things above, not on earthly things. [3]For you died, and your life is now hidden with Christ in God. [4]When Christ, who is your[f] life, appears, then you also will appear with him in glory.

[5]Put to death, therefore, whatever belongs to your earthly nature: sexual immorality, impurity, lust, evil

---

[a] 8 Or the basic principles; also in verse 20
[b] 11 In contexts like this, the Greek word for flesh (sarx) refers to the sinful state of human beings, often presented as a power in opposition to the Spirit; also in verse 13.
[c] 11 Or put off in the circumcision of
[d] 13 Some manuscripts us   [e] 15 Or them in him   [f] 4 Some manuscripts our

desires and greed, which is idolatry. [6]Because of these, the wrath of God is coming.[a] [7]You used to walk in these ways, in the life you once lived. [8]But now you must also rid yourselves of all such things as these: anger, rage, malice, slander, and filthy language from your lips. [9]Do not lie to each other, since you have taken off your old self with its practices [10]and have put on the new self, which is being renewed in knowledge in the image of its Creator. [11]Here there is no Gentile or Jew, circumcised or uncircumcised, barbarian, Scythian, slave or free, but Christ is all, and is in all.

[12]Therefore, as God's chosen people, holy and dearly loved, clothe yourselves with compassion, kindness, humility, gentleness and patience. [13]Bear with each other and forgive one another if any of you has a grievance against someone. Forgive as the Lord forgave you. [14]And over all these virtues put on love, which binds them all together in perfect unity.

[15]Let the peace of Christ rule in your hearts, since as members of one body you were called to peace. And be thankful. [16]Let the message of Christ dwell among you richly as you teach and admonish one another with all wisdom through psalms, hymns, and songs from the Spirit, singing to God with gratitude in your hearts. [17]And whatever you do, whether in word or deed, do it all in the name of the Lord Jesus, giving thanks to God the Father through him.

Instructions for Christian Households

[18]Wives, submit yourselves to your husbands, as is fitting in the Lord.

[19]Husbands, love your wives and do not be harsh with them.

[20]Children, obey your parents in everything, for this pleases the Lord.

[21]Fathers,[b] do not embitter your children, or they will become discouraged.

[22]Slaves, obey your earthly masters in everything; and do it, not only when their eye is on you and to curry their favor, but with sincerity of heart and reverence for the Lord. [23]Whatever you do, work at it with all your heart, as working for the Lord, not for human masters, [24]since you know that you will receive an inheritance from the Lord as a reward. It is the Lord Christ you are serving. [25]Anyone who does wrong will be repaid for their wrongs, and there is no favoritism.

4 Masters, provide your slaves with what is right and fair, because you know that you also have a Master in heaven.

Further Instructions

[2]Devote yourselves to prayer, being watchful and thankful. [3]And pray for us, too, that God may open a door for our message, so that we may proclaim the mystery of Christ, for which I am in chains. [4]Pray that I may proclaim it clearly, as I should. [5]Be wise in the way you act toward outsiders; make the most of every opportunity. [6]Let your conversation be always full of grace, seasoned with salt, so that you may know how to answer everyone.

Final Greetings

[7]Tychicus will tell you all the news about me. He is a dear brother, a faithful minister and fellow servant[c] in the Lord. [8]I am sending him to you for the express purpose that you may know about our[d] circumstances and that he may encourage your hearts. [9]He is

---

[a] 6 Some early manuscripts *coming on those who are disobedient*   [b] 21 Or *Parents*   [c] 7 Or *slave*; also in verse 12   [d] 8 Some manuscripts *that he may know about your*

coming with Onesimus, our faithful and dear brother, who is one of you. They will tell you everything that is happening here.

[10] My fellow prisoner Aristarchus sends you his greetings, as does Mark, the cousin of Barnabas. (You have received instructions about him; if he comes to you, welcome him.) [11] Jesus, who is called Justus, also sends greetings. These are the only Jews[a] among my co-workers for the kingdom of God, and they have proved a comfort to me. [12] Epaphras, who is one of you and a servant of Christ Jesus, sends greetings. He is always wrestling in prayer for you, that you may stand firm in all the will of God, mature and fully assured. [13] I vouch for him that he is working hard for you and for those at Laodicea and Hierapolis. [14] Our dear friend Luke, the doctor, and Demas send greetings. [15] Give my greetings to the brothers and sisters at Laodicea, and to Nympha and the church in her house.

[16] After this letter has been read to you, see that it is also read in the church of the Laodiceans and that you in turn read the letter from Laodicea.

[17] Tell Archippus: "See to it that you complete the ministry you have received in the Lord."

[18] I, Paul, write this greeting in my own hand. Remember my chains. Grace be with you.

1 Thessalonians

1 Paul, Silas[b] and Timothy,

To the church of the Thessalonians in God the Father and the Lord Jesus Christ:

Grace and peace to you.

Thanksgiving for the Thessalonians' Faith

[2] We always thank God for all of you and continually mention you in our prayers. [3] We remember before our God and Father your work produced by faith, your labor prompted by love, and your endurance inspired by hope in our Lord Jesus Christ.

[4] For we know, brothers and sisters[c] loved by God, that he has chosen you, [5] because our gospel came to you not simply with words but also with power, with the Holy Spirit and deep conviction. You know how we lived among you for your sake. [6] You became imitators of us and of the Lord, for you welcomed the message in the midst of severe suffering with the joy given by the Holy Spirit. [7] And so you became a model to all the believers in Macedonia and Achaia. [8] The Lord's message rang out from you not only in Macedonia and Achaia — your faith in God has become known everywhere. Therefore we do not need to say anything about

---

[a] *11* Greek only ones of the circumcision group
[b] *1* Greek *Silvanus*, a variant of *Silas*   [c] *4* The Greek word for *brothers and sisters* (*adelphoi*) refers here to believers, both men and women, as part of God's family; also in 2:1, 9, 14, 17; 3:7; 4:1, 10, 13; 5:1, 4, 12, 14, 25, 27.

it, [9]for they themselves report what kind of reception you gave us. They tell how you turned to God from idols to serve the living and true God, [10]and to wait for his Son from heaven, whom he raised from the dead — Jesus, who rescues us from the coming wrath.

Paul's Ministry in Thessalonica

2 You know, brothers and sisters, that our visit to you was not without results. [2]We had previously suffered and been treated outrageously in Philippi, as you know, but with the help of our God we dared to tell you his gospel in the face of strong opposition. [3]For the appeal we make does not spring from error or impure motives, nor are we trying to trick you. [4]On the contrary, we speak as those approved by God to be entrusted with the gospel. We are not trying to please people but God, who tests our hearts. [5]You know we never used flattery, nor did we put on a mask to cover up greed — God is our witness. [6]We were not looking for praise from people, not from you or anyone else, even though as apostles of Christ we could have asserted our authority. [7]Instead, we were like young children[a] among you.

Just as a nursing mother cares for her children, [8]so we cared for you. Because we loved you so much, we were delighted to share with you not only the gospel of God but our lives as well. [9]Surely you remember, brothers and sisters, our toil and hardship; we worked night and day in order not to be a burden to anyone while we preached the gospel of God to you. [10]You are witnesses, and so is God, of how holy, righteous and blameless we were among you who believed. [11]For you know that we dealt with each of you as a father deals with his own children, [12]encouraging, comforting and urging you to live lives worthy of God, who calls you into his kingdom and glory.

[13]And we also thank God continually because, when you received the word of God, which you heard from us, you accepted it not as a human word, but as it actually is, the word of God, which is indeed at work in you who believe. [14]For you, brothers and sisters, became imitators of God's churches in Judea, which are in Christ Jesus: You suffered from your own people the same things those churches suffered from the Jews [15]who killed the Lord Jesus and the prophets and also drove us out. They displease God and are hostile to everyone [16]in their effort to keep us from speaking to the Gentiles so that they may be saved. In this way they always heap up their sins to the limit. The wrath of God has come upon them at last.[b]

Paul's Longing to See the Thessalonians

[17]But, brothers and sisters, when we were orphaned by being separated from you for a short time (in person, not in thought), out of our intense longing we made every effort to see you. [18]For we wanted to come to you — certainly I, Paul, did, again and again — but Satan blocked our way. [19]For what is our hope, our joy, or the crown in which we will glory in the presence of our Lord Jesus when he comes? Is it not you? [20]Indeed, you are our glory and joy.

3 So when we could stand it no longer, we thought it best to be left by ourselves in Athens. [2]We sent Timothy, who is our brother and co-

---

[a] 7 Some manuscripts *were gentle*   [b] 16 Or *them fully*

worker in God's service in spreading the gospel of Christ, to strengthen and encourage you in your faith, ³so that no one would be unsettled by these trials. For you know quite well that we are destined for them. ⁴In fact, when we were with you, we kept telling you that we would be persecuted. And it turned out that way, as you well know. ⁵For this reason, when I could stand it no longer, I sent to find out about your faith. I was afraid that in some way the tempter had tempted you and that our labors might have been in vain.

Timothy's Encouraging Report

⁶But Timothy has just now come to us from you and has brought good news about your faith and love. He has told us that you always have pleasant memories of us and that you long to see us, just as we also long to see you. ⁷Therefore, brothers and sisters, in all our distress and persecution we were encouraged about you because of your faith. ⁸For now we really live, since you are standing firm in the Lord. ⁹How can we thank God enough for you in return for all the joy we have in the presence of our God because of you? ¹⁰Night and day we pray most earnestly that we may see you again and supply what is lacking in your faith.

¹¹Now may our God and Father himself and our Lord Jesus clear the way for us to come to you. ¹²May the Lord make your love increase and overflow for each other and for everyone else, just as ours does for you. ¹³May he strengthen your hearts so that you will be blameless and holy in the presence of our God and Father when our Lord Jesus comes with all his holy ones.

Living to Please God

4 As for other matters, brothers and sisters, we instructed you how to live in order to please God, as in fact you are living. Now we ask you and urge you in the Lord Jesus to do this more and more. ²For you know what instructions we gave you by the authority of the Lord Jesus.

³It is God's will that you should be sanctified: that you should avoid sexual immorality; ⁴that each of you should learn to control your own body*ᵃ* in a way that is holy and honorable, ⁵not in passionate lust like the pagans, who do not know God; ⁶and that in this matter no one should wrong or take advantage of a brother or sister.*ᵇ* The Lord will punish all those who commit such sins, as we told you and warned you before. ⁷For God did not call us to be impure, but to live a holy life. ⁸Therefore, anyone who rejects this instruction does not reject a human being but God, the very God who gives you his Holy Spirit.

⁹Now about your love for one another we do not need to write to you, for you yourselves have been taught by God to love each other. ¹⁰And in fact, you do love all of God's family throughout Macedonia. Yet we urge you, brothers and sisters, to do so more and more, ¹¹and to make it your ambition to lead a quiet life: You should mind your own business and work with your hands, just as we told you, ¹²so that your daily life may win the respect of outsiders and so that you will not be dependent on anybody.

ᵃ 4 Or *learn to live with your own wife;* or *learn to acquire a wife*   *ᵇ 6* The Greek word for *brother or sister (adelphos)* refers here to a believer, whether man or woman, as part of God's family.

Believers Who Have Died

¹³Brothers and sisters, we do not want you to be uninformed about those who sleep in death, so that you do not grieve like the rest of mankind, who have no hope. ¹⁴For we believe that Jesus died and rose again, and so we believe that God will bring with Jesus those who have fallen asleep in him. ¹⁵According to the Lord's word, we tell you that we who are still alive, who are left until the coming of the Lord, will certainly not precede those who have fallen asleep. ¹⁶For the Lord himself will come down from heaven, with a loud command, with the voice of the archangel and with the trumpet call of God, and the dead in Christ will rise first. ¹⁷After that, we who are still alive and are left will be caught up together with them in the clouds to meet the Lord in the air. And so we will be with the Lord forever. ¹⁸Therefore encourage one another with these words.

The Day of the Lord

5 Now, brothers and sisters, about times and dates we do not need to write to you, ²for you know very well that the day of the Lord will come like a thief in the night. ³While people are saying, "Peace and safety," destruction will come on them suddenly, as labor pains on a pregnant woman, and they will not escape.

⁴But you, brothers and sisters, are not in darkness so that this day should surprise you like a thief. ⁵You are all children of the light and children of the day. We do not belong to the night or to the darkness. ⁶So then, let us not be like others, who are asleep, but let us be awake and sober. ⁷For those who sleep, sleep at night, and those who get drunk, get drunk at night. ⁸But since we belong to the day, let us be sober, putting on faith and love as a breastplate, and the hope of salvation as a helmet. ⁹For God did not appoint us to suffer wrath but to receive salvation through our Lord Jesus Christ. ¹⁰He died for us so that, whether we are awake or asleep, we may live together with him. ¹¹Therefore encourage one another and build each other up, just as in fact you are doing.

Final Instructions

¹²Now we ask you, brothers and sisters, to acknowledge those who work hard among you, who care for you in the Lord and who admonish you. ¹³Hold them in the highest regard in love because of their work. Live in peace with each other. ¹⁴And we urge you, brothers and sisters, warn those who are idle and disruptive, encourage the disheartened, help the weak, be patient with everyone. ¹⁵Make sure that nobody pays back wrong for wrong, but always strive to do what is good for each other and for everyone else.

¹⁶Rejoice always, ¹⁷pray continually, ¹⁸give thanks in all circumstances; for this is God's will for you in Christ Jesus.

¹⁹Do not quench the Spirit. ²⁰Do not treat prophecies with contempt ²¹but test them all; hold on to what is good, ²²reject every kind of evil.

²³May God himself, the God of peace, sanctify you through and through. May your whole spirit, soul and body be kept blameless at the coming of our Lord Jesus Christ. ²⁴The one who calls you is faithful, and he will do it.

²⁵Brothers and sisters, pray for us. ²⁶Greet all God's people with a holy kiss. ²⁷I charge you before the Lord to have this letter read to all the brothers and sisters.

²⁸The grace of our Lord Jesus Christ be with you.

2 Thessalonians

1 Paul, Silas[a] and Timothy,

To the church of the Thessalonians in God our Father and the Lord Jesus Christ:

²Grace and peace to you from God the Father and the Lord Jesus Christ.

Thanksgiving and Prayer

³We ought always to thank God for you, brothers and sisters,[b] and rightly so, because your faith is growing more and more, and the love all of you have for one another is increasing. ⁴Therefore, among God's churches we boast about your perseverance and faith in all the persecutions and trials you are enduring.

⁵All this is evidence that God's judgment is right, and as a result you will be counted worthy of the kingdom of God, for which you are suffering. ⁶God is just: He will pay back trouble to those who trouble you ⁷and give relief to you who are troubled, and to us as well. This will happen when the Lord Jesus is revealed from heaven in blazing fire with his powerful angels. ⁸He will punish those who do not know God and do not obey the gospel of our Lord Jesus. ⁹They will be punished with everlasting destruction and shut out from the presence of the Lord and from the glory of his might ¹⁰on the day he comes to be glorified in his holy people and to be marveled at among all those who have believed. This includes you, because you believed our testimony to you.

¹¹With this in mind, we constantly pray for you, that our God may make you worthy of his calling, and that by his power he may bring to fruition your every desire for goodness and your every deed prompted by faith. ¹²We pray this so that the name of our Lord Jesus may be glorified in you, and you in him, according to the grace of our God and the Lord Jesus Christ.[c]

The Man of Lawlessness

2 Concerning the coming of our Lord Jesus Christ and our being gathered to him, we ask you, brothers and sisters, ²not to become easily unsettled or alarmed by the teaching allegedly from us — whether by a prophecy or by word of mouth or by letter — asserting that the day of the Lord has already come. ³Don't let anyone deceive you in any way, for that day will not come until the rebellion occurs and the man of lawlessness[d] is revealed, the man doomed to destruction. ⁴He will oppose and will exalt himself over everything that is called God or is worshiped, so that he sets himself up in God's temple, proclaiming himself to be God.

⁵Don't you remember that when I was with you I used to tell you these things? ⁶And now you know what is holding him back, so that he may be revealed at the proper time. ⁷For the secret power of lawlessness is already at work; but the one who now holds it back will continue to do so till he is taken out of the way. ⁸And then the lawless one will be revealed, whom

---

[a] 1 Greek *Silvanus*, a variant of *Silas*   [b] 3 The Greek word for *brothers and sisters* (*adelphoi*) refers here to believers, both men and women, as part of God's family; also in 2:1, 13, 15; 3:1, 6, 13.   [c] 12 Or *God and Lord, Jesus Christ*   [d] 3 Some manuscripts *sin*

the Lord Jesus will overthrow with the breath of his mouth and destroy by the splendor of his coming. 9The coming of the lawless one will be in accordance with how Satan works. He will use all sorts of displays of power through signs and wonders that serve the lie, 10and all the ways that wickedness deceives those who are perishing. They perish because they refused to love the truth and so be saved. 11For this reason God sends them a powerful delusion so that they will believe the lie 12and so that all will be condemned who have not believed the truth but have delighted in wickedness.

Stand Firm

13But we ought always to thank God for you, brothers and sisters loved by the Lord, because God chose you as firstfruits[a] to be saved through the sanctifying work of the Spirit and through belief in the truth. 14He called you to this through our gospel, that you might share in the glory of our Lord Jesus Christ.

15So then, brothers and sisters, stand firm and hold fast to the teachings[b] we passed on to you, whether by word of mouth or by letter.

16May our Lord Jesus Christ himself and God our Father, who loved us and by his grace gave us eternal encouragement and good hope, 17encourage your hearts and strengthen you in every good deed and word.

Request for Prayer

3 As for other matters, brothers and sisters, pray for us that the message of the Lord may spread rapidly and be honored, just as it was with you. 2And pray that we may be delivered from wicked and evil people, for not everyone has faith. 3But the Lord

is faithful, and he will strengthen you and protect you from the evil one. 4We have confidence in the Lord that you are doing and will continue to do the things we command. 5May the Lord direct your hearts into God's love and Christ's perseverance.

Warning Against Idleness

6In the name of the Lord Jesus Christ, we command you, brothers and sisters, to keep away from every believer who is idle and disruptive and does not live according to the teaching[c] you received from us. 7For you yourselves know how you ought to follow our example. We were not idle when we were with you, 8nor did we eat anyone's food without paying for it. On the contrary, we worked night and day, laboring and toiling so that we would not be a burden to any of you. 9We did this, not because we do not have the right to such help, but in order to offer ourselves as a model for you to imitate. 10For even when we were with you, we gave you this rule: "The one who is unwilling to work shall not eat."

11We hear that some among you are idle and disruptive. They are not busy; they are busybodies. 12Such people we command and urge in the Lord Jesus Christ to settle down and earn the food they eat. 13And as for you, brothers and sisters, never tire of doing what is good.

14Take special note of anyone who does not obey our instruction in this letter. Do not associate with them, in order that they may feel ashamed. 15Yet do not regard them as an enemy, but warn them as you would a fellow believer.

---

a 13 Some manuscripts *because from the beginning God chose you*   *b 15* Or *traditions*   *c 6* Or *tradition*

Final Greetings

16Now may the Lord of peace himself give you peace at all times and in every way. The Lord be with all of you.

17I, Paul, write this greeting in my own hand, which is the distinguishing mark in all my letters. This is how I write.

18The grace of our Lord Jesus Christ be with you all.

1 Timothy

1 Paul, an apostle of Christ Jesus by the command of God our Savior and of Christ Jesus our hope,

2To Timothy my true son in the faith:

Grace, mercy and peace from God the Father and Christ Jesus our Lord.

Timothy Charged to Oppose False Teachers

3As I urged you when I went into Macedonia, stay there in Ephesus so that you may command certain people not to teach false doctrines any longer 4or to devote themselves to myths and endless genealogies. Such things promote controversial speculations rather than advancing God's work—which is by faith. 5The goal of this command is love, which comes from a pure heart and a good conscience and a sincere faith. 6Some have departed from these and have turned to meaningless talk. 7They want to be teachers of the law, but they do not know what they are talking about or what they so confidently affirm.

8We know that the law is good if one uses it properly. 9We also know that the law is made not for the righteous but for lawbreakers and rebels, the ungodly and sinful, the unholy and irreligious, for those who kill their fathers or mothers, for murderers, 10for the sexually immoral, for those practicing homosexuality, for slave traders and liars and perjurers — and for whatever else is contrary to the sound doctrine 11that conforms to the gospel concerning the glory of the blessed God, which he entrusted to me.

The Lord's Grace to Paul

12I thank Christ Jesus our Lord, who has given me strength, that he considered me trustworthy, appointing me to his service. 13Even though I was once a blasphemer and a persecutor and a violent man, I was shown mercy because I acted in ignorance and unbelief. 14The grace of our Lord was poured out on me abundantly, along with the faith and love that are in Christ Jesus.

15Here is a trustworthy saying that deserves full acceptance: Christ Jesus came into the world to save sinners — of whom I am the worst. 16But for that very reason I was shown mercy so that in me, the worst of sinners, Christ Jesus might display his immense patience as an example for those who would believe in him and receive eternal life. [17]Now to the King eternal, immortal, invisible, the only God, be honor and glory for ever and ever. Amen.

The Charge to Timothy Renewed

[18]Timothy, my son, I am giving you this command in keeping with the prophecies once made about you, so that by recalling them you may fight the battle well, [19]holding on to faith and a good conscience, which some have rejected and so have suffered shipwreck with regard to the faith. [20]Among them are Hymenaeus and Alexander, whom I have handed over to Satan to be taught not to blaspheme.

Instructions on Worship

2 I urge, then, first of all, that petitions, prayers, intercession and thanksgiving be made for all people — [2]for kings and all those in authority, that we may live peaceful and quiet lives in all godliness and holiness. [3]This is good, and pleases God our Savior, [4]who wants all people to be saved and to come to a knowledge of the truth. [5]For there is one God and one mediator between God and mankind, the man Christ Jesus, [6]who gave himself as a ransom for all people. This has now been witnessed to at the proper time. [7]And for this purpose I was appointed a herald and an apostle — I am telling the truth, I am not lying — and a true and faithful teacher of the Gentiles.

[8]Therefore I want the men everywhere to pray, lifting up holy hands without anger or disputing. [9]I also want the women to dress modestly, with decency and propriety, adorning themselves, not with elaborate hairstyles or gold or pearls or expensive clothes, [10]but with good deeds, appropriate for women who profess to worship God.

[11]A woman[a] should learn in quietness and full submission. [12]I do not permit a woman to teach or to assume authority over a man;[b] she must be quiet. [13]For Adam was formed first, then Eve. [14]And Adam was not the one deceived; it was the woman who was deceived and became a sinner. [15]But women[c] will be saved through childbearing — if they continue in faith, love and holiness with propriety.

Qualifications for Overseers and Deacons

3 Here is a trustworthy saying: Whoever aspires to be an overseer desires a noble task. [2]Now the overseer is to be above reproach, faithful to his wife, temperate, self-controlled, respectable, hospitable, able to teach, [3]not given to drunkenness, not violent but gentle, not quarrelsome, not a lover of money. [4]He must manage his own family well and see that his children obey him, and he must do so in a manner worthy of full[d] respect. [5](If anyone does not know how to manage his own family, how can he take care of God's church?) [6]He must not be a recent convert, or he may become conceited and fall under the same judgment as the devil. [7]He must also have a good reputation with outsiders, so that he will not fall into disgrace and into the devil's trap.

[8]In the same way, deacons[e] are to be worthy of respect, sincere, not indulging in much wine, and not pursu-

---

a 11 Or *wife; also in verse 12*   *b* 12 Or *over her husband*   *c* 15 Greek *she*   *d* 4 Or *him with proper*   *e* 8 The word *deacons* refers here to Christians designated to serve with the overseers/elders of the church in a variety of ways; similarly in verse 12; and in Romans 16:1 and Phil. 1:1.

ing dishonest gain. 9They must keep hold of the deep truths of the faith with a clear conscience. 10They must first be tested; and then if there is nothing against them, let them serve as deacons.

11In the same way, the women*a* are to be worthy of respect, not malicious talkers but temperate and trustworthy in everything.

12A deacon must be faithful to his wife and must manage his children and his household well. 13Those who have served well gain an excellent standing and great assurance in their faith in Christ Jesus.

Reasons for Paul's Instructions

14Although I hope to come to you soon, I am writing you these instructions so that, 15if I am delayed, you will know how people ought to conduct themselves in God's household, which is the church of the living God, the pillar and foundation of the truth. 16Beyond all question, the mystery from which true godliness springs is great:

He appeared in the flesh,
    was vindicated by the Spirit,*b*
was seen by angels,
    was preached among the
        nations,
was believed on in the world,
    was taken up in glory.

4 The Spirit clearly says that in later times some will abandon the faith and follow deceiving spirits and things taught by demons. 2Such teachings come through hypocritical liars, whose consciences have been seared as with a hot iron. 3They forbid people to marry and order them to abstain from certain foods, which God created to be received with thanks-

giving by those who believe and who know the truth. 4For everything God created is good, and nothing is to be rejected if it is received with thanksgiving, 5because it is consecrated by the word of God and prayer.

6If you point these things out to the brothers and sisters,*c* you will be a good minister of Christ Jesus, nourished on the truths of the faith and of the good teaching that you have followed. 7Have nothing to do with godless myths and old wives' tales; rather, train yourself to be godly. 8For physical training is of some value, but godliness has value for all things, holding promise for both the present life and the life to come. 9This is a trustworthy saying that deserves full acceptance. 10That is why we labor and strive, because we have put our hope in the living God, who is the Savior of all people, and especially of those who believe.

11Command and teach these things. 12Don't let anyone look down on you because you are young, but set an example for the believers in speech, in conduct, in love, in faith and in purity. 13Until I come, devote yourself to the public reading of Scripture, to preaching and to teaching. 14Do not neglect your gift, which was given you through prophecy when the body of elders laid their hands on you.

15Be diligent in these matters; give yourself wholly to them, so that everyone may see your progress. 16Watch your life and doctrine closely. Persevere in them, because if you do, you will save both yourself and your hearers.

---

a 11 Possibly deacons' wives or women who are deacons   *b* 16 Or *vindicated in spirit*
c 6 The Greek word for *brothers and sisters* (*adelphoi*) refers here to believers, both men and women, as part of God's family.

Widows, Elders and Slaves

5 Do not rebuke an older man harshly, but exhort him as if he were your father. Treat younger men as brothers, ²older women as mothers, and younger women as sisters, with absolute purity.

³Give proper recognition to those widows who are really in need. ⁴But if a widow has children or grandchildren, these should learn first of all to put their religion into practice by caring for their own family and so repaying their parents and grandparents, for this is pleasing to God. ⁵The widow who is really in need and left all alone puts her hope in God and continues night and day to pray and to ask God for help. ⁶But the widow who lives for pleasure is dead even while she lives. ⁷Give the people these instructions, so that no one may be open to blame. ⁸Anyone who does not provide for their relatives, and especially for their own household, has denied the faith and is worse than an unbeliever.

⁹No widow may be put on the list of widows unless she is over sixty, has been faithful to her husband, ¹⁰and is well known for her good deeds, such as bringing up children, showing hospitality, washing the feet of the Lord's people, helping those in trouble and devoting herself to all kinds of good deeds.

¹¹As for younger widows, do not put them on such a list. For when their sensual desires overcome their dedication to Christ, they want to marry. ¹²Thus they bring judgment on themselves, because they have broken their first pledge. ¹³Besides, they get into the habit of being idle and going about from house to house. And not only do they become idlers, but also busybodies who talk nonsense, saying things they ought not to. ¹⁴So I counsel younger widows to marry, to have children, to manage their homes and to give the enemy no opportunity for slander. ¹⁵Some have in fact already turned away to follow Satan.

¹⁶If any woman who is a believer has widows in her care, she should continue to help them and not let the church be burdened with them, so that the church can help those widows who are really in need.

¹⁷The elders who direct the affairs of the church well are worthy of double honor, especially those whose work is preaching and teaching. ¹⁸For Scripture says, "Do not muzzle an ox while it is treading out the grain,"ᵃ and "The worker deserves his wages."ᵇ ¹⁹Do not entertain an accusation against an elder unless it is brought by two or three witnesses. ²⁰But those elders who are sinning you are to reprove before everyone, so that the others may take warning. ²¹I charge you, in the sight of God and Christ Jesus and the elect angels, to keep these instructions without partiality, and to do nothing out of favoritism.

²²Do not be hasty in the laying on of hands, and do not share in the sins of others. Keep yourself pure.

²³Stop drinking only water, and use a little wine because of your stomach and your frequent illnesses.

²⁴The sins of some are obvious, reaching the place of judgment ahead of them; the sins of others trail behind them. ²⁵In the same way, good deeds are obvious, and even those that are not obvious cannot remain hidden forever.

6 All who are under the yoke of slavery should consider their masters worthy of full respect, so that God's

---

ᵃ 18 Deut. 25:4   ᵇ 18 Luke 10:7

name and our teaching may not be slandered. [2]Those who have believing masters should not show them disrespect just because they are fellow believers. Instead, they should serve them even better because their masters are dear to them as fellow believers and are devoted to the welfare[a] of their slaves.

False Teachers and the Love of Money

These are the things you are to teach and insist on. [3]If anyone teaches otherwise and does not agree to the sound instruction of our Lord Jesus Christ and to godly teaching, [4]they are conceited and understand nothing. They have an unhealthy interest in controversies and quarrels about words that result in envy, strife, malicious talk, evil suspicions [5]and constant friction between people of corrupt mind, who have been robbed of the truth and who think that godliness is a means to financial gain.

[6]But godliness with contentment is great gain. [7]For we brought nothing into the world, and we can take nothing out of it. [8]But if we have food and clothing, we will be content with that. [9]Those who want to get rich fall into temptation and a trap and into many foolish and harmful desires that plunge people into ruin and destruction. [10]For the love of money is a root of all kinds of evil. Some people, eager for money, have wandered from the faith and pierced themselves with many griefs.

Final Charge to Timothy

[11]But you, man of God, flee from all this, and pursue righteousness,

godliness, faith, love, endurance and gentleness. [12]Fight the good fight of the faith. Take hold of the eternal life to which you were called when you made your good confession in the presence of many witnesses. [13]In the sight of God, who gives life to everything, and of Christ Jesus, who while testifying before Pontius Pilate made the good confession, I charge you [14]to keep this command without spot or blame until the appearing of our Lord Jesus Christ, [15]which God will bring about in his own time — God, the blessed and only Ruler, the King of kings and Lord of lords, [16]who alone is immortal and who lives in unapproachable light, whom no one has seen or can see. To him be honor and might forever. Amen.

[17]Command those who are rich in this present world not to be arrogant nor to put their hope in wealth, which is so uncertain, but to put their hope in God, who richly provides us with everything for our enjoyment. [18]Command them to do good, to be rich in good deeds, and to be generous and willing to share. [19]In this way they will lay up treasure for themselves as a firm foundation for the coming age, so that they may take hold of the life that is truly life.

[20]Timothy, guard what has been entrusted to your care. Turn away from godless chatter and the opposing ideas of what is falsely called knowledge, [21]which some have professed and in so doing have departed from the faith.

Grace be with you all.

---

[a] 2 Or *and benefit from the service*

2 Timothy

1 Paul, an apostle of Christ Jesus by the will of God, in keeping with the promise of life that is in Christ Jesus,

²To Timothy, my dear son:

Grace, mercy and peace from God the Father and Christ Jesus our Lord.

Thanksgiving

³I thank God, whom I serve, as my ancestors did, with a clear conscience, as night and day I constantly remember you in my prayers. ⁴Recalling your tears, I long to see you, so that I may be filled with joy. ⁵I am reminded of your sincere faith, which first lived in your grandmother Lois and in your mother Eunice and, I am persuaded, now lives in you also.

Appeal for Loyalty to Paul and the Gospel

⁶For this reason I remind you to fan into flame the gift of God, which is in you through the laying on of my hands. ⁷For the Spirit God gave us does not make us timid, but gives us power, love and self-discipline. ⁸So do not be ashamed of the testimony about our Lord or of me his prisoner. Rather, join with me in suffering for the gospel, by the power of God. ⁹He has saved us and called us to a holy life — not because of anything we have done but because of his own purpose and grace. This grace was given us in Christ Jesus before the beginning of time, ¹⁰but it has now been revealed through the appearing of our Savior, Christ Jesus, who has destroyed death and has brought life and immortality to light through the gospel. ¹¹And of this gospel I was ap-pointed a herald and an apostle and a teacher. ¹²That is why I am suffering as I am. Yet this is no cause for shame, because I know whom I have believed, and am convinced that he is able to guard what I have entrusted to him until that day.

¹³What you heard from me, keep as the pattern of sound teaching, with faith and love in Christ Jesus. ¹⁴Guard the good deposit that was entrusted to you — guard it with the help of the Holy Spirit who lives in us.

Examples of Disloyalty and Loyalty

¹⁵You know that everyone in the province of Asia has deserted me, including Phygelus and Hermogenes.

¹⁶May the Lord show mercy to the household of Onesiphorus, because he often refreshed me and was not ashamed of my chains. ¹⁷On the contrary, when he was in Rome, he searched hard for me until he found me. ¹⁸May the Lord grant that he will find mercy from the Lord on that day! You know very well in how many ways he helped me in Ephesus.

The Appeal Renewed

2 You then, my son, be strong in the grace that is in Christ Jesus. ²And the things you have heard me say in the presence of many witnesses entrust to reliable people who will also be qualified to teach others. ³Join with me in suffering, like a good soldier of Christ Jesus. ⁴No one serving as a soldier gets entangled in civilian affairs, but rather tries to please his commanding officer. ⁵Similarly, anyone who competes as an athlete does not receive the victor's crown except by competing according to the rules. 6The hardworking farmer should be the first to receive a share of the crops. 7Reflect on what I am saying, for the Lord will give you insight into all this.

8Remember Jesus Christ, raised from the dead, descended from David. This is my gospel, 9for which I am suffering even to the point of being chained like a criminal. But God's word is not chained. 10Therefore I endure everything for the sake of the elect, that they too may obtain the salvation that is in Christ Jesus, with eternal glory.

11Here is a trustworthy saying:

If we died with him,
    we will also live with him;
12 if we endure,
    we will also reign with him.
If we disown him,
    he will also disown us;
13 if we are faithless,
    he remains faithful,
    for he cannot disown himself.

Dealing With False Teachers

14Keep reminding God's people of these things. Warn them before God against quarreling about words; it is of no value, and only ruins those who listen. 15Do your best to present yourself to God as one approved, a worker who does not need to be ashamed and who correctly handles the word of truth. 16Avoid godless chatter, because those who indulge in it will become more and more ungodly. 17Their teaching will spread like gangrene. Among them are Hymenaeus and Philetus, 18who have departed from the truth. They say that the resurrection has already taken place, and they destroy the faith of some. 19Nevertheless, God's solid foundation stands firm, sealed with this inscription: "The Lord knows those who are his," and, "Everyone who confesses the name of the Lord must turn away from wickedness."

20In a large house there are articles not only of gold and silver, but also of wood and clay; some are for special purposes and some for common use. 21Those who cleanse themselves from the latter will be instruments for special purposes, made holy, useful to the Master and prepared to do any good work.

22Flee the evil desires of youth and pursue righteousness, faith, love and peace, along with those who call on the Lord out of a pure heart. 23Don't have anything to do with foolish and stupid arguments, because you know they produce quarrels. 24And the Lord's servant must not be quarrelsome but must be kind to everyone, able to teach, not resentful. 25Opponents must be gently instructed, in the hope that God will grant them repentance leading them to a knowledge of the truth, 26and that they will come to their senses and escape from the trap of the devil, who has taken them captive to do his will.

3 But mark this: There will be terrible times in the last days. 2People will be lovers of themselves, lovers of money, boastful, proud, abusive, disobedient to their parents, ungrateful, unholy, 3without love, unforgiving, slanderous, without self-control, brutal, not lovers of the good, 4treacherous, rash, conceited, lovers of pleasure rather than lovers of God— 5having a form of godliness but denying its power. Have nothing to do with such people.

6They are the kind who worm their way into homes and gain control over gullible women, who are loaded down with sins and are swayed by all kinds of evil desires, 7always learning but never able to come to a knowledge of the truth. 8Just as Jannes and Jambres opposed Moses, so also these teachers oppose the truth. They are men of depraved minds, who, as far as the faith is concerned, are rejected. 9But they will not get very far because, as in the case of those men, their folly will be clear to everyone.

A Final Charge to Timothy

10You, however, know all about my teaching, my way of life, my purpose, faith, patience, love, endurance, 11persecutions, sufferings — what kinds of things happened to me in Antioch, Iconium and Lystra, the persecutions I endured. Yet the Lord rescued me from all of them. 12In fact, everyone who wants to live a godly life in Christ Jesus will be persecuted, 13while evildoers and impostors will go from bad to worse, deceiving and being deceived. 14But as for you, continue in what you have learned and have become convinced of, because you know those from whom you learned it, 15and how from infancy you have known the Holy Scriptures, which are able to make you wise for salvation through faith in Christ Jesus. 16All Scripture is God-breathed and is useful for teaching, rebuking, correcting and training in righteousness, 17so that the servant of Goda may be thoroughly equipped for every good work.

4 In the presence of God and of Christ Jesus, who will judge the living and the dead, and in view of his appearing and his kingdom, I give you this charge: 2Preach the word; be prepared in season and out of season; correct, rebuke and encourage — with great patience and careful instruction. 3For the time will come when

people will not put up with sound doctrine. Instead, to suit their own desires, they will gather around them a great number of teachers to say what their itching ears want to hear. 4They will turn their ears away from the truth and turn aside to myths. 5But you, keep your head in all situations, endure hardship, do the work of an evangelist, discharge all the duties of your ministry.

6For I am already being poured out like a drink offering, and the time for my departure is near. 7I have fought the good fight, I have finished the race, I have kept the faith. 8Now there is in store for me the crown of righteousness, which the Lord, the righteous Judge, will award to me on that day — and not only to me, but also to all who have longed for his appearing.

Personal Remarks

9Do your best to come to me quickly, 10for Demas, because he loved this world, has deserted me and has gone to Thessalonica. Crescens has gone to Galatia, and Titus to Dalmatia. 11Only Luke is with me. Get Mark and bring him with you, because he is helpful to me in my ministry. 12I sent Tychicus to Ephesus. 13When you come, bring the cloak that I left with Carpus at Troas, and my scrolls, especially the parchments.

14Alexander the metalworker did me a great deal of harm. The Lord will repay him for what he has done. 15You too should be on your guard against him, because he strongly opposed our message.

16At my first defense, no one came to my support, but everyone deserted me. May it not be held against them.

a 17 Or that you, a man of God,

17But the Lord stood at my side and gave me strength, so that through me the message might be fully proclaimed and all the Gentiles might hear it. And I was delivered from the lion's mouth. 18The Lord will rescue me from every evil attack and will bring me safely to his heavenly kingdom. To him be glory for ever and ever. Amen.

Final Greetings

19Greet Priscilla[a] and Aquila and the household of Onesiphorus. 20Erastus stayed in Corinth, and I left Trophimus sick in Miletus. 21Do your best to get here before winter. Eubulus greets you, and so do Pudens, Linus, Claudia and all the brothers and sisters.[b]

22The Lord be with your spirit. Grace be with you all.

Titus

1 Paul, a servant of God and an apostle of Jesus Christ to further the faith of God's elect and their knowledge of the truth that leads to godliness — 2in the hope of eternal life, which God, who does not lie, promised before the beginning of time, 3and which now at his appointed season he has brought to light through the preaching entrusted to me by the command of God our Savior,

4To Titus, my true son in our common faith:

Grace and peace from God the Father and Christ Jesus our Savior.

Appointing Elders Who Love What Is Good

5The reason I left you in Crete was that you might put in order what was left unfinished and appoint[c] elders in every town, as I directed you. 6An elder must be blameless, faithful to his wife, a man whose children believe[d] and are not open to the charge of being wild and disobedient. 7Since an overseer manages God's household,

he must be blameless — not overbearing, not quick-tempered, not given to drunkenness, not violent, not pursuing dishonest gain. 8Rather, he must be hospitable, one who loves what is good, who is self-controlled, upright, holy and disciplined. 9He must hold firmly to the trustworthy message as it has been taught, so that he can encourage others by sound doctrine and refute those who oppose it.

Rebuking Those Who Fail to Do Good

10For there are many rebellious people, full of meaningless talk and deception, especially those of the circumcision group. 11They must be silenced, because they are disrupting whole households by teaching things they ought not to teach — and that for the sake of dishonest gain. 12One of Crete's own prophets has said it:

---

[a] 19 Greek Prisca, a variant of Priscilla
[b] 21 The Greek word for brothers and sisters (adelphoi) refers here to believers, both men and women, as part of God's family.   [c] 5 Or ordain   [d] 6 Or children are trustworthy

"Cretans are always liars, evil brutes, lazy gluttons."ᵍ ¹³This saying is true. Therefore rebuke them sharply, so that they will be sound in the faith ¹⁴and will pay no attention to Jewish myths or to the merely human commands of those who reject the truth. ¹⁵To the pure, all things are pure, but to those who are corrupted and do not believe, nothing is pure. In fact, both their minds and consciences are corrupted. ¹⁶They claim to know God, but by their actions they deny him. They are detestable, disobedient and unfit for doing anything good.

Doing Good for the Sake of the Gospel

2 You, however, must teach what is appropriate to sound doctrine. ²Teach the older men to be temperate, worthy of respect, self-controlled, and sound in faith, in love and in endurance.

³Likewise, teach the older women to be reverent in the way they live, not to be slanderers or addicted to much wine, but to teach what is good. ⁴Then they can urge the younger women to love their husbands and children, ⁵to be self-controlled and pure, to be busy at home, to be kind, and to be subject to their husbands, so that no one will malign the word of God.

⁶Similarly, encourage the young men to be self-controlled. ⁷In everything set them an example by doing what is good. In your teaching show integrity, seriousness ⁸and soundness of speech that cannot be condemned, so that those who oppose you may be ashamed because they have nothing bad to say about us.

⁹Teach slaves to be subject to their masters in everything, to try to please them, not to talk back to them, ¹⁰and not to steal from them,

but to show that they can be fully trusted, so that in every way they will make the teaching about God our Savior attractive.

¹¹For the grace of God has appeared that offers salvation to all people. ¹²It teaches us to say "No" to ungodliness and worldly passions, and to live self-controlled, upright and godly lives in this present age, ¹³while we wait for the blessed hope — the appearing of the glory of our great God and Savior, Jesus Christ, ¹⁴who gave himself for us to redeem us from all wickedness and to purify for himself a people that are his very own, eager to do what is good.

¹⁵These, then, are the things you should teach. Encourage and rebuke with all authority. Do not let anyone despise you.

Saved in Order to Do Good

3 Remind the people to be subject to rulers and authorities, to be obedient, to be ready to do whatever is good, ²to slander no one, to be peaceable and considerate, and always to be gentle toward everyone.

³At one time we too were foolish, disobedient, deceived and enslaved by all kinds of passions and pleasures. We lived in malice and envy, being hated and hating one another. ⁴But when the kindness and love of God our Savior appeared, ⁵he saved us, not because of righteous things we had done, but because of his mercy. He saved us through the washing of rebirth and renewal by the Holy Spirit, ⁶whom he poured out on us generously through Jesus Christ our Savior, ⁷so that, having been justified by his grace, we might become heirs having the hope of eternal life. ⁸This is a trustworthy saying. And I

ᵍ 12 From the Cretan philosopher Epimenides

want you to stress these things, so that those who have trusted in God may be careful to devote themselves to doing what is good. These things are excellent and profitable for everyone.

⁹But avoid foolish controversies and genealogies and arguments and quarrels about the law, because these are unprofitable and useless. ¹⁰Warn a divisive person once, and then warn them a second time. After that, have nothing to do with them. ¹¹You may be sure that such people are warped and sinful; they are self-condemned.

Final Remarks

¹²As soon as I send Artemas or Tychicus to you, do your best to come to me at Nicopolis, because I have decided to winter there. ¹³Do everything you can to help Zenas the lawyer and Apollos on their way and see that they have everything they need. ¹⁴Our people must learn to devote themselves to doing what is good, in order to provide for urgent needs and not live unproductive lives.

¹⁵Everyone with me sends you greetings. Greet those who love us in the faith.

Grace be with you all.

Philemon

¹Paul, a prisoner of Christ Jesus, and Timothy our brother,

To Philemon our dear friend and fellow worker — ²also to Apphia our sister and Archippus our fellow soldier — and to the church that meets in your home:

³Grace and peace to you*ᵃ* from God our Father and the Lord Jesus Christ.

Thanksgiving and Prayer

⁴I always thank my God as I remember you in my prayers, ⁵because I hear about your love for all his holy people and your faith in the Lord Jesus. ⁶I pray that your partnership with us in the faith may be effective in deepening your understanding of every good thing we share for the sake of Christ. ⁷Your love has given me great joy and encouragement, be-

cause you, brother, have refreshed the hearts of the Lord's people.

Paul's Plea for Onesimus

⁸Therefore, although in Christ I could be bold and order you to do what you ought to do, ⁹yet I prefer to appeal to you on the basis of love. It is as none other than Paul — an old man and now also a prisoner of Christ Jesus — ¹⁰that I appeal to you for my son Onesimus,*ᵇ* who became my son while I was in chains. ¹¹Formerly he was useless to you, but now he has become useful both to you and to me.

¹²I am sending him — who is my very heart — back to you. ¹³I would have liked to keep him with me

---

ᵃ 3 The Greek is plural; also in verses 22 and 25; elsewhere in this letter "you" is singular.
ᵇ 10 *Onesimus* means *useful*.

so that he could take your place in helping me while I am in chains for the gospel. [14]But I did not want to do anything without your consent, so that any favor you do would not seem forced but would be voluntary. [15]Perhaps the reason he was separated from you for a little while was that you might have him back forever— [16]no longer as a slave, but better than a slave, as a dear brother. He is very dear to me but even dearer to you, both as a fellow man and as a brother in the Lord.

[17]So if you consider me a partner, welcome him as you would welcome me. [18]If he has done you any wrong or owes you anything, charge it to me. [19]I, Paul, am writing this with my own hand. I will pay it back— not to mention that you owe me your very self. [20]I do wish, brother, that I may have some benefit from you in the Lord; refresh my heart in Christ. [21]Confident of your obedience, I write to you, knowing that you will do even more than I ask.

[22]And one thing more: Prepare a guest room for me, because I hope to be restored to you in answer to your prayers.

[23]Epaphras, my fellow prisoner in Christ Jesus, sends you greetings. [24]And so do Mark, Aristarchus, Demas and Luke, my fellow workers.

[25]The grace of the Lord Jesus Christ be with your spirit.

Hebrews

God's Final Word: His Son

1 In the past God spoke to our ancestors through the prophets at many times and in various ways, [2]but in these last days he has spoken to us by his Son, whom he appointed heir of all things, and through whom also he made the universe. [3]The Son is the radiance of God's glory and the exact representation of his being, sustaining all things by his powerful word. After he had provided purification for sins, he sat down at the right hand of the Majesty in heaven. [4]So he became as much superior to the angels as the name he has inherited is superior to theirs.

The Son Superior to Angels

[5]For to which of the angels did God ever say,

> "You are my Son;
>   today I have become your
>   Father"[a]?

Or again,

> "I will be his Father,
>   and he will be my Son"[b]?

[6]And again, when God brings his firstborn into the world, he says,

> "Let all God's angels worship him."[c]

---

[a] 5 Psalm 2:7   [b] 5 2 Samuel 7:14; 1 Chron. 17:13
[c] 6 Deut. 32:43 (see Dead Sea Scrolls and Septuagint)

[7] In speaking of the angels he says,

"He makes his angels spirits,
and his servants flames of
fire."[a]

[8] But about the Son he says,

"Your throne, O God, will last for
ever and ever;
a scepter of justice will be the
scepter of your kingdom.
[9] You have loved righteousness
and hated wickedness;
therefore God, your God,
has set you above your
companions
by anointing you with the oil
of joy."[b]

[10] He also says,

"In the beginning, Lord, you laid
the foundations of the
earth,
and the heavens are the work
of your hands.
[11] They will perish, but you remain;
they will all wear out like a
garment.
[12] You will roll them up like a robe;
like a garment they will be
changed.
But you remain the same,
and your years will never end."[c]

[13] To which of the angels did God
ever say,

"Sit at my right hand
until I make your enemies
a footstool for your feet"[d]?

[14] Are not all angels ministering spirits
sent to serve those who will inherit
salvation?

Warning to Pay Attention

2 We must pay the most careful
attention, therefore, to what we
have heard, so that we do not drift
away. [2] For since the message spoken
through angels was binding, and every violation and disobedience received its just punishment, [3] how
shall we escape if we ignore so great
a salvation? This salvation, which
was first announced by the Lord, was
confirmed to us by those who heard
him. [4] God also testified to it by signs,
wonders and various miracles, and
by gifts of the Holy Spirit distributed
according to his will.

Jesus Made Fully Human

[5] It is not to angels that he has subjected the world to come, about which
we are speaking. [6] But there is a place
where someone has testified:

"What is mankind that you are
mindful of them,
a son of man that you care for
him?
[7] You made them a little[e] lower
than the angels;
you crowned them with glory
and honor
[8]   and put everything under
their feet."[f,g]

In putting everything under them,[h]
God left nothing that is not subject
to them.[h] Yet at present we do not
see everything subject to them.[h] [9] But
we do see Jesus, who was made lower than the angels for a little while,
now crowned with glory and honor
because he suffered death, so that by
the grace of God he might taste death
for everyone.

[10] In bringing many sons and
daughters to glory, it was fitting

---

[a] 7 Psalm 104:4   [b] 9 Psalm 45:6,7
[c] 12 Psalm 102:25-27   [d] 13 Psalm 110:1   [e] 7 Or
them for a little while   [f] 6-8 Psalm 8:4-6
[g] 7,8 Or 'You made him a little lower than the
angels;/ you crowned him with glory and
honor/ [g]and put everything under his feet."
[h] 8 Or him

that God, for whom and through whom everything exists, should make the pioneer of their salvation perfect through what he suffered. 11Both the one who makes people holy and those who are made holy are of the same family. So Jesus is not ashamed to call them brothers and sisters.ª 12He says,

"I will declare your name to my
     brothers and sisters;
  in the assembly I will sing
     your praises."b

13And again,

"I will put my trust in him."c

And again he says,

"Here am I, and the children God
     has given me."d

14Since the children have flesh and blood, he too shared in their humanity so that by his death he might break the power of him who holds the power of death — that is, the devil — 15and free those who all their lives were held in slavery by their fear of death. 16For surely it is not angels he helps, but Abraham's descendants. 17For this reason he had to be made like them,e fully human in every way, in order that he might become a merciful and faithful high priest in service to God, and that he might make atonement for the sins of the people. 18Because he himself suffered when he was tempted, he is able to help those who are being tempted.

Jesus Greater Than Moses

3 Therefore, holy brothers and sisters, who share in the heavenly calling, fix your thoughts on Jesus, whom we acknowledge as our apostle and high priest. 2He was faithful to the one who appointed him, just

as Moses was faithful in all God's house. 3Jesus has been found worthy of greater honor than Moses, just as the builder of a house has greater honor than the house itself. 4For every house is built by someone, but God is the builder of everything. 5"Moses was faithful as a servant in all God's house,f bearing witness to what would be spoken by God in the future. 6But Christ is faithful as the Son over God's house. And we are his house, if indeed we hold firmly to our confidence and the hope in which we glory.

Warning Against Unbelief

7So, as the Holy Spirit says:

"Today, if you hear his voice,
8   do not harden your hearts
  as you did in the rebellion,
     during the time of testing in
        the wilderness,
9 where your ancestors tested and
     tried me,
  though for forty years they
     saw what I did.
10 That is why I was angry with that
     generation;
  I said, 'Their hearts are always
     going astray,
  and they have not known my
     ways.'
11 So I declared on oath in my
     anger,
  'They shall never enter my
     rest.' "g

12See to it, brothers and sisters, that none of you has a sinful, unbelieving heart that turns away from the living

---

ª 11 The Greek word for *brothers and sisters* (*adelphoi*) refers here to believers, both men and women, as part of God's family; also in verse 12; and in 3:1, 12; 10:19; 13:22.
b 12 Psalm 22:22   c 13 Isaiah 8:17
d 13 Isaiah 8:18   e 17 Or *like his brothers*
f 5 Num. 12:7   g 11 Psalm 95:7-11

God. ¹³But encourage one another daily, as long as it is called "Today," so that none of you may be hardened by sin's deceitfulness. ¹⁴We have come to share in Christ, if indeed we hold our original conviction firmly to the very end. ¹⁵As has just been said:

> "Today, if you hear his voice,
>   do not harden your hearts
>   as you did in the rebellion."ᵃ

¹⁶Who were they who heard and rebelled? Were they not all those Moses led out of Egypt? ¹⁷And with whom was he angry for forty years? Was it not with those who sinned, whose bodies perished in the wilderness? ¹⁸And to whom did God swear that they would never enter his rest if not to those who disobeyed? ¹⁹So we see that they were not able to enter, because of their unbelief.

A Sabbath-Rest for the People of God

4 Therefore, since the promise of entering his rest still stands, let us be careful that none of you be found to have fallen short of it. ²For we also have had the good news proclaimed to us, just as they did; but the message they heard was of no value to them, because they did not share the faith of those who obeyed.ᵇ ³Now we who have believed enter that rest, just as God has said,

> "So I declared on oath in my
>   anger,
>   'They shall never enter my
>   rest.'"ᶜ

And yet his works have been finished since the creation of the world. ⁴For somewhere he has spoken about the seventh day in these words: "On the seventh day God rested from all his works."ᵈ ⁵And again in the passage above he says, "They shall never enter my rest."

⁶Therefore since it still remains for some to enter that rest, and since those who formerly had the good news proclaimed to them did not go in because of their disobedience, ⁷God again set a certain day, calling it "Today." This he did when a long time later he spoke through David, as in the passage already quoted:

> "Today, if you hear his voice,
>   do not harden your hearts."ᵃ

⁸For if Joshua had given them rest, God would not have spoken later about another day. ⁹There remains, then, a Sabbath-rest for the people of God; ¹⁰for anyone who enters God's rest also rests from their works,ᵉ just as God did from his. ¹¹Let us, therefore, make every effort to enter that rest, so that no one will perish by following their example of disobedience.

¹²For the word of God is alive and active. Sharper than any double-edged sword, it penetrates even to dividing soul and spirit, joints and marrow; it judges the thoughts and attitudes of the heart. ¹³Nothing in all creation is hidden from God's sight. Everything is uncovered and laid bare before the eyes of him to whom we must give account.

Jesus the Great High Priest

¹⁴Therefore, since we have a great high priest who has ascended into heaven,ᶠ Jesus the Son of God, let us hold firmly to the faith we profess. ¹⁵For we do not have a high priest

---

who is unable to empathize with our weaknesses, but we have one who has been tempted in every way, just as we are — yet he did not sin. ¹⁶Let us then approach God's throne of grace with confidence, so that we may receive mercy and find grace to help us in our time of need.

5 Every high priest is selected from among the people and is appointed to represent the people in matters related to God, to offer gifts and sacrifices for sins. ²He is able to deal gently with those who are ignorant and are going astray, since he himself is subject to weakness. ³This is why he has to offer sacrifices for his own sins, as well as for the sins of the people. ⁴And no one takes this honor on himself, but he receives it when called by God, just as Aaron was.

⁵In the same way, Christ did not take on himself the glory of becoming a high priest. But God said to him,

> "You are my Son;
>   today I have become your
>   Father."ᵃ

⁶And he says in another place,

> "You are a priest forever,
>   in the order of Melchizedek."ᵇ

⁷During the days of Jesus' life on earth, he offered up prayers and petitions with fervent cries and tears to the one who could save him from death, and he was heard because of his reverent submission. ⁸Son though he was, he learned obedience from what he suffered ⁹and, once made perfect, he became the source of eternal salvation for all who obey him ¹⁰and was designated by God to be high priest in the order of Melchizedek.

Warning Against Falling Away

¹¹We have much to say about this, but it is hard to make it clear to you because you no longer try to understand. ¹²In fact, though by this time you ought to be teachers, you need someone to teach you the elementary truths of God's word all over again. You need milk, not solid food! ¹³Anyone who lives on milk, being still an infant, is not acquainted with the teaching about righteousness. ¹⁴But solid food is for the mature, who by constant use have trained themselves to distinguish good from evil.

6 Therefore let us move beyond the elementary teachings about Christ and be taken forward to maturity, not laying again the foundation of repentance from acts that lead to death,ᶜ and of faith in God, ²instruction about cleansing rites,ᵈ the laying on of hands, the resurrection of the dead, and eternal judgment. ³And God permitting, we will do so.

⁴It is impossible for those who have once been enlightened, who have tasted the heavenly gift, who have shared in the Holy Spirit, ⁵who have tasted the goodness of the word of God and the powers of the coming age ⁶and who have fallenᵉ away, to be brought back to repentance. To their loss they are crucifying the Son of God all over again and subjecting him to public disgrace. ⁷Land that drinks in the rain often falling on it and that produces a crop useful to those for whom it is farmed receives the blessing of God. ⁸But land that produces thorns and thistles is worthless and is in danger of being cursed. In the end it will be burned.

⁹Even though we speak like this,

ᵃ 5 Psalm 2:7   ᵇ 6 Psalm 110:4   ᶜ 1 Or from useless rituals   ᵈ 2 Or about baptisms   ᵉ 6 Or age, ᶠif they fall dear friends, we are convinced of better things in your case — the things that have to do with salvation. [10]God is not unjust; he will not forget your work and the love you have shown him as you have helped his people and continue to help them. [11]We want each of you to show this same diligence to the very end, so that what you hope for may be fully realized. [12]We do not want you to become lazy, but to imitate those who through faith and patience inherit what has been promised.

The Certainty of God's Promise

[13]When God made his promise to Abraham, since there was no one greater for him to swear by, he swore by himself, [14]saying, "I will surely bless you and give you many descendants."[a] [15]And so after waiting patiently, Abraham received what was promised.

[16]People swear by someone greater than themselves, and the oath confirms what is said and puts an end to all argument. [17]Because God wanted to make the unchanging nature of his purpose very clear to the heirs of what was promised, he confirmed it with an oath. [18]God did this so that, by two unchangeable things in which it is impossible for God to lie, we who have fled to take hold of the hope set before us may be greatly encouraged. [19]We have this hope as an anchor for the soul, firm and secure. It enters the inner sanctuary behind the curtain, [20]where our forerunner, Jesus, has entered on our behalf. He has become a high priest forever, in the order of Melchizedek.

Melchizedek the Priest

7 This Melchizedek was king of Salem and priest of God Most High. He met Abraham returning from the defeat of the kings and blessed him, [2]and Abraham gave him a tenth of everything. First, the name Melchizedek means "king of righteousness"; then also, "king of Salem" means "king of peace." [3]Without father or mother, without genealogy, without beginning of days or end of life, resembling the Son of God, he remains a priest forever.

[4]Just think how great he was: Even the patriarch Abraham gave him a tenth of the plunder! [5]Now the law requires the descendants of Levi who become priests to collect a tenth from the people — that is, from their fellow Israelites — even though they also are descended from Abraham. [6]This man, however, did not trace his descent from Levi, yet he collected a tenth from Abraham and blessed him who had the promises. [7]And without doubt the lesser is blessed by the greater. [8]In the one case, the tenth is collected by people who die; but in the other case, by him who is declared to be living. [9]One might even say that Levi, who collects the tenth, paid the tenth through Abraham, [10]because when Melchizedek met Abraham, Levi was still in the body of his ancestor.

Jesus Like Melchizedek

[11]If perfection could have been attained through the Levitical priesthood — and indeed the law given to the people established that priesthood — why was there still need for another priest to come, one in the order of Melchizedek, not in the order of Aaron? [12]For when the priesthood is changed, the law must be changed also. [13]He of whom these things are said belonged to a different tribe, and no one from that tribe has ever served

---

[a] 14 Gen. 22:17

at the altar. [14]For it is clear that our Lord descended from Judah, and in regard to that tribe Moses said nothing about priests. [15]And what we have said is even more clear if another priest like Melchizedek appears, [16]one who has become a priest not on the basis of a regulation as to his ancestry but on the basis of the power of an indestructible life. [17]For it is declared:

> "You are a priest forever,
>   in the order of Melchizedek."[a]

[18]The former regulation is set aside because it was weak and useless [19](for the law made nothing perfect), and a better hope is introduced, by which we draw near to God.

[20]And it was not without an oath! Others became priests without any oath, [21]but he became a priest with an oath when God said to him:

> "The Lord has sworn
>   and will not change his mind:
>   'You are a priest forever.' "[a]

[22]Because of this oath, Jesus has become the guarantor of a better covenant.

[23]Now there have been many of those priests, since death prevented them from continuing in office; [24]but because Jesus lives forever, he has a permanent priesthood. [25]Therefore he is able to save completely[b] those who come to God through him, because he always lives to intercede for them.

[26]Such a high priest truly meets our need — one who is holy, blameless, pure, set apart from sinners, exalted above the heavens. [27]Unlike the other high priests, he does not need to offer sacrifices day after day, first for his own sins, and then for the sins of the people. He sacrificed for their sins once for all when he offered himself.

[28]For the law appoints as high priests men in all their weakness; but the oath, which came after the law, appointed the Son, who has been made perfect forever.

The High Priest of a New Covenant

8 Now the main point of what we are saying is this: We do have such a high priest, who sat down at the right hand of the throne of the Majesty in heaven, [2]and who serves in the sanctuary, the true tabernacle set up by the Lord, not by a mere human being.

[3]Every high priest is appointed to offer both gifts and sacrifices, and so it was necessary for this one also to have something to offer. [4]If he were on earth, he would not be a priest, for there are already priests who offer the gifts prescribed by the law. [5]They serve at a sanctuary that is a copy and shadow of what is in heaven. This is why Moses was warned when he was about to build the tabernacle: "See to it that you make everything according to the pattern shown you on the mountain."[c] [6]But in fact the ministry Jesus has received is as superior to theirs as the covenant of which he is mediator is superior to the old one, since the new covenant is established on better promises.

[7]For if there had been nothing wrong with that first covenant, no place would have been sought for another. [8]But God found fault with the people and said[d]:

> "The days are coming, declares
>   the Lord,
> when I will make a new
>   covenant

---

[a] 17,21 Psalm 110:4   [b] 25 Or forever
[c] 5 Exodus 25:40   [d] 8 Some manuscripts may be translated fault and said to the people.

with the people of Israel
and with the people of Judah.
⁹ It will not be like the covenant
I made with their ancestors
when I took them by the hand
to lead them out of Egypt,
because they did not remain
faithful to my covenant,
and I turned away from them,
declares the Lord.
¹⁰ This is the covenant I will
establish with the people
of Israel
after that time, declares the
Lord.
I will put my laws in their minds
and write them on their
hearts.
I will be their God,
and they will be my people.
¹¹ No longer will they teach their
neighbor,
or say to one another, 'Know
the Lord,'
because they will all know me,
from the least of them to the
greatest.
¹² For I will forgive their
wickedness
and will remember their sins
no more."ᵃ

¹³ By calling this covenant "new,"
he has made the first one obsolete;
and what is obsolete and outdated
will soon disappear.

Worship in the Earthly Tabernacle

9 Now the first covenant had regulations for worship and also an earthly sanctuary. ² A tabernacle was set up. In its first room were the lampstand and the table with its consecrated bread; this was called the Holy Place. ³ Behind the second curtain was a room called the Most Holy Place, ⁴ which had the golden altar of

incense and the gold-covered ark of the covenant. This ark contained the gold jar of manna, Aaron's staff that had budded, and the stone tablets of the covenant. ⁵ Above the ark were the cherubim of the Glory, overshadowing the atonement cover. But we cannot discuss these things in detail now.

⁶ When everything had been arranged like this, the priests entered regularly into the outer room to carry on their ministry. ⁷ But only the high priest entered the inner room, and that only once a year, and never without blood, which he offered for himself and for the sins the people had committed in ignorance. ⁸ The Holy Spirit was showing by this that the way into the Most Holy Place had not yet been disclosed as long as the first tabernacle was still functioning. ⁹ This is an illustration for the present time, indicating that the gifts and sacrifices being offered were not able to clear the conscience of the worshiper. ¹⁰ They are only a matter of food and drink and various ceremonial washings — external regulations applying until the time of the new order.

The Blood of Christ

¹¹ But when Christ came as high priest of the good things that are now already here,ᵇ he went through the greater and more perfect tabernacle that is not made with human hands, that is to say, is not a part of this creation. ¹² He did not enter by means of the blood of goats and calves; but he entered the Most Holy Place once for all by his own blood, thus obtainingᶜ eternal redemption. ¹³ The blood of goats and bulls and the ashes of a heifer sprinkled on those

---

ᵃ 12 Jer. 31:31-34   ᵇ 11 Some early manuscripts are to come   ᶜ 12 Or blood, having obtained who are ceremonially unclean sanctify them so that they are outwardly clean. 14How much more, then, will the blood of Christ, who through the eternal Spirit offered himself unblemished to God, cleanse our consciences from acts that lead to death,ᵃ so that we may serve the living God!

15For this reason Christ is the mediator of a new covenant, that those who are called may receive the promised eternal inheritance — now that he has died as a ransom to set them free from the sins committed under the first covenant.

16In the case of a will,ᵇ it is necessary to prove the death of the one who made it, 17because a will is in force only when somebody has died; it never takes effect while the one who made it is living. 18This is why even the first covenant was not put into effect without blood. 19When Moses had proclaimed every command of the law to all the people, he took the blood of calves, together with water, scarlet wool and branches of hyssop, and sprinkled the scroll and all the people. 20He said, "This is the blood of the covenant, which God has commanded you to keep."ᶜ 21In the same way, he sprinkled with the blood both the tabernacle and everything used in its ceremonies. 22In fact, the law requires that nearly everything be cleansed with blood, and without the shedding of blood there is no forgiveness.

23It was necessary, then, for the copies of the heavenly things to be purified with these sacrifices, but the heavenly things themselves with better sacrifices than these. 24For Christ did not enter a sanctuary made with human hands that was only a copy of the true one; he entered heaven itself, now to appear for us in God's presence. 25Nor did he enter heaven to offer himself again and again, the way the high priest enters the Most Holy Place every year with blood that is not his own. 26Otherwise Christ would have had to suffer many times since the creation of the world. But he has appeared once for all at the culmination of the ages to do away with sin by the sacrifice of himself. 27Just as people are destined to die once, and after that to face judgment, 28so Christ was sacrificed once to take away the sins of many; and he will appear a second time, not to bear sin, but to bring salvation to those who are waiting for him.

Christ's Sacrifice Once for All

10 The law is only a shadow of the good things that are coming — not the realities themselves. For this reason it can never, by the same sacrifices repeated endlessly year after year, make perfect those who draw near to worship. 2Otherwise, would they not have stopped being offered? For the worshipers would have been cleansed once for all, and would no longer have felt guilty for their sins. 3But those sacrifices are an annual reminder of sins. 4It is impossible for the blood of bulls and goats to take away sins.

5Therefore, when Christ came into the world, he said:

"Sacrifice and offering you did
    not desire,
  but a body you prepared for
    me;
6with burnt offerings and sin
    offerings
  you were not pleased.

ᵃ 14 Or *from useless rituals*   ᵇ 16 Same Greek word as *covenant*; also in verse 17   ᶜ 20 Exodus 24:8

7 Then I said, 'Here I am — it is
    written about me in the
    scroll —
I have come to do your will,
    my God.'"ᵃ

8 First he said, "Sacrifices and offerings, burnt offerings and sin offerings you did not desire, nor were you
pleased with them" — though they
were offered in accordance with the
law. 9 Then he said, "Here I am, I have
come to do your will." He sets aside
the first to establish the second. 10 And
by that will, we have been made holy
through the sacrifice of the body of
Jesus Christ once for all.

11 Day after day every priest stands
and performs his religious duties;
again and again he offers the same
sacrifices, which can never take away
sins. 12 But when this priest had offered for all time one sacrifice for
sins, he sat down at the right hand
of God, 13 and since that time he waits
for his enemies to be made his footstool. 14 For by one sacrifice he has
made perfect forever those who are
being made holy.

15 The Holy Spirit also testifies to
us about this. First he says:

16 "This is the covenant I will make
    with them
    after that time, says the
        Lord.
I will put my laws in their
    hearts,
    and I will write them on their
        minds."ᵇ

17 Then he adds:

"Their sins and lawless acts
I will remember no
    more."ᶜ

18 And where these have been forgiven, sacrifice for sin is no longer
necessary.

A Call to Persevere in Faith

19 Therefore, brothers and sisters,
since we have confidence to enter the
Most Holy Place by the blood of Jesus,
20 by a new and living way opened
for us through the curtain, that is,
his body, 21 and since we have a great
priest over the house of God, 22 let us
draw near to God with a sincere heart
and with the full assurance that faith
brings, having our hearts sprinkled to
cleanse us from a guilty conscience
and having our bodies washed with
pure water. 23 Let us hold unswerv-
ingly to the hope we profess, for he
who promised is faithful. 24 And let
us consider how we may spur one another on toward love and good deeds,
25 not giving up meeting together, as
some are in the habit of doing, but encouraging one another — and all the
more as you see the Day approaching.

26 If we deliberately keep on sinning after we have received the
knowledge of the truth, no sacrifice
for sins is left, 27 but only a fearful expectation of judgment and of raging
fire that will consume the enemies of
God. 28 Anyone who rejected the law
of Moses died without mercy on the
testimony of two or three witnesses.
29 How much more severely do you
think someone deserves to be punished who has trampled the Son of
God underfoot, who has treated as
an unholy thing the blood of the covenant that sanctified them, and who
has insulted the Spirit of grace? 30 For
we know him who said, "It is mine to
avenge; I will repay,"ᵈ and again, "The
Lord will judge his people."ᵉ 31 It is a
dreadful thing to fall into the hands of
the living God.

ᵃ 7 Psalm 40:6-8 (see Septuagint)
ᵇ 16 Jer. 31:33   ᶜ 17 Jer. 31:34
ᵈ 30 Deut. 32:35   ᵉ 30 Deut. 32:36; Psalm
135:14

³²Remember those earlier days after you had received the light, when you endured in a great conflict full of suffering. ³³Sometimes you were publicly exposed to insult and persecution; at other times you stood side by side with those who were so treated. ³⁴You suffered along with those in prison and joyfully accepted the confiscation of your property, because you knew that you yourselves had better and lasting possessions. ³⁵So do not throw away your confidence; it will be richly rewarded.

³⁶You need to persevere so that when you have done the will of God, you will receive what he has promised. ³⁷For,

"In just a little while,
    he who is coming will come
    and will not delay."ᵃ

³⁸And,

"But my righteousᵇ one will live
    by faith.
And I take no pleasure
    in the one who shrinks back."ᶜ

³⁹But we do not belong to those who shrink back and are destroyed, but to those who have faith and are saved.

Faith in Action

11 Now faith is confidence in what we hope for and assurance about what we do not see. ²This is what the ancients were commended for.

³By faith we understand that the universe was formed at God's command, so that what is seen was not made out of what was visible.

⁴By faith Abel brought God a better offering than Cain did. By faith he was commended as righteous, when God spoke well of his offerings. And by faith Abel still speaks, even though he is dead.

⁵By faith Enoch was taken from this life, so that he did not experience death: "He could not be found, because God had taken him away."ᵈ For before he was taken, he was commended as one who pleased God. ⁶And without faith it is impossible to please God, because anyone who comes to him must believe that he exists and that he rewards those who earnestly seek him.

⁷By faith Noah, when warned about things not yet seen, in holy fear built an ark to save his family. By his faith he condemned the world and became heir of the righteousness that is in keeping with faith.

⁸By faith Abraham, when called to go to a place he would later receive as his inheritance, obeyed and went, even though he did not know where he was going. ⁹By faith he made his home in the promised land like a stranger in a foreign country; he lived in tents, as did Isaac and Jacob, who were heirs with him of the same promise. ¹⁰For he was looking forward to the city with foundations, whose architect and builder is God. ¹¹And by faith even Sarah, who was past childbearing age, was enabled to bear children because sheᵉ considered him faithful who had made the promise. ¹²And so from this one man, and he as good as dead, came descendants as numerous as the stars in the sky and as countless as the sand on the seashore.

¹³All these people were still living by faith when they died. They did not receive the things promised;

ᵃ 37 Isaiah 26:20; Hab. 2:3   ᵇ 38 Some early manuscripts *But the righteous*   ᶜ 38 Hab. 2:4 (see Septuagint)   ᵈ 5 Gen. 5:24   ᵉ 11 Or By faith Abraham, even though he was too old to have children — and Sarah herself was not able to conceive — was enabled to become a father because he they only saw them and welcomed them from a distance, admitting that they were foreigners and strangers on earth. ¹⁴People who say such things show that they are looking for a country of their own. ¹⁵If they had been thinking of the country they had left, they would have had opportunity to return. ¹⁶Instead, they were longing for a better country — a heavenly one. Therefore God is not ashamed to be called their God, for he has prepared a city for them.

¹⁷By faith Abraham, when God tested him, offered Isaac as a sacrifice. He who had embraced the promises was about to sacrifice his one and only son, ¹⁸even though God had said to him, "It is through Isaac that your offspring will be reckoned."ᵃ ¹⁹Abraham reasoned that God could even raise the dead, and so in a manner of speaking he did receive Isaac back from death.

²⁰By faith Isaac blessed Jacob and Esau in regard to their future.

²¹By faith Jacob, when he was dying, blessed each of Joseph's sons, and worshiped as he leaned on the top of his staff.

²²By faith Joseph, when his end was near, spoke about the exodus of the Israelites from Egypt and gave instructions concerning the burial of his bones.

²³By faith Moses' parents hid him for three months after he was born, because they saw he was no ordinary child, and they were not afraid of the king's edict.

²⁴By faith Moses, when he had grown up, refused to be known as the son of Pharaoh's daughter. ²⁵He chose to be mistreated along with the people of God rather than to enjoy the fleeting pleasures of sin. ²⁶He regarded disgrace for the sake of Christ as

of greater value than the treasures of Egypt, because he was looking ahead to his reward. ²⁷By faith he left Egypt, not fearing the king's anger; he persevered because he saw him who is invisible. ²⁸By faith he kept the Passover and the application of blood, so that the destroyer of the firstborn would not touch the firstborn of Israel.

²⁹By faith the people passed through the Red Sea as on dry land; but when the Egyptians tried to do so, they were drowned.

³⁰By faith the walls of Jericho fell, after the army had marched around them for seven days.

³¹By faith the prostitute Rahab, because she welcomed the spies, was not killed with those who were disobedient.ᵇ

³²And what more shall I say? I do not have time to tell about Gideon, Barak, Samson and Jephthah, about David and Samuel and the prophets, ³³who through faith conquered kingdoms, administered justice, and gained what was promised; who shut the mouths of lions, ³⁴quenched the fury of the flames, and escaped the edge of the sword; whose weakness was turned to strength; and who became powerful in battle and routed foreign armies. ³⁵Women received back their dead, raised to life again. There were others who were tortured, refusing to be released so that they might gain an even better resurrection. ³⁶Some faced jeers and flogging, and even chains and imprisonment. ³⁷They were put to death by stoning;ᶜ they were sawed in two; they were killed by the sword. They went about in sheepskins and goatskins, destitute, persecuted and

---

ᵃ 18 Gen. 21:12   ᵇ 31 Or unbelieving
ᶜ 37 Some early manuscripts stoning; they were put to the test;

mistreated — ³⁸the world was not
worthy of them. They wandered in
deserts and mountains, living in
caves and in holes in the ground.

³⁹These were all commended for
their faith, yet none of them received
what had been promised, ⁴⁰since God
had planned something better for us
so that only together with us would
they be made perfect.

12 Therefore, since we are surrounded by such a great cloud
of witnesses, let us throw off everything that hinders and the sin that so
easily entangles. And let us run with
perseverance the race marked out for
us, ²fixing our eyes on Jesus, the pioneer and perfecter of faith. For the joy
set before him he endured the cross,
scorning its shame, and sat down at
the right hand of the throne of God.
³Consider him who endured such opposition from sinners, so that you
will not grow weary and lose heart.

God Disciplines His Children

⁴In your struggle against sin, you
have not yet resisted to the point of
shedding your blood. ⁵And have you
completely forgotten this word of encouragement that addresses you as
a father addresses his son? It says,

"My son, do not make light of the
     Lord's discipline,
 and do not lose heart when he
     rebukes you,
⁶because the Lord disciplines the
     one he loves,
 and he chastens everyone he
     accepts as his son."ᵃ

⁷Endure hardship as discipline;
God is treating you as his children.
For what children are not disciplined
by their father? ⁸If you are not disciplined — and everyone undergoes
discipline — then you are not legit-

imate, not true sons and daughters
at all. ⁹Moreover, we have all had human fathers who disciplined us and
we respected them for it. How much
more should we submit to the Father
of spirits and live! ¹⁰They disciplined
us for a little while as they thought
best; but God disciplines us for our
good, in order that we may share in
his holiness. ¹¹No discipline seems
pleasant at the time, but painful. Later on, however, it produces a harvest
of righteousness and peace for those
who have been trained by it.

¹²Therefore, strengthen your feeble arms and weak knees. ¹³"Make
level paths for your feet,"ᵇ so that
the lame may not be disabled, but
rather healed.

Warning and Encouragement

¹⁴Make every effort to live in peace
with everyone and to be holy; without holiness no one will see the Lord.
¹⁵See to it that no one falls short of the
grace of God and that no bitter root
grows up to cause trouble and defile
many. ¹⁶See that no one is sexually
immoral, or is godless like Esau, who
for a single meal sold his inheritance
rights as the oldest son. ¹⁷Afterward,
as you know, when he wanted to inherit this blessing, he was rejected.
Even though he sought the blessing
with tears, he could not change what
he had done.

The Mountain of Fear and
the Mountain of Joy

¹⁸You have not come to a mountain
that can be touched and that is burning with fire; to darkness, gloom and
storm; ¹⁹to a trumpet blast or to such
a voice speaking words that those
who heard it begged that no further

ᵃ 5,6 Prov. 3:11,12 (see Septuagint)
ᵇ 13 Prov. 4:26

word be spoken to them, [20]because they could not bear what was commanded: "If even an animal touches the mountain, it must be stoned to death."[a] [21]The sight was so terrifying that Moses said, "I am trembling with fear."[b]

[22]But you have come to Mount Zion, to the city of the living God, the heavenly Jerusalem. You have come to thousands upon thousands of angels in joyful assembly, [23]to the church of the firstborn, whose names are written in heaven. You have come to God, the Judge of all, to the spirits of the righteous made perfect, [24]to Jesus the mediator of a new covenant, and to the sprinkled blood that speaks a better word than the blood of Abel.

[25]See to it that you do not refuse him who speaks. If they did not escape when they refused him who warned them on earth, how much less will we, if we turn away from him who warns us from heaven? [26]At that time his voice shook the earth, but now he has promised, "Once more I will shake not only the earth but also the heavens."[c] [27]The words "once more" indicate the removing of what can be shaken — that is, created things — so that what cannot be shaken may remain.

[28]Therefore, since we are receiving a kingdom that cannot be shaken, let us be thankful, and so worship God acceptably with reverence and awe, [29]for our "God is a consuming fire."[d]

Concluding Exhortations

13 Keep on loving one another as brothers and sisters. [2]Do not forget to show hospitality to strangers, for by so doing some people have shown hospitality to angels without knowing it. [3]Continue to remember those in prison as if you were together with them in prison, and those who are mistreated as if you yourselves were suffering.

[4]Marriage should be honored by all, and the marriage bed kept pure, for God will judge the adulterer and all the sexually immoral. [5]Keep your lives free from the love of money and be content with what you have, because God has said,

"Never will I leave you;
    never will I forsake you."[e]

[6]So we say with confidence,

"The Lord is my helper; I will not
        be afraid.
    What can mere mortals do to
        me?"[f]

[7]Remember your leaders, who spoke the word of God to you. Consider the outcome of their way of life and imitate their faith. [8]Jesus Christ is the same yesterday and today and forever.

[9]Do not be carried away by all kinds of strange teachings. It is good for our hearts to be strengthened by grace, not by eating ceremonial foods, which is of no benefit to those who do so. [10]We have an altar from which those who minister at the tabernacle have no right to eat.

[11]The high priest carries the blood of animals into the Most Holy Place as a sin offering, but the bodies are burned outside the camp. [12]And so Jesus also suffered outside the city gate to make the people holy through his own blood. [13]Let us, then, go to him outside the camp, bearing the disgrace he bore. [14]For here we do not have an enduring city, but we are looking for the city that is to come.

---

[a] 20 Exodus 19:12,13   [b] 21 See Deut. 9:19.
[c] 26 Haggai 2:6   [d] 29 Deut. 4:24
[e] 5 Deut. 31:6   [f] 6 Psalm 118:6,7

¹⁵Through Jesus, therefore, let us continually offer to God a sacrifice of praise — the fruit of lips that openly profess his name. ¹⁶And do not forget to do good and to share with others, for with such sacrifices God is pleased.

¹⁷Have confidence in your leaders and submit to their authority, because they keep watch over you as those who must give an account. Do this so that their work will be a joy, not a burden, for that would be of no benefit to you.

¹⁸Pray for us. We are sure that we have a clear conscience and desire to live honorably in every way. ¹⁹I particularly urge you to pray so that I may be restored to you soon.

Benediction and Final Greetings

²⁰Now may the God of peace, who through the blood of the eternal covenant brought back from the dead our Lord Jesus, that great Shepherd of the sheep, ²¹equip you with everything good for doing his will, and may he work in us what is pleasing to him, through Jesus Christ, to whom be glory for ever and ever. Amen.

²²Brothers and sisters, I urge you to bear with my word of exhortation, for in fact I have written to you quite briefly.

²³I want you to know that our brother Timothy has been released. If he arrives soon, I will come with him to see you.

²⁴Greet all your leaders and all the Lord's people. Those from Italy send you their greetings.

²⁵Grace be with you all.

James

1 James, a servant of God and of the Lord Jesus Christ,

To the twelve tribes scattered among the nations:

Greetings.

Trials and Temptations

²Consider it pure joy, my brothers and sisters,ᵃ whenever you face trials of many kinds, ³because you know that the testing of your faith produces perseverance. ⁴Let perseverance finish its work so that you may be mature and complete, not lacking anything. ⁵If any of you lacks wisdom, you should ask God, who gives generously to all without finding fault, and it will be given to you. ⁶But when you ask, you must believe and not doubt, because the one who doubts is like a wave of the sea, blown and tossed by the wind. ⁷That person should not expect to receive anything from the Lord. ⁸Such a person is double-minded and unstable in all they do.

⁹Believers in humble circumstances ought to take pride in their high position. ¹⁰But the rich should take

---

ᵃ *2* The Greek word for *brothers and sisters* (*adelphoi*) refers here to believers, both men and women, as part of God's family; also in verses 16 and 19; and in 2:1, 5, 14; 3:10, 12; 4:11; 5:7, 9, 10, 12, 19.

pride in their humiliation — since they will pass away like a wild flower. [11]For the sun rises with scorching heat and withers the plant; its blossom falls and its beauty is destroyed. In the same way, the rich will fade away even while they go about their business.

[12]Blessed is the one who perseveres under trial because, having stood the test, that person will receive the crown of life that the Lord has promised to those who love him.

[13]When tempted, no one should say, "God is tempting me." For God cannot be tempted by evil, nor does he tempt anyone; [14]but each person is tempted when they are dragged away by their own evil desire and enticed. [15]Then, after desire has conceived, it gives birth to sin; and sin, when it is full-grown, gives birth to death.

[16]Don't be deceived, my dear brothers and sisters. [17]Every good and perfect gift is from above, coming down from the Father of the heavenly lights, who does not change like shifting shadows. [18]He chose to give us birth through the word of truth, that we might be a kind of firstfruits of all he created.

Listening and Doing

[19]My dear brothers and sisters, take note of this: Everyone should be quick to listen, slow to speak and slow to become angry, [20]because human anger does not produce the righteousness that God desires. [21]Therefore, get rid of all moral filth and the evil that is so prevalent and humbly accept the word planted in you, which can save you.

[22]Do not merely listen to the word, and so deceive yourselves. Do what it says. [23]Anyone who listens to the word but does not do what it says is like someone who looks at his face in a mirror [24]and, after looking at himself, goes away and immediately forgets what he looks like. [25]But whoever looks intently into the perfect law that gives freedom, and continues in it — not forgetting what they have heard, but doing it — they will be blessed in what they do.

[26]Those who consider themselves religious and yet do not keep a tight rein on their tongues deceive themselves, and their religion is worthless. [27]Religion that God our Father accepts as pure and faultless is this: to look after orphans and widows in their distress and to keep oneself from being polluted by the world.

Favoritism Forbidden

2 My brothers and sisters, believers in our glorious Lord Jesus Christ must not show favoritism. [2]Suppose a man comes into your meeting wearing a gold ring and fine clothes, and a poor man in filthy old clothes also comes in. [3]If you show special attention to the man wearing fine clothes and say, "Here's a good seat for you," but say to the poor man, "You stand there" or "Sit on the floor by my feet," [4]have you not discriminated among yourselves and become judges with evil thoughts?

[5]Listen, my dear brothers and sisters: Has not God chosen those who are poor in the eyes of the world to be rich in faith and to inherit the kingdom he promised those who love him? [6]But you have dishonored the poor. Is it not the rich who are exploiting you? Are they not the ones who are dragging you into court? [7]Are they not the ones who are blaspheming the noble name of him to whom you belong?

[8]If you really keep the royal law

found in Scripture, "Love your neighbor as yourself,"[a] you are doing right. [9]But if you show favoritism, you sin and are convicted by the law as lawbreakers. [10]For whoever keeps the whole law and yet stumbles at just one point is guilty of breaking all of it. [11]For he who said, "You shall not commit adultery,"[b] also said, "You shall not murder."[c] If you do not commit adultery but do commit murder, you have become a lawbreaker.

[12]Speak and act as those who are going to be judged by the law that gives freedom, [13]because judgment without mercy will be shown to anyone who has not been merciful. Mercy triumphs over judgment.

Faith and Deeds

[14]What good is it, my brothers and sisters, if someone claims to have faith but has no deeds? Can such faith save them? [15]Suppose a brother or a sister is without clothes and daily food. [16]If one of you says to them, "Go in peace; keep warm and well fed," but does nothing about their physical needs, what good is it? [17]In the same way, faith by itself, if it is not accompanied by action, is dead.

[18]But someone will say, "You have faith; I have deeds."

Show me your faith without deeds, and I will show you my faith by my deeds. [19]You believe that there is one God. Good! Even the demons believe that — and shudder.

[20]You foolish person, do you want evidence that faith without deeds is useless[d]? [21]Was not our father Abraham considered righteous for what he did when he offered his son Isaac on the altar? [22]You see that his faith and his actions were working together, and his faith was made complete by what he did. [23]And the scripture was fulfilled that says, "Abraham believed God, and it was credited to him as righteousness,"[e] and he was called God's friend. [24]You see that a person is considered righteous by what they do and not by faith alone.

[25]In the same way, was not even Rahab the prostitute considered righteous for what she did when she gave lodging to the spies and sent them off in a different direction? [26]As the body without the spirit is dead, so faith without deeds is dead.

Taming the Tongue

3 Not many of you should become teachers, my fellow believers, because you know that we who teach will be judged more strictly. [2]We all stumble in many ways. Anyone who is never at fault in what they say is perfect, able to keep their whole body in check.

[3]When we put bits into the mouths of horses to make them obey us, we can turn the whole animal. [4]Or take ships as an example. Although they are so large and are driven by strong winds, they are steered by a very small rudder wherever the pilot wants to go. [5]Likewise, the tongue is a small part of the body, but it makes great boasts. Consider what a great forest is set on fire by a small spark. [6]The tongue also is a fire, a world of evil among the parts of the body. It corrupts the whole body, sets the whole course of one's life on fire, and is itself set on fire by hell.

[7]All kinds of animals, birds, reptiles and sea creatures are being tamed and have been tamed by mankind, [8]but no human being can tame the tongue. It is a restless evil, full of deadly poison.

[a] 8 Lev. 19:18   [b] 11 Exodus 20:14; Deut. 5:18   [c] 11 Exodus 20:13; Deut. 5:17   [d] 20 Some early manuscripts *dead*   [e] 23 Gen. 15:6

⁹With the tongue we praise our Lord and Father, and with it we curse human beings, who have been made in God's likeness. ¹⁰Out of the same mouth come praise and cursing. My brothers and sisters, this should not be. ¹¹Can both fresh water and salt water flow from the same spring? ¹²My brothers and sisters, can a fig tree bear olives, or a grapevine bear figs? Neither can a salt spring produce fresh water.

Two Kinds of Wisdom

¹³Who is wise and understanding among you? Let them show it by their good life, by deeds done in the humility that comes from wisdom. ¹⁴But if you harbor bitter envy and selfish ambition in your hearts, do not boast about it or deny the truth. ¹⁵Such "wisdom" does not come down from heaven but is earthly, unspiritual, demonic. ¹⁶For where you have envy and selfish ambition, there you find disorder and every evil practice. ¹⁷But the wisdom that comes from heaven is first of all pure; then peace-loving, considerate, submissive, full of mercy and good fruit, impartial and sincere. ¹⁸Peacemakers who sow in peace reap a harvest of righteousness.

Submit Yourselves to God

4 What causes fights and quarrels among you? Don't they come from your desires that battle within you? ²You desire but do not have, so you kill. You covet but you cannot get what you want, so you quarrel and fight. You do not have because you do not ask God. ³When you ask, you do not receive, because you ask with wrong motives, that you may spend what you get on your pleasures. ⁴You adulterous people,ᵃ don't

you know that friendship with the world means enmity against God? Therefore, anyone who chooses to be a friend of the world becomes an enemy of God. ⁵Or do you think Scripture says without reason that he jealously longs for the spirit he has caused to dwell in us?ᵇ ⁶But he gives us more grace. That is why Scripture says:

"God opposes the proud
  but shows favor to the
  humble."ᶜ

⁷Submit yourselves, then, to God. Resist the devil, and he will flee from you. ⁸Come near to God and he will come near to you. Wash your hands, you sinners, and purify your hearts, you double-minded. ⁹Grieve, mourn and wail. Change your laughter to mourning and your joy to gloom. ¹⁰Humble yourselves before the Lord, and he will lift you up.

¹¹Brothers and sisters, do not slander one another. Anyone who speaks against a brother or sisterᵈ or judges them speaks against the law and judges it. When you judge the law, you are not keeping it, but sitting in judgment on it. ¹²There is only one Lawgiver and Judge, the one who is able to save and destroy. But you—who are you to judge your neighbor?

Boasting About Tomorrow

¹³Now listen, you who say, "Today or tomorrow we will go to this or that city, spend a year there, carry on business and make money." ¹⁴Why, you do not even know what will happen

---

ᵃ 4 An allusion to covenant unfaithfulness; see Hosea 3:1. ᵇ 5 Or that the spirit he caused to dwell in us envies intensely; or that the Spirit he caused to dwell in us longs jealously ᶜ 6 Prov. 3:34 ᵈ 11 The Greek word for brother or sister (adelphos) refers here to a believer, whether man or woman, as part of God's family.

tomorrow. What is your life? You are a mist that appears for a little while and then vanishes. [15]Instead, you ought to say, "If it is the Lord's will, we will live and do this or that." [16]As it is, you boast in your arrogant schemes. All such boasting is evil. [17]If anyone, then, knows the good they ought to do and doesn't do it, it is sin for them.

Warning to Rich Oppressors

5 Now listen, you rich people, weep and wail because of the misery that is coming on you. [2]Your wealth has rotted, and moths have eaten your clothes. [3]Your gold and silver are corroded. Their corrosion will testify against you and eat your flesh like fire. You have hoarded wealth in the last days. [4]Look! The wages you failed to pay the workers who mowed your fields are crying out against you. The cries of the harvesters have reached the ears of the Lord Almighty. [5]You have lived on earth in luxury and self-indulgence. You have fattened yourselves in the day of slaughter.[a] [6]You have condemned and murdered the innocent one, who was not opposing you.

Patience in Suffering

[7]Be patient, then, brothers and sisters, until the Lord's coming. See how the farmer waits for the land to yield its valuable crop, patiently waiting for the autumn and spring rains. [8]You too, be patient and stand firm, because the Lord's coming is near. [9]Don't grumble against one another, brothers and sisters, or you will be judged. The Judge is standing at the door!

[10]Brothers and sisters, as an example of patience in the face of suffer-

ing, take the prophets who spoke in the name of the Lord. [11]As you know, we count as blessed those who have persevered. You have heard of Job's perseverance and have seen what the Lord finally brought about. The Lord is full of compassion and mercy.

[12]Above all, my brothers and sisters, do not swear — not by heaven or by earth or by anything else. All you need to say is a simple "Yes" or "No." Otherwise you will be condemned.

The Prayer of Faith

[13]Is anyone among you in trouble? Let them pray. Is anyone happy? Let them sing songs of praise. [14]Is anyone among you sick? Let them call the elders of the church to pray over them and anoint them with oil in the name of the Lord. [15]And the prayer offered in faith will make the sick person well; the Lord will raise them up. If they have sinned, they will be forgiven. [16]Therefore confess your sins to each other and pray for each other so that you may be healed. The prayer of a righteous person is powerful and effective.

[17]Elijah was a human being, even as we are. He prayed earnestly that it would not rain, and it did not rain on the land for three and a half years. [18]Again he prayed, and the heavens gave rain, and the earth produced its crops.

[19]My brothers and sisters, if one of you should wander from the truth and someone should bring that person back, [20]remember this: Whoever turns a sinner from the error of their way will save them from death and cover over a multitude of sins.

---

[a] 5 Or yourselves as in a day of feasting

1 Peter

1 Peter, an apostle of Jesus Christ,

To God's elect, exiles scattered throughout the provinces of Pontus, Galatia, Cappadocia, Asia and Bithynia, ²who have been chosen according to the foreknowledge of God the Father, through the sanctifying work of the Spirit, to be obedient to Jesus Christ and sprinkled with his blood:

Grace and peace be yours in abundance.

Praise to God for a Living Hope

³Praise be to the God and Father of our Lord Jesus Christ! In his great mercy he has given us new birth into a living hope through the resurrection of Jesus Christ from the dead, ⁴and into an inheritance that can never perish, spoil or fade. This inheritance is kept in heaven for you, ⁵who through faith are shielded by God's power until the coming of the salvation that is ready to be revealed in the last time. ⁶In all this you greatly rejoice, though now for a little while you may have had to suffer grief in all kinds of trials. ⁷These have come so that the proven genuineness of your faith — of greater worth than gold, which perishes even though refined by fire — may result in praise, glory and honor when Jesus Christ is revealed. ⁸Though you have not seen him, you love him; and even though you do not see him now, you believe in him and are filled with an inexpressible and glorious joy, ⁹for you are receiving the end result of your faith, the salvation of your souls.

¹⁰Concerning this salvation, the prophets, who spoke of the grace that was to come to you, searched intently and with the greatest care, ¹¹trying to find out the time and circumstances to which the Spirit of Christ in them was pointing when he predicted the sufferings of the Messiah and the glories that would follow. ¹²It was revealed to them that they were not serving themselves but you, when they spoke of the things that have now been told you by those who have preached the gospel to you by the Holy Spirit sent from heaven. Even angels long to look into these things.

Be Holy

¹³Therefore, with minds that are alert and fully sober, set your hope on the grace to be brought to you when Jesus Christ is revealed at his coming. ¹⁴As obedient children, do not conform to the evil desires you had when you lived in ignorance. ¹⁵But just as he who called you is holy, so be holy in all you do; ¹⁶for it is written: "Be holy, because I am holy."ᵃ

¹⁷Since you call on a Father who judges each person's work impartially, live out your time as foreigners here in reverent fear. ¹⁸For you know that it was not with perishable things such as silver or gold that you were redeemed from the empty way of life handed down to you from your ancestors, ¹⁹but with the precious blood of Christ, a lamb without blemish or defect. ²⁰He was chosen before the creation of the world, but was revealed in these last times for your sake. ²¹Through him you believe in God, who raised him from the dead

---

ᵃ *16* Lev. 11:44,45; 19:2

and glorified him, and so your faith and hope are in God.

²²Now that you have purified yourselves by obeying the truth so that you have sincere love for each other, love one another deeply, from the heart.ᵒ ²³For you have been born again, not of perishable seed, but of imperishable, through the living and enduring word of God. ²⁴For,

> "All people are like grass,
>   and all their glory is like the
>   flowers of the field;
> the grass withers and the flowers
>   fall,
> ²⁵   but the word of the Lord
>   endures forever."ᵇ

And this is the word that was preached to you.

2 Therefore, rid yourselves of all malice and all deceit, hypocrisy, envy, and slander of every kind. ²Like newborn babies, crave pure spiritual milk, so that by it you may grow up in your salvation, ³now that you have tasted that the Lord is good.

The Living Stone and a Chosen People

⁴As you come to him, the living Stone — rejected by humans but chosen by God and precious to him — ⁵you also, like living stones, are being built into a spiritual houseᶜ for a holy priesthood, offering spiritual sacrifices acceptable to God through Jesus Christ. ⁶For in Scripture it says:

> "See, I lay a stone in Zion,
>   a chosen and precious
>   cornerstone,
> and the one who trusts in him
>   will never be put to shame."ᵈ

⁷Now to you who believe, this stone is precious. But to those who do not believe,

> "The stone the builders rejected
>   has become the cornerstone,"ᵉ

⁸and,

> "A stone that causes people to
>   stumble
> and a rock that makes them
>   fall."ᶠ

They stumble because they disobey the message — which is also what they were destined for.

⁹But you are a chosen people, a royal priesthood, a holy nation, God's special possession, that you may declare the praises of him who called you out of darkness into his wonderful light. ¹⁰Once you were not a people, but now you are the people of God; once you had not received mercy, but now you have received mercy.

Living Godly Lives in a Pagan Society

¹¹Dear friends, I urge you, as foreigners and exiles, to abstain from sinful desires, which wage war against your soul. ¹²Live such good lives among the pagans that, though they accuse you of doing wrong, they may see your good deeds and glorify God on the day he visits us.

¹³Submit yourselves for the Lord's sake to every human authority: whether to the emperor, as the supreme authority, ¹⁴or to governors, who are sent by him to punish those who do wrong and to commend those who do right. ¹⁵For it is God's will that by doing good you should silence the ignorant talk of foolish people. ¹⁶Live as free people, but do not use your freedom as a cover-up for evil; live as God's slaves. ¹⁷Show proper respect to

---

ᵒ 22 Some early manuscripts *from a pure heart*   ᵇ 25 Isaiah 40:6-8 (see Septuagint)   ᶜ 5 Or *into a temple of the Spirit*   ᵈ 6 Isaiah 28:16   ᵉ 7 Psalm 118:22   ᶠ 8 Isaiah 8:14

everyone, love the family of believers, fear God, honor the emperor.

[18] Slaves, in reverent fear of God submit yourselves to your masters, not only to those who are good and considerate, but also to those who are harsh. [19] For it is commendable if someone bears up under the pain of unjust suffering because they are conscious of God. [20] But how is it to your credit if you receive a beating for doing wrong and endure it? But if you suffer for doing good and you endure it, this is commendable before God. [21] To this you were called, because Christ suffered for you, leaving you an example, that you should follow in his steps.

[22] "He committed no sin,
    and no deceit was found in his
        mouth."[a]

[23] When they hurled their insults at him, he did not retaliate; when he suffered, he made no threats. Instead, he entrusted himself to him who judges justly. [24] "He himself bore our sins" in his body on the cross, so that we might die to sins and live for righteousness; "by his wounds you have been healed." [25] For "you were like sheep going astray,"[b] but now you have returned to the Shepherd and Overseer of your souls.

3 Wives, in the same way submit yourselves to your own husbands so that, if any of them do not believe the word, they may be won over without words by the behavior of their wives, [2] when they see the purity and reverence of your lives. [3] Your beauty should not come from outward adornment, such as elaborate hairstyles and the wearing of gold jewelry or fine clothes. [4] Rather, it should be that of your inner self, the unfading beauty of a gentle and quiet spirit,

which is of great worth in God's sight. [5] For this is the way the holy women of the past who put their hope in God used to adorn themselves. They submitted themselves to their own husbands, [6] like Sarah, who obeyed Abraham and called him her lord. You are her daughters if you do what is right and do not give way to fear.

[7] Husbands, in the same way be considerate as you live with your wives, and treat them with respect as the weaker partner and as heirs with you of the gracious gift of life, so that nothing will hinder your prayers.

Suffering for Doing Good

[8] Finally, all of you, be like-minded, be sympathetic, love one another, be compassionate and humble. [9] Do not repay evil with evil or insult with insult. On the contrary, repay evil with blessing, because to this you were called so that you may inherit a blessing. [10] For,

"Whoever would love life
    and see good days
must keep their tongue from evil
    and their lips from deceitful
        speech.
[11] They must turn from evil and do
    good;
    they must seek peace and
        pursue it.
[12] For the eyes of the Lord are on
    the righteous
    and his ears are attentive to
        their prayer,
but the face of the Lord is against
    those who do evil."[c]

[13] Who is going to harm you if you are eager to do good? [14] But even if you should suffer for what is right, you are blessed. "Do not fear their

---

[a] 22 Isaiah 53:9   [b] 24,25 Isaiah 53:4,5,6 (see Septuagint)   [c] 12 Psalm 34:12-16

threats⁰; do not be frightened."ᵇ ¹⁵But in your hearts revere Christ as Lord. Always be prepared to give an answer to everyone who asks you to give the reason for the hope that you have. But do this with gentleness and respect, ¹⁶keeping a clear conscience, so that those who speak maliciously against your good behavior in Christ may be ashamed of their slander. ¹⁷For it is better, if it is God's will, to suffer for doing good than for doing evil. ¹⁸For Christ also suffered once for sins, the righteous for the unrighteous, to bring you to God. He was put to death in the body but made alive in the Spirit. ¹⁹After being made alive,ᶜ he went and made proclamation to the imprisoned spirits — ²⁰to those who were disobedient long ago when God waited patiently in the days of Noah while the ark was being built. In it only a few people, eight in all, were saved through water, ²¹and this water symbolizes baptism that now saves you also — not the removal of dirt from the body but the pledge of a clear conscience toward God.ᵈ It saves you by the resurrection of Jesus Christ, ²²who has gone into heaven and is at God's right hand — with angels, authorities and powers in submission to him.

Living for God

4 Therefore, since Christ suffered in his body, arm yourselves also with the same attitude, because whoever suffers in the body is done with sin. ²As a result, they do not live the rest of their earthly lives for evil human desires, but rather for the will of God. ³For you have spent enough time in the past doing what pagans choose to do — living in debauchery, lust, drunkenness, orgies, carous-

ing and detestable idolatry. ⁴They are surprised that you do not join them in their reckless, wild living, and they heap abuse on you. ⁵But they will have to give account to him who is ready to judge the living and the dead. ⁶For this is the reason the gospel was preached even to those who are now dead, so that they might be judged according to human standards in regard to the body, but live according to God in regard to the spirit.

⁷The end of all things is near. Therefore be alert and of sober mind so that you may pray. ⁸Above all, love each other deeply, because love covers over a multitude of sins. ⁹Offer hospitality to one another without grumbling. ¹⁰Each of you should use whatever gift you have received to serve others, as faithful stewards of God's grace in its various forms. ¹¹If anyone speaks, they should do so as one who speaks the very words of God. If anyone serves, they should do so with the strength God provides, so that in all things God may be praised through Jesus Christ. To him be the glory and the power for ever and ever. Amen.

Suffering for Being a Christian

¹²Dear friends, do not be surprised at the fiery ordeal that has come on you to test you, as though something strange were happening to you. ¹³But rejoice inasmuch as you participate in the sufferings of Christ, so that you may be overjoyed when his glory is revealed. ¹⁴If you are insulted because of the name of Christ, you are blessed, for the Spirit of glory and

---

ᵃ 14 Or fear what they fear   ᵇ 14 Isaiah 8:12
ᶜ 18,19 Or but made alive in the spirit, ¹⁹in which also   ᵈ 21 Or but an appeal to God for a clear conscience

of God rests on you. ¹⁵If you suffer, it should not be as a murderer or thief or any other kind of criminal, or even as a meddler. ¹⁶However, if you suffer as a Christian, do not be ashamed, but praise God that you bear that name. ¹⁷For it is time for judgment to begin with God's household; and if it begins with us, what will the outcome be for those who do not obey the gospel of God? ¹⁸And,

"If it is hard for the righteous to
be saved,
what will become of the
ungodly and the
sinner?"^a

¹⁹So then, those who suffer according to God's will should commit themselves to their faithful Creator and continue to do good.

To the Elders and the Flock

5 To the elders among you, I appeal as a fellow elder and a witness of Christ's sufferings who also will share in the glory to be revealed: ²Be shepherds of God's flock that is under your care, watching over them — not because you must, but because you are willing, as God wants you to be; not pursuing dishonest gain, but eager to serve; ³not lording it over those entrusted to you, but being examples to the flock. ⁴And when the Chief Shepherd appears, you will receive the crown of glory that will never fade away.

⁵In the same way, you who are younger, submit yourselves to your elders. All of you, clothe yourselves with humility toward one another, because,

"God opposes the proud
but shows favor to the
humble."^b

⁶Humble yourselves, therefore, under God's mighty hand, that he may lift you up in due time. ⁷Cast all your anxiety on him because he cares for you.

⁸Be alert and of sober mind. Your enemy the devil prowls around like a roaring lion looking for someone to devour. ⁹Resist him, standing firm in the faith, because you know that the family of believers throughout the world is undergoing the same kind of sufferings.

¹⁰And the God of all grace, who called you to his eternal glory in Christ, after you have suffered a little while, will himself restore you and make you strong, firm and steadfast. ¹¹To him be the power for ever and ever. Amen.

Final Greetings

¹²With the help of Silas,^c whom I regard as a faithful brother, I have written to you briefly, encouraging you and testifying that this is the true grace of God. Stand fast in it.

¹³She who is in Babylon, chosen together with you, sends you her greetings, and so does my son Mark. ¹⁴Greet one another with a kiss of love.

Peace to all of you who are in Christ.

^a 18 Prov. 11:31 (see Septuagint)   ^b 5 Prov. 3:34
^c 12 Greek Silvanus, a variant of Silas

2 Peter

1 Simon Peter, a servant and apostle of Jesus Christ,

To those who through the righteousness of our God and Savior Jesus Christ have received a faith as precious as ours:

²Grace and peace be yours in abundance through the knowledge of God and of Jesus our Lord.

Confirming One's Calling and Election

³His divine power has given us everything we need for a godly life through our knowledge of him who called us by his own glory and goodness. ⁴Through these he has given us his very great and precious promises, so that through them you may participate in the divine nature, having escaped the corruption in the world caused by evil desires.

⁵For this very reason, make every effort to add to your faith goodness; and to goodness, knowledge; ⁶and to knowledge, self-control; and to self-control, perseverance; and to perseverance, godliness; ⁷and to godliness, mutual affection; and to mutual affection, love. ⁸For if you possess these qualities in increasing measure, they will keep you from being ineffective and unproductive in your knowledge of our Lord Jesus Christ. ⁹But whoever does not have them is nearsighted and blind, forgetting that they have been cleansed from their past sins.

¹⁰Therefore, my brothers and sisters,ᵃ make every effort to confirm your calling and election. For if you do these things, you will never stumble, ¹¹and you will receive a rich welcome into the eternal kingdom of our Lord and Savior Jesus Christ.

Prophecy of Scripture

¹²So I will always remind you of these things, even though you know them and are firmly established in the truth you now have. ¹³I think it is right to refresh your memory as long as I live in the tent of this body, ¹⁴because I know that I will soon put it aside, as our Lord Jesus Christ has made clear to me. ¹⁵And I will make every effort to see that after my departure you will always be able to remember these things.

¹⁶For we did not follow cleverly devised stories when we told you about the coming of our Lord Jesus Christ in power, but we were eyewitnesses of his majesty. ¹⁷He received honor and glory from God the Father when the voice came to him from the Majestic Glory, saying, "This is my Son, whom I love; with him I am well pleased."ᵇ ¹⁸We ourselves heard this voice that came from heaven when we were with him on the sacred mountain.

¹⁹We also have the prophetic message as something completely reliable, and you will do well to pay attention to it, as to a light shining in a dark place, until the day dawns and the morning star rises in your hearts. ²⁰Above all, you must understand that no prophecy of Scripture came about by the prophet's own interpretation of things. ²¹For prophecy never had its origin in the human will,

---

ᵃ 10 The Greek word for *brothers and sisters* (*adelphoi*) refers here to believers, both men and women, as part of God's family.
ᵇ 17 Matt. 17:5; Mark 9:7; Luke 9:35

but prophets, though human, spoke from God as they were carried along by the Holy Spirit.

False Teachers and Their Destruction

2 But there were also false prophets among the people, just as there will be false teachers among you. They will secretly introduce destructive heresies, even denying the sovereign Lord who bought them — bringing swift destruction on themselves. ²Many will follow their depraved conduct and will bring the way of truth into disrepute. ³In their greed these teachers will exploit you with fabricated stories. Their condemnation has long been hanging over them, and their destruction has not been sleeping.

⁴For if God did not spare angels when they sinned, but sent them to hell,ᵃ putting them in chains of darknessᵇ to be held for judgment; ⁵if he did not spare the ancient world when he brought the flood on its ungodly people, but protected Noah, a preacher of righteousness, and seven others; ⁶if he condemned the cities of Sodom and Gomorrah by burning them to ashes, and made them an example of what is going to happen to the ungodly; ⁷and if he rescued Lot, a righteous man, who was distressed by the depraved conduct of the lawless ⁸(for that righteous man, living among them day after day, was tormented in his righteous soul by the lawless deeds he saw and heard) — ⁹if this is so, then the Lord knows how to rescue the godly from trials and to hold the unrighteous for punishment on the day of judgment. ¹⁰This is especially true of those who follow the corrupt desire of the fleshᶜ and despise authority.

Bold and arrogant, they are not afraid to heap abuse on celestial beings; ¹¹yet even angels, although they are stronger and more powerful, do not heap abuse on such beings when bringing judgment on them fromᵈ the Lord. ¹²But these people blaspheme in matters they do not understand. They are like unreasoning animals, creatures of instinct, born only to be caught and destroyed, and like animals they too will perish.

¹³They will be paid back with harm for the harm they have done. Their idea of pleasure is to carouse in broad daylight. They are blots and blemishes, reveling in their pleasures while they feast with you.ᵉ ¹⁴With eyes full of adultery, they never stop sinning; they seduce the unstable; they are experts in greed — an accursed brood! ¹⁵They have left the straight way and wandered off to follow the way of Balaam son of Bezer,ᶠ who loved the wages of wickedness. ¹⁶But he was rebuked for his wrongdoing by a donkey — an animal without speech — who spoke with a human voice and restrained the prophet's madness.

¹⁷These people are springs without water and mists driven by a storm. Blackest darkness is reserved for them. ¹⁸For they mouth empty, boastful words and, by appealing to the lustful desires of the flesh, they entice people who are just escaping from those who live in error. ¹⁹They promise them freedom, while they themselves are slaves of depravity — for "people are slaves to whatever has

---

ᵃ 4 Greek *Tartarus* ᵇ 4 Some manuscripts *in gloomy dungeons* ᶜ 10 In contexts like this, the Greek word for *flesh (sarx)* refers to the sinful state of human beings, often presented as a power in opposition to the Spirit; also in verse 18. ᵈ 11 Many manuscripts *beings in the presence of* ᵉ 13 Some manuscripts *their love feasts* ᶠ 15 Greek *Bosor* mastered them." 20If they have escaped the corruption of the world by knowing our Lord and Savior Jesus Christ and are again entangled in it and are overcome, they are worse off at the end than they were at the beginning. 21It would have been better for them not to have known the way of righteousness, than to have known it and then to turn their backs on the sacred command that was passed on to them. 22Of them the proverbs are true: "A dog returns to its vomit,"ᵃ and, "A sow that is washed returns to her wallowing in the mud."

The Day of the Lord

3 Dear friends, this is now my second letter to you. I have written both of them as reminders to stimulate you to wholesome thinking. 2I want you to recall the words spoken in the past by the holy prophets and the command given by our Lord and Savior through your apostles.

3Above all, you must understand that in the last days scoffers will come, scoffing and following their own evil desires. 4They will say, "Where is this 'coming' he promised? Ever since our ancestors died, everything goes on as it has since the beginning of creation." 5But they deliberately forget that long ago by God's word the heavens came into being and the earth was formed out of water and by water. 6By these waters also the world of that time was deluged and destroyed. 7By the same word the present heavens and earth are reserved for fire, being kept for the day of judgment and destruction of the ungodly.

8But do not forget this one thing, dear friends: With the Lord a day is like a thousand years, and a thousand years are like a day. 9The Lord is not slow in keeping his promise, as some understand slowness. Instead he is patient with you, not wanting anyone to perish, but everyone to come to repentance.

10But the day of the Lord will come like a thief. The heavens will disappear with a roar; the elements will be destroyed by fire, and the earth and everything done in it will be laid bare.ᵇ

11Since everything will be destroyed in this way, what kind of people ought you to be? You ought to live holy and godly lives 12as you look forward to the day of God and speed its coming.ᶜ That day will bring about the destruction of the heavens by fire, and the elements will melt in the heat. 13But in keeping with his promise we are looking forward to a new heaven and a new earth, where righteousness dwells.

14So then, dear friends, since you are looking forward to this, make every effort to be found spotless, blameless and at peace with him. 15Bear in mind that our Lord's patience means salvation, just as our dear brother Paul also wrote you with the wisdom that God gave him. 16He writes the same way in all his letters, speaking in them of these matters. His letters contain some things that are hard to understand, which ignorant and unstable people distort, as they do the other Scriptures, to their own destruction.

17Therefore, dear friends, since you have been forewarned, be on your guard so that you may not be carried away by the error of the lawless and fall from your secure position. 18But grow in the grace and knowledge of our Lord and Savior Jesus Christ. To him be glory both now and forever! Amen.

ᵃ 22 Prov. 26:11   ᵇ 10 Some manuscripts be burned up   ᶜ 12 Or as you wait eagerly for the day of God to come

1 John

The Incarnation of the Word of Life

1 That which was from the beginning, which we have heard, which we have seen with our eyes, which we have looked at and our hands have touched — this we proclaim concerning the Word of life. ²The life appeared; we have seen it and testify to it, and we proclaim to you the eternal life, which was with the Father and has appeared to us. ³We proclaim to you what we have seen and heard, so that you also may have fellowship with us. And our fellowship is with the Father and with his Son, Jesus Christ. ⁴We write this to make our[a] joy complete.

Light and Darkness, Sin and Forgiveness

⁵This is the message we have heard from him and declare to you: God is light; in him there is no darkness at all. ⁶If we claim to have fellowship with him and yet walk in the darkness, we lie and do not live out the truth. ⁷But if we walk in the light, as he is in the light, we have fellowship with one another, and the blood of Jesus, his Son, purifies us from all[b] sin.

⁸If we claim to be without sin, we deceive ourselves and the truth is not in us. ⁹If we confess our sins, he is faithful and just and will forgive us our sins and purify us from all unrighteousness. ¹⁰If we claim we have not sinned, we make him out to be a liar and his word is not in us.

2 My dear children, I write this to you so that you will not sin. But if anybody does sin, we have an ad-vocate with the Father — Jesus Christ, the Righteous One. ²He is the atoning sacrifice for our sins, and not only for ours but also for the sins of the whole world.

Love and Hatred for Fellow Believers

³We know that we have come to know him if we keep his commands. ⁴Whoever says, "I know him," but does not do what he commands is a liar, and the truth is not in that person. ⁵But if anyone obeys his word, love for God[c] is truly made complete in them. This is how we know we are in him: ⁶Whoever claims to live in him must live as Jesus did.

⁷Dear friends, I am not writing you a new command but an old one, which you have had since the beginning. This old command is the message you have heard. ⁸Yet I am writing you a new command; its truth is seen in him and in you, because the darkness is passing and the true light is already shining.

⁹Anyone who claims to be in the light but hates a brother or sister[d] is still in the darkness. ¹⁰Anyone who loves their brother and sister[e] lives in the light, and there is nothing in them to make them stumble. ¹¹But anyone who hates a brother or sister

---

is in the darkness and walks around in the darkness. They do not know where they are going, because the darkness has blinded them.

Reasons for Writing

¹² I am writing to you, dear children,
because your sins have been forgiven on account of his name.
¹³ I am writing to you, fathers,
because you know him who is from the beginning.
I am writing to you, young men,
because you have overcome the evil one.

¹⁴ I write to you, dear children,
because you know the Father.
I write to you, fathers,
because you know him who is from the beginning.
I write to you, young men,
because you are strong,
and the word of God lives in you,
and you have overcome the evil one.

On Not Loving the World

¹⁵ Do not love the world or anything in the world. If anyone loves the world, love for the Father[a] is not in them. ¹⁶ For everything in the world — the lust of the flesh, the lust of the eyes, and the pride of life — comes not from the Father but from the world. ¹⁷ The world and its desires pass away, but whoever does the will of God lives forever.

Warnings Against Denying the Son

¹⁸ Dear children, this is the last hour; and as you have even heard that the antichrist is coming, even now many antichrists have come. This is how we know it is the last hour. ¹⁹ They went out from us, but they did not really belong to us. For if they had belonged to us, they would have remained with us; but their going showed that none of them belonged to us.

²⁰ But you have an anointing from the Holy One, and all of you know the truth.[b] ²¹ I do not write to you because you do not know the truth, but because you do know it and because no lie comes from the truth. ²² Who is the liar? It is whoever denies that Jesus is the Christ. Such a person is the antichrist — denying the Father and the Son. ²³ No one who denies the Son has the Father; whoever acknowledges the Son has the Father also.

²⁴ As for you, see that what you have heard from the beginning remains in you. If it does, you also will remain in the Son and in the Father. ²⁵ And this is what he promised us — eternal life.

²⁶ I am writing these things to you about those who are trying to lead you astray. ²⁷ As for you, the anointing you received from him remains in you, and you do not need anyone to teach you. But as his anointing teaches you about all things and as that anointing is real, not counterfeit — just as it has taught you, remain in him.

God's Children and Sin

²⁸ And now, dear children, continue in him, so that when he appears we may be confident and unashamed before him at his coming.

²⁹ If you know that he is righteous, you know that everyone who does what is right has been born of him.

3 See what great love the Father has lavished on us, that we should be called children of God! And that is what we are! The reason the world

---

[a] 15 Or world, the Father's love   [b] 20 Some manuscripts and you know all things

does not know us is that it did not know him. ²Dear friends, now we are children of God, and what we will be has not yet been made known. But we know that when Christ appears,ᵃ we shall be like him, for we shall see him as he is. ³All who have this hope in him purify themselves, just as he is pure.

⁴Everyone who sins breaks the law; in fact, sin is lawlessness. ⁵But you know that he appeared so that he might take away our sins. And in him is no sin. ⁶No one who lives in him keeps on sinning. No one who continues to sin has either seen him or known him.

⁷Dear children, do not let anyone lead you astray. The one who does what is right is righteous, just as he is righteous. ⁸The one who does what is sinful is of the devil, because the devil has been sinning from the beginning. The reason the Son of God appeared was to destroy the devil's work. ⁹No one who is born of God will continue to sin, because God's seed remains in them; they cannot go on sinning, because they have been born of God. ¹⁰This is how we know who the children of God are and who the children of the devil are: Anyone who does not do what is right is not God's child, nor is anyone who does not love their brother and sister.

More on Love and Hatred

¹¹For this is the message you heard from the beginning: We should love one another. ¹²Do not be like Cain, who belonged to the evil one and murdered his brother. And why did he murder him? Because his own actions were evil and his brother's were righteous. ¹³Do not be surprised, my brothers and sisters,ᵇ if the world hates you. ¹⁴We know that we have

passed from death to life, because we love each other. Anyone who does not love remains in death. ¹⁵Anyone who hates a brother or sister is a murderer, and you know that no murderer has eternal life residing in him.

¹⁶This is how we know what love is: Jesus Christ laid down his life for us. And we ought to lay down our lives for our brothers and sisters. ¹⁷If anyone has material possessions and sees a brother or sister in need but has no pity on them, how can the love of God be in that person? ¹⁸Dear children, let us not love with words or speech but with actions and in truth.

¹⁹This is how we know that we belong to the truth and how we set our hearts at rest in his presence: ²⁰If our hearts condemn us, we know that God is greater than our hearts, and he knows everything. ²¹Dear friends, if our hearts do not condemn us, we have confidence before God ²²and receive from him anything we ask, because we keep his commands and do what pleases him. ²³And this is his command: to believe in the name of his Son, Jesus Christ, and to love one another as he commanded us. ²⁴The one who keeps God's commands lives in him, and he in them. And this is how we know that he lives in us: We know it by the Spirit he gave us.

On Denying the Incarnation

4 Dear friends, do not believe every spirit, but test the spirits to see whether they are from God, because many false prophets have gone out into the world. ²This is how you can recognize the Spirit of God: Every spirit that acknowledges that Jesus

---

ᵃ 2 Or when it is made known   ᵇ 13 The Greek word for brothers and sisters (adelphoi) refers here to believers, both men and women, as part of God's family; also in verse 16.

Christ has come in the flesh is from God, ³but every spirit that does not acknowledge Jesus is not from God. This is the spirit of the antichrist, which you have heard is coming and even now is already in the world.

⁴You, dear children, are from God and have overcome them, because the one who is in you is greater than the one who is in the world. ⁵They are from the world and therefore speak from the viewpoint of the world, and the world listens to them. ⁶We are from God, and whoever knows God listens to us; but whoever is not from God does not listen to us. This is how we recognize the Spirit*ᵃ* of truth and the spirit of falsehood.

God's Love and Ours

⁷Dear friends, let us love one another, for love comes from God. Everyone who loves has been born of God and knows God. ⁸Whoever does not love does not know God, because God is love. ⁹This is how God showed his love among us: He sent his one and only Son into the world that we might live through him. ¹⁰This is love: not that we loved God, but that he loved us and sent his Son as an atoning sacrifice for our sins. ¹¹Dear friends, since God so loved us, we also ought to love one another. ¹²No one has ever seen God; but if we love one another, God lives in us and his love is made complete in us.

¹³This is how we know that we live in him and he in us: He has given us of his Spirit. ¹⁴And we have seen and testify that the Father has sent his Son to be the Savior of the world. ¹⁵If anyone acknowledges that Jesus is the Son of God, God lives in them and they in God. ¹⁶And so we know and rely on the love God has for us.

God is love. Whoever lives in love lives in God, and God in them. ¹⁷This is how love is made complete among

us so that we will have confidence on the day of judgment: In this world we are like Jesus. ¹⁸There is no fear in love. But perfect love drives out fear, because fear has to do with punishment. The one who fears is not made perfect in love.

¹⁹We love because he first loved us. ²⁰Whoever claims to love God yet hates a brother or sister is a liar. For whoever does not love their brother and sister, whom they have seen, cannot love God, whom they have not seen. ²¹And he has given us this command: Anyone who loves God must also love their brother and sister.

Faith in the Incarnate Son of God

5 Everyone who believes that Jesus is the Christ is born of God, and everyone who loves the father loves his child as well. ²This is how we know that we love the children of God: by loving God and carrying out his commands. ³In fact, this is love for God: to keep his commands. And his commands are not burdensome, ⁴for everyone born of God overcomes the world. This is the victory that has overcome the world, even our faith. ⁵Who is it that overcomes the world? Only the one who believes that Jesus is the Son of God.

⁶This is the one who came by water and blood — Jesus Christ. He did not come by water only, but by water and blood. And it is the Spirit who testifies, because the Spirit is the truth. ⁷For there are three that testify: ⁸theᵇ Spirit, the water and the blood; and the three are in agreement. ⁹We accept

---

ᵃ 6 Or spirit   ᵇ 7,8 Late manuscripts of the Vulgate testify in heaven: the Father, the Word and the Holy Spirit, and these three are one. ᵍAnd there are three that testify on earth: the (not found in any Greek manuscript before the fourteenth century) human testimony, but God's testimony is greater because it is the testimony of God, which he has given about his Son. ¹⁰Whoever believes in the Son of God accepts this testimony. Whoever does not believe God has made him out to be a liar, because they have not believed the testimony God has given about his Son. ¹¹And this is the testimony: God has given us eternal life, and this life is in his Son. ¹²Whoever has the Son has life; whoever does not have the Son of God does not have life.

Concluding Affirmations

¹³I write these things to you who believe in the name of the Son of God so that you may know that you have eternal life. ¹⁴This is the confidence we have in approaching God: that if we ask anything according to his will, he hears us. ¹⁵And if we know that he hears us — whatever we ask — we know that we have what we asked of him.

¹⁶If you see any brother or sister commit a sin that does not lead to death, you should pray and God will give them life. I refer to those whose sin does not lead to death. There is a sin that leads to death. I am not saying that you should pray about that. ¹⁷All wrongdoing is sin, and there is sin that does not lead to death.

¹⁸We know that anyone born of God does not continue to sin; the One who was born of God keeps them safe, and the evil one cannot harm them. ¹⁹We know that we are children of God, and that the whole world is under the control of the evil one. ²⁰We know also that the Son of God has come and has given us understanding, so that we may know him who is true. And we are in him who is true by being in his Son Jesus Christ. He is the true God and eternal life.

²¹Dear children, keep yourselves from idols.

2 John

¹The elder,

To the lady chosen by God and to her children, whom I love in the truth — and not I only, but also all who know the truth — ²because of the truth, which lives in us and will be with us forever:

³Grace, mercy and peace from God the Father and from Jesus Christ, the Father's Son, will be with us in truth and love.

⁴It has given me great joy to find some of your children walking in the truth, just as the Father commanded us. ⁵And now, dear lady, I am not writing you a new command but one we have had from the beginning. I ask that we love one another. ⁶And this is love: that we walk in obedience to his commands. As you have heard from the beginning, his command is that you walk in love.

⁷I say this because many deceivers, who do not acknowledge Jesus Christ as coming in the flesh, have gone out into the world. Any such person is the deceiver and the antichrist. ⁸Watch out that you do not

lose what we[a] have worked for, but that you may be rewarded fully. [9]Anyone who runs ahead and does not continue in the teaching of Christ does not have God; whoever continues in the teaching has both the Father and the Son. [10]If anyone comes to you and does not bring this teaching, do not take them into your house or welcome them. [11]Anyone who welcomes them shares in their wicked work.

[12]I have much to write to you, but I do not want to use paper and ink. Instead, I hope to visit you and talk with you face to face, so that our joy may be complete.

[13]The children of your sister, who is chosen by God, send their greetings.

3 John

[1]The elder,

To my dear friend Gaius, whom I love in the truth.

[2]Dear friend, I pray that you may enjoy good health and that all may go well with you, even as your soul is getting along well. [3]It gave me great joy when some believers came and testified about your faithfulness to the truth, telling how you continue to walk in it. [4]I have no greater joy than to hear that my children are walking in the truth.

[5]Dear friend, you are faithful in what you are doing for the brothers and sisters,[b] even though they are strangers to you. [6]They have told the church about your love. Please send them on their way in a manner that honors God. [7]It was for the sake of the Name that they went out, receiving no help from the pagans. [8]We ought therefore to show hospitality to such people so that we may work together for the truth.

[9]I wrote to the church, but Diotrephes, who loves to be first, will not welcome us. [10]So when I come, I will call attention to what he is doing, spreading malicious nonsense about us. Not satisfied with that, he even refuses to welcome other believers. He also stops those who want to do so and puts them out of the church. [11]Dear friend, do not imitate what is evil but what is good. Anyone who does what is good is from God. Anyone who does what is evil has not seen God. [12]Demetrius is well spoken of by everyone — and even by the truth itself. We also speak well of him, and you know that our testimony is true.

[13]I have much to write to you, but I do not want to do so with pen and ink. [14]I hope to see you soon, and we will talk face to face.

Peace to you. The friends here send their greetings. Greet the friends there by name.

---

[a] 8 Some manuscripts *you*   [b] 5 The Greek word for *brothers and sisters* (*adelphoi*) refers here to believers, both men and women, as part of God's family.

Jude

[1] Jude, a servant of Jesus Christ and a brother of James,

To those who have been called, who are loved in God the Father and kept for[a] Jesus Christ:

[2] Mercy, peace and love be yours in abundance.

The Sin and Doom of Ungodly People

[3] Dear friends, although I was very eager to write to you about the salvation we share, I felt compelled to write and urge you to contend for the faith that was once for all entrusted to God's holy people. [4] For certain individuals whose condemnation was written about[b] long ago have secretly slipped in among you. They are ungodly people, who pervert the grace of our God into a license for immorality and deny Jesus Christ our only Sovereign and Lord.

[5] Though you already know all this, I want to remind you that the Lord[c] at one time delivered his people out of Egypt, but later destroyed those who did not believe. [6] And the angels who did not keep their positions of authority but abandoned their proper dwelling — these he has kept in darkness, bound with everlasting chains for judgment on the great Day. [7] In a similar way, Sodom and Gomorrah and the surrounding towns gave themselves up to sexual immorality and perversion. They serve as an example of those who suffer the punishment of eternal fire.

[8] In the very same way, on the strength of their dreams these ungodly people pollute their own bodies, reject authority and heap abuse on celestial beings. [9] But even the archangel Michael, when he was disputing with the devil about the body of Moses, did not himself dare to condemn him for slander but said, "The Lord rebuke you!"[d] [10] Yet these people slander whatever they do not understand, and the very things they do understand by instinct — as irrational animals do — will destroy them.

[11] Woe to them! They have taken the way of Cain; they have rushed for profit into Balaam's error; they have been destroyed in Korah's rebellion.

[12] These people are blemishes at your love feasts, eating with you without the slightest qualm — shepherds who feed only themselves. They are clouds without rain, blown along by the wind; autumn trees, without fruit and uprooted — twice dead. [13] They are wild waves of the sea, foaming up their shame; wandering stars, for whom blackest darkness has been reserved forever.

[14] Enoch, the seventh from Adam, prophesied about them: "See, the Lord is coming with thousands upon thousands of his holy ones [15] to judge everyone, and to convict all of them of all the ungodly acts they have committed in their ungodliness, and of all the defiant words ungodly sinners have spoken against him."[e] [16] These people are grumblers and faultfinders;

---

[a] *1 Or by; or in*   [b] *4 Or individuals who were marked out for condemnation*   [c] *5 Some early manuscripts Jesus*   [d] *9 Jude is alluding to the Jewish Testament of Moses (approximately the first century A.D.).*   [e] *14,15 From the Jewish First Book of Enoch (approximately the first century B.C.).*

they follow their own evil desires; they boast about themselves and flatter others for their own advantage.

A Call to Persevere

[17]But, dear friends, remember what the apostles of our Lord Jesus Christ foretold. [18]They said to you, "In the last times there will be scoffers who will follow their own ungodly desires." [19]These are the people who divide you, who follow mere natural instincts and do not have the Spirit.

[20]But you, dear friends, by building yourselves up in your most holy faith and praying in the Holy Spirit, [21]keep yourselves in God's love as you wait for the mercy of our Lord Jesus Christ to bring you to eternal life.

[22]Be merciful to those who doubt; [23]save others by snatching them from the fire; to others show mercy, mixed with fear — hating even the clothing stained by corrupted flesh.[a]

Doxology

[24]To him who is able to keep you from stumbling and to present you before his glorious presence without fault and with great joy — [25]to the only God our Savior be glory, majesty, power and authority, through Jesus Christ our Lord, before all ages, now and forevermore! Amen.

Revelation

Prologue

1 The revelation from Jesus Christ, which God gave him to show his servants what must soon take place. He made it known by sending his angel to his servant John, [2]who testifies to everything he saw — that is, the word of God and the testimony of Jesus Christ. [3]Blessed is the one who reads aloud the words of this prophecy, and blessed are those who hear it and take to heart what is written in it, because the time is near.

Greetings and Doxology

[4]John,

To the seven churches in the province of Asia:

Grace and peace to you from him who is, and who was, and who is to come, and from the seven spirits[b] before his throne, [5]and from Jesus Christ, who is the faithful witness, the firstborn from the dead, and the ruler of the kings of the earth.

To him who loves us and has freed us from our sins by his blood, [6]and has made us to be a kingdom and priests to serve his God and Father — to him be glory and power for ever and ever! Amen.

[7]"Look, he is coming with the
    clouds,"[c]
and "every eye will see him,

---

[a] 22,23 The Greek manuscripts of these verses vary at several points.   [b] 4 That is, the sevenfold Spirit   [c] 7 Daniel 7:13

even those who pierced him";
    and all peoples on earth "will
        mourn because of him."[a]
            So shall it be! Amen.

[8]"I am the Alpha and the Omega," says the Lord God, "who is, and who was, and who is to come, the Almighty."

John's Vision of Christ

[9]I, John, your brother and companion in the suffering and kingdom and patient endurance that are ours in Jesus, was on the island of Patmos because of the word of God and the testimony of Jesus. [10]On the Lord's Day I was in the Spirit, and I heard behind me a loud voice like a trumpet, [11]which said: "Write on a scroll what you see and send it to the seven churches: to Ephesus, Smyrna, Pergamum, Thyatira, Sardis, Philadelphia and Laodicea."

[12]I turned around to see the voice that was speaking to me. And when I turned I saw seven golden lampstands, [13]and among the lampstands was someone like a son of man,[b] dressed in a robe reaching down to his feet and with a golden sash around his chest. [14]The hair on his head was white like wool, as white as snow, and his eyes were like blazing fire. [15]His feet were like bronze glowing in a furnace, and his voice was like the sound of rushing waters. [16]In his right hand he held seven stars, and coming out of his mouth was a sharp, double-edged sword. His face was like the sun shining in all its brilliance.

[17]When I saw him, I fell at his feet as though dead. Then he placed his right hand on me and said: "Do not be afraid. I am the First and the Last. [18]I am the Living One; I was dead, and now look, I am alive for ever and

ever! And I hold the keys of death and Hades.

[19]"Write, therefore, what you have seen, what is now and what will take place later. [20]The mystery of the seven stars that you saw in my right hand and of the seven golden lampstands is this: The seven stars are the angels[c] of the seven churches, and the seven lampstands are the seven churches.

To the Church in Ephesus

2 "To the angel[d] of the church in Ephesus write:

These are the words of him who holds the seven stars in his right hand and walks among the seven golden lampstands. [2]I know your deeds, your hard work and your perseverance. I know that you cannot tolerate wicked people, that you have tested those who claim to be apostles but are not, and have found them false. [3]You have persevered and have endured hardships for my name, and have not grown weary.

[4]Yet I hold this against you: You have forsaken the love you had at first. [5]Consider how far you have fallen! Repent and do the things you did at first. If you do not repent, I will come to you and remove your lampstand from its place. [6]But you have this in your favor: You hate the practices of the Nicolaitans, which I also hate.

[7]Whoever has ears, let them hear what the Spirit says to the churches. To the one who is victorious, I will give the right to eat

---

[a] 7 Zech. 12:10   [b] 13 See Daniel 7:13.
[c] 20 Or messengers   [d] 1 Or messenger; also in verses 8, 12 and 18

from the tree of life, which is in the paradise of God.

To the Church in Smyrna

8"To the angel of the church in Smyrna write:

These are the words of him who is the First and the Last, who died and came to life again. 9I know your afflictions and your poverty — yet you are rich! I know about the slander of those who say they are Jews and are not, but are a synagogue of Satan. 10Do not be afraid of what you are about to suffer. I tell you, the devil will put some of you in prison to test you, and you will suffer persecution for ten days. Be faithful, even to the point of death, and I will give you life as your victor's crown.

11Whoever has ears, let them hear what the Spirit says to the churches. The one who is victorious will not be hurt at all by the second death.

To the Church in Pergamum

12"To the angel of the church in Pergamum write:

These are the words of him who has the sharp, double-edged sword. 13I know where you live — where Satan has his throne. Yet you remain true to my name. You did not renounce your faith in me, not even in the days of Antipas, my faithful witness, who was put to death in your city — where Satan lives.

14Nevertheless, I have a few things against you: There are some among you who hold to the teaching of Balaam, who taught Balak to entice the Israelites to sin so that they ate food sacrificed to idols and committed sexual immorality. 15Likewise, you also have those who hold to the teaching of the Nicolaitans. 16Repent therefore! Otherwise, I will soon come to you and will fight against them with the sword of my mouth.

17Whoever has ears, let them hear what the Spirit says to the churches. To the one who is victorious, I will give some of the hidden manna. I will also give that person a white stone with a new name written on it, known only to the one who receives it.

To the Church in Thyatira

18"To the angel of the church in Thyatira write:

These are the words of the Son of God, whose eyes are like blazing fire and whose feet are like burnished bronze. 19I know your deeds, your love and faith, your service and perseverance, and that you are now doing more than you did at first.

20Nevertheless, I have this against you: You tolerate that woman Jezebel, who calls herself a prophet. By her teaching she misleads my servants into sexual immorality and the eating of food sacrificed to idols. 21I have given her time to repent of her immorality, but she is unwilling. 22So I will cast her on a bed of suffering, and I will make those who commit adultery with her suffer intensely, unless they repent of her ways. 23I will strike her children dead. Then all the churches will know that I am he who searches hearts and minds, and I will repay each of you according to your deeds.

²⁴Now I say to the rest of you in Thyatira, to you who do not hold to her teaching and have not learned Satan's so-called deep secrets, 'I will not impose any other burden on you, ²⁵except to hold on to what you have until I come.'

²⁶To the one who is victorious and does my will to the end, I will give authority over the nations — ²⁷that one 'will rule them with an iron scepter and will dash them to pieces like pottery'ᵃ — just as I have received authority from my Father. ²⁸I will also give that one the morning star. ²⁹Whoever has ears, let them hear what the Spirit says to the churches.

To the Church in Sardis

3 "To the angelᵇ of the church in Sardis write:

These are the words of him who holds the seven spiritsᶜ of God and the seven stars. I know your deeds; you have a reputation of being alive, but you are dead. ²Wake up! Strengthen what remains and is about to die, for I have found your deeds unfinished in the sight of my God. ³Remember, therefore, what you have received and heard; hold it fast, and repent. But if you do not wake up, I will come like a thief, and you will not know at what time I will come to you.

⁴Yet you have a few people in Sardis who have not soiled their clothes. They will walk with me, dressed in white, for they are worthy. ⁵The one who is victorious will, like them, be dressed in white. I will never blot out the name of that person from the book of life, but will acknowledge that name before my Father and his angels. ⁶Whoever has ears, let them hear what the Spirit says to the churches.

To the Church in Philadelphia

⁷"To the angel of the church in Philadelphia write:

These are the words of him who is holy and true, who holds the key of David. What he opens no one can shut, and what he shuts no one can open. ⁸I know your deeds. See, I have placed before you an open door that no one can shut. I know that you have little strength, yet you have kept my word and have not denied my name. ⁹I will make those who are of the synagogue of Satan, who claim to be Jews though they are not, but are liars — I will make them come and fall down at your feet and acknowledge that I have loved you. ¹⁰Since you have kept my command to endure patiently, I will also keep you from the hour of trial that is going to come on the whole world to test the inhabitants of the earth.

¹¹I am coming soon. Hold on to what you have, so that no one will take your crown. ¹²The one who is victorious I will make a pillar in the temple of my God. Never again will they leave it. I will write on them the name of my God and the name of the city of my God, the new Jerusalem, which is coming down out of heaven from my God; and I will also write on them my new

---

ᵃ 27 Psalm 2:9   ᵇ 1 Or *messenger*; also in verses 7 and 14   ᶜ 1 That is, the sevenfold Spirit name. [13]Whoever has ears, let them hear what the Spirit says to the churches.

To the Church in Laodicea

[14]"To the angel of the church in Laodicea write:

These are the words of the Amen, the faithful and true witness, the ruler of God's creation. [15]I know your deeds, that you are neither cold nor hot. I wish you were either one or the other! [16]So, because you are lukewarm — neither hot nor cold — I am about to spit you out of my mouth. [17]You say, 'I am rich; I have acquired wealth and do not need a thing.' But you do not realize that you are wretched, pitiful, poor, blind and naked. [18]I counsel you to buy from me gold refined in the fire, so you can become rich; and white clothes to wear, so you can cover your shameful nakedness; and salve to put on your eyes, so you can see.

[19]Those whom I love I rebuke and discipline. So be earnest and repent. [20]Here I am! I stand at the door and knock. If anyone hears my voice and opens the door, I will come in and eat with that person, and they with me.

[21]To the one who is victorious, I will give the right to sit with me on my throne, just as I was victorious and sat down with my Father on his throne. [22]Whoever has ears, let them hear what the Spirit says to the churches."

The Throne in Heaven

4 After this I looked, and there before me was a door standing open in heaven. And the voice I had first heard speaking to me like a trumpet said, "Come up here, and I will show you what must take place after this." [2]At once I was in the Spirit, and there before me was a throne in heaven with someone sitting on it. [3]And the one who sat there had the appearance of jasper and ruby. A rainbow that shone like an emerald encircled the throne. [4]Surrounding the throne were twenty-four other thrones, and seated on them were twenty-four elders. They were dressed in white and had crowns of gold on their heads. [5]From the throne came flashes of lightning, rumblings and peals of thunder. In front of the throne, seven lamps were blazing. These are the seven spirits[a] of God. [6]Also in front of the throne there was what looked like a sea of glass, clear as crystal.

In the center, around the throne, were four living creatures, and they were covered with eyes, in front and in back. [7]The first living creature was like a lion, the second was like an ox, the third had a face like a man, the fourth was like a flying eagle. [8]Each of the four living creatures had six wings and was covered with eyes all around, even under its wings. Day and night they never stop saying:

" 'Holy, holy, holy
    is the Lord God Almighty,'[b]
who was, and is, and is to come."

[9]Whenever the living creatures give glory, honor and thanks to him who sits on the throne and who lives for ever and ever, [10]the twenty-four elders fall down before him who sits on the throne and worship him who lives for ever and ever. They lay their crowns before the throne and say:

---

[a] 5 That is, the sevenfold Spirit
[b] 8 Isaiah 6:3

[11] "You are worthy, our Lord
          and God,
     to receive glory and honor
          and power,
     for you created all things,
          and by your will they were
          created
          and have their being."

The Scroll and the Lamb

5 Then I saw in the right hand of him
who sat on the throne a scroll with
writing on both sides and sealed with
seven seals. [2] And I saw a mighty angel
proclaiming in a loud voice, "Who is
worthy to break the seals and open
the scroll?" [3] But no one in heaven
or on earth or under the earth could
open the scroll or even look inside
it. [4] I wept and wept because no one
was found who was worthy to open
the scroll or look inside. [5] Then one of
the elders said to me, "Do not weep!
See, the Lion of the tribe of Judah,
the Root of David, has triumphed.
He is able to open the scroll and its
seven seals."

[6] Then I saw a Lamb, looking as if it
had been slain, standing at the center
of the throne, encircled by the four
living creatures and the elders. The
Lamb had seven horns and seven
eyes, which are the seven spirits[a] of
God sent out into all the earth. [7] He
went and took the scroll from the
right hand of him who sat on the
throne. [8] And when he had taken
it, the four living creatures and the
twenty-four elders fell down before
the Lamb. Each one had a harp and
they were holding golden bowls full
of incense, which are the prayers of
God's people. [9] And they sang a new
song, saying:

     "You are worthy to take the
          scroll
          and to open its seals,

because you were slain,
     and with your blood you
          purchased for God
     persons from every tribe and
          language and people and
          nation.
[10] You have made them to be a
          kingdom and priests to
          serve our God,
     and they will reign[b] on the
          earth."

[11] Then I looked and heard the
voice of many angels, numbering
thousands upon thousands, and ten
thousand times ten thousand. They
encircled the throne and the living
creatures and the elders. [12] In a loud
voice they were saying:

     "Worthy is the Lamb, who was
          slain,
     to receive power and wealth
          and wisdom and strength
          and honor and glory and
          praise!"

[13] Then I heard every creature in
heaven and on earth and under the
earth and on the sea, and all that is
in them, saying:

     "To him who sits on the throne
          and to the Lamb
     be praise and honor and glory
          and power,
          for ever and ever!"

[14] The four living creatures said,
"Amen," and the elders fell down
and worshiped.

The Seals

6 I watched as the Lamb opened
the first of the seven seals. Then I
heard one of the four living creatures
say in a voice like thunder, "Come!"

---

[a] 6 That is, the sevenfold Spirit   [b] 10 Some
manuscripts *they reign*

²I looked, and there before me was a white horse! Its rider held a bow, and he was given a crown, and he rode out as a conqueror bent on conquest.

³When the Lamb opened the second seal, I heard the second living creature say, "Come!" ⁴Then another horse came out, a fiery red one. Its rider was given power to take peace from the earth and to make people kill each other. To him was given a large sword.

⁵When the Lamb opened the third seal, I heard the third living creature say, "Come!" I looked, and there before me was a black horse! Its rider was holding a pair of scales in his hand. ⁶Then I heard what sounded like a voice among the four living creatures, saying, "Two pounds*a* of wheat for a day's wages,*b* and six pounds*c* of barley for a day's wages,*b* and do not damage the oil and the wine!"

⁷When the Lamb opened the fourth seal, I heard the voice of the fourth living creature say, "Come!" I looked, and there before me was a pale horse! Its rider was named Death, and Hades was following close behind him. They were given power over a fourth of the earth to kill by sword, famine and plague, and by the wild beasts of the earth.

⁹When he opened the fifth seal, I saw under the altar the souls of those who had been slain because of the word of God and the testimony they had maintained. ¹⁰They called out in a loud voice, "How long, Sovereign Lord, holy and true, until you judge the inhabitants of the earth and avenge our blood?" ¹¹Then each of them was given a white robe, and they were told to wait a little longer, until the full number of their fellow servants, their brothers and sisters,*d* were killed just as they had been.

¹²I watched as he opened the sixth seal. There was a great earthquake. The sun turned black like sackcloth made of goat hair, the whole moon turned blood red, ¹³and the stars in the sky fell to earth, as figs drop from a fig tree when shaken by a strong wind. ¹⁴The heavens receded like a scroll being rolled up, and every mountain and island was removed from its place.

¹⁵Then the kings of the earth, the princes, the generals, the rich, the mighty, and everyone else, both slave and free, hid in caves and among the rocks of the mountains. ¹⁶They called to the mountains and the rocks, "Fall on us and hide us*e* from the face of him who sits on the throne and from the wrath of the Lamb! ¹⁷For the great day of their*f* wrath has come, and who can withstand it?"

144,000 Sealed

7 After this I saw four angels standing at the four corners of the earth, holding back the four winds of the earth to prevent any wind from blowing on the land or on the sea or on any tree. ²Then I saw another angel coming up from the east, having the seal of the living God. He called out in a loud voice to the four angels who had been given power to harm the land and the sea: ³"Do not harm the land or the sea or the trees until we put a seal on the foreheads of the servants of our God." ⁴Then I heard the number of those who were sealed: 144,000 from all the tribes of Israel.

---

a 6 Or about 1 kilogram   *b* 6 Greek *a denarius*   *c* 6 Or about 3 kilograms
d 11 The Greek word for *brothers and sisters* (*adelphoi*) refers here to believers, both men and women, as part of God's family; also in 12:10; 19:10.   *e* 16 See Hosea 10:8.
f 17 Some manuscripts *his*

⁵ From the tribe of Judah 12,000
    were sealed,
  from the tribe of Reuben 12,000,
  from the tribe of Gad 12,000,
⁶ from the tribe of Asher 12,000,
  from the tribe of Naphtali
    12,000,
  from the tribe of Manasseh
    12,000,
⁷ from the tribe of Simeon 12,000,
  from the tribe of Levi 12,000,
  from the tribe of Issachar 12,000,
⁸ from the tribe of Zebulun 12,000,
  from the tribe of Joseph 12,000,
  from the tribe of Benjamin
    12,000.

The Great Multitude in White Robes

⁹ After this I looked, and there before me was a great multitude that no one could count, from every nation, tribe, people and language, standing before the throne and before the Lamb. They were wearing white robes and were holding palm branches in their hands. ¹⁰ And they cried out in a loud voice:

  "Salvation belongs to our God,
  who sits on the throne,
  and to the Lamb."

¹¹ All the angels were standing around the throne and around the elders and the four living creatures. They fell down on their faces before the throne and worshiped God, ¹² saying:

  "Amen!
  Praise and glory
  and wisdom and thanks and
    honor
  and power and strength
  be to our God for ever and ever.
  Amen!"

¹³ Then one of the elders asked me, "These in white robes—who are they, and where did they come from?"

¹⁴ I answered, "Sir, you know."
  And he said, "These are they who have come out of the great tribulation; they have washed their robes and made them white in the blood of the Lamb. ¹⁵ Therefore,

  "they are before the throne of
    God
  and serve him day and night
    in his temple;
  and he who sits on the throne
    will shelter them with his
    presence.
¹⁶ 'Never again will they hunger;
    never again will they thirst.
  The sun will not beat down on
    them,'ᵃ
    nor any scorching heat.
¹⁷ For the Lamb at the center of the
    throne
  will be their shepherd;
  'he will lead them to springs of
    living water.'ᵃ
  'And God will wipe away every
    tear from their eyes.'ᵇ"

The Seventh Seal and the Golden Censer

8 When he opened the seventh seal, there was silence in heaven for about half an hour.

² And I saw the seven angels who stand before God, and seven trumpets were given to them.

³ Another angel, who had a golden censer, came and stood at the altar. He was given much incense to offer, with the prayers of all God's people, on the golden altar in front of the throne. ⁴ The smoke of the incense, together with the prayers of God's people, went up before God from the angel's hand. ⁵ Then the angel took the censer, filled it with fire from the altar, and hurled it on the earth; and

---

ᵃ 16,17 Isaiah 49:10   ᵇ 17 Isaiah 25:8

there came peals of thunder, rumblings, flashes of lightning and an earthquake.

The Trumpets

⁶Then the seven angels who had the seven trumpets prepared to sound them.

⁷The first angel sounded his trumpet, and there came hail and fire mixed with blood, and it was hurled down on the earth. A third of the earth was burned up, a third of the trees were burned up, and all the green grass was burned up.

⁸The second angel sounded his trumpet, and something like a huge mountain, all ablaze, was thrown into the sea. A third of the sea turned into blood, ⁹a third of the living creatures in the sea died, and a third of the ships were destroyed.

¹⁰The third angel sounded his trumpet, and a great star, blazing like a torch, fell from the sky on a third of the rivers and on the springs of water — ¹¹the name of the star is Wormwood.ᵃ A third of the waters turned bitter, and many people died from the waters that had become bitter.

¹²The fourth angel sounded his trumpet, and a third of the sun was struck, a third of the moon, and a third of the stars, so that a third of them turned dark. A third of the day was without light, and also a third of the night.

¹³As I watched, I heard an eagle that was flying in midair call out in a loud voice: "Woe! Woe! Woe to the inhabitants of the earth, because of the trumpet blasts about to be sounded by the other three angels!"

9 The fifth angel sounded his trumpet, and I saw a star that had fallen from the sky to the earth. The star was given the key to the shaft of the Abyss. ²When he opened the Abyss, smoke rose from it like the smoke from a gigantic furnace. The sun and sky were darkened by the smoke from the Abyss. ³And out of the smoke locusts came down on the earth and were given power like that of scorpions of the earth. ⁴They were told not to harm the grass of the earth or any plant or tree, but only those people who did not have the seal of God on their foreheads. ⁵They were not allowed to kill them but only to torture them for five months. And the agony they suffered was like that of the sting of a scorpion when it strikes. ⁶During those days people will seek death but will not find it; they will long to die, but death will elude them.

⁷The locusts looked like horses prepared for battle. On their heads they wore something like crowns of gold, and their faces resembled human faces. ⁸Their hair was like women's hair, and their teeth were like lions' teeth. ⁹They had breastplates like breastplates of iron, and the sound of their wings was like the thundering of many horses and chariots rushing into battle. ¹⁰They had tails with stingers, like scorpions, and in their tails they had power to torment people for five months. ¹¹They had as king over them the angel of the Abyss, whose name in Hebrew is Abaddon and in Greek is Apollyon (that is, Destroyer).

¹²The first woe is past; two other woes are yet to come.

¹³The sixth angel sounded his trumpet, and I heard a voice coming from the four horns of the golden altar that is before God. ¹⁴It said to the sixth angel who had the trumpet, "Release the four angels who are bound at the great river Euphrates."

ᵃ 11 Wormwood is a bitter substance.

¹⁵And the four angels who had been kept ready for this very hour and day and month and year were released to kill a third of mankind. ¹⁶The number of the mounted troops was twice ten thousand times ten thousand. I heard their number.

¹⁷The horses and riders I saw in my vision looked like this: Their breastplates were fiery red, dark blue, and yellow as sulfur. The heads of the horses resembled the heads of lions, and out of their mouths came fire, smoke and sulfur. ¹⁸A third of mankind was killed by the three plagues of fire, smoke and sulfur that came out of their mouths. ¹⁹The power of the horses was in their mouths and in their tails; for their tails were like snakes, having heads with which they inflict injury.

²⁰The rest of mankind who were not killed by these plagues still did not repent of the work of their hands; they did not stop worshiping demons, and idols of gold, silver, bronze, stone and wood — idols that cannot see or hear or walk. ²¹Nor did they repent of their murders, their magic arts, their sexual immorality or their thefts.

The Angel and the Little Scroll

10 Then I saw another mighty angel coming down from heaven. He was robed in a cloud, with a rainbow above his head; his face was like the sun, and his legs were like fiery pillars. ²He was holding a little scroll, which lay open in his hand. He planted his right foot on the sea and his left foot on the land, ³and he gave a loud shout like the roar of a lion. When he shouted, the voices of the seven thunders spoke. ⁴And when the seven thunders spoke, I was about to write; but I heard a voice from heaven say, "Seal up what the seven thunders have said and do not write it down."

⁵Then the angel I had seen standing on the sea and on the land raised his right hand to heaven. ⁶And he swore by him who lives for ever and ever, who created the heavens and all that is in them, the earth and all that is in it, and the sea and all that is in it, and said, "There will be no more delay! ⁷But in the days when the seventh angel is about to sound his trumpet, the mystery of God will be accomplished, just as he announced to his servants the prophets."

⁸Then the voice that I had heard from heaven spoke to me once more: "Go, take the scroll that lies open in the hand of the angel who is standing on the sea and on the land."

⁹So I went to the angel and asked him to give me the little scroll. He said to me, "Take it and eat it. It will turn your stomach sour, but 'in your mouth it will be as sweet as honey.'ᵃ" ¹⁰I took the little scroll from the angel's hand and ate it. It tasted as sweet as honey in my mouth, but when I had eaten it, my stomach turned sour. ¹¹Then I was told, "You must prophesy again about many peoples, nations, languages and kings."

The Two Witnesses

11 I was given a reed like a measuring rod and was told, "Go and measure the temple of God and the altar, with its worshipers. ²But exclude the outer court; do not measure it, because it has been given to the Gentiles. They will trample on the holy city for 42 months. ³And I will appoint my two witnesses, and they will prophesy for 1,260 days, clothed in sackcloth. ⁴They are "the two olive trees" and the two lampstands, and "they stand before the Lord of the earth."ᵇ ⁵If anyone tries to harm

---

ᵃ 9 Ezek. 3:3   ᵇ 4 See Zech. 4:3,11,14.

them, fire comes from their mouths and devours their enemies. This is how anyone who wants to harm them must die. [6]They have power to shut up the heavens so that it will not rain during the time they are prophesying; and they have power to turn the waters into blood and to strike the earth with every kind of plague as often as they want.

[7]Now when they have finished their testimony, the beast that comes up from the Abyss will attack them, and overpower and kill them. [8]Their bodies will lie in the public square of the great city — which is figuratively called Sodom and Egypt — where also their Lord was crucified. [9]For three and a half days some from every people, tribe, language and nation will gaze on their bodies and refuse them burial. [10]The inhabitants of the earth will gloat over them and will celebrate by sending each other gifts, because these two prophets had tormented those who live on the earth.

[11]But after the three and a half days the breath[a] of life from God entered them, and they stood on their feet, and terror struck those who saw them. [12]Then they heard a loud voice from heaven saying to them, "Come up here." And they went up to heaven in a cloud, while their enemies looked on.

[13]At that very hour there was a severe earthquake and a tenth of the city collapsed. Seven thousand people were killed in the earthquake, and the survivors were terrified and gave glory to the God of heaven.

[14]The second woe has passed; the third woe is coming soon.

The Seventh Trumpet

[15]The seventh angel sounded his trumpet, and there were loud voices in heaven, which said:

"The kingdom of the world has
    become
  the kingdom of our Lord and
    of his Messiah,
and he will reign for ever and
    ever."

[16]And the twenty-four elders, who were seated on their thrones before God, fell on their faces and worshiped God, [17]saying:

"We give thanks to you, Lord God
    Almighty,
  the One who is and who was,
because you have taken your
    great power
  and have begun to reign.
[18]The nations were angry,
  and your wrath has come.
The time has come for judging
    the dead,
  and for rewarding your
    servants the prophets
and your people who revere your
    name,
  both great and small —
and for destroying those who
    destroy the earth."

[19]Then God's temple in heaven was opened, and within his temple was seen the ark of his covenant. And there came flashes of lightning, rumblings, peals of thunder, an earthquake and a severe hailstorm.

The Woman and the Dragon

12 A great sign appeared in heaven: a woman clothed with the sun, with the moon under her feet and a crown of twelve stars on her head. [2]She was pregnant and cried out in pain as she was about to give birth. [3]Then another sign appeared in heaven: an enormous red dragon with seven heads and ten horns and

---

[a] 11 Or *Spirit* (see Ezek. 37:5,14)

seven crowns on its heads. [4]Its tail swept a third of the stars out of the sky and flung them to the earth. The dragon stood in front of the woman who was about to give birth, so that it might devour her child the moment he was born. [5]She gave birth to a son, a male child, who "will rule all the nations with an iron scepter."[a] And her child was snatched up to God and to his throne. [6]The woman fled into the wilderness to a place prepared for her by God, where she might be taken care of for 1,260 days.

[7]Then war broke out in heaven. Michael and his angels fought against the dragon, and the dragon and his angels fought back. [8]But he was not strong enough, and they lost their place in heaven. [9]The great dragon was hurled down — that ancient serpent called the devil, or Satan, who leads the whole world astray. He was hurled to the earth, and his angels with him.

[10]Then I heard a loud voice in heaven say:

"Now have come the salvation
        and the power
    and the kingdom of our
        God,
    and the authority of his
        Messiah.
For the accuser of our brothers
        and sisters,
    who accuses them before
        our God day and night,
    has been hurled down.
[11]They triumphed over him
    by the blood of the Lamb
    and by the word of their
        testimony;
they did not love their lives so
        much
    as to shrink from death.
[12]Therefore rejoice, you heavens
    and you who dwell in them!

But woe to the earth and the sea,
    because the devil has gone
        down to you!
He is filled with fury,
    because he knows that his
        time is short."

[13]When the dragon saw that he had been hurled to the earth, he pursued the woman who had given birth to the male child. [14]The woman was given the two wings of a great eagle, so that she might fly to the place prepared for her in the wilderness, where she would be taken care of for a time, times and half a time, out of the serpent's reach. [15]Then from his mouth the serpent spewed water like a river, to overtake the woman and sweep her away with the torrent. [16]But the earth helped the woman by opening its mouth and swallowing the river that the dragon had spewed out of his mouth. [17]Then the dragon was enraged at the woman and went off to wage war against the rest of her offspring — those who keep God's commands and hold fast their testimony about Jesus.

The Beast out of the Sea

13 The dragon[b] stood on the shore of the sea. And I saw a beast coming out of the sea. It had ten horns and seven heads, with ten crowns on its horns, and on each head a blasphemous name. [2]The beast I saw resembled a leopard, but had feet like those of a bear and a mouth like that of a lion. The dragon gave the beast his power and his throne and great authority. [3]One of the heads of the beast seemed to have had a fatal wound, but the fatal wound had been healed. The whole world was filled with wonder and followed the

---

[a] 5 Psalm 2:9   [b] 1 Some manuscripts *And I*

beast. ⁴People worshiped the dragon because he had given authority to the beast, and they also worshiped the beast and asked, "Who is like the beast? Who can wage war against it?"

⁵The beast was given a mouth to utter proud words and blasphemies and to exercise its authority for forty-two months. ⁶It opened its mouth to blaspheme God, and to slander his name and his dwelling place and those who live in heaven. ⁷It was given power to wage war against God's holy people and to conquer them. And it was given authority over every tribe, people, language and nation. ⁸All inhabitants of the earth will worship the beast — all whose names have not been written in the Lamb's book of life, the Lamb who was slain from the creation of the world.ᵃ

⁹Whoever has ears, let them hear.

¹⁰ "If anyone is to go into captivity,
        into captivity they will go.
    If anyone is to be killedᵇ with the
        sword,
        with the sword they will be
            killed."ᶜ

This calls for patient endurance and faithfulness on the part of God's people.

The Beast out of the Earth

¹¹Then I saw a second beast, coming out of the earth. It had two horns like a lamb, but it spoke like a dragon. ¹²It exercised all the authority of the first beast on its behalf, and made the earth and its inhabitants worship the first beast, whose fatal wound had been healed. ¹³And it performed great signs, even causing fire to come down from heaven to the earth in full view of the people. ¹⁴Because of the signs it was given power to perform on behalf of the first beast, it deceived the inhabitants of the earth. It ordered them to set up an image in honor of the beast who was wounded by the sword and yet lived. ¹⁵The second beast was given power to give breath to the image of the first beast, so that the image could speak and cause all who refused to worship the image to be killed. ¹⁶It also forced all people, great and small, rich and poor, free and slave, to receive a mark on their right hands or on their foreheads, ¹⁷so that they could not buy or sell unless they had the mark, which is the name of the beast or the number of its name.

¹⁸This calls for wisdom. Let the person who has insight calculate the number of the beast, for it is the number of a man.ᵈ That number is 666.

The Lamb and the 144,000

14 Then I looked, and there before me was the Lamb, standing on Mount Zion, and with him 144,000 who had his name and his Father's name written on their foreheads. ²And I heard a sound from heaven like the roar of rushing waters and like a loud peal of thunder. The sound I heard was like that of harpists playing their harps. ³And they sang a new song before the throne and before the four living creatures and the elders. No one could learn the song except the 144,000 who had been redeemed from the earth. ⁴These are those who did not defile themselves with women, for they remained virgins. They follow the Lamb wherever he goes. They were purchased from among mankind and offered as firstfruits to God and the Lamb. ⁵No lie was found in their mouths; they are blameless.

ᵃ 8 Or *written from the creation of the world in the book of life belonging to the Lamb who was slain*   ᵇ 10 Some manuscripts *anyone kills*   ᶜ 10 Jer. 15:2   ᵈ 18 Or *is humanity's number*

The Three Angels

[6]Then I saw another angel flying in midair, and he had the eternal gospel to proclaim to those who live on the earth — to every nation, tribe, language and people. [7]He said in a loud voice, "Fear God and give him glory, because the hour of his judgment has come. Worship him who made the heavens, the earth, the sea and the springs of water."

[8]A second angel followed and said, "'Fallen! Fallen is Babylon the Great,'[a] which made all the nations drink the maddening wine of her adulteries."

[9]A third angel followed them and said in a loud voice: "If anyone worships the beast and its image and receives its mark on their forehead or on their hand, [10]they, too, will drink the wine of God's fury, which has been poured full strength into the cup of his wrath. They will be tormented with burning sulfur in the presence of the holy angels and of the Lamb. [11]And the smoke of their torment will rise for ever and ever. There will be no rest day or night for those who worship the beast and its image, or for anyone who receives the mark of its name." [12]This calls for patient endurance on the part of the people of God who keep his commands and remain faithful to Jesus.

[13]Then I heard a voice from heaven say, "Write this: Blessed are the dead who die in the Lord from now on."

"Yes," says the Spirit, "they will rest from their labor, for their deeds will follow them."

Harvesting the Earth and Trampling the Winepress

[14]I looked, and there before me was a white cloud, and seated on the cloud was one like a son of man[b] with a crown of gold on his head and a sharp sickle in his hand. [15]Then another angel came out of the temple and called in a loud voice to him who was sitting on the cloud, "Take your sickle and reap, because the time to reap has come, for the harvest of the earth is ripe." [16]So he who was seated on the cloud swung his sickle over the earth, and the earth was harvested.

[17]Another angel came out of the temple in heaven, and he too had a sharp sickle. [18]Still another angel, who had charge of the fire, came from the altar and called in a loud voice to him who had the sharp sickle, "Take your sharp sickle and gather the clusters of grapes from the earth's vine, because its grapes are ripe." [19]The angel swung his sickle on the earth, gathered its grapes and threw them into the great winepress of God's wrath. [20]They were trampled in the winepress outside the city, and blood flowed out of the press, rising as high as the horses' bridles for a distance of 1,600 stadia.[c]

Seven Angels With Seven Plagues

15 I saw in heaven another great and marvelous sign: seven angels with the seven last plagues — last, because with them God's wrath is completed. [2]And I saw what looked like a sea of glass glowing with fire and, standing beside the sea, those who had been victorious over the beast and its image and over the number of its name. They held harps given them by God [3]and sang the song of God's servant Moses and of the Lamb:

"Great and marvelous are your deeds,
    Lord God Almighty.

---

[a] 8 Isaiah 21:9   [b] 14 See Daniel 7:13.
[c] 20 That is, about 180 miles or about 300 kilometers

Just and true are your ways,
        King of the nations.ᵃ
⁴ Who will not fear you, Lord,
        and bring glory to your name?
For you alone are holy.
All nations will come
        and worship before you,
for your righteous acts have been
        revealed."ᵇ

⁵After this I looked, and I saw in
heaven the temple — that is, the tabernacle of the covenant law — and
it was opened. ⁶Out of the temple
came the seven angels with the seven
plagues. They were dressed in clean,
shining linen and wore golden sashes
around their chests. ⁷Then one of the
four living creatures gave to the sev-
en angels seven golden bowls filled
with the wrath of God, who lives for
ever and ever. ⁸And the temple was
filled with smoke from the glory of
God and from his power, and no one
could enter the temple until the sev-
en plagues of the seven angels were
completed.

The Seven Bowls of God's Wrath

16 Then I heard a loud voice from
the temple saying to the seven
angels, "Go, pour out the seven bowls
of God's wrath on the earth."

²The first angel went and poured
out his bowl on the land, and ugly, fes-
tering sores broke out on the people
who had the mark of the beast and
worshiped its image.

³The second angel poured out his
bowl on the sea, and it turned into
blood like that of a dead person, and
every living thing in the sea died.

⁴The third angel poured out his
bowl on the rivers and springs of water, and they became blood. ⁵Then
I heard the angel in charge of the
waters say:

"You are just in these judgments,
        O Holy One,
you who are and who were;
⁶ for they have shed the blood of
        your holy people and your
        prophets,
and you have given them
        blood to drink as they
        deserve."

⁷And I heard the altar respond:

"Yes, Lord God Almighty,
        true and just are your
        judgments."

⁸The fourth angel poured out his
bowl on the sun, and the sun was
allowed to scorch people with fire.
⁹They were seared by the intense heat
and they cursed the name of God, who
had control over these plagues, but
they refused to repent and glorify
him.

¹⁰The fifth angel poured out his
bowl on the throne of the beast, and
its kingdom was plunged into darkness. People gnawed their tongues in
agony ¹¹and cursed the God of heaven
because of their pains and their sores,
but they refused to repent of what
they had done.

¹²The sixth angel poured out his
bowl on the great river Euphrates,
and its water was dried up to prepare
the way for the kings from the East.
¹³Then I saw three impure spirits that
looked like frogs; they came out of
the mouth of the dragon, out of the
mouth of the beast and out of the
mouth of the false prophet. ¹⁴They
are demonic spirits that perform
signs, and they go out to the kings
of the whole world, to gather them
for the battle on the great day of God
Almighty.

ᵃ 3 Some manuscripts *ages*   ᵇ 3,4 Phrases in
this song are drawn from Psalm 111:2,3;
Deut. 32:4; Jer. 10:7; Psalms 86:9; 98:2.

¹⁵"Look, I come like a thief! Blessed is the one who stays awake and remains clothed, so as not to go naked and be shamefully exposed."

¹⁶Then they gathered the kings together to the place that in Hebrew is called Armageddon.

¹⁷The seventh angel poured out his bowl into the air, and out of the temple came a loud voice from the throne, saying, "It is done!" ¹⁸Then there came flashes of lightning, rumblings, peals of thunder and a severe earthquake. No earthquake like it has ever occurred since mankind has been on earth, so tremendous was the quake. ¹⁹The great city split into three parts, and the cities of the nations collapsed. God remembered Babylon the Great and gave her the cup filled with the wine of the fury of his wrath. ²⁰Every island fled away and the mountains could not be found. ²¹From the sky huge hailstones, each weighing about a hundred pounds,ᵃ fell on people. And they cursed God on account of the plague of hail, because the plague was so terrible.

Babylon, the Prostitute on the Beast

17 One of the seven angels who had the seven bowls came and said to me, "Come, I will show you the punishment of the great prostitute, who sits by many waters. ²With her the kings of the earth committed adultery, and the inhabitants of the earth were intoxicated with the wine of her adulteries."

³Then the angel carried me away in the Spirit into a wilderness. There I saw a woman sitting on a scarlet beast that was covered with blasphemous names and had seven heads and ten horns. ⁴The woman was dressed in purple and scarlet, and was glittering with gold, precious stones and pearls. She held a golden cup in her hand, filled with abominable things and the filth of her adulteries. ⁵The name written on her forehead was a mystery:

BABYLON THE GREAT
THE MOTHER OF PROSTITUTES
AND OF THE ABOMINATIONS OF THE
EARTH.

⁶I saw that the woman was drunk with the blood of God's holy people, the blood of those who bore testimony to Jesus.

When I saw her, I was greatly astonished. ⁷Then the angel said to me: "Why are you astonished? I will explain to you the mystery of the woman and of the beast she rides, which has the seven heads and ten horns. ⁸The beast, which you saw, once was, now is not, and yet will come up out of the Abyss and go to its destruction. The inhabitants of the earth whose names have not been written in the book of life from the creation of the world will be astonished when they see the beast, because it once was, now is not, and yet will come.

⁹"This calls for a mind with wisdom. The seven heads are seven hills on which the woman sits. ¹⁰They are also seven kings. Five have fallen, one is, the other has not yet come; but when he does come, he must remain for only a little while. ¹¹The beast who once was, and now is not, is an eighth king. He belongs to the seven and is going to his destruction.

¹²"The ten horns you saw are ten kings who have not yet received a kingdom, but who for one hour will receive authority as kings along with the beast. ¹³They have one purpose

---

ᵃ 21 Or about 45 kilograms

and will give their power and authority to the beast. [14]They will wage war against the Lamb, but the Lamb will triumph over them because he is Lord of lords and King of kings — and with him will be his called, chosen and faithful followers."

[15]Then the angel said to me, "The waters you saw, where the prostitute sits, are peoples, multitudes, nations and languages. [16]The beast and the ten horns you saw will hate the prostitute. They will bring her to ruin and leave her naked; they will eat her flesh and burn her with fire. [17]For God has put it into their hearts to accomplish his purpose by agreeing to hand over to the beast their royal authority, until God's words are fulfilled. [18]The woman you saw is the great city that rules over the kings of the earth."

Lament Over Fallen Babylon

18 After this I saw another angel coming down from heaven. He had great authority, and the earth was illuminated by his splendor. [2]With a mighty voice he shouted:

"'Fallen! Fallen is Babylon the
        Great!'[a]
    She has become a dwelling for
        demons
    and a haunt for every impure
        spirit,
        a haunt for every unclean bird,
        a haunt for every unclean and
            detestable animal.
[3] For all the nations have drunk
        the maddening wine of her
        adulteries.
    The kings of the earth
        committed adultery with
        her,
        and the merchants of the
            earth grew rich from her
            excessive luxuries."

Warning to Escape Babylon's Judgment

[4]Then I heard another voice from heaven say:

"'Come out of her, my people,'[b]
        so that you will not share in
            her sins,
        so that you will not receive any
            of her plagues;
[5] for her sins are piled up to heaven,
        and God has remembered her
            crimes.
[6] Give back to her as she has given;
        pay her back double for what
            she has done.
    Pour her a double portion
        from her own cup.
[7] Give her as much torment and
        grief
        as the glory and luxury she
            gave herself.
    In her heart she boasts,
        'I sit enthroned as queen.
    I am not a widow;[c]
        I will never mourn.'
[8] Therefore in one day her plagues
        will overtake her:
    death, mourning and famine.
    She will be consumed by fire,
        for mighty is the Lord God who
            judges her.

Threefold Woe Over Babylon's Fall

[9]"When the kings of the earth who committed adultery with her and shared her luxury see the smoke of her burning, they will weep and mourn over her. [10]Terrified at her torment, they will stand far off and cry:

"'Woe! Woe to you, great city,
        you mighty city of Babylon!
    In one hour your doom has
        come!'

---

[a] 2 Isaiah 21:9   [b] 4 Jer. 51:45   [c] 7 See Isaiah 47:7,8.

¹¹"The merchants of the earth will weep and mourn over her because no one buys their cargoes anymore—¹²cargoes of gold, silver, precious stones and pearls; fine linen, purple, silk and scarlet cloth; every sort of citron wood, and articles of every kind made of ivory, costly wood, bronze, iron and marble; ¹³cargoes of cinnamon and spice, of incense, myrrh and frankincense, of wine and olive oil, of fine flour and wheat; cattle and sheep; horses and carriages; and human beings sold as slaves.

¹⁴"They will say, 'The fruit you longed for is gone from you. All your luxury and splendor have vanished, never to be recovered.' ¹⁵The merchants who sold these things and gained their wealth from her will stand far off, terrified at her torment. They will weep and mourn ¹⁶and cry out:

> "'Woe! Woe to you, great city,
>   dressed in fine linen, purple
>   and scarlet,
> and glittering with gold,
>   precious stones and
>   pearls!
> ¹⁷ In one hour such great wealth
>   has been brought to ruin!'

"Every sea captain, and all who travel by ship, the sailors, and all who earn their living from the sea, will stand far off. ¹⁸When they see the smoke of her burning, they will exclaim, 'Was there ever a city like this great city?' ¹⁹They will throw dust on their heads, and with weeping and mourning cry out:

> "'Woe! Woe to you, great city,
>   where all who had ships on
>   the sea
>   became rich through her
>   wealth!
> In one hour she has been brought
>   to ruin!'

²⁰ "Rejoice over her, you heavens!
    Rejoice, you people of God!
    Rejoice, apostles and prophets!
For God has judged her
    with the judgment she
        imposed on you."

The Finality of Babylon's Doom

²¹Then a mighty angel picked up a boulder the size of a large millstone and threw it into the sea, and said:

> "With such violence
>   the great city of Babylon will be
>   thrown down,
>   never to be found again.
> ²² The music of harpists and
>   musicians, pipers and
>   trumpeters,
>   will be heard in you
>   again.
> No worker of any trade
>   will ever be found in you again.
> The sound of a millstone
>   will never be heard in you
>   again.
> ²³ The light of a lamp
>   will never shine in you again.
> The voice of bridegroom and
>   bride
>   will never be heard in you
>   again.
> Your merchants were the world's
>   important people.
> By your magic spell all the
>   nations were led astray.
> ²⁴ In her was found the blood of
>   prophets and of God's holy
>   people,
>   of all who have been
>   slaughtered on the earth."

Threefold Hallelujah Over Babylon's Fall

19 After this I heard what sounded like the roar of a great multitude in heaven shouting:

"Hallelujah!
Salvation and glory and power
        belong to our God,
2   for true and just are his
        judgments.
He has condemned the great
        prostitute
    who corrupted the earth by
        her adulteries.
He has avenged on her the blood
    of his servants."

3And again they shouted:

"Hallelujah!
The smoke from her goes up for
    ever and ever."

4The twenty-four elders and the
four living creatures fell down and
worshiped God, who was seated on
the throne. And they cried:

"Amen, Hallelujah!"

5Then a voice came from the
throne, saying:

"Praise our God,
    all you his servants,
you who fear him,
    both great and small!"

6Then I heard what sounded like
a great multitude, like the roar of
rushing waters and like loud peals
of thunder, shouting:

"Hallelujah!
    For our Lord God Almighty
        reigns.
7Let us rejoice and be glad
    and give him glory!
For the wedding of the Lamb has
        come,
    and his bride has made herself
        ready.
8Fine linen, bright and clean,
    was given her to wear."
(Fine linen stands for the righteous
acts of God's holy people.)

9Then the angel said to me, "Write
this: Blessed are those who are invited
to the wedding supper of the Lamb!"
And he added, "These are the true
words of God."

10At this I fell at his feet to worship
him. But he said to me, "Don't do that!
I am a fellow servant with you and
with your brothers and sisters who
hold to the testimony of Jesus. Worship God! For it is the Spirit of prophecy who bears testimony to Jesus."

The Heavenly Warrior Defeats the Beast

11I saw heaven standing open and
there before me was a white horse,
whose rider is called Faithful and
True. With justice he judges and
wages war. 12His eyes are like blazing fire, and on his head are many
crowns. He has a name written on
him that no one knows but he himself. 13He is dressed in a robe dipped
in blood, and his name is the Word
of God. 14The armies of heaven were
following him, riding on white horses
and dressed in fine linen, white and
clean. 15Coming out of his mouth is
a sharp sword with which to strike
down the nations. "He will rule them
with an iron scepter."a He treads the
winepress of the fury of the wrath of
God Almighty. 16On his robe and on
his thigh he has this name written:

KING OF KINGS AND LORD OF LORDS.

17And I saw an angel standing in
the sun, who cried in a loud voice to
all the birds flying in midair, "Come,
gather together for the great supper
of God, 18so that you may eat the flesh
of kings, generals, and the mighty,
of horses and their riders, and the
flesh of all people, free and slave,
great and small."

a 15 Psalm 2:9

¹⁹Then I saw the beast and the kings of the earth and their armies gathered together to wage war against the rider on the horse and his army. ²⁰But the beast was captured, and with it the false prophet who had performed the signs on its behalf. With these signs he had deluded those who had received the mark of the beast and worshiped its image. The two of them were thrown alive into the fiery lake of burning sulfur. ²¹The rest were killed with the sword coming out of the mouth of the rider on the horse, and all the birds gorged themselves on their flesh.

The Thousand Years

20 And I saw an angel coming down out of heaven, having the key to the Abyss and holding in his hand a great chain. ²He seized the dragon, that ancient serpent, who is the devil, or Satan, and bound him for a thousand years. ³He threw him into the Abyss, and locked and sealed it over him, to keep him from deceiving the nations anymore until the thousand years were ended. After that, he must be set free for a short time.

⁴I saw thrones on which were seated those who had been given authority to judge. And I saw the souls of those who had been beheaded because of their testimony about Jesus and because of the word of God. They*ᵃ* had not worshiped the beast or its image and had not received its mark on their foreheads or their hands. They came to life and reigned with Christ a thousand years. ⁵(The rest of the dead did not come to life until the thousand years were ended.) This is the first resurrection. ⁶Blessed and holy are those who share in the first resurrection. The second death has no power over

them, but they will be priests of God and of Christ and will reign with him for a thousand years.

The Judgment of Satan

⁷When the thousand years are over, Satan will be released from his prison ⁸and will go out to deceive the nations in the four corners of the earth — Gog and Magog — and to gather them for battle. In number they are like the sand on the seashore. ⁹They marched across the breadth of the earth and surrounded the camp of God's people, the city he loves. But fire came down from heaven and devoured them. ¹⁰And the devil, who deceived them, was thrown into the lake of burning sulfur, where the beast and the false prophet had been thrown. They will be tormented day and night for ever and ever.

The Judgment of the Dead

¹¹Then I saw a great white throne and him who was seated on it. The earth and the heavens fled from his presence, and there was no place for them. ¹²And I saw the dead, great and small, standing before the throne, and books were opened. Another book was opened, which is the book of life. The dead were judged according to what they had done as recorded in the books. ¹³The sea gave up the dead that were in it, and death and Hades gave up the dead that were in them, and each person was judged according to what they had done. ¹⁴Then death and Hades were thrown into the lake of fire. The lake of fire is the second death. ¹⁵Anyone whose name was not found written in the book of life was thrown into the lake of fire.

ᵃ 4 Or God; I also saw those who

A New Heaven and a New Earth

21 Then I saw "a new heaven and a new earth,"[a] for the first heaven and the first earth had passed away, and there was no longer any sea. [2]I saw the Holy City, the new Jerusalem, coming down out of heaven from God, prepared as a bride beautifully dressed for her husband. [3]And I heard a loud voice from the throne saying, "Look! God's dwelling place is now among the people, and he will dwell with them. They will be his people, and God himself will be with them and be their God. [4]'He will wipe every tear from their eyes. There will be no more death'[b] or mourning or crying or pain, for the old order of things has passed away."

[5]He who was seated on the throne said, "I am making everything new!" Then he said, "Write this down, for these words are trustworthy and true."

[6]He said to me: "It is done. I am the Alpha and the Omega, the Beginning and the End. To the thirsty I will give water without cost from the spring of the water of life. [7]Those who are victorious will inherit all this, and I will be their God and they will be my children. [8]But the cowardly, the unbelieving, the vile, the murderers, the sexually immoral, those who practice magic arts, the idolaters and all liars — they will be consigned to the fiery lake of burning sulfur. This is the second death."

The New Jerusalem, the Bride of the Lamb

[9]One of the seven angels who had the seven bowls full of the seven last plagues came and said to me, "Come, I will show you the bride, the wife of the Lamb." [10]And he carried me away in the Spirit to a mountain great and high, and showed me the Holy City, Jerusalem, coming down out of heaven from God. [11]It shone with the glory of God, and its brilliance was like that of a very precious jewel, like a jasper, clear as crystal. [12]It had a great, high wall with twelve gates, and with twelve angels at the gates. On the gates were written the names of the twelve tribes of Israel. [13]There were three gates on the east, three on the north, three on the south and three on the west. [14]The wall of the city had twelve foundations, and on them were the names of the twelve apostles of the Lamb.

[15]The angel who talked with me had a measuring rod of gold to measure the city, its gates and its walls. [16]The city was laid out like a square, as long as it was wide. He measured the city with the rod and found it to be 12,000 stadia[c] in length, and as wide and high as it is long. [17]The angel measured the wall using human measurement, and it was 144 cubits[d] thick.[e] [18]The wall was made of jasper, and the city of pure gold, as pure as glass. [19]The foundations of the city walls were decorated with every kind of precious stone. The first foundation was jasper, the second sapphire, the third agate, the fourth emerald, [20]the fifth onyx, the sixth ruby, the seventh chrysolite, the eighth beryl, the ninth topaz, the tenth turquoise, the eleventh jacinth, and the twelfth amethyst.[f] [21]The twelve gates were twelve pearls, each gate made of a single pearl. The great street of the

---

[a] 1 Isaiah 65:17   [b] 4 Isaiah 25:8   [c] 16 That is, about 1,400 miles or about 2,200 kilometers   [d] 17 That is, about 200 feet or about 65 meters   [e] 17 Or high   [f] 20 The precise identification of some of these precious stones is uncertain.

city was of gold, as pure as transparent glass.

²²I did not see a temple in the city, because the Lord God Almighty and the Lamb are its temple. ²³The city does not need the sun or the moon to shine on it, for the glory of God gives it light, and the Lamb is its lamp. ²⁴The nations will walk by its light, and the kings of the earth will bring their splendor into it. ²⁵On no day will its gates ever be shut, for there will be no night there. ²⁶The glory and honor of the nations will be brought into it. ²⁷Nothing impure will ever enter it, nor will anyone who does what is shameful or deceitful, but only those whose names are written in the Lamb's book of life.

Eden Restored

22 Then the angel showed me the river of the water of life, as clear as crystal, flowing from the throne of God and of the Lamb ²down the middle of the great street of the city. On each side of the river stood the tree of life, bearing twelve crops of fruit, yielding its fruit every month. And the leaves of the tree are for the healing of the nations. ³No longer will there be any curse. The throne of God and of the Lamb will be in the city, and his servants will serve him. ⁴They will see his face, and his name will be on their foreheads. ⁵There will be no more night. They will not need the light of a lamp or the light of the sun, for the Lord God will give them light. And they will reign for ever and ever.

John and the Angel

⁶The angel said to me, "These words are trustworthy and true. The Lord, the God who inspires the prophets, sent his angel to show his servants the things that must soon take place."

⁷"Look, I am coming soon! Blessed is the one who keeps the words of the prophecy written in this scroll."

⁸I, John, am the one who heard and saw these things. And when I had heard and seen them, I fell down to worship at the feet of the angel who had been showing them to me. ⁹But he said to me, "Don't do that! I am a fellow servant with you and with your fellow prophets and with all who keep the words of this scroll. Worship God!"

¹⁰Then he told me, "Do not seal up the words of the prophecy of this scroll, because the time is near. ¹¹Let the one who does wrong continue to do wrong; let the vile person continue to be vile; let the one who does right continue to do right; and let the holy person continue to be holy."

Epilogue: Invitation and Warning

¹²"Look, I am coming soon! My reward is with me, and I will give to each person according to what they have done. ¹³I am the Alpha and the Omega, the First and the Last, the Beginning and the End.

¹⁴"Blessed are those who wash their robes, that they may have the right to the tree of life and may go through the gates into the city. ¹⁵Outside are the dogs, those who practice magic arts, the sexually immoral, the murderers, the idolaters and everyone who loves and practices falsehood.

¹⁶"I, Jesus, have sent my angel to give youᵃ this testimony for the churches. I am the Root and the Offspring of David, and the bright Morning Star."

¹⁷The Spirit and the bride say, "Come!" And let the one who hears

ᵃ *16* The Greek is plural.

say, "Come!" Let the one who is thirsty come; and let the one who wishes take the free gift of the water of life.

[18]I warn everyone who hears the words of the prophecy of this scroll: If anyone adds anything to them, God will add to that person the plagues described in this scroll. [19]And if anyone takes words away from this scroll of prophecy, God will take away from that person any share in the tree of life and in the Holy City, which are described in this scroll.

[20]He who testifies to these things says, "Yes, I am coming soon."

Amen. Come, Lord Jesus.

[21]The grace of the Lord Jesus be with God's people. Amen.

Psalms and Proverbs

Psalms

BOOK I

Psalms 1 – 41

Psalm 1

¹Blessed is the one
    who does not walk in step with
        the wicked
or stand in the way that sinners
        take
or sit in the company of
        mockers,
²but whose delight is in the law of
        the LORD,
    and who meditates on his law
        day and night.
³That person is like a tree planted
        by streams of water,
    which yields its fruit in
        season
and whose leaf does not wither —
    whatever they do prospers.

⁴Not so the wicked!
    They are like chaff
    that the wind blows away.
⁵Therefore the wicked will not
        stand in the judgment,
    nor sinners in the assembly of
        the righteous.

⁶For the LORD watches over the
        way of the righteous,
    but the way of the wicked leads
        to destruction.

Psalm 2

¹Why do the nations conspire[a]
    and the peoples plot in
        vain?

²The kings of the earth rise up
    and the rulers band together
        against the LORD and against
        his anointed, saying,
³"Let us break their chains
    and throw off their
        shackles."

⁴The One enthroned in heaven
        laughs;
    the Lord scoffs at them.
⁵He rebukes them in his anger
    and terrifies them in his
        wrath, saying,
⁶"I have installed my king
    on Zion, my holy mountain."

⁷I will proclaim the LORD's decree:

He said to me, "You are my son;
    today I have become your
        father.
⁸Ask me,
    and I will make the nations
        your inheritance,
    the ends of the earth your
        possession.
⁹You will break them with a rod
        of iron[b];
    you will dash them to pieces
        like pottery."

¹⁰Therefore, you kings, be wise;
    be warned, you rulers of the
        earth.
¹¹Serve the LORD with fear
    and celebrate his rule with
        trembling.
¹²Kiss his son, or he will be angry
    and your way will lead to your
        destruction,

---

[a] *1* Hebrew; Septuagint *rage*   [b] *9 Or will rule
them with an iron scepter* (see Septuagint and
Syriac)

for his wrath can flare up in a
      moment.
  Blessed are all who take refuge
      in him.

Psalm 3[a]

*A psalm of David. When he fled
from his son Absalom.*

1 LORD, how many are my foes!
      How many rise up against me!
2 Many are saying of me,
      "God will not deliver him."[b]

3 But you, LORD, are a shield
      around me,
  my glory, the One who lifts my
      head high.
4 I call out to the LORD,
      and he answers me from his
      holy mountain.

5 I lie down and sleep;
      I wake again, because the LORD
      sustains me.
6 I will not fear though tens of
      thousands
      assail me on every side.

7 Arise, LORD!
      Deliver me, my God!
  Strike all my enemies on the jaw;
      break the teeth of the wicked.

8 From the LORD comes
      deliverance.
  May your blessing be on your
      people.

Psalm 4[c]

*For the director of music. With stringed
instruments. A psalm of David.*

1 Answer me when I call to you,
      my righteous God.
  Give me relief from my distress;
      have mercy on me and hear my
      prayer.

2 How long will you people turn my
      glory into shame?
  How long will you love
      delusions and seek false
      gods[d]?[e]
3 Know that the LORD has set apart
      his faithful servant for
      himself;
  the LORD hears when I call to
      him.

4 Tremble and[f] do not sin;
      when you are on your beds,
      search your hearts and be
      silent.
5 Offer the sacrifices of the
      righteous
      and trust in the LORD.

6 Many, LORD, are asking, "Who will
      bring us prosperity?"
  Let the light of your face shine
      on us.
7 Fill my heart with joy
      when their grain and new wine
      abound.

8 In peace I will lie down and sleep,
      for you alone, LORD,
      make me dwell in safety.

Psalm 5[g]

*For the director of music. For
pipes. A psalm of David.*

1 Listen to my words, LORD,
      consider my lament.
2 Hear my cry for help,
      my King and my God,
      for to you I pray.

---

[a] In Hebrew texts 3:1-8 is numbered 3:2-9.
[b] 2 The Hebrew has *Selah* (a word of uncertain meaning) here and at the end of verses 4 and 8.   [c] In Hebrew texts 4:1-8 is numbered 4:2-9.   [d] 2 Or *seek lies*   [e] 2 The Hebrew has *Selah* (a word of uncertain meaning) here and at the end of verse 4.   [f] 4 Or *In your anger* (see Septuagint)   [g] In Hebrew texts 5:1-12 is numbered 5:2-13.

³ In the morning, LORD, you hear my voice;
  in the morning I lay my requests before you
  and wait expectantly.
⁴ For you are not a God who is pleased with wickedness;
  with you, evil people are not welcome.
⁵ The arrogant cannot stand in your presence.
You hate all who do wrong;
⁶   you destroy those who tell lies.
  The bloodthirsty and deceitful you, LORD, detest.
⁷ But I, by your great love, can come into your house;
in reverence I bow down toward your holy temple.

⁸ Lead me, LORD, in your righteousness
  because of my enemies —
  make your way straight before me.
⁹ Not a word from their mouth can be trusted;
  their heart is filled with malice.
Their throat is an open grave;
  with their tongues they tell lies.
¹⁰ Declare them guilty, O God!
  Let their intrigues be their downfall.
Banish them for their many sins,
  for they have rebelled against you.
¹¹ But let all who take refuge in you be glad;
  let them ever sing for joy.
Spread your protection over them,
  that those who love your name may rejoice in you.

¹² Surely, LORD, you bless the righteous;
  you surround them with your favor as with a shield.

Psalm 6 [a]

For the director of music. With stringed instruments. According to sheminith. [b] *A psalm of David.*

¹ LORD, do not rebuke me in your anger
  or discipline me in your wrath.
² Have mercy on me, LORD, for I am faint;
  heal me, LORD, for my bones are in agony.
³ My soul is in deep anguish.
  How long, LORD, how long?

⁴ Turn, LORD, and deliver me;
  save me because of your unfailing love.
⁵ Among the dead no one proclaims your name.
  Who praises you from the grave?

⁶ I am worn out from my groaning.

  All night long I flood my bed with weeping
  and drench my couch with tears.
⁷ My eyes grow weak with sorrow;
  they fail because of all my foes.

⁸ Away from me, all you who do evil,
  for the LORD has heard my weeping.
⁹ The LORD has heard my cry for mercy;
  the LORD accepts my prayer.
¹⁰ All my enemies will be overwhelmed with shame and anguish;
  they will turn back and suddenly be put to shame.

---

[a] In Hebrew texts 6:1-10 is numbered 6:2-11.
[b] Title: Probably a musical term

Psalm 7[a]

*A shiggaion[b] of David, which he sang to
the LORD concerning Cush, a Benjamite.*

[1] LORD my God, I take refuge in
you;
    save and deliver me from all
      who pursue me,
[2] or they will tear me apart like a
lion
    and rip me to pieces with no
      one to rescue me.

[3] LORD my God, if I have done this
    and there is guilt on my
      hands —
[4] if I have repaid my ally with evil
    or without cause have robbed
      my foe —
[5] then let my enemy pursue and
      overtake me;
    let him trample my life to the
      ground
    and make me sleep in the
      dust.[c]

[6] Arise, LORD, in your anger;
    rise up against the rage of my
      enemies.
    Awake, my God; decree justice.
[7] Let the assembled peoples gather
      around you,
    while you sit enthroned over
      them on high.
[8]   Let the LORD judge the
      peoples.
    Vindicate me, LORD, according to
      my righteousness,
    according to my integrity,
      O Most High.
[9] Bring to an end the violence of
      the wicked
    and make the righteous
      secure —
    you, the righteous God
      who probes minds and hearts.

[10] My shield[d] is God Most High,
    who saves the upright in heart.

[11] God is a righteous judge,
    a God who displays his wrath
      every day.
[12] If he does not relent,
    he[e] will sharpen his sword;
    he will bend and string his
      bow.
[13] He has prepared his deadly
      weapons;
    he makes ready his flaming
      arrows.

[14] Whoever is pregnant with evil
    conceives trouble and gives
      birth to disillusionment.
[15] Whoever digs a hole and scoops
      it out
    falls into the pit they have
      made.
[16] The trouble they cause recoils on
      them;
    their violence comes down on
      their own heads.

[17] I will give thanks to the
      LORD because of his
      righteousness;
    I will sing the praises of the
      name of the LORD Most
      High.

Psalm 8[f]

*For the director of music. According
to gittith.[g] A psalm of David.*

[1] LORD, our Lord,
    how majestic is your name in
      all the earth!

You have set your glory
    in the heavens.

---

[a] In Hebrew texts 7:1-17 is numbered 7:2-18.
[b] Title: Probably a literary or musical term
[c] 5 The Hebrew has *Selah* (a word of uncertain
meaning) here.   [d] 10 Or *sovereign*   [e] 12 Or
If anyone does not repent, / God   [f] In Hebrew
texts 8:1-9 is numbered 8:2-10.   [g] Title:
Probably a musical term

² Through the praise of children
and infants
you have established a
stronghold against your
enemies,
to silence the foe and the
avenger.
³ When I consider your
heavens,
the work of your fingers,
the moon and the stars,
which you have set in place,
⁴ what is mankind that you are
mindful of them,
human beings that you care
for them?ᵃ

⁵ You have made themᵇ a little
lower than the angelsᶜ
and crowned themᵇ with glory
and honor.
⁶ You made them rulers over the
works of your hands;
you put everything under
theirᵈ feet:
⁷ all flocks and herds,
and the animals of the wild,
⁸ the birds in the sky,
and the fish in the sea,
all that swim the paths of the
seas.

⁹ LORD, our Lord,
how majestic is your name in
all the earth!

Psalm 9ᵉ,ᶠ

*For the director of music. To the tune of
"The Death of the Son." A psalm of David.*

¹ I will give thanks to you, LORD,
with all my heart;
I will tell of all your wonderful
deeds.
² I will be glad and rejoice in you;
I will sing the praises of your
name, O Most High.

³ My enemies turn back;
they stumble and perish
before you.
⁴ For you have upheld my right
and my cause,
sitting enthroned as the
righteous judge.
⁵ You have rebuked the nations
and destroyed the wicked;
you have blotted out their
name for ever and ever.
⁶ Endless ruin has overtaken my
enemies,
you have uprooted their
cities;
even the memory of them has
perished.

⁷ The LORD reigns forever;
he has established his throne
for judgment.
⁸ He rules the world in
righteousness
and judges the peoples with
equity.
⁹ The LORD is a refuge for the
oppressed,
a stronghold in times of
trouble.
¹⁰ Those who know your name
trust in you,
for you, LORD, have never
forsaken those who seek
you.

¹¹ Sing the praises of the LORD,
enthroned in Zion;
proclaim among the nations
what he has done.

ᵃ 4 Or *what is a human being that you are
mindful of him, / a son of man that you care for
him?* ᵇ 5 Or *him* ᶜ 5 Or *than God*
ᵈ 6 Or *made him ruler . . . ; / . . . his* ᵉ Psalms
9 and 10 may originally have been a single
acrostic poem in which alternating lines
began with the successive letters of the
Hebrew alphabet. In the Septuagint they
constitute one psalm. ᶠ In Hebrew texts 9:1-
20 is numbered 9:2-21.

12 For he who avenges blood
    remembers;
  he does not ignore the cries of
    the afflicted.

13 LORD, see how my enemies
    persecute me!
  Have mercy and lift me up
    from the gates of death,
14 that I may declare your praises
    in the gates of Daughter Zion,
  and there rejoice in your
    salvation.

15 The nations have fallen into the
    pit they have dug;
  their feet are caught in the net
    they have hidden.
16 The LORD is known by his acts of
    justice;
  the wicked are ensnared by
    the work of their
    hands.ᵃ
17 The wicked go down to the realm
    of the dead,
  all the nations that forget God.
18 But God will never forget the
    needy;
  the hope of the afflicted will
    never perish.

19 Arise, LORD, do not let mortals
    triumph;
  let the nations be judged in
    your presence.
20 Strike them with terror, LORD;
  let the nations know they are
    only mortal.

Psalm 10ᵇ

1 Why, LORD, do you stand far off?
  Why do you hide yourself in
    times of trouble?

2 In his arrogance the wicked man
    hunts down the weak,
  who are caught in the schemes
    he devises.

3 He boasts about the cravings of
    his heart;
  he blesses the greedy and
    reviles the LORD.
4 In his pride the wicked man does
    not seek him;
  in all his thoughts there is no
    room for God.
5 His ways are always prosperous;
  your laws are rejected
    byᶜ him;
  he sneers at all his enemies.
6 He says to himself, "Nothing will
    ever shake me."
  He swears, "No one will ever
    do me harm."

7 His mouth is full of lies and
    threats;
  trouble and evil are under his
    tongue.
8 He lies in wait near the villages;
  from ambush he murders the
    innocent.
  His eyes watch in secret for his
    victims;
9   like a lion in cover he lies in
    wait.
  He lies in wait to catch the
    helpless;
  he catches the helpless and
    drags them off in his net.
10 His victims are crushed, they
    collapse;
  they fall under his strength.
11 He says to himself, "God will
    never notice;
  he covers his face and never
    sees."

ᵃ 16 The Hebrew has *Higgaion* and *Selah* (words of uncertain meaning) here; *Selah* occurs also at the end of verse 20.   ᵇ Psalms 9 and 10 may originally have been a single acrostic poem in which alternating lines began with the successive letters of the Hebrew alphabet. In the Septuagint they constitute one psalm.   ᶜ 5 See Septuagint; Hebrew / *they are haughty, and your laws are far from*

12 Arise, LORD! Lift up your hand,
    O God.
  Do not forget the helpless.
13 Why does the wicked man revile
    God?
  Why does he say to himself,
    "He won't call me to account"?
14 But you, God, see the trouble of
    the afflicted;
  you consider their grief and
    take it in hand.
  The victims commit themselves
    to you;
  you are the helper of the
    fatherless.
15 Break the arm of the wicked
    man;
  call the evildoer to account for
    his wickedness
  that would not otherwise be
    found out.

16 The LORD is King for ever and
    ever;
  the nations will perish from
    his land.
17 You, LORD, hear the desire of the
    afflicted;
  you encourage them, and you
    listen to their cry,
18 defending the fatherless and the
    oppressed,
  so that mere earthly mortals
    will never again strike terror.

Psalm 11

For the director of music. Of David.

1 In the LORD I take refuge.
  How then can you say to me:
    "Flee like a bird to your
      mountain.
2 For look, the wicked bend their
    bows;
  they set their arrows against
    the strings
  to shoot from the shadows
    at the upright in heart.

3 When the foundations are being
    destroyed,
  what can the righteous do?"

4 The LORD is in his holy temple;
  the LORD is on his heavenly
    throne.
  He observes everyone on earth;
  his eyes examine them.
5 The LORD examines the
    righteous,
  but the wicked, those who love
    violence,
  he hates with a passion.
6 On the wicked he will rain
  fiery coals and burning sulfur;
  a scorching wind will be their
    lot.

7 For the LORD is righteous,
  he loves justice;
  the upright will see his face.

Psalm 12 [a]

*For the director of music. According
to sheminith.[b] A psalm of David.*

1 Help, LORD, for no one is faithful
    anymore;
  those who are loyal have
    vanished from the human
    race.
2 Everyone lies to their neighbor;
  they flatter with their lips
  but harbor deception in their
    hearts.

3 May the LORD silence all
  flattering lips
  and every boastful tongue —
4 those who say,
  "By our tongues we will
    prevail;
  our own lips will defend us —
  who is lord over us?"

---

5 "Because the poor are plundered
        and the needy groan,
    I will now arise," says the LORD.
    "I will protect them from
        those who malign them."

6 And the words of the LORD are
        flawless,
    like silver purified in a
        crucible,
    like gold[d] refined seven
        times.

7 You, LORD, will keep the needy
        safe
    and will protect us forever
        from the wicked,

8 who freely strut about
    when what is vile is honored
        by the human race.

Psalm 13[b]

*For the director of music.
A psalm of David.*

1 How long, LORD? Will you forget
        me forever?
    How long will you hide your
        face from me?

2 How long must I wrestle with my
        thoughts
    and day after day have sorrow
        in my heart?
    How long will my enemy
        triumph over me?

3 Look on me and answer, LORD
        my God.
    Give light to my eyes, or I will
        sleep in death,

4 and my enemy will say, "I have
        overcome him,"
    and my foes will rejoice when I
        fall.

5 But I trust in your unfailing
        love;
    my heart rejoices in your
        salvation.

6 I will sing the LORD's praise,
    for he has been good to me.

Psalm 14

For the director of music. Of David.

1 The fool[c] says in his heart,
        "There is no God."
    They are corrupt, their deeds are
        vile;
    there is no one who does good.

2 The LORD looks down from
        heaven
    on all mankind
    to see if there are any who
        understand,
    any who seek God.

3 All have turned away, all have
        become corrupt;
    there is no one who does good,
        not even one.

4 Do all these evildoers know
        nothing?

    They devour my people as
        though eating bread;
    they never call on the LORD.

5 But there they are, overwhelmed
        with dread,
    for God is present in the
        company of the righteous.

6 You evildoers frustrate the plans
        of the poor,
    but the LORD is their refuge.

7 Oh, that salvation for Israel
        would come out of Zion!
    When the LORD restores his
        people,
    let Jacob rejoice and Israel be
        glad!

---

[d] 6 Probable reading of the original Hebrew
text; Masoretic Text *earth* · [b] In Hebrew texts
13:1-6 is numbered 13:2-6. · [c] 1 The Hebrew
words rendered *fool* in Psalms denote one
who is morally deficient.

Psalm 15

A psalm of David.

¹ LORD, who may dwell in your
      sacred tent?
   Who may live on your holy
      mountain?

² The one whose walk is
      blameless,
   who does what is righteous,
   who speaks the truth from
      their heart;
³ whose tongue utters no
      slander,
   who does no wrong to a
      neighbor,
   and casts no slur on others;
⁴ who despises a vile person
   but honors those who fear
      the LORD;
   who keeps an oath even when
      it hurts,
   and does not change their
      mind;
⁵ who lends money to the poor
      without interest;
   who does not accept a bribe
      against the innocent.

Whoever does these things
   will never be shaken.

Psalm 16

A miktam[a] of David.

¹ Keep me safe, my God,
   for in you I take refuge.

² I say to the LORD, "You are my
      Lord;
   apart from you I have no good
      thing."
³ I say of the holy people who are
      in the land,
   "They are the noble ones
      in whom is all my
      delight."

⁴ Those who run after other gods
      will suffer more and more.
   I will not pour out libations of
      blood to such gods
   or take up their names on my
      lips.

⁵ LORD, you alone are my portion
      and my cup;
   you make my lot secure.
⁶ The boundary lines have fallen
      for me in pleasant places;
   surely I have a delightful
      inheritance.

⁷ I will praise the LORD, who
      counsels me;
   even at night my heart
      instructs me.
⁸ I keep my eyes always on the
      LORD.
   With him at my right hand,
   I will not be shaken.

⁹ Therefore my heart is glad and
      my tongue rejoices;
   my body also will rest secure,
¹⁰ because you will not abandon me
      to the realm of the dead,
   nor will you let your faithful[b]
      one see decay.
¹¹ You make known to me the path
      of life;
   you will fill me with joy in
      your presence,
   with eternal pleasures at your
      right hand.

Psalm 17

A prayer of David.

¹ Hear me, LORD, my plea is just;
   listen to my cry.
   Hear my prayer —
   it does not rise from deceitful
      lips.

---
a Title: Probably a literary or musical term
b 10 Or holy

² Let my vindication come from
 you;
 may your eyes see what is
  right.

³ Though you probe my heart,
 though you examine me at
  night and test me,
 you will find that I have planned
  no evil;
 my mouth has not
  transgressed.
⁴ Though people tried to bribe me,
 I have kept myself from the
  ways of the violent
 through what your lips have
  commanded.
⁵ My steps have held to your paths;
 my feet have not stumbled.

⁶ I call on you, my God, for you will
  answer me;
 turn your ear to me and hear
  my prayer.
⁷ Show me the wonders of your
  great love,
 you who save by your right
  hand
 those who take refuge in you
  from their foes.
⁸ Keep me as the apple of your eye;
 hide me in the shadow of your
  wings
⁹ from the wicked who are out to
  destroy me,
 from my mortal enemies who
  surround me.

¹⁰ They close up their callous hearts,
 and their mouths speak with
  arrogance.
¹¹ They have tracked me down, they
  now surround me,
 with eyes alert, to throw me to
  the ground.
¹² They are like a lion hungry for
  prey,
 like a fierce lion crouching in
  cover.

¹³ Rise up, LORD, confront them,
  bring them down;
 with your sword rescue me
  from the wicked.
¹⁴ By your hand save me from such
  people, LORD,
 from those of this world whose
  reward is in this life.
May what you have stored up
 for the wicked fill their
  bellies;
 may their children gorge
  themselves on it,
 and may there be leftovers for
  their little ones.

¹⁵ As for me, I will be vindicated
 and will see your face;
 when I awake, I will be
  satisfied with seeing your
  likeness.

Psalm 18ᵃ

*For the director of music. Of David
the servant of the LORD. He sang
to the LORD the words of this song
when the LORD delivered him from
the hand of all his enemies and
from the hand of Saul. He said:*

¹ I love you, LORD, my strength.

² The LORD is my rock, my fortress
  and my deliverer;
 my God is my rock, in whom I
  take refuge,
 my shieldᵇ and the hornᶜ
  of my salvation, my
  stronghold.

³ I called to the LORD, who is
  worthy of praise,
 and I have been saved from
  my enemies.

ᵃ In Hebrew texts 18:1-50 is numbered 18:2-51.
ᵇ *2* Or *sovereign* ᶜ *2 Horn* here symbolizes
strength.

⁴ The cords of death entangled me;
　　the torrents of destruction
　　　overwhelmed me.
⁵ The cords of the grave coiled
　　around me;
　　the snares of death confronted
　　　me.

⁶ In my distress I called to the
　　Lord;
　　I cried to my God for help.
From his temple he heard my
　　voice;
　　my cry came before him, into
　　　his ears.
⁷ The earth trembled and quaked,
　　and the foundations of the
　　　mountains shook;
　　they trembled because he was
　　　angry.
⁸ Smoke rose from his nostrils;
　　consuming fire came from his
　　　mouth,
　　burning coals blazed out of it.
⁹ He parted the heavens and came
　　down;
　　dark clouds were under his
　　　feet.
¹⁰ He mounted the cherubim and
　　flew;
　　he soared on the wings of the
　　　wind.
¹¹ He made darkness his covering,
　　his canopy around him —
　　the dark rain clouds of the sky.
¹² Out of the brightness of
　　his presence clouds
　　　advanced,
　　with hailstones and bolts of
　　　lightning.
¹³ The Lord thundered from
　　heaven;
　　the voice of the Most High
　　　resounded.ᵃ
¹⁴ He shot his arrows and scattered
　　the enemy,
　　with great bolts of lightning
　　　he routed them.

¹⁵ The valleys of the sea were
　　exposed
　　and the foundations of the
　　　earth laid bare
　at your rebuke, Lord,
　　at the blast of breath from
　　　your nostrils.
¹⁶ He reached down from on high
　　and took hold of me;
　　he drew me out of deep
　　　waters.
¹⁷ He rescued me from my
　　powerful enemy,
　　from my foes, who were too
　　　strong for me.
¹⁸ They confronted me in the day of
　　my disaster,
　　but the Lord was my support.
¹⁹ He brought me out into a
　　spacious place;
　　he rescued me because he
　　　delighted in me.

²⁰ The Lord has dealt with
　　me according to my
　　　righteousness;
　　according to the cleanness
　　　of my hands he has
　　　rewarded me.
²¹ For I have kept the ways of the
　　Lord;
　　I am not guilty of turning
　　　from my God.
²² All his laws are before me;
　　I have not turned away from
　　　his decrees.
²³ I have been blameless before
　　him
　　and have kept myself from sin.
²⁴ The Lord has rewarded
　　me according to my
　　　righteousness,
　　according to the cleanness of
　　　my hands in his sight.

ᵃ 13 Some Hebrew manuscripts and Septuagint
(see also 2 Samuel 22:14); most Hebrew
manuscripts *resounded, / amid hailstones and
bolts of lightning*

²⁵ To the faithful you show yourself
      faithful,
    to the blameless you show
      yourself blameless,
²⁶ to the pure you show yourself
      pure,
    but to the devious you show
      yourself shrewd.
²⁷ You save the humble
    but bring low those whose
      eyes are haughty.
²⁸ You, LORD, keep my lamp burning;
    my God turns my darkness
      into light.
²⁹ With your help I can advance
      against a troopᵃ;
    with my God I can scale a wall.

³⁰ As for God, his way is perfect:
      The LORD's word is flawless;
    he shields all who take refuge
      in him.
³¹ For who is God besides the LORD?
    And who is the Rock except
      our God?
³² It is God who arms me with
      strength
    and keeps my way secure.
³³ He makes my feet like the feet of
      a deer;
    he causes me to stand on the
      heights.
³⁴ He trains my hands for battle;
    my arms can bend a bow of
      bronze.
³⁵ You make your saving help my
      shield,
    and your right hand sustains
      me;
    your help has made me great.
³⁶ You provide a broad path for my
      feet,
    so that my ankles do not give
      way.

³⁷ I pursued my enemies and
      overtook them;
    I did not turn back till they
      were destroyed.

³⁸ I crushed them so that they
      could not rise;
    they fell beneath my feet.
³⁹ You armed me with strength for
      battle;
    you humbled my adversaries
      before me.
⁴⁰ You made my enemies turn their
      backs in flight,
    and I destroyed my foes.
⁴¹ They cried for help, but there
      was no one to save
      them—
    to the LORD, but he did not
      answer.
⁴² I beat them as fine as windblown
      dust;
    I trampled themᵇ like mud in
      the streets.
⁴³ You have delivered me from the
      attacks of the people;
    you have made me the head
      of nations.
    People I did not know now serve
      me,
⁴⁴   foreigners cower before me;
    as soon as they hear of me,
      they obey me.
⁴⁵ They all lose heart;
    they come trembling from
      their strongholds.

⁴⁶ The LORD lives! Praise be to my
      Rock!
    Exalted be God my Savior!
⁴⁷ He is the God who avenges me,
    who subdues nations under
      me,
⁴⁸   who saves me from my
      enemies.
    You exalted me above my
      foes;
    from a violent man you
      rescued me.

ᵃ 29 Or *can run through a barricade*
ᵇ 42 Many Hebrew manuscripts, Septuagint,
Syriac and Targum (see also 2 Samuel 22:43);
Masoretic Text *I poured them out*

⁴⁹ Therefore I will praise you, LORD,
  among the nations;
  I will sing the praises of your
    name.

⁵⁰ He gives his king great victories;
  he shows unfailing love to his
    anointed,
  to David and to his
    descendants forever.

Psalm 19[a]

For the director of music.
A psalm of David.

¹ The heavens declare the glory of
    God;
  the skies proclaim the work of
    his hands.
² Day after day they pour forth
    speech;
  night after night they reveal
    knowledge.
³ They have no speech, they use no
    words;
  no sound is heard from them.
⁴ Yet their voice[b] goes out into all
    the earth,
  their words to the ends of the
    world.
  In the heavens God has pitched a
    tent for the sun.
⁵   It is like a bridegroom coming
    out of his chamber,
  like a champion rejoicing to
    run his course.
⁶ It rises at one end of the heavens
  and makes its circuit to the
    other;
  nothing is deprived of its
    warmth.

⁷ The law of the LORD is perfect,
  refreshing the soul.
  The statutes of the LORD are
    trustworthy,
  making wise the simple.

⁸ The precepts of the LORD are
    right,
  giving joy to the heart.
  The commands of the LORD are
    radiant,
  giving light to the eyes.
⁹ The fear of the LORD is pure,
  enduring forever.
  The decrees of the LORD are firm,
  and all of them are righteous.

¹⁰ They are more precious than gold,
  than much pure gold;
  they are sweeter than honey,
  than honey from the
    honeycomb.
¹¹ By them your servant is warned;
  in keeping them there is great
    reward.
¹² But who can discern their own
    errors?
  Forgive my hidden faults.
¹³ Keep your servant also from
    willful sins;
  may they not rule over me.
  Then I will be blameless,
  innocent of great
    transgression.

¹⁴ May these words of my mouth
  and this meditation of my
    heart
  be pleasing in your sight,
  LORD, my Rock and my
    Redeemer.

Psalm 20[c]

For the director of music.
A psalm of David.

¹ May the LORD answer you when
  you are in distress;
  may the name of the God of
    Jacob protect you.

---

[a] In Hebrew texts 19:1-14 is numbered 19:2-15.
[b] 4 Septuagint, Jerome and Syriac; Hebrew *measuring line*   [c] In Hebrew texts 20:1-9 is numbered 20:2-10.

2 May he send you help from the
     sanctuary
  and grant you support from
     Zion.
3 May he remember all your
     sacrifices
  and accept your burnt
     offerings.[a]
4 May he give you the desire of your
     heart
  and make all your plans
     succeed.
5 May we shout for joy over your
     victory
  and lift up our banners in the
     name of our God.

  May the LORD grant all your
     requests.

6 Now this I know:
     The LORD gives victory to his
        anointed.
  He answers him from his
     heavenly sanctuary
  with the victorious power of his
     right hand.
7 Some trust in chariots and some
     in horses,
  but we trust in the name of the
     LORD our God.
8 They are brought to their knees
     and fall,
  but we rise up and stand firm.
9 LORD, give victory to the king!
  Answer us when we call!

Psalm 21[b]

For the director of music. A psalm of David.

1 The king rejoices in your strength,
     LORD.
  How great is his joy in the
     victories you give!

2 You have granted him his heart's
     desire
  and have not withheld the
     request of his lips.[a]

3 You came to greet him with rich
     blessings
  and placed a crown of pure
     gold on his head.
4 He asked you for life, and you
     gave it to him —
  length of days, for ever and
     ever.
5 Through the victories you gave,
     his glory is great;
  you have bestowed on him
     splendor and majesty.
6 Surely you have granted him
     unending blessings
  and made him glad with the
     joy of your presence.
7 For the king trusts in the LORD;
  through the unfailing love of
     the Most High
  he will not be shaken.

8 Your hand will lay hold on all
     your enemies;
  your right hand will seize your
     foes.
9 When you appear for battle,
  you will burn them up as in a
     blazing furnace.
  The LORD will swallow them up
     in his wrath,
  and his fire will consume
     them.
10 You will destroy their
     descendants from the
        earth,
  their posterity from mankind.
11 Though they plot evil against
     you
  and devise wicked schemes,
     they cannot succeed.
12 You will make them turn their
     backs
  when you aim at them with
     drawn bow.

---

[a] 3,2 The Hebrew has *Selah* (a word of
uncertain meaning) here.   [b] In Hebrew texts
21:1-13 is numbered 21:2-14.

¹³ Be exalted in your strength,
    LORD;
  we will sing and praise your
    might.

Psalm 22[a]

*For the director of music. To the tune
  of "The Doe of the Morning."
  A psalm of David.*

¹ My God, my God, why have you
    forsaken me?
  Why are you so far from
    saving me,
  so far from my cries of
    anguish?
² My God, I cry out by day, but you
    do not answer,
  by night, but I find no rest.[b]

³ Yet you are enthroned as the
    Holy One;
  you are the one Israel praises.[c]
⁴ In you our ancestors put their
    trust;
  they trusted and you delivered
    them.
⁵ To you they cried out and were
    saved;
  in you they trusted and were
    not put to shame.

⁶ But I am a worm and not a man,
  scorned by everyone, despised
    by the people.
⁷ All who see me mock me;
  they hurl insults, shaking their
    heads.
⁸ "He trusts in the LORD," they say,
  "let the LORD rescue him.
  Let him deliver him,
  since he delights in him."

⁹ Yet you brought me out of the
    womb;
  you made me trust in you,
  even at my mother's
    breast.

¹⁰ From birth I was cast on you;
  from my mother's womb you
    have been my God.

¹¹ Do not be far from me,
  for trouble is near
  and there is no one to help.

¹² Many bulls surround me;
  strong bulls of Bashan
    encircle me.
¹³ Roaring lions that tear their prey
  open their mouths wide
    against me.
¹⁴ I am poured out like water,
  and all my bones are out of
    joint.
  My heart has turned to wax;
  it has melted within me.
¹⁵ My mouth[d] is dried up like a
    potsherd,
  and my tongue sticks to the
    roof of my mouth;
  you lay me in the dust of
    death.

¹⁶ Dogs surround me,
  a pack of villains encircles me;
  they pierce[e] my hands and my
    feet.
¹⁷ All my bones are on display;
  people stare and gloat over
    me.
¹⁸ They divide my clothes among
    them
  and cast lots for my garment.

¹⁹ But you, LORD, do not be far
    from me.
  You are my strength; come
    quickly to help me.

---

[a] In Hebrew texts 22:1-31 is numbered 22:2-32.
[b] 2 Or *night, and am not silent*   [c] 3 Or *Yet
you are holy, / enthroned on the praises of
Israel*   [d] 15 Probable reading of the original
Hebrew text; Masoretic Text *strength*
[e] 16 Dead Sea Scrolls and some manuscripts of
the Masoretic Text, Septuagint and Syriac;
most manuscripts of the Masoretic Text *me, /
like a lion*

²⁰ Deliver me from the sword,
    my precious life from the
        power of the dogs.
²¹ Rescue me from the mouth of
        the lions;
    save me from the horns of the
        wild oxen.

²² I will declare your name to my
        people;
    in the assembly I will praise
        you.
²³ You who fear the LORD, praise
        him!
    All you descendants of Jacob,
        honor him!
    Revere him, all you
        descendants of Israel!
²⁴ For he has not despised or
        scorned
    the suffering of the afflicted
        one;
    he has not hidden his face from
        him
    but has listened to his cry for
        help.

²⁵ From you comes the theme of
        my praise in the great
        assembly;
    before those who fear you*ᵃ* I
        will fulfill my vows.
²⁶ The poor will eat and be
        satisfied;
    those who seek the LORD will
        praise him —
    may your hearts live
        forever!

²⁷ All the ends of the earth
    will remember and turn to
        the LORD,
    and all the families of the
        nations
    will bow down before him,
²⁸ for dominion belongs to the
        LORD
    and he rules over the
        nations.

²⁹ All the rich of the earth will feast
        and worship;
    all who go down to the dust
        will kneel before him —
    those who cannot keep
        themselves alive.
³⁰ Posterity will serve him;
    future generations will be told
        about the Lord.
³¹ They will proclaim his
        righteousness,
    declaring to a people yet
        unborn:
    He has done it!

Psalm 23

A psalm of David.

¹ The LORD is my shepherd,
    I lack nothing.
²   He makes me lie down in
        green pastures,
    he leads me beside quiet
        waters,
³   he refreshes my soul.
    He guides me along the right
        paths
    for his name's sake.
⁴ Even though I walk
        through the darkest
        valley,ᵇ
    I will fear no evil,
        for you are with me;
    your rod and your staff,
        they comfort me.

⁵ You prepare a table before me
    in the presence of my
        enemies.
    You anoint my head with oil;
        my cup overflows.
⁶ Surely your goodness and love
        will follow me
    all the days of my life,

ᵃ 25 Hebrew *him*   *ᵇ 4* Or *the valley of the
shadow of death*

and I will dwell in the house of
the LORD
forever.

Psalm 24

Of David. A psalm.

¹ The earth is the LORD's, and
everything in it,
the world, and all who live in
it;
² for he founded it on the seas
and established it on the
waters.

³ Who may ascend the mountain
of the LORD?
Who may stand in his holy
place?
⁴ The one who has clean hands
and a pure heart,
who does not trust in an idol
or swear by a false god.ᵃ

⁵ They will receive blessing from
the LORD
and vindication from God
their Savior.
⁶ Such is the generation of those
who seek him,
who seek your face, God of
Jacob.ᵇ,ᶜ

⁷ Lift up your heads, you gates;
be lifted up, you ancient doors,
that the King of glory may
come in.
⁸ Who is this King of glory?
The LORD strong and mighty,
the LORD mighty in battle.
⁹ Lift up your heads, you gates;
lift them up, you ancient
doors,
that the King of glory may
come in.
¹⁰ Who is he, this King of glory?
The LORD Almighty —
he is the King of glory.

Psalm 25ᵈ

Of David.

¹ In you, LORD my God,
I put my trust.

² I trust in you;
do not let me be put to
shame,
nor let my enemies triumph
over me.
³ No one who hopes in you
will ever be put to shame,
but shame will come on those
who are treacherous without
cause.

⁴ Show me your ways, LORD,
teach me your paths.
⁵ Guide me in your truth and
teach me,
for you are God my Savior,
and my hope is in you all day
long.
⁶ Remember, LORD, your great
mercy and love,
for they are from of old.
⁷ Do not remember the sins of
my youth
and my rebellious ways;
according to your love
remember me,
for you, LORD, are good.

⁸ Good and upright is the
LORD;
therefore he instructs sinners
in his ways.
⁹ He guides the humble in what
is right
and teaches them his way.

ᵃ 4 Or *swear falsely*   ᵇ 6 Two Hebrew
manuscripts and Syriac (see also Septuagint);
most Hebrew manuscripts *face, Jacob*
ᶜ 6 The Hebrew has *Selah* (a word of uncertain
meaning) here and at the end of verse 10.
ᵈ This psalm is an acrostic poem, the verses of
which begin with the successive letters of the
Hebrew alphabet.

¹⁰ All the ways of the LORD are
    loving and faithful
  toward those who keep the
    demands of his covenant.
¹¹ For the sake of your name,
    LORD,
  forgive my iniquity, though it
    is great.
¹² Who, then, are those who fear
    the LORD?
  He will instruct them in the
    ways they should
    choose.ᵃ
¹³ They will spend their days in
    prosperity,
  and their descendants will
    inherit the land.
¹⁴ The LORD confides in those who
    fear him;
  he makes his covenant known
    to them.
¹⁵ My eyes are ever on the LORD,
  for only he will release my feet
    from the snare.

¹⁶ Turn to me and be gracious to
    me,
  for I am lonely and afflicted.
¹⁷ Relieve the troubles of my heart
  and free me from my anguish.
¹⁸ Look on my affliction and my
    distress
  and take away all my sins.
¹⁹ See how numerous are my
    enemies
  and how fiercely they
    hate me!

²⁰ Guard my life and rescue me;
  do not let me be put to shame,
  for I take refuge in you.
²¹ May integrity and uprightness
    protect me,
  because my hope, LORD,ᵇ is
    in you.

²² Deliver Israel, O God,
  from all their troubles!

Psalm 26

Of David.

¹ Vindicate me, LORD,
  for I have led a blameless life;
  I have trusted in the LORD
    and have not faltered.
² Test me, LORD, and try me,
  examine my heart and my
    mind;
³ for I have always been mindful
    of your unfailing love
  and have lived in reliance on
    your faithfulness.

⁴ I do not sit with the deceitful,
  nor do I associate with
    hypocrites.
⁵ I abhor the assembly of evildoers
  and refuse to sit with the
    wicked.
⁶ I wash my hands in innocence,
  and go about your altar, LORD,
⁷ proclaiming aloud your praise
  and telling of all your
    wonderful deeds.

⁸ LORD, I love the house where you
    live,
  the place where your glory
    dwells.
⁹ Do not take away my soul along
    with sinners,
  my life with those who are
    bloodthirsty,
¹⁰ in whose hands are wicked
    schemes,
  whose right hands are full of
    bribes.
¹¹ I lead a blameless life;
  deliver me and be merciful to
    me.
¹² My feet stand on level ground;
  in the great congregation I will
    praise the LORD.

ᵃ 12 Or *ways he chooses*   ᵇ 21 Septuagint;
Hebrew does not have LORD.

Psalm 27

Of David.

[1] The LORD is my light and my
    salvation —
  whom shall I fear?
  The LORD is the stronghold of my
    life —
  of whom shall I be afraid?

[2] When the wicked advance
      against me
    to devour[a] me,
  it is my enemies and my foes
    who will stumble and fall.
[3] Though an army besiege me,
    my heart will not fear;
  though war break out
      against me,
    even then I will be confident.

[4] One thing I ask from the LORD,
    this only do I seek:
  that I may dwell in the house of
      the LORD
    all the days of my life,
  to gaze on the beauty of the LORD
    and to seek him in his temple.
[5] For in the day of trouble
    he will keep me safe in his
      dwelling;
  he will hide me in the shelter of
      his sacred tent
    and set me high upon a rock.

[6] Then my head will be exalted
    above the enemies who
      surround me;
  at his sacred tent I will sacrifice
      with shouts of joy;
  I will sing and make music to
      the LORD.

[7] Hear my voice when I call, LORD;
    be merciful to me and
      answer me.
[8] My heart says of you, "Seek his
      face!"
  Your face, LORD, I will seek.

[9] Do not hide your face from me,
    do not turn your servant away
      in anger;
  you have been my helper.
  Do not reject me or forsake me,
    God my Savior.
[10] Though my father and mother
      forsake me,
    the LORD will receive me.
[11] Teach me your way, LORD;
    lead me in a straight path
      because of my oppressors.
[12] Do not turn me over to the desire
      of my foes,
    for false witnesses rise up
      against me,
    spouting malicious
      accusations.

[13] I remain confident of this:
    I will see the goodness of the
      LORD
    in the land of the living.
[14] Wait for the LORD;
    be strong and take heart
    and wait for the LORD.

Psalm 28

Of David.

[1] To you, LORD, I call;
    you are my Rock,
    do not turn a deaf ear
      to me.
  For if you remain silent,
    I will be like those who go
      down to the pit.
[2] Hear my cry for mercy
    as I call to you for help,
  as I lift up my hands
    toward your Most Holy Place.

[3] Do not drag me away with the
      wicked,
    with those who do evil,

---

[a] 2 Or *slander*

who speak cordially with their
neighbors
but harbor malice in their
hearts.
⁴ Repay them for their deeds
and for their evil work;
repay them for what their hands
have done
and bring back on them what
they deserve.

⁵ Because they have no regard for
the deeds of the LORD
and what his hands have done,
he will tear them down
and never build them up
again.

⁶ Praise be to the LORD,
for he has heard my cry for
mercy.
⁷ The LORD is my strength and my
shield;
my heart trusts in him, and he
helps me.
My heart leaps for joy,
and with my song I praise him.

⁸ The LORD is the strength of his
people,
a fortress of salvation for his
anointed one.
⁹ Save your people and bless your
inheritance;
be their shepherd and carry
them forever.

Psalm 29

A psalm of David.

¹ Ascribe to the LORD, you
heavenly beings,
ascribe to the LORD glory and
strength.
² Ascribe to the LORD the glory due
his name;
worship the LORD in the
splendor of his* holiness.

³ The voice of the LORD is over the
waters;
the God of glory thunders,
the LORD thunders over the
mighty waters.
⁴ The voice of the LORD is powerful;
the voice of the LORD is
majestic.
⁵ The voice of the LORD breaks the
cedars;
the LORD breaks in pieces the
cedars of Lebanon.
⁶ He makes Lebanon leap like a
calf,
Sirion* like a young wild ox.
⁷ The voice of the LORD strikes
with flashes of lightning.
⁸ The voice of the LORD shakes the
desert;
the LORD shakes the Desert of
Kadesh.
⁹ The voice of the LORD twists the
oaks*
and strips the forests bare.
And in his temple all cry, "Glory!"

¹⁰ The LORD sits enthroned over the
flood;
the LORD is enthroned as King
forever.
¹¹ The LORD gives strength to his
people;
the LORD blesses his people
with peace.

Psalm 30*

*A psalm. A song. For the dedication
of the temple.* Of David.*

¹ I will exalt you, LORD,
for you lifted me out of the
depths
and did not let my enemies
gloat over me.

---

a 2 Or LORD *with the splendor of*   *b* 6 That is,
Mount Hermon   *c* 9 Or LORD *makes the deer
give birth*   *d* In Hebrew texts 30:1-12 is
numbered 30:2-13.   *e* Title: Or *palace*

² LORD my God, I called to you for
        help,
    and you healed me.
³ You, LORD, brought me up
        from the realm of the
        dead;
    you spared me from going
        down to the pit.

⁴ Sing the praises of the LORD,
        you his faithful people;
    praise his holy name.
⁵ For his anger lasts only a
        moment,
    but his favor lasts a lifetime;
weeping may stay for the
        night,
    but rejoicing comes in the
        morning.

⁶ When I felt secure, I said,
    "I will never be shaken."
⁷ LORD, when you favored me,
    you made my royal mountain*a*
        stand firm;
but when you hid your face,
    I was dismayed.

⁸ To you, LORD, I called;
    to the Lord I cried for
        mercy:
⁹ "What is gained if I am
        silenced,
    if I go down to the pit?
Will the dust praise you?
    Will it proclaim your
        faithfulness?
¹⁰ Hear, LORD, and be merciful
        to me;
    LORD, be my help."

¹¹ You turned my wailing into
        dancing;
    you removed my sackcloth
        and clothed me with joy,
¹² that my heart may sing your
        praises and not be silent.
LORD my God, I will praise you
    forever.

Psalm 31*b*

For the director of music.
A psalm of David.

¹ In you, LORD, I have taken
        refuge;
    let me never be put to
        shame;
    deliver me in your
        righteousness.
² Turn your ear to me,
    come quickly to my rescue;
be my rock of refuge,
    a strong fortress to save me.
³ Since you are my rock and my
        fortress,
    for the sake of your name lead
        and guide me.
⁴ Keep me free from the trap that
        is set for me,
    for you are my refuge.
⁵ Into your hands I commit my
        spirit;
    deliver me, LORD, my faithful
        God.

⁶ I hate those who cling to
        worthless idols;
    as for me, I trust in the
        LORD.
⁷ I will be glad and rejoice in
        your love,
    for you saw my affliction
        and knew the anguish of my
        soul.
⁸ You have not given me into the
        hands of the enemy
    but have set my feet in a
        spacious place.

⁹ Be merciful to me, LORD, for
        I am in distress;
    my eyes grow weak with
        sorrow,
    my soul and body with grief.

---

a 7 That is, Mount Zion   *b* In Hebrew texts
31:1-24 is numbered 31:2-25.

¹⁰ My life is consumed by anguish
      and my years by groaning;
   my strength fails because of my
      affliction,ᵃ
   and my bones grow weak.
¹¹ Because of all my enemies,
      I am the utter contempt of my
         neighbors
   and an object of dread to my
         closest friends —
   those who see me on the street
      flee from me.
¹² I am forgotten as though I were
      dead;
   I have become like broken
      pottery.
¹³ For I hear many whispering,
      "Terror on every side!"
   They conspire against me
      and plot to take my life.
¹⁴ But I trust in you, LORD;
      I say, "You are my God."
¹⁵ My times are in your hands;
      deliver me from the hands of
         my enemies,
   from those who pursue me.
¹⁶ Let your face shine on your
      servant;
   save me in your unfailing love.
¹⁷ Let me not be put to shame, LORD,
      for I have cried out to you;
   but let the wicked be put to
      shame
   and be silent in the realm of
      the dead.
¹⁸ Let their lying lips be silenced,
      for with pride and contempt
   they speak arrogantly against
      the righteous.

¹⁹ How abundant are the good
      things
   that you have stored up for
      those who fear you,
   that you bestow in the sight of all,
      on those who take refuge in
         you.

²⁰ In the shelter of your presence
      you hide them
   from all human intrigues;
   you keep them safe in your
      dwelling
   from accusing tongues.

²¹ Praise be to the LORD,
      for he showed me the wonders
         of his love
   when I was in a city under
      siege.
²² In my alarm I said,
      "I am cut off from your sight!"
   Yet you heard my cry for mercy
      when I called to you for help.

²³ Love the LORD, all his faithful
      people!
   The LORD preserves those who
      are true to him,
   but the proud he pays back in
      full.
²⁴ Be strong and take heart,
      all you who hope in the LORD.

Psalm 32

*Of David. A maskil.*ᵇ

¹ Blessed is the one
      whose transgressions are
         forgiven,
   whose sins are covered.
² Blessed is the one
      whose sin the LORD does not
         count against them
   and in whose spirit is no
      deceit.

³ When I kept silent,
      my bones wasted away
   through my groaning all day
      long.
⁴ For day and night
      your hand was heavy on me;

ᵃ 10 Or guilt   ᵇ Title: Probably a literary or
musical term

my strength was sapped
    as in the heat of summer.[a]

⁵ Then I acknowledged my sin to
        you
    and did not cover up my
        iniquity.
I said, "I will confess
    my transgressions to the LORD."
And you forgave
    the guilt of my sin.

⁶ Therefore let all the faithful pray
        to you
    while you may be found;
surely the rising of the mighty
        waters
    will not reach them.
⁷ You are my hiding place;
    you will protect me from
        trouble
    and surround me with songs of
        deliverance.

⁸ I will instruct you and teach you
        in the way you should go;
    I will counsel you with my
        loving eye on you.
⁹ Do not be like the horse or the
        mule,
    which have no understanding
but must be controlled by bit and
        bridle
    or they will not come to you.
¹⁰ Many are the woes of the wicked,
    but the LORD's unfailing love
        surrounds the one who trusts
        in him.
¹¹ Rejoice in the LORD and be glad,
        you righteous;
    sing, all you who are upright in
        heart!

Psalm 33

¹ Sing joyfully to the LORD, you
        righteous;
    it is fitting for the upright to
        praise him.

² Praise the LORD with the harp;
    make music to him on the
        ten-stringed lyre.
³ Sing to him a new song;
    play skillfully, and shout for joy.

⁴ For the word of the LORD is right
        and true;
    he is faithful in all he does.
⁵ The LORD loves righteousness and
        justice;
    the earth is full of his unfailing
        love.

⁶ By the word of the LORD the
        heavens were made,
    their starry host by the breath
        of his mouth.
⁷ He gathers the waters of the sea
        into jars[b];
    he puts the deep into
        storehouses.
⁸ Let all the earth fear the LORD;
    let all the people of the world
        revere him.
⁹ For he spoke, and it came to be;
    he commanded, and it stood
        firm.

¹⁰ The LORD foils the plans of the
        nations;
    he thwarts the purposes of the
        peoples.
¹¹ But the plans of the LORD stand
        firm forever,
    the purposes of his heart
        through all generations.

¹² Blessed is the nation whose God is
        the LORD,
    the people he chose for his
        inheritance.
¹³ From heaven the LORD looks down
        and sees all mankind;
¹⁴ from his dwelling place he
        watches
    all who live on earth—

---

[a] 4 The Hebrew has *Selah* (a word of uncertain
meaning) here and at the end of verses 5 and 7.
[b] 7 Or *sea as into a heap*

¹⁵ he who forms the hearts of all,
   who considers everything they
      do.

¹⁶ No king is saved by the size of his
      army;
   no warrior escapes by his great
      strength.
¹⁷ A horse is a vain hope for
      deliverance;
   despite all its great strength it
      cannot save.
¹⁸ But the eyes of the LORD are on
      those who fear him,
   on those whose hope is in his
      unfailing love,
¹⁹ to deliver them from death
   and keep them alive in
      famine.

²⁰ We wait in hope for the LORD;
   he is our help and our
      shield.
²¹ In him our hearts rejoice,
   for we trust in his holy name.
²² May your unfailing love be with
      us, LORD,
   even as we put our hope in
      you.

Psalm 34^{a,b}

*Of David. When he pretended to
be insane before Abimelek, who
drove him away, and he left.*

¹ I will extol the LORD at all times;
   his praise will always be on my
      lips.
² I will glory in the LORD;
   let the afflicted hear and
      rejoice.
³ Glorify the LORD with me;
   let us exalt his name together.

⁴ I sought the LORD, and he
      answered me;
   he delivered me from all my
      fears.

⁵ Those who look to him are
      radiant;
   their faces are never covered
      with shame.
⁶ This poor man called, and the
      LORD heard him;
   he saved him out of all his
      troubles.
⁷ The angel of the LORD encamps
      around those who fear
      him,
   and he delivers them.

⁸ Taste and see that the LORD is
      good;
   blessed is the one who takes
      refuge in him.
⁹ Fear the LORD, you his holy
      people,
   for those who fear him lack
      nothing.
¹⁰ The lions may grow weak and
      hungry,
   but those who seek the LORD
      lack no good thing.
¹¹ Come, my children, listen to me;
   I will teach you the fear of the
      LORD.
¹² Whoever of you loves life
   and desires to see many good
      days,
¹³ keep your tongue from evil
   and your lips from telling lies.
¹⁴ Turn from evil and do good;
   seek peace and pursue it.

¹⁵ The eyes of the LORD are on the
      righteous,
   and his ears are attentive to
      their cry;
¹⁶ but the face of the LORD is
      against those who do evil,
   to blot out their name from
      the earth.

---

^a This psalm is an acrostic poem, the verses of
which begin with the successive letters of the
Hebrew alphabet.   ^b In Hebrew texts 34:1-22
is numbered 34:2-23.

17 The righteous cry out, and the
     LORD hears them;
   he delivers them from all
       their troubles.
18 The LORD is close to the
       brokenhearted
   and saves those who are
       crushed in spirit.

19 The righteous person may have
       many troubles,
   but the LORD delivers him
       from them all;
20 he protects all his bones,
   not one of them will be
       broken.

21 Evil will slay the wicked;
   the foes of the righteous will
       be condemned.
22 The LORD will rescue his
       servants;
   no one who takes refuge
       in him will be
       condemned.

Psalm 35

Of David.

1 Contend, LORD, with those who
       contend with me;
   fight against those who fight
       against me.
2 Take up shield and armor;
   arise and come to my aid.
3 Brandish spear and javelin[a]
       against those who
       pursue me.
   Say to me,
       "I am your salvation."

4 May those who seek my
       life
   be disgraced and put to
       shame;
   may those who plot my
       ruin
   be turned back in dismay.

5 May they be like chaff before the
       wind,
   with the angel of the LORD
       driving them away;
6 may their path be dark and
       slippery,
   with the angel of the LORD
       pursuing them.

7 Since they hid their net for me
       without cause
   and without cause dug a pit
       for me,
8 may ruin overtake them by
       surprise—
   may the net they hid entangle
       them,
   may they fall into the pit, to
       their ruin.
9 Then my soul will rejoice in the
       LORD
   and delight in his salvation.
10 My whole being will exclaim,
       "Who is like you, LORD?
   You rescue the poor from those
       too strong for them,
   the poor and needy from those
       who rob them."

11 Ruthless witnesses come
       forward;
   they question me on things
       I know nothing about.
12 They repay me evil for good
   and leave me like one
       bereaved.
13 Yet when they were ill, I put on
       sackcloth
   and humbled myself with
       fasting.
   When my prayers returned to me
       unanswered,
14   I went about mourning
       as though for my friend or
       brother.
   I bowed my head in grief
       as though weeping for my
       mother.

---

a 3 Or and block the way

15 But when I stumbled, they
        gathered in glee;
    assailants gathered against me
        without my knowledge.
    They slandered me without
        ceasing.
16 Like the ungodly they
        maliciously mocked;[a]
    they gnashed their teeth at
        me.

17 How long, Lord, will you look on?
    Rescue me from their ravages,
        my precious life from these
        lions.
18 I will give you thanks in the great
        assembly;
    among the throngs I will
        praise you.

19 Do not let those gloat over me
        who are my enemies without
        cause;
    do not let those who hate me
        without reason
    maliciously wink the eye.
20 They do not speak peaceably,
        but devise false accusations
        against those who live quietly
        in the land.
21 They sneer at me and say, "Aha!
        Aha!
    With our own eyes we have
        seen it."

22 LORD, you have seen this; do not
        be silent.
    Do not be far from me, Lord.
23 Awake, and rise to my defense!
    Contend for me, my God and
        Lord.
24 Vindicate me in your
        righteousness, LORD my
        God;
    do not let them gloat over me.
25 Do not let them think, "Aha, just
        what we wanted!"
    or say, "We have swallowed
        him up."

26 May all who gloat over my
        distress
    be put to shame and confusion;
    may all who exalt themselves
        over me
    be clothed with shame and
        disgrace.
27 May those who delight in my
        vindication
    shout for joy and gladness;
    may they always say, "The LORD
        be exalted,
    who delights in the well-being
        of his servant."

28 My tongue will proclaim your
        righteousness,
    your praises all day long.

Psalm 36[b]

*For the director of music. Of David
the servant of the LORD.*

1 I have a message from God in my
        heart
    concerning the sinfulness of
        the wicked:[c]
    There is no fear of God
        before their eyes.

2 In their own eyes they flatter
        themselves
    too much to detect or hate
        their sin.
3 The words of their mouths are
        wicked and deceitful;
    they fail to act wisely or do
        good.
4 Even on their beds they plot evil;
    they commit themselves to a
        sinful course
    and do not reject what is wrong.

---

[a] 16 Septuagint; Hebrew may mean *Like an
ungodly circle of mockers.*   [b] In Hebrew texts
36:1-12 is numbered 36:2-13.   [c] 1 Or *A message
from God: The transgression of the wicked /
resides in their hearts.*

⁵ Your love, LORD, reaches to the
heavens,
    your faithfulness to the skies.
⁶ Your righteousness is like the
highest mountains,
    your justice like the great deep.
    You, LORD, preserve both
people and animals.
⁷ How priceless is your unfailing
love, O God!
    People take refuge in the
shadow of your wings.
⁸ They feast on the abundance of
your house;
    you give them drink from your
river of delights.
⁹ For with you is the fountain of
life;
    in your light we see light.

¹⁰ Continue your love to those who
know you,
    your righteousness to the
upright in heart.
¹¹ May the foot of the proud not
come against me,
    nor the hand of the wicked
drive me away.
¹² See how the evildoers lie
fallen —
    thrown down, not able to rise!

Psalm 37ᵃ

Of David.

¹ Do not fret because of those who
are evil
    or be envious of those who do
wrong;
² for like the grass they will soon
wither,
    like green plants they will
soon die away.

³ Trust in the LORD and do good;
    dwell in the land and enjoy
safe pasture.

⁴ Take delight in the LORD,
    and he will give you the
desires of your heart.

⁵ Commit your way to the LORD;
    trust in him and he will do
this:
⁶ He will make your righteous
reward shine like the
dawn,
    your vindication like the
noonday sun.

⁷ Be still before the LORD
    and wait patiently for him;
do not fret when people succeed
in their ways,
    when they carry out their
wicked schemes.

⁸ Refrain from anger and turn
from wrath;
    do not fret — it leads only to
evil.
⁹ For those who are evil will be
destroyed,
    but those who hope in the
LORD will inherit the land.

¹⁰ A little while, and the wicked will
be no more;
    though you look for them,
they will not be found.
¹¹ But the meek will inherit the
land
    and enjoy peace and prosperity.

¹² The wicked plot against the
righteous
    and gnash their teeth at them;
¹³ but the Lord laughs at the
wicked,
    for he knows their day is
coming.

¹⁴ The wicked draw the sword
    and bend the bow

ᵃ This psalm is an acrostic poem, the stanzas of
which begin with the successive letters of the
Hebrew alphabet.

to bring down the poor and
needy,
    to slay those whose ways are
    upright.
¹⁵ But their swords will pierce their
own hearts,
    and their bows will be
    broken.

¹⁶ Better the little that the
righteous have
    than the wealth of many
    wicked;
¹⁷ for the power of the wicked will
be broken,
    but the LORD upholds the
    righteous.

¹⁸ The blameless spend their days
under the LORD's care,
    and their inheritance will
    endure forever.
¹⁹ In times of disaster they will not
wither;
    in days of famine they will
    enjoy plenty.

²⁰ But the wicked will perish:
    Though the LORD's enemies
    are like the flowers of the
    field,
    they will be consumed, they
    will go up in smoke.

²¹ The wicked borrow and do not
repay,
    but the righteous give
    generously;
²² those the LORD blesses will
inherit the land,
    but those he curses will be
    destroyed.

²³ The LORD makes firm the steps
of the one who delights in
him;
²⁴ though he may stumble, he will
not fall,
    for the LORD upholds him with
    his hand.

²⁵ I was young and now I am old,
    yet I have never seen the
    righteous forsaken
    or their children begging
    bread.
²⁶ They are always generous and
lend freely;
    their children will be a
    blessing.ᵃ

²⁷ Turn from evil and do good;
    then you will dwell in the land
    forever.
²⁸ For the LORD loves the just
    and will not forsake his
    faithful ones.

    Wrongdoers will be completely
    destroyedᵇ;
    the offspring of the wicked
    will perish.
²⁹ The righteous will inherit the
land
    and dwell in it forever.

³⁰ The mouths of the righteous
utter wisdom,
    and their tongues speak what
    is just.
³¹ The law of their God is in their
hearts;
    their feet do not slip.

³² The wicked lie in wait for the
righteous,
    intent on putting them to
    death;
³³ but the LORD will not leave
    them in the power of the
    wicked
    or let them be condemned
    when brought to trial.

³⁴ Hope in the LORD
    and keep his way.

ᵃ 26 Or freely; / the names of their children will
be used in blessings (see Gen. 48:20); or freely; /
others will see that their children are blessed
ᵇ 28 See Septuagint; Hebrew They will be
protected forever

He will exalt you to inherit the
    land;
  when the wicked are
      destroyed, you will see it.

³⁵ I have seen a wicked and ruthless
    man
  flourishing like a luxuriant
      native tree,
³⁶ but he soon passed away and was
    no more;
  though I looked for him, he
      could not be found.

³⁷ Consider the blameless, observe
    the upright;
  a future awaits those who seek
      peace.ᵃ
³⁸ But all sinners will be destroyed;
  there will be no futureᵇ for the
      wicked.

³⁹ The salvation of the righteous
    comes from the LORD;
  he is their stronghold in time
      of trouble.
⁴⁰ The LORD helps them and
    delivers them;
  he delivers them from the
      wicked and saves them,
  because they take refuge in
      him.

Psalm 38ᶜ

A psalm of David. A petition.

¹ LORD, do not rebuke me in your
    anger
  or discipline me in your wrath.
² Your arrows have pierced me,
  and your hand has come down
      on me.
³ Because of your wrath there is no
    health in my body;
  there is no soundness in my
      bones because of my sin.
⁴ My guilt has overwhelmed me
  like a burden too heavy to bear.

⁵ My wounds fester and are
    loathsome
  because of my sinful folly.
⁶ I am bowed down and brought
    very low;
  all day long I go about
      mourning.
⁷ My back is filled with searing
    pain;
  there is no health in my body.
⁸ I am feeble and utterly crushed;
  I groan in anguish of heart.

⁹ All my longings lie open before
    you, Lord;
  my sighing is not hidden from
      you.
¹⁰ My heart pounds, my strength
    fails me;
  even the light has gone from
      my eyes.
¹¹ My friends and companions
    avoid me because of my
      wounds;
  my neighbors stay far away.
¹² Those who want to kill me set
    their traps,
  those who would harm me talk
      of my ruin;
  all day long they scheme and
      lie.

¹³ I am like the deaf, who cannot
    hear,
  like the mute, who cannot
      speak;
¹⁴ I have become like one who does
    not hear,
  whose mouth can offer no
      reply.
¹⁵ LORD, I wait for you;
  you will answer, Lord my God.
¹⁶ For I said, "Do not let them gloat
  or exalt themselves over me
      when my feet slip."

ᵃ 37 Or upright; / those who seek peace will have
posterity   ᵇ 38 Or posterity   ᶜ In Hebrew
texts 38:1-22 are numbered 38:2-23.

17 For I am about to fall,
   and my pain is ever with me.
18 I confess my iniquity;
   I am troubled by my sin.
19 Many have become my enemies
      without cause[a];
   those who hate me without
      reason are numerous.
20 Those who repay my good with
      evil
   lodge accusations against me,
      though I seek only to do what
      is good.

21 LORD, do not forsake me;
   do not be far from me, my God.
22 Come quickly to help me,
   my Lord and my Savior.

Psalm 39[b]

*For the director of music. For
Jeduthun. A psalm of David.*

1 I said, "I will watch my ways
   and keep my tongue from sin;
   I will put a muzzle on my mouth
      while in the presence of the
      wicked."
2 So I remained utterly silent,
   not even saying anything
      good.
   But my anguish increased;
3   my heart grew hot within me.
   While I meditated, the fire
      burned;
   then I spoke with my tongue:

4 "Show me, LORD, my life's end
   and the number of my days;
   let me know how fleeting my
      life is.
5 You have made my days a mere
      handbreadth;
   the span of my years is as
      nothing before you.
   Everyone is but a breath,
      even those who seem secure.[c]

6 "Surely everyone goes around like
      a mere phantom;
   in vain they rush about,
      heaping up wealth
   without knowing whose it will
      finally be.

7 "But now, Lord, what do I look for?
   My hope is in you.
8 Save me from all my
      transgressions;
   do not make me the scorn of
      fools.
9 I was silent; I would not open my
      mouth,
   for you are the one who has
      done this.
10 Remove your scourge from me;
   I am overcome by the blow of
      your hand.
11 When you rebuke and discipline
      anyone for their sin,
   you consume their wealth like a
      moth —
   surely everyone is but a breath.

12 "Hear my prayer, LORD,
   listen to my cry for help;
   do not be deaf to my weeping.
   I dwell with you as a foreigner,
      a stranger, as all my ancestors
      were.
13 Look away from me, that I may
      enjoy life again
   before I depart and am no more."

Psalm 40[d]

*For the director of music.
Of David. A psalm.*

1 I waited patiently for the LORD;
   he turned to me and heard my
      cry.

---

[a] 19 One Dead Sea Scrolls manuscript;
Masoretic Text *my vigorous enemies*   [b] In
Hebrew texts 39:1-13 is numbered 39:2-14.
[c] 5 The Hebrew has *Selah* (a word of uncertain
meaning) here and at the end of verse 11.
[d] In Hebrew texts 40:1-17 is numbered 40:2-18.

²He lifted me out of the slimy pit,
   out of the mud and mire;
he set my feet on a rock
   and gave me a firm place to
      stand.
³He put a new song in my mouth,
   a hymn of praise to our God.
Many will see and fear the LORD
   and put their trust in him.

⁴Blessed is the one
   who trusts in the LORD,
who does not look to the proud,
   to those who turn aside to false
      gods.ᵃ
⁵Many, LORD my God,
   are the wonders you have done,
   the things you planned for us.
None can compare with you;
   were I to speak and tell of your
      deeds,
   they would be too many to
      declare.

⁶Sacrifice and offering you did not
      desire —
   but my ears you have
      openedᵇ —
   burnt offerings and sin
      offeringsᶜ you did not
      require.
⁷Then I said, "Here I am, I have
      come —
   it is written about me in the
      scroll.ᵈ
⁸I desire to do your will, my God;
   your law is within my heart."

⁹I proclaim your saving acts in the
      great assembly;
   I do not seal my lips, LORD,
      as you know.
¹⁰I do not hide your righteousness
      in my heart;
   I speak of your faithfulness and
      your saving help.
I do not conceal your love and
      your faithfulness
   from the great assembly.

¹¹Do not withhold your mercy from
      me, LORD;
   may your love and faithfulness
      always protect me.
¹²For troubles without number
      surround me;
   my sins have overtaken me,
      and I cannot see.
They are more than the hairs of
      my head,
   and my heart fails within me.
¹³Be pleased to save me, LORD;
   come quickly, LORD, to help me.

¹⁴May all who want to take my life
   be put to shame and confusion;
may all who desire my ruin
   be turned back in disgrace.
¹⁵May those who say to me, "Aha!
      Aha!"
   be appalled at their own
      shame.
¹⁶But may all who seek you
   rejoice and be glad in you;
may those who long for your
      saving help always say,
   "The LORD is great!"

¹⁷But as for me, I am poor and
      needy;
   may the Lord think of me.
You are my help and my
      deliverer;
   you are my God, do not delay.

Psalm 41ᵉ

For the director of music.
A psalm of David.

¹Blessed are those who have
      regard for the weak;
   the LORD delivers them in
      times of trouble.

ᵃ 4 Or *to lies*   ᵇ 6 Hebrew; some Septuagint
manuscripts *but a body you have prepared for
me*   ᶜ 6 Or *purification offerings*   ᵈ 7 Or
come / with the scroll written for me   ᵉ In
Hebrew texts 41:1-13 is numbered 41:2-14.

2 The LORD protects and preserves
them —
they are counted among the
blessed in the land —
he does not give them over to
the desire of their foes.
3 The LORD sustains them on their
sickbed
and restores them from their
bed of illness.

4 I said, "Have mercy on me,
LORD;
heal me, for I have sinned
against you."
5 My enemies say of me in malice,
"When will he die and his
name perish?"
6 When one of them comes to see
me,
he speaks falsely, while his
heart gathers slander;
then he goes out and spreads
it around.

7 All my enemies whisper together
against me;
they imagine the worst for me,
saying,
8 "A vile disease has afflicted him;
he will never get up from the
place where he lies."
9 Even my close friend,
someone I trusted,
one who has shared my bread,
has turned[a] against me.

10 But may you have mercy on me,
LORD;
raise me up, that I may repay
them.
11 I know that you are pleased with
me,
for my enemy does not
triumph over me.
12 Because of my integrity you
uphold me
and set me in your presence
forever.

13 Praise be to the LORD, the God of
Israel,
from everlasting to
everlasting.
Amen and Amen.

BOOK II

Psalms 42 – 72

Psalm 42[b,c]

*For the director of music. A maskil[d]
of the Sons of Korah.*

1 As the deer pants for streams of
water,
so my soul pants for you, my
God.
2 My soul thirsts for God, for the
living God.
When can I go and meet with
God?
3 My tears have been my food
day and night,
while people say to me all day
long,
"Where is your God?"
4 These things I remember
as I pour out my soul:
how I used to go to the house of
God
under the protection of the
Mighty One[e]
with shouts of joy and praise
among the festive throng.

5 Why, my soul, are you downcast?
Why so disturbed within me?

---

[a] 9 Hebrew *has lifted up his heel*   [b] In many
Hebrew manuscripts Psalms 42 and 43
constitute one psalm.   [c] In Hebrew texts
42:1-11 is numbered 42:2-12.   [d] Title: Probably
a literary or musical term   [e] 4 See
Septuagint and Syriac; the meaning of the
Hebrew for this line is uncertain.

Put your hope in God,
    for I will yet praise him,
      my Savior and my God.

[6] My soul is downcast within me;
    therefore I will remember you
from the land of the Jordan,
    the heights of Hermon — from
      Mount Mizar.
[7] Deep calls to deep
    in the roar of your waterfalls;
all your waves and breakers
    have swept over me.

[8] By day the LORD directs his love,
    at night his song is with me —
      a prayer to the God of my life.

[9] I say to God my Rock,
    "Why have you forgotten me?
Why must I go about mourning,
      oppressed by the enemy?"
[10] My bones suffer mortal agony
    as my foes taunt me,
saying to me all day long,
    "Where is your God?"

[11] Why, my soul, are you downcast?
    Why so disturbed within me?
Put your hope in God,
    for I will yet praise him,
      my Savior and my God.

Psalm 43[a]

[1] Vindicate me, my God,
    and plead my cause
      against an unfaithful nation.
Rescue me from those who are
      deceitful and wicked.
[2] You are God my stronghold.
    Why have you rejected me?
Why must I go about mourning,
      oppressed by the enemy?
[3] Send me your light and your
      faithful care,
    let them lead me;
let them bring me to your holy
      mountain,
    to the place where you dwell.

[4] Then I will go to the altar of God,
    to God, my joy and my delight.
I will praise you with the lyre,
    O God, my God.

[5] Why, my soul, are you downcast?
    Why so disturbed within me?
Put your hope in God,
    for I will yet praise him,
      my Savior and my God.

Psalm 44[b]

For the director of music. Of the
Sons of Korah. A maskil.[c]

[1] We have heard it with our ears,
    O God;
    our ancestors have told us
what you did in their days,
    in days long ago.
[2] With your hand you drove out
      the nations
    and planted our ancestors;
you crushed the peoples
    and made our ancestors
      flourish.
[3] It was not by their sword that
      they won the land,
    nor did their arm bring them
      victory;
it was your right hand, your
      arm,
    and the light of your face, for
      you loved them.

[4] You are my King and my God,
    who decrees[d] victories for
      Jacob.
[5] Through you we push back our
      enemies;
    through your name we
      trample our foes.

---

[a] In many Hebrew manuscripts Psalms 42 and
43 constitute one psalm.   [b] In Hebrew texts
44:1-26 is numbered 44:2-27.   [c] Title:
Probably a literary or musical term
[d] 4 Septuagint, Aquila and Syriac; Hebrew
King, O God; / command

6 I put no trust in my bow,
  my sword does not bring me
    victory;
7 but you give us victory over our
    enemies,
  you put our adversaries to
    shame.

8 In God we make our boast all day
    long,
  and we will praise your name
    forever.[a]

9 But now you have rejected and
    humbled us;
  you no longer go out with our
    armies.
10 You made us retreat before the
    enemy,
  and our adversaries have
    plundered us.
11 You gave us up to be devoured
    like sheep
  and have scattered us among
    the nations.
12 You sold your people for a
    pittance,
  gaining nothing from their sale.

13 You have made us a reproach to
    our neighbors,
  the scorn and derision of those
    around us.
14 You have made us a byword
    among the nations;
  the peoples shake their heads at
    us.
15 I live in disgrace all day long,
  and my face is covered with
    shame
16 at the taunts of those who
    reproach and revile me,
  because of the enemy, who is
    bent on revenge.

17 All this came upon us,
  though we had not forgotten
    you;
  we had not been false to your
    covenant.

18 Our hearts had not turned back;
  our feet had not strayed from
    your path.
19 But you crushed us and made us
    a haunt for jackals;
  you covered us over with deep
    darkness.

20 If we had forgotten the name of
    our God
  or spread out our hands to a
    foreign god,
21 would not God have discovered it,
  since he knows the secrets of
    the heart?
22 Yet for your sake we face death all
    day long;
  we are considered as sheep to
    be slaughtered.

23 Awake, Lord! Why do you sleep?
  Rouse yourself! Do not reject
    us forever.
24 Why do you hide your face
  and forget our misery and
    oppression?

25 We are brought down to the dust;
  our bodies cling to the ground.
26 Rise up and help us;
  rescue us because of your
    unfailing love.

Psalm 45[b]

*For the director of music. To the
tune of "Lilies." Of the Sons of Korah.
A maskil.[c] A wedding song.*

1 My heart is stirred by a noble
    theme
  as I recite my verses for the
    king;
  my tongue is the pen of a
    skillful writer.

---

[a] 8 The Hebrew has *Selah* (a word of uncertain
meaning) here. [b] In Hebrew texts 45:1-17 is
numbered 45:2-18. [c] Title: Probably a
literary or musical term

² You are the most excellent of men
and your lips have been
anointed with grace,
since God has blessed you
forever.

³ Gird your sword on your side, you
mighty one;
clothe yourself with splendor
and majesty.

⁴ In your majesty ride forth
victoriously
in the cause of truth, humility
and justice;
let your right hand achieve
awesome deeds.

⁵ Let your sharp arrows pierce
the hearts of the king's
enemies;
let the nations fall beneath
your feet.

⁶ Your throne, O God,ᵃ will last for
ever and ever;
a scepter of justice will be the
scepter of your kingdom.

⁷ You love righteousness and hate
wickedness;
therefore God, your God,
has set you above your
companions
by anointing you with the oil of
joy.

⁸ All your robes are fragrant with
myrrh and aloes and
cassia;
from palaces adorned with
ivory
the music of the strings makes
you glad.

⁹ Daughters of kings are among
your honored women;
at your right hand is the royal
bride in gold of Ophir.

¹⁰ Listen, daughter, and pay careful
attention:
Forget your people and your
father's house.

¹¹ Let the king be enthralled by
your beauty;
honor him, for he is your lord.

¹² The city of Tyre will come with a
gift,ᵇ
people of wealth will seek your
favor.

¹³ All glorious is the princess within
her chamber;
her gown is interwoven with
gold.

¹⁴ In embroidered garments she is
led to the king;
her virgin companions follow
her—
those brought to be with her.

¹⁵ Led in with joy and gladness,
they enter the palace of the
king.

¹⁶ Your sons will take the place of
your fathers;
you will make them princes
throughout the land.

¹⁷ I will perpetuate your memory
through all generations;
therefore the nations will
praise you for ever and
ever.

Psalm 46ᶜ

*For the director of music. Of the Sons of
Korah. According to* alamoth.ᵈ *A song.*

¹ God is our refuge and strength,
an ever-present help in
trouble.

² Therefore we will not fear,
though the earth give
way
and the mountains fall into
the heart of the sea,

ᵃ 6 Here the king is addressed as God's
representative.   ᵇ 12 Or *A Tyrian robe is
among the gifts*   ᶜ In Hebrew texts 46:1-11 is
numbered 46:2-12.   ᵈ Title: Probably a
musical term

³ though its waters roar and foam
and the mountains quake with
their surging.ᵃ

⁴ There is a river whose streams
make glad the city of God,
the holy place where the Most
High dwells.
⁵ God is within her, she will not
fall;
God will help her at break of
day.
⁶ Nations are in uproar, kingdoms
fall;
he lifts his voice, the earth
melts.

⁷ The LORD Almighty is with us;
the God of Jacob is our fortress.

⁸ Come and see what the LORD has
done,
the desolations he has brought
on the earth.
⁹ He makes wars cease
to the ends of the earth.
He breaks the bow and shatters
the spear;
he burns the shieldsᵇ with fire.
¹⁰ He says, "Be still, and know that I
am God;
I will be exalted among the
nations,
I will be exalted in the earth."

¹¹ The LORD Almighty is with us;
the God of Jacob is our fortress.

Psalm 47ᶜ

*For the director of music. Of the
Sons of Korah. A psalm.*

¹ Clap your hands, all you nations;
shout to God with cries of joy.

² For the LORD Most High is
awesome,
the great King over all the
earth.

³ He subdued nations under us,
peoples under our feet.
⁴ He chose our inheritance for us,
the pride of Jacob, whom he
loved.ᵈ

⁵ God has ascended amid shouts of
joy,
the LORD amid the sounding of
trumpets.
⁶ Sing praises to God, sing praises;
sing praises to our King, sing
praises.
⁷ For God is the King of all the
earth;
sing to him a psalm of praise.

⁸ God reigns over the nations;
God is seated on his holy
throne.
⁹ The nobles of the nations
assemble
as the people of the God of
Abraham,
for the kingsᵉ of the earth belong
to God;
he is greatly exalted.

Psalm 48ᶠ

A song. A psalm of the Sons of Korah.

¹ Great is the LORD, and most
worthy of praise,
in the city of our God, his holy
mountain.

² Beautiful in its loftiness,
the joy of the whole earth,
like the heights of Zaphonᵍ is
Mount Zion,
the city of the Great King.

ᵃ *3* The Hebrew has *Selah* (a word of uncertain
meaning) here and at the end of verses 7
and 11.   ᵇ *9* Or *chariots*   ᶜ In Hebrew texts
47:1-9 is numbered 47:2-10.   ᵈ *4* The Hebrew
has *Selah* (a word of uncertain meaning) here.
ᵉ *9* Or *shields*   ᶠ In Hebrew texts 48:1-14 is
numbered 48:2-15.   ᵍ *2* *Zaphon* was the most
sacred mountain of the Canaanites.

³ God is in her citadels;
   he has shown himself to be
      her fortress.

⁴ When the kings joined forces,
   when they advanced
      together,
⁵ they saw her and were
      astounded;
   they fled in terror.
⁶ Trembling seized them there,
   pain like that of a woman in
      labor.
⁷ You destroyed them like ships
      of Tarshish
   shattered by an east wind.

⁸ As we have heard,
   so we have seen
      in the city of the LORD
         Almighty,
   in the city of our God:
      God makes her secure
         forever.^a

⁹ Within your temple, O God,
   we meditate on your unfailing
      love.
¹⁰ Like your name, O God,
   your praise reaches to the
      ends of the earth;
   your right hand is filled with
      righteousness.
¹¹ Mount Zion rejoices,
   the villages of Judah
      are glad
   because of your judgments.

¹² Walk about Zion, go around
      her,
   count her towers,
¹³ consider well her ramparts,
   view her citadels,
   that you may tell of them
      to the next generation.

¹⁴ For this God is our God for ever
      and ever;
   he will be our guide even to
      the end.

Psalm 49^b

*For the director of music. Of the
Sons of Korah. A psalm.*

¹ Hear this, all you peoples;
   listen, all who live in this
      world,
² both low and high,
   rich and poor alike:
³ My mouth will speak words of
      wisdom;
   the meditation of my
      heart will give you
         understanding.
⁴ I will turn my ear to a proverb;
   with the harp I will expound
      my riddle:

⁵ Why should I fear when evil days
      come,
   when wicked deceivers
      surround me —
⁶ those who trust in their wealth
   and boast of their great riches?
⁷ No one can redeem the life of
      another
   or give to God a ransom for
      them —
⁸ the ransom for a life is costly,
   no payment is ever enough —
⁹ so that they should live on
      forever
   and not see decay.
¹⁰ For all can see that the wise die,
   that the foolish and the
      senseless also perish,
   leaving their wealth to others.
¹¹ Their tombs will remain their
      houses^c forever,
   their dwellings for endless
      generations,
   though they had^d named lands
      after themselves.

---

^a 8 The Hebrew has *Selah* (a word of uncertain
meaning) here.   ^b In Hebrew texts 49:1-20 is
numbered 49:2-21.   ^c 11 Septuagint and Syriac;
Hebrew *In their thoughts their houses will
remain*   ^d 11 Or *generations, / for they have*

¹² People, despite their wealth, do
not endure;
　　they are like the beasts that
　　　perish.

¹³ This is the fate of those who trust
in themselves,
　　and of their followers,
　　　who approve their
　　　　sayings.^a
¹⁴ They are like sheep and are
destined to die;
　　death will be their
　　　shepherd
　　(but the upright will prevail
　　　over them in the
　　　morning).
　　Their forms will decay in the
　　　grave,
　　far from their princely
　　　mansions.
¹⁵ But God will redeem me from
the realm of the dead;
　　he will surely take me to
　　　himself.
¹⁶ Do not be overawed when
others grow rich,
　　when the splendor of their
　　　houses increases;
¹⁷ for they will take nothing
with them when they
　　die,
　　their splendor will not
　　　descend with them.
¹⁸ Though while they live they
count themselves
　　blessed —
　　and people praise you when
　　　you prosper —
¹⁹ they will join those who have
gone before them,
　　who will never again see the
　　　light of life.

²⁰ People who have wealth but
lack understanding
　　are like the beasts that
　　　perish.

Psalm 50

A psalm of Asaph.

¹ The Mighty One, God, the LORD,
speaks and summons the earth
　　from the rising of the sun to
　　　where it sets.
² From Zion, perfect in beauty,
　　God shines forth.
³ Our God comes
　　and will not be silent;
　　a fire devours before him,
　　and around him a tempest
　　　rages.
⁴ He summons the heavens above,
　　and the earth, that he may
　　　judge his people:
⁵ "Gather to me this consecrated
people,
　　who made a covenant with me
　　　by sacrifice."
⁶ And the heavens proclaim his
righteousness,
　　for he is a God of justice.^{b,c}

⁷ "Listen, my people, and I will
speak;
　　I will testify against you,
　　　Israel:
　　I am God, your God.
⁸ I bring no charges against you
concerning your sacrifices
　　or concerning your burnt
　　　offerings, which are ever
　　　before me.
⁹ I have no need of a bull from
your stall
　　or of goats from your pens,
¹⁰ for every animal of the forest is
mine,
　　and the cattle on a thousand
　　　hills.

---

^a 13 The Hebrew has *Selah* (a word of uncertain
meaning) here and at the end of verse 15.
^b 6 With a different word division of the
Hebrew; Masoretic Text *for God himself is
judge*　　^c 6 The Hebrew has *Selah* (a word of
uncertain meaning) here.

¹¹ I know every bird in the
mountains,
and the insects in the fields
are mine.
¹² If I were hungry I would not tell
you,
for the world is mine, and all
that is in it.
¹³ Do I eat the flesh of bulls
or drink the blood of
goats?

¹⁴ "Sacrifice thank offerings
to God,
fulfill your vows to the Most
High,
¹⁵ and call on me in the day of
trouble;
I will deliver you, and you will
honor me."

¹⁶ But to the wicked person, God
says:

"What right have you to recite
my laws
or take my covenant on your
lips?
¹⁷ You hate my instruction
and cast my words behind
you.
¹⁸ When you see a thief, you join
with him;
you throw in your lot with
adulterers.
¹⁹ You use your mouth for evil
and harness your tongue to
deceit.
²⁰ You sit and testify against your
brother
and slander your own
mother's son.
²¹ When you did these things and
I kept silent,
you thought I was exactly* like
you.
But I now arraign you
and set my accusations before
you.

²² "Consider this, you who forget
God,
or I will tear you to pieces,
with no one to rescue
you:
²³ Those who sacrifice thank
offerings honor me,
and to the blameless* I will
show my salvation."

Psalm 51*

*For the director of music. A psalm
of David. When the prophet Nathan came
to him after David had committed
adultery with Bathsheba.*

¹ Have mercy on me, O God,
according to your unfailing
love;
according to your great
compassion
blot out my transgressions.
² Wash away all my iniquity
and cleanse me from my sin.

³ For I know my transgressions,
and my sin is always before
me.
⁴ Against you, you only, have I
sinned
and done what is evil in your
sight;
so you are right in your verdict
and justified when you judge.
⁵ Surely I was sinful at birth,
sinful from the time my
mother conceived me.
⁶ Yet you desired faithfulness even
in the womb;
you taught me wisdom in that
secret place.

---

* 21 Or thought the 'I AM' was   * 23 Probable
reading of the original Hebrew text; the
meaning of the Masoretic Text for this phrase
is uncertain.   * In Hebrew texts 51:1-19 is
numbered 51:3-21.

⁷ Cleanse me with hyssop, and I
will be clean;
wash me, and I will be whiter
than snow.
⁸ Let me hear joy and gladness;
let the bones you have crushed
rejoice.
⁹ Hide your face from my sins
and blot out all my iniquity.

¹⁰ Create in me a pure heart,
O God,
and renew a steadfast spirit
within me.
¹¹ Do not cast me from your
presence
or take your Holy Spirit from
me.
¹² Restore to me the joy of your
salvation
and grant me a willing spirit,
to sustain me.

¹³ Then I will teach transgressors
your ways,
so that sinners will turn back
to you.
¹⁴ Deliver me from the guilt of
bloodshed, O God,
you who are God my Savior,
and my tongue will sing of
your righteousness.
¹⁵ Open my lips, Lord,
and my mouth will declare
your praise.
¹⁶ You do not delight in sacrifice,
or I would bring it;
you do not take pleasure in
burnt offerings.
¹⁷ My sacrifice, O God, is*ᵃ* a broken
spirit;
a broken and contrite
heart
you, God, will not despise.

¹⁸ May it please you to prosper
Zion,
to build up the walls of
Jerusalem.

¹⁹ Then you will delight in the
sacrifices of the righteous,
in burnt offerings offered
whole;
then bulls will be offered on
your altar.

Psalm 52ᵇ

*For the director of music. A maskilᶜ
of David. When Doeg the Edomite had
gone to Saul and told him: "David has
gone to the house of Ahimelek."*

¹ Why do you boast of evil, you
mighty hero?
Why do you boast all day
long,
you who are a disgrace in the
eyes of God?
² You who practice deceit,
your tongue plots destruction;
it is like a sharpened razor.
³ You love evil rather than good,
falsehood rather than
speaking the truth.ᵈ
⁴ You love every harmful word,
you deceitful tongue!

⁵ Surely God will bring you down
to everlasting ruin:
He will snatch you up and
pluck you from your tent;
he will uproot you from the
land of the living.
⁶ The righteous will see and fear;
they will laugh at you, saying,
⁷ "Here now is the man
who did not make God his
stronghold
but trusted in his great wealth
and grew strong by destroying
others!"

ᵃ 17 Or *The sacrifices of God are*   ᵇ In Hebrew
texts 52:1-9 is numbered 52:3-11.   ᶜ Title:
Probably a literary or musical term   ᵈ 3 The
Hebrew has *Selah* (a word of uncertain
meaning) here and at the end of verse 5.

8 But I am like an olive tree
    flourishing in the house of
        God;
I trust in God's unfailing love
    for ever and ever.
9 For what you have done I will
    always praise you
    in the presence of your faithful
        people.
And I will hope in your name,
    for your name is good.

Psalm 53 [a]

*For the director of music. According
to mahalath.[b] A maskil[c] of David.*

1 The fool says in his heart,
    "There is no God."
They are corrupt, and their ways
    are vile;
there is no one who does
    good.

2 God looks down from heaven
    on all mankind
to see if there are any who
    understand,
    any who seek God.
3 Everyone has turned away, all
    have become corrupt;
there is no one who does
    good,
    not even one.

4 Do all these evildoers know
    nothing?

They devour my people as
    though eating bread;
they never call on God.
5 But there they are, overwhelmed
    with dread,
    where there was nothing to
        dread.
God scattered the bones of those
    who attacked you;
you put them to shame, for
    God despised them.

6 Oh, that salvation for Israel
    would come out
        of Zion!
When God restores his
    people,
    let Jacob rejoice and Israel be
        glad!

Psalm 54 [d]

*For the director of music. With stringed
instruments. A maskil[c] of David. When
the Ziphites had gone to Saul and said,
"Is not David hiding among us?"*

1 Save me, O God, by your name;
    vindicate me by your might.
2 Hear my prayer, O God;
    listen to the words of my
        mouth.

3 Arrogant foes are attacking me;
    ruthless people are trying to
        kill me —
    people without regard for
        God.[e]

4 Surely God is my help;
    the Lord is the one who
        sustains me.

5 Let evil recoil on those who
    slander me;
    in your faithfulness destroy
        them.

6 I will sacrifice a freewill offering
    to you;
    I will praise your name, LORD,
        for it is good.
7 You have delivered me from all
    my troubles,
    and my eyes have looked in
        triumph on my foes.

---

a In Hebrew texts 53:1-6 is numbered 53:2-7.
b Title: Probably a musical term   c Title:
Probably a literary or musical term   d In
Hebrew texts 54:1-7 is numbered 54:3-9.
e 3 The Hebrew has *Selah* (a word of uncertain
meaning) here.

Psalm 55[a]

*For the director of music. With stringed
instruments. A maskil[b] of David.*

[1] Listen to my prayer, O God,
  do not ignore my plea;
[2]   hear me and answer me.
My thoughts trouble me and I am
    distraught
[3]   because of what my enemy is
    saying,
  because of the threats of the
    wicked;
for they bring down suffering on
    me
  and assail me in their anger.

[4] My heart is in anguish within me;
  the terrors of death have fallen
    on me.
[5] Fear and trembling have beset
    me;
  horror has overwhelmed me.
[6] I said, "Oh, that I had the wings
    of a dove!
  I would fly away and be at rest.
[7] I would flee far away
  and stay in the desert;[c]
[8] I would hurry to my place of
    shelter,
  far from the tempest and
    storm."

[9] Lord, confuse the wicked,
  confound their words,
for I see violence and strife in
    the city.
[10] Day and night they prowl about
    on its walls;
  malice and abuse are within it.
[11] Destructive forces are at work in
    the city;
  threats and lies never leave its
    streets.

[12] If an enemy were insulting me,
  I could endure it;
if a foe were rising against me,
  I could hide.

[13] But it is you, a man like myself,
  my companion, my close
    friend,
[14] with whom I once enjoyed sweet
    fellowship
  at the house of God,
as we walked about
  among the worshipers.

[15] Let death take my enemies by
    surprise;
  let them go down alive to the
    realm of the dead,
  for evil finds lodging among
    them.

[16] As for me, I call to God,
  and the LORD saves me.
[17] Evening, morning and noon
  I cry out in distress,
  and he hears my voice.
[18] He rescues me unharmed
  from the battle waged against
    me,
  even though many oppose me.
[19] God, who is enthroned from of
    old,
  who does not change —
he will hear them and humble
    them,
  because they have no fear of
    God.

[20] My companion attacks his friends;
  he violates his covenant.
[21] His talk is smooth as butter,
  yet war is in his heart;
his words are more soothing
    than oil,
  yet they are drawn swords.

[22] Cast your cares on the LORD
  and he will sustain you;
he will never let
  the righteous be shaken.

---

[a] In Hebrew texts 55:1-23 is numbered 55:2-24.
[b] Title: Probably a literary or musical term
[c] 7 The Hebrew has *Selah* (a word of uncertain
meaning) here and in the middle of verse 19.

23 But you, God, will bring down the
wicked
　into the pit of decay;
the bloodthirsty and deceitful
　will not live out half their days.

But as for me, I trust in you.

Psalm 56[a]

*For the director of music. To the
tune of "A Dove on Distant Oaks."
Of David. A miktam.[b] When the
Philistines had seized him in Gath.*

1 Be merciful to me, my God,
　for my enemies are in hot
　　pursuit;
all day long they press their
　attack.
2 My adversaries pursue me all day
　long;
　in their pride many are
　　attacking me.

3 When I am afraid, I put my trust
　in you.
4 　In God, whose word I praise —
in God I trust and am not afraid.
　What can mere mortals do to
　　me?

5 All day long they twist my words;
　all their schemes are for my
　　ruin.
6 They conspire, they lurk,
　they watch my steps,
　hoping to take my life.
7 Because of their wickedness do
　not[c] let them escape;
　in your anger, God, bring the
　　nations down.

8 Record my misery;
　list my tears on your scroll[d] —
　are they not in your record?
9 Then my enemies will turn back
　when I call for help.
　By this I will know that God is
　　for me.

10 In God, whose word I praise,
　in the LORD, whose word I
　　praise —
11 in God I trust and am not afraid.
　What can man do to me?

12 I am under vows to you,
　my God;
I will present my thank
　offerings to you.
13 For you have delivered me from
　death
and my feet from stumbling,
that I may walk before God
　in the light of life.

Psalm 57[e]

*For the director of music. To the tune of
"Do Not Destroy." Of David. A miktam.[b]
When he had fled from Saul into the cave.*

1 Have mercy on me, my God, have
　mercy on me,
　for in you I take refuge.
I will take refuge in the shadow
　of your wings
until the disaster has passed.

2 I cry out to God Most High,
　to God, who vindicates me.
3 He sends from heaven and
　saves me,
rebuking those who hotly
　pursue me —[f]
God sends forth his love and
　his faithfulness.

4 I am in the midst of lions;
　I am forced to dwell among
　ravenous beasts —

---

[a] In Hebrew texts 56:1-13 is numbered 56:2-14.
[b] Title: Probably a literary or musical term
[c] 7 Probable reading of the original Hebrew
text; Masoretic Text does not have *do not.*
[d] 8 Or *misery; / put my tears in your wineskin*
[e] In Hebrew texts 57:1-11 is numbered 57:2-12.
[f] 3 The Hebrew has *Selah* (a word of uncertain
meaning) here and at the end of verse 6.

men whose teeth are spears and
    arrows,
  whose tongues are sharp
    swords.

5 Be exalted, O God, above the
    heavens;
  let your glory be over all the
    earth.

6 They spread a net for my feet —
    I was bowed down in distress.
  They dug a pit in my path —
    but they have fallen into it
    themselves.

7 My heart, O God, is steadfast,
    my heart is steadfast;
  I will sing and make music.
8 Awake, my soul!
  Awake, harp and lyre!
    I will awaken the dawn.

9 I will praise you, Lord, among
    the nations;
  I will sing of you among the
    peoples.
10 For great is your love, reaching
    to the heavens;
  your faithfulness reaches to
    the skies.

11 Be exalted, O God, above the
    heavens;
  let your glory be over all the
    earth.

Psalm 58ᵃ

*For the director of music. To the tune of
"Do Not Destroy." Of David. A miktam.ᵇ*

1 Do you rulers indeed speak
    justly?
  Do you judge people with
    equity?
2 No, in your heart you devise
    injustice,
  and your hands mete out
    violence on the earth.

3 Even from birth the wicked go
    astray;
  from the womb they are
    wayward, spreading
    lies.
4 Their venom is like the venom
    of a snake,
  like that of a cobra that has
    stopped its ears,
5 that will not heed the tune of
    the charmer,
  however skillful the
    enchanter may be.

6 Break the teeth in their mouths,
    O God;
  LORD, tear out the fangs of
    those lions!
7 Let them vanish like water that
    flows away;
  when they draw the bow,
    let their arrows fall
    short.
8 May they be like a slug that
    melts away as it moves
    along,
  like a stillborn child that
    never sees the sun.

9 Before your pots can feel the
    heat of the thorns —
  whether they be green or
    dry — the wicked will be
    swept away.ᶜ
10 The righteous will be glad when
    they are avenged,
  when they dip their feet in
    the blood of the
    wicked.
11 Then people will say,
    "Surely the righteous still are
    rewarded;
  surely there is a God who
    judges the earth."

ᵃ In Hebrew texts 58:1-11 is numbered 58:2-12.
ᵇ Title: Probably a literary or musical term
ᶜ 9 The meaning of the Hebrew for this
verse is uncertain.

Psalm 59[a]

For the director of music. To the tune
of "Do Not Destroy." Of David.
A miktam.[b] When Saul had sent
men to watch David's house
in order to kill him.

[1] Deliver me from my enemies,
  O God;
  be my fortress against
    those who are
    attacking me.
[2] Deliver me from evildoers
  and save me from those
    who are after my
    blood.

[3] See how they lie in wait
  for me!
  Fierce men conspire against
    me
  for no offense or sin of mine,
    LORD.
[4] I have done no wrong, yet
    they are ready to
    attack me.
  Arise to help me; look on
    my plight!
[5] You, LORD God Almighty,
    you who are the God of
    Israel,
  rouse yourself to punish all
    the nations;
  show no mercy to wicked
    traitors.[c]

[6] They return at evening,
    snarling like dogs,
  and prowl about the city.
[7] See what they spew from their
    mouths—
  the words from their lips are
    sharp as swords,
  and they think, "Who can
    hear us?"
[8] But you laugh at them,
    LORD;
  you scoff at all those
    nations.

[9] You are my strength, I watch
    for you;
  you, God, are my fortress,
[10]   my God on whom I can
    rely.

God will go before me
  and will let me gloat over
    those who slander
    me.
[11] But do not kill them, Lord our
    shield,[d]
  or my people will forget.
In your might uproot them
  and bring them down.
[12] For the sins of their mouths,
  for the words of their lips,
  let them be caught in their
    pride.
For the curses and lies they
    utter,
[13]   consume them in your
    wrath,
  consume them till they are
    no more.
Then it will be known to the
  ends of the earth
  that God rules over Jacob.

[14] They return at evening,
    snarling like dogs,
  and prowl about the city.
[15] They wander about for food
  and howl if not satisfied.
[16] But I will sing of your strength,
  in the morning I will sing of
    your love;
for you are my fortress,
  my refuge in times of trouble.

[17] You are my strength, I sing
    praise to you;
  you, God, are my fortress,
  my God on whom I can rely.

[a] In Hebrew texts 59:1-17 are numbered 59:2-18.
[b] Title: Probably a literary or musical term
[c] 5 The Hebrew has *Selah* (a word of uncertain
meaning) here and at the end of verse 13.
[d] 11 Or *sovereign*

Psalm 60[a]

*For the director of music. To the
tune of "The Lily of the Covenant."
A miktam[b] of David. For teaching.
When he fought Aram Naharaim[c] and
Aram Zobah,[d] and when Joab returned
and struck down twelve thousand
Edomites in the Valley of Salt.*

1 You have rejected us, God, and
     burst upon us;
   you have been angry — now
     restore us!
2 You have shaken the land and
     torn it open;
   mend its fractures, for it is
     quaking.
3 You have shown your people
     desperate times;
   you have given us wine that
     makes us stagger.
4 But for those who fear you, you
     have raised a banner
   to be unfurled against the
     bow.[e]

5 Save us and help us with your
     right hand,
   that those you love may be
     delivered.
6 God has spoken from his
     sanctuary:
   "In triumph I will parcel out
     Shechem
   and measure off the Valley of
     Sukkoth.
7 Gilead is mine, and Manasseh is
     mine;
   Ephraim is my helmet,
     Judah is my scepter.
8 Moab is my washbasin,
   on Edom I toss my sandal;
   over Philistia I shout in
     triumph."

9 Who will bring me to the
     fortified city?
   Who will lead me to Edom?

10 Is it not you, God, you who have
     now rejected us
   and no longer go out with our
     armies?
11 Give us aid against the enemy,
   for human help is
     worthless.
12 With God we will gain the
     victory,
   and he will trample down our
     enemies.

Psalm 61[f]

*For the director of music. With
stringed instruments. Of David.*

1 Hear my cry, O God;
   listen to my prayer.

2 From the ends of the earth I call
     to you,
   I call as my heart grows faint;
   lead me to the rock that is
     higher than I.
3 For you have been my refuge,
   a strong tower against the foe.

4 I long to dwell in your tent
     forever
   and take refuge in the shelter
     of your wings.[e]
5 For you, God, have heard my
     vows;
   you have given me the
     heritage of those who fear
     your name.

6 Increase the days of the king's
     life,
   his years for many
     generations.

---

[a] In Hebrew texts 60:1-12 is numbered 60:3-14.
[b] Title: Probably a literary or musical term
[c] Title: That is, Arameans of Northwest
Mesopotamia   [d] Title: That is, Arameans of
central Syria   [e] 4 The Hebrew has *Selah* (a
word of uncertain meaning) here.   [f] In
Hebrew texts 61:1-8 is numbered 61:2-9.

7 May he be enthroned in God's
presence forever;
appoint your love and
faithfulness to protect
him.

8 Then I will ever sing in praise of
your name
and fulfill my vows day after
day.

Psalm 62[a]

*For the director of music. For
Jeduthun. A psalm of David.*

1 Truly my soul finds rest in God;
my salvation comes from
him.
2 Truly he is my rock and my
salvation;
he is my fortress, I will never
be shaken.

3 How long will you assault me?
Would all of you throw me
down —
this leaning wall, this tottering
fence?
4 Surely they intend to topple me
from my lofty place;
they take delight in lies.
With their mouths they bless,
but in their hearts they curse.[b]

5 Yes, my soul, find rest in God;
my hope comes from him.
6 Truly he is my rock and my
salvation;
he is my fortress, I will not be
shaken.
7 My salvation and my honor
depend on God[c];
he is my mighty rock, my
refuge.
8 Trust in him at all times, you
people;
pour out your hearts to him,
for God is our refuge.

9 Surely the lowborn are but a
breath,
the highborn are but a lie.
If weighed on a balance, they are
nothing;
together they are only a
breath.
10 Do not trust in extortion
or put vain hope in stolen
goods;
though your riches increase,
do not set your heart on them.

11 One thing God has spoken,
two things I have heard:
"Power belongs to you, God,
12   and with you, Lord, is
unfailing love";
and, "You reward everyone
according to what they have
done."

Psalm 63[d]

*A psalm of David. When he was
in the Desert of Judah.*

1 You, God, are my God,
earnestly I seek you;
I thirst for you,
my whole being longs for you,
in a dry and parched land
where there is no water.

2 I have seen you in the sanctuary
and beheld your power and
your glory.
3 Because your love is better than
life,
my lips will glorify you.
4 I will praise you as long as I live,
and in your name I will lift up
my hands.

---

[a] In Hebrew texts 62:1-12 is numbered 62:2-13.
[b] 4 The Hebrew has *Selah* (a word of uncertain
meaning) here and at the end of verse 8.
[c] 7 Or / *God Most High is my salvation and my
honor*   [d] In Hebrew texts 63:1-11 is numbered
63:2-12.

⁵ I will be fully satisfied as with
the richest of foods;
with singing lips my mouth
will praise you.

⁶ On my bed I remember you;
I think of you through the
watches of the night.

⁷ Because you are my help,
I sing in the shadow of your
wings.

⁸ I cling to you;
your right hand upholds me.

⁹ Those who want to kill me will
be destroyed;
they will go down to the
depths of the earth.

¹⁰ They will be given over to the
sword
and become food for jackals.

¹¹ But the king will rejoice in God;
all who swear by God will glory
in him,
while the mouths of liars will
be silenced.

Psalm 64ᵃ

*For the director of music.
A psalm of David.*

¹ Hear me, my God, as I voice my
complaint;
protect my life from the threat
of the enemy.

² Hide me from the conspiracy of
the wicked,
from the plots of evildoers.

³ They sharpen their tongues like
swords
and aim cruel words like
deadly arrows.

⁴ They shoot from ambush at the
innocent;
they shoot suddenly, without
fear.

⁵ They encourage each other in
evil plans,
they talk about hiding their
snares;
they say, "Who will see itᵇ?"

⁶ They plot injustice and say,
"We have devised a perfect
plan!"
Surely the human mind and
heart are cunning.

⁷ But God will shoot them with his
arrows;
they will suddenly be struck
down.

⁸ He will turn their own tongues
against them
and bring them to ruin;
all who see them will shake
their heads in scorn.

⁹ All people will fear;
they will proclaim the works
of God
and ponder what he has
done.

¹⁰ The righteous will rejoice in the
Lᴏʀᴅ
and take refuge in him;
all the upright in heart will
glory in him!

Psalm 65ᶜ

*For the director of music.
A psalm of David. A song.*

¹ Praise awaitsᵈ you, our God, in
Zion;
to you our vows will be
fulfilled.

² You who answer prayer,
to you all people will come.

ᵃ In Hebrew texts 64:1-10 is numbered 64:2-11.
ᵇ 5 Or *us*   ᶜ In Hebrew texts 65:1-13 is
numbered 65:2-14.   ᵈ 1 Or *befits*; the
meaning of the Hebrew for this word is
uncertain.

³ When we were overwhelmed
by sins,
you forgave^a our
transgressions.

⁴ Blessed are those you choose
and bring near to live in your
courts!
We are filled with the good
things of your house,
of your holy temple.

⁵ You answer us with awesome
and righteous deeds,
God our Savior,
the hope of all the ends of the
earth
and of the farthest seas,

⁶ who formed the mountains by
your power,
having armed yourself with
strength,

⁷ who stilled the roaring of the
seas,
the roaring of their waves,
and the turmoil of the
nations.

⁸ The whole earth is filled with
awe at your wonders;
where morning dawns, where
evening fades,
you call forth songs of joy.

⁹ You care for the land and water
it;
you enrich it abundantly.
The streams of God are filled
with water
to provide the people with
grain,
for so you have ordained it.^b

¹⁰ You drench its furrows and level
its ridges;
you soften it with showers and
bless its crops.

¹¹ You crown the year with your
bounty,
and your carts overflow with
abundance.

¹² The grasslands of the wilderness
overflow;
the hills are clothed with
gladness.

¹³ The meadows are covered with
flocks
and the valleys are mantled
with grain;
they shout for joy and sing.

Psalm 66

For the director of music.
A song. A psalm.

¹ Shout for joy to God, all the earth!
²   Sing the glory of his name;
make his praise glorious.

³ Say to God, "How awesome are
your deeds!
So great is your power
that your enemies cringe
before you.

⁴ All the earth bows down to you;
they sing praise to you,
they sing the praises of your
name."^c

⁵ Come and see what God has
done,
his awesome deeds for
mankind!

⁶ He turned the sea into dry land,
they passed through the
waters on foot—
come, let us rejoice in him.

⁷ He rules forever by his power,
his eyes watch the nations—
let not the rebellious rise up
against him.

⁸ Praise our God, all peoples,
let the sound of his praise be
heard;

---

^a 3 Or *made atonement for*   ^b 9 Or *for that is how you prepare the land*   ^c 4 The Hebrew has *Selah* (a word of uncertain meaning) here and at the end of verses 7 and 15.

9 he has preserved our lives
    and kept our feet from
        slipping.
10 For you, God, tested us;
    you refined us like silver.
11 You brought us into prison
    and laid burdens on our backs.
12 You let people ride over our
        heads;
    we went through fire and
        water,
    but you brought us to a place
        of abundance.

13 I will come to your temple with
        burnt offerings
    and fulfill my vows to you—
14 vows my lips promised and my
        mouth spoke
    when I was in trouble.
15 I will sacrifice fat animals to you
    and an offering of rams;
    I will offer bulls and goats.

16 Come and hear, all you who fear
        God;
    let me tell you what he has
        done for me.
17 I cried out to him with my
        mouth;
    his praise was on my tongue.
18 If I had cherished sin in my heart,
    the Lord would not have
        listened;
19 but God has surely listened
    and has heard my prayer.
20 Praise be to God,
    who has not rejected my prayer
    or withheld his love from me!

Psalm 67[a]

*For the director of music. With stringed
instruments. A psalm. A song.*

1 May God be gracious to us and
        bless us
    and make his face shine
        on us—[b]

2 so that your ways may be known
        on earth,
    your salvation among all
        nations.

3 May the peoples praise you, God;
    may all the peoples praise you.
4 May the nations be glad and sing
        for joy,
    for you rule the peoples with
        equity
    and guide the nations of the
        earth.
5 May the peoples praise you, God;
    may all the peoples praise you.

6 The land yields its harvest;
    God, our God, blesses us.
7 May God bless us still,
    so that all the ends of the earth
        will fear him.

Psalm 68[c]

*For the director of music.
Of David. A psalm. A song.*

1 May God arise, may his enemies
        be scattered;
    may his foes flee before him.
2 May you blow them away like
        smoke—
    as wax melts before the fire,
    may the wicked perish before
        God.
3 But may the righteous be glad
    and rejoice before God;
    may they be happy and joyful.

4 Sing to God, sing in praise of his
        name,
    extol him who rides on the
        clouds[d];
    rejoice before him—his name
        is the Lord.

---

[a] In Hebrew texts 67:1-7 is numbered 67:2-8.
[b] 1 The Hebrew has *Selah* (a word of uncertain
meaning) here and at the end of verse 4.   [c] In
Hebrew texts 68:1-35 is numbered 68:2-36.
[d] 4 Or *name, / prepare the way for him who rides
through the deserts*

⁵ A father to the fatherless, a
　　defender of widows,
　is God in his holy dwelling.
⁶ God sets the lonely in families,ᵃ
　he leads out the prisoners with
　　singing;
　but the rebellious live in a
　　sun-scorched land.

⁷ When you, God, went out before
　　your people,
　when you marched through
　　the wilderness,ᵇ
⁸ the earth shook, the heavens
　　poured down rain,
　before God, the One of
　　Sinai,
　before God, the God of
　　Israel.
⁹ You gave abundant showers,
　　O God;
　you refreshed your weary
　　inheritance.
¹⁰ Your people settled in it,
　and from your bounty, God,
　　you provided for the poor.

¹¹ The Lord announces the word,
　and the women who proclaim
　　it are a mighty throng:
¹² "Kings and armies flee in
　　haste;
　the women at home divide
　　the plunder.
¹³ Even while you sleep among
　　the sheep pens,ᶜ
　the wings of my dove are
　　sheathed with silver,
　its feathers with shining
　　gold."
¹⁴ When the Almightyᵈ scattered
　　the kings in the land,
　it was like snow fallen on
　　Mount Zalmon.

¹⁵ Mount Bashan, majestic
　　mountain,
　Mount Bashan, rugged
　　mountain,

¹⁶ why gaze in envy, you rugged
　　mountain,
　at the mountain where God
　　chooses to reign,
　where the LORD himself will
　　dwell forever?
¹⁷ The chariots of God are tens of
　　thousands
　and thousands of thousands;
　the Lord has come from Sinai
　　into his sanctuary.ᵉ
¹⁸ When you ascended on high,
　you took many captives;
　you received gifts from people,
　even fromᶠ the rebellious —
　that you,ᵍ LORD God, might
　　dwell there.

¹⁹ Praise be to the Lord, to God our
　　Savior,
　who daily bears our burdens.
²⁰ Our God is a God who saves;
　from the Sovereign LORD
　　comes escape from death.
²¹ Surely God will crush the heads
　　of his enemies,
　the hairy crowns of those who
　　go on in their sins.
²² The Lord says, "I will bring them
　　from Bashan;
　I will bring them from the
　　depths of the sea,
²³ that your feet may wade in the
　　blood of your foes,
　while the tongues of your dogs
　　have their share."

²⁴ Your procession, God, has come
　　into view,
　the procession of my God and
　　King into the sanctuary.

ᵃ 6 Or *the desolate in a homeland*　ᵇ 7 The Hebrew has *Selah* (a word of uncertain meaning) here and at the end of verses 19 and 32.　ᶜ 13 Or *the campfires; or the saddlebags*　ᵈ 14 Hebrew *Shaddai*　ᵉ 17 Probable reading of the original Hebrew text; Masoretic Text *Lord is among them at Sinai in holiness*　ᶠ 18 Or *gifts for people, / even*　ᵍ 18 Or *they*

²⁵ In front are the singers, after
        them the musicians;
    with them are the young
        women playing the
        timbrels.
²⁶ Praise God in the great
        congregation;
    praise the LORD in the
        assembly of Israel.
²⁷ There is the little tribe of
        Benjamin, leading
        them,
    there the great throng of
        Judah's princes,
    and there the princes of
        Zebulun and of Naphtali.

²⁸ Summon your power, God^a;
    show us your strength, our
        God, as you have done
        before.
²⁹ Because of your temple at
        Jerusalem
    kings will bring you gifts.
³⁰ Rebuke the beast among the
        reeds,
    the herd of bulls among the
        calves of the nations.
    Humbled, may the beast bring
        bars of silver.
    Scatter the nations who
        delight in war.
³¹ Envoys will come from Egypt;
    Cush^b will submit herself to
        God.

³² Sing to God, you kingdoms
        of the earth,
    sing praise to the Lord,
³³ to him who rides across the
        highest heavens, the
        ancient heavens,
    who thunders with mighty
        voice.
³⁴ Proclaim the power of God,
    whose majesty is over Israel,
    whose power is in the
        heavens.

³⁵ You, God, are awesome in your
        sanctuary;
    the God of Israel gives power
        and strength to his
        people.

Praise be to God!

Psalm 69^c

*For the director of music. To the
tune of "Lilies." Of David.*

¹ Save me, O God,
    for the waters have come up to
        my neck.
² I sink in the miry depths,
    where there is no foothold.
    I have come into the deep
        waters;
    the floods engulf me.
³ I am worn out calling for
        help;
    my throat is parched.
    My eyes fail,
    looking for my God.
⁴ Those who hate me without
        reason
    outnumber the hairs of my
        head;
    many are my enemies without
        cause,
    those who seek to destroy me.
    I am forced to restore
    what I did not steal.

⁵ You, God, know my folly;
    my guilt is not hidden from
        you.

⁶ Lord, the LORD Almighty,
    may those who hope in you
    not be disgraced because
        of me;

---

^a 28 Many Hebrew manuscripts, Septuagint
and Syriac; most Hebrew manuscripts *Your
God has summoned power for you*   ^b 31 That
is, the upper Nile region   ^c In Hebrew texts
69:1-36 is numbered 69:2-37.

God of Israel,
  may those who seek you
    not be put to shame because
      of me.
7 For I endure scorn for your sake,
  and shame covers my face.
8 I am a foreigner to my own
    family,
  a stranger to my own mother's
    children;
9 for zeal for your house consumes
    me,
  and the insults of those who
    insult you fall on me.
10 When I weep and fast,
  I must endure scorn;
11 when I put on sackcloth,
  people make sport of me.
12 Those who sit at the gate
    mock me,
  and I am the song of the
    drunkards.

13 But I pray to you, LORD,
  in the time of your favor;
in your great love, O God,
  answer me with your sure
    salvation.
14 Rescue me from the mire,
  do not let me sink;
deliver me from those who hate
    me,
  from the deep waters.
15 Do not let the floodwaters
    engulf me
  or the depths swallow
    me up
  or the pit close its mouth
    over me.

16 Answer me, LORD, out of the
    goodness of your love;
  in your great mercy turn
    to me.
17 Do not hide your face from your
    servant;
  answer me quickly, for I am
    in trouble.

18 Come near and rescue me;
  deliver me because of my foes.

19 You know how I am scorned,
    disgraced and shamed;
  all my enemies are before you.
20 Scorn has broken my heart
    and has left me helpless;
  I looked for sympathy, but there
      was none,
  for comforters, but I found
    none.
21 They put gall in my food
  and gave me vinegar for my
    thirst.

22 May the table set before them
    become a snare;
  may it become retribution
    and[a] a trap.
23 May their eyes be darkened so
    they cannot see,
  and their backs be bent
    forever.
24 Pour out your wrath on them;
  let your fierce anger overtake
    them.
25 May their place be deserted;
  let there be no one to dwell in
    their tents.
26 For they persecute those you
    wound
  and talk about the pain of
    those you hurt.
27 Charge them with crime upon
    crime;
  do not let them share in your
    salvation.
28 May they be blotted out of the
    book of life
  and not be listed with the
    righteous.

29 But as for me, afflicted and in
    pain—
  may your salvation, God,
    protect me.

---

a 22 Or snare / and their fellowship become

30 I will praise God's name in song
    and glorify him with
        thanksgiving.
31 This will please the LORD more
        than an ox,
    more than a bull with its horns
        and hooves.
32 The poor will see and be glad —
    you who seek God, may your
        hearts live!
33 The LORD hears the needy
    and does not despise his
        captive people.

34 Let heaven and earth praise him,
    the seas and all that move in
        them,
35 for God will save Zion
    and rebuild the cities of Judah.
Then people will settle there and
        possess it;
36   the children of his servants will
        inherit it,
    and those who love his name
        will dwell there.

Psalm 70[a]

*For the director of music.
Of David. A petition.*

1 Hasten, O God, to save me;
    come quickly, LORD, to help
        me.

2 May those who want to take my
        life
    be put to shame and confusion;
may all who desire my ruin
    be turned back in disgrace.
3 May those who say to me, "Aha!
        Aha!"
    turn back because of their
        shame.
4 But may all who seek you
    rejoice and be glad in you;
may those who long for your
        saving help always say,
    "The LORD is great!"

5 But as for me, I am poor and
        needy;
    come quickly to me, O God.
You are my help and my
        deliverer;
    LORD, do not delay.

Psalm 71

1 In you, LORD, I have taken refuge;
    let me never be put to shame.
2 In your righteousness, rescue me
        and deliver me;
    turn your ear to me and
        save me.
3 Be my rock of refuge,
    to which I can always go;
give the command to save me,
    for you are my rock and my
        fortress.
4 Deliver me, my God, from the
        hand of the wicked,
    from the grasp of those who
        are evil and cruel.

5 For you have been my hope,
        Sovereign LORD,
    my confidence since my youth.
6 From birth I have relied on you;
    you brought me forth from my
        mother's womb.
    I will ever praise you.
7 I have become a sign to many;
    you are my strong refuge.
8 My mouth is filled with your
        praise,
    declaring your splendor all
        day long.

9 Do not cast me away when
        I am old;
    do not forsake me when my
        strength is gone.
10 For my enemies speak
        against me;
    those who wait to kill me
        conspire together.

---

[a] In Hebrew texts 70:1-5 is numbered 70:2-6.

¹¹ They say, "God has forsaken him;
    pursue him and seize him,
    for no one will rescue him."
¹² Do not be far from me, my God;
    come quickly, God, to help me.
¹³ May my accusers perish in
        shame;
    may those who want to harm
        me
    be covered with scorn and
        disgrace.

¹⁴ As for me, I will always have
        hope;
    I will praise you more and
        more.

¹⁵ My mouth will tell of your
        righteous deeds,
    of your saving acts all day
        long —
    though I know not how to
        relate them all.
¹⁶ I will come and proclaim your
        mighty acts, Sovereign
        LORD;
    I will proclaim your righteous
        deeds, yours alone.
¹⁷ Since my youth, God, you have
        taught me,
    and to this day I declare your
        marvelous deeds.
¹⁸ Even when I am old and gray,
    do not forsake me, my God,
    till I declare your power to the
        next generation,
    your mighty acts to all who are
        to come.

¹⁹ Your righteousness, God, reaches
        to the heavens,
    you who have done great
        things.
    Who is like you, God?
²⁰ Though you have made me see
        troubles,
    many and bitter,
    you will restore my life again;

from the depths of the earth
    you will again bring me up.
²¹ You will increase my honor
    and comfort me once more.

²² I will praise you with the harp
    for your faithfulness, my God;
    I will sing praise to you with the
        lyre,
    Holy One of Israel.
²³ My lips will shout for joy
    when I sing praise to you —
    I whom you have delivered.
²⁴ My tongue will tell of your
        righteous acts
    all day long,
    for those who wanted to harm
        me
    have been put to shame and
        confusion.

Psalm 72

Of Solomon.

¹ Endow the king with your justice,
        O God,
    the royal son with your
        righteousness.
² May he judge your people in
        righteousness,
    your afflicted ones with
        justice.

³ May the mountains bring
        prosperity to the people,
    the hills the fruit of
        righteousness.
⁴ May he defend the afflicted
        among the people
    and save the children of the
        needy;
    may he crush the oppressor.
⁵ May he endure[a] as long as the
        sun,
    as long as the moon, through
        all generations.

ᵃ 5 Septuagint; Hebrew *You will be feared*

⁶ May he be like rain falling on a
mown field,
  like showers watering the
  earth.
⁷ In his days may the righteous
flourish
  and prosperity abound till the
  moon is no more.

⁸ May he rule from sea to sea
  and from the River^a to the ends
  of the earth.
⁹ May the desert tribes bow before
him
  and his enemies lick the dust.
¹⁰ May the kings of Tarshish and of
distant shores
  bring tribute to him.
  May the kings of Sheba and Seba
  present him gifts.
¹¹ May all kings bow down to him
  and all nations serve him.

¹² For he will deliver the needy who
cry out,
  the afflicted who have no one
  to help.
¹³ He will take pity on the weak and
the needy
  and save the needy from death.
¹⁴ He will rescue them from
  oppression and violence,
  for precious is their blood in his
  sight.

¹⁵ Long may he live!
  May gold from Sheba be given
  him.
  May people ever pray for him
  and bless him all day long.
¹⁶ May grain abound throughout the
land;
  on the tops of the hills may it
  sway.
  May the crops flourish like
  Lebanon
  and thrive^b like the grass of the
  field.
¹⁷ May his name endure forever;
  may it continue as long as the
  sun.

Then all nations will be blessed
  through him,^c
  and they will call him blessed.

¹⁸ Praise be to the LORD God, the
  God of Israel,
  who alone does marvelous
  deeds.
¹⁹ Praise be to his glorious name
  forever;
  may the whole earth be filled
  with his glory.
  Amen and Amen.

²⁰ This concludes the prayers
  of David son of Jesse.

BOOK III

Psalms 73 – 89

Psalm 73

A psalm of Asaph.

¹ Surely God is good to Israel,
  to those who are pure
  in heart.

² But as for me, my feet had almost
slipped;
  I had nearly lost my foothold.
³ For I envied the arrogant
  when I saw the prosperity of
  the wicked.

⁴ They have no struggles;
  their bodies are healthy and
  strong.^d

---

^a 8 That is, the Euphrates   ^b 16 Probable
reading of the original Hebrew text; Masoretic
Text *Lebanon, / from the city*   ^c 17 Or *will use
his name in blessings* (see Gen. 48:20)
^d 4 With a different word division of the
Hebrew; Masoretic Text *struggles at their
death; / their bodies are healthy*

⁵ They are free from common
       human burdens;
    they are not plagued by
       human ills.
⁶ Therefore pride is their
       necklace;
    they clothe themselves with
       violence.
⁷ From their callous hearts comes
       iniquity*ᵃ*;
    their evil imaginations have
       no limits.
⁸ They scoff, and speak with
       malice;
    with arrogance they threaten
       oppression.
⁹ Their mouths lay claim to
       heaven,
    and their tongues take
       possession of the
       earth.
¹⁰ Therefore their people turn to
       them
    and drink up waters in
       abundance.*ᵇ*
¹¹ They say, "How would God
       know?
    Does the Most High know
       anything?"

¹² This is what the wicked are
       like —
    always free of care, they go
       on amassing wealth.

¹³ Surely in vain I have kept my
       heart pure
    and have washed my hands in
       innocence.
¹⁴ All day long I have been
       afflicted,
    and every morning brings
       new punishments.

¹⁵ If I had spoken out like that,
    I would have betrayed your
       children.
¹⁶ When I tried to understand all
       this,
    it troubled me deeply

¹⁷ till I entered the sanctuary of
       God;
    then I understood their final
       destiny.

¹⁸ Surely you place them on
       slippery ground;
    you cast them down to ruin.
¹⁹ How suddenly are they
       destroyed,
    completely swept away by
       terrors!
²⁰ They are like a dream when one
       awakes;
    when you arise, Lord,
    you will despise them as
       fantasies.

²¹ When my heart was grieved
    and my spirit embittered,
²² I was senseless and ignorant;
    I was a brute beast before you.

²³ Yet I am always with you;
    you hold me by my right hand.
²⁴ You guide me with your counsel,
    and afterward you will take
       me into glory.
²⁵ Whom have I in heaven
       but you?
    And earth has nothing I desire
       besides you.
²⁶ My flesh and my heart may fail,
    but God is the strength of my
       heart
    and my portion forever.

²⁷ Those who are far from you will
       perish;
    you destroy all who are
       unfaithful to you.
²⁸ But as for me, it is good to be
       near God.
    I have made the Sovereign
       LORD my refuge;
    I will tell of all your deeds.

ᵃ 7 Syriac (see also Septuagint); Hebrew *Their
eyes bulge with fat*   ᵇ 10 The meaning of the
Hebrew for this verse is uncertain.

Psalm 74

A maskil[a] of Asaph.

¹ O God, why have you rejected us
    forever?
  Why does your anger smolder
    against the sheep of your
    pasture?
² Remember the nation you
    purchased long ago,
  the people of your inheritance,
    whom you redeemed —
  Mount Zion, where you dwelt.
³ Turn your steps toward these
    everlasting ruins,
  all this destruction the enemy
    has brought on the
    sanctuary.

⁴ Your foes roared in the place
    where you met with us;
  they set up their standards as
    signs.
⁵ They behaved like men wielding
    axes
  to cut through a thicket of
    trees.
⁶ They smashed all the carved
    paneling
  with their axes and hatchets.
⁷ They burned your sanctuary to
    the ground;
  they defiled the dwelling place
    of your Name.
⁸ They said in their hearts,
    "We will crush them
    completely!"
  They burned every place
    where God was worshiped
    in the land.

⁹ We are given no signs from God;
  no prophets are left,
  and none of us knows how
    long this will be.
¹⁰ How long will the enemy mock
    you, God?
  Will the foe revile your name
    forever?

¹¹ Why do you hold back your hand,
    your right hand?
  Take it from the folds of your
    garment and destroy
    them!

¹² But God is my King from long
    ago;
  he brings salvation on the
    earth.

¹³ It was you who split open the sea
    by your power;
  you broke the heads of the
    monster in the waters.
¹⁴ It was you who crushed the
    heads of Leviathan
  and gave it as food to the
    creatures of the desert.
¹⁵ It was you who opened up
    springs and streams;
  you dried up the ever-flowing
    rivers.
¹⁶ The day is yours, and yours also
    the night;
  you established the sun and
    moon.
¹⁷ It was you who set all the
    boundaries of the earth;
  you made both summer and
    winter.

¹⁸ Remember how the enemy has
    mocked you, LORD,
  how foolish people have
    reviled your name.
¹⁹ Do not hand over the life of your
    dove to wild beasts;
  do not forget the lives of your
    afflicted people forever.
²⁰ Have regard for your covenant,
  because haunts of violence
    fill the dark places of the
    land.
²¹ Do not let the oppressed retreat
    in disgrace;
  may the poor and needy praise
    your name.

ᵃ Title: Probably a literary or musical term

²² Rise up, O God, and defend your
cause;
    remember how fools mock you
    all day long.
²³ Do not ignore the clamor of your
adversaries,
    the uproar of your enemies,
    which rises continually.

Psalm 75[a]

*For the director of music. To
the tune of "Do Not Destroy."
A psalm of Asaph. A song.*

¹ We praise you, God,
    we praise you, for your Name
    is near;
    people tell of your wonderful
    deeds.

² You say, "I choose the appointed
time;
    it is I who judge with equity.
³ When the earth and all its people
quake,
    it is I who hold its pillars
    firm.[b]
⁴ To the arrogant I say, 'Boast no
more,'
    and to the wicked, 'Do not lift
    up your horns.[c]
⁵ Do not lift your horns against
heaven;
    do not speak so defiantly.'"

⁶ No one from the east or the west
    or from the desert can exalt
    themselves.
⁷ It is God who judges:
    He brings one down, he exalts
    another.
⁸ In the hand of the LORD is a cup
    full of foaming wine mixed
    with spices;
    he pours it out, and all the
    wicked of the earth
    drink it down to its very dregs.

⁹ As for me, I will declare this
forever;
    I will sing praise to the God of
    Jacob,
¹⁰ who says, "I will cut off the horns
    of all the wicked,
    but the horns of the righteous
    will be lifted up."

Psalm 76[d]

*For the director of music. With stringed
instruments. A psalm of Asaph. A song.*

¹ God is renowned in Judah;
    in Israel his name is great.
² His tent is in Salem,
    his dwelling place in Zion.
³ There he broke the flashing
arrows,
    the shields and the swords, the
    weapons of war.[e]

⁴ You are radiant with light,
    more majestic than mountains
    rich with game.
⁵ The valiant lie plundered,
    they sleep their last sleep;
    not one of the warriors
    can lift his hands.
⁶ At your rebuke, God of Jacob,
    both horse and chariot lie
    still.

⁷ It is you alone who are to be
feared.
    Who can stand before you
    when you are angry?
⁸ From heaven you pronounced
judgment,
    and the land feared and was
    quiet —

---

[a] In Hebrew texts 75:1-10 is numbered 75:2-11.
[b] 3 The Hebrew has *Selah* (a word of uncertain meaning) here.   [c] 4 *Horns* here symbolize strength; also in verses 5 and 10.   [d] In Hebrew texts 76:1-12 is numbered 76:2-13.
[e] 3 The Hebrew has *Selah* (a word of uncertain meaning) here and at the end of verse 9.

9 when you, God, rose up to judge,
　　to save all the afflicted of the
　　land.
10 Surely your wrath against
　　mankind brings you
　　praise,
　　and the survivors of your
　　wrath are restrained.[a]

11 Make vows to the LORD your God
　　and fulfill them;
　　let all the neighboring lands
　　bring gifts to the One to be
　　feared.
12 He breaks the spirit of rulers;
　　he is feared by the kings of the
　　earth.

Psalm 77[b]

*For the director of music. For
Jeduthun. Of Asaph. A psalm.*

1 I cried out to God for help;
　　I cried out to God to hear me.
2 When I was in distress, I sought
　　the Lord;
　　at night I stretched out
　　untiring hands,
　　and I would not be comforted.

3 I remembered you, God, and I
　　groaned;
　　I meditated, and my spirit
　　grew faint.[c]
4 You kept my eyes from
　　closing;
　　I was too troubled to speak.
5 I thought about the former
　　days,
　　the years of long ago;
6 I remembered my songs in the
　　night.
　　My heart meditated and my
　　spirit asked:

7 "Will the Lord reject forever?
　　Will he never show his favor
　　again?

8 Has his unfailing love vanished
　　forever?
　　Has his promise failed for all
　　time?
9 Has God forgotten to be
　　merciful?
　　Has he in anger withheld his
　　compassion?"

10 Then I thought, "To this I will
　　appeal:
　　the years when the Most High
　　stretched out his right
　　hand.
11 I will remember the deeds of the
　　LORD;
　　yes, I will remember your
　　miracles of long ago.
12 I will consider all your works
　　and meditate on all your
　　mighty deeds."

13 Your ways, God, are holy.
　　What god is as great as our
　　God?
14 You are the God who performs
　　miracles;
　　you display your power among
　　the peoples.
15 With your mighty arm you
　　redeemed your people,
　　the descendants of Jacob and
　　Joseph.
16 The waters saw you, God,
　　the waters saw you and
　　writhed;
　　the very depths were
　　convulsed.
17 The clouds poured down water,
　　the heavens resounded with
　　thunder;
　　your arrows flashed back and
　　forth.

---

[a] 10 Or *Surely the wrath of mankind brings you
praise, / and with the remainder of wrath you
arm yourself*　　[b] In Hebrew texts 77:1-20 is
numbered 77:2-21.　　[c] 3 The Hebrew has *Selah*
(a word of uncertain meaning) here and at the
end of verses 9 and 15.

¹⁸ Your thunder was heard in the
whirlwind,
your lightning lit up the world;
the earth trembled and
quaked.
¹⁹ Your path led through the sea,
your way through the mighty
waters,
though your footprints were
not seen.

²⁰ You led your people like a flock
by the hand of Moses and
Aaron.

Psalm 78

A maskil[a] of Asaph.

¹ My people, hear my teaching;
listen to the words of my
mouth.
² I will open my mouth with a
parable;
I will utter hidden things,
things from of old—
³ things we have heard and known,
things our ancestors have told
us.
⁴ We will not hide them from their
descendants;
we will tell the next generation
the praiseworthy deeds of the
LORD,
his power, and the wonders he
has done.
⁵ He decreed statutes for Jacob
and established the law in
Israel,
which he commanded our
ancestors
to teach their children,
⁶ so the next generation would
know them,
even the children yet to be
born,
and they in turn would tell
their children.

⁷ Then they would put their trust
in God
and would not forget his deeds
but would keep his commands.
⁸ They would not be like their
ancestors—
a stubborn and rebellious
generation,
whose hearts were not loyal to
God,
whose spirits were not faithful
to him.

⁹ The men of Ephraim, though
armed with bows,
turned back on the day of
battle;
¹⁰ they did not keep God's covenant
and refused to live by his law.
¹¹ They forgot what he had done,
the wonders he had shown
them.
¹² He did miracles in the sight of
their ancestors
in the land of Egypt, in the
region of Zoan.
¹³ He divided the sea and led them
through;
he made the water stand up
like a wall.
¹⁴ He guided them with the cloud by
day
and with light from the fire all
night.
¹⁵ He split the rocks in the
wilderness
and gave them water as
abundant as the seas;
¹⁶ he brought streams out of a rocky
crag
and made water flow down like
rivers.
¹⁷ But they continued to sin against
him,
rebelling in the wilderness
against the Most High.

ᵃ Title: Probably a literary or musical term

18 They willfully put God to the test
by demanding the food they
craved.
19 They spoke against God;
they said, "Can God really
spread a table in the
wilderness?
20 True, he struck the rock,
and water gushed out,
streams flowed abundantly,
but can he also give us bread?
Can he supply meat for his
people?"
21 When the LORD heard them, he
was furious;
his fire broke out against
Jacob,
and his wrath rose against
Israel,
22 for they did not believe in God
or trust in his deliverance.
23 Yet he gave a command to the
skies above
and opened the doors of the
heavens;
24 he rained down manna for the
people to eat,
he gave them the grain of
heaven.
25 Human beings ate the bread of
angels;
he sent them all the food they
could eat.
26 He let loose the east wind from
the heavens
and by his power made the
south wind blow.
27 He rained meat down on them
like dust,
birds like sand on the
seashore.
28 He made them come down
inside their camp,
all around their tents.
29 They ate till they were gorged —
he had given them what they
craved.
30 But before they turned from
what they craved,
even while the food was still in
their mouths,
31 God's anger rose against them;
he put to death the sturdiest
among them,
cutting down the young men
of Israel.
32 In spite of all this, they kept on
sinning;
in spite of his wonders, they
did not believe.
33 So he ended their days in futility
and their years in terror.
34 Whenever God slew them, they
would seek him;
they eagerly turned to him
again.
35 They remembered that God was
their Rock,
that God Most High was their
Redeemer.
36 But then they would flatter him
with their mouths,
lying to him with their
tongues;
37 their hearts were not loyal to
him,
they were not faithful to his
covenant.
38 Yet he was merciful;
he forgave their iniquities
and did not destroy them.
Time after time he restrained his
anger
and did not stir up his full
wrath.
39 He remembered that they were
but flesh,
a passing breeze that does not
return.
40 How often they rebelled against
him in the wilderness
and grieved him in the
wasteland!

⁴¹ Again and again they put God to
    the test;
  they vexed the Holy One of
    Israel.
⁴² They did not remember his
    power —
  the day he redeemed them
    from the oppressor,
⁴³ the day he displayed his signs in
    Egypt,
  his wonders in the region of
    Zoan.
⁴⁴ He turned their river into blood;
  they could not drink from
    their streams.
⁴⁵ He sent swarms of flies that
    devoured them,
  and frogs that devastated
    them.
⁴⁶ He gave their crops to the
    grasshopper,
  their produce to the locust.
⁴⁷ He destroyed their vines with
    hail
  and their sycamore-figs with
    sleet.
⁴⁸ He gave over their cattle to the
    hail,
  their livestock to bolts of
    lightning.
⁴⁹ He unleashed against them his
    hot anger,
  his wrath, indignation and
    hostility —
  a band of destroying angels.
⁵⁰ He prepared a path for his anger;
  he did not spare them from
    death
  but gave them over to the
    plague.
⁵¹ He struck down all the firstborn
    of Egypt,
  the firstfruits of manhood in
    the tents of Ham.
⁵² But he brought his people out
    like a flock;
  he led them like sheep
    through the wilderness.

⁵³ He guided them safely, so they
    were unafraid;
  but the sea engulfed their
    enemies.
⁵⁴ And so he brought them to the
    border of his holy land,
  to the hill country his right
    hand had taken.
⁵⁵ He drove out nations before
    them
  and allotted their lands to
    them as an inheritance;
  he settled the tribes of Israel
    in their homes.
⁵⁶ But they put God to the test
  and rebelled against the Most
    High;
  they did not keep his statutes.
⁵⁷ Like their ancestors they were
    disloyal and faithless,
  as unreliable as a faulty bow.
⁵⁸ They angered him with their
    high places;
  they aroused his jealousy with
    their idols.
⁵⁹ When God heard them, he was
    furious;
  he rejected Israel completely.
⁶⁰ He abandoned the tabernacle of
    Shiloh,
  the tent he had set up among
    humans.
⁶¹ He sent the ark of his might into
    captivity,
  his splendor into the hands of
    the enemy.
⁶² He gave his people over to the
    sword;
  he was furious with his
    inheritance.
⁶³ Fire consumed their young men,
  and their young women had
    no wedding songs;
⁶⁴ their priests were put to the
    sword,
  and their widows could not
    weep.

⁶⁵ Then the Lord awoke as from
   sleep,
     as a warrior wakes from the
       stupor of wine.
⁶⁶ He beat back his enemies;
     he put them to everlasting
       shame.
⁶⁷ Then he rejected the tents of
   Joseph,
     he did not choose the tribe of
       Ephraim;
⁶⁸ but he chose the tribe of Judah,
     Mount Zion, which he loved.
⁶⁹ He built his sanctuary like the
   heights,
     like the earth that he
       established forever.
⁷⁰ He chose David his servant
     and took him from the sheep
       pens;
⁷¹ from tending the sheep he
   brought him
     to be the shepherd of his
       people Jacob,
       of Israel his inheritance.
⁷² And David shepherded them
     with integrity of heart;
       with skillful hands he led
         them.

Psalm 79

A psalm of Asaph.

¹ O God, the nations have invaded
   your inheritance;
     they have defiled your holy
       temple,
     they have reduced Jerusalem
       to rubble.
² They have left the dead bodies of
   your servants
     as food for the birds of
       the sky,
     the flesh of your own people
       for the animals of the
         wild.

³ They have poured out blood like
   water
     all around Jerusalem,
     and there is no one to bury the
       dead.
⁴ We are objects of contempt to
   our neighbors,
     of scorn and derision to those
       around us.

⁵ How long, LORD? Will you be
   angry forever?
     How long will your jealousy
       burn like fire?
⁶ Pour out your wrath on the
   nations
     that do not acknowledge you,
   on the kingdoms
     that do not call on your
       name;
⁷ for they have devoured Jacob
     and devastated his homeland.

⁸ Do not hold against us the sins
     of past generations;
     may your mercy come quickly
       to meet us,
     for we are in desperate need.

⁹ Help us, God our Savior,
     for the glory of your name;
   deliver us and forgive our sins
     for your name's sake.
¹⁰ Why should the nations say,
     "Where is their God?"

Before our eyes, make known
   among the nations
     that you avenge the
       outpoured blood of your
         servants.
¹¹ May the groans of the prisoners
     come before you;
     with your strong arm preserve
       those condemned
         to die.
¹² Pay back into the laps of our
   neighbors seven times
     the contempt they have hurled
       at you, Lord.

¹³ Then we your people, the sheep
    of your pasture,
    will praise you forever;
  from generation to generation
    we will proclaim your
    praise.

Psalm 80[a]

*For the director of music. To the tune of
"The Lilies of the Covenant."
Of Asaph. A psalm.*

¹ Hear us, Shepherd of Israel,
    you who lead Joseph like
    a flock.
  You who sit enthroned between
    the cherubim,
    shine forth ² before Ephraim,
    Benjamin and Manasseh.
  Awaken your might;
    come and save us.

³ Restore us, O God;
    make your face shine
    on us,
    that we may be saved.

⁴ How long, LORD God Almighty,
    will your anger smolder
    against the prayers of your
    people?
⁵ You have fed them with the
    bread of tears;
  you have made them drink
    tears by the bowlful.
⁶ You have made us an object
    of derision[b] to our
    neighbors,
  and our enemies mock us.

⁷ Restore us, God Almighty;
    make your face shine
    on us,
    that we may be saved.

⁸ You transplanted a vine from
    Egypt;
  you drove out the nations
    and planted it.

⁹ You cleared the ground for it,
    and it took root and filled the
    land.
¹⁰ The mountains were covered
    with its shade,
  the mighty cedars with its
    branches.
¹¹ Its branches reached as far as the
    Sea,[c]
  its shoots as far as the River.[d]

¹² Why have you broken down its
    walls
  so that all who pass by pick its
    grapes?
¹³ Boars from the forest ravage it,
  and insects from the fields
    feed on it.

¹⁴ Return to us, God Almighty!
  Look down from heaven and
    see!
  Watch over this vine,
¹⁵   the root your right hand has
    planted,
  the son[e] you have raised up for
    yourself.

¹⁶ Your vine is cut down, it is
    burned with fire;
  at your rebuke your people
    perish.
¹⁷ Let your hand rest on the man at
    your right hand,
  the son of man you have
    raised up for yourself.
¹⁸ Then we will not turn away from
    you;
  revive us, and we will call on
    your name.

¹⁹ Restore us, LORD God Almighty;
    make your face shine on us,
    that we may be saved.

---

[a] In Hebrew texts 80:1-19 is numbered 80:2-20.
[b] 6 Probable reading of the original Hebrew
text; Masoretic Text *contention*
[c] 11 Probably the Mediterranean   [d] 11 That is,
the Euphrates   [e] 15 Or *branch*

Psalm 81[a]

For the director of music. According to gittith.[b] Of Asaph.

[1] Sing for joy to God our strength;
    shout aloud to the God of
        Jacob!
[2] Begin the music, strike the
        timbrel,
    play the melodious harp and
        lyre.

[3] Sound the ram's horn at the New
        Moon,
    and when the moon is full, on
        the day of our festival;
[4] this is a decree for Israel,
    an ordinance of the God of
        Jacob.
[5] When God went out against
        Egypt,
    he established it as a statute
        for Joseph.

I heard an unknown voice say:

[6] "I removed the burden from
        their shoulders;
    their hands were set free from
        the basket.
[7] In your distress you called and I
        rescued you,
    I answered you out of a
        thundercloud;
    I tested you at the waters of
        Meribah.[c]
[8] Hear me, my people, and I will
        warn you —
    if you would only listen to me,
        Israel!
[9] You shall have no foreign god
        among you;
    you shall not worship any god
        other than me.
[10] I am the LORD your God,
    who brought you up out of
        Egypt.
    Open wide your mouth and I will
        fill it.

[11] "But my people would not listen
        to me;
    Israel would not submit to me.
[12] So I gave them over to their
        stubborn hearts
    to follow their own devices.

[13] "If my people would only listen
        to me,
    if Israel would only follow my
        ways,
[14] how quickly I would subdue their
        enemies
    and turn my hand against
        their foes!
[15] Those who hate the LORD would
        cringe before him,
    and their punishment would
        last forever.
[16] But you would be fed with the
        finest of wheat;
    with honey from the rock I
        would satisfy you."

Psalm 82

A psalm of Asaph.

[1] God presides in the great
        assembly;
    he renders judgment among
        the "gods":

[2] "How long will you[d] defend the
        unjust
    and show partiality to the
        wicked?[c]
[3] Defend the weak and the
        fatherless;
    uphold the cause of the poor
        and the oppressed.
[4] Rescue the weak and the needy;
    deliver them from the hand of
        the wicked.

---

[a] In Hebrew texts 81:1-16 is numbered 81:2-17.
[b] Title: Probably a musical term   [c] 7 The Hebrew has *Selah* (a word of uncertain meaning) here.   [d] 2 The Hebrew is plural.

5 "The 'gods' know nothing, they
       understand nothing.
   They walk about in darkness;
       all the foundations of the
       earth are shaken.

6 "I said, 'You are "gods";
   you are all sons of the Most
       High.'
7 But you will die like mere
       mortals;
   you will fall like every other
       ruler."

8 Rise up, O God, judge the earth,
   for all the nations are your
       inheritance.

Psalm 83[a]

A song. A psalm of Asaph.

1 O God, do not remain silent;
   do not turn a deaf ear,
   do not stand aloof, O God.
2 See how your enemies growl,
   how your foes rear their
       heads.
3 With cunning they conspire
       against your people;
   they plot against those you
       cherish.
4 "Come," they say, "let us destroy
       them as a nation,
   so that Israel's name is
       remembered no more."

5 With one mind they plot
       together;
   they form an alliance against
       you —
6 the tents of Edom and the
       Ishmaelites,
   of Moab and the Hagrites,
7 Byblos, Ammon and Amalek,
   Philistia, with the people of
       Tyre.
8 Even Assyria has joined them
   to reinforce Lot's descendants.[b]

9 Do to them as you did to Midian,
   as you did to Sisera and Jabin at
       the river Kishon,
10 who perished at Endor
   and became like dung on the
       ground.
11 Make their nobles like Oreb and
       Zeeb,
   all their princes like Zebah and
       Zalmunna,
12 who said, "Let us take possession
   of the pasturelands of God."

13 Make them like tumbleweed, my
       God,
   like chaff before the wind.
14 As fire consumes the forest
   or a flame sets the mountains
       ablaze,
15 so pursue them with your tempest
   and terrify them with your
       storm.
16 Cover their faces with shame,
       Lord,
   so that they will seek your
       name.

17 May they ever be ashamed and
       dismayed;
   may they perish in disgrace.
18 Let them know that you, whose
       name is the Lord —
   that you alone are the Most
       High over all the earth.

Psalm 84[c]

*For the director of music. According to
gittith.[d] Of the Sons of Korah. A psalm.*

1 How lovely is your dwelling place,
   Lord Almighty!
2 My soul yearns, even faints,
   for the courts of the Lord;

---

[a] In Hebrew texts 83:1-18 is numbered 83:2-19.
[b] *8* The Hebrew has *Selah* (a word of uncertain
meaning) here.   [c] In Hebrew texts 84:1-12 is
numbered 84:2-13.   [d] Title: Probably a
musical term

my heart and my flesh cry out
for the living God.
³ Even the sparrow has found a
home,
and the swallow a nest for
herself,
where she may have her
young—
a place near your altar,
LORD Almighty, my King and
my God.
⁴ Blessed are those who dwell in
your house;
they are ever praising you.ᵃ

⁵ Blessed are those whose strength
is in you,
whose hearts are set on
pilgrimage.
⁶ As they pass through the Valley
of Baka,
they make it a place of springs;
the autumn rains also cover it
with pools.ᵇ
⁷ They go from strength to
strength,
till each appears before God in
Zion.

⁸ Hear my prayer, LORD God
Almighty;
listen to me, God of Jacob.
⁹ Look on our shield,ᶜ O God;
look with favor on your
anointed one.

¹⁰ Better is one day in your courts
than a thousand elsewhere;
I would rather be a doorkeeper in
the house of my God
than dwell in the tents of the
wicked.
¹¹ For the LORD God is a sun and
shield;
the LORD bestows favor and
honor;
no good thing does he withhold
from those whose walk is
blameless.

¹² LORD Almighty,
blessed is the one who trusts
in you.

Psalm 85ᵈ

*For the director of music. Of the
Sons of Korah. A psalm.*

¹ You, LORD, showed favor to your
land;
you restored the fortunes of
Jacob.
² You forgave the iniquity of your
people
and covered all their sins.ᵉ
³ You set aside all your wrath
and turned from your fierce
anger.

⁴ Restore us again, God our Savior,
and put away your displeasure
toward us.
⁵ Will you be angry with us forever?
Will you prolong your anger
through all generations?
⁶ Will you not revive us again,
that your people may rejoice
in you?
⁷ Show us your unfailing love,
LORD,
and grant us your salvation.

⁸ I will listen to what God the LORD
says;
he promises peace to his
people, his faithful
servants—
but let them not turn to folly.
⁹ Surely his salvation is near those
who fear him,
that his glory may dwell in our
land.

ᵃ 4 The Hebrew has *Selah* (a word of uncertain
meaning) here and at the end of verse 8.
ᵇ 6 Or *blessings*   ᶜ 9 Or *sovereign*   ᵈ In
Hebrew texts 85:1-13 is numbered 85:2-14.
ᵉ 2 The Hebrew has *Selah* (a word of uncertain
meaning) here.

¹⁰ Love and faithfulness meet
     together;
   righteousness and peace kiss
     each other.
¹¹ Faithfulness springs forth from
     the earth,
   and righteousness looks down
     from heaven.
¹² The LORD will indeed give what
     is good,
   and our land will yield its
     harvest.
¹³ Righteousness goes before
     him
   and prepares the way for his
     steps.

Psalm 86

A prayer of David.

¹ Hear me, LORD, and answer me,
   for I am poor and needy.
² Guard my life, for I am faithful
     to you;
   save your servant who trusts
     in you.
 You are my God; ³have mercy on
     me, Lord,
   for I call to you all day long.
⁴ Bring joy to your servant,
     Lord,
   for I put my trust in you.

⁵ You, Lord, are forgiving and
     good,
   abounding in love to all who
     call to you.
⁶ Hear my prayer, LORD;
   listen to my cry for mercy.
⁷ When I am in distress, I call to
     you,
   because you answer me.

⁸ Among the gods there is none
     like you, Lord;
   no deeds can compare with
     yours.

⁹ All the nations you have
     made
   will come and worship before
     you, Lord;
   they will bring glory to your
     name.
¹⁰ For you are great and do
     marvelous deeds;
   you alone are God.

¹¹ Teach me your way, LORD,
   that I may rely on your
     faithfulness;
 give me an undivided heart,
   that I may fear your name.
¹² I will praise you, Lord my God,
   with all my heart;
   I will glorify your name
     forever.
¹³ For great is your love
     toward me;
   you have delivered me from
     the depths,
   from the realm of the dead.

¹⁴ Arrogant foes are attacking me,
     O God;
   ruthless people are trying to
     kill me —
   they have no regard for
     you.
¹⁵ But you, Lord, are a
     compassionate and
     gracious God,
   slow to anger, abounding in
     love and faithfulness.
¹⁶ Turn to me and have mercy on
     me;
   show your strength in behalf
     of your servant;
 save me, because I serve you
   just as my mother did.
¹⁷ Give me a sign of your
     goodness,
   that my enemies may see it
     and be put to shame,
   for you, LORD, have helped me
     and comforted me.

Psalm 87

Of the Sons of Korah. A psalm. A song.

¹ He has founded his city on the
holy mountain.
² The LORD loves the gates
of Zion
more than all the other
dwellings of Jacob.

³ Glorious things are said of you,
city of God:ᵃ
⁴ "I will record Rahabᵇ and
Babylon
among those who
acknowledge me —
Philistia too, and Tyre, along
with Cushᶜ —
and will say, 'This one was
born in Zion.'"ᵈ
⁵ Indeed, of Zion it will be said,
"This one and that one were
born in her,
and the Most High himself will
establish her."
⁶ The LORD will write in the
register of the peoples:
"This one was born in Zion."
⁷ As they make music they will
sing,
"All my fountains are in you."

Psalm 88ᵉ

*A song. A psalm of the Sons
of Korah. For the director of music.
According to* mahalath leannoth.ᶠ
A maskilᵍ *of Heman the Ezrahite.*

¹ LORD, you are the God who
saves me;
day and night I cry out to you.
² May my prayer come before you;
turn your ear to my cry.

³ I am overwhelmed with troubles
and my life draws near to
death.

⁴ I am counted among those who
go down to the pit;
I am like one without strength.
⁵ I am set apart with the dead,
like the slain who lie in the
grave,
whom you remember no more,
who are cut off from your care.
⁶ You have put me in the lowest
pit,
in the darkest depths.
⁷ Your wrath lies heavily on me;
you have overwhelmed me
with all your waves.ᵇ
⁸ You have taken from me my
closest friends
and have made me repulsive
to them.
I am confined and cannot escape;
⁹   my eyes are dim with grief.

I call to you, LORD, every day;
I spread out my hands to you.
¹⁰ Do you show your wonders to the
dead?
Do their spirits rise up and
praise you?
¹¹ Is your love declared in the
grave,
your faithfulness in
Destructionⁱ?
¹² Are your wonders known in the
place of darkness,
or your righteous deeds in the
land of oblivion?

ᵃ *3* The Hebrew has *Selah* (a word of uncertain
meaning) here and at the end of verse 6.
ᵇ *4* A poetic name for Egypt   ᶜ *4* That is, the
upper Nile region   ᵈ *4* Or *"I will record
concerning those who acknowledge me: / 'This
one was born in Zion.' / Hear this, Rahab and
Babylon, / and you too, Philistia, Tyre and
Cush."*   ᵉ In Hebrew texts 88:1-18 is
numbered 88:2-19.   ᶠ Title: Possibly a tune,
"The Suffering of Affliction"   ᵍ Title:
Probably a literary or musical term   ᵇ *7* The
Hebrew has *Selah* (a word of uncertain
meaning) here and at the end of verse 10.
ⁱ *11* Hebrew *Abaddon*

¹³ But I cry to you for help, LORD;
    in the morning my prayer
        comes before you.
¹⁴ Why, LORD, do you reject me
    and hide your face from me?

¹⁵ From my youth I have suffered
        and been close to death;
    I have borne your terrors and
        am in despair.
¹⁶ Your wrath has swept over me;
    your terrors have destroyed me.
¹⁷ All day long they surround me
        like a flood;
    they have completely
        engulfed me.
¹⁸ You have taken from me friend
        and neighbor —
    darkness is my closest friend.

Psalm 89ᵃ

A maskilᵇ of Ethan the Ezrahite.

¹ I will sing of the LORD's great
        love forever;
    with my mouth I will make
        your faithfulness known
        through all generations.
² I will declare that your love
        stands firm forever,
    that you have established your
        faithfulness in heaven
        itself.
³ You said, "I have made a
        covenant with my chosen
        one,
    I have sworn to David my
        servant,
⁴ 'I will establish your line forever
    and make your throne
        firm through all
        generations.'"ᶜ

⁵ The heavens praise your
        wonders, LORD,
    your faithfulness too, in the
        assembly of the holy ones.

⁶ For who in the skies above can
        compare with the LORD?
    Who is like the LORD among
        the heavenly beings?
⁷ In the council of the holy ones
        God is greatly feared;
    he is more awesome than all
        who surround him.
⁸ Who is like you, LORD God
        Almighty?
    You, LORD, are mighty,
        and your faithfulness
        surrounds you.

⁹ You rule over the surging sea;
    when its waves mount up, you
        still them.
¹⁰ You crushed Rahab like one of
        the slain;
    with your strong arm you
        scattered your enemies.
¹¹ The heavens are yours, and yours
        also the earth;
    you founded the world and all
        that is in it.
¹² You created the north and the
        south;
    Tabor and Hermon sing for joy
        at your name.
¹³ Your arm is endowed with
        power;
    your hand is strong, your right
        hand exalted.

¹⁴ Righteousness and justice are
        the foundation of your
        throne;
    love and faithfulness go before
        you.
¹⁵ Blessed are those who have
        learned to acclaim you,
    who walk in the light of your
        presence, LORD.

ᵃ In Hebrew texts 89:1-52 is numbered 89:2-53.
ᵇ Title: Probably a literary or musical term
ᶜ 4 The Hebrew has *Selah* (a word of uncertain
meaning) here and at the end of verses 37, 45
and 48.

¹⁶ They rejoice in your name all day
long;
they celebrate your
righteousness.
¹⁷ For you are their glory and
strength,
and by your favor you exalt our
horn.[a]
¹⁸ Indeed, our shield[b] belongs to the
LORD,
our king to the Holy One of
Israel.

¹⁹ Once you spoke in a vision,
to your faithful people you said:
"I have bestowed strength on a
warrior;
I have raised up a young man
from among the people.
²⁰ I have found David my servant;
with my sacred oil I have
anointed him.
²¹ My hand will sustain him;
surely my arm will strengthen
him.
²² The enemy will not get the better
of him;
the wicked will not oppress
him.
²³ I will crush his foes before him
and strike down his
adversaries.
²⁴ My faithful love will be with him,
and through my name his
horn[c] will be exalted.
²⁵ I will set his hand over the sea,
his right hand over the rivers.
²⁶ He will call out to me, 'You are my
Father,
my God, the Rock my Savior.'
²⁷ And I will appoint him to be my
firstborn,
the most exalted of the kings of
the earth.
²⁸ I will maintain my love to him
forever,
and my covenant with him will
never fail.

²⁹ I will establish his line forever,
his throne as long as the
heavens endure.

³⁰ "If his sons forsake my law
and do not follow my statutes,
³¹ if they violate my decrees
and fail to keep my commands,
³² I will punish their sin with the
rod,
their iniquity with flogging;
³³ but I will not take my love from
him,
nor will I ever betray my
faithfulness.
³⁴ I will not violate my covenant
or alter what my lips have
uttered.
³⁵ Once for all, I have sworn by my
holiness—
and I will not lie to David—
³⁶ that his line will continue forever
and his throne endure before
me like the sun;
³⁷ it will be established forever like
the moon,
the faithful witness in the sky."

³⁸ But you have rejected, you have
spurned,
you have been very angry with
your anointed one.
³⁹ You have renounced the
covenant with your
servant
and have defiled his crown in
the dust.
⁴⁰ You have broken through all his
walls
and reduced his strongholds to
ruins.
⁴¹ All who pass by have plundered
him;
he has become the scorn of his
neighbors.

---

[a] 17 *Horn* here symbolizes strong one.   [b] 18 Or *sovereign*   [c] 24 *Horn* here symbolizes strength.

⁴² You have exalted the right hand
of his foes;
you have made all his enemies
rejoice.
⁴³ Indeed, you have turned back
the edge of his sword
and have not supported him in
battle.
⁴⁴ You have put an end to his
splendor
and cast his throne to the
ground.
⁴⁵ You have cut short the days of
his youth;
you have covered him with a
mantle of shame.

⁴⁶ How long, LORD? Will you hide
yourself forever?
How long will your wrath burn
like fire?
⁴⁷ Remember how fleeting is my
life.
For what futility you have
created all humanity!
⁴⁸ Who can live and not see
death,
or who can escape the power
of the grave?
⁴⁹ Lord, where is your former great
love,
which in your faithfulness you
swore to David?
⁵⁰ Remember, Lord, how your
servant has[a] been
mocked,
how I bear in my heart the
taunts of all the nations,
⁵¹ the taunts with which your
enemies, LORD, have
mocked,
with which they have mocked
every step of your
anointed one.

⁵² Praise be to the LORD forever!
Amen and Amen.

BOOK IV

Psalms 90 – 106

Psalm 90

A prayer of Moses the man of God.

¹ Lord, you have been our dwelling
place
throughout all generations.
² Before the mountains were born
or you brought forth the whole
world,
from everlasting to everlasting
you are God.

³ You turn people back to dust,
saying, "Return to dust, you
mortals."
⁴ A thousand years in your sight
are like a day that has just
gone by,
or like a watch in the night.
⁵ Yet you sweep people away in the
sleep of death —
they are like the new grass of
the morning:
⁶ In the morning it springs up new,
but by evening it is dry and
withered.

⁷ We are consumed by your anger
and terrified by your
indignation.
⁸ You have set our iniquities
before you,
our secret sins in the light of
your presence.
⁹ All our days pass away under
your wrath;
we finish our years with a
moan.
¹⁰ Our days may come to seventy
years,
or eighty, if our strength
endures;

---

^a 50 Or *your servants have*

yet the best of them are but
  trouble and sorrow,
    for they quickly pass, and we
      fly away.
[11] If only we knew the power of
  your anger!
    Your wrath is as great as the
      fear that is your due.
[12] Teach us to number our days,
  that we may gain a heart of
    wisdom.

[13] Relent, LORD! How long will it be?
  Have compassion on your
    servants.
[14] Satisfy us in the morning with
  your unfailing love,
    that we may sing for joy and
      be glad all our days.
[15] Make us glad for as many days as
  you have afflicted us,
    for as many years as we have
      seen trouble.
[16] May your deeds be shown to your
  servants,
    your splendor to their
      children.

[17] May the favor[a] of the Lord our
  God rest on us;
    establish the work of our
      hands for us —
    yes, establish the work of our
      hands.

Psalm 91

[1] Whoever dwells in the shelter of
  the Most High
    will rest in the shadow of the
      Almighty.[b]
[2] I will say of the LORD, "He is my
  refuge and my fortress,
    my God, in whom I trust."

[3] Surely he will save you
  from the fowler's snare
    and from the deadly
      pestilence.

[4] He will cover you with his
  feathers,
    and under his wings you will
      find refuge;
    his faithfulness will be your
      shield and rampart.
[5] You will not fear the terror of
  night,
    nor the arrow that flies
      by day,
[6] nor the pestilence that stalks in
  the darkness,
    nor the plague that destroys at
      midday.
[7] A thousand may fall at your side,
  ten thousand at your right
    hand,
    but it will not come near you.
[8] You will only observe with your
  eyes
    and see the punishment of the
      wicked.

[9] If you say, "The LORD is my
  refuge,"
    and you make the Most High
      your dwelling,
[10] no harm will overtake you,
  no disaster will come near
    your tent.
[11] For he will command his angels
  concerning you
    to guard you in all your ways;
[12] they will lift you up in their
  hands,
    so that you will not strike your
      foot against a stone.
[13] You will tread on the lion and
  the cobra;
    you will trample the great lion
      and the serpent.

[14] "Because he[c] loves me," says the
  LORD, "I will rescue him;
    I will protect him, for he
      acknowledges my name.

---

[a] 17 Or beauty   [b] 1 Hebrew Shaddai
[c] 14 That is, probably the king

¹⁵ He will call on me, and I will
answer him;
I will be with him in trouble,
I will deliver him and honor
him.
¹⁶ With long life I will satisfy him
and show him my salvation."

Psalm 92ᵃ

A psalm. A song. For the Sabbath day.

¹ It is good to praise the LORD
and make music to your name,
O Most High,
² proclaiming your love in the
morning
and your faithfulness at night,
³ to the music of the ten-stringed
lyre
and the melody of the harp.

⁴ For you make me glad by your
deeds, LORD;
I sing for joy at what your
hands have done.
⁵ How great are your works, LORD,
how profound your thoughts!
⁶ Senseless people do not know,
fools do not understand,
⁷ that though the wicked spring up
like grass
and all evildoers flourish,
they will be destroyed forever.

⁸ But you, LORD, are forever exalted.

⁹ For surely your enemies, LORD,
surely your enemies will
perish;
all evildoers will be scattered.
¹⁰ You have exalted my hornᵇ like
that of a wild ox;
fine oils have been poured on
me.
¹¹ My eyes have seen the defeat of
my adversaries;
my ears have heard the rout of
my wicked foes.

¹² The righteous will flourish like a
palm tree,
they will grow like a cedar of
Lebanon;
¹³ planted in the house of the
LORD,
they will flourish in the courts
of our God.
¹⁴ They will still bear fruit in old
age,
they will stay fresh and green,
¹⁵ proclaiming, "The LORD is
upright;
he is my Rock, and there is no
wickedness in him."

Psalm 93

¹ The LORD reigns, he is robed in
majesty;
the LORD is robed in majesty
and armed with
strength;
indeed, the world is
established, firm and
secure.
² Your throne was established
long ago;
you are from all eternity.

³ The seas have lifted up, LORD,
the seas have lifted up their
voice;
the seas have lifted up their
pounding waves.
⁴ Mightier than the thunder of the
great waters,
mightier than the breakers
of the sea —
the LORD on high is mighty.

⁵ Your statutes, LORD, stand
firm;
holiness adorns your house
for endless days.

ᵃ In Hebrew texts 92:1-15 is numbered 92:2-16.
ᵇ 10 *Horn* here symbolizes strength.

Psalm 94

¹ The LORD is a God who avenges.
  O God who avenges, shine
    forth.
² Rise up, Judge of the earth;
  pay back to the proud what
    they deserve.
³ How long, LORD, will the wicked,
  how long will the wicked be
    jubilant?

⁴ They pour out arrogant words;
  all the evildoers are full of
    boasting.
⁵ They crush your people, LORD;
  they oppress your inheritance.
⁶ They slay the widow and the
    foreigner;
  they murder the fatherless.
⁷ They say, "The LORD does not see;
  the God of Jacob takes no
    notice."

⁸ Take notice, you senseless ones
    among the people;
  you fools, when will you
    become wise?
⁹ Does he who fashioned the ear
    not hear?
  Does he who formed the eye
    not see?
¹⁰ Does he who disciplines nations
    not punish?
  Does he who teaches mankind
    lack knowledge?
¹¹ The LORD knows all human plans;
  he knows that they are futile.

¹² Blessed is the one you discipline,
    LORD,
  the one you teach from your
    law;
¹³ you grant them relief from days
    of trouble,
  till a pit is dug for the wicked.
¹⁴ For the LORD will not reject his
    people;
  he will never forsake his
    inheritance.

¹⁵ Judgment will again be founded
    on righteousness,
  and all the upright in heart will
    follow it.

¹⁶ Who will rise up for me against
    the wicked?
  Who will take a stand for me
    against evildoers?
¹⁷ Unless the LORD had given me
    help,
  I would soon have dwelt in the
    silence of death.
¹⁸ When I said, "My foot is slipping,"
  your unfailing love, LORD,
    supported me.
¹⁹ When anxiety was great within
    me,
  your consolation brought me
    joy.

²⁰ Can a corrupt throne be allied
    with you —
  a throne that brings on misery
    by its decrees?
²¹ The wicked band together against
    the righteous
  and condemn the innocent to
    death.
²² But the LORD has become my
    fortress,
  and my God the rock in whom I
    take refuge.
²³ He will repay them for their sins
  and destroy them for their
    wickedness;
  the LORD our God will destroy
    them.

Psalm 95

¹ Come, let us sing for joy to the
    LORD;
  let us shout aloud to the Rock
    of our salvation.
² Let us come before him with
    thanksgiving
  and extol him with music and
    song.

³ For the LORD is the great God,
  the great King above all gods.
⁴ In his hand are the depths of the
  earth,
    and the mountain peaks belong
      to him.
⁵ The sea is his, for he made it,
  and his hands formed the dry
    land.

⁶ Come, let us bow down in
  worship,
    let us kneel before the LORD our
      Maker;
⁷ for he is our God
  and we are the people of his
    pasture,
      the flock under his care.

Today, if only you would hear his
  voice,
⁸ "Do not harden your hearts as you
  did at Meribah,ᵃ
    as you did that day at Massahᵇ
      in the wilderness,
⁹ where your ancestors tested me;
  they tried me, though they had
    seen what I did.
¹⁰ For forty years I was angry with
  that generation;
    I said, 'They are a people whose
      hearts go astray,
        and they have not known my
          ways.'
¹¹ So I declared on oath in my anger,
  'They shall never enter my
    rest.'"

Psalm 96

¹ Sing to the LORD a new song;
  sing to the LORD, all the earth.
² Sing to the LORD, praise his name;
  proclaim his salvation day after
    day.
³ Declare his glory among the
  nations,
    his marvelous deeds among all
      peoples.

⁴ For great is the LORD and most
  worthy of praise;
    he is to be feared above all
      gods.
⁵ For all the gods of the nations are
  idols,
    but the LORD made the
      heavens.
⁶ Splendor and majesty are before
  him;
    strength and glory are in his
      sanctuary.

⁷ Ascribe to the LORD, all you
  families of nations,
    ascribe to the LORD glory and
      strength.
⁸ Ascribe to the LORD the glory due
  his name;
    bring an offering and come
      into his courts.
⁹ Worship the LORD in the
  splendor of hisᶜ holiness;
    tremble before him, all the
      earth.
¹⁰ Say among the nations, "The
  LORD reigns."
    The world is firmly
      established, it cannot be
        moved;
    he will judge the peoples with
      equity.

¹¹ Let the heavens rejoice, let the
  earth be glad;
    let the sea resound, and all
      that is in it.
¹² Let the fields be jubilant, and
  everything in them;
    let all the trees of the forest
      sing for joy.
¹³ Let all creation rejoice before the
  LORD, for he comes,
    he comes to judge the
      earth.

ᵃ 8 *Meribah* means *quarreling.*   ᵇ 8 *Massah*
means *testing.*   ᶜ 9 Or LORD *with the
splendor of*

He will judge the world in
    righteousness
    and the peoples in his
       faithfulness.

Psalm 97

1 The LORD reigns, let the earth be
    glad;
    let the distant shores rejoice.
2 Clouds and thick darkness
    surround him;
    righteousness and justice are
       the foundation of his
       throne.
3 Fire goes before him
    and consumes his foes on
       every side.
4 His lightning lights up the world;
    the earth sees and trembles.
5 The mountains melt like wax
    before the LORD,
    before the Lord of all the
       earth.
6 The heavens proclaim his
    righteousness,
    and all peoples see his glory.

7 All who worship images are put
    to shame,
    those who boast in idols —
    worship him, all you gods!

8 Zion hears and rejoices
    and the villages of Judah are
       glad
    because of your judgments,
       LORD.
9 For you, LORD, are the Most High
    over all the earth;
    you are exalted far above all
       gods.
10 Let those who love the LORD hate
    evil,
    for he guards the lives of his
       faithful ones
    and delivers them from the
       hand of the wicked.

11 Light shines[a] on the righteous
    and joy on the upright in heart.
12 Rejoice in the LORD, you who are
    righteous,
    and praise his holy name.

Psalm 98

A psalm.

1 Sing to the LORD a new song,
    for he has done marvelous
       things;
    his right hand and his holy arm
    have worked salvation for him.
2 The LORD has made his salvation
    known
    and revealed his righteousness
       to the nations.
3 He has remembered his love
    and his faithfulness to Israel;
    all the ends of the earth have
       seen
    the salvation of our God.

4 Shout for joy to the LORD, all the
    earth,
    burst into jubilant song with
       music;
5 make music to the LORD with the
    harp,
    with the harp and the sound of
       singing,
6 with trumpets and the blast of
    the ram's horn —
    shout for joy before the LORD,
       the King.

7 Let the sea resound, and
    everything in it,
    the world, and all who live
       in it.
8 Let the rivers clap their hands,
    let the mountains sing
       together for joy;

---

[a] *11* One Hebrew manuscript and ancient
versions (see also 112:4); most Hebrew
manuscripts *Light is sown*

9 let them sing before the LORD,
　for he comes to judge the
　　earth.
He will judge the world in
　righteousness
and the peoples with
　equity.

Psalm 99

1 The LORD reigns,
　let the nations tremble;
he sits enthroned between the
　cherubim,
　let the earth shake.
2 Great is the LORD in Zion;
　he is exalted over all the
　　nations.
3 Let them praise your great and
　awesome name —
　he is holy.

4 The King is mighty, he loves
　justice —
　you have established equity;
in Jacob you have done
　what is just and right.
5 Exalt the LORD our God
　and worship at his footstool;
　he is holy.

6 Moses and Aaron were among
　his priests,
　Samuel was among those who
　　called on his name;
they called on the LORD
　and he answered them.
7 He spoke to them from the pillar
　of cloud;
　they kept his statutes and the
　　decrees he gave them.

8 LORD our God,
　you answered them;
you were to Israel a forgiving
　God,
　though you punished their
　　misdeeds.ᵃ

9 Exalt the LORD our God
　and worship at his holy
　　mountain,
　for the LORD our God is holy.

Psalm 100

A psalm. For giving grateful praise.

1 Shout for joy to the LORD, all the
　earth.
2　Worship the LORD with
　gladness;
　come before him with joyful
　　songs.
3 Know that the LORD is God.
　It is he who made us, and we
　　are hisᵇ;
　we are his people, the sheep of
　　his pasture.

4 Enter his gates with thanksgiving
　and his courts with praise;
　give thanks to him and praise
　　his name.
5 For the LORD is good and his love
　endures forever;
　his faithfulness continues
　　through all generations.

Psalm 101

Of David. A psalm.

1 I will sing of your love and
　justice;
　to you, LORD, I will sing praise.
2 I will be careful to lead a
　blameless life —
　when will you come to me?

I will conduct the affairs of my
　house
　with a blameless heart.
3 I will not look with approval
　on anything that is vile.

ᵃ 8 Or God, / a avenger of the wrongs done to
them　ᵇ 3 Or and not we ourselves

I hate what faithless people do;
　I will have no part in it.
[4] The perverse of heart shall be far
　　from me;
　I will have nothing to do with
　　what is evil.

[5] Whoever slanders their neighbor
　　in secret,
　I will put to silence;
whoever has haughty eyes and a
　　proud heart,
　I will not tolerate.

[6] My eyes will be on the faithful in
　　the land,
　that they may dwell with me;
the one whose walk is blameless
　will minister to me.

[7] No one who practices deceit
　will dwell in my house;
no one who speaks falsely
　will stand in my presence.

[8] Every morning I will put to
　　silence
　all the wicked in the land;
I will cut off every evildoer
　from the city of the LORD.

Psalm 102[a]

*A prayer of an afflicted person
who has grown weak and pours
out a lament before the LORD.*

[1] Hear my prayer, LORD;
　let my cry for help come to you.
[2] Do not hide your face from me
　when I am in distress.
Turn your ear to me;
　when I call, answer me quickly.

[3] For my days vanish like smoke;
　my bones burn like glowing
　　embers.
[4] My heart is blighted and withered
　　like grass;
　I forget to eat my food.

[5] In my distress I groan aloud
　and am reduced to skin and
　　bones.
[6] I am like a desert owl,
　like an owl among the
　　ruins.
[7] I lie awake; I have become
　like a bird alone on a roof.
[8] All day long my enemies
　　taunt me;
　those who rail against me use
　　my name as a curse.
[9] For I eat ashes as my food
　and mingle my drink with
　　tears
[10] because of your great wrath,
　for you have taken me up
　　and thrown me aside.
[11] My days are like the evening
　　shadow;
　I wither away like grass.

[12] But you, LORD, sit enthroned
　　forever;
　your renown endures through
　　all generations.
[13] You will arise and have
　　compassion on Zion,
　for it is time to show favor
　　to her;
　the appointed time has
　　come.
[14] For her stones are dear to your
　　servants;
　her very dust moves them to
　　pity.
[15] The nations will fear the name
　　of the LORD,
　all the kings of the earth will
　　revere your glory.
[16] For the LORD will rebuild Zion
　and appear in his glory.
[17] He will respond to the prayer
　　of the destitute;
　he will not despise their
　　plea.

[a] In Hebrew texts 102:1-28 is numbered 102:2-29.

¹⁸ Let this be written for a future generation,
  that a people not yet created may praise the LORD:
¹⁹ "The LORD looked down from his sanctuary on high,
  from heaven he viewed the earth,
²⁰ to hear the groans of the prisoners
  and release those condemned to death."
²¹ So the name of the LORD will be declared in Zion
  and his praise in Jerusalem
²² when the peoples and the kingdoms
  assemble to worship the LORD.

²³ In the course of my life[a] he broke my strength;
  he cut short my days.
²⁴ So I said:
  "Do not take me away, my God, in the midst of my days;
  your years go on through all generations.
²⁵ In the beginning you laid the foundations of the earth,
  and the heavens are the work of your hands.
²⁶ They will perish, but you remain;
  they will all wear out like a garment.
  Like clothing you will change them
  and they will be discarded.
²⁷ But you remain the same,
  and your years will never end.
²⁸ The children of your servants will live in your presence;
  their descendants will be established before you."

Psalm 103

Of David.

¹ Praise the LORD, my soul;
  all my inmost being, praise his holy name.
² Praise the LORD, my soul,
  and forget not all his benefits—
³ who forgives all your sins
  and heals all your diseases,
⁴ who redeems your life from the pit
  and crowns you with love and compassion,
⁵ who satisfies your desires with good things
  so that your youth is renewed like the eagle's.

⁶ The LORD works righteousness
  and justice for all the oppressed.
⁷ He made known his ways to Moses,
  his deeds to the people of Israel:
⁸ The LORD is compassionate and gracious,
  slow to anger, abounding in love.
⁹ He will not always accuse,
  nor will he harbor his anger forever;
¹⁰ he does not treat us as our sins deserve
  or repay us according to our iniquities.
¹¹ For as high as the heavens are above the earth,
  so great is his love for those who fear him;
¹² as far as the east is from the west,
  so far has he removed our transgressions from us.

---

[a] 23 Or *By his power*

¹³ As a father has compassion on
     his children,
  so the LORD has compassion
     on those who fear him;
¹⁴ for he knows how we are formed,
  he remembers that we are
     dust.
¹⁵ The life of mortals is like grass,
  they flourish like a flower of
     the field;
¹⁶ the wind blows over it and it is
     gone,
  and its place remembers it no
     more.
¹⁷ But from everlasting to
     everlasting
  the LORD's love is with those
     who fear him,
  and his righteousness
     with their children's
     children —
¹⁸ with those who keep his
     covenant
  and remember to obey his
     precepts.

¹⁹ The LORD has established his
     throne in heaven,
  and his kingdom rules over all.

²⁰ Praise the LORD, you his angels,
  you mighty ones who do his
     bidding,
  who obey his word.
²¹ Praise the LORD, all his heavenly
     hosts,
  you his servants who do his
     will.
²² Praise the LORD, all his works
  everywhere in his dominion.

  Praise the LORD, my soul.

Psalm 104

¹ Praise the LORD, my soul.

LORD my God, you are very great;
  you are clothed with splendor
     and majesty.

² The LORD wraps himself in light
     as with a garment;
  he stretches out the heavens
     like a tent
³ and lays the beams of his
     upper chambers on their
     waters.

He makes the clouds his
     chariot
  and rides on the wings of the
     wind.
⁴ He makes winds his
     messengers,ᵃ
  flames of fire his servants.

⁵ He set the earth on its
     foundations;
  it can never be moved.
⁶ You covered it with the watery
     depths as with
     a garment;
  the waters stood above the
     mountains.
⁷ But at your rebuke the waters
     fled,
  at the sound of your thunder
     they took to flight;
⁸ they flowed over the
     mountains,
  they went down into the
     valleys,
  to the place you assigned for
     them.
⁹ You set a boundary they cannot
     cross;
  never again will they cover
     the earth.

¹⁰ He makes springs pour water
     into the ravines;
  it flows between the
     mountains.
¹¹ They give water to all the beasts
     of the field;
  the wild donkeys quench their
     thirst.

ᵃ 4 Or *angels*

12 The birds of the sky nest by the
       waters;
    they sing among the branches.
13 He waters the mountains from
       his upper chambers;
    the land is satisfied by the
       fruit of his work.
14 He makes grass grow for the
       cattle,
    and plants for people to
       cultivate—
    bringing forth food from the
       earth:
15 wine that gladdens human
       hearts,
    oil to make their faces shine,
    and bread that sustains their
       hearts.
16 The trees of the LORD are well
       watered,
    the cedars of Lebanon that he
       planted.
17 There the birds make their
       nests;
    the stork has its home in the
       junipers.
18 The high mountains belong to
       the wild goats;
    the crags are a refuge for the
       hyrax.

19 He made the moon to mark the
       seasons,
    and the sun knows when to go
       down.
20 You bring darkness, it becomes
       night,
    and all the beasts of the forest
       prowl.
21 The lions roar for their prey
    and seek their food from God.
22 The sun rises, and they steal
       away;
    they return and lie down in
       their dens.
23 Then people go out to their
       work,
    to their labor until evening.

24 How many are your works,
       LORD!
    In wisdom you made them all;
    the earth is full of your
       creatures.
25 There is the sea, vast and
       spacious,
    teeming with creatures
       beyond number—
    living things both large and
       small.
26 There the ships go to and fro,
    and Leviathan, which you
       formed to frolic there.

27 All creatures look to you
    to give them their food at the
       proper time.
28 When you give it to them,
    they gather it up;
    when you open your hand,
    they are satisfied with good
       things.
29 When you hide your face,
    they are terrified;
    when you take away their
       breath,
    they die and return to the
       dust.
30 When you send your Spirit,
    they are created,
    and you renew the face of the
       ground.

31 May the glory of the LORD endure
       forever;
    may the LORD rejoice in his
       works—
32 he who looks at the earth, and it
       trembles,
    who touches the mountains,
       and they smoke.

33 I will sing to the LORD all my life;
    I will sing praise to my God as
       long as I live.
34 May my meditation be pleasing
       to him,
    as I rejoice in the LORD.

35 But may sinners vanish from the
　　earth
　　　and the wicked be no more.

Praise the LORD, my soul.

Praise the LORD.[a]

Psalm 105

1 Give praise to the LORD, proclaim
　　his name;
　　　make known among the
　　　　nations what he has done.
2 Sing to him, sing praise to him;
　　tell of all his wonderful acts.
3 Glory in his holy name;
　　let the hearts of those who seek
　　　the LORD rejoice.
4 Look to the LORD and his
　　strength;
　　seek his face always.

5 Remember the wonders he has
　　done,
　　his miracles, and the judgments
　　　he pronounced,
6 you his servants, the descendants
　　of Abraham,
　　his chosen ones, the children
　　　of Jacob.
7 He is the LORD our God;
　　his judgments are in all the
　　　earth.

8 He remembers his covenant
　　forever,
　　the promise he made, for a
　　　thousand generations,
9 the covenant he made with
　　Abraham,
　　the oath he swore to Isaac.
10 He confirmed it to Jacob as a
　　decree,
　　to Israel as an everlasting
　　　covenant:
11 "To you I will give the land of
　　Canaan
　　as the portion you will inherit."

12 When they were but few in
　　number,
　　few indeed, and strangers
　　　in it,
13 they wandered from nation to
　　nation,
　　from one kingdom to another.
14 He allowed no one to oppress
　　them;
　　for their sake he rebuked
　　　kings:
15 "Do not touch my anointed
　　ones;
　　do my prophets no harm."

16 He called down famine on the
　　land
　　and destroyed all their
　　　supplies of food;
17 and he sent a man before
　　them —
　　Joseph, sold as a slave.
18 They bruised his feet with
　　shackles,
　　his neck was put in irons,
19 till what he foretold came to
　　pass,
　　till the word of the LORD
　　　proved him true.
20 The king sent and released him,
　　the ruler of peoples set him
　　　free.
21 He made him master of his
　　household,
　　ruler over all he possessed,
22 to instruct his princes as he
　　pleased
　　and teach his elders wisdom.

23 Then Israel entered Egypt;
　　Jacob resided as a foreigner in
　　　the land of Ham.
24 The LORD made his people very
　　fruitful;
　　he made them too numerous
　　　for their foes,

---

[a] 35 Hebrew *Hallelu Yah*; in the Septuagint this
line stands at the beginning of Psalm 105.

25 whose hearts he turned to hate
      his people,
   to conspire against his
      servants.
26 He sent Moses his servant,
   and Aaron, whom he had
      chosen.
27 They performed his signs among
      them,
   his wonders in the land of
      Ham.
28 He sent darkness and made the
      land dark—
   for had they not rebelled
      against his words?
29 He turned their waters into
      blood,
   causing their fish to die.
30 Their land teemed with frogs,
   which went up into the
      bedrooms of their rulers.
31 He spoke, and there came
      swarms of flies,
   and gnats throughout their
      country.
32 He turned their rain into hail,
   with lightning throughout
      their land;
33 he struck down their vines and
      fig trees
   and shattered the trees of their
      country.
34 He spoke, and the locusts came,
   grasshoppers without
      number;
35 they ate up every green thing in
      their land,
   ate up the produce of their
      soil.
36 Then he struck down all the
      firstborn in their land,
   the firstfruits of all their
      manhood.
37 He brought out Israel, laden with
      silver and gold,
   and from among their tribes
      no one faltered.

38 Egypt was glad when they left,
   because dread of Israel had
      fallen on them.
39 He spread out a cloud as a
      covering,
   and a fire to give light at night.
40 They asked, and he brought
      them quail;
   he fed them well with the
      bread of heaven.
41 He opened the rock, and water
      gushed out;
   it flowed like a river in the
      desert.

42 For he remembered his holy
      promise
   given to his servant Abraham.
43 He brought out his people with
      rejoicing,
   his chosen ones with shouts
      of joy;
44 he gave them the lands of the
      nations,
   and they fell heir to what
      others had toiled for—
45 that they might keep his
      precepts
   and observe his laws.

   Praise the Lord.[a]

Psalm 106

1 Praise the Lord.[b]

   Give thanks to the Lord, for he
      is good;
   his love endures forever.

2 Who can proclaim the mighty
      acts of the Lord
   or fully declare his praise?
3 Blessed are those who act
      justly,
   who always do what is right.

---

[a] 45 Hebrew *Hallelu Yah*   [b] 1 Hebrew *Hallelu
Yah*; also in verse 48

4 Remember me, LORD, when
    you show favor to your
    people,
  come to my aid when you save
    them,
5 that I may enjoy the prosperity
    of your chosen ones,
  that I may share in the joy of
    your nation
  and join your inheritance in
    giving praise.

6 We have sinned, even as our
    ancestors did;
  we have done wrong and acted
    wickedly.
7 When our ancestors were in
    Egypt,
  they gave no thought to your
    miracles;
  they did not remember your
    many kindnesses,
  and they rebelled by the sea,
    the Red Sea.^a
8 Yet he saved them for his name's
    sake,
  to make his mighty power
    known.
9 He rebuked the Red Sea, and it
    dried up;
  he led them through the
    depths as through a
    desert.
10 He saved them from the hand
    of the foe;
  from the hand of the enemy
    he redeemed them.
11 The waters covered their
    adversaries;
  not one of them survived.
12 Then they believed his
    promises
  and sang his praise.
13 But they soon forgot what he had
    done
  and did not wait for his plan
    to unfold.

14 In the desert they gave in to their
    craving;
  in the wilderness they put God
    to the test.
15 So he gave them what they asked
    for,
  but sent a wasting disease
    among them.
16 In the camp they grew envious of
    Moses
  and of Aaron, who was
    consecrated to the LORD.
17 The earth opened up and
    swallowed Dathan;
  it buried the company of
    Abiram.
18 Fire blazed among their followers;
  a flame consumed the wicked.
19 At Horeb they made a calf
  and worshiped an idol cast
    from metal.
20 They exchanged their glorious
    God
  for an image of a bull, which
    eats grass.
21 They forgot the God who saved
    them,
  who had done great things in
    Egypt,
22 miracles in the land of Ham
  and awesome deeds by the Red
    Sea.
23 So he said he would destroy
    them—
  had not Moses, his chosen one,
  stood in the breach before him
  to keep his wrath from
    destroying them.
24 Then they despised the pleasant
    land;
  they did not believe his
    promise.
25 They grumbled in their tents
  and did not obey the LORD.

^a 7 Or *the Sea of Reeds*; also in verses 9 and 22

²⁶ So he swore to them with
uplifted hand
that he would make them fall
in the wilderness,
²⁷ make their descendants fall
among the nations
and scatter them throughout
the lands.

²⁸ They yoked themselves to the
Baal of Peor
and ate sacrifices offered to
lifeless gods;
²⁹ they aroused the LORD's anger by
their wicked deeds,
and a plague broke out among
them.
³⁰ But Phinehas stood up and
intervened,
and the plague was checked.
³¹ This was credited to him as
righteousness
for endless generations to
come.

³² By the waters of Meribah they
angered the LORD,
and trouble came to Moses
because of them;
³³ for they rebelled against the
Spirit of God,
and rash words came from
Moses' lips.ᵃ

³⁴ They did not destroy the
peoples
as the LORD had commanded
them,
³⁵ but they mingled with the
nations
and adopted their customs.
³⁶ They worshiped their idols,
which became a snare to them.
³⁷ They sacrificed their sons
and their daughters to false
gods.
³⁸ They shed innocent blood,
the blood of their sons and
daughters,

whom they sacrificed to the idols
of Canaan,
and the land was desecrated
by their blood.
³⁹ They defiled themselves by what
they did;
by their deeds they prostituted
themselves.

⁴⁰ Therefore the LORD was angry
with his people
and abhorred his inheritance.
⁴¹ He gave them into the hands of
the nations,
and their foes ruled over them.
⁴² Their enemies oppressed them
and subjected them to their
power.
⁴³ Many times he delivered them,
but they were bent on
rebellion
and they wasted away in their
sin.
⁴⁴ Yet he took note of their distress
when he heard their cry;
⁴⁵ for their sake he remembered his
covenant
and out of his great love he
relented.
⁴⁶ He caused all who held them
captive
to show them mercy.

⁴⁷ Save us, LORD our God,
and gather us from the
nations,
that we may give thanks to your
holy name
and glory in your praise.

⁴⁸ Praise be to the LORD, the God of
Israel,
from everlasting to
everlasting.

Let all the people say, "Amen!"

Praise the LORD.

ᵃ 33 Or against his spirit, / and rash words
came from his lips

BOOK V

Psalms 107 – 150

Psalm 107

¹ Give thanks to the LORD, for he is
good;
  his love endures forever.

² Let the redeemed of the LORD tell
their story —
  those he redeemed from the
hand of the foe,
³ those he gathered from the
lands,
  from east and west, from north
and south.ᵃ

⁴ Some wandered in desert
wastelands,
  finding no way to a city where
they could settle.
⁵ They were hungry and thirsty,
  and their lives ebbed away.
⁶ Then they cried out to the LORD
in their trouble,
  and he delivered them from
their distress.
⁷ He led them by a straight way
  to a city where they could
settle.
⁸ Let them give thanks to the LORD
for his unfailing love
  and his wonderful deeds for
mankind,
⁹ for he satisfies the thirsty
  and fills the hungry with good
things.

¹⁰ Some sat in darkness, in utter
darkness,
  prisoners suffering in iron
chains,
¹¹ because they rebelled against
God's commands
  and despised the plans of the
Most High.

¹² So he subjected them to bitter
labor;
  they stumbled, and there was
no one to help.
¹³ Then they cried to the LORD in
their trouble,
  and he saved them from their
distress.
¹⁴ He brought them out of
darkness, the utter
darkness,
  and broke away their chains.
¹⁵ Let them give thanks to the LORD
for his unfailing love
  and his wonderful deeds for
mankind,
¹⁶ for he breaks down gates of
bronze
  and cuts through bars of iron.

¹⁷ Some became fools through their
rebellious ways
  and suffered affliction because
of their iniquities.
¹⁸ They loathed all food
  and drew near the gates of
death.
¹⁹ Then they cried to the LORD in
their trouble,
  and he saved them from their
distress.
²⁰ He sent out his word and healed
them;
  he rescued them from the
grave.
²¹ Let them give thanks to the LORD
for his unfailing love
  and his wonderful deeds for
mankind.
²² Let them sacrifice thank offerings
  and tell of his works with
songs of joy.

²³ Some went out on the sea in
ships;
  they were merchants on the
mighty waters.

ᵃ 3 Hebrew north and the sea

24 They saw the works of the LORD,
   his wonderful deeds in the
      deep.
25 For he spoke and stirred up a
      tempest
   that lifted high the waves.
26 They mounted up to the heavens
      and went down to the
         depths;
   in their peril their courage
      melted away.
27 They reeled and staggered like
      drunkards;
   they were at their wits' end.
28 Then they cried out to the LORD
      in their trouble,
   and he brought them out of
      their distress.
29 He stilled the storm to a whisper;
   the waves of the sea[a] were
      hushed.
30 They were glad when it grew
      calm,
   and he guided them to their
      desired haven.
31 Let them give thanks to the LORD
      for his unfailing love
   and his wonderful deeds for
      mankind.
32 Let them exalt him in the
      assembly of the people
   and praise him in the council
      of the elders.

33 He turned rivers into a desert,
   flowing springs into thirsty
      ground,
34 and fruitful land into a salt waste,
   because of the wickedness of
      those who lived there.
35 He turned the desert into pools
      of water
   and the parched ground into
      flowing springs;
36 there he brought the hungry to
      live,
   and they founded a city where
      they could settle.

37 They sowed fields and planted
      vineyards
   that yielded a fruitful harvest;
38 he blessed them, and their
      numbers greatly
         increased,
   and he did not let their herds
      diminish.

39 Then their numbers decreased,
      and they were humbled
   by oppression, calamity and
      sorrow;
40 he who pours contempt on nobles
   made them wander in a
      trackless waste.
41 But he lifted the needy out of
      their affliction
   and increased their families
      like flocks.
42 The upright see and rejoice,
   but all the wicked shut their
      mouths.

43 Let the one who is wise heed
      these things
   and ponder the loving deeds of
      the LORD.

Psalm 108[b]

A song. A psalm of David.

1 My heart, O God, is steadfast;
   I will sing and make music
      with all my soul.
2 Awake, harp and lyre!
   I will awaken the dawn.
3 I will praise you, LORD, among the
      nations;
   I will sing of you among the
      peoples.
4 For great is your love, higher than
      the heavens;
   your faithfulness reaches to
      the skies.

---

[a] 29 Dead Sea Scrolls; Masoretic Text / *their
waves*   [b] In Hebrew texts 108:1-13 is
numbered 108:2-14.

5 Be exalted, O God, above the
heavens;
    let your glory be over all the
    earth.

6 Save us and help us with your
right hand,
    that those you love may be
    delivered.
7 God has spoken from his
sanctuary:
    "In triumph I will parcel out
    Shechem
    and measure off the Valley of
    Sukkoth.
8 Gilead is mine, Manasseh is mine;
    Ephraim is my helmet,
    Judah is my scepter.
9 Moab is my washbasin,
    on Edom I toss my sandal;
    over Philistia I shout in
    triumph."

10 Who will bring me to the fortified
city?
    Who will lead me to Edom?
11 Is it not you, God, you who have
rejected us
    and no longer go out with our
    armies?
12 Give us aid against the enemy,
    for human help is worthless.
13 With God we will gain the victory,
    and he will trample down our
    enemies.

Psalm 109

For the director of music.
Of David. A psalm.

1 My God, whom I praise,
    do not remain silent,
2 for people who are wicked and
deceitful
    have opened their mouths
    against me;
    they have spoken against me
    with lying tongues.

3 With words of hatred they
surround me;
    they attack me without cause.
4 In return for my friendship they
accuse me,
    but I am a man of prayer.
5 They repay me evil for good,
    and hatred for my friendship.

6 Appoint someone evil to oppose
my enemy;
    let an accuser stand at his
    right hand.
7 When he is tried, let him be
found guilty,
    and may his prayers condemn
    him.
8 May his days be few;
    may another take his place of
    leadership.
9 May his children be fatherless
    and his wife a widow.
10 May his children be wandering
beggars;
    may they be driven[e] from their
    ruined homes.
11 May a creditor seize all he
has;
    may strangers plunder the
    fruits of his labor.
12 May no one extend kindness to
him
    or take pity on his fatherless
    children.
13 May his descendants be cut
off,
    their names blotted out from
    the next generation.
14 May the iniquity of his fathers
be remembered before
the LORD;
    may the sin of his mother
    never be blotted out.
15 May their sins always remain
before the LORD,
    that he may blot out their
    name from the earth.

e 10 Septuagint; Hebrew sought

16 For he never thought of doing a
        kindness,
    but hounded to death the poor
        and the needy and the
        brokenhearted.
17 He loved to pronounce a curse —
        may it come back on him.
    He found no pleasure in
        blessing —
    may it be far from him.
18 He wore cursing as his garment;
    it entered into his body like
        water,
    into his bones like oil.
19 May it be like a cloak wrapped
        about him,
    like a belt tied forever around
        him.
20 May this be the LORD's payment
        to my accusers,
    to those who speak evil of me.

21 But you, Sovereign LORD,
    help me for your name's sake;
    out of the goodness of your
        love, deliver me.
22 For I am poor and needy,
    and my heart is wounded
        within me.
23 I fade away like an evening
        shadow;
    I am shaken off like a locust.
24 My knees give way from fasting;
    my body is thin and gaunt.
25 I am an object of scorn to my
        accusers;
    when they see me, they shake
        their heads.

26 Help me, LORD my God;
    save me according to your
        unfailing love.
27 Let them know that it is your
        hand,
    that you, LORD, have done it.
28 While they curse, may you bless;
    may those who attack me be
        put to shame,
    but may your servant rejoice.

29 May my accusers be clothed with
        disgrace
    and wrapped in shame as in a
        cloak.
30 With my mouth I will greatly
        extol the LORD;
    in the great throng of
        worshipers I will praise
        him.
31 For he stands at the right hand of
        the needy,
    to save their lives from those
        who would condemn
        them.

Psalm 110

Of David. A psalm.

1 The LORD says to my lord:[a]

    "Sit at my right hand
    until I make your enemies
        a footstool for your feet."

2 The LORD will extend your mighty
        scepter from Zion, saying,
    "Rule in the midst of your
        enemies!"
3 Your troops will be willing
    on your day of battle.
    Arrayed in holy splendor,
        your young men will come to
            you
        like dew from the morning's
            womb.[b]

4 The LORD has sworn
    and will not change his mind:
    "You are a priest forever,
        in the order of Melchizedek."

5 The Lord is at your right hand[c];
    he will crush kings on the day
        of his wrath.

---

1 Or Lord   3 The meaning of the Hebrew
for this sentence is uncertain.   5 Or My
lord is at your right hand, LORD

⁶ He will judge the nations, heaping
   up the dead
  and crushing the rulers of the
   whole earth.
⁷ He will drink from a brook along
   the way,ᵃ
  and so he will lift his head high.

Psalm 111ᵇ

¹ Praise the LORD.ᶜ

 I will extol the LORD with all my
   heart
  in the council of the upright
   and in the assembly.

² Great are the works of the LORD;
   they are pondered by all who
   delight in them.
³ Glorious and majestic are his
   deeds,
  and his righteousness endures
   forever.
⁴ He has caused his wonders to be
   remembered;
  the LORD is gracious and
   compassionate.
⁵ He provides food for those who
   fear him;
  he remembers his covenant
   forever.
⁶ He has shown his people the
   power of his works,
  giving them the lands of other
   nations.
⁷ The works of his hands are
   faithful and just;
  all his precepts are trustworthy.
⁸ They are established for ever and
   ever,
  enacted in faithfulness and
   uprightness.
⁹ He provided redemption for his
   people;
  he ordained his covenant
   forever—
  holy and awesome is his name.

¹⁰ The fear of the LORD is the
    beginning of wisdom;
   all who follow his precepts
    have good understanding.
   To him belongs eternal
    praise.

Psalm 112ᵇ

¹ Praise the LORD.ᶜ

 Blessed are those who fear the
   LORD,
  who find great delight in his
   commands.

² Their children will be mighty in
   the land;
  the generation of the upright
   will be blessed.
³ Wealth and riches are in their
   houses,
  and their righteousness
   endures forever.
⁴ Even in darkness light dawns
   for the upright,
  for those who are gracious
   and compassionate and
   righteous.
⁵ Good will come to those who
   are generous and lend
   freely,
  who conduct their affairs with
   justice.

⁶ Surely the righteous will never
   be shaken;
  they will be remembered
   forever.
⁷ They will have no fear of bad
   news;
  their hearts are steadfast,
   trusting in the LORD.

ᵃ 7 The meaning of the Hebrew for this clause
is uncertain.   ᵇ This psalm is an acrostic
poem, the lines of which begin with the
successive letters of the Hebrew alphabet.
ᶜ 1 Hebrew *Hallelu Yah*

⁸ Their hearts are secure, they will
    have no fear;
  in the end they will look in
      triumph on their foes.
⁹ They have freely scattered their
    gifts to the poor,
  their righteousness endures
      forever;
  their horn[a] will be lifted high
      in honor.
¹⁰ The wicked will see and be vexed,
    they will gnash their teeth and
      waste away;
  the longings of the wicked will
      come to nothing.

Psalm 113

¹ Praise the LORD.[b]

  Praise the LORD, you his servants;
    praise the name of the LORD.
² Let the name of the LORD be
    praised,
  both now and forevermore.
³ From the rising of the sun to the
    place where it sets,
  the name of the LORD is to be
      praised.

⁴ The LORD is exalted over all the
    nations,
  his glory above the heavens.
⁵ Who is like the LORD our God,
  the One who sits enthroned on
      high,
⁶ who stoops down to look
  on the heavens and the earth?

⁷ He raises the poor from the dust
  and lifts the needy from the
      ash heap;
⁸ he seats them with princes,
  with the princes of his people.
⁹ He settles the childless woman in
    her home
  as a happy mother of children.

  Praise the LORD.

Psalm 114

¹ When Israel came out of Egypt,
  Jacob from a people of foreign
      tongue,
² Judah became God's sanctuary,
  Israel his dominion.

³ The sea looked and fled,
  the Jordan turned back;
⁴ the mountains leaped like rams,
  the hills like lambs.

⁵ Why was it, sea, that you fled?
  Why, Jordan, did you turn
      back?
⁶ Why, mountains, did you leap
    like rams,
  you hills, like lambs?

⁷ Tremble, earth, at the presence
    of the Lord,
  at the presence of the God of
      Jacob,
⁸ who turned the rock into a pool,
  the hard rock into springs of
      water.

Psalm 115

¹ Not to us, LORD, not to us
  but to your name be the glory,
  because of your love and
      faithfulness.

² Why do the nations say,
  "Where is their God?"
³ Our God is in heaven;
  he does whatever pleases him.
⁴ But their idols are silver and
    gold,
  made by human hands.
⁵ They have mouths, but cannot
    speak,
  eyes, but cannot see.
⁶ They have ears, but cannot hear,
  noses, but cannot smell.

ᵃ 9 *Horn* here symbolizes dignity.
ᵇ 1 Hebrew *Hallelu Yah*; also in verse 9

⁷ They have hands, but cannot
  feel,
    feet, but cannot walk,
    nor can they utter a sound
      with their throats.
⁸ Those who make them will be
  like them,
    and so will all who trust in
    them.

⁹ All you Israelites, trust in the
  LORD —
    he is their help and shield.
¹⁰ House of Aaron, trust in the
  LORD —
    he is their help and shield.
¹¹ You who fear him, trust in the
  LORD —
    he is their help and shield.

¹² The LORD remembers us and will
  bless us:
    He will bless his people
    Israel,
    he will bless the house of
    Aaron,
¹³ he will bless those who fear the
  LORD —
    small and great alike.

¹⁴ May the LORD cause you to
  flourish,
    both you and your children.
¹⁵ May you be blessed by the
  LORD,
    the Maker of heaven and
    earth.

¹⁶ The highest heavens belong to
  the LORD,
    but the earth he has given to
    mankind.
¹⁷ It is not the dead who praise the
  LORD,
    those who go down to the
    place of silence;
¹⁸ it is we who extol the LORD,
    both now and forevermore.

Praise the LORD.ᵃ

Psalm 116

¹ I love the LORD, for he heard my
  voice;
    he heard my cry for mercy.
² Because he turned his ear to me,
    I will call on him as long as I
    live.

³ The cords of death entangled me,
    the anguish of the grave came
    over me;
    I was overcome by distress and
    sorrow.
⁴ Then I called on the name of the
  LORD:
    "LORD, save me!"

⁵ The LORD is gracious and
  righteous;
    our God is full of compassion.
⁶ The LORD protects the unwary;
    when I was brought low, he
    saved me.

⁷ Return to your rest, my soul,
    for the LORD has been good to
    you.

⁸ For you, LORD, have delivered me
  from death,
    my eyes from tears,
    my feet from stumbling,
⁹ that I may walk before the LORD
    in the land of the living.

¹⁰ I trusted in the LORD when I said,
    "I am greatly afflicted";
¹¹ in my alarm I said,
    "Everyone is a liar."

¹² What shall I return to the LORD
    for all his goodness to me?
¹³ I will lift up the cup of salvation
    and call on the name of the
    LORD.
¹⁴ I will fulfill my vows to the LORD
    in the presence of all his people.

ᵃ 18 Hebrew *Hallelu Yah*

15 Precious in the sight of the LORD
    is the death of his faithful
       servants.
16 Truly I am your servant, LORD;
    I serve you just as my mother
       did;
    you have freed me from my
       chains.
17 I will sacrifice a thank offering to
       you
    and call on the name of the
       LORD.
18 I will fulfill my vows to the LORD
    in the presence of all his
       people,
19 in the courts of the house of the
       LORD —
    in your midst, Jerusalem.

    Praise the LORD.[a]

Psalm 117

1 Praise the LORD, all you nations;
    extol him, all you peoples.
2 For great is his love toward us,
    and the faithfulness of the
       LORD endures forever.

    Praise the LORD.[a]

Psalm 118

1 Give thanks to the LORD, for he is
       good;
    his love endures forever.

2 Let Israel say:
    "His love endures forever."
3 Let the house of Aaron say:
    "His love endures forever."
4 Let those who fear the LORD say:
    "His love endures forever."

5 When hard pressed, I cried to the
       LORD;
    he brought me into a spacious
       place.

6 The LORD is with me; I will not be
       afraid.
    What can mere mortals do
       to me?
7 The LORD is with me; he is my
       helper.
    I look in triumph on my
       enemies.

8 It is better to take refuge in the
       LORD
    than to trust in humans.
9 It is better to take refuge in the
       LORD
    than to trust in princes.
10 All the nations surrounded me,
    but in the name of the LORD I
       cut them down.
11 They surrounded me on every
       side,
    but in the name of the LORD I
       cut them down.
12 They swarmed around me like
       bees,
    but they were consumed
       as quickly as burning
       thorns;
    in the name of the LORD I cut
       them down.
13 I was pushed back and about to
       fall,
    but the LORD helped me.
14 The LORD is my strength and my
       defense[b];
    he has become my salvation.

15 Shouts of joy and victory
    resound in the tents of the
       righteous:
    "The LORD's right hand has done
       mighty things!
16   The LORD's right hand is lifted
       high;
    the LORD's right hand has done
       mighty things!"
17 I will not die but live,
    and will proclaim what the
       LORD has done.

---

[a] 19 Hebrew *Hallelu Yah*   [b] 14 Or *song*

18 The LORD has chastened me
    severely,
    but he has not given me over
      to death.
19 Open for me the gates of the
      righteous;
    I will enter and give thanks to
      the LORD.
20 This is the gate of the LORD
    through which the righteous
      may enter.
21 I will give you thanks, for you
      answered me;
    you have become my
      salvation.

22 The stone the builders
      rejected
    has become the cornerstone;
23 the LORD has done this,
    and it is marvelous in our
      eyes.
24 The LORD has done it this very
      day;
    let us rejoice today and be
      glad.

25 LORD, save us!
    LORD, grant us success!

26 Blessed is he who comes in the
      name of the LORD.
    From the house of the LORD
    we bless you.ᵃ
27 The LORD is God,
    and he has made his light
      shine on us.
    With boughs in hand, join in the
      festal procession
    upᵇ to the horns of the
      altar.

28 You are my God, and I will praise
      you;
    you are my God, and I will
      exalt you.

29 Give thanks to the LORD, for he
      is good;
    his love endures forever.

Psalm 119ᶜ

א Aleph

1 Blessed are those whose ways are
      blameless,
    who walk according to the law
      of the LORD.
2 Blessed are those who keep his
      statutes
    and seek him with all their
      heart —
3 they do no wrong
    but follow his ways.
4 You have laid down precepts
    that are to be fully obeyed.
5 Oh, that my ways were steadfast
    in obeying your decrees!
6 Then I would not be put to
      shame
    when I consider all your
      commands.
7 I will praise you with an upright
      heart
    as I learn your righteous laws.
8 I will obey your decrees;
    do not utterly forsake me.

ב Beth

9 How can a young person stay on
      the path of purity?
    By living according to your
      word.
10 I seek you with all my heart;
    do not let me stray from your
      commands.
11 I have hidden your word in my
      heart
    that I might not sin against you.
12 Praise be to you, LORD;
    teach me your decrees.

ᵃ 26 The Hebrew is plural.   ᵇ 27 Or Bind the
festal sacrifice with ropes / and take it   ᶜ This
psalm is an acrostic poem, the stanzas of
which begin with successive letters of the
Hebrew alphabet; moreover, the verses of each
stanza begin with the same letter of the
Hebrew alphabet.

13 With my lips I recount
 all the laws that come from
 your mouth.
14 I rejoice in following your statutes
 as one rejoices in great riches.
15 I meditate on your precepts
 and consider your ways.
16 I delight in your decrees;
 I will not neglect your word.

ג Gimel

17 Be good to your servant while I
 live,
 that I may obey your word.
18 Open my eyes that I may see
 wonderful things in your law.
19 I am a stranger on earth;
 do not hide your commands
 from me.
20 My soul is consumed with longing
 for your laws at all times.
21 You rebuke the arrogant, who are
 accursed,
 those who stray from your
 commands.
22 Remove from me their scorn and
 contempt,
 for I keep your statutes.
23 Though rulers sit together and
 slander me,
 your servant will meditate on
 your decrees.
24 Your statutes are my delight;
 they are my counselors.

ד Daleth

25 I am laid low in the dust;
 preserve my life according to
 your word.
26 I gave an account of my ways and
 you answered me;
 teach me your decrees.
27 Cause me to understand the way
 of your precepts,
 that I may meditate on your
 wonderful deeds.

28 My soul is weary with sorrow;
 strengthen me according to
 your word.
29 Keep me from deceitful ways;
 be gracious to me and teach
 me your law.
30 I have chosen the way of
 faithfulness;
 I have set my heart on your
 laws.
31 I hold fast to your statutes, LORD;
 do not let me be put to shame.
32 I run in the path of your
 commands,
 for you have broadened my
 understanding.

ה He

33 Teach me, LORD, the way of your
 decrees,
 that I may follow it to the
 end.[a]
34 Give me understanding, so that I
 may keep your law
 and obey it with all my heart.
35 Direct me in the path of your
 commands,
 for there I find delight.
36 Turn my heart toward your
 statutes
 and not toward selfish gain.
37 Turn my eyes away from
 worthless things;
 preserve my life according to
 your word.[b]
38 Fulfill your promise to your
 servant,
 so that you may be feared.
39 Take away the disgrace I dread,
 for your laws are good.
40 How I long for your precepts!
 In your righteousness
 preserve my life.

---

[a] 33 Or follow it for its reward
[b] 37 Two manuscripts of the Masoretic Text
and Dead Sea Scrolls; most manuscripts of the
Masoretic Text *life in your way*

ו Waw

41 May your unfailing love come to
      me, LORD,
   your salvation, according to
      your promise;
42 then I can answer anyone who
      taunts me,
   for I trust in your word.
43 Never take your word of truth
      from my mouth,
   for I have put my hope in
      your laws.
44 I will always obey your law,
   for ever and ever.
45 I will walk about in freedom,
   for I have sought out your
      precepts.
46 I will speak of your statutes
      before kings
   and will not be put to
      shame,
47 for I delight in your commands
   because I love them.
48 I reach out for your commands,
      which I love,
   that I may meditate on your
      decrees.

ז Zayin

49 Remember your word to your
      servant,
   for you have given me hope.
50 My comfort in my suffering is
      this:
   Your promise preserves my
      life.
51 The arrogant mock me
      unmercifully,
   but I do not turn from your
      law.
52 I remember, LORD, your ancient
      laws,
   and I find comfort in them.
53 Indignation grips me because
      of the wicked,
   who have forsaken your law.

54 Your decrees are the theme of my
      song
   wherever I lodge.
55 In the night, LORD, I remember
      your name,
   that I may keep your law.
56 This has been my practice:
   I obey your precepts.

ח Heth

57 You are my portion, LORD;
   I have promised to obey your
      words.
58 I have sought your face with all
      my heart;
   be gracious to me according to
      your promise.
59 I have considered my ways
   and have turned my steps to
      your statutes.
60 I will hasten and not delay
   to obey your commands.
61 Though the wicked bind me with
      ropes,
   I will not forget your law.
62 At midnight I rise to give you
      thanks
   for your righteous laws.
63 I am a friend to all who fear you,
   to all who follow your precepts.
64 The earth is filled with your love,
      LORD;
   teach me your decrees.

ט Teth

65 Do good to your servant
   according to your word, LORD.
66 Teach me knowledge and good
      judgment,
   for I trust your commands.
67 Before I was afflicted I went
      astray,
   but now I obey your word.
68 You are good, and what you do is
      good;
   teach me your decrees.

⁶⁹ Though the arrogant have
  smeared me with lies,
 I keep your precepts with all
  my heart.
⁷⁰ Their hearts are callous and
  unfeeling,
 but I delight in your law.
⁷¹ It was good for me to be afflicted
 so that I might learn your
  decrees.
⁷² The law from your mouth is more
  precious to me
 than thousands of pieces of
  silver and gold.

י Yodh

⁷³ Your hands made me and
  formed me;
 give me understanding to
  learn your commands.
⁷⁴ May those who fear you rejoice
  when they see me,
 for I have put my hope in your
  word.
⁷⁵ I know, LORD, that your laws are
  righteous,
 and that in faithfulness you
  have afflicted me.
⁷⁶ May your unfailing love be my
  comfort,
 according to your promise to
  your servant.
⁷⁷ Let your compassion come to me
  that I may live,
 for your law is my delight.
⁷⁸ May the arrogant be put to shame
  for wronging me without
  cause;
 but I will meditate on your
  precepts.
⁷⁹ May those who fear you turn
  to me,
 those who understand your
  statutes.
⁸⁰ May I wholeheartedly follow your
  decrees,
 that I may not be put to shame.

כ Kaph

⁸¹ My soul faints with longing for
  your salvation,
 but I have put my hope in your
  word.
⁸² My eyes fail, looking for your
  promise;
 I say, "When will you comfort
  me?"
⁸³ Though I am like a wineskin in
  the smoke,
 I do not forget your decrees.
⁸⁴ How long must your servant wait?
 When will you punish my
  persecutors?
⁸⁵ The arrogant dig pits to trap me,
 contrary to your law.
⁸⁶ All your commands are
  trustworthy;
 help me, for I am being
  persecuted without cause.
⁸⁷ They almost wiped me from the
  earth,
 but I have not forsaken your
  precepts.
⁸⁸ In your unfailing love preserve
  my life,
 that I may obey the statutes of
  your mouth.

ל Lamedh

⁸⁹ Your word, LORD, is eternal;
 it stands firm in the heavens.
⁹⁰ Your faithfulness continues
  through all generations;
 you established the earth, and
  it endures.
⁹¹ Your laws endure to this day,
 for all things serve you.
⁹² If your law had not been my
  delight,
 I would have perished in my
  affliction.
⁹³ I will never forget your precepts,
 for by them you have
  preserved my life.

94 Save me, for I am yours;
    I have sought out your
        precepts.
95 The wicked are waiting to destroy
        me,
    but I will ponder your statutes.
96 To all perfection I see a limit,
    but your commands are
        boundless.

מ Mem

97 Oh, how I love your law!
    I meditate on it all day long.
98 Your commands are always with
        me
    and make me wiser than my
        enemies.
99 I have more insight than all my
        teachers,
    for I meditate on your statutes.
100 I have more understanding than
        the elders,
    for I obey your precepts.
101 I have kept my feet from every
        evil path
    so that I might obey your word.
102 I have not departed from your
        laws,
    for you yourself have taught
        me.
103 How sweet are your words to my
        taste,
    sweeter than honey to my
        mouth!
104 I gain understanding from your
        precepts;
    therefore I hate every wrong
        path.

נ Nun

105 Your word is a lamp for my feet,
    a light on my path.
106 I have taken an oath and
        confirmed it,
    that I will follow your
        righteous laws.

107 I have suffered much;
    preserve my life, LORD,
        according to your word.
108 Accept, LORD, the willing praise
        of my mouth,
    and teach me your laws.
109 Though I constantly take my life
        in my hands,
    I will not forget your law.
110 The wicked have set a snare
        for me,
    but I have not strayed from
        your precepts.
111 Your statutes are my heritage
        forever;
    they are the joy of my heart.
112 My heart is set on keeping your
        decrees
    to the very end.[a]

ס Samekh

113 I hate double-minded people,
    but I love your law.
114 You are my refuge and my
        shield;
    I have put my hope in your
        word.
115 Away from me, you evildoers,
    that I may keep the commands
        of my God!
116 Sustain me, my God, according to
        your promise, and I will
        live;
    do not let my hopes be dashed.
117 Uphold me, and I will be
        delivered;
    I will always have regard for
        your decrees.
118 You reject all who stray from
        your decrees,
    for their delusions come to
        nothing.
119 All the wicked of the earth you
        discard like dross;
    therefore I love your statutes.

_____
a 112 Or decrees / for their enduring reward

120 My flesh trembles in fear of you;
    I stand in awe of your laws.

ע Ayin

121 I have done what is righteous and
    just;
    do not leave me to my
        oppressors.
122 Ensure your servant's well-being;
    do not let the arrogant oppress
        me.
123 My eyes fail, looking for your
        salvation,
    looking for your righteous
        promise.
124 Deal with your servant according
        to your love
    and teach me your decrees.
125 I am your servant; give me
        discernment
    that I may understand your
        statutes.
126 It is time for you to act, LORD;
    your law is being broken.
127 Because I love your commands
    more than gold, more than
        pure gold,
128 and because I consider all your
        precepts right,
    I hate every wrong path.

פ Pe

129 Your statutes are wonderful;
    therefore I obey them.
130 The unfolding of your words
        gives light;
    it gives understanding to the
        simple.
131 I open my mouth and pant,
    longing for your commands.
132 Turn to me and have mercy
        on me,
    as you always do to those who
        love your name.
133 Direct my footsteps according to
        your word;
    let no sin rule over me.

134 Redeem me from human
        oppression,
    that I may obey your precepts.
135 Make your face shine on your
        servant
    and teach me your decrees.
136 Streams of tears flow from my
        eyes,
    for your law is not obeyed.

צ Tsadhe

137 You are righteous, LORD,
    and your laws are right.
138 The statutes you have laid down
        are righteous;
    they are fully trustworthy.
139 My zeal wears me out,
    for my enemies ignore your
        words.
140 Your promises have been
        thoroughly tested,
    and your servant loves
        them.
141 Though I am lowly and
        despised,
    I do not forget your precepts.
142 Your righteousness is everlasting
    and your law is true.
143 Trouble and distress have come
        upon me,
    but your commands give me
        delight.
144 Your statutes are always
        righteous;
    give me understanding that I
        may live.

ק Qoph

145 I call with all my heart; answer
        me, LORD,
    and I will obey your decrees.
146 I call out to you; save me
    and I will keep your statutes.
147 I rise before dawn and cry for
        help;
    I have put my hope in your
        word.

148 My eyes stay open through the
watches of the night,
that I may meditate on your
promises.
149 Hear my voice in accordance with
your love;
preserve my life, LORD,
according to your laws.
150 Those who devise wicked
schemes are near,
but they are far from your law.
151 Yet you are near, LORD,
and all your commands are
true.
152 Long ago I learned from your
statutes
that you established them to
last forever.

ר Resh

153 Look on my suffering and
deliver me,
for I have not forgotten your
law.
154 Defend my cause and redeem me;
preserve my life according to
your promise.
155 Salvation is far from the wicked,
for they do not seek out your
decrees.
156 Your compassion, LORD, is great;
preserve my life according to
your laws.
157 Many are the foes who
persecute me,
but I have not turned from
your statutes.
158 I look on the faithless with
loathing,
for they do not obey your
word.
159 See how I love your precepts;
preserve my life, LORD, in
accordance with your love.
160 All your words are true;
all your righteous laws are
eternal.

ש Sin and Shin

161 Rulers persecute me without
cause,
but my heart trembles at your
word.
162 I rejoice in your promise
like one who finds great spoil.
163 I hate and detest falsehood
but I love your law.
164 Seven times a day I praise you
for your righteous laws.
165 Great peace have those who love
your law,
and nothing can make them
stumble.
166 I wait for your salvation, LORD,
and I follow your commands.
167 I obey your statutes,
for I love them greatly.
168 I obey your precepts and your
statutes,
for all my ways are known to
you.

ת Taw

169 May my cry come before you,
LORD;
give me understanding
according to your word.
170 May my supplication come
before you;
deliver me according to your
promise.
171 May my lips overflow with
praise,
for you teach me your decrees.
172 May my tongue sing of your
word,
for all your commands are
righteous.
173 May your hand be ready to
help me,
for I have chosen your
precepts.
174 I long for your salvation, LORD,
and your law gives me delight.

175 Let me live that I may praise you,
    and may your laws sustain me.
176 I have strayed like a lost sheep.
    Seek your servant,
    for I have not forgotten your
        commands.

Psalm 120

A song of ascents.

1 I call on the LORD in my distress,
    and he answers me.
2 Save me, LORD,
    from lying lips
    and from deceitful tongues.

3 What will he do to you,
    and what more besides,
    you deceitful tongue?
4 He will punish you with a
        warrior's sharp arrows,
    with burning coals of the
        broom bush.

5 Woe to me that I dwell in
        Meshek,
    that I live among the tents of
        Kedar!
6 Too long have I lived
    among those who hate peace.
7 I am for peace;
    but when I speak, they are for
        war.

Psalm 121

A song of ascents.

1 I lift up my eyes to the
        mountains —
    where does my help come
        from?
2 My help comes from the LORD,
    the Maker of heaven and earth.

3 He will not let your foot slip —
    he who watches over you will
        not slumber;

4 indeed, he who watches over
        Israel
    will neither slumber nor
        sleep.

5 The LORD watches over you —
    the LORD is your shade at your
        right hand;
6 the sun will not harm you by day,
    nor the moon by night.

7 The LORD will keep you from all
        harm —
    he will watch over your life;
8 the LORD will watch over your
        coming and going
    both now and forevermore.

Psalm 122

A song of ascents. Of David.

1 I rejoiced with those who said
        to me,
    "Let us go to the house of the
        LORD."
2 Our feet are standing
    in your gates, Jerusalem.

3 Jerusalem is built like a city
    that is closely compacted
        together.
4 That is where the tribes go up —
    the tribes of the LORD —
    to praise the name of the LORD
    according to the statute given
        to Israel.
5 There stand the thrones for
        judgment,
    the thrones of the house
        of David.

6 Pray for the peace of Jerusalem:
    "May those who love you be
        secure.
7 May there be peace within your
        walls
    and security within your
        citadels."

8 For the sake of my family and
friends,
I will say, "Peace be within
you."
9 For the sake of the house of the
LORD our God,
I will seek your prosperity.

Psalm 123

A song of ascents.

1 I lift up my eyes to you,
to you who sit enthroned in
heaven.
2 As the eyes of slaves look to the
hand of their master,
as the eyes of a female slave
look to the hand of her
mistress,
so our eyes look to the LORD
our God,
till he shows us his mercy.

3 Have mercy on us, LORD, have
mercy on us,
for we have endured no end
of contempt.
4 We have endured no end
of ridicule from the
arrogant,
of contempt from the
proud.

Psalm 124

A song of ascents. Of David.

1 If the LORD had not been on our
side —
let Israel say —
2 if the LORD had not been on our
side
when people attacked us,
3 they would have swallowed us
alive
when their anger flared
against us;

4 the flood would have engulfed us,
the torrent would have swept
over us,
5 the raging waters
would have swept us away.

6 Praise be to the LORD,
who has not let us be torn by
their teeth.
7 We have escaped like a bird
from the fowler's snare;
the snare has been broken,
and we have escaped.
8 Our help is in the name of the
LORD,
the Maker of heaven and
earth.

Psalm 125

A song of ascents.

1 Those who trust in the LORD are
like Mount Zion,
which cannot be shaken but
endures forever.
2 As the mountains surround
Jerusalem,
so the LORD surrounds his
people
both now and forevermore.

3 The scepter of the wicked will
not remain
over the land allotted to the
righteous,
for then the righteous might use
their hands to do evil.

4 LORD, do good to those who are
good,
to those who are upright in
heart.
5 But those who turn to crooked
ways
the LORD will banish with the
evildoers.

Peace be on Israel.

Psalm 126

A song of ascents.

¹ When the Lord restored the
    fortunes of[a] Zion,
  we were like those who
    dreamed.[b]
² Our mouths were filled with
    laughter,
  our tongues with songs
    of joy.
  Then it was said among the
    nations,
  "The Lord has done great
    things for them."
³ The Lord has done great things
    for us,
  and we are filled with joy.

⁴ Restore our fortunes,[c] Lord,
  like streams in the Negev.
⁵ Those who sow with tears
  will reap with songs of joy.
⁶ Those who go out weeping,
  carrying seed to sow,
  will return with songs of joy,
  carrying sheaves with them.

Psalm 127

A song of ascents. Of Solomon.

¹ Unless the Lord builds the
    house,
  the builders labor in vain.
  Unless the Lord watches over
    the city,
  the guards stand watch in
    vain.
² In vain you rise early
  and stay up late,
  toiling for food to eat —
  for he grants sleep to[d] those
    he loves.

³ Children are a heritage from the
    Lord,
  offspring a reward from him.

⁴ Like arrows in the hands of a
    warrior
  are children born in one's
    youth.
⁵ Blessed is the man
  whose quiver is full of
    them.
  They will not be put to
    shame
  when they contend with
    their opponents in
    court.

Psalm 128

A song of ascents.

¹ Blessed are all who fear the
    Lord,
  who walk in obedience
    to him.
² You will eat the fruit of your
    labor;
  blessings and prosperity will
    be yours.
³ Your wife will be like a fruitful
    vine
  within your house;
  your children will be like olive
    shoots
  around your table.
⁴ Yes, this will be the blessing
  for the man who fears the
    Lord.

⁵ May the Lord bless you from
    Zion;
  may you see the prosperity
    of Jerusalem
  all the days of your life.
⁶ May you live to see your
    children's children —
  peace be on Israel.

---

[a] 1 Or *Lord brought back the captives to*   [b] 1 Or *those restored to health*   [c] 4 Or *Bring back our captives*   [d] 2 Or *eat* — / *for while they sleep he provides for*

Psalm 129

A song of ascents.

1 "They have greatly oppressed me
    from my youth,"
    let Israel say;
2 "they have greatly oppressed me
    from my youth,
    but they have not gained the
      victory over me.
3 Plowmen have plowed my back
    and made their furrows long.
4 But the LORD is righteous;
    he has cut me free from the
      cords of the wicked."

5 May all who hate Zion
    be turned back in shame.
6 May they be like grass on the
    roof,
    which withers before it can
      grow;
7 a reaper cannot fill his hands
    with it,
    nor one who gathers fill his
      arms.
8 May those who pass by not say to
    them,
    "The blessing of the LORD be
      on you;
    we bless you in the name of
      the LORD."

Psalm 130

A song of ascents.

1 Out of the depths I cry to you,
    LORD;
2   Lord, hear my voice.
    Let your ears be attentive
    to my cry for mercy.

3 If you, LORD, kept a record of sins,
    Lord, who could stand?
4 But with you there is forgiveness,
    so that we can, with reverence,
    serve you.

5 I wait for the LORD, my whole
    being waits,
    and in his word I put my hope.
6 I wait for the Lord
    more than watchmen wait for
      the morning,
    more than watchmen wait for
      the morning.

7 Israel, put your hope in the LORD,
    for with the LORD is unfailing
      love
    and with him is full
      redemption.
8 He himself will redeem Israel
    from all their sins.

Psalm 131

A song of ascents. Of David.

1 My heart is not proud, LORD,
    my eyes are not haughty;
    I do not concern myself with
      great matters
    or things too wonderful for
      me.
2 But I have calmed and quieted
    myself,
    I am like a weaned child with
      its mother;
    like a weaned child I am
      content.

3 Israel, put your hope in the LORD
    both now and forevermore.

Psalm 132

A song of ascents.

1 LORD, remember David
    and all his self-denial.

2 He swore an oath to the LORD,
    he made a vow to the Mighty
      One of Jacob:
3 "I will not enter my house
    or go to my bed,

⁴ I will allow no sleep to my
  eyes
    or slumber to my eyelids,
⁵ till I find a place for the LORD,
    a dwelling for the Mighty One
      of Jacob."

⁶ We heard it in Ephrathah,
    we came upon it in the fields
      of Jaar:ᵃ
⁷ "Let us go to his dwelling
    place,
    let us worship at his footstool,
      saying,
⁸ 'Arise, LORD, and come to your
    resting place,
    you and the ark of your
      might.
⁹ May your priests be clothed with
    your righteousness;
    may your faithful people sing
      for joy.'"

¹⁰ For the sake of your servant
    David,
    do not reject your anointed
      one.
¹¹ The LORD swore an oath to David,
    a sure oath he will not revoke:
    "One of your own descendants
      I will place on your throne.
¹² If your sons keep my covenant
    and the statutes I teach them,
    then their sons will sit
      on your throne for ever and
        ever."

¹³ For the LORD has chosen Zion,
    he has desired it for his
      dwelling, saying,
¹⁴ "This is my resting place for
    ever and ever;
    here I will sit enthroned, for I
      have desired it.
¹⁵ I will bless her with abundant
    provisions;
    her poor I will satisfy with
      food.

¹⁶ I will clothe her priests with
    salvation,
    and her faithful people will
      ever sing for joy.
¹⁷ "Here I will make a hornᵇ grow
    for David
    and set up a lamp for my
      anointed one.
¹⁸ I will clothe his enemies with
    shame,
    but his head will be adorned
      with a radiant crown."

Psalm 133

A song of ascents. Of David.

¹ How good and pleasant it is
    when God's people live
      together in unity!

² It is like precious oil poured on
    the head,
    running down on the
      beard,
    running down on Aaron's
      beard,
    down on the collar of his
      robe.
³ It is as if the dew of Hermon
    were falling on Mount Zion.
    For there the LORD bestows his
      blessing,
    even life forevermore.

Psalm 134

A song of ascents.

¹ Praise the LORD, all you servants
    of the LORD
    who minister by night in the
      house of the LORD.

ᵃ 6 Or *heard of it in Ephrathah, / we found it in
the fields of Jearim.* (See 1 Chron. 13:5,6) (And
no quotation marks around verses 7-9)
ᵇ 17 *Horn* here symbolizes strong one, that is,
king.

² Lift up your hands in the
     sanctuary
   and praise the LORD.

³ May the LORD bless you from
     Zion,
   he who is the Maker of heaven
     and earth.

Psalm 135

¹ Praise the LORD.ᵃ

Praise the name of the LORD;
   praise him, you servants of the
     LORD,
² you who minister in the house of
     the LORD,
   in the courts of the house of
     our God.

³ Praise the LORD, for the LORD is
     good;
   sing praise to his name, for
     that is pleasant.
⁴ For the LORD has chosen Jacob
     to be his own,
   Israel to be his treasured
     possession.

⁵ I know that the LORD is great,
   that our Lord is greater than
     all gods.
⁶ The LORD does whatever pleases
     him,
   in the heavens and on the
     earth,
   in the seas and all their depths.
⁷ He makes clouds rise from the
     ends of the earth;
   he sends lightning with the
     rain
   and brings out the wind from
     his storehouses.

⁸ He struck down the firstborn of
     Egypt,
   the firstborn of people and
     animals.

⁹ He sent his signs and wonders
     into your midst, Egypt,
   against Pharaoh and all his
     servants.
¹⁰ He struck down many nations
   and killed mighty kings —
¹¹ Sihon king of the Amorites,
   Og king of Bashan,
   and all the kings of
     Canaan —
¹² and he gave their land as an
     inheritance,
   an inheritance to his people
     Israel.

¹³ Your name, LORD, endures
     forever,
   your renown, LORD, through
     all generations.
¹⁴ For the LORD will vindicate his
     people
   and have compassion on his
     servants.

¹⁵ The idols of the nations are
     silver and gold,
   made by human hands.
¹⁶ They have mouths, but cannot
     speak,
   eyes, but cannot see.
¹⁷ They have ears, but cannot
     hear,
   nor is there breath in their
     mouths.
¹⁸ Those who make them will be
     like them,
   and so will all who trust in
     them.

¹⁹ All you Israelites, praise the
     LORD;
   house of Aaron, praise the
     LORD;
²⁰ house of Levi, praise the
     LORD;
   you who fear him, praise the
     LORD.

ᵃ 1 Hebrew *Hallelu Yah*; also in verses 3 and 21

²¹ Praise be to the Lord from Zion,
to him who dwells in
Jerusalem.

Praise the Lord.

Psalm 136

¹ Give thanks to the Lord, for he is
good.
His love endures forever.
² Give thanks to the God of gods.
His love endures forever.
³ Give thanks to the Lord of lords:
His love endures forever.

⁴ to him who alone does great
wonders,
His love endures forever.
⁵ who by his understanding made
the heavens,
His love endures forever.
⁶ who spread out the earth upon
the waters,
His love endures forever.
⁷ who made the great lights —
His love endures forever.
⁸ the sun to govern the day,
His love endures forever.
⁹ the moon and stars to govern the
night;
His love endures forever.

¹⁰ to him who struck down the
firstborn of Egypt
His love endures forever.
¹¹ and brought Israel out from
among them
His love endures forever.
¹² with a mighty hand and
outstretched arm;
His love endures forever.

¹³ to him who divided the Red Sea*
asunder
His love endures forever.
¹⁴ and brought Israel through the
midst of it,
His love endures forever.

¹⁵ but swept Pharaoh and his army
into the Red Sea;
His love endures forever.
¹⁶ to him who led his people
through the wilderness;
His love endures forever.
¹⁷ to him who struck down great
kings,
His love endures forever.
¹⁸ and killed mighty kings —
His love endures forever.
¹⁹ Sihon king of the Amorites
His love endures forever.
²⁰ and Og king of Bashan —
His love endures forever.
²¹ and gave their land as an
inheritance,
His love endures forever.
²² an inheritance to his servant
Israel.
His love endures forever.

²³ He remembered us in our low
estate
His love endures forever.
²⁴ and freed us from our enemies.
His love endures forever.
²⁵ He gives food to every creature.
His love endures forever.

²⁶ Give thanks to the God of heaven.
His love endures forever.

Psalm 137

¹ By the rivers of Babylon we sat
and wept
when we remembered Zion.
² There on the poplars
we hung our harps,
³ for there our captors asked us for
songs,
our tormentors demanded
songs of joy;
they said, "Sing us one of the
songs of Zion!"

a 13 Or the Sea of Reeds; also in verse 15

⁴ How can we sing the songs of
the LORD
while in a foreign land?
⁵ If I forget you, Jerusalem,
may my right hand forget its
skill.
⁶ May my tongue cling to the roof
of my mouth
if I do not remember you,
if I do not consider Jerusalem
my highest joy.
⁷ Remember, LORD, what the
Edomites did
on the day Jerusalem fell.
"Tear it down," they cried,
"tear it down to its
foundations!"
⁸ Daughter Babylon, doomed to
destruction,
happy is the one who repays
you
according to what you have
done to us.
⁹ Happy is the one who seizes your
infants
and dashes them against the
rocks.

Psalm 138

Of David.

¹ I will praise you, LORD, with all
my heart;
before the "gods" I will sing
your praise.
² I will bow down toward your
holy temple
and will praise your name
for your unfailing love and
your faithfulness,
for you have so exalted your
solemn decree
that it surpasses your fame.
³ When I called, you answered
me;
you greatly emboldened me.

⁴ May all the kings of the earth
praise you, LORD,
when they hear what you have
decreed.
⁵ May they sing of the ways of the
LORD,
for the glory of the LORD is
great.
⁶ Though the LORD is exalted, he
looks kindly on the lowly;
though lofty, he sees them
from afar.
⁷ Though I walk in the midst of
trouble,
you preserve my life.
You stretch out your hand
against the anger of my
foes;
with your right hand you save
me.
⁸ The LORD will vindicate me;
your love, LORD, endures
forever—
do not abandon the works of
your hands.

Psalm 139

For the director of music.
Of David. A psalm.

¹ You have searched me, LORD,
and you know me.
² You know when I sit and when I
rise;
you perceive my thoughts
from afar.
³ You discern my going out and
my lying down;
you are familiar with all my
ways.
⁴ Before a word is on my tongue
you, LORD, know it completely.
⁵ You hem me in behind and
before,
and you lay your hand upon
me.

⁶ Such knowledge is too wonderful
    for me,
  too lofty for me to attain.

⁷ Where can I go from your Spirit?
  Where can I flee from your
    presence?
⁸ If I go up to the heavens, you are
    there;
  if I make my bed in the
    depths, you are there.
⁹ If I rise on the wings of the dawn,
  if I settle on the far side of the
    sea,
¹⁰ even there your hand will guide
    me,
  your right hand will hold me
    fast.
¹¹ If I say, "Surely the darkness will
    hide me
  and the light become night
    around me,"
¹² even the darkness will not be
    dark to you;
  the night will shine like the
    day,
  for darkness is as light to you.

¹³ For you created my inmost
    being;
  you knit me together in my
    mother's womb.
¹⁴ I praise you because I am
    fearfully and wonderfully
    made;
  your works are wonderful,
  I know that full well.
¹⁵ My frame was not hidden from
    you
  when I was made in the secret
    place,
  when I was woven together in
    the depths of the earth.
¹⁶ Your eyes saw my unformed
    body;
  all the days ordained for me
    were written in your book
  before one of them came to be.

¹⁷ How precious to me are your
    thoughts,ᵃ God!
  How vast is the sum of
    them!
¹⁸ Were I to count them,
  they would outnumber the
    grains of sand —
  when I awake, I am still with
    you.

¹⁹ If only you, God, would slay the
    wicked!
  Away from me, you who are
    bloodthirsty!
²⁰ They speak of you with evil
    intent;
  your adversaries misuse your
    name.
²¹ Do I not hate those who hate you,
    LORD,
  and abhor those who are in
    rebellion against you?
²² I have nothing but hatred for
    them;
  I count them my enemies.
²³ Search me, God, and know my
    heart;
  test me and know my anxious
    thoughts.
²⁴ See if there is any offensive way
    in me,
  and lead me in the way
    everlasting.

Psalm 140ᵇ

For the director of music.
A psalm of David.

¹ Rescue me, LORD, from
    evildoers;
  protect me from the violent,
² who devise evil plans in their
    hearts
  and stir up war every day.

ᵃ 17 Or *How amazing are your thoughts
concerning me*   ᵇ In Hebrew texts 140:1-13 is
numbered 140:2-14.

3 They make their tongues as
      sharp as a serpent's;
   the poison of vipers is on their
      lips.ᵃ

4 Keep me safe, LORD, from the
      hands of the wicked;
   protect me from the violent,
      who devise ways to trip my
      feet.
5 The arrogant have hidden a
      snare for me;
   they have spread out the cords
      of their net
   and have set traps for me
      along my path.

6 I say to the LORD, "You are my
      God."
   Hear, LORD, my cry for mercy.
7 Sovereign LORD, my strong
      deliverer,
   you shield my head in the day
      of battle.
8 Do not grant the wicked their
      desires, LORD;
   do not let their plans succeed.

9 Those who surround me proudly
      rear their heads;
   may the mischief of their lips
      engulf them.
10 May burning coals fall on them;
      may they be thrown into the
      fire,
   into miry pits, never to rise.
11 May slanderers not be
      established in the land;
   may disaster hunt down the
      violent.

12 I know that the LORD secures
      justice for the poor
   and upholds the cause of the
      needy.
13 Surely the righteous will praise
      your name,
   and the upright will live in
      your presence.

Psalm 141

A psalm of David.

1 I call to you, LORD, come quickly
      to me;
   hear me when I call to you.
2 May my prayer be set before you
      like incense;
   may the lifting up of my
      hands be like the evening
      sacrifice.

3 Set a guard over my mouth,
      LORD;
   keep watch over the door of
      my lips.
4 Do not let my heart be drawn to
      what is evil
   so that I take part in wicked
      deeds
   along with those who are
      evildoers;
   do not let me eat their
      delicacies.

5 Let a righteous man strike me —
      that is a kindness;
   let him rebuke me — that is oil
      on my head.
   My head will not refuse it,
      for my prayer will still be
      against the deeds of
      evildoers.

6 Their rulers will be thrown down
      from the cliffs,
   and the wicked will learn
      that my words were well
      spoken.
7 They will say, "As one plows
      and breaks up the
      earth,
   so our bones have been
      scattered at the mouth
      of the grave."

ᵃ 3 The Hebrew has *Selah* (a word of uncertain
meaning) here and at the end of verses 5
and 8.

8 But my eyes are fixed on you,
        Sovereign LORD;
    in you I take refuge — do not
        give me over to death.
9 Keep me safe from the traps set
        by evildoers,
    from the snares they have laid
        for me.
10 Let the wicked fall into their own
        nets,
    while I pass by in safety.

Psalm 142[a]

*A maskil[b] of David. When he
was in the cave. A prayer.*

1 I cry aloud to the LORD;
    I lift up my voice to the LORD
        for mercy.
2 I pour out before him my
        complaint;
    before him I tell my trouble.

3 When my spirit grows faint
        within me,
    it is you who watch over my
        way.
    In the path where I walk
        people have hidden a snare for
        me.
4 Look and see, there is no one at
        my right hand;
    no one is concerned for me.
    I have no refuge;
        no one cares for my life.

5 I cry to you, LORD;
    I say, "You are my refuge,
        my portion in the land of the
        living."

6 Listen to my cry,
    for I am in desperate need;
    rescue me from those who
        pursue me,
    for they are too strong for me.
7 Set me free from my prison,
    that I may praise your name.

Then the righteous will gather
        about me
    because of your goodness to
        me.

Psalm 143

A psalm of David.

1 LORD, hear my prayer,
    listen to my cry for mercy;
    in your faithfulness and
        righteousness
    come to my relief.
2 Do not bring your servant into
        judgment,
    for no one living is righteous
        before you.

3 The enemy pursues me,
    he crushes me to the ground;
    he makes me dwell in the
        darkness
    like those long dead.
4 So my spirit grows faint within
        me;
    my heart within me is
        dismayed.

5 I remember the days of long
        ago;
    I meditate on all your works
    and consider what your hands
        have done.
6 I spread out my hands to you;
    I thirst for you like a parched
        land.[c]

7 Answer me quickly, LORD;
    my spirit fails.
    Do not hide your face from me
    or I will be like those who go
        down to the pit.
8 Let the morning bring me word
    of your unfailing love,
    for I have put my trust in you.

---

[a] In Hebrew texts 142:1-7 is numbered 142:2-8.
[b] Title: Probably a literary or musical term
[c] 6 The Hebrew has *Selah* (a word of uncertain
meaning) here.

Show me the way I should go,
    for to you I entrust my life.
9 Rescue me from my enemies,
        LORD,
    for I hide myself in you.
10 Teach me to do your will,
    for you are my God;
may your good Spirit
    lead me on level ground.

11 For your name's sake, LORD,
        preserve my life;
in your righteousness, bring
        me out of trouble.
12 In your unfailing love, silence my
        enemies;
    destroy all my foes,
    for I am your servant.

Psalm 144

Of David.

1 Praise be to the LORD my Rock,
    who trains my hands for war,
    my fingers for battle.
2 He is my loving God and my
        fortress,
    my stronghold and my
        deliverer,
    my shield, in whom I take refuge,
    who subdues peoples^a under
        me.

3 LORD, what are human beings
        that you care for them,
    mere mortals that you think of
        them?
4 They are like a breath;
    their days are like a fleeting
        shadow.

5 Part your heavens, LORD, and
        come down;
    touch the mountains, so that
        they smoke.
6 Send forth lightning and scatter
        the enemy;
    shoot your arrows and rout
        them.

7 Reach down your hand from on
        high;
    deliver me and rescue me
    from the mighty waters,
    from the hands of foreigners
8 whose mouths are full of lies,
    whose right hands are
        deceitful.

9 I will sing a new song to you, my
        God;
    on the ten-stringed lyre I will
        make music to you,
10 to the One who gives victory to
        kings,
    who delivers his servant
        David.

From the deadly sword ¹¹deliver
        me;
    rescue me from the hands of
        foreigners
whose mouths are full of lies,
    whose right hands are
        deceitful.

12 Then our sons in their youth
    will be like well-nurtured
        plants,
and our daughters will be like
        pillars
    carved to adorn a palace.
13 Our barns will be filled
    with every kind of provision.
Our sheep will increase by
        thousands,
    by tens of thousands in our
        fields;
14   our oxen will draw heavy
        loads.^b
There will be no breaching of
        walls,
    no going into captivity,
    no cry of distress in our streets.

---

^a 2 Many manuscripts of the Masoretic Text,
Dead Sea Scrolls, Aquila, Jerome and Syriac;
most manuscripts of the Masoretic Text
subdues my people   ^b 14 Or *our chieftains
will be firmly established*

¹⁵ Blessed is the people of whom
        this is true;
    blessed is the people whose
        God is the LORD.

Psalm 145[a]

A psalm of praise. Of David.

¹ I will exalt you, my God the King;
    I will praise your name for
        ever and ever.
² Every day I will praise you
    and extol your name for ever
        and ever.

³ Great is the LORD and most
        worthy of praise;
    his greatness no one can
        fathom.
⁴ One generation commends your
        works to another;
    they tell of your mighty acts.
⁵ They speak of the glorious
        splendor of your
        majesty—
    and I will meditate on your
        wonderful works.[b]
⁶ They tell of the power of your
        awesome works—
    and I will proclaim your great
        deeds.
⁷ They celebrate your abundant
        goodness
    and joyfully sing of your
        righteousness.

⁸ The LORD is gracious and
        compassionate,
    slow to anger and rich in love.

⁹ The LORD is good to all;
    he has compassion on all he
        has made.

¹⁰ All your works praise you, LORD;
    your faithful people extol you.
¹¹ They tell of the glory of your
        kingdom
    and speak of your might,

¹² so that all people may know
        of your mighty acts
    and the glorious splendor
        of your kingdom.
¹³ Your kingdom is an everlasting
        kingdom,
    and your dominion
        endures through all
        generations.

The LORD is trustworthy in all
        he promises
    and faithful in all he does.[c]
¹⁴ The LORD upholds all who fall
    and lifts up all who are bowed
        down.
¹⁵ The eyes of all look to you,
    and you give them their food
        at the proper time.
¹⁶ You open your hand
    and satisfy the desires of every
        living thing.

¹⁷ The LORD is righteous in all his
        ways
    and faithful in all he does.
¹⁸ The LORD is near to all who call
        on him,
    to all who call on him in
        truth.
¹⁹ He fulfills the desires of those
        who fear him;
    he hears their cry and saves
        them.
²⁰ The LORD watches over all who
        love him,
    but all the wicked he will
        destroy.

---

[a] This psalm is an acrostic poem, the verses of
which (including verse 13b) begin with the
successive letters of the Hebrew alphabet.
[b] 5 Dead Sea Scrolls and Syriac (see also
Septuagint); Masoretic Text *On the glorious
splendor of your majesty / and on your
wonderful works I will meditate*
[c] 13 One manuscript of the Masoretic Text,
Dead Sea Scrolls and Syriac (see also
Septuagint); most manuscripts of the
Masoretic Text do not have the last two lines
of verse 13.

²¹ My mouth will speak in praise of
the LORD.
Let every creature praise his
holy name
for ever and ever.

Psalm 146

¹ Praise the LORD.ᵃ

Praise the LORD, my soul.

² I will praise the LORD all my
life;
I will sing praise to my God as
long as I live.
³ Do not put your trust in princes,
in human beings, who cannot
save.
⁴ When their spirit departs, they
return to the ground;
on that very day their plans
come to nothing.
⁵ Blessed are those whose help is
the God of Jacob,
whose hope is in the LORD
their God.
⁶ He is the Maker of heaven and
earth,
the sea, and everything in
them—
he remains faithful forever.
⁷ He upholds the cause of the
oppressed
and gives food to the hungry.
The LORD sets prisoners free,
⁸   the LORD gives sight to the
blind,
the LORD lifts up those who are
bowed down,
the LORD loves the righteous.
⁹ The LORD watches over the
foreigner
and sustains the fatherless and
the widow,
but he frustrates the ways of
the wicked.

¹⁰ The LORD reigns forever,
your God, O Zion, for all
generations.

Praise the LORD.

Psalm 147

¹ Praise the LORD.ᵇ

How good it is to sing praises to
our God,
how pleasant and fitting to
praise him!

² The LORD builds up Jerusalem;
he gathers the exiles of Israel.
³ He heals the brokenhearted
and binds up their wounds.
⁴ He determines the number of
the stars
and calls them each by name.
⁵ Great is our Lord and mighty in
power;
his understanding has no
limit.
⁶ The LORD sustains the humble
but casts the wicked to the
ground.
⁷ Sing to the LORD with grateful
praise;
make music to our God on the
harp.
⁸ He covers the sky with clouds;
he supplies the earth with rain
and makes grass grow on the
hills.
⁹ He provides food for the cattle
and for the young ravens when
they call.
¹⁰ His pleasure is not in the
strength of the horse,
nor his delight in the legs of
the warrior;

ᵃ 1 Hebrew *Hallelu Yah*; also in verse 10
ᵇ 1 Hebrew *Hallelu Yah*; also in verse 20

[11] the LORD delights in those who
   fear him,
      who put their hope in his
         unfailing love.

[12] Extol the LORD, Jerusalem;
   praise your God, Zion.

[13] He strengthens the bars of your
   gates
      and blesses your people within
         you.

[14] He grants peace to your borders
   and satisfies you with the finest
      of wheat.

[15] He sends his command to the
   earth;
      his word runs swiftly.

[16] He spreads the snow like wool
   and scatters the frost like
      ashes.

[17] He hurls down his hail like
   pebbles.
      Who can withstand his icy blast?

[18] He sends his word and melts
   them;
      he stirs up his breezes, and the
         waters flow.

[19] He has revealed his word
   to Jacob,
      his laws and decrees to Israel.

[20] He has done this for no other
   nation;
      they do not know his laws.[a]

   Praise the LORD.

Psalm 148

[1] Praise the LORD.[b]

   Praise the LORD from the heavens;
      praise him in the heights above.

[2] Praise him, all his angels;
   praise him, all his heavenly
      hosts.

[3] Praise him, sun and moon;
   praise him, all you shining
      stars.

[4] Praise him, you highest heavens
   and you waters above the
      skies.

[5] Let them praise the name of the
   LORD,
      for at his command they were
         created,

[6] and he established them for ever
   and ever —
      he issued a decree that will
         never pass away.

[7] Praise the LORD from the earth,
   you great sea creatures and all
      ocean depths,

[8] lightning and hail, snow and
   clouds,
      stormy winds that do his
         bidding,

[9] you mountains and all hills,
   fruit trees and all cedars,

[10] wild animals and all cattle,
   small creatures and flying
      birds,

[11] kings of the earth and all
   nations,
      you princes and all rulers on
         earth,

[12] young men and women,
   old men and children.

[13] Let them praise the name of the
   LORD,
      for his name alone is exalted;
         his splendor is above the earth
            and the heavens.

[14] And he has raised up for his
   people a horn,[c]
      the praise of all his faithful
         servants,
      of Israel, the people close to
         his heart.

   Praise the LORD.

---

[a] 20 Masoretic Text; Dead Sea Scrolls and
Septuagint *nation; / he has not made his laws
known to them*   [b] 1 Hebrew *Hallelu Yah*; also
in verse 14   [c] 14 *Horn* here symbolizes
strength.

Psalm 149

[1] Praise the LORD.[a]

Sing to the LORD a new song,
    his praise in the assembly
      of his faithful people.

[2] Let Israel rejoice in their
    Maker;
    let the people of Zion be glad
      in their King.
[3] Let them praise his name with
    dancing
    and make music to him with
      timbrel and harp.
[4] For the LORD takes delight in his
    people;
    he crowns the humble with
      victory.
[5] Let his faithful people rejoice in
    this honor
    and sing for joy on their
      beds.

[6] May the praise of God be in their
    mouths
    and a double-edged sword in
      their hands,
[7] to inflict vengeance on the
    nations
    and punishment on the
      peoples,
[8] to bind their kings with
    fetters,
    their nobles with shackles
      of iron,
[9] to carry out the sentence written
    against them—
    this is the glory of all his
      faithful people.

Praise the LORD.

Psalm 150

[1] Praise the LORD.[b]

Praise God in his sanctuary;
    praise him in his mighty
      heavens.
[2] Praise him for his acts of power;
    praise him for his surpassing
      greatness.
[3] Praise him with the sounding of
    the trumpet,
    praise him with the harp and
      lyre,
[4] praise him with timbrel and
    dancing,
    praise him with the strings
      and pipe,
[5] praise him with the clash of
    cymbals,
    praise him with resounding
      cymbals.

[6] Let everything that has breath
    praise the LORD.

Praise the LORD.

---

[a] 1 Hebrew *Hallelu Yah*; also in verse 9
[b] 1 Hebrew *Hallelu Yah*; also in verse 6

Proverbs

Purpose and Theme

1 The proverbs of Solomon son of David, king of Israel:

2 for gaining wisdom and instruction;
  for understanding words of insight;
3 for receiving instruction in prudent behavior,
  doing what is right and just and fair;
4 for giving prudence to those who are simple,[a]
  knowledge and discretion to the young —
5 let the wise listen and add to their learning,
  and let the discerning get guidance —
6 for understanding proverbs and parables,
  the sayings and riddles of the wise.[b]
7 The fear of the LORD is the beginning of knowledge,
  but fools[c] despise wisdom and instruction.

Prologue: Exhortations to Embrace Wisdom

Warning Against the Invitation of Sinful Men

8 Listen, my son, to your father's instruction
  and do not forsake your mother's teaching.
9 They are a garland to grace your head
  and a chain to adorn your neck.
10 My son, if sinful men entice you,
  do not give in to them.
11 If they say, "Come along with us;
  let's lie in wait for innocent blood,
  let's ambush some harmless soul;
12 let's swallow them alive, like the grave,
  and whole, like those who go down to the pit;
13 we will get all sorts of valuable things
  and fill our houses with plunder;
14 cast lots with us;
  we will all share the loot" —
15 my son, do not go along with them,
  do not set foot on their paths;
16 for their feet rush into evil,
  they are swift to shed blood.
17 How useless to spread a net
  where every bird can see it!
18 These men lie in wait for their own blood;
  they ambush only themselves!

---

[a] 4 The Hebrew word rendered *simple* in Proverbs denotes a person who is gullible, without moral direction and inclined to evil.
[b] 6 Or *understanding a proverb, namely, a parable, / and the sayings of the wise, their riddles*   [c] 7 The Hebrew words rendered *fool* in Proverbs, and often elsewhere in the Old Testament, denote a person who is morally deficient.

19 Such are the paths of all who go
        after ill-gotten gain;
    it takes away the life of those
        who get it.

Wisdom's Rebuke

20 Out in the open wisdom calls
        aloud,
    she raises her voice in the
        public square;
21 on top of the wall[a] she cries out,
    at the city gate she makes her
        speech:

22 "How long will you who are
        simple love your simple
        ways?
    How long will mockers delight
        in mockery
    and fools hate knowledge?
23 Repent at my rebuke!
    Then I will pour out my
        thoughts to you,
    I will make known to you my
        teachings.
24 But since you refuse to listen
        when I call
    and no one pays attention
        when I stretch out my
        hand,
25 since you disregard all my
        advice
    and do not accept my rebuke,
26 I in turn will laugh when disaster
        strikes you;
    I will mock when calamity
        overtakes you —
27 when calamity overtakes you
        like a storm,
    when disaster sweeps over you
        like a whirlwind,
    when distress and trouble
        overwhelm you.

28 "Then they will call to me but I
        will not answer;
    they will look for me but will
        not find me,

29 since they hated knowledge
        and did not choose to fear the
        LORD.
30 Since they would not accept my
        advice
    and spurned my rebuke,
31 they will eat the fruit of their
        ways
    and be filled with the fruit of
        their schemes.
32 For the waywardness of the
        simple will kill them,
    and the complacency of fools
        will destroy them;
33 but whoever listens to me will
        live in safety
    and be at ease, without fear of
        harm."

Moral Benefits of Wisdom

2 My son, if you accept my words
    and store up my commands
        within you,
2 turning your ear to wisdom
    and applying your heart to
        understanding —
3 indeed, if you call out for insight
    and cry aloud for
        understanding,
4 and if you look for it as for silver
    and search for it as for hidden
        treasure,
5 then you will understand the
        fear of the LORD
    and find the knowledge of
        God.
6 For the LORD gives wisdom;
    from his mouth come
        knowledge and
        understanding.
7 He holds success in store for the
        upright,
    he is a shield to those whose
        walk is blameless,

---

a 21 Septuagint; Hebrew / at noisy street
corners

8 for he guards the course of the just
and protects the way of his faithful ones.

9 Then you will understand what is right and just
and fair — every good path.

10 For wisdom will enter your heart,
and knowledge will be pleasant to your soul.

11 Discretion will protect you,
and understanding will guard you.

12 Wisdom will save you from the ways of wicked men,
from men whose words are perverse,

13 who have left the straight paths to walk in dark ways,

14 who delight in doing wrong
and rejoice in the perverseness of evil,

15 whose paths are crooked
and who are devious in their ways.

16 Wisdom will save you also from the adulterous woman,
from the wayward woman with her seductive words,

17 who has left the partner of her youth
and ignored the covenant she made before God.[a]

18 Surely her house leads down to death
and her paths to the spirits of the dead.

19 None who go to her return
or attain the paths of life.

20 Thus you will walk in the ways of the good
and keep to the paths of the righteous.

21 For the upright will live in the land,
and the blameless will remain in it;

22 but the wicked will be cut off from the land,
and the unfaithful will be torn from it.

Wisdom Bestows Well-Being

3 My son, do not forget my teaching,
but keep my commands in your heart,

2 for they will prolong your life many years
and bring you peace and prosperity.

3 Let love and faithfulness never leave you;
bind them around your neck,
write them on the tablet of your heart.

4 Then you will win favor and a good name
in the sight of God and man.

5 Trust in the LORD with all your heart
and lean not on your own understanding;

6 in all your ways submit to him,
and he will make your paths straight.[b]

7 Do not be wise in your own eyes;
fear the LORD and shun evil.

8 This will bring health to your body
and nourishment to your bones.

a 17 Or covenant of her God   b 6 Or will direct your paths

⁹ Honor the LORD with your
wealth,
with the firstfruits of all your
crops;
¹⁰ then your barns will be filled to
overflowing,
and your vats will brim over
with new wine.

¹¹ My son, do not despise the LORD's
discipline,
and do not resent his
rebuke,
¹² because the LORD disciplines
those he loves,
as a father the son he delights
in.ᵃ

¹³ Blessed are those who find
wisdom,
those who gain
understanding,
¹⁴ for she is more profitable than
silver
and yields better returns than
gold.
¹⁵ She is more precious than
rubies;
nothing you desire can
compare with her.
¹⁶ Long life is in her right
hand;
in her left hand are riches
and honor.
¹⁷ Her ways are pleasant ways,
and all her paths are peace.
¹⁸ She is a tree of life to those who
take hold of her;
those who hold her fast will
be blessed.

¹⁹ By wisdom the LORD laid the
earth's foundations,
by understanding he set the
heavens in place;
²⁰ by his knowledge the watery
depths were divided,
and the clouds let drop the
dew.

²¹ My son, do not let wisdom and
understanding out of
your sight,
preserve sound judgment and
discretion;
²² they will be life for you,
an ornament to grace your
neck.
²³ Then you will go on your way in
safety,
and your foot will not
stumble.
²⁴ When you lie down, you will not
be afraid;
when you lie down, your sleep
will be sweet.
²⁵ Have no fear of sudden disaster
or of the ruin that overtakes
the wicked,
²⁶ for the LORD will be at your side
and will keep your foot from
being snared.

²⁷ Do not withhold good from those
to whom it is due,
when it is in your power
to act.
²⁸ Do not say to your neighbor,
"Come back tomorrow and I'll
give it to you" —
when you already have it with
you.
²⁹ Do not plot harm against your
neighbor,
who lives trustfully near you.
³⁰ Do not accuse anyone for no
reason —
when they have done you no
harm.

³¹ Do not envy the violent
or choose any of their ways.
³² For the LORD detests the perverse
but takes the upright into his
confidence.

ᵃ 12 Hebrew; Septuagint loves, / and he
chastens everyone he accepts as his child

33 The LORD's curse is on the house
   of the wicked,
   but he blesses the home of the
   righteous.
34 He mocks proud mockers
   but shows favor to the humble
   and oppressed.
35 The wise inherit honor,
   but fools get only shame.

Get Wisdom at Any Cost

4 Listen, my sons, to a father's
   instruction;
   pay attention and gain
   understanding.
2 I give you sound learning,
   so do not forsake my
   teaching.
3 For I too was a son to my
   father,
   still tender, and cherished by
   my mother.
4 Then he taught me, and he said
   to me,
   "Take hold of my words with
   all your heart;
   keep my commands, and you
   will live.
5 Get wisdom, get understanding;
   do not forget my words or turn
   away from them.
6 Do not forsake wisdom, and she
   will protect you;
   love her, and she will watch
   over you.
7 The beginning of wisdom is this:
   Get[a] wisdom.
   Though it cost all you have,[b]
   get understanding.
8 Cherish her, and she will exalt
   you;
   embrace her, and she will
   honor you.
9 She will give you a garland to
   grace your head
   and present you with a
   glorious crown."

10 Listen, my son, accept what I say,
   and the years of your life will
   be many.
11 I instruct you in the way of
   wisdom
   and lead you along straight
   paths.
12 When you walk, your steps will
   not be hampered;
   when you run, you will not
   stumble.
13 Hold on to instruction, do not let
   it go;
   guard it well, for it is your life.
14 Do not set foot on the path of the
   wicked
   or walk in the way of evildoers.
15 Avoid it, do not travel on it;
   turn from it and go on your
   way.
16 For they cannot rest until they do
   evil;
   they are robbed of sleep till
   they make someone
   stumble.
17 They eat the bread of wickedness
   and drink the wine of violence.
18 The path of the righteous is like
   the morning sun,
   shining ever brighter till the
   full light of day.
19 But the way of the wicked is like
   deep darkness;
   they do not know what makes
   them stumble.
20 My son, pay attention to what I
   say;
   turn your ear to my words.
21 Do not let them out of your sight,
   keep them within your heart;
22 for they are life to those who find
   them
   and health to one's whole
   body.

---

[a] 7 Or *Wisdom is supreme; therefore get*
[b] 7 Or *wisdom. / Whatever else you get*

23 Above all else, guard your
    heart,
  for everything you do flows
    from it.
24 Keep your mouth free of
    perversity;
  keep corrupt talk far from
    your lips.
25 Let your eyes look straight
    ahead;
  fix your gaze directly before
    you.
26 Give careful thought to the[a]
    paths for your feet
  and be steadfast in all your
    ways.
27 Do not turn to the right or the
    left;
  keep your foot from evil.

Warning Against Adultery

5 My son, pay attention to my
    wisdom,
  turn your ear to my words of
    insight,
2 that you may maintain
    discretion
  and your lips may preserve
    knowledge.
3 For the lips of the adulterous
    woman drip honey,
  and her speech is smoother
    than oil;
4 but in the end she is bitter as
    gall,
  sharp as a double-edged
    sword.
5 Her feet go down to death;
  her steps lead straight to the
    grave.
6 She gives no thought to the way
    of life;
  her paths wander aimlessly,
  but she does not know it.

7 Now then, my sons, listen to me;
  do not turn aside from what I
    say.

8 Keep to a path far from her,
  do not go near the door of her
    house,
9 lest you lose your honor
    to others
  and your dignity[b] to one who
    is cruel,
10 lest strangers feast on your
    wealth
  and your toil enrich the house
    of another.
11 At the end of your life you will
    groan,
  when your flesh and body are
    spent.
12 You will say, "How I hated
    discipline!
  How my heart spurned
    correction!
13 I would not obey my teachers
  or turn my ear to my
    instructors.
14 And I was soon in serious
    trouble
  in the assembly of God's
    people."

15 Drink water from your own
    cistern,
  running water from your own
    well.
16 Should your springs overflow in
    the streets,
  your streams of water in the
    public squares?
17 Let them be yours alone,
  never to be shared with
    strangers.
18 May your fountain be blessed,
  and may you rejoice in the
    wife of your youth.
19 A loving doe, a graceful deer —
  may her breasts satisfy you
    always,
  may you ever be intoxicated
    with her love.

---

[a] 26 Or *Make level*   [b] 9 Or *years*

20 Why, my son, be intoxicated with
     another man's wife?
   Why embrace the bosom of a
     wayward woman?

21 For your ways are in full view
     of the LORD,
   and he examines all your
     paths.
22 The evil deeds of the wicked
     ensnare them;
   the cords of their sins hold
     them fast.
23 For lack of discipline they will
     die,
   led astray by their own great
     folly.

Warnings Against Folly

6 My son, if you have put
        up security for your
        neighbor,
   if you have shaken hands in
     pledge for a stranger,
2 you have been trapped by what
     you said,
   ensnared by the words of your
     mouth.
3 So do this, my son, to free
     yourself,
   since you have fallen into your
     neighbor's hands:
   Go — to the point of
     exhaustion — [a]
   and give your neighbor no
     rest!
4 Allow no sleep to your eyes,
   no slumber to your eyelids.
5 Free yourself, like a gazelle from
     the hand of the hunter,
   like a bird from the snare of
     the fowler.

6 Go to the ant, you sluggard;
   consider its ways and be
     wise!
7 It has no commander,
   no overseer or ruler,

8 yet it stores its provisions in
     summer
   and gathers its food at harvest.

9 How long will you lie there, you
     sluggard?
   When will you get up from your
     sleep?
10 A little sleep, a little slumber,
   a little folding of the hands to
     rest —
11 and poverty will come on you like
     a thief
   and scarcity like an armed man.

12 A troublemaker and a villain,
   who goes about with a corrupt
     mouth,
13 who winks maliciously with his
     eye,
   signals with his feet
   and motions with his fingers,
14 who plots evil with deceit in his
     heart —
   he always stirs up conflict.
15 Therefore disaster will overtake
     him in an instant;
   he will suddenly be
     destroyed — without
     remedy.

16 There are six things the LORD
     hates,
   seven that are detestable to
     him:
17   haughty eyes,
   a lying tongue,
   hands that shed innocent
     blood,
18   a heart that devises wicked
     schemes,
   feet that are quick to rush
     into evil,
19   a false witness who pours out
     lies
   and a person who stirs
     up conflict in the
     community.

---

[a] 3 Or Go and humble yourself,

Warning Against Adultery

20 My son, keep your father's
command
and do not forsake your
mother's teaching.
21 Bind them always on your
heart;
fasten them around your
neck.
22 When you walk, they will guide
you;
when you sleep, they will
watch over you;
when you awake, they will
speak to you.
23 For this command is a lamp,
this teaching is a light,
and correction and instruction
are the way to life,
24 keeping you from your
neighbor's wife,
from the smooth talk of a
wayward woman.

25 Do not lust in your heart after
her beauty
or let her captivate you with
her eyes.

26 For a prostitute can be had for a
loaf of bread,
but another man's wife preys
on your very life.
27 Can a man scoop fire into his lap
without his clothes being
burned?
28 Can a man walk on hot coals
without his feet being
scorched?
29 So is he who sleeps with another
man's wife;
no one who touches her will
go unpunished.

30 People do not despise a thief if
he steals
to satisfy his hunger when he
is starving.

31 Yet if he is caught, he must pay
sevenfold,
though it costs him all the
wealth of his house.
32 But a man who commits adultery
has no sense;
whoever does so destroys
himself.
33 Blows and disgrace are his
lot,
and his shame will never be
wiped away.

34 For jealousy arouses a husband's
fury,
and he will show no mercy
when he takes revenge.
35 He will not accept any
compensation;
he will refuse a bribe, however
great it is.

Warning Against the Adulterous Woman

7 My son, keep my words
and store up my commands
within you.
2 Keep my commands and you
will live;
guard my teachings as the
apple of your eye.
3 Bind them on your fingers;
write them on the tablet
of your heart.
4 Say to wisdom, "You are my
sister,"
and to insight, "You are my
relative."
5 They will keep you from the
adulterous woman,
from the wayward woman
with her seductive
words.

6 At the window of my
house
I looked down through
the lattice.

⁷ I saw among the simple,
  I noticed among the young
    men,
  a youth who had no sense.
⁸ He was going down the street
    near her corner,
  walking along in the direction
    of her house
⁹ at twilight, as the day was
    fading,
  as the dark of night set in.

¹⁰ Then out came a woman to meet
    him,
  dressed like a prostitute and
    with crafty intent.
¹¹ (She is unruly and defiant,
  her feet never stay at home;
¹² now in the street, now in the
    squares,
  at every corner she lurks.)
¹³ She took hold of him and kissed
    him
  and with a brazen face she
    said:

¹⁴ "Today I fulfilled my vows,
  and I have food from my
    fellowship offering at
    home.
¹⁵ So I came out to meet you;
  I looked for you and have
    found you!
¹⁶ I have covered my bed
  with colored linens from
    Egypt.
¹⁷ I have perfumed my bed
  with myrrh, aloes and
    cinnamon.
¹⁸ Come, let's drink deeply of love
    till morning;
  let's enjoy ourselves with love!
¹⁹ My husband is not at home;
  he has gone on a long journey.
²⁰ He took his purse filled with
    money
  and will not be home till full
    moon."

²¹ With persuasive words she led
    him astray;
  she seduced him with her
    smooth talk.
²² All at once he followed her
  like an ox going to the
    slaughter,
  like a deer[a] stepping into a
    noose[b]
²³   till an arrow pierces his
    liver,
  like a bird darting into a
    snare,
  little knowing it will cost him
    his life.

²⁴ Now then, my sons, listen
    to me;
  pay attention to what I say.
²⁵ Do not let your heart turn to her
    ways
  or stray into her paths.
²⁶ Many are the victims she has
    brought down;
  her slain are a mighty throng.
²⁷ Her house is a highway to the
    grave,
  leading down to the chambers
    of death.

Wisdom's Call

8 Does not wisdom call out?
  Does not understanding raise
    her voice?
² At the highest point along the
    way,
  where the paths meet, she
    takes her stand;
³ beside the gate leading into the
    city,
  at the entrance, she cries
    aloud:
⁴ "To you, O people, I call out;
  I raise my voice to all
    mankind.

---

[a] 22 Syriac (see also Septuagint); Hebrew *fool*
[b] 22 The meaning of the Hebrew for this line is uncertain.

5 You who are simple, gain
        prudence;
    you who are foolish, set your
        hearts on it.[a]
6 Listen, for I have trustworthy
        things to say;
    I open my lips to speak what is
        right.
7 My mouth speaks what is true,
    for my lips detest wickedness.
8 All the words of my mouth are
        just;
    none of them is crooked or
        perverse.
9 To the discerning all of them are
        right;
    they are upright to those who
        have found knowledge.
10 Choose my instruction instead
        of silver,
    knowledge rather than choice
        gold,
11 for wisdom is more precious
        than rubies,
    and nothing you desire can
        compare with her.

12 "I, wisdom, dwell together with
        prudence;
    I possess knowledge and
        discretion.
13 To fear the LORD is to hate evil;
    I hate pride and arrogance,
        evil behavior and perverse
        speech.
14 Counsel and sound judgment
        are mine;
    I have insight, I have power.
15 By me kings reign
    and rulers issue decrees that
        are just;
16 by me princes govern,
    and nobles — all who rule on
        earth.[b]
17 I love those who love me,
    and those who seek me
        find me.

18 With me are riches and honor,
        enduring wealth and
        prosperity.
19 My fruit is better than fine gold;
    what I yield surpasses choice
        silver.
20 I walk in the way of
        righteousness,
    along the paths of justice,
21 bestowing a rich inheritance on
        those who love me
    and making their treasuries
        full.

22 "The LORD brought me forth as
        the first of his works,[c,d]
    before his deeds of old;
23 I was formed long ages ago,
    at the very beginning, when
        the world came to be.
24 When there were no watery
        depths, I was given birth,
    when there were no springs
        overflowing with water;
25 before the mountains were
        settled in place,
    before the hills, I was given
        birth,
26 before he made the world or its
        fields
    or any of the dust of the
        earth.
27 I was there when he set the
        heavens in place,
    when he marked out the
        horizon on the face of the
        deep,
28 when he established the clouds
        above
    and fixed securely the
        fountains of the deep,

---

[a] 5 Septuagint; Hebrew *foolish, instruct your
minds*   [b] 16 Some Hebrew manuscripts and
Septuagint; other Hebrew manuscripts *all
righteous rulers*   [c] 22 Or *way*; or *dominion*
[d] 22 Or *The LORD possessed me at the beginning
of his work*; or *The LORD brought me forth at
the beginning of his work*

²⁹ when he gave the sea its
boundary
so the waters would not
overstep his command,
and when he marked out the
foundations of the
earth.
³⁰ Then I was constantly[a] at his
side.
I was filled with delight day after
day,
rejoicing always in his
presence,
³¹ rejoicing in his whole world
and delighting in mankind.

³² "Now then, my children, listen
to me;
blessed are those who keep
my ways.
³³ Listen to my instruction and be
wise;
do not disregard it.
³⁴ Blessed are those who listen
to me,
watching daily at my doors,
waiting at my doorway.
³⁵ For those who find me find
life
and receive favor from the
LORD.
³⁶ But those who fail to find me
harm themselves;
all who hate me love death."

Invitations of Wisdom and Folly

9 Wisdom has built her house;
she has set up[b] its seven
pillars.
² She has prepared her meat and
mixed her wine;
she has also set her table.
³ She has sent out her servants,
and she calls
from the highest point of
the city,

⁴ "Let all who are simple come
to my house!"
To those who have no sense she
says,
⁵ "Come, eat my food
and drink the wine I have
mixed.
⁶ Leave your simple ways and you
will live;
walk in the way of insight."

⁷ Whoever corrects a mocker
invites insults;
whoever rebukes the wicked
incurs abuse.
⁸ Do not rebuke mockers or they
will hate you;
rebuke the wise and they will
love you.
⁹ Instruct the wise and they will be
wiser still;
teach the righteous and they
will add to their
learning.

¹⁰ The fear of the LORD is the
beginning of wisdom,
and knowledge of the Holy
One is understanding.
¹¹ For through wisdom[c] your days
will be many,
and years will be added to your
life.
¹² If you are wise, your wisdom will
reward you;
if you are a mocker, you alone
will suffer.

¹³ Folly is an unruly woman;
she is simple and knows
nothing.
¹⁴ She sits at the door of her house,
on a seat at the highest point
of the city,

---

[a] 30 Or was the artisan; or was a little child
[b] 1 Septuagint, Syriac and Targum; Hebrew has hewn out   [c] 11 Septuagint, Syriac and Targum; Hebrew me

15 calling out to those who
        pass by,
    who go straight on their
        way,
16 "Let all who are simple come
        to my house!"
    To those who have no sense she
        says,
17 "Stolen water is sweet;
        food eaten in secret is
        delicious!"
18 But little do they know that the
        dead are there,
    that her guests are deep in the
        realm of the dead.

Proverbs of Solomon

10 The proverbs of Solomon:

    A wise son brings joy to his
        father,
    but a foolish son brings grief
        to his mother.

2 Ill-gotten treasures have no
        lasting value,
    but righteousness delivers
        from death.

3 The LORD does not let the
        righteous go hungry,
    but he thwarts the craving
        of the wicked.

4 Lazy hands make for poverty,
    but diligent hands bring
        wealth.

5 He who gathers crops in summer
        is a prudent son,
    but he who sleeps during
        harvest is a disgraceful
        son.

6 Blessings crown the head of the
        righteous,
    but violence overwhelms the
        mouth of the wicked.[a]

7 The name of the righteous is
        used in blessings,[b]
    but the name of the wicked
        will rot.

8 The wise in heart accept
        commands,
    but a chattering fool comes
        to ruin.

9 Whoever walks in integrity walks
        securely,
    but whoever takes crooked
        paths will be found
        out.

10 Whoever winks maliciously
        causes grief,
    and a chattering fool comes
        to ruin.

11 The mouth of the righteous is
        a fountain of life,
    but the mouth of the wicked
        conceals violence.

12 Hatred stirs up conflict,
    but love covers over all
        wrongs.

13 Wisdom is found on the lips of
        the discerning,
    but a rod is for the back
        of one who has no
        sense.

14 The wise store up knowledge,
    but the mouth of a fool invites
        ruin.

15 The wealth of the rich is their
        fortified city,
    but poverty is the ruin of the
        poor.

16 The wages of the righteous
        is life,
    but the earnings of the wicked
        are sin and death.

---

*a 6 Or righteous, / but the mouth of the wicked
conceals violence*   *b 7 See Gen. 48:20.*

17 Whoever heeds discipline shows
     the way to life,
   but whoever ignores
     correction leads others
     astray.

18 Whoever conceals hatred with
     lying lips
   and spreads slander is a fool.

19 Sin is not ended by multiplying
     words,
   but the prudent hold their
     tongues.

20 The tongue of the righteous is
     choice silver,
   but the heart of the wicked is
     of little value.

21 The lips of the righteous nourish
     many,
   but fools die for lack of sense.

22 The blessing of the LORD brings
     wealth,
   without painful toil for it.

23 A fool finds pleasure in wicked
     schemes,
   but a person of understanding
     delights in wisdom.

24 What the wicked dread will
     overtake them;
   what the righteous desire will
     be granted.

25 When the storm has swept by,
     the wicked are gone,
   but the righteous stand firm
     forever.

26 As vinegar to the teeth and
     smoke to the eyes,
   so are sluggards to those who
     send them.

27 The fear of the LORD adds length
     to life,
   but the years of the wicked are
     cut short.

28 The prospect of the righteous
     is joy,
   but the hopes of the wicked
     come to nothing.

29 The way of the LORD is a refuge
     for the blameless,
   but it is the ruin of those who
     do evil.

30 The righteous will never be
     uprooted,
   but the wicked will not remain
     in the land.

31 From the mouth of the righteous
     comes the fruit of
     wisdom,
   but a perverse tongue will be
     silenced.

32 The lips of the righteous know
     what finds favor,
   but the mouth of the wicked
     only what is perverse.

11 The LORD detests dishonest
     scales,
   but accurate weights find favor
     with him.

2 When pride comes, then comes
     disgrace,
   but with humility comes
     wisdom.

3 The integrity of the upright
     guides them,
   but the unfaithful are destroyed
     by their duplicity.

4 Wealth is worthless in the day
     of wrath,
   but righteousness delivers
     from death.

5 The righteousness of the
     blameless makes their
     paths straight,
   but the wicked are brought
     down by their own
     wickedness.

6 The righteousness of the upright
    delivers them,
  but the unfaithful are trapped
    by evil desires.

7 Hopes placed in mortals die with
    them;
  all the promise of[a] their power
    comes to nothing.

8 The righteous person is rescued
    from trouble,
  and it falls on the wicked
    instead.

9 With their mouths the godless
    destroy their neighbors,
  but through knowledge the
    righteous escape.

10 When the righteous prosper,
    the city rejoices;
  when the wicked perish, there
    are shouts of joy.

11 Through the blessing of the
    upright a city is
    exalted,
  but by the mouth of the
    wicked it is destroyed.

12 Whoever derides their neighbor
    has no sense,
  but the one who has
    understanding holds their
    tongue.

13 A gossip betrays a confidence,
  but a trustworthy person
    keeps a secret.

14 For lack of guidance a nation
    falls,
  but victory is won through
    many advisers.

15 Whoever puts up security for
    a stranger will surely
    suffer,
  but whoever refuses to shake
    hands in pledge is
    safe.

16 A kindhearted woman gains
    honor,
  but ruthless men gain only
    wealth.

17 Those who are kind benefit
    themselves,
  but the cruel bring ruin on
    themselves.

18 A wicked person earns deceptive
    wages,
  but the one who sows
    righteousness reaps a
    sure reward.

19 Truly the righteous attain life,
  but whoever pursues evil finds
    death.

20 The LORD detests those whose
    hearts are perverse,
  but he delights in those whose
    ways are blameless.

21 Be sure of this: The wicked will
    not go unpunished,
  but those who are righteous
    will go free.

22 Like a gold ring in a pig's snout
    is a beautiful woman who
    shows no discretion.

23 The desire of the righteous ends
    only in good,
  but the hope of the wicked
    only in wrath.

24 One person gives freely, yet gains
    even more;
  another withholds unduly, but
    comes to poverty.

25 A generous person will prosper;
  whoever refreshes others will
    be refreshed.

---

[a] 7 Two Hebrew manuscripts; most Hebrew
manuscripts, Vulgate, Syriac and Targum
*When the wicked die, their hope perishes; / all
they expected from*

26 People curse the one who hoards
grain,
but they pray God's blessing
on the one who is willing
to sell.

27 Whoever seeks good finds
favor,
but evil comes to one who
searches for it.

28 Those who trust in their riches
will fall,
but the righteous will thrive
like a green leaf.

29 Whoever brings ruin on their
family will inherit only
wind,
and the fool will be servant
to the wise.

30 The fruit of the righteous is a
tree of life,
and the one who is wise saves
lives.

31 If the righteous receive their due
on earth,
how much more the ungodly
and the sinner!

12 Whoever loves discipline loves
knowledge,
but whoever hates correction
is stupid.

2 Good people obtain favor from
the LORD,
but he condemns those who
devise wicked schemes.

3 No one can be established
through wickedness,
but the righteous cannot be
uprooted.

4 A wife of noble character is her
husband's crown,
but a disgraceful wife is like
decay in his bones.

5 The plans of the righteous are
just,
but the advice of the wicked
is deceitful.

6 The words of the wicked lie in
wait for blood,
but the speech of the upright
rescues them.

7 The wicked are overthrown and
are no more,
but the house of the righteous
stands firm.

8 A person is praised according to
their prudence,
and one with a warped mind
is despised.

9 Better to be a nobody and yet
have a servant
than pretend to be somebody
and have no food.

10 The righteous care for the needs
of their animals,
but the kindest acts of the
wicked are cruel.

11 Those who work their land will
have abundant food,
but those who chase fantasies
have no sense.

12 The wicked desire the stronghold
of evildoers,
but the root of the righteous
endures.

13 Evildoers are trapped by their
sinful talk,
and so the innocent escape
trouble.

14 From the fruit of their lips
people are filled with
good things,
and the work of their hands
brings them reward.

15 The way of fools seems right to
them,
but the wise listen to advice.

16 Fools show their annoyance at
    once,
  but the prudent overlook an
    insult.

17 An honest witness tells the truth,
  but a false witness tells lies.

18 The words of the reckless pierce
    like swords,
  but the tongue of the wise
    brings healing.

19 Truthful lips endure forever,
  but a lying tongue lasts only a
    moment.

20 Deceit is in the hearts of those
    who plot evil,
  but those who promote peace
    have joy.

21 No harm overtakes the
    righteous,
  but the wicked have their fill
    of trouble.

22 The LORD detests lying lips,
  but he delights in people who
    are trustworthy.

23 The prudent keep their
    knowledge to themselves,
  but a fool's heart blurts out
    folly.

24 Diligent hands will rule,
  but laziness ends in forced
    labor.

25 Anxiety weighs down the heart,
  but a kind word cheers it up.

26 The righteous choose their
    friends carefully,
  but the way of the wicked
    leads them astray.

27 The lazy do not roast[a] any
    game,
  but the diligent feed on the
    riches of the hunt.

28 In the way of righteousness there
    is life;
  along that path is immortality.

13 A wise son heeds his father's
    instruction,
  but a mocker does not respond
    to rebukes.

2 From the fruit of their lips
    people enjoy good things,
  but the unfaithful have an
    appetite for violence.

3 Those who guard their lips
    preserve their lives,
  but those who speak rashly
    will come to ruin.

4 A sluggard's appetite is never
    filled,
  but the desires of the diligent
    are fully satisfied.

5 The righteous hate what is false,
  but the wicked make
    themselves a stench
  and bring shame on
    themselves.

6 Righteousness guards the person
    of integrity,
  but wickedness overthrows
    the sinner.

7 One person pretends to be rich,
    yet has nothing;
  another pretends to be poor,
    yet has great wealth.

8 A person's riches may ransom
    their life,
  but the poor cannot respond
    to threatening rebukes.

9 The light of the righteous shines
    brightly,
  but the lamp of the wicked is
    snuffed out.

---

a 27 The meaning of the Hebrew for this word
is uncertain.

[10] Where there is strife, there is
     pride,
  but wisdom is found in those
     who take advice.

[11] Dishonest money dwindles away,
  but whoever gathers money
     little by little makes it
     grow.

[12] Hope deferred makes the heart
     sick,
  but a longing fulfilled is a tree
     of life.

[13] Whoever scorns instruction will
     pay for it,
  but whoever respects a
     command is rewarded.

[14] The teaching of the wise is a
     fountain of life,
  turning a person from the
     snares of death.

[15] Good judgment wins favor,
  but the way of the unfaithful
     leads to their destruction.[a]

[16] All who are prudent act with[b]
     knowledge,
  but fools expose their folly.

[17] A wicked messenger falls into
     trouble,
  but a trustworthy envoy brings
     healing.

[18] Whoever disregards discipline
     comes to poverty and
     shame,
  but whoever heeds correction
     is honored.

[19] A longing fulfilled is sweet to the
     soul,
  but fools detest turning from
     evil.

[20] Walk with the wise and become
     wise,
  for a companion of fools
     suffers harm.

[21] Trouble pursues the sinner,
  but the righteous are rewarded
     with good things.

[22] A good person leaves an
     inheritance for their
     children's children,
  but a sinner's wealth is stored
     up for the righteous.

[23] An unplowed field produces food
     for the poor,
  but injustice sweeps it
     away.

[24] Whoever spares the rod hates
     their children,
  but the one who loves their
     children is careful to
     discipline them.

[25] The righteous eat to their hearts'
     content,
  but the stomach of the wicked
     goes hungry.

14 The wise woman builds her
        house,
  but with her own hands the
     foolish one tears hers
     down.

[2] Whoever fears the LORD walks
     uprightly,
  but those who despise him
     are devious in their
     ways.

[3] A fool's mouth lashes out with
     pride,
  but the lips of the wise protect
     them.

[4] Where there are no oxen, the
     manger is empty,
  but from the strength of
     an ox come abundant
     harvests.

---

[a] 15 Septuagint and Syriac; the meaning of the
Hebrew for this phrase is uncertain.   [b] 16 Or
prudent protect themselves through

5 An honest witness does not
deceive,
but a false witness pours out
lies.

6 The mocker seeks wisdom and
finds none,
but knowledge comes easily to
the discerning.

7 Stay away from a fool,
for you will not find
knowledge on their lips.

8 The wisdom of the prudent is
to give thought to their
ways,
but the folly of fools is
deception.

9 Fools mock at making amends
for sin,
but goodwill is found among
the upright.

10 Each heart knows its own
bitterness,
and no one else can share its
joy.

11 The house of the wicked will be
destroyed,
but the tent of the upright will
flourish.

12 There is a way that appears to be
right,
but in the end it leads to
death.

13 Even in laughter the heart may
ache,
and rejoicing may end in grief.

14 The faithless will be fully repaid
for their ways,
and the good rewarded for
theirs.

15 The simple believe anything,
but the prudent give thought
to their steps.

16 The wise fear the LORD and shun
evil,
but a fool is hotheaded and yet
feels secure.

17 A quick-tempered person does
foolish things,
and the one who devises evil
schemes is hated.

18 The simple inherit folly,
but the prudent are crowned
with knowledge.

19 Evildoers will bow down in
the presence of the
good,
and the wicked at the gates
of the righteous.

20 The poor are shunned even by
their neighbors,
but the rich have many
friends.

21 It is a sin to despise one's
neighbor,
but blessed is the one who
is kind to the needy.

22 Do not those who plot evil go
astray?
But those who plan what
is good find*a* love and
faithfulness.

23 All hard work brings a
profit,
but mere talk leads only
to poverty.

24 The wealth of the wise is their
crown,
but the folly of fools yields
folly.

25 A truthful witness saves
lives,
but a false witness is
deceitful.

---

a 22 Or show

²⁶ Whoever fears the Lᴏʀᴅ has a
     secure fortress,
   and for their children it will be
     a refuge.

²⁷ The fear of the Lᴏʀᴅ is a fountain
     of life,
   turning a person from the
     snares of death.

²⁸ A large population is a king's
     glory,
   but without subjects a prince
     is ruined.

²⁹ Whoever is patient has great
     understanding,
   but one who is quick-tempered
     displays folly.

³⁰ A heart at peace gives life to the
     body,
   but envy rots the bones.

³¹ Whoever oppresses the poor
     shows contempt for their
     Maker,
   but whoever is kind to the
     needy honors God.

³² When calamity comes, the
     wicked are brought down,
   but even in death the
     righteous seek refuge in
     God.

³³ Wisdom reposes in the heart of
     the discerning
   and even among fools she lets
     herself be known.ᵃ

³⁴ Righteousness exalts a nation,
   but sin condemns any people.

³⁵ A king delights in a wise servant,
   but a shameful servant
     arouses his fury.

15 A gentle answer turns away
     wrath,
   but a harsh word stirs up
     anger.

² The tongue of the wise adorns
     knowledge,
   but the mouth of the fool
     gushes folly.

³ The eyes of the Lᴏʀᴅ are
     everywhere,
   keeping watch on the wicked
     and the good.

⁴ The soothing tongue is a tree of
     life,
   but a perverse tongue crushes
     the spirit.

⁵ A fool spurns a parent's discipline,
   but whoever heeds correction
     shows prudence.

⁶ The house of the righteous
     contains great treasure,
   but the income of the wicked
     brings ruin.

⁷ The lips of the wise spread
     knowledge,
   but the hearts of fools are not
     upright.

⁸ The Lᴏʀᴅ detests the sacrifice of
     the wicked,
   but the prayer of the upright
     pleases him.

⁹ The Lᴏʀᴅ detests the way of the
     wicked,
   but he loves those who pursue
     righteousness.

¹⁰ Stern discipline awaits anyone
     who leaves the path;
   the one who hates correction
     will die.

¹¹ Death and Destructionᵇ lie open
     before the Lᴏʀᴅ —
   how much more do human
     hearts!

ᵃ 33 Hebrew; Septuagint and Syriac
*discerning / but in the heart of fools she is not
known*   ᵇ 11 Hebrew *Abaddon*

¹² Mockers resent correction,
    so they avoid the wise.

¹³ A happy heart makes the face
      cheerful,
    but heartache crushes the
      spirit.

¹⁴ The discerning heart seeks
      knowledge,
    but the mouth of a fool feeds
      on folly.

¹⁵ All the days of the oppressed are
      wretched,
    but the cheerful heart has a
      continual feast.

¹⁶ Better a little with the fear of the
      LORD
    than great wealth with
      turmoil.

¹⁷ Better a small serving of
      vegetables with love
    than a fattened calf with
      hatred.

¹⁸ A hot-tempered person stirs up
      conflict,
    but the one who is patient
      calms a quarrel.

¹⁹ The way of the sluggard is
      blocked with thorns,
    but the path of the upright is a
      highway.

²⁰ A wise son brings joy to his
      father,
    but a foolish man despises his
      mother.

²¹ Folly brings joy to one who has
      no sense,
    but whoever has
      understanding keeps a
      straight course.

²² Plans fail for lack of counsel,
    but with many advisers they
      succeed.

²³ A person finds joy in giving an
      apt reply—
    and how good is a timely
      word!

²⁴ The path of life leads upward for
      the prudent
    to keep them from going
      down to the realm of the
      dead.

²⁵ The LORD tears down the house
      of the proud,
    but he sets the widow's
      boundary stones
      in place.

²⁶ The LORD detests the thoughts of
      the wicked,
    but gracious words are pure in
      his sight.

²⁷ The greedy bring ruin to their
      households,
    but the one who hates bribes
      will live.

²⁸ The heart of the righteous
      weighs its answers,
    but the mouth of the wicked
      gushes evil.

²⁹ The LORD is far from the wicked,
    but he hears the prayer of the
      righteous.

³⁰ Light in a messenger's eyes
      brings joy to the heart,
    and good news gives health to
      the bones.

³¹ Whoever heeds life-giving
      correction
    will be at home among the
      wise.

³² Those who disregard discipline
      despise themselves,
    but the one who heeds
      correction gains
      understanding.

33 Wisdom's instruction is to fear
the LORD,
and humility comes before
honor.

16

To humans belong the plans
of the heart,
but from the LORD comes the
proper answer of the
tongue.

2 All a person's ways seem pure to
them,
but motives are weighed by
the LORD.

3 Commit to the LORD whatever
you do,
and he will establish your
plans.

4 The LORD works out everything
to its proper end —
even the wicked for a day of
disaster.

5 The LORD detests all the proud of
heart.
Be sure of this: They will not
go unpunished.

6 Through love and faithfulness
sin is atoned for;
through the fear of the LORD
evil is avoided.

7 When the LORD takes pleasure in
anyone's way,
he causes their enemies to
make peace with them.

8 Better a little with righteousness
than much gain with injustice.

9 In their hearts humans plan their
course,
but the LORD establishes their
steps.

10 The lips of a king speak as an
oracle,
and his mouth does not betray
justice.

11 Honest scales and balances
belong to the LORD;
all the weights in the bag are
of his making.

12 Kings detest wrongdoing,
for a throne is established
through righteousness.

13 Kings take pleasure in honest
lips;
they value the one who speaks
what is right.

14 A king's wrath is a messenger of
death,
but the wise will appease it.

15 When a king's face brightens, it
means life;
his favor is like a rain cloud in
spring.

16 How much better to get wisdom
than gold,
to get insight rather than
silver!

17 The highway of the upright
avoids evil;
those who guard their ways
preserve their lives.

18 Pride goes before destruction,
a haughty spirit before a fall.

19 Better to be lowly in spirit along
with the oppressed
than to share plunder with the
proud.

20 Whoever gives heed to
instruction prospers,[a]
and blessed is the one who
trusts in the LORD.

21 The wise in heart are called
discerning,
and gracious words promote
instruction.[b]

---

[a] 20 Or *whoever speaks prudently finds what is good* [b] 21 Or *words make a person persuasive*

474

22 Prudence is a fountain of life to
the prudent,
but folly brings punishment to
fools.

23 The hearts of the wise make their
mouths prudent,
and their lips promote
instruction.[a]

24 Gracious words are
a honeycomb,
sweet to the soul and healing
to the bones.

25 There is a way that appears to be
right,
but in the end it leads to
death.

26 The appetite of laborers works
for them;
their hunger drives them on.

27 A scoundrel plots evil,
and on their lips it is like a
scorching fire.

28 A perverse person stirs up
conflict,
and a gossip separates close
friends.

29 A violent person entices their
neighbor
and leads them down a path
that is not good.

30 Whoever winks with their eye is
plotting perversity;
whoever purses their lips is
bent on evil.

31 Gray hair is a crown of
splendor;
it is attained in the way of
righteousness.

32 Better a patient person than a
warrior,
one with self-control than one
who takes a city.

33 The lot is cast into the lap,
but its every decision is from
the LORD.

17 Better a dry crust with peace
and quiet
than a house full of feasting,
with strife.

2 A prudent servant will rule over
a disgraceful son
and will share the inheritance
as one of the family.

3 The crucible for silver and the
furnace for gold,
but the LORD tests the
heart.

4 A wicked person listens to
deceitful lips;
a liar pays attention to a
destructive tongue.

5 Whoever mocks the poor shows
contempt for their
Maker;
whoever gloats over disaster
will not go unpunished.

6 Children's children are a crown
to the aged,
and parents are the pride of
their children.

7 Eloquent lips are unsuited to a
godless fool —
how much worse lying lips to
a ruler!

8 A bribe is seen as a charm by the
one who gives it;
they think success will come
at every turn.

9 Whoever would foster love
covers over an offense,
but whoever repeats the
matter separates close
friends.

---

[a] 23 Or prudent / and make their lips persuasive

¹⁰ A rebuke impresses a discerning
person
more than a hundred lashes
a fool.

¹¹ Evildoers foster rebellion against
God;
the messenger of death will
be sent against them.

¹² Better to meet a bear robbed of
her cubs
than a fool bent on folly.

¹³ Evil will never leave the house
of one who pays back evil for
good.

¹⁴ Starting a quarrel is like
breaching a dam;
so drop the matter before a
dispute breaks out.

¹⁵ Acquitting the guilty and
condemning the
innocent—
the LORD detests them
both.

¹⁶ Why should fools have money
in hand to buy wisdom,
when they are not able to
understand it?

¹⁷ A friend loves at all times,
and a brother is born for a
time of adversity.

¹⁸ One who has no sense shakes
hands in pledge
and puts up security for a
neighbor.

¹⁹ Whoever loves a quarrel loves
sin;
whoever builds a high gate
invites destruction.

²⁰ One whose heart is corrupt does
not prosper;
one whose tongue is perverse
falls into trouble.

²¹ To have a fool for a child brings
grief;
there is no joy for the parent
of a godless fool.

²² A cheerful heart is good
medicine,
but a crushed spirit dries up
the bones.

²³ The wicked accept bribes in
secret
to pervert the course of
justice.

²⁴ A discerning person keeps
wisdom in view,
but a fool's eyes wander to the
ends of the earth.

²⁵ A foolish son brings grief to his
father
and bitterness to the mother
who bore him.

²⁶ If imposing a fine on the
innocent is not good,
surely to flog honest officials
is not right.

²⁷ The one who has knowledge uses
words with restraint,
and whoever has
understanding is even-
tempered.

²⁸ Even fools are thought wise if
they keep silent,
and discerning if they hold
their tongues.

18 An unfriendly person pursues
selfish ends
and against all sound
judgment starts
quarrels.

² Fools find no pleasure in
understanding
but delight in airing their own
opinions.

3 When wickedness comes, so does
    contempt,
  and with shame comes
    reproach.

4 The words of the mouth are deep
    waters,
  but the fountain of wisdom is
    a rushing stream.

5 It is not good to be partial to the
    wicked
  and so deprive the innocent
    of justice.

6 The lips of fools bring them
    strife,
  and their mouths invite a
    beating.

7 The mouths of fools are their
    undoing,
  and their lips are a snare to
    their very lives.

8 The words of a gossip are like
    choice morsels;
  they go down to the inmost
    parts.

9 One who is slack in his
    work
  is brother to one who
    destroys.

10 The name of the LORD is a
    fortified tower;
  the righteous run to it and are
    safe.

11 The wealth of the rich is their
    fortified city;
  they imagine it a wall too high
    to scale.

12 Before a downfall the heart is
    haughty,
  but humility comes before
    honor.

13 To answer before listening —
  that is folly and shame.

14 The human spirit can endure in
    sickness,
  but a crushed spirit who can
    bear?

15 The heart of the discerning
    acquires knowledge,
  for the ears of the wise seek it
    out.

16 A gift opens the way
  and ushers the giver into the
    presence of the great.

17 In a lawsuit the first to speak
    seems right,
  until someone comes forward
    and cross-examines.

18 Casting the lot settles disputes
  and keeps strong opponents
    apart.

19 A brother wronged is more
    unyielding than a
    fortified city;
  disputes are like the barred
    gates of a citadel.

20 From the fruit of their mouth
    a person's stomach is
    filled;
  with the harvest of their lips
    they are satisfied.

21 The tongue has the power of life
    and death,
  and those who love it will eat
    its fruit.

22 He who finds a wife finds what
    is good
  and receives favor from the
    LORD.

23 The poor plead for mercy,
  but the rich answer harshly.

24 One who has unreliable friends
    soon comes to ruin,
  but there is a friend who sticks
    closer than a brother.

19 Better the poor whose walk is
blameless
than a fool whose lips are
perverse.

² Desire without knowledge is not
good —
how much more will hasty feet
miss the way!

³ A person's own folly leads to
their ruin,
yet their heart rages against
the LORD.

⁴ Wealth attracts many friends,
but even the closest friend of
the poor person deserts
them.

⁵ A false witness will not go
unpunished,
and whoever pours out lies
will not go free.

⁶ Many curry favor with a ruler,
and everyone is the friend of
one who gives gifts.

⁷ The poor are shunned by all their
relatives —
how much more do their
friends avoid them!
Though the poor pursue them
with pleading,
they are nowhere to be found.ᵃ

⁸ The one who gets wisdom loves
life;
the one who cherishes
understanding will soon
prosper.

⁹ A false witness will not go
unpunished,
and whoever pours out lies
will perish.

¹⁰ It is not fitting for a fool to live
in luxury —
how much worse for a slave to
rule over princes!

¹¹ A person's wisdom yields
patience;
it is to one's glory to overlook
an offense.

¹² A king's rage is like the roar of a
lion,
but his favor is like dew on the
grass.

¹³ A foolish child is a father's ruin,
and a quarrelsome wife
is like
the constant dripping of a
leaky roof.

¹⁴ Houses and wealth are inherited
from parents,
but a prudent wife is from the
LORD.

¹⁵ Laziness brings on deep sleep,
and the shiftless go hungry.

¹⁶ Whoever keeps commandments
keeps their life,
but whoever shows contempt
for their ways will die.

¹⁷ Whoever is kind to the poor
lends to the LORD,
and he will reward them for
what they have done.

¹⁸ Discipline your children, for in
that there is hope;
do not be a willing party to
their death.

¹⁹ A hot-tempered person must pay
the penalty;
rescue them, and you will have
to do it again.

²⁰ Listen to advice and accept
discipline,
and at the end you will be
counted among the
wise.

ᵃ 7 The meaning of the Hebrew for this
sentence is uncertain.

²¹ Many are the plans in a person's
heart,
  but it is the LORD's purpose
    that prevails.

²² What a person desires is
  unfailing love^a;
  better to be poor than a liar.

²³ The fear of the LORD leads to life;
  then one rests content,
    untouched by trouble.

²⁴ A sluggard buries his hand in the
  dish;
  he will not even bring it back
    to his mouth!

²⁵ Flog a mocker, and the simple
  will learn prudence;
  rebuke the discerning, and
    they will gain knowledge.

²⁶ Whoever robs their father and
  drives out their mother
  is a child who brings shame
    and disgrace.

²⁷ Stop listening to instruction, my
  son,
  and you will stray from the
    words of knowledge.

²⁸ A corrupt witness mocks at
  justice,
  and the mouth of the wicked
    gulps down evil.

²⁹ Penalties are prepared for
  mockers,
  and beatings for the backs of
    fools.

20 Wine is a mocker and beer a
  brawler;
  whoever is led astray by them
    is not wise.

² A king's wrath strikes terror like
  the roar of a lion;
  those who anger him forfeit
    their lives.

³ It is to one's honor to avoid strife,
  but every fool is quick to
    quarrel.

⁴ Sluggards do not plow in
  season;
  so at harvest time they look
    but find nothing.

⁵ The purposes of a person's heart
  are deep waters,
  but one who has insight draws
    them out.

⁶ Many claim to have unfailing
  love,
  but a faithful person who can
    find?

⁷ The righteous lead blameless
  lives;
  blessed are their children after
    them.

⁸ When a king sits on his throne to
  judge,
  he winnows out all evil with
    his eyes.

⁹ Who can say, "I have kept my
  heart pure;
  I am clean and without sin"?

¹⁰ Differing weights and differing
  measures —
  the LORD detests them both.

¹¹ Even small children are known
  by their actions,
  so is their conduct really pure
    and upright?

¹² Ears that hear and eyes that
  see —
  the LORD has made them both.

¹³ Do not love sleep or you will
  grow poor;
  stay awake and you will have
    food to spare.

^a 22 Or Greed is a person's shame

¹⁴ "It's no good, it's no good!" says
the buyer —
then goes off and boasts about
the purchase.

¹⁵ Gold there is, and rubies in
abundance,
but lips that speak knowledge
are a rare jewel.

¹⁶ Take the garment of one who
puts up security for a
stranger;
hold it in pledge if it is done
for an outsider.

¹⁷ Food gained by fraud tastes
sweet,
but one ends up with a mouth
full of gravel.

¹⁸ Plans are established by seeking
advice;
so if you wage war, obtain
guidance.

¹⁹ A gossip betrays a confidence;
so avoid anyone who talks too
much.

²⁰ If someone curses their father or
mother,
their lamp will be snuffed out
in pitch darkness.

²¹ An inheritance claimed too soon
will not be blessed at the end.

²² Do not say, "I'll pay you back for
this wrong!"
Wait for the LORD, and he will
avenge you.

²³ The LORD detests differing
weights,
and dishonest scales do not
please him.

²⁴ A person's steps are directed by
the LORD.
How then can anyone
understand their own
way?

²⁵ It is a trap to dedicate something
rashly
and only later to consider
one's vows.

²⁶ A wise king winnows out the
wicked;
he drives the threshing wheel
over them.

²⁷ The human spirit is*ª* the lamp
of the LORD
that sheds light on one's
inmost being.

²⁸ Love and faithfulness keep a
king safe;
through love his throne is
made secure.

²⁹ The glory of young men is their
strength,
gray hair the splendor of the
old.

³⁰ Blows and wounds scrub away
evil,
and beatings purge the inmost
being.

21 In the LORD's hand the king's
heart is a stream of
water
that he channels toward all
who please him.

² A person may think their own
ways are right,
but the LORD weighs the
heart.

³ To do what is right and just
is more acceptable to the LORD
than sacrifice.

⁴ Haughty eyes and a proud
heart —
the unplowed field of
the wicked — produce
sin.

ª 27 Or *A person's words are*

⁵ The plans of the diligent lead to
      profit
   as surely as haste leads to
      poverty.

⁶ A fortune made by a lying
      tongue
   is a fleeting vapor and a deadly
      snare.ᵃ

⁷ The violence of the wicked will
      drag them away,
   for they refuse to do what is
      right.

⁸ The way of the guilty is
      devious,
   but the conduct of the
      innocent is upright.

⁹ Better to live on a corner of the
      roof
   than share a house with a
      quarrelsome wife.

¹⁰ The wicked crave evil;
   their neighbors get no mercy
      from them.

¹¹ When a mocker is punished, the
      simple gain wisdom;
   by paying attention to the wise
      they get knowledge.

¹² The Righteous Oneᵇ takes note
      of the house of the
      wicked
   and brings the wicked to ruin.

¹³ Whoever shuts their ears to the
      cry of the poor
   will also cry out and not be
      answered.

¹⁴ A gift given in secret soothes
      anger,
   and a bribe concealed in the
      cloak pacifies great wrath.

¹⁵ When justice is done, it brings
      joy to the righteous
   but terror to evildoers.

¹⁶ Whoever strays from the path
      of prudence
   comes to rest in the company
      of the dead.

¹⁷ Whoever loves pleasure will
      become poor;
   whoever loves wine and olive
      oil will never be rich.

¹⁸ The wicked become a ransom for
      the righteous,
   and the unfaithful for the
      upright.

¹⁹ Better to live in a desert
   than with a quarrelsome and
      nagging wife.

²⁰ The wise store up choice food and
      olive oil,
   but fools gulp theirs down.

²¹ Whoever pursues righteousness
      and love
   finds life, prosperityᶜ and
      honor.

²² One who is wise can go up against
      the city of the mighty
   and pull down the stronghold
      in which they trust.

²³ Those who guard their mouths
      and their tongues
   keep themselves from
      calamity.

²⁴ The proud and arrogant
      person — "Mocker" is his
      name —
   behaves with insolent fury.

²⁵ The craving of a sluggard will be
      the death of him,
   because his hands refuse to
      work.

ᵃ 6 Some Hebrew manuscripts, Septuagint
and Vulgate; most Hebrew manuscripts *vapor
for those who seek death*   ᵇ 12 Or *The
righteous person*   ᶜ 21 Or *righteousness*

26 All day long he craves for more,
but the righteous give without
sparing.

27 The sacrifice of the wicked is
detestable —
how much more so when
brought with evil intent!

28 A false witness will perish,
but a careful listener will
testify successfully.

29 The wicked put up a bold front,
but the upright give thought
to their ways.

30 There is no wisdom, no insight,
no plan
that can succeed against the
Lord.

31 The horse is made ready for the
day of battle,
but victory rests with the
Lord.

22 A good name is more
desirable than great
riches;
to be esteemed is better than
silver or gold.

2 Rich and poor have this in
common:
The Lord is the Maker of them
all.

3 The prudent see danger and take
refuge,
but the simple keep going and
pay the penalty.

4 Humility is the fear of the Lord;
its wages are riches and honor
and life.

5 In the paths of the wicked are
snares and pitfalls,
but those who would preserve
their life stay far from
them.

6 Start children off on the way they
should go,
and even when they are old
they will not turn from it.

7 The rich rule over the poor,
and the borrower is slave to
the lender.

8 Whoever sows injustice reaps
calamity,
and the rod they wield in fury
will be broken.

9 The generous will themselves be
blessed,
for they share their food with
the poor.

10 Drive out the mocker, and out
goes strife;
quarrels and insults are ended.

11 One who loves a pure heart and
who speaks with grace
will have the king for a friend.

12 The eyes of the Lord keep watch
over knowledge,
but he frustrates the words of
the unfaithful.

13 The sluggard says, "There's a lion
outside!
I'll be killed in the public
square!"

14 The mouth of an adulterous
woman is a deep pit;
a man who is under the Lord's
wrath falls into it.

15 Folly is bound up in the heart of
a child,
but the rod of discipline will
drive it far away.

16 One who oppresses the poor to
increase his wealth
and one who gives gifts to
the rich — both come to
poverty.

Thirty Sayings
of the Wise

Saying 1

17 Pay attention and turn your ear
    to the sayings of the wise;
  apply your heart to what I
    teach,
18 for it is pleasing when you keep
    them in your heart
  and have all of them ready on
    your lips.
19 So that your trust may be in the
    LORD,
  I teach you today, even you.
20 Have I not written thirty sayings
    for you,
  sayings of counsel and
    knowledge,
21 teaching you to be honest and to
    speak the truth,
  so that you bring back truthful
    reports
  to those you serve?

Saying 2

22 Do not exploit the poor because
    they are poor
  and do not crush the needy in
    court,
23 for the LORD will take up their
    case
  and will exact life for life.

Saying 3

24 Do not make friends with a hot-
    tempered person,
  do not associate with one
    easily angered,
25 or you may learn their ways
  and get yourself ensnared.

Saying 4

26 Do not be one who shakes hands
    in pledge
  or puts up security for debts;
27 if you lack the means to pay,
  your very bed will be snatched
    from under you.

Saying 5

28 Do not move an ancient boundary
    stone
  set up by your ancestors.

Saying 6

29 Do you see someone skilled in
    their work?
  They will serve before kings;
  they will not serve before
    officials of low rank.

Saying 7

23 When you sit to dine with a
    ruler,
  note well what[a] is before you,
2 and put a knife to your throat
  if you are given to gluttony.
3 Do not crave his delicacies,
  for that food is deceptive.

Saying 8

4 Do not wear yourself out to get
    rich;
  do not trust your own
    cleverness.
5 Cast but a glance at riches, and
    they are gone,
  for they will surely sprout wings
  and fly off to the sky like an
    eagle.

Saying 9

6 Do not eat the food of a
    begrudging host,
  do not crave his delicacies;
7 for he is the kind of person
  who is always thinking about
    the cost.[b]

---

[a] 1 Or who   [b] 7 Or for as he thinks within
himself, / so he is; or for as he puts on a feast, /
so he is

"Eat and drink," he says to you,
  but his heart is not with you.
8 You will vomit up the little you
    have eaten
  and will have wasted your
    compliments.

Saying 10

9 Do not speak to fools,
  for they will scorn your
    prudent words.

Saying 11

10 Do not move an ancient
    boundary stone
  or encroach on the fields of
    the fatherless,
11 for their Defender is strong;
  he will take up their case
    against you.

Saying 12

12 Apply your heart to instruction
  and your ears to words of
    knowledge.

Saying 13

13 Do not withhold discipline from
    a child;
  if you punish them with the
    rod, they will not die.
14 Punish them with the rod
  and save them from death.

Saying 14

15 My son, if your heart is wise,
  then my heart will be glad
    indeed;
16 my inmost being will rejoice
  when your lips speak what is
    right.

Saying 15

17 Do not let your heart envy
    sinners,
  but always be zealous for the
    fear of the LORD.

18 There is surely a future hope for
    you,
  and your hope will not be cut
    off.

Saying 16

19 Listen, my son, and be wise,
  and set your heart on the right
    path:
20 Do not join those who drink too
    much wine
  or gorge themselves on
    meat,
21 for drunkards and gluttons
    become poor,
  and drowsiness clothes them
    in rags.

Saying 17

22 Listen to your father, who gave
    you life,
  and do not despise your
    mother when she is old.
23 Buy the truth and do not sell it —
  wisdom, instruction and
    insight as well.
24 The father of a righteous child
    has great joy;
  a man who fathers a wise son
    rejoices in him.
25 May your father and mother
    rejoice;
  may she who gave you birth be
    joyful!

Saying 18

26 My son, give me your heart
  and let your eyes delight in my
    ways,
27 for an adulterous woman is a
    deep pit,
  and a wayward wife is a
    narrow well.
28 Like a bandit she lies in wait
  and multiplies the unfaithful
    among men.

Saying 19

29 Who has woe? Who has sorrow?
    Who has strife? Who has
        complaints?
    Who has needless bruises?
        Who has bloodshot
        eyes?
30 Those who linger over wine,
    who go to sample bowls of
        mixed wine.
31 Do not gaze at wine when it is
        red,
    when it sparkles in the cup,
    when it goes down smoothly!
32 In the end it bites like a snake
    and poisons like a viper.
33 Your eyes will see strange
        sights,
    and your mind will imagine
        confusing things.
34 You will be like one sleeping on
        the high seas,
    lying on top of the rigging.
35 "They hit me," you will say, "but
        I'm not hurt!
    They beat me, but I don't feel
        it!
    When will I wake up
        so I can find another
        drink?"

Saying 20

24 Do not envy the wicked,
    do not desire their company;
2 for their hearts plot violence,
    and their lips talk about
        making trouble.

Saying 21

3 By wisdom a house is built,
    and through understanding it
        is established;
4 through knowledge its rooms
        are filled
    with rare and beautiful
        treasures.

Saying 22

5 The wise prevail through great
        power,
    and those who have
        knowledge muster their
        strength.
6 Surely you need guidance to
        wage war,
    and victory is won through
        many advisers.

Saying 23

7 Wisdom is too high for fools;
    in the assembly at the gate
        they must not open their
        mouths.

Saying 24

8 Whoever plots evil
    will be known as a schemer.
9 The schemes of folly are sin,
    and people detest a mocker.

Saying 25

10 If you falter in a time of
        trouble,
    how small is your strength!
11 Rescue those being led away to
        death;
    hold back those staggering
        toward slaughter.
12 If you say, "But we knew nothing
        about this,"
    does not he who weighs the
        heart perceive it?
    Does not he who guards your life
        know it?
    Will he not repay everyone
        according to what they
        have done?

Saying 26

13 Eat honey, my son, for it is good;
    honey from the comb is sweet
        to your taste.

¹⁴ Know also that wisdom is like
honey for you:
If you find it, there is a future
hope for you,
and your hope will not be cut
off.

Saying 27

¹⁵ Do not lurk like a thief near the
house of the righteous,
do not plunder their dwelling
place;
¹⁶ for though the righteous fall
seven times, they rise
again,
but the wicked stumble when
calamity strikes.

Saying 28

¹⁷ Do not gloat when your enemy
falls;
when they stumble, do not let
your heart rejoice,
¹⁸ or the LORD will see and
disapprove
and turn his wrath away from
them.

Saying 29

¹⁹ Do not fret because of evildoers
or be envious of the wicked,
²⁰ for the evildoer has no future
hope,
and the lamp of the wicked
will be snuffed out.

Saying 30

²¹ Fear the LORD and the king, my
son,
and do not join with rebellious
officials,
²² for those two will send sudden
destruction on them,
and who knows what
calamities they can
bring?

Further Sayings
of the Wise

²³ These also are sayings of the wise:

To show partiality in judging is
not good:
²⁴ Whoever says to the guilty, "You
are innocent,"
will be cursed by peoples and
denounced by nations.
²⁵ But it will go well with those who
convict the guilty,
and rich blessing will come on
them.

²⁶ An honest answer
is like a kiss on the lips.

²⁷ Put your outdoor work in order
and get your fields ready;
after that, build your house.

²⁸ Do not testify against your
neighbor without
cause—
would you use your lips to
mislead?
²⁹ Do not say, "I'll do to them as
they have done to me;
I'll pay them back for what
they did."

³⁰ I went past the field of a
sluggard,
past the vineyard of someone
who has no sense;
³¹ thorns had come up everywhere,
the ground was covered with
weeds,
and the stone wall was in
ruins.
³² I applied my heart to what I
observed
and learned a lesson from
what I saw:
³³ A little sleep, a little slumber,
a little folding of the hands to
rest—

³⁴ and poverty will come on you
    like a thief
and scarcity like an armed
    man.

More Proverbs of Solomon

25 These are more proverbs of Solomon, compiled by the men of Hezekiah king of Judah:

² It is the glory of God to conceal
    a matter;
to search out a matter is the
    glory of kings.
³ As the heavens are high and the
    earth is deep,
so the hearts of kings are
    unsearchable.

⁴ Remove the dross from the
    silver,
and a silversmith can produce
    a vessel;
⁵ remove wicked officials from the
    king's presence,
and his throne will be
    established through
    righteousness.

⁶ Do not exalt yourself in the
    king's presence,
and do not claim a place
    among his great men;
⁷ it is better for him to say to you,
    "Come up here,"
than for him to humiliate you
    before his nobles.

What you have seen with your
    eyes
⁸ do not bring^a hastily to
    court,
for what will you do in the
    end
    if your neighbor puts you to
    shame?

⁹ If you take your neighbor to
    court,
do not betray another's
    confidence,
¹⁰ or the one who hears it may
    shame you
and the charge against you
    will stand.

¹¹ Like apples^b of gold in settings of
    silver
is a ruling rightly given.
¹² Like an earring of gold or an
    ornament of fine gold
is the rebuke of a wise judge to
    a listening ear.

¹³ Like a snow-cooled drink at
    harvest time
is a trustworthy messenger to
    the one who sends him;
he refreshes the spirit of his
    master.
¹⁴ Like clouds and wind without
    rain
is one who boasts of gifts
    never given.

¹⁵ Through patience a ruler can be
    persuaded,
and a gentle tongue can break
    a bone.

¹⁶ If you find honey, eat just
    enough —
too much of it, and you will
    vomit.
¹⁷ Seldom set foot in your
    neighbor's house —
too much of you, and they will
    hate you.

¹⁸ Like a club or a sword or a sharp
    arrow
is one who gives false
    testimony against a
    neighbor.

---

^a 7,8 Or nobles / on whom you had set your eyes. / ⁸Do not go   ^b 11 Or possibly apricots

¹⁹ Like a broken tooth or a lame
       foot
    is reliance on the unfaithful in
       a time of trouble.
²⁰ Like one who takes away a
       garment on a cold day,
    or like vinegar poured on a
       wound,
    is one who sings songs to a
       heavy heart.
²¹ If your enemy is hungry, give
       him food to eat;
    if he is thirsty, give him water
       to drink.
²² In doing this, you will heap
       burning coals on his head,
    and the LORD will reward you.
²³ Like a north wind that brings
       unexpected rain
    is a sly tongue — which
       provokes a horrified look.
²⁴ Better to live on a corner of the
       roof
    than share a house with a
       quarrelsome wife.
²⁵ Like cold water to a weary soul
    is good news from a distant
       land.
²⁶ Like a muddied spring or a
       polluted well
    are the righteous who give way
       to the wicked.
²⁷ It is not good to eat too much
       honey,
    nor is it honorable to search
       out matters that are too
       deep.
²⁸ Like a city whose walls are
       broken through
    is a person who lacks self-
       control.

26 Like snow in summer or rain
       in harvest,
    honor is not fitting for a fool.

² Like a fluttering sparrow or a
       darting swallow,
    an undeserved curse does not
       come to rest.
³ A whip for the horse, a bridle for
       the donkey,
    and a rod for the backs of
       fools!
⁴ Do not answer a fool according to
       his folly,
    or you yourself will be just like
       him.
⁵ Answer a fool according to his
       folly,
    or he will be wise in his own
       eyes.
⁶ Sending a message by the hands
       of a fool
    is like cutting off one's feet or
       drinking poison.
⁷ Like the useless legs of one who
       is lame
    is a proverb in the mouth of a
       fool.
⁸ Like tying a stone in a sling
    is the giving of honor to a fool.
⁹ Like a thornbush in a drunkard's
       hand
    is a proverb in the mouth of a
       fool.
¹⁰ Like an archer who wounds at
       random
    is one who hires a fool or any
       passer-by.
¹¹ As a dog returns to its vomit,
    so fools repeat their folly.
¹² Do you see a person wise in their
       own eyes?
    There is more hope for a fool
       than for them.
¹³ A sluggard says, "There's a lion in
       the road,
    a fierce lion roaming the
       streets!"
¹⁴ As a door turns on its hinges,
    so a sluggard turns on his bed.

¹⁵ A sluggard buries his hand in the dish;
   he is too lazy to bring it back to his mouth.
¹⁶ A sluggard is wiser in his own eyes
   than seven people who answer discreetly.

¹⁷ Like one who grabs a stray dog by the ears
   is someone who rushes into a quarrel not their own.
¹⁸ Like a maniac shooting flaming arrows of death
¹⁹ is one who deceives their neighbor
   and says, "I was only joking!"

²⁰ Without wood a fire goes out;
   without a gossip a quarrel dies down.
²¹ As charcoal to embers and as wood to fire,
   so is a quarrelsome person for kindling strife.
²² The words of a gossip are like choice morsels;
   they go down to the inmost parts.

²³ Like a coating of silver dross on earthenware
   are fervent⁰ lips with an evil heart.
²⁴ Enemies disguise themselves with their lips,
   but in their hearts they harbor deceit.
²⁵ Though their speech is charming, do not believe them,
   for seven abominations fill their hearts.
²⁶ Their malice may be concealed by deception,
   but their wickedness will be exposed in the assembly.

²⁷ Whoever digs a pit will fall into it;
   if someone rolls a stone, it will roll back on them.
²⁸ A lying tongue hates those it hurts,
   and a flattering mouth works ruin.

27 Do not boast about tomorrow, for you do not know what a day may bring.

² Let someone else praise you, and not your own mouth;
   an outsider, and not your own lips.

³ Stone is heavy and sand a burden,
   but a fool's provocation is heavier than both.

⁴ Anger is cruel and fury overwhelming,
   but who can stand before jealousy?

⁵ Better is open rebuke than hidden love.

⁶ Wounds from a friend can be trusted,
   but an enemy multiplies kisses.

⁷ One who is full loathes honey from the comb,
   but to the hungry even what is bitter tastes sweet.

⁸ Like a bird that flees its nest is anyone who flees from home.

⁹ Perfume and incense bring joy to the heart,
   and the pleasantness of a friend springs from their heartfelt advice.

⁰ 23 Hebrew; Septuagint *smooth*

¹⁰ Do not forsake your friend or a
    friend of your family,
  and do not go to your relative's
    house when disaster
    strikes you —
  better a neighbor nearby than
    a relative far away.

¹¹ Be wise, my son, and bring joy to
    my heart;
  then I can answer anyone who
    treats me with contempt.

¹² The prudent see danger and take
    refuge,
  but the simple keep going and
    pay the penalty.

¹³ Take the garment of one who
    puts up security for a
    stranger;
  hold it in pledge if it is done
    for an outsider.

¹⁴ If anyone loudly blesses their
    neighbor early in the
    morning,
  it will be taken as a curse.

¹⁵ A quarrelsome wife is like the
    dripping
  of a leaky roof in a rainstorm;

¹⁶ restraining her is like restraining
    the wind
  or grasping oil with the hand.

¹⁷ As iron sharpens iron,
  so one person sharpens
    another.

¹⁸ The one who guards a fig tree
    will eat its fruit,
  and whoever protects their
    master will be honored.

¹⁹ As water reflects the face,
  so one's life reflects the heart.ᵃ

²⁰ Death and Destructionᵇ are never
    satisfied,
  and neither are human eyes.

²¹ The crucible for silver and the
    furnace for gold,
  but people are tested by their
    praise.

²² Though you grind a fool in a
    mortar,
  grinding them like grain with
    a pestle,
  you will not remove their folly
    from them.

²³ Be sure you know the condition
    of your flocks,
  give careful attention to your
    herds;

²⁴ for riches do not endure forever,
  and a crown is not secure for
    all generations.

²⁵ When the hay is removed and
    new growth appears
  and the grass from the hills is
    gathered in,

²⁶ the lambs will provide you with
    clothing,
  and the goats with the price of
    a field.

²⁷ You will have plenty of goats'
    milk to feed your family
  and to nourish your female
    servants.

28 The wicked flee though no
    one pursues,
  but the righteous are as bold
    as a lion.

² When a country is rebellious, it
    has many rulers,
  but a ruler with discernment
    and knowledge maintains
    order.

³ A rulerᶜ who oppresses the
    poor
  is like a driving rain that
    leaves no crops.

ᵃ 19 Or so others reflect your heart back to you
ᵇ 20 Hebrew *Abaddon*   ᶜ 3 Or *A poor person*

⁴ Those who forsake instruction
     praise the wicked,
  but those who heed it resist
     them.

⁵ Evildoers do not understand
     what is right,
  but those who seek the LORD
     understand it fully.

⁶ Better the poor whose walk is
     blameless
  than the rich whose ways are
     perverse.

⁷ A discerning son heeds
     instruction,
  but a companion of
     gluttons disgraces his
     father.

⁸ Whoever increases wealth by
     taking interest or profit
     from the poor
  amasses it for another, who
     will be kind to the
     poor.

⁹ If anyone turns a deaf ear to my
     instruction,
  even their prayers are
     detestable.

¹⁰ Whoever leads the upright along
      an evil path
   will fall into their own
      trap,
   but the blameless will receive
      a good inheritance.

¹¹ The rich are wise in their own
      eyes;
   one who is poor and
      discerning sees how
      deluded they are.

¹² When the righteous triumph,
      there is great elation;
   but when the wicked rise to
      power, people go into
      hiding.

¹³ Whoever conceals their sins does
      not prosper,
   but the one who confesses and
      renounces them finds
      mercy.

¹⁴ Blessed is the one who always
      trembles before God,
   but whoever hardens their
      heart falls into trouble.

¹⁵ Like a roaring lion or a charging
      bear
   is a wicked ruler over a
      helpless people.

¹⁶ A tyrannical ruler practices
      extortion,
   but one who hates ill-gotten
      gain will enjoy a long
      reign.

¹⁷ Anyone tormented by the guilt
      of murder
   will seek refuge in the
      grave;
   let no one hold them back.

¹⁸ The one whose walk is blameless
      is kept safe,
   but the one whose ways are
      perverse will fall into the
      pit.ᵃ

¹⁹ Those who work their land will
      have abundant food,
   but those who chase fantasies
      will have their fill of
      poverty.

²⁰ A faithful person will be richly
      blessed,
   but one eager to get rich will
      not go unpunished.

²¹ To show partiality is not
      good—
   yet a person will do wrong for
      a piece of bread.

ᵃ 18 Syriac (see Septuagint); Hebrew *into one*

22 The stingy are eager to get
        rich
    and are unaware that poverty
        awaits them.

23 Whoever rebukes a person will
        in the end gain favor
    rather than one who has a
        flattering tongue.

24 Whoever robs their father or
        mother
    and says, "It's not wrong,"
    is partner to one who
        destroys.

25 The greedy stir up conflict,
    but those who trust in the
        LORD will prosper.

26 Those who trust in themselves
        are fools,
    but those who walk in wisdom
        are kept safe.

27 Those who give to the poor will
        lack nothing,
    but those who close their eyes
        to them receive many
        curses.

28 When the wicked rise to power,
        people go into hiding;
    but when the wicked perish,
        the righteous thrive.

29 Whoever remains stiff-
        necked after many
        rebukes
    will suddenly be destroyed —
        without remedy.

2 When the righteous thrive,
        the people rejoice;
    when the wicked rule, the
        people groan.

3 A man who loves wisdom brings
        joy to his father,
    but a companion of prostitutes
        squanders his wealth.

4 By justice a king gives a country
        stability,
    but those who are greedy for[a]
        bribes tear it down.

5 Those who flatter their
        neighbors
    are spreading nets for their
        feet.

6 Evildoers are snared by their
        own sin,
    but the righteous shout for joy
        and are glad.

7 The righteous care about justice
        for the poor,
    but the wicked have no such
        concern.

8 Mockers stir up a city,
    but the wise turn away anger.

9 If a wise person goes to court
        with a fool,
    the fool rages and scoffs, and
        there is no peace.

10 The bloodthirsty hate a person
        of integrity
    and seek to kill the upright.

11 Fools give full vent to their
        rage,
    but the wise bring calm in the
        end.

12 If a ruler listens to lies,
    all his officials become
        wicked.

13 The poor and the oppressor have
        this in common:
    The LORD gives sight to the
        eyes of both.

14 If a king judges the poor with
        fairness,
    his throne will be established
        forever.

---

[a] 4 Or who give

¹⁵ A rod and a reprimand impart
      wisdom,
   but a child left undisciplined
      disgraces its mother.

¹⁶ When the wicked thrive, so does
      sin,
   but the righteous will see their
      downfall.

¹⁷ Discipline your children, and
      they will give you
      peace;
   they will bring you the
      delights you desire.

¹⁸ Where there is no revelation,
      people cast off restraint;
   but blessed is the one
      who heeds wisdom's
      instruction.

¹⁹ Servants cannot be corrected by
      mere words;
   though they understand, they
      will not respond.

²⁰ Do you see someone who speaks
      in haste?
   There is more hope for a fool
      than for them.

²¹ A servant pampered from youth
      will turn out to be insolent.

²² An angry person stirs up conflict,
   and a hot-tempered person
      commits many sins.

²³ Pride brings a person low,
   but the lowly in spirit gain
      honor.

²⁴ The accomplices of thieves are
      their own enemies;
   they are put under oath and
      dare not testify.

²⁵ Fear of man will prove to be a
      snare,
   but whoever trusts in the Lord
      is kept safe.

²⁶ Many seek an audience with a
      ruler,
   but it is from the Lord that
      one gets justice.

²⁷ The righteous detest the
      dishonest;
   the wicked detest the upright.

Sayings of Agur

30 The sayings of Agur son of Ja-
      keh — an inspired utterance.

This man's utterance to Ithiel:

"I am weary, God,
   but I can prevail.ᵃ
² Surely I am only a brute, not a
      man;
   I do not have human
      understanding.
³ I have not learned wisdom,
   nor have I attained to the
      knowledge of the Holy
      One.
⁴ Who has gone up to heaven and
      come down?
   Whose hands have gathered
      up the wind?
   Who has wrapped up the waters
      in a cloak?
   Who has established all the
      ends of the earth?
   What is his name, and what is
      the name of his son?
   Surely you know!

⁵ "Every word of God is flawless;
   he is a shield to those who take
      refuge in him.
⁶ Do not add to his words,
   or he will rebuke you and
      prove you a liar.

ᵃ 1 With a different word division of the
Hebrew; Masoretic Text *utterance to Ithiel, / to
Ithiel and Ukal:*

7 "Two things I ask of you,
    LORD;
  do not refuse me before
    I die:
8 Keep falsehood and lies far from
    me;
  give me neither poverty nor
    riches,
  but give me only my daily
    bread.
9 Otherwise, I may have too much
    and disown you
  and say, 'Who is the LORD?'
  Or I may become poor and
    steal,
  and so dishonor the name of
    my God.

10 "Do not slander a servant to their
    master,
  or they will curse you, and you
    will pay for it.

11 "There are those who curse their
    fathers
  and do not bless their
    mothers;
12 those who are pure in their own
    eyes
  and yet are not cleansed of
    their filth;
13 those whose eyes are ever so
    haughty,
  whose glances are so
    disdainful;
14 those whose teeth are swords
  and whose jaws are set with
    knives
  to devour the poor from the
    earth
  and the needy from among
    mankind.

15 "The leech has two daughters.
    'Give! Give!' they cry.

  "There are three things that are
    never satisfied,
  four that never say, 'Enough!':

16 the grave, the barren womb,
  land, which is never satisfied
    with water,
  and fire, which never says,
    'Enough!'

17 "The eye that mocks a father,
  that scorns an aged mother,
  will be pecked out by the ravens
    of the valley,
  will be eaten by the vultures.

18 "There are three things that are
    too amazing for me,
  four that I do not understand:
19 the way of an eagle in the sky,
  the way of a snake on a rock,
  the way of a ship on the high
    seas,
  and the way of a man with a
    young woman.

20 "This is the way of an adulterous
    woman:
  She eats and wipes her mouth
  and says, 'I've done nothing
    wrong.'

21 "Under three things the earth
    trembles,
  under four it cannot bear up:
22 a servant who becomes king,
  a godless fool who gets plenty
    to eat,
23 a contemptible woman who gets
    married,
  and a servant who displaces
    her mistress.

24 "Four things on earth are small,
  yet they are extremely wise:
25 Ants are creatures of little
    strength,
  yet they store up their food in
    the summer;
26 hyraxes are creatures of little
    power,
  yet they make their home in
    the crags;

²⁷ locusts have no king,
  yet they advance together in
      ranks;
²⁸ a lizard can be caught with the
      hand,
  yet it is found in kings'
      palaces.

²⁹ "There are three things that are
      stately in their stride,
  four that move with stately
      bearing:
³⁰ a lion, mighty among beasts,
  who retreats before nothing;
³¹ a strutting rooster, a he-goat,
  and a king secure against
      revolt.ᵃ

³² "If you play the fool and exalt
      yourself,
  or if you plan evil,
  clap your hand over your
      mouth!
³³ For as churning cream produces
      butter,
  and as twisting the nose
      produces blood,
  so stirring up anger produces
      strife."

Sayings of King Lemuel

31 The sayings of King Lemuel — an
  inspired utterance his mother
taught him.

² Listen, my son! Listen, son of my
      womb!
  Listen, my son, the answer to
      my prayers!
³ Do not spend your strengthᵇ on
      women,
  your vigor on those who ruin
      kings.

⁴ It is not for kings, Lemuel —
  it is not for kings to drink
      wine,
  not for rulers to crave beer,

⁵ lest they drink and forget what
      has been decreed,
  and deprive all the oppressed
      of their rights.
⁶ Let beer be for those who are
      perishing,
  wine for those who are in
      anguish!
⁷ Let them drink and forget their
      poverty
  and remember their misery no
      more.

⁸ Speak up for those who cannot
      speak for themselves,
  for the rights of all who are
      destitute.
⁹ Speak up and judge fairly;
  defend the rights of the poor
      and needy.

Epilogue: The Wife of Noble Character

¹⁰ ᶜ A wife of noble character who
      can find?
  She is worth far more than
      rubies.
¹¹ Her husband has full confidence
      in her
  and lacks nothing of value.
¹² She brings him good, not harm,
  all the days of her life.
¹³ She selects wool and flax
  and works with eager hands.
¹⁴ She is like the merchant ships,
  bringing her food from afar.
¹⁵ She gets up while it is still night;
  she provides food for her
      family
  and portions for her female
      servants.

ᵃ 31 The meaning of the Hebrew for this
phrase is uncertain.   ᵇ 3 Or wealth
ᶜ 10 Verses 10-31 are an acrostic poem, the
verses of which begin with the successive
letters of the Hebrew alphabet.

16 She considers a field and buys it;
    out of her earnings she plants
        a vineyard.
17 She sets about her work
    vigorously;
    her arms are strong for her
        tasks.
18 She sees that her trading is
    profitable,
    and her lamp does not go out
        at night.
19 In her hand she holds the distaff
    and grasps the spindle with
        her fingers.
20 She opens her arms to the
    poor
    and extends her hands to the
        needy.
21 When it snows, she has no fear
    for her household;
    for all of them are clothed in
        scarlet.
22 She makes coverings for her
    bed;
    she is clothed in fine linen and
        purple.
23 Her husband is respected at the
    city gate,
    where he takes his seat
        among the elders of the
        land.

24 She makes linen garments and
    sells them,
    and supplies the merchants
        with sashes.
25 She is clothed with strength and
    dignity;
    she can laugh at the days to
        come.
26 She speaks with wisdom,
    and faithful instruction is
        on her tongue.
27 She watches over the affairs
    of her household
    and does not eat the bread
        of idleness.
28 Her children arise and call her
    blessed;
    her husband also, and he
        praises her:
29 "Many women do noble
    things,
    but you surpass them all."
30 Charm is deceptive, and beauty
    is fleeting;
    but a woman who fears the
        LORD is to be praised.
31 Honor her for all that her hands
    have done,
    and let her works bring
        her praise at the city
        gate.

Table of Weights and Measures

	BIBLICAL UNIT	APPROXIMATE AMERICAN EQUIVALENT	APPROXIMATE METRIC EQUIVALENT
Weights	talent (60 minas)	75 pounds	34 kilograms
	mina (50 shekels)	1 ¼ pounds	560 grams
	shekel (2 bekas)	⅖ ounce	11.5 grams
	pim (⅔ shekel)	¼ ounce	7.8 grams
	beka (10 gerahs)	⅕ ounce	5.7 grams
	gerah	1/50 ounce	0.6 gram
	daric	⅓ ounce	8.4 grams
Length	cubit	18 inches	45 centimeters
	span	9 inches	23 centimeters
	handbreadth	3 inches	7.5 centimeters
	stadion (pl. stadia)	600 feet	183 meters
Capacity *Dry Measure*	cor [homer] (10 ephahs)	6 bushels	220 liters
	lethek (5 ephahs)	3 bushels	110 liters
	ephah (10 omers)	⅗ bushel	22 liters
	seah (⅓ ephah)	7 quarts	7.5 liters
	omer (1/10 ephah)	2 quarts	2 liters
	cab (1/18 ephah)	1 quart	1 liter
Liquid Measure	bath (1 ephah)	6 gallons	22 liters
	hin (⅙ bath)	1 gallon	3.8 liters
	log (1/72 bath)	⅓ quart	0.3 liter

The figures of the table are calculated on the basis of a shekel equaling 11.5 grams, a cubit equaling 18 inches and an ephah equaling 22 liters. The quart referred to is either a dry quart (slightly larger than a liter) or a liquid quart (slightly smaller than a liter), whichever is applicable. The ton referred to in the footnotes is the American ton of 2,000 pounds. These weights are calculated relative to the particular commodity involved. Accordingly, the same measure of capacity in the text may be converted into different weights in the footnotes.

This table is based upon the best available information, but it is not intended to be mathematically precise; like the measurement equivalents in the footnotes, it merely gives approximate amounts and distances. Weights and measures differed somewhat at various times and places in the ancient world. There is uncertainty particularly about the ephah and the bath; further discoveries may shed more light on these units of capacity.

A Word About the NIV

The goal of the New International Version (NIV) is to enable English-speaking people from around the world to read and hear God's eternal Word in their own language. Our work as translators is motivated by our conviction that the Bible is God's Word in written form. We believe that the Bible contains the divine answer to the deepest needs of humanity, sheds unique light on our path in a dark world and sets forth the way to our eternal well-being. Out of these deep convictions, we have sought to recreate as far as possible the experience of the original audience — blending transparency to the original text with accessibility for the millions of English speakers around the world. We have prioritized accuracy, clarity and literary quality with the goal of creating a translation suitable for public and private reading, evangelism, teaching, preaching, memorizing and liturgical use. We have also sought to preserve a measure of continuity with the long tradition of translating the Scriptures into English.

The complete NIV Bible was first published in 1978. It was a completely new translation made by over a hundred scholars working directly from the best available Hebrew, Aramaic and Greek texts. The translators came from the United States, Great Britain, Canada, Australia and New Zealand, giving the translation an international scope. They were from many denominations and churches — including Anglican, Assemblies of God, Baptist, Brethren, Christian Reformed, Church of Christ, Evangelical Covenant, Evangelical Free, Lutheran, Mennonite, Methodist, Nazarene, Presbyterian, Wesleyan and others. This breadth of denominational and theological perspective helped to safeguard the translation from sectarian bias. For these reasons, and by the grace of God, the NIV has gained a wide readership in all parts of the English-speaking world.

The work of translating the Bible is never finished. As good as they are, English translations must be regularly updated so that they will continue to communicate accurately the meaning of God's Word. Updates are needed in order to reflect the latest developments in our understanding of the biblical world and its languages and to keep pace with changes in English usage. Recognizing, then, that the NIV would retain its ability to communicate God's Word accurately only if it were regularly updated, the original translators established the Committee on Bible Translation (CBT). The Committee is a self-perpetuating group of biblical scholars charged with keeping abreast of advances in biblical scholarship and changes in English and issuing periodic updates to the NIV. The CBT is an independent, self-governing body and has sole responsibility for the NIV text. The Committee mirrors the original group of translators in its diverse international and denominational makeup and in its unifying commitment to the Bible as God's inspired Word.

In obedience to its mandate, the Committee has issued periodic updates to the NIV. An initial revision was released in 1984. A more thorough revision process was completed in 2005, resulting in the separately published TNIV.

The updated NIV you now have in your hands builds on both the original NIV and the TNIV and represents the latest effort of the Committee to articulate God's unchanging Word in the way the original authors might have said it had they been speaking in English to the global English-speaking audience today.

Translation Philosophy

The Committee's translating work has been governed by three widely accepted principles about the way people use words and about the way we understand them.

First, the meaning of words is determined by the way that users of the language actually use them at any given time. For the biblical languages, therefore, the Committee utilizes the best and most recent scholarship on the way Hebrew, Aramaic and Greek words were being used in biblical times. At the same time, the Committee carefully studies the state of modern English. Good translation is like good communication: one must know the target audience so that the appropriate choices can be made about which English words to use to represent the original words of Scripture. From its inception, the NIV has had as its target the general English-speaking population all over the world, the "International" in its title reflecting this concern. The aim of the Committee is to put the Scriptures into natural English that will communicate effectively with the broadest possible audience of English speakers.

Modern technology has enhanced the Committee's ability to choose the right English words to convey the meaning of the original text. The field of computational linguistics harnesses the power of computers to provide broadly applicable and current data about the state of the language. Translators can now access huge databases of modern English to better understand the current meaning and usage of key words. The Committee utilized this resource in preparing the 2011 edition of the NIV. An area of especially rapid and significant change in English is the way certain nouns and pronouns are used to refer to human beings. The Committee therefore requested experts in computational linguistics at Collins Dictionaries to pose some key questions about this usage to its database of English — the largest in the world, with over 4.4 billion words, gathered from several English-speaking countries and including both spoken and written English. (The Collins Study, called "The Development and Use of Gender Language in Contemporary English," can be accessed at *http://www.thenivbible.com/about-the-niv/about-the-2011-edition/*.) The study revealed that the most popular words to describe the human race in modern U.S. English were "humanity," "man" and "mankind." The Committee then used this data in the updated NIV, choosing from among these three words (and occasionally others also) depending on the context.

A related issue creates a larger problem for modern translations: the move away from using the third-person masculine singular pronouns — "he/him/his" — to refer to men and women equally. This usage does persist in some forms of English, and this revision therefore occasionally uses these pronouns in a generic sense. But the tendency, recognized in day-to-day usage and confirmed by the Collins study, is away from the generic use of "he," "him" and "his." In recognition of this shift in language and in an effort to translate into the natural English that people are actually using, this revision of the NIV generally uses other constructions when the biblical text is plainly addressed to men and women equally. The reader will encounter especially frequently a "they," "their" or "them" to express a generic singular idea. Thus, for instance, Mark 8:36 reads: "What good is it for someone to gain the whole world, yet forfeit their soul?" This generic use of the "distributive" or "singular" they/them/their has been used for many centuries by respected writers of English and has now become established as standard English, spoken and written, all over the world.

A second linguistic principle that feeds into the Committee's translation work is that meaning is found not in individual words, as vital as they are, but in larger clusters: phrases, clauses, sentences, discourses. Translation is not, as many people think, a matter of word substitution: English word *x* in place of Hebrew word *y*. Translators must first determine the meaning of the words of the biblical languages in the context of the passage and then select English words that accurately communicate that meaning to modern listeners and readers. This means that accurate translation will not always reflect the exact structure of the original language. To be sure, there is debate over the degree to which translators should try to preserve the "form" of the original text in English. From the beginning, the NIV has taken a mediating position on this issue. The manual produced when the translation that became the NIV was first being planned states: "If the Greek or Hebrew syntax has a good parallel in modern English, it should be used. But if there is no good parallel, the English syntax appropriate to the meaning of the original is to be chosen." It is fine, in other words, to carry over the form of the biblical languages into English — but not at the expense of natural expression. The principle that meaning resides in larger clusters of words means that the Committee has not insisted on a "word-for-word" approach to translation. We certainly believe that every word of Scripture is inspired by God and therefore to be carefully studied to determine what God is saying to us. It is for this reason that the Committee labors over every single word of the original texts, working hard to determine how each of those words contributes to what the text is saying. Ultimately, however, it is how these individual words function in combination with other words that determines meaning.

A third linguistic principle guiding the Committee in its translation work is the recognition that words have a spectrum of meaning. It is popular to define a word by using another word, or "gloss," to substitute for it. This substitute word is then sometimes called the "literal" meaning of a word. In fact, however, words have a range of possible meanings. Those meanings will vary depending on the context, and words in one language will usually not occupy the same semantic range as words in another language. The Committee therefore studies each original word of Scripture in its context to identify its meaning in a particular verse and then chooses an appropriate English word (or phrase) to represent it. It is impossible, then, to translate any given Hebrew, Aramaic or Greek word with the same English word all the time. The

Committee does try to translate related occurrences of a word in the original languages with the same English word in order to preserve the connection for the English reader. But the Committee generally privileges clear natural meaning over a concern with consistency in rendering particular words.

Textual Basis

For the Old Testament the standard Hebrew text, the Masoretic Text as published in the latest edition of *Biblia Hebraica*, has been used throughout. The Masoretic Text tradition contains marginal notations that offer variant readings. These have sometimes been followed instead of the text itself. Because such instances involve variants within the Masoretic tradition, they have not been indicated in the textual notes. In a few cases, words in the basic consonantal text have been divided differently than in the Masoretic Text. Such cases are usually indicated in the textual footnotes. The Dead Sea Scrolls contain biblical texts that represent an earlier stage of the transmission of the Hebrew text. They have been consulted, as have been the Samaritan Pentateuch and the ancient scribal traditions concerning deliberate textual changes. The translators also consulted the more important early versions. Readings from these versions, the Dead Sea Scrolls and the scribal traditions were occasionally followed where the Masoretic Text seemed doubtful and where accepted principles of textual criticism showed that one or more of these textual witnesses appeared to provide the correct reading. In rare cases, the translators have emended the Hebrew text where it appears to have become corrupted at an even earlier stage of its transmission. These departures from the Masoretic Text are also indicated in the textual footnotes. Sometimes the vowel indicators (which are later additions to the basic consonantal text) found in the Masoretic Text did not, in the judgment of the translators, represent the correct vowels for the original text. Accordingly, some words have been read with a different set of vowels. These instances are usually not indicated in the footnotes.

The Greek text used in translating the New Testament has been an eclectic one, based on the latest editions of the Nestle-Aland/United Bible Societies' Greek New Testament. The translators have made their choices among the variant readings in accordance with widely accepted principles of New Testament textual criticism. Footnotes call attention to places where uncertainty remains.

The New Testament authors, writing in Greek, often quote the Old Testament from its ancient Greek version, the Septuagint. This is one reason why some of the Old Testament quotations in the NIV New Testament are not identical to the corresponding passages in the NIV Old Testament. Such quotations in the New Testament are indicated with the footnote "(see Septuagint)."

Footnotes and Formatting

Footnotes in this version are of several kinds, most of which need no explanation. Those giving alternative translations begin with "Or" and generally introduce the alternative with the last word preceding it in the text, except when it is a single-word alternative. When poetry is quoted in a footnote a slash mark indicates a line division.

It should be noted that references to diseases, minerals, flora and fauna, architectural details, clothing, jewelry, musical instruments and other articles cannot always be identified with precision. Also, linear measurements and measures of capacity can only be approximated (see the Table of Weights and Measures). Although *Selah*, used mainly in the Psalms, is probably a musical term, its meaning is uncertain. Since it may interrupt reading and distract the reader, this word has not been kept in the English text, but every occurrence has been signaled by a footnote.

As an aid to the reader, sectional headings have been inserted. They are not to be regarded as part of the biblical text and are not intended for oral reading. It is the Committee's hope that these headings may prove more helpful to the reader than the traditional chapter divisions, which were introduced long after the Bible was written.

Sometimes the chapter and/or verse numbering in English translations of the Old Testament differs from that found in published Hebrew texts. This is particularly the case in the Psalms, where the traditional titles are included in the Hebrew verse numbering. Such differences are indicated in the footnotes at the bottom of the page. In the New Testament, verse numbers that marked off portions of the traditional English text not supported by the best Greek manuscripts now appear in brackets, with a footnote indicating the text that has been omitted (see, for example, Matthew 17:[21]).

Mark 16:9 – 20 and John 7:53 — 8:11, although long accorded virtually equal status with the rest of the Gospels in which they stand, have a questionable standing in the textual history of the New Testament, as noted in the bracketed annotations with which they are set off. A different typeface has been chosen for these passages to indicate their uncertain status.

Basic formatting of the text, such as lining the poetry, paragraphing (both prose and poetry), setting up of (administrative-like) lists, indenting letters and lengthy prayers within narratives and the insertion of sectional headings, has been the work of the Committee. However, the choice between single-column and double-column formats has been left to the publishers. Also the issuing of "red-letter" editions is a publisher's choice — one that the Committee does not endorse.

The Committee has again been reminded that every human effort is flawed — including this revision of the NIV. We trust, however, that many will find in it an improved representation of the Word of God, through which they hear his call to faith in our Lord Jesus Christ and to service in his kingdom. We offer this version of the Bible to him in whose name and for whose glory it has been made.

The Committee on Bible Translation

The ABCs of Salvation

A   **All** people are sinners.
All have sinned and fall short of the glory of God.   —Romans 3:23

B   The **Bible** is God's word of love and salvation.
But these are written that you may believe that Jesus is the
Messiah, the Son of God, and that by believing you may have
life in his name.   —John 20:31

C   The **condition** of sinners is serious.
All will be condemned who have not believed the truth but have delighted in wickedness.   —2 Thessalonians 2:12

D   Christ **died** to save sinners.
While we were still sinners, Christ died for us.   —Romans 5:8

E   **Everyone** who believes will have **eternal** life.
Whoever believes in [Jesus] shall not perish but have
eternal life.   —John 3:16

F   We are saved through **faith**.
For in the gospel the righteousness of God is revealed — a righteousness that is by faith from first to last, just as it is written: "The righteous will live by faith."   —Romans 1:17

G   **Good works** will not save you.
For it is by grace you have been saved, through faith — and this is
not from yourselves, it is the gift of God — not by works, so that no
one can boast.   —Ephesians 2:8–9

H   **Hell** and punishment await unbelievers.
He will punish those who do not know God and do not obey the
gospel of our Lord Jesus. They will be punished with everlasting
destruction and shut out from the presence of the Lord and from the
glory of his might.   —2 Thessalonians 1:8–9

I   Nothing is **impossible** for God.
For no word from God will ever fail.   —Luke 1:37

J There is **joy** in heaven over one sinner who repents.

"There is rejoicing in the presence of the angels of God over one sinner who repents."
—*Luke 15:10*

K If we trust God, he will **keep** us from sin.

[Give praise] to him who is able to keep you from stumbling and to present you before his glorious presence without fault and with great joy.
—*Jude 24*

L God **loves** sinners and wants to save them.

For God so loved the world that he gave his one and only Son, that whoever believes in him shall not perish but have eternal life.
—*John 3:16*

M God has **mercy** on unbelievers.

For God has bound everyone over to disobedience so that he may have mercy on them all.
—*Romans 11:32*

N Jesus is the only **name** by which we can be saved.

Salvation is found in no one else, for there is no other name under heaven given to mankind by which we must be saved.   —*Acts 4:12*

O We show God we love him by **obeying** his commandments.

This is love for God: to keep his commands. And his commands are not burdensome.
—*1 John 5:3*

P God is **patient** with unbelievers.

The Lord is not slow in keeping his promise, as some understand slowness. Instead he is patient with you, not wanting anyone to perish, but everyone to come to repentance.   —*2 Peter 3:9*

Q Those who don't believe should **quickly** decide to follow Jesus.

I tell you, now is the time of God's favor, now is the day of salvation.
—*2 Corinthians 6:2*

R Christians have a reason to **rejoice**.

"Rejoice that your names are written in heaven."
—*Luke 10:20*

S The Bible, the **Scriptures**, can teach us how to be saved.

From infancy you have known the Holy Scriptures, which are able to make you wise for salvation through faith in Christ Jesus.
—*2 Timothy 3:15*

T We should give **thanks** to God for the wonderful gift of salvation.

Thanks be to God for his indescribable gift!   —*2 Corinthians 9:15*

U The Holy Spirit helps us **understand** God's Word.

What we have received is not the spirit of the world, but the Spirit who is from God, so that we may understand what God has freely given us.
—*1 Corinthians 2:12*

V Jesus has gained **victory** over death for us.

When the perishable has been clothed with the imperishable, and the mortal with immortality, then the saying that is written will come true: "Death has been swallowed up in victory." —*1 Corinthians 15:54*

W **Whoever** calls on Jesus will be saved.

"Everyone who calls on the name of the Lord will be saved."
—*Acts 2:21*

Y God loves **you** so much he calls you his child.

See what great love the Father has lavished on us, that we should be called children of God! And that is what we are!
—*1 John 3:1*

A NOTE REGARDING THE TYPE

This Bible was set in the Zondervan NIV Typeface, commissioned by Zondervan, a division of HarperCollins Christian Publishing, and designed in Aarhus, Denmark, by Klaus E. Krogh and Heidi Rand Sørensen of 2K/DENMARK. The design takes inspiration from the vision of the New International Version (NIV) to be a modern translation that gives the reader the most accurate Bible text possible, reflects the very best of biblical scholarship, and uses contemporary global English. The designers of the Zondervan NIV Typeface sought to reflect this rich, half-century-old tradition of accuracy, readability, and clarity while also embodying the best advancements in modern Bible typography. The result is a distinctive, open Bible typeface that is uncompromisingly beautiful, clear, readable at any size, and perfectly suited to the New International Version.

Understanding Jesus' Identity and Mission

"Stretch out your hand to heal and perform miraculous signs and wonders through the name of your holy servant Jesus." Acts 4:30 (read Acts 4:23-31)

What happened after the crucifixion of Jesus that changed the minds of the disciples, who had denied, disobeyed and deserted Jesus? Very simply, what happened is similar to what Jesus experienced at his baptism, when he heard the Father declare, "This is my Son, whom I love; with him I am well pleased" (Matthew 3:17), and was launched into his public ministry—it was confirmed to them that Jesus was who they had hoped he was.

And who exactly was he? Jesus knew he was the person appointed by God to execute the climactic saving act of God in human history. He had been authorized by God, empowered by God, he spoke for God, and he was directed by God to do this task. So what Jesus said, God said. What Jesus did was the work of God.

Jesus believed he was on a divine mission to redeem the people of God. The implication is that the people of God were lost and that God had to do something—as he had always done—to intervene and set them back on the right track. But there was a difference this time. This was the last time. This was the last chance.

Did Jesus believe he was the Son of God, the Anointed One of God? The answer is yes. Did he see himself as the Son of Man? The answer is yes. Did he see himself as the Messiah? Yes, that's the way he viewed himself. Did he believe that anybody less than God could save the world? No.

As Dr. William Lane Craig once wrote, "Here is a man who thought of himself as the Son of God in a unique sense, who claimed to act and speak with divine authority, who held himself to be a worker of miracles, and who believed that people's eternal destiny hinged on whether or not they believed in him."[1][2]

---

[1] William Lane Craig, *Reasonable Faith* (Westchester, IL: Crossway, 1994), 252.
[2] Adapted from an interview with Dr. Ben Witherington III

Was Jesus' Tomb Empty?

"When they had carried out all that was written about him, they took him down from the tree and laid him in a tomb. But God raised him from the dead." Acts 13:29–30 (read Acts 13:26-41)

The enduring symbol of Easter—the vacant tomb of Jesus—is a historical reality. The empty grave is reported or implied in extremely early sources—Mark's Gospel and the early Christian creed recorded in 1 Corinthians 15:3–7—which date so close to the event that they are highly unlikely to have been products of legend.

The fact that the Gospels report that women discovered the empty tomb bolsters the story's authenticity. The site of Jesus' tomb was known to both Christian and Jew alike, so skeptics could have checked it.

In fact, there's no record that anybody—not even the Roman authorities or Jewish leaders—ever claimed that the tomb still contained Jesus' body. Instead, they were forced to invent the absurd story that the disciples, despite having no motive or opportunity, had stolen the body (see Matthew 28:11–15)—a theory that not even today's most skeptical critic believes.

What's more, the resurrection was the central proclamation of the early church from the very beginning. The ancient creed from 1 Corinthians 15:3–7 mentions specific individuals who encountered the risen Christ, and Paul even challenged first-century doubters to talk with these individuals personally to determine the truth of the matter for themselves.

The book of Acts is littered with extremely early affirmations of Jesus' resurrection, while the Gospels describe numerous encounters in detail. British theologian Michael Green concludes, "The appearances of Jesus are as well authenticated as anything in antiquity ... There can be no rational doubt that they occurred."[1]

---

[1] Michael Green, *The Empty Cross of Jesus* (Downers Grove, IL: InterVarsity, 1984), 97, cited in Ankerberg and Weldon, *Knowing the Truth About the Resurrection* (Eugene, OR: Harvest House, 1996), 22.